Passing the Keys

Passing the Keys

MODERN CARDINALS, CONCLAVES, AND THE ELECTION OF THE NEXT POPE

FRANCIS A. BURKLE-YOUNG

MADISON BOOKS

Lanham · New York · Oxford

Published by Madison Books
4720 Boston Way
Lanham, Maryland 20706

12 Hid's Copse Road
Cumnor Hill, Oxford OX2 9JJ, England

Distributed by National Book Network

Library of Congress Cataloging-in-Publication Data

Burkle-Young, Francis A.
    Passing the keys : modern cardinals, conclaves, and the election
of the next pope / Francis A. Burkle-Young
        p.   cm.
    Includes bibliographical references and index.
    ISBN 1-56833-130-4 (cloth : alk. paper)
    1. Popes—Election—History—20th century. 2. Papacy—History—
20th century. I. Title.
BX1805.B87 1999   99-29538
262'.13—dc21   CIP

⊖™ *The paper used in this publication meets the minimum requirements of*
American National Standard for Information Sciences—Permanence of
Paper for Printed Library Materials, ANSI/NISO Z39.48–1992.
Manufactured in the United Stated of America.

To the Memory of

ELLEN LOUISE BURKLE YOUNG

September 1, 1905—January 30, 1979

Contents

Acknowledgments

I wish to thank Dr. George Allan Cate, Richard E. Cullen, and Laurence S. Galvin for the dozens of hours they contributed to retrieving materials for me, reading the manuscript, and aiding me generally in the task of finishing this book. Without their help, this study could never have been completed. I thank Mariuz R. Grabek for assistance with materials in the Polish language, and Saundra Rose Maley for help with some library collections. I owe a larger debt than these thanks can repay to Fra Raphael Brown, O.F.M., who first introduced me to the study of the College of Cardinals when I was a young student at the Library of Congress, forty years ago. I also thank the late Professor Dr. Hermann Everard Schüssler for his half-decade of guidance and advice on ecclesiastical history when I was his graduate student in the 1970s. I am indebted to William S. Peterson for designing the book.

Among many collections, both in the United States and Europe, I have been most grateful for access to the Library of Congress and the Mullen Library at the Catholic University of America.

I also would like to thank those who gave me interviews over the years or were willing to have less formal, but extensive private conversations with me. It always is sad when valuable sources cannot be acknowledged openly and with profusion, but I am precluded by custom from doing that for a work such as this one.

Finally, I am grateful for years of tolerance for cardinals and for advice, for training in scholarly research techniques, for reading and criticizing my writing, and for decades of complete support, to Ellen Louise Burkle Young.

Foreword

Papal elections are human, not divine, events. They are conducted by a group of men who have reached the second highest level in a global insitution of almost a billion members and to which they have devoted themselves since youth. While the specific details of each conclave are different, each also reflects a commonality of experience on the part of the men who have participated in them.

This book surveys the conclave system in the modern history of the Catholic Church and recounts the details of how recent popes have been elected. It then goes on to explore whether these past elections have lessons and precedents which may apply to the election of the next pope.

Those who have the suffrage have frequent opportunities to express their political, social, and economic opinions. In some developed democracies, voters often can make significant choices every year, in national, provincial or state, and local elections. And most modern voters do not regard the casting of a ballot as the supreme moment of their public or professional lives. A cardinal, by contrast, realizes that his opportunity to vote comes usually only once or twice in a lifetime, and that casting the ballot is the single most important act he will perform in the course of the life he has chosen. His vote, and the votes of his colleagues, determine who will become absolute monarch for life over the institution that the cardinal regards as the greatest and most important in the world. This is not to say that cardinals always vote for one of their number for entirely weighty reasons, because personality plays at least as much of a part in being a successful candidate for the papacy as heavier considerations of policy, government, or personal holiness. But all the cardinals are well aware that the act of voting for a new pope is the single most important privilege and obligation of the office of the cardinalate. Indeed, today there is no other reason, administrative or theological, for the office to exist at all—most cardinals who live outside Rome are residential archbishops in no way different from many others of the same rank, and most of the curial cardinals in Rome head offices, or dicastries, which could be led just as easily by others with different titles. Fundamentally, the cardinals exist, as vital functionaries of the Church, solely for the purpose of being a part of the body of electors that chooses the pope. As with every other human insitution, the essential humanity of its members does not change, although times and external circumstances and questions do.

Perhaps, then, from the experiences of other modern conclaves, we can discern some of the principles which will operate in the next one.

This book is not, in the proper meaning of the term, a history of the conclaves from 1878. The writing of good history must be based entirely on primary sources, and, if possible, all of those sources that are relevant to the events under examination. It is for this reason that there are few historical works that have been written on topics after World War I that have much enduring value at all. Many, if not most, of the primary materials that are required for such work are not yet available to serious scholars. Many are still classified by governments and other institutions, and are, therefore, generally unavailable. Many others remain in the private papers of the participants in the major events of this century—papers which, all too often, lie in the hands of relatives or decendants of the participants, who are unwilling to open them to detailed scrutiny. Just now, after the close of the Cold War, with the opening of a number of Russian archives and collections, both governmental and private, we are coming, finally, to a more well-rounded understanding of World War I—an event which closed more than eighty years ago. This truth, it must be said, often does not sit well with the way in which history is studied and practiced in America today. The great majority of doctorates in history granted today are written by graduate students on topics in twentieth-century history—topics whose essential primary sources remain closed.

For example, American universities have granted almost four thousand doctorates for dissertations on World War II, yet most of the primary materials—especially on the most sensitive, and, therefore, interesting topics—remain classified by the governments that generated them. How valuable can such studies be, when much of the material that is relevant to a balanced historical approach has never been seen? This error of "presentism" is rife among American writers today, academic or not.

Passing the Keys is a narrative with a historical perspective, and should not be regarded as an academic work subject to the accusation of "presentism." All the modern popes, especially Pius XII, Paul VI, and John Paul II, have inveighed powerfully against anyone who attempts to learn the secrets of modern papal elections, and they have imposed spiritual penalties, on anyone who reveals anything, that are meant to be the most frightening imaginable. For this reason, few participants, from the cardinals to the least members of the staffs, have been willing to talk about the actions behind the key at all. A few, of course, have written memoranda for their own recall—although this, too, is now forbidden—and a very few others have written or spoken publicly about the events in which they have participated (for which, if they are Catholic, they incurred an excommunication so thorough that it can be lifted only by the pope)! From these meager but valuable gleanings, approached through the eyes of an experienced observer of the College of Cardinals, it is possible to know something about modern conclaves; perhaps just enough to take some lessons from the experiences of the past and, from them—and from the lives and work of the cardinals who have elected, and will elect, popes—determine something useful about the forces in the next conclave and the pope it will produce.

Francis A. Burkle-Young
Washington, D.C.

Introduction

As billions of people today troop to the polls in rites of democracy, either in form or in substance, it is worth recalling that the choice of this planet's foremost Christian leader is the oldest process of election by secret ballot still maintained in the world. It was not always so. In the beginning, the leader of the Christian community in Rome may have been chosen either by his predecessor or by popular voice. By the close of the second century, however, the latter system prevailed, and Rome's bishop was chosen in the same manner as other bishops in the Christian world. The danger that two or more popular prelates might be hailed as bishop at the same time, thus provoking schism, emerged as early as 217, in the dual election of Calixtus I and Hyppolytus. Nevertheless, election by popular acclamation continued to be the lawful method of providing a pope for hundreds of years, up to the early eleventh century.

In this first thousand years of papal succession, the rôle of the city's Christian community was usurped on several occasions. By the early eleventh century, the papacy had, in fact, become a pawn of the local feudal nobility, to be handed out to a retainer or scion of whatever family happened to control the city at the moment. The situation became so scandalous that the Emperor Henry III finally intervened, and, in 1046 at the Synod of Sutri, he began a series of appointed German popes. These six, who followed in rapid succession, were no better at easing the troubles of Rome than were the Italian feudal creatures who preceded them.

In the spring of 1058, a sudden uprising of Roman barons precipitated the solution to this problem. The barons seized an unsettled moment at the death of Stephen X to install Joannes Mincius, cardinal-bishop of Velletri, as Benedict X. The principal papal advisor during the past three reigns, the cardinal-archdeacon Hildebrand, returned to Rome and vehemently opposed Benedict, who seemed on the threshold of returning the papacy to the lawlessness of former decades. Hildebrand overthrew his rival, which led to the installation of the reform-minded bishop of Florence, Gerardus, as Pope Nicholas II, on January 24, 1059.

Just seventy-nine days later, on April 13, the new pope issued the first constitution on papal elections, *In nomine Domini*. It sought to eliminate forever popular factionalism, baronial imposition, and German interference, alike. It made the cardinal-bishops the sole electors of the pope, and required that the cardinal-priests and cardinal-deacons adhere to their decision as soon as they knew of it. Since that time, no papal election with any pretense of validity has been carried out without the presence of cardinals, and, because of their rôle in choosing the popes, their stature steadily increased until, by the mid-twelfth century, they occupied a place in the Western Church second only to that of the pope himself, a position they retain today.

This is not to say that the Roman cardinals were unimportant figures before 1059. By the early third century, Rome had at least twenty-five recognized centers of Christian worship, called titles, which were under the care of resident priests. These ancestors of modern parishes increased in importance after the legal fetters were removed from Christian worship by the Edict of Milan in 312, and the resident caretakers soon became a separate group of important members of the Roman clergy—the cardinal-priests. Shortly thereafter, a group of fourteen men emerged as the cardinal-deacons. These functionaries were the supervisors of the *diaconiæ*—a unique group of institutions in Rome, one in each of the civic regions established by the Emperor Hadrian—where charity was dispensed, care for the traveler and the sick provided, and, later, local Christian administration carried out. Gradually, too, the residential bishops in Rome's nearby suburbs came into more and more contact with their senior colleague in the Eternal City. Eventually, they became permanent fixtures at the papal court as the cardinal-bishops. Their number varied, but by the twelfth century became fixed at six, a number which has been exceeded only twice, briefly, down to the present time.

Important as these groups of cardinals were in and near Rome, they soon transcended their local rôle to become major figures of the Western Church. As the Roman empire in the West decayed and collapsed, it brought down with it the whole apparatus of civil administration and law which had provided more than three centuries of order and stability in the civilized Western world. There was no organization ready to fill this void, either in Rome itself or in the rest of the western lands of the old empire. Step by step, the populace of the city, now almost wholly Christian, turned for government to the one remaining figure who commanded nearly universal respect, their bishop, the pope. Elsewhere in the western portions of the empire, there was a similar growth in episcopal responsibility and power. Who, then, would settle disputes between bishops, or between a bishop and some new feudatory? The unique leader, in the north and west of the old empire at least, was the nearest of the four ancient patriarchs, the pope. There was no one to whom the popes could pass this new burden of authority, even if they had wished to do so—as surely Leo I must have so wished when he, and a few members of the papal court, faced Attila the Hun in 452 and persuaded him not to sack Rome.

The work of the papal administration became so great that the cardinal-priests and cardinal-deacons gradually were drawn into the papal court, the curia, as the principal assistants of the pope, while their old offices of pastors and civic administrators were left in the hands of vicars and delegates. Eventually, the cardinal-bishops, too, were absorbed into the Roman bureaucracy and were seen less and less in the small towns near Rome which had been their principal administrative charge. By the eleventh century, a church had supplanted each of the old *diaconiæ* as the seat of each cardinal-deacon, and to this day each new cardinal-deacon is assigned to a church that once was associated with, or is a successor to, a *diaconia*; each cardinal-bishop holds, in name, one of the old suburban dioceses; and each cardinal-priest is the formal pastor of a designated Roman parish, still called a title.

The lasting power of Nicholas II's election constitution, *In nomine Domini*, was tested often after 1059. Only once, however, was the document wholly superseded. On April 22, 1073, at the funeral of Alexander II, large numbers of the crowd began to shout, "let Hildebrand be pope, the papacy to Hildebrand." The popular demonstration reached such proportions that the cardinals could only hastily ratify the accession of Gregory VII, the very reformer who stood behind Nicholas II in the first place. Another test of the rôle of cardinals as papal electors came with the death of Gelasius II at the great medieval abbey of Cluny on January 28, 1119. Driven from Rome by an uprising of Roman barons, the pope had only six of the nearly sixty living cardinals with him when he died. In order to provide no opportunity for local Roman politics to plunge the Church once more into chaos, these six proceeded to elect a new pope at once, though none of them were cardinal-bishops. Their choice, Guy de Bourgogne, was installed on February 2 as Calixtus II. The cardinals in Rome immediately ratified his elevation as soon as they were notified. Thus a crisis was averted and, at the same time, the right of all the cardinals to participate in the election of the pope was established in a difficult situation. From this time forward, at least, the cardinals of all three ranks seem to have participated equally in the choice of the pope, though not always with the harmony displayed in 1119. In 1130, and again in 1159, schisms were begun because of disputes among the cardinals over the papal election, with the eventual enthronement of two popes on each occasion. The right of all three cardinalitial ranks to an equal voice was finally confirmed by Alexander III in 1179, at the Third Lateran Council, by the constitution *Licet de vitanda.* This document also required the winning candidate for the throne to obtain a two-thirds majority of all the cardinals present, so as to obviate forever a nearly equal split in the College which could bring about a double elevation, such as that which had marred Alexander's own rise in 1159.

As the cardinals rose in importance, their number gradually diminished. Those holding the rank and sharing in the very considerable revenues of the College did everything in their power to persuade succeeding popes to name few, if any, new cardinals, since the incorporation of new members involved a redistribution of wealth and power, with proportionately less for each member in an enlarged College. At the time of the enthronement of Innocent III in 1198, there seems to have been between twenty-five and thirty cardinals, including Konrad von Wittelsbach, the first cardinal in history to hold the rank while living elsewhere than Rome. Even this number, though, was probably only half the size of the membership a half-century before. By the death of Gregory IX, on August 22, 1241, the number of cardinals had sunk to fifteen. Internal wrangling among the electors kept the papal chair vacant until October 25, when Cardinal Gaufrido Castiglione became Celestine IV. Celestine, however, died after only sixteen days as pope. The internal fighting resumed, and by the time Cardinal Sinibaldo Fieschi was elected Pope Innocent IV—more than a year and a half later, on June 25, 1243—the College's eleven survivors had become scandals to the entire Western world. Innocent and his immediate successors, moreover, did nothing to remedy the situation. Alexander IV (1254–1261) created only one new cardinal in a six-and-a-half year reign.

The death of Clement IV, on November 29, 1268, began the final crisis that was to be resolved by the foundation of the conclave system. For more than two years, the cardinals wrangled bitterly among themselves in the episcopal palace at Viterbo, where Clement had died. Two of the cardinals themselves died in the interim, and a third became so ill and disgusted that he resigned his rights as an elector and left. The personal pleas of the kings of France and Sicily did nothing to hasten matters. Finally, Viterbo's mayor, backed by his townspeople, took drastic action. First, the cardinals were confined to the palace and, when this produced no result, their food supply was curtailed. At last, the mayor ordered part of the palace roof stripped away, to expose the cardinals to the weather. Only then were the sixteen electors persuaded to act. They chose six of their number as a committee to reach a decision by compromise. The six proclaimed Tedaldo Visconti, archdeacon of Liege, as the new pope on September 1, 1271. The papacy had been vacant for six more days than a thousand. The man they chose was not only not a cardinal, a somewhat common occurrence in the Middle Ages, but was not even in Europe. When Visconti was notified suddenly that he was pope, he was at Acre in Palestine in the company of the future Edward I of England, who was there on a sort of mini-crusade. The new pope called himself Gregory X and speedily returned to Italy. Later, he summoned the Second Council of Lyons where, in 1274, he issued the constitution *Ubi periculum*.

In his prescription for the troubles of papal elections, Gregory laid down that the cardinals were to wait for ten days after a pope's death for any of their number who might be absent to join them. They were then to enter a common room in the place where the late pope had died—or in the nearest town free from any ecclesiastical censure, at least—and remain shut up together under lock and key, *cum clavis*, until they chose a new pope. If they went three days without a decision, their meals, passed to them through a grate, were to be reduced to only one dish at midday and another in the evening. If five more days passed with no result, their food was to be cut back to bread, water, and a little wine. Gregory pressed the cardinals with one more strong inducement to a speedy election—the cardinals were to receive no revenues of any kind during a vacancy. Gregory further laid on the local population of whatever place happened to be the site of an election the duty of seeing to it that all the provisions of *Ubi periculum* were met. Thus, the word and the institution—conclave—entered the world at the same moment.

Gregory X's provisions, in addition to being the first legislation to force a rapid papal election, were among the most forceful and most useful in the history of the Church. Unfortunately, there were four papal deaths in the two years following Gregory's own end in January, 1276. The first two elections, carried out to the letter of *Ubi periculum*, were models of speed. The first took only one day and the second only nine days. The second of the new popes, Adrian V, expressed enormous dissatisfaction with the conclave system—as well he might, since his health was completely undermined by its rigors, however short. Adrian died thirty-eight days after his election, before he could do anything to modify the system. His successor, the Church's only Portuguese pope, John XXI, elected after a conclave of eleven days, immediately abolished Gregory's laws. As might have been expected, the next vacancy, after John's reign of less than a year, lasted one hundred eighty-nine days.

One area of reform which Gregory X had not tackled seriously was the administrative problem caused by the dwindling number of cardinals. The election of four cardinals, one after another in 1276–1277, their sudden deaths, and the fact that none of them elevated any new members to the College finally reduced the number of living cardinals to seven, one of whom took no part in the elections at all.

For more than half a year after the death of John XXI, six superannu-ated churchmen sat and glared at each other. When they finally realized that they might all die before they could reach an accord, they compro-mised by electing the oldest of their number, Cardinal Giovanni Gaetano Orsini, a Roman noble who chose to be called Nicholas III, on November 25, 1277. Now there were six.

Nicholas did, at least, appoint nine more cardinals in his three-year reign, and the College was never reduced again to so small a membership as six.

Nevertheless, the next few elections were nearly all characterized by long delays. On July 5, 1294, the College ended one impasse of more than two years by dragging an aged, ignorant hermit, Pietro del Murrone, from his retreat and forcing the crown on his head as Celestine V. Before be-coming the last pope to abdicate, after a pontificate of four months, Celes-tine not only created thirteen new cardinals but also reimposed Gregory X's law of elections. Celestine's resignation, therefore, was followed by a vacancy of only eleven days. The new pope, Boniface VIII, incorporated the provisions of *Ubi periculum* into canon law, and since that time all the popes have been chosen within the framework of the conclave, though the actual procedures for electing them has been much modified through the ages.

Celestine V's creation of cardinals in 1294 was a mixed blessing for the Church, for more than half were French and several others had close ties with the French king of Naples, who dominated much of the hermit's brief reign. After Boniface VIII, and after the brief seven-month reign of his suc-cessor, Benedict XI, these French and francophile cardinals brought off a major coup by electing Bertrand de Got, the archbishop of Bordeaux, on June 5, 1305. De Got was not a cardinal, but he was the brother of one of Celestine's cardinals, now dead. When he was notified at Bordeaux of his election, de Got chose the name Clement V and announced his intention to cross the Alps at once. His health, however, was simply not up to the journey. He wandered around southern France for some time, and finally came to rest at Avignon, where he was joined by the cardinals who had elected him. In a reign of nearly nine years, Clement created twenty-four new cardinals, a number unprecedented in nearly a century, but all of them except one were French. Moreover, six of them were papal nephews and one other a great-nephew. Thus, when Clement died, sixteen of the two dozen living cardinals were French. They proceeded to force the election of one of their own, Jacques d'Euse of Cahors, who, as John XXII, contin-ued Clement's policy of packing the College with papal relatives and other

Frenchmen. This brought the papacy firmly into a seventy-five year period in Avignon, during which the city of Rome decayed. The "Babylonian Captivity" of the papacy was followed by an even more disastrous trouble—the Great Schism.

One of the few memorable acts of Clement V was his election constitution, *Ne Romani*, of 1311. In it, Clement decreed that the papal election must take place in the diocese where the late pope had died, thus ensuring that the next conclave would take place in Avignon. But Clement also made it quite clear that every cardinal, unless fully deposed from office for crime, was entitled to be present in the conclave and to have an active vote. This provision remained a fundamental part of the law of papal elections until 1970, when it was altered by Paul VI. On November 21 of that year, Paul VI issued the motu proprio *Ingravescentem Ætatem* which deprived all the cardinals who were over the age of eighty at the death of the pope of the right to vote in the next conclave. This decision, which overturned a custom that was almost seven hundred years old, had important consequences in the two elections in 1978 and will have an even greater effect in the coming conclave.

During the Avignonese period, a curious formality made its appearance in the conclave. This was the "election capitulation." In order to keep as much power in the hands of the College as possible, the cardinals would draw up collectively, and then subscribe to, a document which restricted, often severely, the papal powers of the one elected. Beginning with Innocent VI, each new pope regularly repudiated his adherence to the capitulation as one of the first acts of the new reign—Innocent rejected the capitulation he had signed in the bull *Solicitudo* in 1353, the year after his election. In spite of these repudiations, the cardinals continued to draw up formal election capitulations at the beginning of each conclave down to the end of the fifteenth century. Although the custom eventually died away, cardinals were often pressed by their colleagues to promise favors or commit themselves to a predetermined policy as a price for the throne. This whole practice finally was condemned by Innocent XII, in the bull *Ecclesiæ Catholicæ* of September 22, 1695. But papal bulls do not, of course, alter either human nature or the mechanisms that apportion human power. As recently as 1922, Cardinal Raffaele Merry del Val, the powerful leader of the conservatives in the conclave, told Achille Ratti, who was about to become Pius XI, that he would bring the whole of the conservative vote to his side in the next ballot, if only Ratti would make certain promises about policy and administration to the conservatives, in turn. To his credit, Ratti refused the bargain, and was elected anyway.

The greatest crisis in the history of the papacy began on March 26,

1378, when Gregory XI, the seventh successive French pope, died in Rome. The cardinals traveling with him were besieged immediately by the Roman people who demanded, if not a Roman pope, at least an Italian one. After trying to forestall the mob, by making the senile Cardinal Francesco Thebaldeschi don papal robes and show himself, the sixteen cardinals, eleven of whom were French, capitulated and elected Bartolomeo Prignano, the archbishop of Bari, who became Urban VI. Urban, the last man elected to the papal chair who was not a cardinal, proved to be a harsh, cruel megalomaniac who terrorized the College. During the following summer, the cardinals found excuses, one by one, to slip away from the papal court. At Anagni, on September 20, thirteen of them formally repudiated the election of Urban, on the grounds that his election had taken place under duress, and then chose one of their number, Robert de Geneve, who called himself Clement VII. The six cardinals who had remained behind in Avignon when Gregory XI went to Italy now promptly acknowledged Clement as the true pope. Clement then returned to Avignon and soon commanded the loyalty of all the surviving cardinals created before 1378. Thus the Great Schism began as an age of two popes; by 1409 a third contender appeared, added to the fray by the work of the Council of Pisa, which had been convoked by a majority of the cardinals from both papal courts expressly to resolve the problem. The reduction of the papacy to its former state of just one occupant finally occurred at the Council of Constance on November 11, 1417, when Cardinal Oddone Colonna became Pope Martin V. At the election of 1417, the cardinals of all three obediences who participated—Rome, Avignon, and Pisa—were joined by six prelates from each of the five "nations" who were represented at the council. The thirty "national" electors were the last non-cardinals to have a voice in the selection of the pope; and they, together with the twenty-four cardinals who also were present, combined to make the largest conclave in two centuries. The number of papal electors in 1417 rivals the number of electors in the increased College of Cardinals of more recent times.

Martin devoted his whole pontificate to the task of restoring papal prestige and power, and was largely successful. His successor, Eugenius IV (1431–1447), almost undid the whole program, however, by placing himself in opposition to the Council of Basel, to which two of the cardinals who had been created by Martin V gave their adherence. After a long series of fruitless negotiations, the council deposed Eugenius from his throne on June 25, 1439. The pope, needless to say, rejected the council's actions, and meditated on several responses. Of these, the most wide-ranging turned out to be the creation of seventeen new cardinals on the following December 18, which more than doubled the size of the College.

The principal criterion employed by the pope in selecting the new princes of the Church was not the traditional one—long, faithful service in the Church's administration. Almost all of the cardinals created in 1439 received the red hat for political rather than religious reasons. The pope made two Greeks cardinals to help to cement a recent, fragile reunion with the Eastern church, while both the French chancellor and a former English chancellor were made cardinals to flatter their respective monarchs and to ensure that those kings did not cast their lot with the Council of Basel. For the same reason, Eugenius also gave red hats to prominent members of the Hungarian, Polish, Portuguese, and Burgundian courts, as well as to representatives of the Genoese and Milanese nobility. He made a cardinal of a young cousin of Charles VII of France, and elevated an important member of the German imperial council, as well. Eugenius also did not forget to honor the old noble families of the Roman vicinity.

In his successful effort to consolidate papal power and to thwart the actions of the Council, Eugenius had executed a revolution of major importance in the history of the Church. It is hard to overstress its significance, both for the conduct of Church government and for the politics of papal elections over the next three and a half centuries.

For several centuries, the great majority of the cardinals had come from the same curial offices as had members of the College from ages past, as well as from the families of the popes. The curial prelates were, for the most part, wholly devoted to the service of the Church, while the papal relatives were concerned for the success and well-being of the uncle, great-uncle, or brother who had made them princes of the Church. Together, as cardinals, they worked willingly as a collegiate body for the benefit of, at least, the College of Cardinals. The medieval members of the College were aware, acutely, of the importance of the cardinalate in the governance of the Church, and former pontiffs usually had elevated new cardinals from the ranks of those already known to the senior cardinals through years of association. By creating so many "crown cardinals," as the servants of kings rather than popes came to be known, Eugenius dealt a blow to the collegiality of the cardinals from which they would never wholly recover. Indeed, the nineteenth century would arrive before the cardinals once more felt themselves united as a body of churchmen in the service of the Church.

Many of those created in 1439 were strangers to those already in the College, and to each other. Just about the only communality they shared was their loyalty to Eugenius in his quarrel with Basel. More significantly, however, this creation was the first time that any pope had given the cardinalate to so many men to reward long and faithful service to secular powers and to local interests rather than to the Church or to the pope himself. Perhaps the most important consequence of this radical change can be seen over the next four centuries, when the red hat of the cardinalate often became simply an ornament given by the pope to those who already possessed great power outside the Church—as was true in the cases of Wolsey, Richelieu, and Mazarin, among many others—and represented to the receiver no real addition to the power and prestige that already were his.

Eugenius's success with this promotion, as well as with his other anti-conciliar policies, was nearly complete. By the end of the reign, the Council of Basel was virtually moribund, and its participants made an unconditional submission to the next pope, Nicholas V. Eugenius's alteration in the nature of the cardinalate manifested itself quickly in the next election, when so many political cardinals were resident outside the papal court at the pope's death that more than a fourth of the College played no rôle at all in selecting Nicholas.

The Italian and Spanish popes of the fifteenth century followed, and amplified, the policy of their French predecessors in using nepotism to fill seats in the College. As a power in Europe second to none, the popes always feared conspiracy and intrigue against themselves and their policies. Without the benefit of the hereditary principle to protect their thrones, each pope faced the task of choosing fully loyal and supportive advisors. But who could be trusted? Each pope quickly learned that members of his own family had the greatest interest in having him enjoy a long, successful pontificate, since, at the very moment of his demise, the major part of their careers of power and influence would come to an end. Reliance on cardinal-nephews became so widespread that, by the end of the fifteenth century, the senior cardinal-nephew in each reign had risen to a status equal to that of a first minister of state. Moreover, each pontiff found that he could stretch the limits established by his predecessors concerning the number of relatives in the College of Cardinals. Martin V had contented himself with elevating one nephew; Eugenius IV had two cardinal-nephews; but Sixtus IV (1472–1484) had no fewer than six.

Beyond the actions of political appointment of royal servants and nepotism in changing the cardinalate and the operations of the conclaves stood a third new policy. In March, 1460, Pius II (1458–1464) admitted the first scion of an Italian ruling princely house to the College in the person of Francesco Gonzaga, younger son of Mantua's ruler, Marchese Luigi III. Within a few years, every important ruling family in the peninsula thought that they were entitled to have at least one member in the College, and soon the College was populated by Sforza from Milan, Medici from Florence, d'Este from Ferrara, and members of the Neapolitan royal family, among others. The conclave which elected Rodrigo de Lançol y Borgia as Pope Alexander VI in 1492 has come down in history as perhaps the most venal of all. Borgia, the wealthiest and most influential cardinal—and himself a cardinal-nephew of Calixtus III—blatantly offered bribes of money, offices, and preferments of all sorts, in his successful bid for the throne. He achieved his highest ambition largely because the revolution in the College begun by Eugenius IV was now complete. The membership consisted no longer of papal bureaucrats but rather was a collection of relatives of former popes, Italian princes, and relatives and servants of Europe's more important kings. To all of these men, the general welfare of the Church was of less importance than the aggrandizement and power each could enjoy through making the right bargain.

During the election of 1492, a half century after the Eugenian revolution, there were twenty-seven living cardinals. Of them, no fewer than ten were the nephews or great-nephews of dead popes; eight were representatives of Italian noble families; four were cardinals who had been elevated on the nomination of kings; and still another was a teenaged boy whose qualification for the office was that his father had once been a loyal general in the service of the papacy. Only four of the twenty-seven could be described, by the greatest stretch of kindness, as churchmen in the service of the Church. And, of that total, four eventually would rise to the papal throne—three cardinal-nephews and an Italian noble.

The shock of the Reformation in the next generation put an end to the worst of these excesses, but the cardinals whose primary loyalty was to the Church itself had their choices for the papal throne limited, in conclaves down to the end of the eighteenth century, by the power of Italian princes, papal relatives, and royal favorites.

Julius II (1503–1513) was the first pope to respond to the public outcry at the corruption which infected both College and conclave, even though he was himself a cardinal-nephew of Sixtus IV. In the bull *Cum tam divino*, dated January 14, 1505, he ordered that never again should simony—the purchase of church office—be countenanced in a conclave. The specific scandal of 1492 was beyond repetition.

Julius II's successor, Leo X (1513–1521), struck the first blow to reduce the threat that was posed by having so much power concentrated in the hands of so few—and those loyal to interests outside the welfare of the Church. For three centuries, the number of cardinals at any time had seldom exceeded two dozen. In response to a conspiracy against his life, in which perhaps a majority of the College was implicated, Leo executed one cardinal, as a warning, and then greatly reduced the power available to each member of the College by holding the first "grand consistory." He nominated thirty-one new cardinals in a single day, July 1, 1517—a number of new cardinals equaled once, by Pius XII in 1946, but never surpassed.

At one stroke, Leo ended forever the practice of the College to work against the promotion of new members. Significantly, it was the much larger and broadened Leonine College which elected the Dutch Adrian VI in the conclave following Leo's death. Adrian became the last non-Italian pope until the election of John Paul II in 1978.

The conclaves held before and after this time, however, were still rather haphazard affairs. The cardinals were locked up together, not very securely on some occasions, and proceeded to negotiate among themselves until a candidate emerged, more often than not in a series of carefully orchestrated compromises, to become the new pope. The first major step at regulating the activities of the electors while in the conclave was a fruit of the Catholic reformation and the spirit of the Council of Trent.

Pius IV (1559–1565), on October 9, 1562, issued the constitution *In eligendis*, which established several new regulations concerning the conclave. For example, at least once each day the cardinals were to vote by secret ballot. After the results were tallied and announced, the electors could, if they wished, hold an *accessus*, a formal action in which each elector could rise at his throne and verbally change his vote in favor of one of those candidates leading in the tally. The cardinals were to be assigned cells according to drawn lots. Communication with anyone outside the conclave was forbidden, though the major ambassadors were permitted to come to the conclave's gates and make formal statements, but only on urgent matters. The prelates who were charged with preserving a conclave's security were instructed to examine all the food taken into the area from the cardinals' kitchens, so that no messages could be smuggled in. The cardinals themselves were ordered to choose some of their number who were to inspect the walls and partitions every day, to protect against any break in security. This legislation of Pius IV was another major evolution on the way to the modern conclave.

Over the following seventy-five years, several more popes enacted far-reaching laws regarding both the College of Cardinals and the conclave. Sixtus V (1585–1590), in the constitutions *Postquam verus* (December 3, 1586) and *Religiosa* (April 13, 1587), fixed the maximum number of cardinals at seventy: six cardinal-bishops, fifty cardinal-priests, and fourteen cardinal-deacons, in imitation of the elders of Moses. This policy continued in effect until 1958. Gregory XV (1621–1623) proclaimed two new constitutions to regulate the cardinals and the conclave, *Æterni Patris* (November 15, 1621) and *Decet Romanum Pontificem* (March 12, 1622). The first of these laid down the fundamental law of conclaves, based in part on

In eligendis, which continues to the present day—although each modern pope has issued a constitution on papal elections which has made minor modifications in its rules and procedures.

Æterni Patris provided that the election of a pope must take place in a conclave at which a written ballot was used, and nowhere else. No cardinal was to vote for himself, and each cardinal was to sign his ballot so that, if necessary, the ballots could be examined after the tally to show that this rule had not been violated. Should an *accessus* be held, it was to be conducted in the form of amendments to the ballots in the same rigorous secrecy which characterized the original poll. Two ballots and two *accessi* would be held daily, the first of each in the morning after Mass, and the others in the evening, after the chanting of the *Veni Creator Spiritus*.

Every cardinal in the conclave was required to attend both voting sessions or face excommunication. Gregory XV further provided that three scrutators would be chosen by lot to count the votes in each session, and three tellers, also chosen by lot, would verify the results. The cardinals were forbidden to make any agreements or compacts, to pass signals or threats of any kind to one another, or to refuse to vote; "but the provisions shall not exclude an exchange of opinion or understanding in the matter of the papal election." This latter phrase left a loophole which allowed political bargaining to continue in the conclaves.

During the course of the sixteenth century, most of the papal elections felt the weight of Spanish influence, because of the preeminent standing of Philip II (1555–1598) in Catholic Europe. In the seventeenth century, France was the main influence, especially in the years of Louis XIV (1643–1715). But, throughout this period, there was a gradual decline in the international political importance of the elections. The pope had ceased to be the major figure in European affairs and the continent's kings regularly ignored Roman pronouncements. By the seventeenth and eighteenth centuries, the concern of the powers of the time was to ensure the election of a pope who would not upset the status quo with sudden pronouncements that had political implications. In order to guarantee this, the German emperors, and the kings of France and Spain, began to claim an unquestioned right to veto the candidacy of any cardinal whom they thought would be against their interests. This right of veto, the *jus exclusivæ*, had been recognized informally since the middle of the sixteenth century, but was accepted openly by the cardinals for the first time in 1721, when the Emperor Charles VI notified the College that he excluded Cardinal Fabrizio Paolucci de' Calboli from the throne. The "right" apparently became dormant, however, by the later eighteenth century, only to appear again, in 1903, with startling results.

The conclaves of 1758 and 1769 turned on a matter of little real importance—whether or not Europe's important nations could secure the election of a pope willing to suppress the Jesuits. By contrast, the conclave of 1774–1775 was a long, grand party hosted by the principal French cardinal, François Joachim de Pierre de Bernis, in which the conclave's precincts were opened on a number of occasions—once to entertain the Emperor Joseph II and his brother, Archduke Leopold, who were traveling in Italy, ostensibly incognito. These revels, which ended in the elevation of Bernis's candidate, Giovanni Angelo Braschi as Pius VI, marked the nadir of the modern conclave system.

An air of seriousness returned in 1800, when thirty-four of the forty-five living cardinals met in Venice to elect a successor to Pius VI. Fearing the wrath of Napoleon, who had forbidden the choice of a new pope without his express permission, the cardinals had assembled in Venice because it was the closest point to Rome at which they could enjoy Austrian protection. It became the last conclave to be held outside the Eternal City. The electors chose Pius VII, a cousin of Pius VI named Barnabà Chiaramonti, who, immediately after his election, invested the secretary of the conclave, Ercole Consalvi, with the cardinalate, a traditional reward for a difficult job well done, and made him secretary of state as well.

Consalvi initiated the operation of the modern papal secretariat of state, and assured to his successors in office a bureaucratic rôle in Church affairs second only to that of the pope. Coincident with this change came the final disappearance of the cardinal-nephews, and although Leo XIII made his brother a cardinal, it was a merited appointment and Giuseppe Pecci did not influence papal affairs.

Pius VII also was the last pope to appoint crown cardinals to the College. After his election, he knew that he had to reach a rapprochement with Napoleon quickly, if he were to avoid the imprisonment to which the Consul had consigned his cousin and predecessor, Pius VI.

After the death of Pius VII in 1823, the Church saw three conclaves in eight years. Two of the popes chosen, Leo XII in 1823 and Gregory XVI in 1831, proved themselves to be among the most spirited reactionaries in Europe. Gregory's successor, Pius IX, elected in 1846, began his career as the youngest pope in more than a century. He instituted a significant number of liberal reforms, but it was too late. Beset by revolution in Rome and ignored abroad, Pius gradually became as much of an intransigent reactionary as his immediate predecessors. He summoned the First Vatican Council in 1870 largely to rubber stamp his later, ultra-conservative policies, including that of papal infallibility.

The history of modern papal elections opens in 1878, with the reaction of the cardinals to the abolition of the States of the Church and the unification of Italy. With their choice, Leo XIII, the first modern pope, comes the beginning of a new movement to bring the Church into the social, political, and economic reality of the industrialized world.

Passing the Keys

I. The Beginnings of the Contemporary Church

From the moment the Royal Italian Army entered Rome, in September, 1870, until the death of Pius IX, seven and a half years later, many people doubted whether there would ever be another conclave. Pius responded to Victor Emmanuel's occupation of Rome by retiring within the Vatican Palace and permitted virtually no intercourse between the members of his court and the bureaucracy of a newly united Italy.

During the last years of his life, no one was more aware than Pius that attempts might be made by the Italian government to thwart the choice of a new pope. Therefore, he put into effect several policies designed to ensure that his death would be followed speedily by the election of his successor. He secretly prepared no fewer than three papal constitutions dealing with conclaves to be made public only on his death.

The first of these, *In hac sublimi*, dated August 21, 1871, was the most far-reaching. In it, he abrogated all the laws regarding conclaves established by his predecessors during the preceding six centuries, should any interference be offered to the cardinals after his death. He directed that the meeting of the conclave need not necessarily take place at the site of his death but rather that a general congregation of cardinals should meet immediately to decide the time and place of the papal election and inform absent cardinals of its decision. Further, Pius instructed that the electoral process was to begin when one half plus one of the living cardinals should meet, even if this were in the first general congregation assembled after his death. Any person who received the adherence of two-thirds of those present would be elected canonically as the new pope, though that might represent the votes of as little as one third of the living cardinals.

In the second constitution, *Licet per apostolicas*, September 8, 1874, Pius confirmed the earlier document but forbade the cardinals to break, in any way, with those traditions which could be observed safely. In addition, he expressly prohibited the Sacred College from exercising papal powers thus forcing them to a quick election, and he demanded strongly that the cardinals maintain secrecy about the electoral proceedings.

In the third and last electoral constitution, *Consulturi*, dated October 10, 1877, Pius ordered that the cardinals should be prepared to break up the conclave and move at once to a new site if their work were impeded in any way. They were empowered to take this action, even if the balloting already had begun. Moreover, though he had wished formerly that his constitutions be first considered by a tribunal made up of the dean, archpriest, and archdeacon of the College of Cardinals, he now desired that all the cardinals be informed of their provisions at once by a public reading immediately after his death.

Of all the steps he took, however, the most far-reaching was his intentional broadening of the membership in the College to include wider representation for non-Italian Catholics. He hoped to reduce, thereby, the possibility that the Italian government would interfere with the deliberations of a body which included, among others, English, French, German, and Spanish nationals. The importance of this policy cannot be overstated, since the steady increase in non-Italian membership has led to a gradual diminution of Italian influence in the selection of the pope from that time to our own, even though the Vatican bureaucracy remains chiefly Italian.

By early 1877, it was clear that the eighty-five-year-old Pius would not live much longer, and the negotiations among the cardinals began in earnest. Cardinal Domenico Bartolini, a Roman endowed with a loud, coarse voice, and immensely fat as well, had risen to become prefect of the Sacred Congregation of Rites. By virtue of his office, as well as his considerable intellectual ability, he had become one of a small handful of powerful cardinals who actually made the day-to-day decisions by which the Church functioned. Bartolini, like many urban peasants who grow up in the streets, had an unerring sense of political manipulation. At the heart of this skill was his staunch protection of everyone whom he called friend. He carefully abided by every arrangement and compromise he ever made and was famous for never breaking his word.

During the early negotiations, Bartolini astutely took advantage of the courtesy calls that other cardinals made on him to sound them out carefully regarding their plans for the next election, a freedom given him by Pius's lifting of the prohibition on electioneering. Cardinals who came to inquire after the patient's health were skillfully drawn into discussions of the relative merits of their colleagues. During the long beginning of this political orchestration, the scarlet-clad Friar Tuck artfully concealed both his motives and his choice for the throne. By the Christmas season, however, Bartolini had decided that he would expend every effort to secure the elevation of Gioacchino Pecci, a senior cardinal who had recently been elevated to the vitally important position of chamberlain of the Church.

The sixty-seven-year-old Pecci was Bartolini's opposite. Sprung from the minor nobility, this tall and spare intellectual had begun his rise in the Church's bureaucracy when he had served a term as papal ambassador to Belgium under Gregory XVI. Though Pius IX had made him bishop of Perugia in 1846 and cardinal in 1853, he had been for years persona non grata at the papal court as a result of a deep and long-standing antipathy between him and Cardinal Giacomo Antonelli, secretary of state for most of Pius's reign. After Antonelli's death in the autumn of 1876, however, the way was clear for Pecci to appear more often in Rome. His talents, long hidden away in provincial administration, now quickly won him preferment. The office of chamberlain was, and is, one of the most powerful in the Church. Among other functions, this prelate, who is always a cardinal, is the interim administrator of the entire Church during a vacancy of the papal chair. On September 21, 1877, Pius IX appointed Pecci to the office.

Toward the end of January, 1878, it became very clear that Pius IX was at the end of his reign; indeed, one Roman paper already had published an erroneous notice of his death. The pope was able to give a public audience on February 2, but, on the following day, he could stand and take a few steps only with assistance. But by the night of the sixth, he was feverish and slightly delirious. On the morning of the seventh, he suffered a brief attack of fever after which he regained his full faculties; but, by this time, the physicians in attendance on him confirmed his own sensations, which indicated his last day. During the course of the morning, the pope was visited by numerous cardinals and prelates. At noon, the pope sent for Cardinal Bilio, so that he could begin his recitation of the prayers for the dying. When the cardinal reached the prayer which begins "Depart, Christian soul," Pius spoke his last words in a firm, strong voice, "yes, depart." Almost immediately afterward the final agony began and, at 5:40 P.M., the pope was dead. The old ceremony of tapping the pontiff's forehead three times with a silver hammer, while calling out his baptismal name, recounted frequently in tales of the deaths of popes, had not been used since the passing of Clement X in 1676; rather the veil covering the face of Pius was lifted three times as Pecci softly said, "Giovanni, Giovanni, Giovanni." After this the chamberlain retired to his own quarters to inspect the documents discovered by his staff and to issue orders that the first general congregation of cardinals would be held on the following morning.

The conclave opened formally on Monday, February 18, at thirty-five minutes past five, when the secretary of the Sacred College, Monsignor Pietro Lasagni, announced "extra omnes," the signal that everyone who was not to be immured must leave. This conclave was the largest one held thus far in the history of the Church, not because there were sixty electors—other conclaves had seen as many—but because the staff of cooks and servants were for the first time included within the conclave walls. In spite of this, and the confusion that was engendered by the fact that this was the first papal election to be held in the Vatican in more than a century, security was perfect. Not a few of those present were impressed by the excellent job done by the chamberlain in preparing the conclave so swiftly.

The actual voting began at eleven on Tuesday morning, and was concluded in an hour. One cardinal had not sealed his ballot at all, and another had used his personal signet for that purpose, so that his coat of arms was stamped visibly on the paper. Nevertheless, in spite of the automatic voiding of the ballot, it was decided to announce the results, to give the College a chance to see if any pattern was emerging. Pecci had received only nineteen votes.

Nevertheless, Bartolini's skill gradually, ballot by ballot, advanced Pecci's candidacy. Wednesday, February 20, 1878, dawned clear and surprisingly warm in Rome. The cardinals had hot chocolate or cafe-au-lait and then made their way, in various states of exhaustion, to the Pauline Chapel where Mass was said at eight o'clock. Afterwards, sixty of them went to the Sistine to begin preparations for the morning scrutiny, which nearly all concerned believed would be the last.

During the counting of the ballots which followed, a ripple of chuckles ran through the chapel when the scrutators read one which was marked "for no one." As the enumeration continued, the chamberlain stood silently at his throne, staring straight ahead. At the conclusion, he had received forty-four votes, three more than the number necessary for election, and the scrutators concluded their work by announcing, "Pecci—electus." Pecci rose, and silence fell in the Sistine. "Since God wills that I assume the papacy, I will not contradict." Di Pietro continued, "By what name will you be known." "That of Leo XIII, out of the deference and gratitude I have always had for Leo XII and the veneration of Saint Leo I have had since my youth," responded the new pope. It was just a few minutes short of one o'clock.

The reign of Leo XIII had begun. When it ended, a quarter century later, Gioacchino Pecci had led the Church firmly, with clear and measured steps, into the modern world, while raising the spiritual prestige of the papacy to a height it had not enjoyed perhaps since the thirteenth century. His reign, second in length only to that of Pius IX in the history of the Church, fully justified the confidence and enthusiasm of Domenico Bartolini, the Roman peasant boy risen to cardinal, who was chiefly responsible for engineering Pecci's rise.

Leo was one of the outstanding popes in the Church's history, but the conduct of the conclave after his death was marred by several political and procedural blunders which virtually suspended, for more than a decade, much of his forward-looking policy of political modernization.

Pius X (1903)

As in 1878, the Sacred College had ample time to consider their duty of election while Leo yet lived. By the early spring of 1903, it was evident that the ninety-three-year-old pope had but a short time to live. Throughout the next several months, Leo was well aware that preliminary negotiations among the cardinals over the choice of his successor were under way. In June, a substantial number of cardinals, prompted by a rumor that the pope was near death, hastened to Rome. Leo used the occasion to summon a general consistory on June 22 at which seven new cardinals were named. At the outset of this session Leo glanced over the assembled College and grimly remarked, "Dear brethren, I am happy to announce to this consistory which I have summoned that this is to be a consistory, and not a conclave." Nevertheless, the pope's pale, emaciated form and his feeble voice gave every indication that the reign soon would end.

During his pontificate Leo gave no hint to the cardinals of his own choice for a successor, but his complex conciliatory political policy, which seemed everywhere successful in raising the popular estimation of the papacy, was administered during the last decade and a half of the reign by one of the ablest of modern cardinal-secretaries of state, Mariano Rampolla del Tindaro. By 1903 the forty-nine-year-old Sicilian, who had once been papal ambassador to Madrid, was generally regarded as the logical choice to follow in the footsteps of Leo.

By late June, the pope was growing visibly more feeble day by day, and quiet but active preparations began for the coming conclave. On July 3, the Vatican's semi-official newspaper, *Osservatore Romano*, published a notice that all the pope's audiences and receptions had been abandoned; this statement was interpreted by many members of the College as the signal to begin preparing for a journey to Rome. On the following day, public word was issued that the pope was indeed seriously ill. On Tuesday, July 7, Luigi Oreglia di Santo Stefano, the dean of the College, ordered that telegrams be dispatched to all the absent cardinals asking them to prepare for the conclave.

In spite of every expectation, Leo held on to life with a serenity and an exercise of will that passed the imaginations of those about him. Several crises during the next two weeks were overcome successfully, and some began to voice the hope that the pontiff might recover. But his strength was exhausted, his constitution shattered, and at 2:45 P.M. on Monday, July 20, he suffered a heart attack which heralded the end. A few minutes before four o'clock, the majordomo of the palace, Gaetano Bisleti, bent over Leo and asked for a blessing. The pope, lucid still, raised his arm in benediction and quietly said, "This is the end," after which he sank back and lost consciousness. It was four o'clock. Four minutes later, without any disturbance at all, he was dead.

Sixty-two of the sixty-four cardinals were in Rome when the conclave formally opened on July 31. Only Pietro Celesia, the decrepit eighty-nine-year-old archbishop of Palermo, and Patrick Francis Moran, the Irish-born archbishop of Sydney, Australia, were absent. Celesia was too ill to leave his palace; Moran was still at sea on his ten-thousand-mile voyage to Rome.

When they arose on the morning of the first of August, the cardinals attended Mass together, after which they had a small breakfast and then entered the Sistine and conducted the first ballot. Mariano Rampolla del Tindaro received twenty-four votes, Girolamo Maria Gotti received seventeen, and Giuseppe Melchiore Sarto, the almost unknown patriarch of Venice, five. At the conclusion of the count, Sarto turned to Lecot, who occupied the adjacent throne, and remarked on his five votes: "They are amusing themselves with my name."

When the cardinals assembled in the Sistine for the afternoon voting, every aspect of the procedure went smoothly. The results for the favorites were: Rampolla, twenty-nine; Gotti, sixteen; and Sarto, ten.

The night of August 1 passed quietly in the conclave, for only one man knew that he would, in the morning, explode a political bombshell that would halt Leo's policies for a decade and bring about a stunning coup for Oreglia and the conservatives. That man was Cardinal Jan Puzyna de Kozielsko, and the bombshell was the specific exclusion of Rampolla from the throne by the Emperor Franz Josef.

The *jus exclusivae*, or right of exclusion, traditionally claimed by Spain, France, and Austria, developed in the sixteenth century when Philip II unofficially informed the cardinals, in several of the conclaves during his long reign, of candidates he found unacceptable. The cardinals of his time, in acceding to his wishes in his self-proclaimed role as protector of the Catholic Church, established a dangerous precedent by tacitly recognizing Philip's right to a voice, however indirect, in the choice of a pope. After Philip's death in 1598, no more was heard of any "right" to exclude a cardinal from the papal throne for almost half a century until, in 1644, Philip IV of Spain revived the pretensions of his grandfather by opposing Cardinal Giulio Sacchetti, a trusted confidant of the recently deceased Pope Urban VIII. Eleven years later, in the next conclave, Sacchetti was again excluded by Spain. On both occasions, many cardinals were troubled by this interference and appealed to their more theologically minded colleagues for opinions on the validity of Spain's actions. In 1655, the Spanish Jesuit, Cardinal Juan de Lugo, wrote a dissertation on the subject while the conclave was still in progress. In it, he affirmed Spain's right to the veto. Apparently, few in the conclave cared that the skilled theologian was a Spanish subject himself. By the end of the century, France had risen to the position of international prominence enjoyed by Spain in the time of Philip II. The French monarch, Louis XIV, expected to receive the same consideration for his wishes as had been granted to former Spanish kings. At the same time, the German emperor was not to be upstaged by either of his southern neighbors, and likewise advanced a claim to the "right of exclusion." Since these three monarchs represented the bulk of the political power that was in the hands of Catholic sovereigns, the members of the College silently agreed to the right of veto being in the hands of these monarchs, and, in 1721, it was formally exercised in writing for the first time, when Cardinal Michael Friedrich von Althaan notified the conclave that the Emperor Charles VI opposed the elevation of the cardinal-secretary of state of Clement XI, Fabrizio Paolucci de' Calboli, although the latter had, at that time, received only fourteen votes out of fifty-eight cast. During the next century and a half, the "right of exclusion" was invoked five more times; by Spain in 1730 and 1830, by Austria in 1800 and 1823, and by France in 1758. Whether the *jus exlusivae* was a valid right or not, it is the case that no cardinal who was subjected to the exclusion ever rose to the throne. In 1878, it was known that Cardinal Luigi Bilio was opposed by both France and Austria but, as he specifically excluded himself from consideration for the throne before the conclave ever began, both of the cardinals who were entrusted with their master's vetoes kept silent. By 1903, most members of the College did not give the prospect of a veto very much thought. Though the *jus exlusivae* was not mentioned, as such, in the legislation of Pius IX concerning the possible coercion of the cardinals, they considered that the legislation banished the question forever. The key error was, of course, that Pius, and some earlier popes as well, had not specifically abolished the "right of exclusion" in their general electoral pronouncements.

On the morning of August 2, the cardinals followed the same routine as they had on the first day of the meeting. Early in the day, Puzyna had drawn Oreglia aside and tried to present a written memorandum to the dean which contained the Emperor's exclusion. Oreglia realized at once what the College would think if he accepted the document officially—namely that he himself was launching an attack to prevent Rampolla's rise. And though stopping Rampolla was his highest ambition for the conclave, Oreglia foresaw that acceptance of the note might well bring about his greatest dread, a backfire of opinion that would lead to a Sicilian Leo XIV.

Following his rebuff by Oreglia, the Polish cardinal-prince then approached the secretary of the conclave, Monsignor Merry del Val, and asked him to take official receipt of the memorandum, but the newly appointed secretary was horrified at the thought and refused categorically to have anything to do with the matter. Puzyna then went to the Sistine, and when his colleagues arrived he began to read his statement aloud. In the conversation and confusion which accompanied the entrance of the cardinals, many could not hear the Pole, while others paid no attention. Puzyna raised his voice considerably, and a sudden silence pervaded Michaelangelo's room as the stunned College listened to the text of the note Oreglia had rejected: "I consider it an honor to have been called by highest command to this commission, to inform Your Eminence, as dean of the Sacred College of the most eminent cardinals and chamberlain of the Holy Roman Church, so that Your Eminence may become aware of, and deign to note in an official manner, in the name and by the authority of His Apostolic Majesty, Franz Josef, Emperor of Austria and King of Hungary, that he wishes to use the ancient rights and privileges of exclusion against my most eminent lord Cardinal Mariano Rampolla del Tindaro."

In the welter of voices which rose following this reading, Oreglia stepped forward and clearly announced, "This communication is not accepted by the conclave in any official manner. No cardinal is to give any consideration whatever to this 'veto' and all are to continue to vote their conscience." Rampolla himself then rose to speak, "I regret that a grave attempt has been made in the matter of a pontifical election against the liberty of the Church and the dignity of the Sacred College by a lay power, and therefore I protest it energetically. As far as my humble person is concerned, I declare that nothing more honorable nor more pleasing to me could have happened."

A blow had been struck against Rampolla's candidacy which assuredly doomed it to fail. Franz Josef, the patriarch of Europe's monarchs and a general supporter of the Church, could not be ignored. Some thought the action of the Austrian emperor was taken upon the request of the Italian government, others thought that Kaiser Wilhelm II might have importuned Vienna for the exclusion of Rampolla. Not one cardinal was sure what his position should be, but all of them knew the that the papacy of

Leo's chief servant would be compromised from its beginning, were he to be elevated.

The hurried switching of votes, because of the change in conservative orientation, was quickly revealed in the morning ballot. Rampolla had twenty-nine votes; but Sarto now received twenty-one.

When the cardinals were assembled for the second scrutiny of the day, they found themselves confronted by Cardinal Louis Adolphe Perraud, the bishop of Autun, who delivered a vigorous tirade against the veto of Rampolla from the middle of the chapel, but his remarks were greeted with silence, and nobody rose to second his opinion. Delayed far past the scheduled hour by the unexpected events of the day, the count was not completed until nearly six thirty. Rampolla now had thirty votes and Sarto received twenty-four.

This ballot marked Rampolla's high tide—but all were convinced that it stood as much for sympathy as for hope. Sarto was nonplussed. After springing from ten to twenty-one votes in the morning scrutiny, he now added three more; and he was the only candidate whose strength was growing from vote to vote. At the end of the count, he turned to Lecot and said in Latin, "My election will be the ruin of the Church." Later, he wandered around the chapel, almost in a daze, saying to various cardinals, "God knows that I am not worthy of the papacy and not fitted to the enormous task; give your vote to someone else. . . . I am not worthy . . . I am not capable . . . forget me." Clearly, he had become panic-stricken. This was no pose. Sarto was so frightened and overwhelmed that he broke down and wept publicly during the course of the evening. This exhibition did not deter the cardinals who supported him. Indeed, one or two who hesitated were now won to his cause by his unfeigned humility, including Anton Fischer of Cologne.

The first scrutiny on Monday, August 3, clearly revealed Rampolla with twenty-seven and Sarto with twenty-four. One cardinal wrote the word nemini on his ballot, a vote for no one. In the afternoon ballot, Sarto surged to thirty-five, while Rampolla's support declined to sixteen.

On Tuesday morning, August 4, after the usual preliminaries were over, produced the fully expected result: Guiseppe Melchiore Sarto had fifty votes, well more than the number needed to elect him; Rampolla had ten, and Girolamo Maria Gotti had two.

At the moment that the revisers announced the results of their search, the result became official. Oreglia, grim visaged as ever, moved to confront Sarto, asking him whether or not he accepted the election. Sarto quoted the words of Jesus in the garden of Gethsemane: "If this cup may not pass away from me, Thy will be done." The dean and chamberlain did not feel that a quotation of Jesus Christ met the constitutional requirements mandated by canon law, and asked again, bluntly and brusquely, "Do you accept?" and Sarto, barely audible, murmured, "I accept." At that moment, the other cardinals reached for the cords at the sides of their thrones so that only the one above number twenty-one remained elevated. Oreglia continued, "By what name will you be called," and Sarto replied, "In memory of the holy popes whose protection I need, and especially in memory of those who, in these latter times, have strenuously endured the persecutions against the Church themselves, I will be called Pius."

There was none of the outbreak of cheers and applause from the cardinals which had greeted the elevation of Leo XIII a quarter of a century before; the oppressive quality of the moment—Sarto's sadness, Oreglia's rudeness—prevented any of that. The cardinals simply went, one by one, to make their first obeisance to the new pope while the chapel doors were opened to admit the masters of ceremonies for the purpose of drawing up the document that ratified the election officially and burning the ballots. It was 11:45 A.M.

The epilogue to the election of 1903 saw the rise of Merry del Val to the position of cardinal-secretary of state, an office that he retained for the entire reign. On January 20, 1904, Pius promulgated the constitution *Commissum nobis* which specifically abolished forever the "right of exclusion." For all that Pius X occupies a special place in the history of the modern Church by reason of his great piety—he was canonized in 1954—the eleven-year reign was itself perhaps the least distinguished of any in the past century. The Romans themselves, almost at once, began to call their bishop "Pio Non Decimo" (Pius the Ninth the Tenth)—and the label got right to the heart of the matter. Pius X, like Pius IX before him, was simply incapable of dealing with the political, social, and intellectual problems of the Church in the modern world. He alienated diplomats, scholars, and governments alike with a conservative intransigence which began at once to reverse the extraordinary goodwill developed by Leo XIII.

The conclave of 1903 left no one happy, Sarto least of all, for of all the modern popes he least desired the throne and was acutely conscious of his own shortcomings. The progressives saw much of Leo's work compromised, especially in France; and the conservatives felt somewhat betrayed by Pius's silent acquiescence to an accommodation with the realities of life in twentieth-century Italy. The brilliant Rampolla was consigned to oblivion.

Benedict XV (1914)

The end of Pius X's life came suddenly and as a direct result of the outbreak of World War I. Pius, like a number of well-informed and prescient men in Europe, had foreseen the outbreak of a major war for several years. As early as 1911, he would often greet his secretary of state, Cardinal Raffaele Merry del Val, with the phrase, "Things are going badly, we shall not get through 1914." At the close of May, 1913, he received the retiring Brazilian ambassador, Dr. Bruno Chaves, and remarked to him, "You are fortunate in returning to your home in Brazil, so you will not be here for the world war."

When 1914 arrived, the pope felt the time of crisis approaching. On May 25, he held his final consistory, at which he created thirteen new cardinals. In his speech from the throne on that occasion, Pius once again spoke of the trend of the European powers toward war. On the afternoon of June 28, when news arrived of the assassination of the heir to the Austrian throne, Franz Ferdinand, and his wife, Sophie Chotek, at Sarajevo, the pope realized that the time had come. He went to his chapel immediately and remained in deep prayer, not just for the dead archduke and his wife, but for peace.

During the following month, he exhorted everywhere for restraint, but in vain. On August 2, the day after hostilities began, he made a universal appeal for peace, which had as little effect as his other efforts. Shortly afterwards, the Austrian ambassador called with a request for a papal blessing for the Austrian army. Exasperated, the pope told him sharply, "I do not bless war, I bless peace."

On the afternoon of Saturday, August 15, Pius had the first symptoms of a sore throat and decided to retire early. Members of the household sent for his two principal physicians, Ettore Marchiafava and Diomede Amici, but, after a brief examination, they concluded that the pope was not gravely ill and they expected his full recovery within a day or two. Pius continued to be ill during Sunday and Monday, however, though he did go to his study table in his bedroom from time to time to continue business.

On Tuesday the eighteenth, Cardinal Merry del Val was not feeling well himself and sent the urgent business of the secretariat of state to the pope in the hands of his principal assistant, Monsignor Nicola Canali. When Canali arrived in the pope's bedroom, Pius said to him, "Tell the cardinal to get well, for when he is ill, I am ill too." During the course of Tuesday, the pope occasionally seemed on the point of complete recovery and little fear existed when he retired for the night. When Pius did not call for his chaplain, Monsignor Bressan, at the usual hour on the morning of the nineteenth, the latter became worried and entered the bedroom on his own initiative. He found Pius in very great pain with a high fever. The doctors were immediately called and arrived to find the pope's lungs greatly congested. By eight o'clock, Merry del Val arrived. When he came, the doctors told him that Pius's condition was very grave indeed. At ten o'clock, Pius had a sudden crisis, and when Merry del Val rushed to the bed, the pope could only grasp his hands and, gasping, cry out, "Eminence . . . Eminence. . . ." The cardinal turned and ordered that Pius be given the sacraments of the dying at once. The pope, realizing his condition, whispered, "I resign myself completely." These were the last coherent words he spoke. At 1:15 on the morning of the twentieth of August, the reign came to an end as Pius quietly passed from sleep to death.

At the moment of Pius' death, the College of Cardinals had sixty-five members, twenty-one of whom had been elevated by Leo XIII and the remainder by Pius X. The circumstances facing the College were among the most difficult ever encountered. No one had any idea how, or if, all the cardinals could to come to Rome for a papal election in the state of war, even though Italy was still neutral. The worry became more acute when it was learned that the train on which the dean of the College, eighty-two-year-old Serafino Vannutelli, was returning to Rome was bombed by terrorists. Nine people were injured, but the first-class carriage on which Vannutelli was riding was undamaged.

While in 1878 and 1903 there had been ample time for the cardinals to test the waters regarding preferences for the throne, such was not the case in 1914. Many of those created earlier in the same year had not yet come to Rome to receive their red hats, and some were completely unknown in the curia. The College was completely unprepared to face a conclave in the opening days of the most devastating war thus far in the history of man. Many of the progressives had hoped, throughout Pius's reign, eventually to enthrone Rampolla, their defeated candidate in the election of 1903. They were now completely disorganized, since Rampolla had died on December 16, 1913—too early for the papacy and too late for those who supported his cause to fix their attentions on another. Moreover, the war overshadowed every other consideration, from the difficulty of English and French cardinals being shut up with their Austrian and German colleagues, to the weighty thoughts that each cardinal gave to the prospect that his country's enemies might triumph in electing a partisan as the next pontiff.

The morning of Monday, August 31, saw the formal beginning of the conclave. At 9:30, the Mass of the Holy Spirit was celebrated in the Pauline Chapel by Domenico Ferrata. This was followed immediately by the *monitio*, the formal address to the cardinals, delivered by the functionary charged traditionally with that task, the papal secretary of Latin Briefs to Princes; at this time it was Monsignor Aurelio Galli.

At five o'clock, after a short rest, the cardinals reassembled in the Pauline Chapel. The *Veni Sancte Spiritus* was chanted and the cardinals began to process to the Sistina, two by two. When the electors arrived, they found the chapel fully prepared for the conclave, ringed by sixty-five thrones with canopies, one for each member of the College, even though eight were absent.

At seven o'clock on the morning of September 1, the cardinals together attended a low Mass, said by Vincenzo Vannutelli, at which all of them received the Eucharist, except Cardinal Benedetto Lorenzelli, archbishop of Lucca, who was gravely ill and kept to his bed. At 9:27 A.M., precisely, the actual voting began. The tally showed two candidates leading with twelve votes each: Pietro Maffi of Pisa and Giacomo della Chiesa of Bologna.

The result was a decided set-back for the integrists at the very opening of the conclave, for no fewer than thirty-two votes out of the fifty-seven cast were for progressive cardinals. Of course, the first ballot of every conclave is a dress rehearsal. Each cardinal pays special attention to his role and his attitude, so as not to embarrass himself or invalidate the voting. Thereafter, with familiarity, the pace proceeds more swiftly. In 1914, the electors found their stride with great celerity. The second ballot, which began at 10:42, lasted only thirteen minutes. When the results were announced and tallied, the progressives could begin to feel somewhat easier in mind, as their favorites began to build up a substantial block of votes: both Pietro Maffi and Giacomo della Chiesa had sixteen.

In the first ballot, thirty-two votes had been given to candidates who clearly were anti-integrist in their thinking. In the second, that number had risen to thirty-six. The progressives were cheered, not only by the narrowing of the field of candidates but also by the increased support their cause was marshalling. The conservatives, meanwhile, could still count on enough votes to bar anyone from the throne who was not of their number, for their candidates had received a total of twenty votes—one more than the one-third necessary to prevent the election of a progressive.

Unlike the 1878 election, when conclavists carried on much of the inter-scrutiny campaigning, by carrying messages back and forth for their masters, the cardinals in 1914 kept every aspect of their political discussions in their own hands. The war raging outside and the constitution of Pius X ruling inside combined to make each elector much more cautious about revealing his convictions or intentions.

When the cardinals reassembled in the Sistine at five o'clock, there was an anxious quality to the meeting that was absent in the morning. Each cardinal surely wondered how the campaigning of the afternoon had affected the chances of the candidate he supported, or of his own opportunity. When it was over, Della Chiesa had eighteen and Maffi, sixteen.

The fourth scrutiny began at 5:45, after only a brief pause. When the results were tallied Della Chiesa now had twenty-one votes, while Maffi had dropped to fourteen. The progressives were moving slowly to unite behind one candidate.

Through the evening after supper, and on into the night, various partisans made efforts on behalf of all the major candidates. The thought uppermost in the minds of the integrists was to defeat the candidacy of Della Chiesa, no matter what they had to undergo, since he was the one cardinal in the College who represented most thoroughly the views and policies of Leo XIII and Rampolla—not only had he been the latter's able under-secretary for many years, but he made no secret of his admiration for his former master.

On the morning of Wednesday, September 2, the cardinals attended a low Mass celebrated by the sacristan of the conclave and then went to the Sistine for the fifth scrutiny, which began at 9:30. Within a half-hour, the scrutiny was over, and Della Chiesa had twenty votes, a loss of one.

At 10:15, the cardinals began the second scrutiny of the day. When the results were announced, Della Chiesa had recovered and moved forward to twenty-seven votes.

By the scrutiny at five o'clock in the afternoon, Della Chiesa's adherents had risen to thirty-one, and on the next ballot he gained another follower. But the conservatives, too, had united behind a single candidate, Domenico Serafini, who received twenty-four votes—only one waverer was left; he had voted for Agostino Richelmy. The conclave was now deadlocked!

As they left the Sistine for supper, the electors knew that they were facing some of the most dangerous moments in the history of the modern Church. Della Chiesa could not attain the thirty- eight votes he needed for election without the support of a few conservatives. The twenty-four supporters of Serafini likewise knew that, if they stood fast with him, they could block the election of any progressive—Della Chiesa or another. If both sides were unaltered in the morning, the fate of the conclave would be clear—either a complete dismantling of the current electoral coalitions followed by a new search for a compromise pope; or a long, bitter conclave which would only grow more polarized inside while Europe was being destroyed outside. In this frame of mind, each cardinal retired to his cell to consider his morning vote.

On the morning of the third of September, again the cardinals did their voting with haste—each desired to know if one of the opposing walls would crack. When the results were announced, the rift, small but critical, plainly was in view, for Della Chiesa now had thirty-four votes to Serafini's twenty-two—Richelmy still retained his one adherent. It seemed that it was the conservatives who were giving way, but would the erosion continue? The cardinals balloted a second time, at 10:21. Now their speed was feverish—the progressives hoped for a quick victory, while the die-hard integrists hoped to stall one more time to give them the opportunity for a last-ditch campaign before the evening scrutinies. In nine minutes it was over: Giacomo Della Chiesa, thirty-eight; Domenico Serafini, eighteen; Agostino Richelmy, one.

The archbishop of Bologna had obtained a majority of just two-thirds. The cardinals turned, to untwist the cords which controlled the canopies over their heads and lower them in the presence of the new supreme pontiff. But the agony was not quite over. A die-hard integrist, unknown today, demanded that the ballots be opened until the tellers verified that Della Chiesa had not voted for himself, which would have invalidated the scrutiny. Della Chiesa made no protest. He sat, cold and tight-lipped, on his throne while the tellers carried out the examination—the last insult he would ever endure publicly in his career. Falconio, Andrieu, and de Laï opened the ballots, one by one, until they found the new pope's—he had voted for Serafini.

Serafino Vannutelli performed his most solemn act as dean of the College of Cardinals. He stepped slowly before Della Chiesa, whose throne was the seventeenth from the altar on the right side. Firmly, he put the age-old question, and Della Chiesa replied that he accepted the election. The dean then asked by what name he would be known. Every new pope for a century and more had taken the time to briefly explain his reasons for choosing the name he did, but this time the reply was abrupt, "Benedictus"—Benedict the Fifteenth. The pope never did explain his choice, but many thought that he chose the name Benedict in honor of Benedict XIV, the last archbishop of Bologna before him to be elected pope. It was now a few minutes before 11:30 A.M.

The vantage of most of a century makes it possible to assess the conclave of 1914 somewhat better than many of its participants did. The six Austro-German cardinals were viewed collectively as the grand electors in the assembly, and so regarded themselves. Gustav Piffl noted in his diary: "Thus, thanks to our perseverance, we Austrians and Germans have succeeded in getting our candidate elected." But if Piffl thought that the efforts of the central European cardinals were to be rewarded with favoritism, he was mistaken. Benedict immediately replaced Merry del Val as secretary of state with Domenico Ferrata, the former nuncio in Paris, and when that cardinal died after only a month in office, Pietro Gasparri was chosen in turn. Thus, the new pope displayed, from the very outset of the reign, a sympathy for France, which belied the Germanophile feelings many French thought he had during the course of World War I. Benedict tried to steer an even, neutral course among the powers, even after Italy entered the war on the side of the allies. Perhaps his greatest public achievement was his seven point proposal for peace, issued on August 1, 1917. The ultimate failure of this proposal was engendered by the firm rejection of the United States, yet the most salient of Wilson's fourteen points derived from Benedict's document.

Benedict's reign saw a substantial diminution of integrist power in the Vatican. He replaced not only Merry del Val but also Nicola Canali and several other conservative members of the secretariat of state, and he began the difficult labor of winning back good diplomatic relations with many governments whose dealings with Pius and Merry del Val had been anything but cordial. Success followed these effects, and, by the end of the reign, the number of countries represented at the Vatican had risen from fourteen to twenty-six, including France.

Since Benedict was only fifty-nine when he came to the throne—one of the six youngest popes in the last two hundred fifty years (John Paul II, at fifty-eight, was another)—his contemporaries predicted a relatively long reign. Indeed, his three modern predecessors who were under sixty when they were elected, Pius VI, Pius VII, and Pius IX, had each reigned for more than twenty years. Such was not the case for Benedict, however. The trouble of his birth and his natural inclination to frailty endowed him with a delicate constitution, even though he always was healthy in adulthood. The essential strength of his constitution was sapped by anxiety and frustration caused by the war. Ultimately, Benedict XV, as well as Pius X, can be considered its casualty.

Pius XI (1922)

Unlike any of the three past reigns, the end of the pontificate of Benedict XV was heralded by several warnings; but no one, except perhaps the pope himself, appeared to notice. The first occurred late in November, 1921, when Benedict was forced to stand for more than half an hour in a cold and damp passage until a functionary could be found with the correct key to unlock a door. Within a day the pope had contracted a cold which seemed impossible for him to shake. By the time the pope gave the annual reception for Roman patricians, on Thursday, January 5, 1922, he was suffering from a wracking cough. When he left this reception, Benedict was overheard to remark, "A cough is the drum of death." One week later, at 6:30 on the morning of January 12, the pope said Mass in the Cappella Matilde for the students of the College of the Propaganda. Those who took communion from Benedict's hands noticed that they were hot and feverish. The address that the pope gave to the students was punctuated by seizures of violent coughing.

By the morning of January 18, the pope was unable to rise and spent the day resting. The following night passed easily for Benedict and, at 5:30 A.M. on Thursday, January 19, he received another visit from his physicians, who spent an hour and a half with him. At the close of this examination, the medical team emerged from the papal bedchamber with an optimistic report. Dr. Amico Bignami stated that "a few days in bed would completely restore the pope's health."

When he finally fell asleep that night, there was every expectation that the improvement in his condition predicted by the doctors would occur and that soon the full pontifical schedule would be met again. Like his predecessor, Pius X, Benedict's end was signalled by a crisis at night while he was alone, for when he awakened on Friday morning he had taken a dramatic turn for the worse; his gasping breath was audible to everyone who came near his door. At the conclusion of Mass, the pontiff expressed a strong desire to receive the last rites, and someone sent Agostino Zampini, the Augustinian titular bishop of Porfireone, the sacristan of the palace, to perform this office—just as he had for Pius X, seven and a half years before. Benedict also had asked for solitude to prepare himself for the final rite of the Church to which he had given his life. Those about him gave him these few minutes of peace, but Bishop Zampini did not have the opportunity of quietly doing his office as he had for Pius X, because by the time his little procession had reached the door of the bedchamber it had been joined by twenty cardinals. At the same time, the little antechamber next to the bedroom had filled with virtually every member of the diplomatic corps then in Rome. Cardinal Oreste Giorgi, the major penitentiary, began the final rites at 11:30. He began to read the profession of faith of the Council of Trent and then that of the First Vatican Council while the pope was being vested, over his night clothes, in rochet, pectoral cross, and stole. By this time, Benedict was too weak to sit up in bed and read the formula, so the profession was repeated, a few words at a time, and the pope thus had time to collect himself sufficiently to answer. After this, Giorgi pronounced a general absolution over his dying leader. As the bedchamber filled with cardinals, Benedict heard one of them say, "Holy Father, worry about nothing, but do just as your doctors tell you." Unable to identify the prelate who had spoken, Benedict, in a clear, firm voice, audible to all, replied, "If it pleases the Lord that I shall work again for his Church, I am ready; if he says, 'Enough,' let His will be done." He then turned to Cardinal Augusto Silj who, as Prefect of the Supreme Tribunal of the Apostolic Signature, was responsible for much of the daily office procedure at the Vatican in Benedict's time. To him the pope said, "I beg you to pray for me to the Virgin of Pompeii." Now the medical team came in for a brief check on how the pontiff was bearing up under the ceremonies of his death. Benedict was raised a little in bed, and his right hand laid upon a gilt-edged scarlet velvet cushion so that the cardinals could come forward singly and kiss his ring for the last time. Throughout the lengthy procession of cardinals, the pope seemed comatose, but when Merry del Val approached, he opened his eyes and said, "Alive or dead, pray for me."

After the members of the College had left, Gasparri returned and spent about twenty minutes in conversation with the pope. It was at this time that the cardinal-secretary of state took charge of the pope's will. Afterwards, Gasparri ordered telegrams to be dispatched to all of the forty-one cardinals who were outside Rome, directing them to prepare for their journey to take part in a conclave. Other messages that announced the pope's serious condition were sent to Vatican diplomats stationed around the world and to members of the Della Chiesa family in Genoa and Piacenza.

In the evening, Benedict received his nephews, Count Giovanni Persico, the son of his beloved elder sister, Giulia, and the Marchese Giuseppe Della Chiesa. He asked them for their prayers and was told in return that the whole world was praying for him. Later, Benedict overheard Dr. Battistini mutter, "Take me away, O Lord, but spare the pope." The pontiff turned toward him and said, "It is you who should go to bed. You are older than I. Go to bed." After another administration of oxygen and injections of camphor, the pope was able to rest somewhat more comfortably during the remainder of the evening of the twentieth, but at two o'clock on Saturday morning he was again awake, and requested viaticum once more. Bishop Zampini now performed the rite for which he had been sent on the preceding evening. After he received communion, Benedict seemed to regain some strength. But, after this short respite, the pope's condition worsened suddenly, and all visitors were dismissed. This crisis, shortly before dawn, left him gasping for breath and in intense pain.

Now the physicians held another consultation to determine if they should try any new measures to ease the pope's passing. At 7:00 A.M., Gasparri came out into the antechamber and said to those present that, in his opinion, death was near.

January 21 is the feast of Saint Agnes, patroness of the Capranica College, where the pope had studied in his youth. Remembering this, Benedict asked that a small statue of the saint, which had been presented to him by students at the College, be brought in and placed so that he might see it. He then gave short audiences to several cardinals, including Vincenzo Vannutelli, the dean of the College; Raffaele Merry del Val; and Camillo Laurenti, the junior member of the College. At eleven o'clock, Benedict asked that the new archbishop of Bologna, Giovanni Battista Nasalli-Rocca di Corneliano, be brought to him. After a time, they were joined by Ersilio Manzani, bishop of Piacenza, for whom the pope also had asked.

Suddenly, a few minutes after noon, the pope suffered a complete relapse. The visitors were hastened away and their place taken by Benedict's doctors. As the pontiff sank into delirium, Dr. Battistini tried to listen to his heart rate, but Benedict strenuously resisted any further handling by the doctors—"I am tired, I am tired, leave me alone. I want rest, I want sleep."

At two o'clock, Benedict suddenly threw back his covers and began to rise, announcing that he intended to resume work, that he had so much to do. Some considerable force was necessary to persuade him to stay where he was. Shortly after this, his delirium became worse but, at about four o'clock, he regained lucidity once more. At this time, Dr. Battistini told him directly that the coming hours would be his last. Benedict's reply was fully in keeping with his life's dedication, "Willingly do we offer our life for the peace of the world." He then sank down on his pillows, from the slight rise he had made while he addressed Battistini, and called for Fra Celidonio, his male nurse. He told the latter that Cardinal Antonio Vico would say the next Mass at the little portable altar, in place of the major domo of the palace, Monsignor Riccardo Sanz de Samper, who was ill. Under no circumstances, continued the pope, was the major domo to be awakened in the morning, for this would cause him to lose the rest he needed to regain his health.

Gradually, the pope's vital signs grew weaker. He drifted off into a fitful sleep. During the course of the evening there was no sudden change in the pope's condition, but it was clear that his struggle was drawing to a close. At about eight o'clock, he awoke and turned to his nephew, Giuseppe, to ask if prayers were really being offered for him. "Not only in Rome, but in all the churches in Italy and the world," was the reply. Again the pope closed his eyes, but at eight thirty he spoke to Nasalli-Rocca, who was standing nearby, "It's too late for you, go to bed." About an hour later, he attempted to rise once more but was restrained gently. Unexpectedly, he then asked what time it was. When he was told that it was nine thirty, he replied, "Well, there is plenty of time before six o'clock." This response was ascribed to another attack of delirium at the time, but later it would achieve great significance for those who had heard it. At 11:15, Benedict made one final effort to rise and, when he sank back, he entered a motionless state which persisted, with one moment's exception, to the end.

Shortly after midnight, Monsignor Migone said another Mass in the antechamber, but this time Benedict paid no heed to the service. At about one in the morning, Dr. Battistini came in and, glancing at the pope, came out at once to tell those clustered about the door that the end had nearly come. By two o'clock, Benedict's face had become waxen, his nose seemingly even more pointed; his mouth had dropped open and the death rattle could be plainly heard throughout the room. Giorgi stepped forward, and, shouting, so as to penetrate the closing curtain of life, cried, "Holiness, bless your relatives." A barely perceptible movement of the right hand could be seen. Again Giorgi shouted, "Holiness, now bless your household." And again there was a slight motion of the hand. Now Giorgi cried, "Holiness, bless the people who desire peace." With a sudden, convulsed jerk Benedict rose to a half-seated position—eyes wide open—and, in a voice which contained the last of his strength, he cried out, "May the blessing of Almighty God, Father, Son, and Holy Spirit, descend on you now and remain forever," as he slowly and deliberately traced the sign of the cross in the air three times in a grand benediction. His whole constitution was now exhausted, and he collapsed backward in a completely moribund state, while the others in the room tried to regain their composure after this splendid moment.

In the room were gathered both of Benedict's nephews, the four doctors, Gasparri and several other cardinals, Nasalli-Rocca, Zampini, and the faithful Migone. They stood and watched the pope's breathing become shallower and more irregular until, at six o'clock, the very hour he had mentioned earlier, Benedict gave a great sigh. Dr. Bignami leaned forward and held a candle near the lips of the pontiff. The flame did not flicker.

A few moments later, Gasparri reentered the bedroom clad in the purple robes of the chamberlain of the Church. While the other cardinals, robed in black, stood clustered around the bed, Gasparri raised the veil which had been placed over Benedict's face and, trembling, called out the dead pope's Christian name three times. He then turned and pronounced the pope truly dead.

Gasparri now began to put into motion steps leading to the holding of the conclave. At the moment of Benedict's death, the Sacred College consisted of sixty-one members, but, on the morning of January 23, the archbishop of Toledo, Enrique Almaraz y Santos, died in his residence at the age of seventy-four, reducing the number of potential electors to sixty. Shortly afterward, the staff of the archbishop of Santiago de Compostella, José María Martín de Herrera y de la Iglesia, at eighty-six the oldest cardinal, announced that their master was too infirm to make the journey to Rome.

The conclave began on Tuesday, February 2. At 9:30, Vannutelli chanted the Mass of the Holy Spirit. After this, Monsignor Aurelio Galli, secretary of the Roman Rota, delivered the election allocution, just as he had done seven years before. At four in the afternoon, the cardinals assembled in the Cappella Paolina. All but one of the fifty-three cardinals in Rome attended—Niccolo Marini, still suffering from an attack of influenza, was assisted by his aides directly into the conclave's precincts and put to bed. The Veni Sancte Spiritus was intoned and the electors then marched to the Sistine to take the oath to preserve the inviolability of the conclave.

By six the next morning, the members of the College were awake and preparing for the day's events. They had their choice of saying Mass themselves or attending another service and receiving communion there. After Mass, the electors assembled in the Sistine for the first and second ballots of the election. Only fifty were present, since Marini was still abed with influenza and Pompilj and Bacilieri stayed away with colds. After the selection of the scrutators, infirmarians, and tellers, the cardinals cast their first vote, and once the infirmarians had collected the votes of their three ill colleagues, the ballots were counted—revealing that the division between the integrists and the progressives had grown no narrower during the pontificate of Benedict XV. The two principal conservative candidates, Raffaele Merry del Val and Pietro La Fontaine, had gathered sixteen votes, while the two main liberals, Pietro Gasparri and Pietro Maffi, commanded eighteen. Among the seven others who received votes, Achille Ratti, the archbishop of Milan, had four. The cardinals then repeated their task, with the result that Raffaele Merry del Val now had eleven votes, while Maffi, Gasparri, and La Fontaine each had ten. Ratti was just behind with nine.

Still a deadlock was looming—twenty solid progressives in the Gasparri-Maffi column and twenty equally solid integrists who supported Merry del Val and La Fontaine. At 12:30, it was over, and the papers burned.

The cardinals adjourned for a midday meal, having agreed to reconvene at 3:30 for the third and fourth ballots. The afternoon's voting produced little substantive change, except that Ratti's followers seemed to be abandonning him, leaving him with only six votes on the third ballot, and five on fourth. By five o'clock, the papers were ready to be burned.

The discussions among the cardinals during the evening are lost in detail but recoverable in substance. It was becoming obvious that a deadlock, similar to that in 1914, would soon be reached. So certain was this that Gasparri sent word that an additional 120,000 lire were to be raised from Church holdings to purchase more provisions for the conclave. Among the conservatives, the falsity of the rumor about La Fontaine's family was learned, and several of those who had abandoned his cause decided to return to his support once more. For the liberals, there was encouragement in the rising tide in favor of Gasparri, and Pietro Maffi's loyalists were pressed urgently to swing to the chamberlain's side, in the hope that a united front on the next ballot might bring the election their way, much as the united progressives had brought about the election of Della Chiesa in 1914.

At 9:30 on Saturday, Mass was held for the electors and was followed by the first ballot. The three cardinals who had been too ill to participate publicly on the day before were now at their thrones, so all the electors were present finally in the Sistine. When the tellers had finished announcing the results of the voting, the products of the previous evening's campaigns were to be seen. All but six of the convinced progressives had now fallen into line behind Gasparri. Five liberals still held with Ratti and one with Maffi. Gasparri's own vote now stood revealed in spite of the official secrecy. He had voted for Ratti, since a vote for himself might have invalidated the scrutiny and he was known not to favor Maffi. The integrists displayed considerable confusion in their ranks, perhaps because of the slander of La Fontaine. When the results of the sixth scrutiny were tallied, Pietro Gasparri had twenty-four votes, the conservative Pietro La Fontaine had thirteen, while Ratti's total fell again to four. Gasparri had now gained the last of Maffi's adherents and had managed even to detach one of Ratti's group—the liberals were beginning to run a strong tide.

When the cardinals reconvened at 3:30 for the seventh ballot, the deadlock had been reached. Pietro Gasparri had twenty-four votes and Pietro La Fontaine had twenty-two. Only one vote remained to Raffaele Merry del Val, who had withdrawn his candidacy officially in favor of La Fontaine. Ratti kept his stalwart four, while Gaetano Bisleti and Camillo Laurenti each received one.

The orientation of twenty-eight liberals to twenty-five conservatives was maintained, but La Fontaine had emerged definitely as the unifying integrist candidate. Gasparri's support had peaked. At the worst, a few of the integrists had thought he might get Ratti's votes at last, but this had not happened. Grimly, the cardinals moved to conduct the eighth scrutiny, the last of the day. The results contained a small but sharp surprise: Pietro

Gasparri still had his twenty-four followers, but La Fontaine had lost a vote to Ratti, who now had five adherents. Three others had received one vote each: Gaetano Bisleti, Basilio Pompilj, and Camillo Laurenti.

Merry del Val's last holdout had moved to the column of another arch-conservative, Pompilj. Otherwise, the results seemed the same—except that Ratti had gained a vote at the expense of La Fontaine, at a moment when minority candidates were supposed to fade! This almost impercepti-ble gain gave several of the cardinals considerable room for thought during the following evening and night.

After all, wasn't Ratti, well, rather harmless. He had been a librarian for years, first at the Ambrosiana in Milan and then at the Vatican, before Benedict had chosen him suddenly to be the envoy to Poland; his job there had been rather successful without raising too many hackles, though his nunciature had ended under something of a cloud, because of internal Pol-ish passions. Benedict had extricated him neatly from an impasse by mak-ing him a cardinal on June 13, 1921, and giving him Milan as an archiepis-copal seat. Ratti was thought to be somewhat progressive, but then who knew much about his views at all, at least in detail. He might make the ideal candidate, though he was the junior cardinal-priest in the College. Then, also, some liberals may have considered, he is the candidate who re-ceives Gasparri's vote and, therefore, he must be quite acceptable to the chamberlain. Ratti was perhaps the man to prevent the election of 1922 from strangling on its own politics.

The fruit of these thoughts showed themselves in the ninth ballot, the first held on the fifth of February: Pietro Gasparri, nineteen; Pietro La Fon-taine, eighteen; Achille Ratti, eleven; Basilio Pompilj, one; Camillo Lau-renti, three; and Oreste Giorgi, one. The results of the next ballot showed the liberals moving firmly to Ratti: Pietro Gasparri, sixteen; Pietro La Fon-taine, eight; Achille Ratti, fourteen; Camillo Laurenti, five; Oreste Giorgi, one; Gennaro Granito Pignatelli di Belmonte, eight; and Donato Sbarretti, one.

La Fontaine's sun seemed to be setting and Ratti's rising as the cardi-nals watched the morning's ballots and tallies being burned. To Gasparri, who well knew Ratti's views, the result was quite satisfactory even though his own candidacy was foundering.

During the recess, Gasparri worked actively but quietly in Ratti's favor, becoming, in the process, the grand elector of 1922. By the next vote, at 3:30, the French had joined the Poles in their support for the Milanese archbishop, and several others from among the chamberlain's adherents were ready to switch, though four were said to favor La Fontaine now. The results of the eleventh ballot exhibited a strong turn to Ratti, although the conservatives had rallied once more behind La Fontaine: Pietro Gasparri, two; Pietro La Fontaine, twenty-three; Achille Ratti, twenty-four; and Camillo Laurenti, four.

The cardinals proceeded to vote again, and then anxiously awaited the tally to see if Ratti could gain any further support from the conservatives or whether the election would founder now on a Ratti–La Fontaine crisis as it had done on the Gasparri–La Fontaine block. The results were: Pietro Gasparri, one; Pietro La Fontaine, twenty-two; Achille Ratti, twenty-seven; and Camillo Laurenti, three.

As the cardinals left the Sistine for their supper, most of them knew that Ratti was about to emerge as the fully acceptable alternative. If the conservatives could be won over, even vote by vote, as had been done by Della Chiesa at the war's start, then Ratti's eventual enthronement was certain. The negotiations among the cardinals that night went on at a more feverish pace than at any time since the death of Benedict. A group of integrists proposed a last ditch rally behind one of their own, perhaps Laurenti, but their choice refused to have anything to do with the move.

In the evening, Merry del Val made one final effort to save the integrity of his bloc. He called upon Ratti in his cell and offered the whole of the integrist vote if only the latter would promise not to reappoint Gasparri as secretary of state. Ratti, realizing that such a bargain might gain him a throne but compromise a reign, curtly refused. Merry del Val was not the only visitor to the Milanese archbishop's cell that evening, however, and many other callers were far more pleasant. They came to meet and converse with the man many of them hardly knew but for whom they would vote in the morning. Ratti's conclavist, Monsignor Carlo Confalonieri, by 1978 himself the dean of the College of Cardinals, recorded his surprise at the stream of cardinals waiting on his master.

When the electors had assembled at 9:30 on the morning of Monday, February 6, the air was filled with expectancy, awaiting the conclusion of the meditations and negotiations carried on the night before. Merry del Val made no move to release his party and his command over them was now to be challenged to the fullest. The voting on the thirteenth ballot revealed a tide for Ratti running at the full: Pietro La Fontaine, eighteen; Achille Ratti, thirty; Gaetano de Laï, one; and Camillo Laurenti, four.

Ratti's cause had pulled together all the progressive votes as well as two of the integrists. Were the two conservative suffrages showing the way? The electors quickly prepared and held the fourteenth scrutiny. Would Ratti be able to win over six more integrists and achieve the throne? When the tally was finished the longest conclave in a century was over: Pietro La Fontaine, nine; Achille Ratti, forty-two; and Camillo Laurenti, two.

One by one, the cardinals lowered the canopies above their thrones until only that above Ratti's remained open. They gathered around the dean, Vincenzo Vannutelli, who was flanked by the archpriest and archdeacon of the College, Michael Logue and Gaetano Bisleti. Vannutelli stepped before the man who had received six more than the two-thirds majority of the votes. "Do you accept the election, canonically made, of yourself as sovereign pontiff?" asked the dean. Ratti composed himself for a moment, and replied, "It must never be said that I refused to submit unreservedly to the will of God. No one shall say that I shrank before a burden that was to be laid on my shoulders. No one shall say that I fail to appreciate the votes of my colleagues. Therefore, in spite of my unworthiness, of which I am deeply conscious, I accept." The cardinals immediately sank to their knees in the presence of the man who, but a few moments before, had been the least of them. "By what name will you be called?" continued Vannutelli. The new pope replied, "Under the pontificate of Pius IX, I was initiated into the Catholic Church and took the first steps in my ecclesiastical career. Pius X called me to Rome. Pius is a name of peace. Therefore, in the desire to devote my endeavors to the work of peace throughout the world, to which my predecessor, Benedict XV, consecrated himself, I choose the name Pius XI."

After a short pause, he continued, "I desire to add one word. I protest in the presence of the members of the Sacred College that it is my heart's desire to safeguard and defend all the rights of the Church and all the prerogatives of the Holy See, and, having said that, I wish that my first benediction should go forth as a symbol of that peace to which humanity aspires, not only to Rome and to Italy, but to all the Church and to the whole world. I will give my benediction from the outer balcony of Saint Peter's." The last of Pius's remarks stunned the cardinals of the integrist party. Not since 1870 had a pope shown himself from the exterior of the basilica, facing the capital of the Italian nation. This decision made all the little overtures of Gasparri insignificant by comparison. The new pontiff was revealing himself at once in a position far more progressive than any but the most liberal members of the College could imagine. At once, several of the conservative cardinals hastened to his side to expostulate and protest, almost violently. To Gaetano de Laï, with an air quite characteristic of the Trojan whose name he had chosen, he said sharply, "Remember, I am no longer a cardinal. I am the Supreme Pontiff now." The stalwart integrists were stunned into silence.

Pius then left his throne to enter the sacristy and don the best fitting of the three sets of papal robes that were held in readiness there. While awaiting the pope's return, Gasparri remarked to those near him, "It took four-

teen rotations, like the stations of the cross, to set the pope firmly upon
Calvary." When Pius returned, he received the first obedience from the
members of the College, after which he prepared to appear on the exterior
loggia.

A procession had been formed a few minutes earlier, and attendants had
gone forward to open the windows onto Saint Peter's Square and unfold a
large tapestry with the papal arms over the railing. The crowd outside,
having seen the white smoke from the burning ballots at 11:35, pressed forward. There was a sudden crush as several thousand people tried to enter
the basilica. They were certain that the first blessing of the new pope
would come from the interior loggia, just as it had for the past three reigns.

A considerable delay now ensued. Then Gaetano Bisleti, the archdeacon, appeared on the interior balcony and announced the election of Pius
XI in the age-old formula. When he was done, a prelate of the pontifical
household stepped forward and made the surprise announcement of the
location from which the pope would deliver his blessing. At once, there
was another convulsive shift in the mass of people, as those inside the basilica tried to regain the favored vantage points they had lost. Then the
bells of the basilica began to peal in honor of the new pontiff. Their sound
was soon being echoed by the bells of every church in the city. Then, to tu-
multuous cheers, Pius appeared on the exterior loggia of the great basilica.
With the peals of bells framing his voice, he delivered his first pontifical
blessing to tens of thousands of jubilant Romans.

At that moment a private train, provided by the Italian government, was
just coming to rest in the Rome station. As Cardinal O'Connell alighted,
he asked one of the prelates who had come to meet him the reason for the
peals. He was told that the ringing was a celebration for the election of the
new pope, Ratti. "Who?" roared "Number One in Boston." "Spell it." As
the surname of the new pope was spelled carefully for the American cardinal's benefit he fumed down the platform and into a waiting car for the
short drive to the palace—he was just one hour too late. When he arrived,
Pius received him at once. The purple face of one of the College's most
vigorous members told the whole story, and within a few days Pius issued
a papal rescript putting forward the time that was to elapse from the death
of a pope to the opening of a conclave from ten to fifteen days. No cardinal
from a distant shore would ever again miss a conclave.

Pius's appearance for his first blessing signalled not only the opening of
a new reign but also signalled a policy which would lead to an accommodation with the Italian government—finally accomplished seven years later
in the Lateran Treaties. Inside the Vatican, the shock of rapid changes was
not done yet. Pius proclaimed at once the reappointment of Gasparri as

secretary of state, without waiting the customary day or two. Gasparri thus became the first secretary of state to retain his office for a substantial period in two reigns; Merry del Val's work was completely undone.

Today, the reign of Pius XI—seventeen years, almost to the day—seems a little lost, a moment of rest after one global war and before the outbreak of the next. But his liberal reign did advance the progressive policies that had begun with Benedict XV, and he carried their spirit forward with others of his own. The retirement of Gasparri in 1930, after the Lateran Treaties had settled the "Roman question" and capped his career, opened the way for the rise of his most trusted lieutenant, Eugenio Pacelli, who served as cardinal-secretary of state during the last nine years of Pius XI's pontificate. The effect that Pacelli had, however, is best judged in terms of his own story.

II. "Ancestral Voices..."

As the mid-1930s approached, Pius XI began to grow weaker and his grasp of the daily management of the Church's affairs began to slacken. In June, 1936, the pope complained for the first time of increasing pain in his legs. This manifestation of pain and weakness at first surprised Pius, who had enjoyed robust good health for decades. In spite of his former profession of librarian, the pope had led a vigorous life before his election, with mountain climbing as his principal hobby. His occasional weakness for a good cigar and a glass of beer was all that disturbed an otherwise exceptional moderation in living. Yet he was now approaching eighty and the infirmities of age had begun to show.

Pius's summer vacation at Castelgandolfo, which he relished each year from 1933 onward, was prolonged in 1936, so as to give him some chance to regain his fading strength. With his return to the Vatican on October 1, Pius resumed his full schedule. Late in November his constitution began to show signs of severe strain, and by December 4 he was gravely ill. The central problem was a disturbance of his heart's rhythm, together with other myocardial difficulties which stemmed from advancing arteriosclerosis. The lessened circulation, together with the varicose veins which affected his left leg particularly, made it impossible for him to walk. A special movable bed was brought in at the pope's insistence so that he could continue working. Throughout the remainder of 1936, Pius remained very weak, but early in the following year he rallied and the improvement in his circulation allowed him to resume almost a full schedule.

Antonio Bacci, then secretary of Latin Briefs to Princes and later cardinal, had an interview with Pius at this time and congratulated the pope on his recovery. He reminded the pontiff that Leo XIII, who indeed had a frail constitution, had lived to be ninety-three. "Let us not pay useless compliments," rejoined the pope. "Do you know why so few live to be ninety?" Bacci, who had maintained an attitude of circumspect reverence to four popes, was lost for an answer. "Because they die sooner," continued Pius. Gradually, throughout 1937, cardiac insufficiency sapped what strength Pius had been able to regain during the earlier enforced rest. The pope had mentioned frequently that he hoped to be spared a long decline and a laborious death like that of Leo XIII, but this wish was not to be.

During the last period of the reign, Pius came to rely more and more on the exceptional abilities of his cardinal-secretary of state, Eugenio Pacelli. After he succeeded Gasparri, in 1930, Pacelli had been entrusted with increasing control over the Church's affairs, more indeed than any of his predecessors for some time past. Pius also ensured that Pacelli became well-known among both foreign cardinals and secular statesmen by sending him repeatedly on foreign missions which, in former reigns, were usually confided to lesser prelates. Visits to Buenos Aires in 1934, Lourdes in 1935, the United States in 1936, Lisieux in 1937, and Budapest in 1938, gave Pacelli a wider exposure to both the modern Church and current affairs than that possessed by any other cardinal of the age.

All of this program of contact and administration can be seen as Pius XI's deliberate effort to groom Pacelli as his successor. Already weak and debilitated to an extent few could have imagined two years before, Pius held his last consistory for the elevation of new cardinals on December 13, 1937. During his homily on that occasion, Pius broke from his prepared text, in which he had reminded the cardinals of his age and the likelihood that this consistory would be his last, to quote a line from the Gospel of John, "There stands one among you whom you do not know." Pius then abruptly continued with the remark of Jesus to Peter, "What is it to you, think only to follow me." This sudden comment on the succession surprised many in attendance and once he had returned to his apartment a number of the prelates asked to whom he had alluded. His ready answer, "To Cardinal Pacelli." Earlier, in 1936, during an audience for Monsignor Domenico Tardini, later himself a cardinal-secretary of state, Pius remarked on Pacelli's visit to the United States, "I make him travel so that he may get to know the world and the world may get to know him. . . he will be a splendid pope." And, in 1935, on Pacelli's name day, Pius had sent his secretary of state a present of a picture of the conferment of the primacy on Saint Peter. Accompanying the picture was the brief note, "Also as an augury for Your Eminence."

Pius moved officially to concentrate the administration of the Church in Pacelli's hands during the *sede vacante*. On April 1, 1935, he appointed Pacelli camerlengo; and on December 13, 1937, in the same consistory in which he delivered his remarks on the succession, Pius also ensured Pacelli's election as camerlengo of the College of Cardinals. This officer, who presides over the business affairs of the College as a whole, is normally an annual appointment, but Pacelli was continued in 1938 and 1939, as well.

In 1938, Pius continued to weaken steadily. The advance of his circulatory problems was accompanied by strong pain which was only partially eased by medication. During this period, the pope was acutely conscious of the rise of political tension in Europe. On September 28, the eve of the Munich conference, he broadcast on the Vatican radio an appeal for peace; but even after the agreement on the following day which seemed to defuse the present crisis, he was no longer to be persuaded that war was avoidable. In October, the injections of cardiac stimulants, which had been discontinued earlier in the year, were resumed. In spite of them, however, Pius suffered two heart attacks on November 25. At the same time there was a notable deterioration in his breathing because of his worsening cardiac condition.

Despite these events, the pope kept to his schedule. On December 18, for example, he participated in celebrations marking the third anniversary of the foundation of the Pontifical Academy of Sciences. His medical advisors, led by Professor Aminta Milani, urged him to lessen his activities, but Pius continued to reject their advice.

Throughout the Christmas season and into the following January, the pope continued to perform his customary schedule of business and ritual; but, by February 1, he was near complete exhaustion. In the evening of that day, one of his male nurses, Brother Faustino Giuli, as soon as he came on duty, was shocked by the signs of Pius's deteriorating condition. Dr. Milani was sent for immediately, and just as immediately ordered the pope to bed. On the following day, the pope participated in the rites of Candlemas; and, on the third, he attended ceremonies marking the fiftieth anniversary of the foundation of the Pontifical Canadian College, but for the most part he was persuaded to rest.

That Pius did not yet realize that his pontificate would end shortly was shown on the fourth, when he issued a summons to the entire Italian episcopate to attend a convocation on the eleventh to coincide with celebrations for the seventeenth anniversary of his coronation. The pope wished to use the occasion to announce a condemnation of the recent policies of Mussolini—a fact confirmed only in 1959 when the Vatican finally released the text of the pope's intended remarks. Also on the fourth, Pius held his last formal papal audience when he received the newly appointed Romanian ambassador, Dr. Nicolas Petresco Comnenius. He also had his last walk in the Vatican gardens. By that evening, the pope's pulse had sunk to forty, but genuine alarm was not evident immediately, in part because Dr. Milani was now himself bedridden with influenza and was not given news of this latest development.

Though he was not strong enough to celebrate mass on the morning of the fifth, Pius did receive communion, and then insisted on being taken to his study for the usual daily meeting with Pacelli. Following this, a group of schoolchildren who had won a local catechism competition was given an audience of about five minutes. After this the pope was once more put to bed.

Monday, February 6, was the seventeenth anniversary of his election. Pius spent it resting quietly, for no audiences had been scheduled on Mondays for some time. In the afternoon, he was examined by two new specialists, Dr. Filippo Rocchi and Dr. Luigi Bonanome, who detected signs of failure in the urinary tract, a new worrisome complication. His temperature had risen to 99.5. By Tuesday, Pius was yet weaker, and, although Pacelli was admitted to the bedroom for a brief business interview, the rest of the day's activities were cancelled. This sudden cancellation was the first real sign given to the public that the pope's condition was indeed serious. Pius insisted on being helped to a chair in his bedroom for a brief change of place, but most of his hours were spent either asleep or lying in bed while one of the chamberlains read to him.

During the following night, the crisis worsened further and the pope experienced some periods of delirium. In order to allay public concern, the Vatican announced on the seventh that Pius was only suffering from a slight cold. When some news of Pius's true condition reached the Roman populace, rumor took over, and, as is usual in such cases, the stories soon became far more alarming than the reality. The pontiff had gone insane; the College of Cardinals would have to become an extraordinary governing body after the pope's recovery; the pope was delirious constantly.

The *Osservatore Romano*, the Vatican's official news source, did little to quell popular fear and doubt on the morning of the eighth. It merely announced that Pius was resting to conserve his strength for the convocation of bishops on the eleventh. Throughout the day, the pope was visited periodically by Doctors Rocchi and Bonanome, who found his condition essentially unchanged. At five o'clock, he was once more put to bed after having spent some hours in his chair. At one point during the day, Pacelli asked Pius if it would not be wise to postpone the convocation to a later time, but the quick, clipped answer was no.

The following night seemed easy enough under the circumstances, even though he was able to get little, if any, sleep. Most of the night was occupied in alternating periods of prayer and rather spirited conversations with his nurse. The physicians' noon examination on the ninth showed a further marked deterioration. The evidences of more cardiac and arterial weakening were very strong, and vascular decomposition had reached an advanced state. The approaching end was now clear, the failing irreversible. Pius was now told at last that there was no hope, and in the afternoon the reporters at the Vatican were finally given the news.

At three o'clock, Pius asked those nearby to recite the rosary with him,

"We must say it now," he repeated several times.

Over the preceding several weeks, Pius had experienced greater and greater periods of intense pain generated by his ever-slowing circulation. On the evening of the ninth, his suffering jagged its way to a crescendo. During the day he had complained several times of intense pain in the region of his bladder, and at about four o'clock he suddenly went limp and fell back in bed while being examined by Dr. Rocchi. His pulse became so faint that the end seemed imminent. Dr. Rocchi at once administered a substantial injection of camphorated oil. Since such a medication, a powerful stimulant, could have caused an instant, powerful increase in the pulse rate and consequent sudden death, Dr. Rocchi had risked his professional career. Pius rallied, however, and began his final hours.

Dr. Rocchi soon came into the papal antechamber to announce that the pope had regained consciousness. Now came a visit from the last group of his staff to see him fully conscious. Pacelli was there, accompanied by his two principal assistants, Domenico Tardini and Giovanni Battista Montini. A few other members of the papal court were admitted, as was Pius's favorite nephew, Franco Ratti. At this time someone recalled that on the previous day the pope had asked his secretary, Carlo Confalonieri, to pray with him at the end. The prayer the pope chose was an old popular invocation. Now the time had come. Confalonieri began, "Jesus, Mary, and Joseph, I give you my heart, my mind, and my soul. Jesus, Mary, and Joseph, help me in my last agony. Jesus, Mary, and Joseph, may. . . ," the secretary gave way completely. Pius looked firmly at Confalonieri, and continued clearly, ". . . may I breathe forth my soul in peace with thee." They were the pope's last words. Shortly after nine, Pius had his last full medical examination, carried out by Doctors Rocchi, Bonanome, and Bianci-Cesar.

At ten o'clock the papal apartments were closed. The male nurse assigned for the night, Brother Pelagio, took up his station in the bedroom, while Dr. Rocchi slept immediately outside. Pius was no longer able to recognize those around him.

The final crisis began shortly after three in the morning of the tenth. For some time, Pius had been comatose but when the nurse noticed a change in the pope's breathing, he called Dr. Rocchi from the next room. Rocchi, responding to the almost nonexistent pulse, again tried injections of stimulants, but this time there was no rally from the aged and weakened body. Rocchi sent for the two papal secretaries, Carlo Confalonieri and Giovanni Venini, and told them that the end was near. The prelates then sent for Pacelli, Franco Ratti, and Cardinal Camillo Caccia Dominioni, the archdeacon of the College. Word also was taken to Dr. Milani, still ill himself, and he too sped to the Vatican.

The Cardinal Grand Penitentiary, Lorenzo Lauri, whose duty it was to administer the last rites to the dying pontiff, could not be found, so the papal sacristan, Monsignor Alfonso Camillo De Romanis, stood by the bed ready to perform the last ceremony for a dying Catholic.

At four o'clock, Vatican radio broadcast the first word of the approaching end to reach the outside world.

At 5:15, the doctor tried another round of stimulants, and now Pius briefly recovered some consciousness. Monsignor De Romanis began his solemn act, while to Pacelli, Pius's closest confidant and right hand, fell the duty of goading the pontiff into one last exercise of supreme religious power. "Holy Father, give us your blessing," called the Secretary of State. Struggling still, Pius began to mumble while his hand rose for a moment from the bed. It was hopeless, and at 5:31 it was over.

The rituals for the body now began. As candles were placed around the deathbed, Pacelli returned to his apartment to don his violet mozzetta and mantelletta. He then returned to Pius's bed, lifted the veil that had been placed over the pope's face, and called out his baptismal name three times: "Achille, Achille, Achille." He then turned and made the formal announcement that the pope was truly dead. At 6:38, the Campanone, the great eleven-ton bell of Saint Peter's, led the tolling that carried the news to the city. In the pope's private chapel, a few steps from the bed, Cardinal Francesco Marchetti-Selvaggiani, the Cardinal Vicar of Rome, began the first mass for the repose of Pius's soul. Monsignor Alberto Serafini, secretary of Apostolic Briefs, began drafting the death certificate for the signatures of Pacelli and the other cardinals at the Vatican.

Within a short time Pacelli, functioning now as camerlengo, since his post as secretary of state had lapsed with Pius's end, was in his office beginning the process of notifying the cardinals of the death and the coming conclave. Of the sixty-two formal messages to be sent, nearly all those to the thirty-five Italians could be delivered in Rome. Those to the curial officials, of course, but also those to Italian archbishops, since they had come for the convocation that would now never take place. Some of the twenty-seven non-Italian cardinals were also near at hand. Eugene Tisserant, the French prefect of the Vatican Library and secretary of the congregation for the Oriental Church, resided in Rome. Also in the city were Jean Verdier, archbishop of Paris; Jean Marie Rodrigue Villeneuve, archbishop of Quebec; and Francisco de Asis Vidal y Barraquer, the archbishop of Tarragona, who had been forced into exile as a result of the Spanish Civil War. The remaining twenty-three messages, however, ranged from the limits of Europe almost to the limits of the globe.

Of the twenty-seven non-Italian cardinals, the largest contingent was the French with six. Besides Tisserant and Verdier, there were three archbishops, Achille Liénart of Lille, Emmanuel Celestin Suhard of Reims, and Pierre Gerlier of Lyon, together with Henri Marie Alfred Baudrillart, the eighty-year-old rector of the Institut Catholique in Paris. Spain had two other archbishops, Pedro Segura y Saenz of Seville and Isidoro Goma y Tomas of Toledo. Germany had three archbishops, Adolf Bertram of Breslau, Michael von Faulhaber of Munich, and Karl Joseph Schulte of Cologne. With them now was Theodor Innitzer of Vienna, who was numbered very willingly among the Germans after the Anschluss. The other European nations with substantial Catholic populations had their traditional representatives: Joseph Ernest van Roey of Malines in Belgium; August Hlond, the Polish Primate; Justinian Georg Seredi of Hungary; Manuel Gonçalves e Cerejeira of Lisbon; Joseph MacRory of Armagh in Ireland; Karl Kaspar of Prague; and the Englishman, Arthur Hinsley. The Canadian Cardinal Villeneuve had five colleagues from the New World: William Henry O'Connell of Boston, the archpriest of the College; Dennis Dougherty of Philadelphia; George William Mundelein of Chicago; Sebastião Leme da Silveira Cintra of Rio de Janeiro; and Santiago Luis Copello of Buenos Aires. Completing the group was Ignace Gabriel Tappouni, the Melkite Patriarch of Antioch, who resided in Beirut.

While the non-Italians were not yet a majority in the College, they were the largest percentage of their kind who were able to participate in the election of a pope since the fourteenth century.

For most of them, the news of Pius's death came to their residences, but a few were found far from home. Cardinal O'Connell, now almost eighty, was enjoying a warm holiday at the Hermitage in Nassau when he received the news on the morning of the tenth. Deprived by distance of voting in 1914 and 1922, it was he who had persuaded Pius XI to extend the time for assembling the conclave from nine to at least fifteen days. Now he was ready. "Number One in Boston," who remarked, "God be with us and here goes for Rome," was fortunate to find the Cunard-White Star liner *Britannic* at Nassau, scheduled to depart at midnight for a two-day run to New York. He immediately booked passage and boarded the ship, abandoning many of his things, including his red hat. It was the beginning of the most momentous period in his life.

While O'Connell hastened to board the *Britannic*, Chicago's Cardinal Mundelein hurriedly collected his things from an interrupted Florida vacation, and within a few hours was safely ensconced in a Pullman northbound on "The Miamian." Mundelein—like Dougherty, who had the benefit of a leisurely drive from Philadelphia to New York—had booked passage on the great Italian liner *Rex*, which was scheduled to sail at noon on the twelfth. A floating palace, the 51,000-ton *Rex* had held the Blue Riband of the Atlantic for the fastest crossing in 1933, and, while no longer the fastest liner on the seas, she was to make Naples in seven days.

The Brazilian Cardinal Leme and the Argentinean Cardinal Copello were equally fortunate. They were both able to sail on the Italian Lines' *Neptunia*. Though only 20,000 tons, the *Neptunia* was the largest and fastest liner connecting Europe with South America. Copello boarded at Buenos Aires on the evening of the eleventh, while Leme embarked when the ship stopped at Rio on the sixteenth.

The *Neptunia* was due in Naples on March 1 and both South American cardinals were aware that a delay of even one day in their passage would cause them to miss the opening of the conclave.

Meanwhile, in Rome, the preparations for the election were going forward. The first general congregation of the College of Cardinals met at 10 A.M. in the Vatican, with thirty-one cardinals in attendance, under the leadership of the dean of the College, the Cardinal Bishop of Ostia and Albano, Gennaro Granito Pignatelli di Belmonte. He was one of only two cardinals who survived from the reign of Pius X, O'Connell being the other. Pignatelli, in spite of his eighty-seven years, pressed forward vigorously with plans and decisions. The first order of business was to listen to a reading of the constitution on the *sede vacante* and the conclave. Then Pacelli ceremonially broke the Fisherman's Ring, the signet of Pius XI. Before continuing with the arrangements for Pius's funeral and the election, the cardinals then received the whole delegation of one hundred seventy Italian bishops who had come to Rome for the now-cancelled convocation. After the bishops had expressed their condolences and departed, the congregation appointed Monsignor Arborio Mella di Sant'Elia, the papal master of the chamber, to be governor of the conclave. They next appointed a committee of three cardinal-deacons who were to supervise the physical arrangements of the conclave. The three cardinals, all Italian, were the sprightly archdeacon of the College, Camillo Caccia Dominioni, the grim Nicola Canali of the Holy Office, and Domenico Mariani. The next order of business was to set the timetable for the funeral ceremonies for Pius XI. The *novemdiali*, the nine days' rites, were to begin on Sunday morning, the twelfth. It was decided that the first six days of ceremonies would be followed by a short delay, with the last three to be held after the arrival of some of the more distant cardinals, so they could participate in the final ceremonies.

The cardinals then took up the question of the date on which the conclave would begin. Pacelli, who led the discussion, was at first anxious to begin at the earliest possible date so that the cardinals would be freed as soon as possible from outside political pressure in a time of world crisis. When it became clear that the two South Americans and O'Connell could not arrive in time, Pacelli withdrew from his earlier position. That this was, in part, because of his great respect for O'Connell is likely. The congregation agreed to postpone consideration of the starting date to a later session.

The *prattiche*, or informal preliminary negotiations among the cardinals, had already begun. For more than a century, no curial cardinal had been elected to the throne, so the earliest discussions centered around the heads of the great Italian archdioceses. There never was a serious question of electing a non-Italian pope, despite the lengthy columns which appeared in newspapers throughout the world discussing such a possibility. The Patriarch of Venice, Adeodato Giovanni Piazza, was too young at 54; and, at 58, Alfredo Ildefonso Schuster of Milan was not a very serious contender. In addition to a slight disability because of his youth, Schuster was thought to be both too close to the policies of Mussolini and too mystical. Giovanni Battista Nasalli-Rocca di Corneliano of Bologna, Alessio Ascalesi of Naples, Maurilio Fossati of Turin, and Luigi Lavitrano of Palermo, were thought to be marginal possibilities only. But the sixty-six-year-old Elia dalla Costa of Florence was another matter. Very ascetic in his daily life, dalla Costa had considerable pastoral experience and was known to view the liberalizing policies of Pius XI with some disfavor. At the same time, he was a vigorous defender of the rights of the Church in the face of Mussolini's recent incursions. The conservatives began to mention his name more and more often in their conversations.

The twenty-seven Italian cardinals in the curia were by no means unified, but the general trend among them was to share the ultraconservative views of Pius X and Merry del Val, under whom most of them had risen to positions of importance. Among these prelates there was talk of advancing the candidacy of one of the "Three Ms," Francesco Marmaggi, Luigi Maglione, or Massimo Massimi.

The last was a member of one of Rome's oldest princely families and could be relied upon to resist any pressure from the upstart Mussolini. Some recalled that when Napoleon had occupied Rome, he confronted an ancestor of the cardinal with the challenging question, "Prince, people tell me that your family claims to be descended from Quintus Fabius Maximus, the great consul. Is this true?" The Prince Massimi of an earlier time replied, just as abruptly, "General, people have been saying so for two thousand years, so there must be something to it!"

While these discussions continued, the Axis powers began a strong attempt to influence the choice of Pius's successor. Neither Hitler nor Mussolini was anxious to see Pius XI's later policies continue. Indeed, Mussolini escaped formidable papal condemnation only because of Pius's death. While few overt moves were made, it became clear that Fascism would prefer one of the more conservative members of the College, one unlikely to pursue the policies of social action which had characterized the last reign.

By Sunday morning, Pius's body had been moved into Saint Peter's for public viewing. Meanwhile, in New York, it was apparent that Mundelein's train would not arrive in time for the normal sailing hour of the *Rex*. The Italian Line announced that it would delay the departure of the liner for two hours while the Pennsylvania Railroad, over whose tracks "The Miamian" travelled from Washington to New York, cleared the northbound main line of all possible conflicting traffic and shortened or cancelled a number of stops. Mundelein's fellow travellers, some of whom gaped and grew angry as their stations whizzed by, were treated to a nearly non-stop run into Pennsylvania Station. At 1:15, the cardinal was met by a delegation of twenty of New York's Finest led by Police Commissioner Louis Valentine. The train had arrived twenty minutes early. Pausing just long enough to kneel and kiss Mundelein's ring, Valentine had the cardinal, his staff, and his luggage put into three cars and taken with sirens sounding to the pier on West Fifty-second Street. At 1:37, the cardinal was on board the Rex and the ship began to get underway.

The *Rex* now gone, O'Connell had to make the best plans he could while pounding up the coast on the *Britannic*. One plan had him sailing on the aged, but still splendid, *Aquitania* to Cherbourg and then travelling overland by train to Rome. This option was rejected, because it was thought that his health might not be able to withstand the long overland journey in Europe. Air transportation on the Continent also was rejected for the same reason. The Italian Line, by now becoming famous for accommodating cardinals, offered him passage on the 25,000-ton *Saturnia*, which was to sail from New York on the fifteenth. They agreed to arrange a meeting at Gibraltar with the *Neptunia*, so that the cardinal could transfer to the faster liner for a direct passage to Naples. This transfer was to be made because the *Saturnia* already had passengers booked for several intermediate stops in the western Mediterranean and the stops at these ports could not be cancelled. Boston's cardinal finally chose this program. When, on Monday the thirteenth, the *Britannic* reached New York, O'Connell also was met by a delegation of police—twenty-six of them under the command of a deputy chief inspector. They rushed him to the Plaza Hotel to await *Saturnia's* departure.

Also on Monday, the general congregation met again and decided to perform the interment of Pius at 4 P.M. on Tuesday afternoon. Achille Liénart, the first of the absent non-Italians to arrive in the Eternal City, was present at that meeting. The congregation received the hereditary prince-marshal of the conclave, Luigi Chigi-Albani della Rovere, who, speaking as Grand Master of the Knights of Saint John, delivered an address of con-dolence. Cardinal Pignatelli, in thanking the prince for his words, asked the Knights of Malta to pray for the gift to the papacy of a "saintly man." The rumors flew. Based on this slight remark, entirely appropriate to the occasion, it was said that the dean opposed the election of a curial cardi-nal. Also in this session of the congregation, the great leaden matrix of the pontifical seal was brought in by Monsignor Pietro Borgia and shattered in an ancient ceremony that had been created to prevent its misuse during a vacancy. Late that evening, three more cardinals arrived in Rome—Seredi, Hinsley, and Suhard.

On Tuesday the fourteenth, the last of the three public requiems in Saint Peter's began at ten o'clock. A half hour later, the general congrega-tion of cardinals met once more. With thirty-six in attendance, the cardi-nals appointed a second committee of three who were to examine the credentials of all those who were to be immured with the electors in the conclave. Federico Tedeschini, Giuseppe Pizzardo, and Domenico Jorio, like the earlier triumvirate, were all members of the curia. During this same session, the cardinals learned from the first committee that the cost for holding the conclave would approach one hundred thousand dollars. In consequence, a number of money-saving expedients were discussed. Cac-cia Dominioni's committee also announced that it had agreed to an earlier suggestion that Vatican radio be given the name of the new pope before the public announcement at Saint Peter's, so that the news could be broadcast internationally as soon as possible.

Soon after 1 P.M., the great doors of the basilica were closed and its staff began to prepare for Pius's entombment. Preceded by a procession of all the members of the papal household, thirty-seven cardinals came to wit-ness the late pope's last journey. The first part of the ceremony, which be-gan just after 4:30, included a recitation of the prayers for the dead and then a reading of the act of burial. Following this, ten of the *sediari*, the men who had the duty of carrying the pope's elevated portable throne, the *sedia gestatoria*, lifted the whole bier, moved it a few feet, and lowered it into the innermost of the three coffins. Then began a series of troublesome delays that lengthened the time planned for the burial. Pius's full comple-ment of pontifical robes were too long and bulky to fit into the coffin easily. His feet had to be raised and the robes folded back under them. After this, Antonio Bacci delivered a brief eulogy and then a copy of his text was

placed in a brass cylinder and put into the inner coffin together with the
traditional three bags of coins, one bag each of gold, silver, and copper;
each containing seventeen coins, one for each year of the reign. Pius's secretaries, Confalonieri and Venini, now came forward and covered the late
pope's face with a veil of white silk. A similar veil was placed over his
hands by Carlo Respighi, who substituted for Arborio Mella di Sant'Elia.
The latter was ill as well as burdened with his new office of governor of the
conclave. Finally, Cardinal Giovanni Battista Nasalli-Rocca di Corneliano
covered the body with a crimson pall. This duty fell to him as the senior
surviving cardinal elevated to the College by Pius XI.

Workmen now came forward to close the three coffins. The first, of
wood, presented no difficulty. After it had been tightly sealed, it was encir-
cled with three ribbons, which were sealed by Pacelli. When the bronze lid
of the second coffin was being sealed with solder, however, the workmen
ran out of the material and someone had to be sent out into the city to purchase more. After more delay, and the placing of ribbons around the
bronze casket, the third coffin, of lead, began to be closed. Now the cardinals made their way down into the crypt to the burial site. While waiting
for the nest of coffins, which weighed nearly half a ton, to be lowered by
pulleys to the crypt level, many of the cardinals knelt to pray at the tomb of
Pius X. A smaller number prayed also at the tomb of Benedict XV. These
two popes, together with Pius XI's old rival, Merry del Val, rested near the
site that Pius had chosen some years before as that of his final repose.

Earlier in the day, when workmen examined the wall before which it
was proposed to inter the pope, a large, forgotten recess was discovered
behind it. Plans were hurriedly made to place the coffins in the recess, un-
opened since the sixteenth century, rather than to surround the pope's remains with a vault on the outside of the wall.

The cardinals in the crypt, accompanied only by Pius's nephew, niece,
and sister-in-law, received the remains and placed them in the niche without ceremony. Then they dispersed into the frigid and dark Roman
evening. Early on Wednesday morning, a construction crew placed panels
of imitation marble in front of the recess and the public was admitted in
groups of twenty to the site.

Also on Wednesday, at 10 A.M. in the Consistorial Hall, the general congregation met again, with thirty-five in attendance. It was found that no
one had ordered the Palatine Guard to vacate its quarters so that the area
could be turned into the conclave's kitchen, and this was now done. Little
additional business was considered, because the cardinals' time was absorbed in preparations to receive the whole of the diplomatic corps on
Thursday. The corps was to make a public expression of condolence

through an address delivered by their dean. And, at last, O'Connell was at sea.

Thursday's meeting in the Consistorial Hall rushed through a number of procedural acts and then admitted the diplomats. It was expected that some reference to the wishes of the Axis powers might be made during the ceremony, because the dean of the diplomatic corps accredited to the Vatican was the German ambassador, Dr. Carl-Ludwig Diego von Bergen. The German's first expressions of sorrow were innocuous enough but near the end of his address he said, "We live and act in one of the most decisive hours of history. We are assisting in the elaboration of a new world, which wants to raise itself upon the ruins of a past that in many things has no longer any reason to exist." Von Bergen then went on to express the desire for a pope who would help in the "peaceful evolution" of this "new world." While the ambassador spoke, a strained atmosphere pervaded the assembly. Some of the cardinals were surprised that neither the British nor the French ambassador voiced any immediate objection. After one other brief paragraph, von Bergen concluded. The aged dean of the College, Cardinal Pignatelli di Belmonte, slowly rose to deliver his reply. He removed his biretta and in a clear, strong voice spoke a few words of formal thanks as demanded by the occasion. As he spoke he became more and more icy and reserved. He concluded, looking at von Bergen, ". . . the Sacred College . . . raises fervent prayers to the Lord that he may deign to concede to His Church, for its good and in the interests of the nations you represent, a supreme shepherd *after His own heart.*" In the ensuing silence the diplomats withdrew to pay a formal visit to the tomb of Pius XI. The other members of the diplomatic corps—except, of course, the Italian ambassador, Pignatti—were indeed upset with von Bergen's remarks, and the next most senior envoy, the Peruvian ambassador, Pablo Mimbala, later delivered a written complaint to von Bergen on behalf of his colleagues.

The arrival of MacRory in the evening brought the number of electors in Rome to forty-one.

On Friday the seventeenth, the center of attention shifted from the Vatican to the church of Sant'Andrea delle Valle. Here the nuncio to Italy, Francesco Borgognini-Duca, later a cardinal, said a requiem before King Victor Emmanuel III, Queen Helena, Mussolini, and the entire Italian cabinet. Friday also saw the first of the Germans to reach Rome, Michael von Faulhaber, the courageous anti-Nazi archbishop of Munich.

On Saturday came the first of the final three masses to be said in Saint Peter's for the soul of Pius XI. The four absolutions at the end of the mass were given by Cardinals von Faulhaber, Vidal y Barraquer, Nasalli-Rocca,

and Alessandro Verde, secretary of the Congregation of Rites and Ceremonies. After the mass, the ninth general congregation assembled to hear
the oaths of a few of the cardinals who had not yet sworn to uphold the
constitutions on conclaves.

At seven in the evening, the *Rex* docked at Naples. Dougherty and
Mundelein went immediately to the special train which the Italian government provided to carry them to Rome. They were again underway within
forty-five minutes of landing. If the realities of the world situation had escaped the attention of the electors from the United States, they were soon
brought back with force. The first sight that met Mundelein's eyes as he
came on deck to land was the large German flag with its swastika flying
from the masthead of the liner *Wilhelm Gustloff*.

Both Americans were greeted cordially on their arrival in Rome by representatives from the Vatican, Italy, and the United States. Dougherty was
driven to the Ambassadors Hotel, his preferred residence when in Rome,
while Mundelein went to the little college of Saint Mary of the Lake, which
he had founded.

During the excitement of the arrival of the first of the Americans, few
gave much attention to the coming of the youngest cardinal, the fifty-one-
year-old Manuel Gonçalves e Cerejeira. But his journey from Lisbon was a
symbol of the changing world. Portugal's cardinal arrived by air.

The second of the final group of masses was chanted by Cardinal
Alessio Ascalesi in Saint Peter's on Sunday morning. The four absolutions
on this occasion were imparted by van Roey, Hlond, Segura y Saenz, and
Seredi. The sensation of the day was provided by Pacelli, however. When
he passed through the courtyard of San Damaso early in the morning he
noticed crews who were continuing to work on the preparations for the
conclave. Sending for the Vatican engineers, he told them indignantly that
since the conclave was still ten days away there was no need for Sunday
work. The crews were sent home.

The brief tenth general congregation met immediately after the mass.
Mundelein took his oath and, after some routine business, the cardinals
dispersed. Sunday also saw the arrival of Karl Joseph Schulte from Cologne and Ignace Gabriel Tappouni from Beirut.

Monday the twentieth saw the last of the final sequence of masses, with
Schuster of Milan officiating and absolutions from Dougherty, Mundelein,
Gonçalves e Cerejeira, and Pacelli. Pacelli's final absolution to his beloved
superior strained his famous reserve to the breaking point, though only a
few in the ceremony noticed it. Forty-five cardinals attended the mass and
the eleventh general congregation which ensued immediately afterward in
the sacristy of the basilica.

All the cardinals who were present and had not yet taken the oath to uphold the election constitution did so at this time, including Dougherty.

Soon after the dispersal of the College, the last French cardinal, Baudrillart, arrived in Rome by train. In the days before he set out, his friends had urged him not to make the journey because of his age, but the eighty-eight-year-old rector stepped from the train seemingly refreshed by his journey.

Tuesday's meeting, the twelfth general congregation, finally saw the opening date of the conclave fixed at March 1. This was done when it seemed highly probable that all sixty-two members of the College would arrive by that time. Only three of the non-Italian cardinals had not yet arrived, O'Connell, Leme, and Copello; but, if the Italian Line maintained the arrangements it had made already, they would be in Rome by the evening of the first.

There had been a general expectation in Rome for some days that for the first time since the thirteenth century all the living cardinals would participate in the election of the pope. That expectation was dimmed somewhat when the Dominican cardinal, Tommaso Pio Boggiani, experienced a worsening of his diabetic condition in addition to an increasing problem with a cataract, and Francesco Marchetti-Selvaggiani had to be put to bed with a badly sprained ankle.

These two cardinals, though bedridden, received visitors and took part in the *prattiche*, which became very active now that all but three members of the College were in Rome or the immediate vicinity.

The consensus in the College was that a general European war, if not one involving the world, was now unavoidable. Although the traditional two wings of the College, conservative and liberal, were still the major divisions, their antagonism seemed muted in this election by the gravity of the world's political crisis. The question which dominated many of the conversations among the cardinals was whether the Church needed a political pope with a wide understanding of world affairs or a religious pope to serve as an example during the coming years of chaos and destruction. Some of the more conservative, still under the inspiration of Merry del Val, thought that Elia dalla Costa of Florence best fitted the latter model, in spite of his blunt and vigorous defense of his sphere of authority in the face of Fascist demands. Though he could never be called strictly neutral, he was comparatively unconcerned with political matters and concentrated his exceedingly pious life in asceticism and the pastoral care of his flock.

Those who championed an experienced diplomat and politician looked to Pacelli first of all, but also considered the abilities of the "Three Ms," two of whom had served in important nunciatures, Luigi Maglione in

Paris and Francesco Marmaggi in Bucharest, Prague, and Warsaw. Massimo Massimi, the third "M," was the curia's most distinguished lawyer.

But Pacelli was the leading candidate among those who favored a pope with extensive political experience and acumen. How could it be otherwise? Pius XI, more than any other pope in centuries, had tried to influence the choice of his successor, and Pacelli was his object. This alone, however, might have been seen as reason enough to reject the camerlengo's candidacy had there not been other violations of custom involved. It was against tradition to elevate the cardinal-secretary of state. Though the office was founded only in the middle of the sixteenth century, there were earlier positions in the curia in which its functions were carried out. In the broadest sense, only Fabio Chigi, who reigned as Alexander VI (1655–1667), and Giulio Rospigliosi, Clement IX (1667–1669), had come to the papal throne from the second ranking administrative position in the Church since the Middle Ages. Moreover, for different reasons, the candidacies of Rampolla, Merry del Val, and Gasparri, had failed in the three conclaves just before this one. Again, custom discouraged the election of a native Roman to the papacy, none having risen since Emilio Altieri was elected as Clement X in 1670—although Michelangelo de' Conti, Innocent XIII (1721–1723), while not a native, did spring from an ancient Roman noble family which had given the Church several popes. To elevate Pacelli, then, would violate not one but a whole library of conclave traditions. Because of this, the world press gave little discussion to his chances, even though he was the best known as well as the most powerful of the cardinals during the *sede vacante*.

Nevertheless, during the *prattiche*, Pacelli emerged as the candidate preferred by nearly all the non-Italian cardinals. Verdier, for example, was recruiting support for the camerlengo almost from the moment of Pius's death. Among the other French, Liénart was an early adherent, as was Gerlier. The latter's support may, indeed, have at first risen out of gratitude because Pacelli had been responsible for his transfer from the relatively obscure diocese of Tarbes to the archdiocese of Lyon, and, hence, his rise to the cardinalate. This was analogous to the support which Suhard at first gave to Maglione, who had secured Suhard's rise from Bayeux to Reims while the former was the nuncio in Paris. However, Maglione had made it perfectly clear during the *prattiche* that he was not a willing candidate for the papal throne. When Pacelli let it be known that Maglione was his choice for secretary of state, Suhard became his adherent also. Baudrillart arrived in Paris already in favor of Pacelli; Villeneuve, who was, like Verdier, in Rome when Pius died, was also an early member of the Pacellian party. Villeneuve, in fact, was heard to predict that Pacelli would become pope and that Maglione would succeed the new pontiff as secretary of state. Other European cardinals came to Rome ready to support the same cause. Van Roey, Hinsley, Cerejeira, Hlond, Seredi, and Kaspar, all had come to know Pacelli during his extensive tours of the past few years or in dealing with him as secretary of state, and all now were in favor of his election. From the other side of the Rhine came Michael von Faulhaber, the leading anti-Nazi in the German hierarchy, to press for the camerlengo's election. Vidal y Barraquer, the liberal exiled Spaniard, was also in Pacelli's favor. Among the major foreign prelates, only the Americans seemed to be an unknown quantity. Pacelli was, however, very close to O'Connell and had gone to Boston in 1936 to open his American visit. The two had met for the first time forty years before at the centenary birthday party for the camerlengo's grandfather. O'Connell had been introduced to the young Roman priest by Ernesto Pacelli, a cousin, who was not only the American's good friend but also, occasionally, his banker.

This tide of support from the non-Italians did not mean that Pacelli had no local partisans. Marchetti-Selvaggiani was an early influential adherent, as were Vincenzo La Puma, the prefect of the Congregation of Religious; Domenico Mariani and Carlo Cremonesi, both also curial cardinals; Pietro Fumasoni-Biondi, the prefect of Propaganda; and Giuseppe Pizzardo, an old colleague who had been consecrated a bishop by Pacelli. Perhaps the most influential of the Roman champions, however, was the dean of the College, Pignatelli di Belmonte, who brought his tremendous prestige to the process of making Pacelli the next pope. Camillo Caccia Dominioni also worked in this cause and, from among the Italian pastors, so did Nasalli-Rocca di Corneliano.

By the end of the *novemdiali* it looked as if Pacelli could expect at least twenty-four or twenty-five votes on the first ballot.

That the camerlengo enjoyed such a large following was a recognition of the growing danger of Fascism in particular. For the first time in several centuries, many of the cardinals were actually fearful lest their votes and deliberation become known to the outside world. In consequence, the committee on credentials put into effect a new system for authorizing admission to the conclave. Formerly, the electors merely had to submit the names of their conclavists and attendants for automatic approval. Now, however, each person had to have a dossier including details of his antecedents, his parents, friends, companions, and records of any contacts he had with legations or embassies. This was done in spite of the fact that each cardinal vouched readily for the integrity of his staff. The new requirements and procedures were announced and approved in the twelfth general congregation on the twenty-first.

On Wednesday morning, the twenty-second, the thirteenth general congregation met. After the regular session, the two standing committees convened together and went on a full tour of the conclave area. They found the work progressing on schedule. Sixty-one apartments had been created, together with a kitchen and considerable space for the attending staff, out of the central core of the Vatican palace. The sixty-second cardinal was Pacelli, who was accorded the privilege of remaining in his old quarters, which were entirely enclosed in the conclave's precincts. Work still needed to be done in the Sistine Chapel, where a wooden floor was being installed to raise the bases of the sixty-two thrones to a level equal to the base of the altar. All the thrones were covered in purple, breaking a tradition of several centuries in which purple thrones were reserved for the cardinals elevated by the pope who had just died and all the others were covered in green. When the work was completed, later in the week, the seating in the chapel was arranged with twenty-seven thrones against each side wall and eight in the rear, facing the altar. The cardinals would be seated according to their order. The dean, Pignatelli, had the first throne nearest to the altar on the left, followed by the other five cardinal-bishops, Donato Sbarretti, the sub-dean of the College and secretary of the Congregation of the Holy Office; Tommaso Pio Boggiani, the chancellor of the Church; Enrico Gasparri, nephew of Pietro and prefect of the Supreme Tribunal of the Apostolic Signature; Francesco Marchetti-Selvaggiani; and Angelo Maria Dolci, a senior diplomat. Throne number seven, proceeding down the left wall, was reserved for O'Connell, the archpriest, followed by the forty-seven other cardinal-priests, down the left, away from the altar, across the back wall, and then towards the altar on the right side. The junior cardinal-priest, Gerlier, was seated beside the junior cardinal-deacon, Giovanni Mercati. The remaining seven cardinal-deacons were then to be seated in ascending order of seniority, with Caccia Dominioni, the archdeacon, occupying throne number sixty-two, adjacent to the altar on the right side. Pacelli was to have throne number twenty-four, while number thirty-three, against the back wall, bore a plaque with the inscription "Pius P. P. XI VI Februar. MCMXXII." In this conclave it would be used by Maurilio Fossati, the archbishop of Turin.

The session of the fourteenth general congregation, on Thursday morning, was a short one with fifty-three cardinals present. After it, the standing committees met twice, once in the morning and again in the afternoon, to continue with the business of readying the conclave precincts and examining the credentials of the staff.

On the morning of the twenty-fourth, Monsignor Carlo Respighi, the prefect of Apostolic Ceremonies, dispatched to each of the cardinals the *intimatio*, the formal invitation to take part in the conclave:

> On Wednesday, March 1, 1939, at 9:30 in the morning, in the Pauline Chapel of the Apostolic Vatican Palace, the Most Eminent and Most Reverend Lord Cardinal Gennaro Granito Pignatelli di Belmonte, Bishop of Ostia and Albano, Dean of the Sacred College, will celebrate a solemn mass of the Holy Spirit. The Most Eminent and Most Reverend Lords Cardinals will attend it wearing their woolen robes with plain rochets and capes of violet silk with ermine fur.
>
> After the mass the prayer *De eligendo Summo Pontifice* will be said.
>
> On the same day, at 1:30 in the afternoon, the Most Eminent and Most Reverend Lords Cardinals, wearing cassocks and mozettas of violet silk with silken sashes of the same color, but without rochets, will gather in the aforesaid chapel. Then, preceded by the cross and singing *Veni Creator*, they will enter in a procession in the order of seniority into the conclave, where all the rest will be performed according to custom.

During the general congregation on Friday morning, cells were allotted to those cardinals who were ill or whose late arrival might find them very tired. Pacelli, as has been mentioned, already had been accorded the right to remain in his apartment and use it as his cell. Now special arrangements were made for Boggiani, Marchetti-Selvaggiani, and Schulte, who were ill, and for O'Connell, Leme, and Copello, who were expected in Rome only in time to make their way into the conclave before the doors were shut. After these considerations, the rest of the cardinals drew lots for their cells.

Saturday's meeting, with fifty-five cardinals present, continued with the cardinals' own last-minute arrangements for the conclave. Besides the three still travelling, and the ill Boggiani and Marchetti-Selvaggiani, two others were absent. Vincenzo La Puma had left Rome to visit his ill sister, who was to die on Sunday; and Sbarretti, whose age of eighty-two counselled him to rest in preparation for the cardinalate's most important duty.

Meanwhile, at sea, the earlier plans for having the *Saturnia* meet the *Neptunia* at Gibraltar were going awry. Storms in the South Atlantic had caused *Neptunia* to drop ten hours behind her schedule. The Argentinian and Brazilian cardinals, who knew that a delay of even hours might mean that they would miss the conclave, were consumed with anxiety. Aboard *Saturnia*, O'Connell also fretted that he might lose the last chance he would ever have to participate in the election of a pope. Normally, O'Connell's ship would have sailed directly from New York to Naples. On this passage, however, stops had been scheduled at Madeira, Teneriffe, in the

Canaries, at Casablanca, Gibraltar, Algiers, and Nice. It did not please the archpriest that he had to sail back-and-forth, up-and-down the western Mediterranean while the days slipped by. Despite the itinerary, though, officials of the Italian Line assured Boston's cardinal that both he and his Latin American colleagues would arrive in time. They even offered assurances that a scheduled stop by the *Neptunia* at Algiers would be cancelled if there were any danger of a late arrival in Naples. On Saturday the twenty-fifth, while *Saturnia* was anchored at Casablanca, O'Connell was handed a cablegram from Pacelli that reassured "Number One" that the conclave would not begin until the evening of March 1. On board *Neptunia*, the problem of lost time was becoming serious. It did not seem that the meeting at Gibraltar could be kept. Captain Iviani of the *Saturnia* radioed to the other liner to change the date and place of the meeting to the twenty-seventh at Algiers. On Monday morning, *Saturnia* entered Algiers harbor and anchored.

All over the Mediterranean basin, the month of February had been exceptionally cold. The reporters who covered the preparations for the conclave remarked on the fact that a new central heating system would prevent the cardinals from the genuine suffering which had been experienced in earlier winter elections. Now, in Algiers, the night of the twenty-seventh came clear and frigid. In the comparative darkness of the harbor *Saturnia* waited. Her passengers walked the decks in short bursts, eyeing the horizon for some sign of a successful rendezvous. Finally, just before ten o'clock, ablaze with lights, *Neptunia* sailed in. O'Connell's luggage was already prepared for transfer, and this was undertaken immediately. The one major pier in the city was neither long enough nor wide enough to accommodate either of the great liners, let alone both at once. Consequently, a series of barges had been lashed together and extended out from shore, each of them being connected to the next by a short plank. This was done for each ship, so that O'Connell first had to make his way to the dock and then outward to the new vessel. The tide was high and the water choppy as the cardinal made his way across the two series of swaying, pitching barges in the night. When he was boarding the *Neptunia* there was a spontaneous eruption of cheers from the passengers who had been with him since New York. Captain Iviani had accompanied O'Connell to the new ship. Now he made his introductions to his colleague and left his formidable charge in new hands. Within an hour *Neptunia* was at sea for Naples.

The meeting of the sixteenth general congregation on Sunday the twenty-sixth saw the number of cardinals in attendance rise to fifty-six, because of La Puma's return; but Monday's meeting had two fewer, because La Puma was again absent attending to the funeral of his sister, while Dolci was indisposed. This meeting saw the formal approval of twelve nuns of the Little Sisters of the Sacred Family as the cooks for the conclave. This order had performed the same services in 1922, which was the first time that any women had been present in the conclave. One wag remarked that he knew now that the conclave would be a short one, as would anyone else who had ever tasted the good sisters's culinary fare.

The same fifty-five cardinals who had been present on Monday also attended the eighteenth and last general congregation on Tuesday. This meeting was devoted to a final review of all the preparations for the coming election. When it concluded, many of the cardinals had their first chance to tour the conclave's precincts, guided by members of the Vatican's architectural staff.

In the afternoon and evening occurred the last negotiations of the *prattiche*. The champions of Pacelli, particularly Verdier, Marchetti-Selvaggiani, Pignatelli, and Caccia Dominioni, had worked assiduously to gain support from the largely conservative administrative cardinals in the curia. Their rounds of calls had attracted little public attention, however, because those whom they were trying to sway had never received wide public notice and, indeed, were often unknown to the public, even in Rome. Men like the prefect of the Congregation of Rites, Carlo Salotti; the secretary of the Consistorial Congregation, Raffaele Carlo Rossi; the retired former nuncio to Austria, Enrico Sibilia; and the eighty-two-year-old secretary of the Apostolic Signature, Federico Cattani Amadori, were not even on the lists of sources carried by many of the reporters who covered Roman events. Nor were they often on the lists of those narrow and self-important figures who sought interviews with cardinals to convey their views on whomever they thought should be elected—"for the good of the Church," of course. But the comparative unknowns were representative of those cardinals who had to be won over twice by those who favored Pacelli. The curial cardinals had to be persuaded that the times demanded a political rather than a pastoral pope, and then they had to be shown that Pacelli was the most suitable candidate with that background.

Another subject in the last discussions of the *prattiche* was the attitude of O'Connell. Though he had never before participated in a conclave, his prestige was enormous. He and Pignatelli were the only two cardinals who survived from the reign of Pius X. Eight cardinals—Sbarretti, Boggiani, Ascalesi, Bertram, von Faulhaber, Dougherty, Vidal y Barraquer, and Schulte—survived from those elevated by Benedict XV, but too many of them were thought to have political liabilities that far outweighed their experience of having participated in the election of 1922, the three Germans, because they were German; Dougherty, because he had not voted in 1922 and was considered too loud and brusque; Vidal y Barraquer, because he was an exile; Sbarretti, who was too feeble; and Boggiani, too ill. So the prestige of seniority and experience rested with Pignatelli and O'Connell. Boston's cardinal, though often outspoken and brash, also had views on the position of the Church in the modern world which were well-thought-out and tested in the crucible of political, Irish New England. The deaths of Baltimore's Gibbons and New York's Hayes, years before, had left O'Connell the unquestioned figure of leadership in Catholic America. The skill of his administration had made the archdiocese of Boston one of the most financially sound and devotedly loyal in the world. So O'Connell came as the Catholic prelate closest to national authority in a country which those who were prescient—Churchill included—knew would play an important, perhaps decisive, rôle in the unfolding of the war to come and the peace which would eventually follow.

Pacelli's friends and foes alike realized that O'Connell's voice in the conclave would be an important one. They knew also of his four decades of friendship with Pius XI's secretary of state, but they could not be sure that friendship and professional respect would be translated into active support in a campaign to win the tiara. They also knew, of course, that he was a disciple of Merry del Val and an old friend of de Laï. So how would this theological and political conservative go?

At seven in the morning of Wednesday, March 1, the *Neptunia* docked at Naples. The two Latin Americans hastened to the train which had been provided for them by the Italian government and were off to Rome within a few minutes. By eleven, they had arrived and were met by a delegation of Vatican officials and an escort provided by the Pontifical Noble Guard—both groups dispatched for the purpose by Pacelli. Since the opening mass of the Holy Spirit, as indicated in the *intimatio*, already was in progess, Leme and Copello went immediately to the conclave precincts to rest in their cells after their long and tedious journey. They would join the others later in the afternoon procession to the Sistine Chapel.

The two cardinals who were still unwell, Boggiani and Marchetti-Selvaggiani, also did not attend the inaugural rites. Later in the day, they each went directly from their residences to the conclave. Forty-six members of the College of Cardinals were present as prescribed, however, when Pignatelli presided at the mass of the Holy Spirit.

O'Connell also disembarked from the *Neptunia* in haste, preceding the other two by several minutes. He was not interested in the special train, perhaps because of unhappy memories of 1922, when a similar special accommodation had brought him to Rome too late. Accompanied by Pacelli's specially-dispatched welcomer, Monsignor Hurley, O'Connell, his attendants, and his luggage, were put into a motorcade of four cars, which left at high speed directly from the pier. It was 8:40 A.M., "Number One" had made it now.

The cardinal from New England felt sufficiently sure of his schedule to stop for a quiet luncheon on the way, and when he arrived in Rome at 2:30 he had himself and his party taken to the Grand Hotel. As he entered his suite he found a new red hat to replace the one he had left in Nassau.

As the cardinals gathered at four o'clock for the procession to the Sistine Chapel, O'Connell arose from his short rest and dressed in the same formal robes worn by the others, but he did not rush to join them. Why expend time and energy in pomp and procession when it was the vote that mattered?

Fifty-nine cardinals marched in slow progress to the Sistine, mostly in pairs but some alone. Boggiani and Marchetti-Selvaggiani were already in their cells. As the cardinals passed by, the more knowledgeable of those on the side identified them for their less well-informed neighbors. Comments were exchanged on the appearance of the electors, their chances, their politics. As some of the popular favorites were spotted, there were the usual ripples of movement in the crowd and the raising of voices. Pietro Boetto, one of the Jesuit cardinals, looked somber in his black robes. Pacelli, walking alone, looked distant and reserved. "There's the pope." "Do you think he can do it?" "I'm sure of it." When Ermenegildo Pellegrinetti, the former nuncio to Belgrade, passed by, one of the ambassadors remarked to Jean Riviere, the counsellor of the French embassy, "There goes somebody with a good chance." "But," replied Riviere, "no one has spoken of him." "That's why he's got a good chance," sententiously replied the envoy.

As the last of the fifty-nine entered the Sistine, the doors were closed. Each cardinal went to his throne and signed the printed copy of the oath to obey the election constitution, whose text he found on the small writing desk in front of it. In order of seniority they then rose, knelt before the altar, read the oath aloud, and delivered the signed copy to the master of ceremonies.

While this process was being conducted, O'Connell arrived at the Vatican in the car which Pacelli had sent. He went through the door at the court of San Damaso and passed along the same ways as his colleagues had done a little time before. Accompanied by Domenico Tardini, one of Pacelli's two closest assistants, he made his way past the crowd which had come to watch the procession. As he went along there were muffled whispers, "Cardinale O'Connell di Boston." Entering the conclave, he asked to be shown to his cell immediately. "Number thirty-four," said one of the attendants, who led him upstairs to the quarters reserved for him by the general congregation of cardinals. The attendant threw open the door; it was the private apartment of the pope. After a few moments, Tardini helped O'Connell don the rest of the set of ceremonial robes for the day. Then they went together down to the Sistine. The sensation caused by his passage outside was considerable, but it was nothing compared to that as he made his entrance into the most famous chapel in the Christian world, near the end of the ceremony of the oath. He had come, he was the last, he was indeed at the fullness of his career and his life. Here, today, the power and the glory, not forever, but amen.

Escorted from the door of the Sistine by the Prince-Marshal Chigi-Albani della Rovere, and by Camillo Serafini, the governor of the Vatican Palace, he was welcomed quickly by the master of ceremonies, Carlo Respighi, who accompanied him to the altar. O'Connell knelt and offered a public prayer of thanksgiving for his safe arrival.

Pignatelli left his throne and came forward, clasped O'Connell, and whispered that his happiness was complete. They stood together now, the last representatives of Pius X in the College. Pacelli also left his throne to congratulate Boston's cardinal on a timely arrival. As he glanced around from his throne, O'Connell thought, "how many of these cardinals have I seen as minor officials in the various offices of the Vatican?"

So there were sixty who emerged from the Sistine after the ceremony. As each cardinal stepped from the chapel, a member of the Noble Guard detached himself from his companions to escort the elector to his assigned cell. The Noble Guard normally attended only the pope, but now each cardinal was a potential sovereign pontiff and entitled to the full honors of his possibility.

About twenty minutes after the last cardinal had left the chapel, a bell was rung and Monsignor Respighi began the process of closing up the conclave by calling out the traditional phrase, "Extra Omnes." The Prince-Marshal on the outside, and Camerlengo Pacelli on the inside, then did a final turn of the area while the Swiss Guard marched through all the passages and threw open all the doors and closures. Pacelli and Chigi-Albani della Rovere met again at 6:15 at the door into the conclave which led from the court of San Damaso. Two minutes later, the door swung closed and the keys were turned on both sides. The election of the pope who would lead Catholicism through to the end of the age of Hitler had begun.

The evening's events included a full supper followed by exchanges of visits among the cardinals. The Pacellians now had one major doubt resolved; O'Connell was with them—and was willing to say so. This was the last open opportunity for active campaigning and it was exercised to the fullest. Only the first ballot on the morrow would reveal how successful Pacelli's friends had been.

On Thursday morning, March 2, the first activity of the day was the arrival of a few items of food that had not been taken in on the previous evening. The rota, the panelled revolving door first used in 1503, through which objects may pass without the exchangers seeing or speaking to each other, was used for this purpose. At nine o'clock, the cardinals who wished to hear Mass went to the Sistine, where Pignatelli was the celebrant. After the low mass was over, the cardinals went to the Hall of the Popes in the Borgia Apartments, which had been converted into a refectory. Here a light, continental breakfast was served.

At ten o'clock, a bell was rung in the court of San Damaso to signal the electors that the voting was about to begin. After the sixty who were to vote in the Sistine had entered, the door was shut against eavesdropping or interruption by the conclavists and staff.

The scrutators and infirmarians were chosen and Pignatelli then got the first ballot under way very speedily. The infirmarians went to the cells of Boggiani and Marchetti-Selvaggiani to collect their ballots, and, when they returned, the tally was begun.

At its conclusion, the results of the efforts of Verdier, Pignatelli, and the others in favor of a strong political pope, were very clear. Pacelli had received thirty-six votes, only six short of election. The other twenty-six had gone to a wide array of candidates, including Elia dalla Costa, Federico Tedeschini, and Luigi Maglione

With a good measure of assurance it is possible to determine the thirty-six who voted for the camerlengo on the first ballot. Verdier, certainly, as well as the rest of the French—Liénart, Gerlier, Suhard, Baudrillart, and Tisserant. The majority of the cardinals who were the unique representatives of their nations, van Roey, Hinsley, Cerejeira, Hlond, Seredi, Kaspar, and Villeneuve. Also Vidal y Barraquer, an outspoken Pacellian, and O'Connell, together with the other two Americans, Dougherty and Mundelein. The two Latin Americans, Leme and Copello, and the German, von Faulhaber, and at least twelve Italians, Pignatelli di Belmonte, Marchetti-Selvaggiani, La Puma, Mariani, Cremonesi, Fumasoni-Biondi, Pizzardo, Caccia Dominioni, Nasalli-Rocca di Corneliano, Maglione, Piazza, and Canali. The remaining four, about whose vote there is less assurance, were probably Bertram, Schulte, Tappouni, and Gasparri.

Quickly the cardinals went about conducting the second vote. As before, the ballots of the two ill cardinals were collected and the tally begun. When this round was concluded the supporters of Pacelli were wreathed with smiles, for he had gained six more votes. His tally stood at forty-two, precisely the number necessary to win. Before the dean, archpriest, and archdeacon could approach Pacelli's throne to ask if he accepted the election, it was necessary to open the second fold of each ballot to determine that Pacelli had not voted for himself. Pacelli understood the possibility of unrest in the Church during crisis and war were it ever suspected that the reigning pope had just barely achieved the throne. He used the pause to make an uncharacteristically blunt appeal for another round of voting, so that the cardinals could reflect on what their actions meant. He would hear of no other way. This was agreed to generally before Pacelli's ballot was reached. He had voted for Tedeschini.

The ballots and tally papers were now collected for burning in the little black iron stove installed at the rear of the chapel. In order to make sure that the color of the smoke was appropriate, wood chips instead of wet straw had been provided for black smoke. When the bundles and chips were set alight, however, the smoke was white, not black. The first wisps of the *sfumata* were visible to the crowd already gathered in the great Piazza di San Pietro at 12:17 P.M., exactly eighteen hours to the minute after the conclave had begun. Inside, there was consternation at the way the burning of the documents was going, and more wood was added to change the color, but, of course, without success. Gradually, the stove began to turn a cherry red. Water was thrown on the flames in great haste and now the smoke became black. Outside, the appearance had changed from white to a light gray after a few minutes. Suddenly, great bouts of black smoke issued and the crowd began to disperse.

After the brief flurry of excitement over the stove, the cardinals adjourned to the refectory for lunch at one o'clock. All except Pacelli. He took his breviary out to the loggia of the court of San Damaso and spent the hour between one and two pacing up and down, performing at the same time his daily priestly obligation. A number of the cardinals saw him there as they returned from their meal. He was an impressive combination of his natural gravity and reserve coupled with extraordinary agitation.

At two o'clock the bell rang once more, for the beginning of the afternoon session. At its sound, Pacelli turned to descend the three steps into the Sistine, lost his footing, and fell heavily onto the solid marble floor. O'Connell, whose sharp wit seldom missed an opportunity, quickly bent down to help Pacelli to his feet; "The Vicar of Jesus Christ, on earth," exclaimed the Bostonian. Pacelli, in fact, sprang to his feet unaided and determined for himself that he had no serious injury, though he was later examined by his own physician, Dr. Riccardo Galeazzi-Lisi, who treated a few bruises.

Once the cardinals were in the Chapel together, the procedures of the morning were put into motion all over again. For Pacelli, the result would be decisive. Either he would be elected by a number clearly greater than the two-thirds required or his flood tide would be over, after having touched election itself. His adherents seemed to have little doubt. Time after time, the three scrutators read the name Pacelli. Forty-two passed, but the cardinals waited until every ballot was checked before making any response. When his name was read for the forty-eighth time it was over. Pignatelli, O'Connell, and Caccia Dominioni, now rose from their thrones and stepped to face the camerlengo. Pignatelli now spoke the ancient formula, "Do you accept the election, canonically made, of yourself as supreme pontiff?" Eugenio Pacelli had now regained his outward composure and replied, "I accept." "By what name do you wish to be known?" continued the dean. "Pius," was the reply. Then he was just barely heard to murmur, "Have pity on me, O God, according to Thy mercy."

The second word Pacelli had uttered as pope reaffirmed a commitment to continue the policies of Pius XI, for the choice of a papal name by such an astute politician and diplomat as Pacelli was meant to have, and did have, instant positive significance. With the word "Pius" clearly heard, the cardinals reached to the sides of their thrones, loosened the cords, and lowered the canopies which had stretched over them. Each arose and, in order of seniority, came forward for the first ceremony of obedience to Pius XII. The new pope spoke a few words to each of them. To Verdier, he expressed his understanding of the rôle the archbishop of Paris had played in the election. Soon, he, together with Pignatelli, Marchetti-Selvaggiani, and O'Connell, were hailed as the grand electors of 1939—those who had led their colleagues to a swift conclusion to the process.

The ballots and tallies were now burned, but with greater care than had been exercised in the morning. The first glimpse of the *sfumata* came at 5:28. Day was already beginning to darken and the color, at first, was not recognizable, but the feeling in the crowd was that the election had ended and no one stirred. At one minute past six, the façade of the basilica was flooded with electric light, the doors leading to the Loggia of Benedictions were opened, and four attendants lowered a great tapestry bearing the arms of Pius IX over the balcony. Some of the conclavists and attendants, who now began to appear at the side windows, were waving white handkerchiefs vigorously. A few in the crowd understood the signal, a white flag, peace, *pace, Pacelli*. Almost at once Cardinal Caccia Dominioni appeared. Microphones, which were used for the announcement of a papal election for the first time in 1939, were turned on and the voice of the archdeacon resounded through the Piazza, "Annuntio vobis, gaudiam mag-

nam, habemus papam. Eminentissimum ac Reverendissimum Dominum
..." He paused to savor the moment, almost too long, ". . . Dominum Eu
..." The crowd exploded into a roar. The two syllables had given it away,
a Roman, one of them, had been chosen at last. ". . . genium, Sanctæ Romanæ Ecclesiæ Cardinalem Pacelli," Caccia Dominioni's voice rose to be
heard over the tremendous demonstration below, "qui sibi nomen impo-
suit Pium Duodecimum." The storm continued unabated, some broke
into a "Te Deum," but most just cheered until they were hoarse. No other
election in this century has been greeted with such a massive outpouring
of popular enthusiasm at Saint Peter's as that of Pius XII. At 6:15 Vatican
radio made the first announcement, making note of the fact that Pius XII
had been chosen on his sixty-third birthday.

Five minutes later, a large group of cardinals was seen to gather at the
windows to the left of the central balcony. The Italian troops who had
been stationed in nearby side streets by Mussolini "in case of disorder"
now came into the upper end of the Piazza and formed up for a formal sa-
lute, thus splitting the rear section of the great crowd into two wings. The
sun had now set behind the basilica and, in the chilly, clear evening, the
whole of Saint Peter's was framed from the rear in a brilliant scarlet radi-
ance. Perhaps this moment already had been imagined by the great architects who had labored on the building—Bramante, Michelangelo,
Fontana, Bernini.

In a few moments more, Pius appeared and delivered his first blessing.
Afterwards, he stood for a time acknowledging the roar from below, then
reentered the basilica to return to the Sistine. The electric lights were
turned off suddenly, the façade was plunged into darkness, and the people
began to depart.

Enthroned once again, Pius received the second obedience of those
who had elected him. As the cardinals prepared to leave, Pius went to the
cell of Marchetti-Selvaggiani. "Holiness," said the cardinal-vicar, attempting to rise. "No," said Pius, motioning the cardinal to lie down, "tonight
let it just be your Francesco to my Eugenio." After a brief visit, Pius returned to the apartment he had occupied for so many years and spoke to
his sisters by telephone, as well as to the provost of the little village of
Desio, the birthplace of Pius XI.

At 7:15, the doors of the conclave were opened. Within fifteen minutes,
all the cardinals had left—only Pius remained. His bags were packed for
what he had hoped would be a holiday in Switzerland; now they would go
on a shorter journey, just upstairs.

Enough time has passed that the question of whether or not the College
chose wisely in 1939 can have something of an objective answer. Pius XII

was able to maintain the independence of the Vatican throughout World War II. A considerable accomplishment, since Napoleon's precedent of the arrest and imprisonment of Pius VI was too close, as the Church views history, to be forgotten or ignored. There is little doubt that if Pius XII had antagonized Hitler much more than he did, he too would have been arrested and the Vatican occupied. As it was, the Church worked throughout the War to ameliorate its effects, where it could.

In the years following the War, Pius's saintly appearance and reserved manner seemed to embody nearly all that the modern world expected to see in a pope. The papacy's prestige in the 1950s was greater than it had been in centuries. When he died in 1958, the results of Pius's chief folly were revealed. He had insisted on keeping too much of the daily management of the Church's affairs in his own hands. For example, as Villeneuve had predicted, Maglione was appointed secretary of state within a few days of Pius's election; but, when he died in 1944, he was not replaced. For fourteen years, Pius XII, like Louis XIV of France before him, was his own first minister of state. Pius also deliberated each step of either policy or procedure with great care. Appointments to minor offices, as well as to great ones, were often not made for months, sometimes years, while the pope considered the merits of various candidates. As Pius's health declined during the last five years of his life, the pace of actual business grew slower and slower while, ironically, the pace of public activity increased. Pius received more groups of pilgrims and professional societies during his last years and months than he ever had during the first fifteen years of his reign. By the end of the reign, the results of Pius's management had become nearly disastrous—there were pressing matters of consequence which had received no attention in years.

Yet the reign as a whole must be judged a success, for the perception of the papacy as western civilization's moral and ethical conscience was never stronger than in the years of Pius XII, and his immediate successor, John XXIII.

III. Aggiornamento

The war for which the College of Cardinals had tried to prepare the Church by electing Pius XII finally began just two days short of his first half year on the throne.

It is unclear just how much of a Germanophile he was before he was sent to Munich as nuncio in 1917, but during his years there, and in his ensuing nunciature in Berlin, from 1925 to 1929, he embraced, both intellectually and æsthetically, German culture and life—Beethoven was his favorite composer, Dürer his favorite artist. His household staff was largely German, from his housekeeper, Mother Pasqualina Lehnert, to his confessor, Father Augustin Bea; and he frequently spoke nearly perfect German not only at home but with others, as well. Perhaps the anecdote which reveals his deep understanding of, and sympathy with, German life is the occasion in which, while nuncio, his car drove through Wittenberg. He asked the driver to stop at the entrance to the Collegiate Church there. He left his car, entered the church, and prayed for a little while at the tomb of Martin Luther, alone and unattended. Of course, we cannot know the nature of his prayer, nor can we ever delineate with precision the nature and range of Pacelli's respect for the great Reformer and his theology, but the private visit to Luther's tomb reveals much about Pius's personality and thinking in itself.

Because of this closeness to German thought and culture, he, like Churchill, was clear-sighted in appreciating how dangerous Hitler was, long before the latter's rise to power. Thus when, as cardinal-secretary of state, he led Pius XI to conclude the concordat of 1933 with the new Chancellor, he made the concessions he did in an effort to preserve some liberty for Catholics under a demonstrably unchristian regime, as his personal notes on the treaty reveal. As the 1930s moved forward, he directed for the pope an increasing pressure against Fascism, but with no positive result. Open and forthright opposition to Hitler finally came in Pius XI's encyclical to the Germans, *Mit brennender Sorge* (*With burning heart*), on March 14, 1937—much of which Pacelli wrote himself. In the following year, he broke personally with the leading prelate in northern Europe, Cardinal Theodor Innitzer, archbishop of Vienna, when the latter openly supported the *Anschluss*. With these, and other anti-fascist actions, it was no surprise that Hitler's official reaction to Pacelli's election was cold and hostile.

Once the war began, with Mussolini only a few minutes by car away from the Vatican, Pius XII determined to hold the Church in a defensive and wary posture for the duration of the war. For the long history of the Church, the memory of Napoleon's order to place Pius VI in a closed carriage and take him to house-arrest in France, where the pontiff died, was too close to be far from daily memory. In an age of total war and surrounded by totalitarian rule, a repetition could come at any moment. To shield the Church from this particular peril, Pius prepared—and signed— an instrument of abdication which was to be published if the Vatican were occupied and his freedom compromised. In this way, Hitler's seizure of his person would simply mean the arrest of Father Pacelli, while the cardinals who were able to meet outside Axis territory would be free to elect his successor canonically. This document remained officially secret for decades, until it was revealed by Cardinal Pietro Palazzini in an interview in January, 1988.

As another part of his defensive posture, Pius announced that he would make no new appointments to the residential hierarchy for the duration of the war, save only for the gravest of reasons, and that he would not hold a consistory for the creation of new cardinals for the same period. Gradually, then, age and death took its toll on the higher reaches of Church government. During the war years, twenty-three cardinals died, including two of the three Americans, O'Connell in Boston and Mundelein in Chicago; two of the three Germans, Schulte in Köln and Bertram in Breslau; and Arthur Hinsley, the only English cardinal. More serious than these, however, were the deaths of two curial officials whose offices Pius never filled. Immediately after his election, the pope had appointed two old and trusted confidants to his own former offices: Luigi Maglione was made cardinal-secretary of state and Lorenzo Lauri was made camerlengo. But both of these prelates had short careers in their new positons. When Lauri died, on October 8, 1941, the office of camerlengo fell vacant once more, and Pius appointed no successor to him for the remainder of the reign. And once Maglione also died, on August 22, 1944, Pius assumed responsibility for the secretariat of state himself, aided by two younger monsignori, Giovanni Battista Montini and Domenico Tardini, and never again filled the office. The latter decision increased the pope's workload immensely, although the diplomatic activities of the secretariat of state were the tasks he enjoyed the most; the consequence of the former decision would leave the organization of the conclave to elect his successor in the hands of the dean of the College, since, for the first time in hundreds of years, the official charged with that responsibility was nonexistent.

By mid-October, 1945, the College was reduced to thirty-eight members, its smallest population since 1517, and yet another death occurred—that of the Jesuit Pietro Boetto, archbishop of Genoa, on January 31, 1946—before the formal creation of Pius's new cardinals.

Pius decided to begin his post-war renewal of the Church with a complete replenishment of the College, one that would, at a single stroke, bring the number of cardinals back to its full strength of seventy, as mandated in Sixtus V's constitution, *Postquam verus*, in 1586. By late October, the pope had completed his list of thirty-two new cardinals, the largest number elevated on a single day in the history of the Church, eclipsing by one the creations of the Grand Consistory of Leo X on July 1, 1517. Members of the curia inquired if the formal consistory for their creation would be held on one of the Ember Days of December, a traditional time for the elevation of new cardinals, as well as for the consecration of bishops and the ordination of priests. Without comment or explanation, Pius responded that the creation would take place on Monday, February 18, 1946. In the light of past curial precedent, it was an unusual day of the week and an unusual date in the year.

Pius XII's Grand Consistory completely reshaped the orientation and outlook of the College in one sweeping revolution. Of the thirty-two, only four were Italian, and only four were curial officials—three of the Italians, Aloisi Masella, Micara, and Bruno, and the Russo-Armenian, Agagianian. For the first time since the early fifteenth century, Italians were reduced to a minority in the College, and curial cardinals had the lowest proportion of the membership in history. The curia was stunned. Since Pius's election, ten curial cardinals had died—Sbarretti, Mariani, Dolci, Lauri, Boggiani, Pellegrinetti, Cattani Amadori, La Puma, Cremonesi, and Maglione, all Italians. Now, only four had been replaced in the College of Cardinals, and one of the newly elevated was a Russian.

No fewer than twenty-seven of the new cardinals were residential archbishops and bishops. Many represented Catholic populations that had never had cardinalitial representation before—from Sydney to Toronto, from China to Peru. The largest single bloc of the new creations was that from the United States, with four. Another characteristic which the new European cardinals shared was their common strong anti-fascist position in the war, including the three Germans, particularly von Galen, and especially Adam Stefan Sapieha, the archbishop of Kraków. The latter, a Polish prince by birth, was now a prince of the Church, and his people's familiar name for him, the "Prince Prince," reflects the honor and dignity in which he was held. His war record and his ecclesiastical stature made him the leading Catholic figure behind the Iron Curtain in the first phase of the Cold War, and this, in turn, brought more prominent attention than would otherwise have been the case to those who were associated with him, including young Father Karol Wojtyła. The new cardinals were:

Gregory Peter XV Agagianian: *Pat. of Cilicia of the Armenians*
John Glennon: *Archbishop of St. Louis*
Benedetto Aloisi Masella: *Pref., Cong. of the Sacraments*
Clemente Micara: *Cardinal-Vicar of Rome*
Adam Stefan Sapieha: *Archbishop of Krakow*
Edward Aloysius Mooney: *Archbishop of Detroit*
Jules Saliège: *Archbishop of Toulouse*
James Charles McGuigan: *Archbishop of Toronto*
Samuel Alfonsus Stritch: *Archbishop of Chicago*
Augustín Parrado y Garcia: *Archbishop of Granada*
Clément Emile Roques: *Archbishop of Rennes*
Jan de Jong: *Archbishop of Utrecht*
Carlos Carmelo de Vasconcellos Motta: *Archbishop of São Paulo*
Pierre Petit de Julleville: *Archbishop of Rouen*
Norman Thomas Gilroy: *Archbishop of Sydney*
Francis Joseph Spellman: *Archbishop of New York*
José María Caro Rodriguez: *Archbishop of Santiago*
Teódosio Clemente de Gouveia: *Archbishop of Lourenço Marques*
Jaime de Barros Câmara: *Archbishop of Rio de Janeiro*
Enrique Pla y Deniel: *Archbishop of Toledo*
Manuel Arteaga y Betancourt: *Archbishop of Havana*
Josef Frings: *Archbishop of Köln*
Juan Gualberto Guevara: *Archbishop of Lima*
Bernard Griffin: *Archbishop of Westminster*
Manuel Arcé y Ochotorena: *Archbishop of Tarragona*
Jozsef Mindszenty: *Archbishop of Esztergom*
Ernesto Ruffini: *Archbishop of Palermo*
Konrad von Preysing-Lichtenegg-Moos: *Archbishop-Bishop of Berlin*
Clemens-August von Galen: *Bishop of Münster*
Antonio Caggiano: *Bishop of Rosario*
Thomas Tien-ken-sin: *Archbishop of Beijing*
Giuseppe Bruno: *Pref. of the Apostolic Signature*

The pomp and splendor of the Grand Consistory was the greatest Europe had seen since the coronation of George VI in 1937, nearly a decade before. The arrival of the new cardinals in Rome; the rounds of dinners, parties, and receptions to honor them; the public consistory itself; the ensuing ceremonies of the opening and closing of the mouths of the new cardinals; their processional visits to their new title churches, all combined to re-illuminate Rome from the gray aftermath of war with its poverty. But the zenith of this splendor was the public consistory of February 18 at which the new cardinals were created formally. Pius never commented on his choice of the date but it seems that his choice was meant to be a gesture of compassion to the devastated ordinary people of Germany, no matter what their background or creed, for it was the three-hundredth anniversary of the death—and, consequently, in Catholic terms, the feast—of Martin Luther. At the same time, the new membership in the College singled out those men in Europe who had remained most distant from Fascism. The three new French cardinals, for example, were the archbishops who had refused most clearly to support the Vichy regime.

Of course, there were a few contretemps, as the new cardinals adjusted to their new stations and to each other. At one reception, bluff, hearty Frank Spellman of New York found himself placed, rather uncomfortably, next to the reserved and subtle Konrad von Preysing of Berlin. Spellman's first few efforts at general conversation met with little success, so he tried ecclesiastical small talk. "I understand, Your Eminence, that when we die our red hats will be suspended by wires from the rooves of our cathedrals until they rot away." Von Preysing bleakly looked at the prosperous American and, doubtless remembering the bombed-out shell of his episcopal seat, responded, "Your Eminence forgets that I have no roof."

The Grand Consistory of Pius XII, with its radical redistribution of membership in the College, is the real beginning of that thirty-year process which transformed Catholicism from the Church of the Council of Trent to the post-Vatican II institution of today. When its effect is combined with Pius's refusal to fill high curial offices, lest the new incumbents quietly work to thwart the papal will in some matters, which produced a destabilization of the curia, the influence of the conservative and integrist wing of the College of Cardinals was dealt a blow from which it never recovered. Pius XII canonized Pius X with great splendor on May 29, 1954, but the ceremony represented real closure to integrist policies rather than a rebirth of Pius X's narrow theology and rigid ideas of archconservative papal government.

Although he had a slight tendency to anemia and a predisposition to contract bronchial infections easily, Pius generally enjoyed steady good health for many decades. Even with the extremely demanding schedule of work he set for himself, Pius showed no lessening of his strength, and suffered no severe bouts of ill health, for the first nine years of his reign. In the days that followed his seventy-second birthday in March 1948, however, he began to complain of difficulties in urination. His personal physician of many years, Doctor Riccardo Galeazzi-Lisi, conducted a full medical examination which revealed a considerable enlargement of the left lobe of the pontiff's prostate. Galeazzi-Lisi—an oculist with limited training as a physician who was prone to somewhat questionable methods of medical treatment—prescribed a regimen of doses of homeopathic medicine combined with alterations in the pope's diet as appropriate for the condition. Perhaps in spite of, rather than because of, this treatment, Pius recovered, but subsequent examinations revealed some cardiovascular sclerosis, particularly in the myocardium, as well as some significant decrease in the elasticity of the wall of the aorta—all of which might be expected in any man of the pope's age.

Suddenly, at the close of August, 1952, Pius was stricken with a severe attack of gastritis. An analysis of the results of his frequent attacks of vomiting showed both traces of blood and elevated levels of stomach acid. In addition, traces of albumin began to appear in the urine, suggesting the onset of kidney dysfunction, and Pius also exhibited some signs of lymphocytosis. As the pope daily became weaker, Galeazzi-Lisi cast about wildly for some cause for these symptoms. Eventually, he decided that Pius had poisoned himself through the overuse of a chromic acid solution that the pope used when he brushed his teeth and massaged his gums. There is no other evidence beyond the doctor's opinion to support this diagnosis, and Pius showed his rejection of the idea by continuing to use this preparation in his personal hygeine. Although he suffered some permanent debility from his illness, Pius did recover and had returned to a full schedule of work by late November.

Although Pius had full confidence in the robustness of his constitution and in his recuperative powers, the long illness of 1952 persuaded him to yield to the growing pressure to name new cardinals. Between the Grand Consistory in 1946 and the closing weeks of 1952, twenty-three cardinals had died, which reduced the membership to forty-six. Among those twenty-three, no fewer than nine were Italian curial cardinals—Enrico Gasparri, Caccia Dominioni, Salotti, Pignatelli di Belmonte, Sibilia, Rossi, Marmaggi, Lavitrano, and Marchetti-Selvaggiani. More and more congregations that customarily were headed by cardinal prefects now were administered by pro-prefects, still other offices that usually were led by cardinals were now under *sostituti*. Because of Pius's well-known desire to concentrate power in his own hands—"I am looking for executors, not collaborators," he once said to his *sostituti* in the secretariat of state, Montini and Tardini—and because of his desire to internationalize the upper reaches of the hierarchy, some curial officials went so far as to think that he might let the number of curial cardinals dwindle to almost nothing, and perhaps with only two or three Italians among that few, were he to reign long enough. This was not entirely an idle fear. By the end of 1952, there were only fourteen curial cardinals left alive, ten of whom had been named to the College by Pius XI. Of the fourteen, four were over eighty and another five were over seventy-five, and all of them were Italian. And, just as alarming for the longer term, two of the five "younger men" were a Frenchman, Tisserant, and a Russian, Agagianian.

Since the cardinalate began as a curial institution in the first place—the first non-curial cardinal in history was Konrad von Wittelsbach, Archbishop of Mainz, son of Otto, Duke of Bavaria, who was created by Alexander III in 1163, six hundred years after the first emergence of the Roman office of cardinal—the possibility that curial representation in the College might actually end, or be reduced to so low a number as to be without influence, was appalling to Vatican officials.

So, when Pius began to rally from his illness in the fall of 1952, nearly the whole of the Vatican bureaucracy united to press the pope, from meeting to meeting, from day to day, to elevate new members to the College, reminding him, as softly as they dared, that there were now twenty-four vacancies, and that his own recent crisis of health made a fresh creation prudent. Pius, of course, also was well aware that seven of the twenty-three who had died since 1946 were his own creations—Glennon, von Galen, Parrado y Garcia, Petit de Julleville, Arcé y Ochotorena, von Preysing, and the great Sapieha. Finally, after protracted discussions through the fall, a final list of twenty-four names was settled and published on November 29. The date for the consistory at which the formal creations would take place was set for January 12, 1953.

Celso Costantini: *Chancellor*
Agosto Alvaro da Silva: *Archbishop of São Salvador da Bahia*
Gaetano Cicognani: *Prefect, Congregation of Rites*
Angelo Giuseppe Roncalli: *Patriarch of Venice*
Valerio Valeri: *Prefect, Cong. of Religious*
Pietro Ciriaci: *Prefect, Cong. of the Council*
Francesco Borgongini Duca: *Vatican administration*
Maurice Feltin: *Archbishop of Paris*
Marcello Mimmi: *Archbishop of Naples*
Carlos María de la Torre: *Archbishop of Quito*
Alojzije Stepinac: *Archbishop of Zagreb*
Georges Grente: *Archbishop-Bishop of Le Mans*
Giuseppe Siri: *Archbishop of Genoa*
John D'Alton: *Archbishop of Armagh*

James Francis Louis McIntyre: *Archbishop of Los Angeles*
Giacomo Lercaro: *Archbishop of Bologna*
Stefan Wyzynski: *Archbishop of Gniezno and Warsaw*
Benjamin de Arriba y Castro: *Archbishop of Tarragona*
Fernando Quiroga y Palacios: *Archbishop of Santiago de Compostella*
Paul-Emile Léger: *Archbishop of Montréal*
Crisanto Luque: *Archbishop of Bogotá*
Valerian Gracias: *Archbishop of Bombay*
Joseph Wendel: *Archbishop of München and Freising*
Alfredo Ottaviani: *Prefect, Congregation of the Holy Office*

At first glance, the fact that six of the twenty-four were Italian curial cardinals, and four others were Italian ordinaries, makes it appear that the curia was, slightly, victorious in reversing Pius's policy with respect to the naming of new cardinals. A longer consideration, however, makes it clear that the "victory" was only partial and rather hollow. Five of the six new curial cardinals were in their late sixties or older—Costantini (76), Cicognani (71), Valeri (69), Borgognini Duca (68), and Ciriaci (67). Only Ottaviani, at sixty-two, was a "younger man."

By contrast, six of the fourteen non-Italians were both young and vigorous by the standards of the College—Léger (48), Wyzynski (51), Wendel (51), Gracias, the first Indian cardinal in history (52), Quiroga y Palacios (52), and Stepinac (54). And of the four Italian residential cardinals, Siri of Genoa was just forty-six and Lercaro of Bologna was an exceptionally energetic sixty-one—and both were pastoral and anti-curial to the core.

The Pacelli were a remarkably long-lived family, and Pius himself may well have expected to see the years of his reign equal those of Leo XIII or Pius IX. If he did think so, and there is some evidence that he did, chance favored his outliving not only all of the older curial cardinals created by Pius XI but also several, if not all, of those he himself had named, both in 1946 and in 1953. As it was, the remaining five years, nine months of Pius's reign saw the deaths of five more of the remaining nine Italian curial cardinals of Pius XI—Nasalli-Rocca di Corneliano, Massimi, Jorio, Mercati, and Piazza—as well as two of the ten he had named: Bruno and Borgognini Duca. Another curial creation of 1953, Celso Costantini, died during the *sede vacante* of 1958, before the conclave opened.

In addition, Pius had more knowledge of the political and diplomatic history of the modern church than all but a few of his contemporaries. He knew well the historical criteria used to select popes, and he knew that, since the death of Clement XII in 1740—blind, incapacitated by gout, and with failing mental powers—the conclaves always had chosen new popes whose age fell within a fairly narrow window from fifty-seven to sixty-eight—old enough to be fully experienced, young enough to have some remaining vigor. The only exception to this rule had been Pius IX, who was fifty-four when he was elected in 1846. Based on this precedent, Pius was confident that perhaps only Agagianian of the curial cardinals would be alive at the end of his reign and could become a serious candidate for the throne. And, indeed, when he died in 1958, at an earlier date than he had expected, four of Pius XI's five surviving curial cardinals were more than eighty: Fumasoni-Biondi (86), Tedeschini (85), Canali (84), and Pizzardo (81); while Tisserant was seventy-four. Similarly, five of the seven curial cardinals he had created were in their mid-seventies or older: Aloisi Masella (79), Micara (79), Cicognani (77), Valeri (75), and Ciriaci (73); only Ottaviani (68) and Agagianian (64) met the modern criterion of age to be *papabili*. The same criterion excluded five of the seven Italian residential ordinaries, as well: Dalla Costa of Florence (86), Fossati of Turin (82), Roncalli of Venice (77), Mimmi of Naples (76), and Ruffini of Palermo (70); only Lercaro of Bologna (68) fell within the "age window," because Siri of Genoa probably was too young at fifty-two.

Can we discern from these figures Pius's purpose in his distribution of membership in the College of Cardinals and his expectations of his successor? Of the Italians and the curial cardinals, he might have expected both Agagianian and Siri to be *papabili* one day, as indeed they were, but it cannot be thought seriously that he was carrying out his revolution specifically to benefit a secretly-chosen name. It can, however, be speculated that he was manipulating the College to produce another result—a non-Italian pope. Indeed, if he had lived for six years longer than he did—well within his own expectations of himself—and had continued the same policies with regard to the College of Cardinals, which almost certainly he would have done, he would have seen the end of eight of the seventeen remaining Italians and only Siri would have been left as a serious Italian candidate; while, by then, several of his non-Italian "younger men" would have met the traditional age criterion very well, including Léger of Montreal, Wyzynski of Warsaw, Gracias of Bombay, Quiroga y Palacios of Santiago de Compostella, and Stepinac of Zagreb. From the background, mind, and spirit of Pius XII who better to lead the church in the titanic struggle against Marxism than an experienced Russian, Croat or Pole; what better signal to the millions of newly evangelized Catholics throughout the world than an Indian pope. Is there any evidence at all that this speculation may be true? William Arthur Purdy recovered just one anecdote about the Grand Consistory, which he included in *The Church on the Move.*

Someone asked Pius about the potential effect of creating thirty-two cardinals of whom only four were Italian. The pope replied, "Well, it might mean that I shall have a foreign successor."

When Pius XI died in 1939, there were sixty-two cardinals, of whom thirty-five were Italian. Twenty-seven of those thirty-five were curial officials, as was the Frenchman, Tisserant, giving the curia forty-five percent of the electorate. Almost twenty years later, when the voting started in 1958, there were fifty-one cardinals, of whom only twelve were curial officials—giving the curial representation only 23.5 percent of the electorate. During those same twenty years, the number of Italian curial cardinals had fallen from twenty-seven to ten. And even of those ten, only one, Alfredo Ottaviani, could be said to hold to political and theological standards comparable to those of the integrists in 1914 and 1922—his motto, *Semper Idem* (*Always the Same*), was one public evidence of this. Moreover, while thirty-five of the sixty-two cardinals in 1939 were Italians, in 1958 only seventeen were. At one-third of the membership, it was the smallest Italian presence in a conclave since the election of Calixtus III in 1455, five hundred years before. This was the ultimate triumph of Pius XII over the forces of integrism and reaction, especially in the Vatican bureaucracy. It was his cardinalitial revolution that set the stage for the powerful *aggiornamento* of John XXIII. When it is recalled that the overwhelming majority of the bishops who sat at the Second Vatican Council, including almost all of the leading Council fathers, were raised to the episcopacy by Pius XII, the full force of his contribution to the making of the modern church can be appreciated.

During the spring and summer of 1953, Pius remained well and strong but, in September, he had, for the first time, a prolonged siege of those hiccoughs which would plague him, and debilitate him, for much of the rest of his life. At the same time, he began to experience pain in his right hand and, eventually, it became so weak that he was no longer able to write for prolonged periods. It was at this time that he began to rely on the typewriter as his principal means of written communication. Galeazzi-Lisi decided, after X-ray examinations, that the cause was an arthritic condition that stemmed from an incident in 1950 when a pilgrim had gripped Pius's hand with too much force. At the time, the strain had seemed slight, but now the doctor ascribed the cause of the present debility to it. While Pius was suffering with these troubles, he developed an abscess between the molar and premolar on the upper right side of his jaw. The pope described this pain as the greatest he had experienced in his life. Eventually, an extraction relieved the condition. Later, during the fall, he also recovered the full use of his right hand. By January, 1954, however, his hiccoughs had increased in both frequency and intensity to the point that the pope was exhausted, nervous, and tired almost continually. In addition, there were evident signs of an increasing gastritis. News of the pope's condition had now become general public knowledge, and thousands of letters containing hundreds of cures for hiccoughs poured into the Vatican.

At about this same time, Monsignor Ludwig Kaas, a specialist in the maintenance and restoration of medieval mosaics who headed the office charged with the care of the mosaics in Saint Peter's, conversed with the pope about the work of the Swiss gerontologist, Paul Niehans, who advocated a rejuvenative treatment of injections of cellular extracts from the hypothalamus and adrenal glands of fetal lambs. Pius was greatly interested in this, as a part of his expectation of a very long pontificate in which he wished to retain his general health and vigor for as long as possible. Galeazzi-Lisi also discussed the Niehans treatments with the pope and expressed his skepticism about them. In spite of his adverse opinion, Galeazzi-Lisi tried a course of the treatment and experienced no ill effects—a fact which he communicated to Pius.

On January 26, 1954, at Pius's own request, Niehans came to the Vatican and administered his cellular injection. The papal reaction was violent, and almost catastrophic. Within a day, Pius was vomiting profusely. The gastric expulsions were black in color, of a very high acidity, and had distinct traces of blood. Soon afterward, blood also appeared in his waste. With rest and careful diet, the pope eventually overcame the consequences of the treatment and its resulting debilitation. By July, his weight had returned to its normal 165 pounds and, now fully recovered, he made his annual journey to the papal summer palace at Castel Gandolfo.

As the summer waned, Pius decided, inexplicably and against all advice, to receive another treatment from Niehans. On September 12, Niehans injected the pope with another ampoulle of the cellular extract and, as those around him feared, the reaction was even more severe and violent. The same symptoms as those Pius had experienced in January were fully evident on the following day, but this time he also exhibited symptoms of a stomach lesion. During October, the gastric disturbances persisted—a burning sensation in his stomach accompanied by frequent gastric spasms and attacks of hiccoughs, now never far away from his daily experience. Galeazzi-Lisi's examinations and X-rays now revealed wide creases in the mucous lining of the stomach that converged to a point in the mesogastric region which, when palpated, produced considerable pain. Once again, Galeazzi-Lisi conducted a full physical and radiological examination. He now discovered that the frequent bouts of hiccoughs had produced a chronic phlegm and had caused a slight separation of the right vocal chord.

As had been the case with the January episode, rest and a carefully regulated diet brought a recuperation and, by the beginning of November, the pope resumed his full working schedule. Once recovered, Pius again asked that Niehans give him another injection of the cellular extract. The pope's peremptory orders could not be ignored, and Niehans came once again and administered a third injection on November 7. On this occasion, the violent reaction to the treatment was delayed for some days, perhaps because Pius's body was developing some tolerance for the foreign matter. Nevertheless, ultimately the reaction appeared once more, in an even more serious and enervating form. The hiccoughs returned, accompanied by a severe burning sensation in his stomach. The episodes of vomiting came again, as well, with the same traces of blood and high acidity.

On the morning of December 2, Pius's condition suddenly worsened dramatically. He became very pale and sank into a semi-stupor. Galeazzi-Lisi found himself beyond mere exasperation when Pius requested him, in a weak voice, to send for Niehans yet again. Within a short time, the situation became so grave that the pope thought himself near death. Messages were dispatched to the other Pacelli in or near Rome to come at once. Galeazzi-Lisi did his utmost to persuade Pius to agree to allow him to call in outside medical consultants. When members of his family also agreed with this course of action, and were strengthened by some of the staff from the secretariat of state, the pope acquiesced.

Seeing that death could supervene at any moment, Galeazzi-Lisi told the pope that, if he wished, he could admit Cardinal Eugene Tisserant, the dean of the College, and Cardinal Nicola Canali, archdeacon of the College, penetentiary major, and for years Pius's chief financial advisor, for a brief audience. At the pope's bedside, they urged the pontiff to hold a consistory in his bedchamber for the purpose of naming new cardinals. Two popes, they reminded him, had held such consistories—Clement IX on November 29, 1669, ten days before his death, and Pius IX on December 28, 1877, forty-one days before his end. Ill as he was, Pius grasped the meaning of their ploy at once, rejected the idea, and then dismissed them.

By 6:00 P.M., the reign seemed nearly over. Pius's features were very strained, his skin and mucous membranes were livid. His stomach was so distended that the abdominal region was rigid and tympanous; he was greatly dehydrated; and his vital signs were ominous—for, although his blood pressure was 130/90, his pulse had increased to 140.

As the evening wore on, the hiccoughs and the attacks of vomiting continued to be very frequent, and the consequence of the latter was green and viscous, with included clots of blood. Galeazzi-Lisi now did another X-ray, this time of the peritoneum, to determine whether or not he also was now dealing with either a perforation of the bowel or an intestinal blockage. The X-ray showed neither. Nevertheless, the alimentary system below the stomach became greatly distended and meteoric.

Just when the last moments seemed as if they could not be far away, around midnight, the hiccoughs ceased, his pulse became slower and more regular, his temperature returned to normal, and his blood pressure dropped to 125/80. Although Pius was unable to sleep for the remainder of the night, there were some periods of relative calm, as the incidents of vomiting became less frequent. From time to time, he had short bouts of the hiccoughs but, by morning, the slow and measured return from the close brush with death continued. Later in the morning, Pius was able to ingest slowly some small amounts of milk, coffee, beer, tea, consommé with fruit juice, some soft egg, vitamins, and even a little champagne. The short medical bulletin released on the evening of December 3 summed up the circumstances well: "Today, the doctor had a consultation about the condition of the Sovereign Pontiff. The improvement of this morning gives the doctors some hope."

Pius's steady improvement continued over the next several days. Some were better than others, and there were recurrences of both the hiccoughs and the vomiting, but, in general, his recovery seemed almost miraculous. He now resumed work on a very light schedule. Each day he recorded a small part of the address that would be played in Santa Maria Maggiore, during the ceremonies on December 8 which marked the end of the Marian Year.

By December 9, the hiccoughs and the burning sensation in his stomach at last disappeared and the pope seemed certain to recover.

A small portable altar had been set up in the antecamera adjacent to his bedroom, and now Pius began each day at seven o'clock by having the doors between the two rooms thrown open while he heard mass. After this, he often was carried to a small chaise, where he would stay for many hours, reading documents and doing other light work, with frequent interruptions for rest. He continued to receive small transfusions of whole blood, to strengthen him and to relieve a slight anemia.

By December 15, Galeazzi-Lisi thought that he was strong enough to withstand a comprehensive physical and radiological examination lasting several hours. A part of this procedure included X-rays of the thorax and of the digestive system. These revealed a lingering, but not critical, gastritis, as well as a small hyatial hernia and evidences of reflux in the esophagus. In the light of the latter evidence, Galeazzi-Lisi ordered that additional pillows be placed on the pope's bed to allow him to sleep in a partially elevated position to prevent a recurrence of the reflux.

At this time, Pius began to take a little exercise through short walks in the open air. His only reaction to this was the appearance of a tingling sensation in his legs at night which disturbed his sleep. But this condition was alleviated easily by alcohol rubs.

A further examination on January 18 showed him still further improved and, on January 20, Galeazzi-Lisi pronounced his patient recoverd. The final encouraging sign was that his weight, which had dropped from his normal 165 to 136 pounds during the worst days of his illness, had risen again to 163.

On Sunday, April 17, 1955, a week after Easter, he was so restored that he was able to preside over the long and tiring service for the beatification of the Chinese martyrs. Although the crisis was over, Pius never forgot how close he had come to death. His general demeanor and character became more nervous and febrile, and he at last believed that his reign might not be as long as he had once expected and that he might not live as long as his relatives. He resumed his full schedule and the even regularity of his life for the next four years, but it was never quite the same.

By 1958, the papal routine for the summer differed little from that of previous years. In spite of his gradually diminishing physical powers, punctuated by more and more frequent bouts of ill health, Pius admitted little variance in his daily schedule of audiences, both with curial staff and with visitors, and his administrative work.

As usual, he moved to Castel Gandolfo in early August to stay for the hotter months of the year, just as he had done each summer since the war's end. Just twelve miles southeast of the limits of Rome itself, amid a small group of towns called the Castelli Romani, the residence is quite different from the usual conception of an Italian summer villa. It is, in fact, a vast and splendid palace whose facilities for papal government are hardly less than the conveniences of the Vatican itself. In early classical times, it was the site of Alba Longa, a citadel and village to which Roman legend ascribed the rôle of mother of many of the Latin cities, including Rome itself.

In the Imperial Age, the Emperor Domitian (81–96) built his own summer residence there, amid a cluster of early ruins and restored ancient temples still visible from the primitive age. Although the place lost its early strategic importance for Rome, its elevation—fourteen hundred feet above sea level—and its position on the shores of little Lake Albano, a water-filled crater in a dormant volcano, has made it a desirable site for centuries. In the twelfth century, a scion of the Genoese Gandolfi family built a castle there, which eventually passed into the hands of the Savelli, the family of Popes Honorius III (1216–1227) and Honorius IV (1285–1287). In 1596, the property fell into the hands of Clement VIII who, eight years later, declared it to be an inalienable part of the papal patrimony. In 1624, less than a year after his election, Urban VIII ordered all of the old structure to be pulled down and replaced by a lavish residence designed by Carlo Maderno, the architectural genius who defined the early Baroque style in Rome. Nearby, at the same time, rose the smaller but equally sumptuous Villa Barberini, the summer residence of Francesco Barberini, Urban's favorite cardinal-nephew. Also close by is the Villa Cibo, a retreat built for the family of Innocent VIII (1484–1492). All three estates are now joined as a single, extraterritorial entity. The papal palace was enlarged and embellished significantly by several popes, notably Alexander VII (1655–1667), Clement XIII (1758–1769), and Pius IX (1846–1878). During its long period of papal disuse, from 1870 to 1929, it fell into disrepair, but, after the Lateran Treaties of 1929 restored it to the popes, Pius XI had its facilities modernized throughout, including both land-line and radio communication with the Vatican. He also moved the Vatican's astronomical observatory to the site in 1936. The papal establishment at Castel Gandolfo, then, is a complex of buildings, joined together by large and elaborate gardens, rather than a simple vacation retreat.

At the summer palace, the pope continued his full round of audiences and receptions for the persons and groups who made the journey out from the city to see him. Of his many engagements, none was more pleasing to him than a performance of Sir Edward Elgar's *Dream of Gerontius*, a setting of the mystical text by Cardinal Newman. Pius seemed spellbound by the power of England's foremost Catholic composer and, when the performance ended, he said quietly to the conductor, Sir John Barbirolli, "My son, that is a sublime masterpiece." The concert was, indeed, a rare refreshing moment from his audiences with hematologists, judges, beekeepers, and executives from the gas industry.

Normally, Pius and his court would move back to Rome as the summer ended. On this occasion, however, his physician, Doctor Riccardo Galeazzi-Lisi, suggested that he prolong his stay for some weeks in the hope that a little more of the life and air of Castel Gandolfo would add to his dwindling store of strength. Throughout the latter part of August and then through September, the members of Pius's staff had noticed a distinct weakening of his physical state, combined with a heightened paleness. In addition, Pius once again was experiencing an increase in those episodes of hiccoughs which had debilitated him so much in 1954. Galeazzi-Lisi's suggestion that the pontiff remain at the summer residence reflected his real concern, especially because Pius always found the two moves each year, to and from Castel Gandolfo, to be extremely trying. Once Pius had acquiesced to the suggestion that he remain in the country, Galeazzi-Lisi thought that he could be free for a few days to attend a conference in Brussels and left his patient in the care of Sister Pasqualina and her squad of four nuns, who made up the immediate household staff of the pope.

At first, it seemed that the pope's condition was stable, at least, but in the last days of September his attacks of hiccoughs increased alarmingly and the ensuing exhaustion and debilitation were sufficient to summon Galeazzi-Lisi back from Belgium.

On the afternoon of Wednesday, October 1, just before Pius's weekly general audience for the public, the Vatican issued a bulletin which stated that the pontiff was suffering from a "slight indisposition" and that he had been advised to reduce his heavy schedule for a time. A few moments later, the pope appeared on the audience balcony, but remained in public for only eight minutes, compared with the half hour or hour that he usually stood there. He dropped his customary words of welcome in several languages and, after acknowledging the cheers of the people for a few moments, imparted his papal blessing and withdrew. Later in the day, official sources elaborated slightly on their earlier announcement and added that the pope was "fatigued" from overwork. In fact, the attacks of hiccoughs had reduced him to near total exhaustion.

Galeazzi-Lisi was back at Castel Gandolfo on Thursday and managed to get his patient to rest quietly for some time. This pause brought a slight rally to the pope's condition. On Friday, October 3, he received a large group of pilgrims who had come from New York to Rome in the company of Cardinal Spellman. While his voice was steady as he spoke to them in English, those closest to him noticed that he fought back attacks of the hiccoughs on several occasions. Following this audience, Pius met privately with Spellman for about twenty minutes. This short audience was the first real signal to the outside world that the pope was seriously ill. He had not seen Spellman for some time, and, in such cases before, their private conversations often lasted for hours. The quick end to their meeting now, and Spellman's later private comments about Pius's state of health and his demanding schedule, were significant. No pope can have a voice in the election of his successor, but each does have two traditional signals by which he can suggest a suitable pontiff for the future. One is the name of the cardinal who stands first in precedence among those in the first creation of the new reign, as John XXIII did in naming Giovanni Battista Montini first among the cardinals he elevated on December 15, 1958—generally, cardinals are ranked in each creation based on their seniority as bishops. In 1946, it was the cardinal-patriarch Krekor Agagianian whose name stood first, but, as a patriarch, his name might be expected to precede those of the prelates who were archbishops or bishops. Another is the prelate to whom the pope gives his own red hat, his own former symbol of the cardinalate, before the custom of presenting the great *galerum rubrum* was abolished by Paul VI. In 1946, Pius presented his to Frank Spellman, the archbishop of New York. Their relationship to one another was as close to that of father and son as can exist between two unrelated men who each occupy offices of great power. Spellman's rapid departure from the presence of his beloved mentor was, therefore, as clear an announcement of Pius's condition as an honest formal bulletin might have been.

Following Spellman's departure, Pius again was persuaded to rest. These periods of relative inactivity did seem to produce some slight improvement, as had been shown by the results of his ease on the night before. He felt so refreshed on the following morning that his scheduled audience with the members of the Italian Society of Plastic Surgeons went ahead as planned. After it concluded, Pius rested once again.

On Sunday, October 5, the pope awoke again with a sense of well-being and recovery. He insisted on carrying forward his full day's schedule, in spite of his recent debilitation. In the morning, he received members of the curial staff and, later, he granted a private audience to Alec Guinness, who was a recent convert to Catholicism. Guinness had been invited to this private papal reception because of several recent triumphs that had elevated him to the first rank of the theatrical world. His period of conversion saw his polished and delicate performance as the Crown Prince in the film adaptation of Ferenc Molnár's play, *A hattyú* (*The Swan*); followed by his powerful evocation of British military pride and honor in *The Bridge on the River Kwai*, for which he received the Oscar for the best performance by an actor; and then his rôle as Gulley Jimson in his own screenplay from Joyce Carey's novel, *The Horse's Mouth*—for this, too, Guinness received an Oscar nomination, for the best screenplay based on material from another medium.

By the conclusion of his brief conversation with the actor, Pius's hiccoughs had returned with such intensity that he often was forced to make prolonged pauses between his words. Guinness was the last person from beyond the papal establishment to see the pope alive. In the evening, after a detailed conversation with the pope about his condition, Galeazzi-Lisi decided that the best course of treatment was a gastric lavage with an alkaline solution, which he proposed to carry out early on the next day. After this decision, Pius retired for the night, again in the hope that rest would prove to be the best cure.

Just after six on the morning of Monday, October 6, Galeazzi-Lisi returned to the pope's apartments, accompanied by Professor Ferdinando Corelli of the University of Rome, a cardiologist who was to administer the lavage, since he had wide experience in this treatment. The two physicians found the pope already awake and dressed, seated in an armchair between the two large windows of his bedroom. Within a few moments, assisted by Sister Pasqualina, the two had prepared all the materials and equipment necessary for the procedure.

Much to the relief of everyone present, the treatment went better than anyone had expected. The pope accepted the intubation without difficulty, and when the alkaline solution was aspirated from his stomach it was seen to be perfectly clear, free from any undigested nutrients or debris and, especially, free from blood.

The pope's evident relief at the smoothness of the procedure and its very favorable outcome left him in unusually high spirits. He remained seated in his armchair while he conducted a good-humored conversation with those present. They all chatted together about the beauty of the estate at Castel Gandolfo and its salubrious climate—so different from the heat and sultriness of Rome, yet so close to the city—and about that most common of all human topics, the weather. "You know Peppe the gardener, downstairs," said the pope. "He knows how to predict the weather. Peppe is never fooled. If you wish to know how the weather will be, do not consult the weather bulletin, ask Peppe. Peppe is more than a human barometer, he is a wine grower. . . ." Pius exhibited rare lightheartedness and began to joke. "Do you know the story of the man who was taken to the hospital because of his enormous belly," he began. "The doctors told him that he had dropsy, but the man, who was a wine grower like Peppe, said to them, 'That is not possible, I always have made my own wine. I never add water. And I don't drink anything else. So where does this water come from that you say you have found in my belly?'"

Suddenly, Pius's expression seemed startled and the color drained from his face. "Professor," he cried out to Galeazzi-Lisi, with a slurring of his speech, "I can hardly speak . . . I can't see anything . . . What is happening to me? Have you shut the windows? Is the weather bad, perhaps? I can't see anything . . . I can't see anything." He tried to raise his hand to his eyes, but could not.

Sister Pasqualina and the two doctors lifted him from the chair and carried him to a divan near his bed. The nun tried to give him some water, but by then the pope was unconscious.

Galeazzi-Lisi now sent for another physician, Professor Pietro Gasbarrini, a gastroenterologist on the faculty of the University of Bologna, to join him in assessing the pope's condition. Gasbarrini came immediately and the two reviewed the condition of the unconscious old man. The present symptoms—a decrease in the reflexes of the pupils of the eyes, accompanied by exaggerated reflexes in his feet, his Achilles tendons, and his patellæ, especially on the left side of his body; muscle spasms, again especially on the left; and the appearance of the Babinsky effect, most marked in the left foot—all suggested that the pope had suffered a severe cerebral thrombosis, a fairly massive stroke. The outward manifestations that occurred before Pius lost consciousness—blindness, aphasia, paresis, and his difficulty with speech and swallowing—seemed to locate the event near the middle cerebral artery.

Galeazzi-Lisi decided at once to undertake a powerful and massive intervention. In rapid order, he administered strong doses of camphor, caffeine, sparteine, aminophylline, and a papaverine homologue called Eupaverin, all of which he had ready from the large store of drugs that had been placed in the residence just in the case of such an emergency. This powerful cocktail of vasodilators and cardiac stimulants, the doctors hoped, would relax the obstructed blood vessels to prevent both further thrombosis and hemorrhage. Immediately afterward, an oxygen tent was brought into the bedroom and placed over the pope, and a glucose drip was started.

Someone suggested, because of the gravity of the situation, that Pius be given extreme unction, the sacrament for those who may die. According to the protocol of the papal household, it was the sacristan, Monsignor Pieter Canisius van Lierde, who should perform that function, but he was at the Vatican and could not be expected to arrive for some time. The pope's immediate staff, who had now gathered outside the door of his bedroom as the alarm spread, included one of the consultors of the Congregation of the Holy Office, the Jesuit Father Wilhelm Hentrich, who was at Castel Gandolfo as a reference assistant to the pope. He was the nearest priest, and was now brought into the bedroom quickly to administer the last rites.

While the pope lay silent, messages were dispatched to both members of the Pacelli family and to those functionaries whose presence was required in case the pope died. The first of these messages was a telegram to Eugene Tisserant, who had been, since 1951, the Cardinal-Bishop of Ostia and Porto and Dean of the Sacred College. In the absence of a camerlengo, it would be his duty to preside formally over the last moments of the pontificate. Tisserant was himself enjoying a brief summer vacation at Nancy in France, his birthplace. Now the French government placed an airliner at his disposal for the fastest possible return to Rome.

Meanwhile, as news of Pius's critical condition moved by word of mouth through the Vatican, and then through Rome, a sense of real panic began to overtake the curia and the rest of the ecclesiastical establishment in Rome. Pius had been on the throne for almost twenty years and his rule had been both autocratic and direct. By 1958, most of those working under him had served no other pope, and they—as is often the case when a subordinate population loses its leader—seemed almost unable to function. After all, the pope was not dead, just incapacitated. What if he were to recover and then disapprove strongly of actions or decisions they had made during the emergency?

The situation was made all the worse because, throughout the morning, the Vatican's official posture was that the reports were all rumor and that nothing of consequence had happened. Finally, at about one o'clock in the afternoon, came a short announcement that the pope was seriously ill. So great was the official paralysis that it had taken nearly five hours from the moment word was received at the Vatican to prepare and release the briefest of announcements.

While the confusion and alarm in Rome continued to rise throughout the late morning and early afternoon, at Castel Gandolfo the pope was making a near-miraculous recovery. The most serious of his symptoms receded in the reverse order of their appearance and soon Pius regained conciousness. His first words were "What has happened? What has occurred?"

A fresh physical examination revealed only one new complication, an obstructed vesicle. To treat this, Galeazzi-Lisi sent for one of Rome's leading urologists, Doctor Ermanno Mingazzini. In addition, Pius was now given an additional dose of camphor as well as injections of atropine and digitalis, and another glucose drip was set up.

By the early evening, the pope was once again completely lucid. He sat up, saying, "I have to work; I have to write; there are people whom I must receive . . . I cannot be ill."

Finally, at 6:30 P.M., the last official bulletin of the day was released at the Vatican. The English text read:

> The conditions of the Holy Father have notably improved as far as the circulatory disturbances of the brain are concerned. Suitable treatment has immediately been begun. The Holy Father's strong constitution has again shown considerable powers of resistance. Further observation is necessary before a final prognosis can be made.

It was almost true.

For the large number of people now clustered in the summer palace, the clearest sign that the pope was now expected to recover was that Monsignor van Lierde, the sacristan, was now present, but he was not asked to administer the last rites to the pontiff again.

The pope now was moved from the divan, on which he had lain all day, to his bed and soon fell asleep. During the night, Galeazzi-Lisi monitored his patient nearly constantly, and continued to administer his medical cocktail of vasodilators and cardiac stimulants. To these were added anti-biotics, because of the probe that Dr. Mingazzini had used to clear the vesicular obstruction. In general, the spirits of those present were high. The only disquieting note was another return of episodes of hiccoughs—the very condition which had lead to the crisis in the first place. Pius awoke for the first time at about four, with a complete absence of his hiccoughs, and then fell asleep again.

When Pius awakened for the second time on the morning of the seventh, at about 9:00, he himself was persuaded that he would overcome the present situation, as well. First, he heard Mass and received communion, and he, and those about him, were delighted when he was able to swallow the wafer, which showed that this faculty, too, had returned. He was able to speak rather clearly, although still not with the precision of enunciation that was his habit.

When one of the nuns pressed forward to inquire, "How do you feel? How to you feel?" he replied, somewhat testily, "Well, completely well." In the first physical examination, which followed the Mass, he took the thermometer from under his arm, read it, and nodded, as if expressing satisfaction with the result. The morning bulletin, released at 7 A.M., read:

> The Holy Father, in general, continues to improve. His sensory apparatus appears completely lucid. There are no signs of motor deficiency. Hiccups reappeared yesterday evening, but disappeared this morning. His temperature, which was 37.5 Centigrade (99 Fahrenheit) yesterday evening, was 37.0 Centigrade (98.6 Fahrenheit) this morning. His pulse was 82 and his breathing normal. His Holiness was able to take food.

Again, the text, drafted by Galeazzi-Lisi, was almost true. The hiccoughs had not disappeared completely, and, as yet, Pius had eaten nothing.

Outside the bedroom, the crowd which had gathered on the previous day remained, while a visitor's register was set up for the throngs of ambassadors, officials of the Italian government, and curial functionaries, including every cardinal in Rome, who came to call and to wish the pope a speedy recovery.

None of these persons was admitted to the sickroom, except Cardinal Tisserant, who had come directly from his landing. At ten o'clock, he spoke privately with Pius for a few moments and, somewhat reassured that this crisis, like the earlier ones, would pass, left the chamber.

A few moments later, Pius was told that Monsignor Angelo Dell'Acqua, the under secretary of state, was one of those who were waiting outside. He insisted on seeing him at once. When Dell'Acqua told him that every where in the world people were praying for his recovery, he expressed great gratification. Dell'Acqua held in his hand some of the thousands of messages of concern which had poured into the Vatican since Pius had become ill. One of them was a radiogram from Frank Spellman, sent from the Greek liner *Olympia* on which the cardinal and his pilgrims were sailing back to New York. Pius insisted that this message be read to him in full, and then he dictated a brief reply: "We feel consoled and comforted in our illness by the tranquil message you have sent to us; and, with the assurance of our sincere gratitude, we impart to you and your pilgrims our paternal and apostolic blessing." It was his last message and his last official act, sent to the man for whom he cared the most. For Spellman, who received this reply by radio in the late afternoon, it was the "paternal" rather than the "apostolic" blessing which signalled that the long affection still stood.

But he was not yet fully lucid, as Dell'Acqua discovered at the end of his interview when the pope abruptly asked him why the audiences for the day had been canceled. He went on to say how much he regretted not being able to receive in public audience the pilgrims who had come to Castel Gandolfo to see him.

After Dell'Acqua left, at 11:30, Pius sat up in bed and took some light nourishment, which included a small serving of tapioca, some fruit juice, and about three ounces of Bordeaux. Later in the afternoon, his sister, Countess Elisabetha Pacelli Rossignani, visited him briefly.

At five o'clock, now fully seated upright in bed, the pope conversed with those about him with considerable animation. He asked Galeazzi-Lisi to play a recording of the first symphony of Beethoven, one of his favorite works, and, while the music played, he moved his right hand gently in keeping with the tempi. When the recording finished, he asked for another, but Galeazzi-Lisi refused him his request on the grounds that he needed to rest. Nevertheless, Pius continued with his conversation. At one point, Galeazzi-Lisi asked what music he preferred. After some reflection, Pius replied, "I like all music, but if I must choose, I would say: Wagner, Beethoven, Bach." He continued to talk about his ideas on music, and on art, in general. "Loving and cultivating music serves both art and religion at the same time. In fact, music, like the other arts, is a gift from God; it stimulates a rejoicing of the spirit, it delights and lifts the soul."

Pius's discourse was interrupted by another clinical examination, followed by more injections of stimulants and vasodilators. By six o'clock, the pope had lain down once again, when he suffered another attack of hiccoughs, although, on this occasion, the episode seemed relatively mild.

This attack was followed by a surge in his blood pressure, which had risen to 170/100 by six-thirty. Another injection, this one of an anti-hypertensive, lowered the figure to 140/85 and the pope was able to rest for a short time.

After a time, he asked for something more to eat, and, at 9:00 P.M., he was given a small serving of semolina with a meat gravy and a cup of sweetened chamomile tea, his favorite evening beverage. Galeazzi-Lisi had recommended it to him years before as a cure for his periodic insomnia and it became a regular part of his evening routine. Suddenly, his voice rose, as he said to one of the attending nuns, "But what are these doctors doing? Have they not disclosed the news? . . . bring me the newspapers!"

Galeazzi-Lisi panicked. He left the bedroom to confer with some of the cardinals and other curial prelates who were outside, urging them to print a false edition of *Osservatore Romano* quickly, one which would be filled with optimistic bulletins about the pope's health. The precedent for this, he said, was the false edition that had been prepared in the last days of Leo XIII and then presented to the dying pope to read. While the officials considered this somewhat bizarre request, Pius fell asleep for the night.

The doctor's reaction had been a surprise to those in the bedroom, but may well have been prompted by his memory of the official bulletin that he had approved for release at 5:30 P.M. The English text read:

> The Holy Father rested quietly this afternoon for three hours. Then he took regular nourishment. His condition in general remains satisfactory. Temperature 37.6 Centigrade (99.7 Fahrenheit). Blood pressure: maximum 130, minimum, 85, pulse 102, breathing 24. The therapeutic program that has been decided upon is being carried out in full.

Optimistic enough, but still embellished with half-truths, like the non-existent "regular nourishment," which the pope would recognize at once.

Although he was quiet, Pius did not fall asleep until nearly 3:00 A.M. In the meanwhile, in order to create the public impression that Pius was receiving the same spiritual treatment as any other ill Catholic, the pastor of the parish which included the summer residence, Father Dino Sella, was brought in to keep a vigil at the pope's bedside.

During the remainder of the night, the medical team remained with the pope. Galeazzi-Lisi, in particular, remained at the bedside, monitoring his patient's condition for any signs of change. At dawn, when he began to awake after his short sleep, Pius experienced cardiac arrhythmia. His respiration increased to twenty-one, his blood pressure rose to 140/80, his pulse reached a rapid 102; and his bladder emptied. Father Sella was rushed from the bedroom at 6:30, lest his observations contradict Galeazzi-Lisi's words.

Again, aggressive treatment seemed to ease the situation when, suddenly, at 7:30, while he was undergoing the morning clinical examination, Pius had a second, more massive, stroke. He immediately lapsed into a coma—his mouth thrown open and breathing labored. He was eased back in his bed and the oxygen tent was once again installed over him.

Galeazzi-Lisi again tried the cocktail of injections he had used forty-seven hours before, but this time there was no response from the failing patient.

A brief consultation among the physicians brought the agreement that the end was near. The Vatican was notified by telephone at once and all those prelates who had left on the evening before, convinced that the worst of the crisis was over, now began to hurry back to Castel Gandolfo. One of the first to arrive was Monsignor van Lierde, who now administered the last rites to the unconscious pope. A few minutes later, Cardinal Tisserant appeared. From that time forward, he would orchestrate the playing out of the drama. The outer offices and reception rooms of the palace were soon filled with crowds of dignitaries and officials. Their vehicles added to a confused welter of traffic outside the residence, and their persons contributed to a growing confusion within.

At noon, Pius's temperature was still a normal 98.6, but his blood pressure again had risen, to 130/80, and his pulse had sped to 115. An hour later, his temperature had begun its final rise and stood at 99.5, while the blood pressure and pulse also were elevated, at 140/90 and 130, respectively. This slight elevation in temperature suggested to Galeazzi-Lisi that the pope had begun to exhibit the symptoms of pneumonia. Only if he were able to arrest this secondary effect would there be any chance for Pius to recover. At two, Galeazzi-Lisi tried a final round of injections in a last effort to save the dying man. Pius received antibiotics as well as digitalis, but Galeazzi-Lisi also administered a large injection of canfoxil. Essentially a soluabilized camphor, canfoxil was a trade preparation of the ammonium salt of d-carboxylic acid that was recognized then as a powerful antibiotic and anti-infective. Usually, it was applied topically in a salve and Galeazzi-Lisi's use of the drug in an injection indicated his growing despair.

By this time, the bedroom was crowded with a large throng of persons. Some, like Tisserant and Clemente Micara, were cardinals who had significant parts to play were the pope to die, or to survive in an incapacitated state. Others, like the sacristan, Pieter Canisius van Lierde; his confessor, Father Augustin Bea, S.J.; and the *maestro di camera*, Federico Callori di Vignale, were prelates charged with specific rituals at the time of the pope's death. The members of the pope's family also clustered about him. His sister, Contessa Elisabetha Pacelli Rossignani, and his three nephews,

Princes Carlo, Giulio, and Marcantonio Pacelli, were close to him, as was Sister Pasqualina, who never was far from the side of the man she had served since his nunciature in Bavaria, forty years before.

The long afternoon and evening were filled with periods of prayer, led by one or another of the prelates, and by periodic physical examinations of the pope, to monitor his journey to death with precision. By three o'clock, the first signs of pneumonia clearly were present, and by four his temperature had reached 100.8. While his blood pressure remained steady at 140/90, his respiration had increased to 36 and his pulse to 140. Another examination, at 4:30 P.M., revealed signs of cardiopulmonary collapse. His pulse remained at 140, but his respiration had now increased to 38. By five o'clock, his respiration had reached 48—his breath was coming in short pants of little more than a second's duration—and his temperature now stood at 101.5, with a pulse of 155 and a blood pressure of 150/90. Any flickering hope that Pius might live was now extinguished.

At six, his blood pressure was elevated to 160/100. At about this time, Pius's right hand moved slightly several times as his last sign of life. Several persons in the room interpreted this as the pope's effort to impart a final blessing, but this was, unfortunately, a romantic label for the final muscle spasm, since he was now deeply comatose.

At 6:30, the room was disturbed by the bustling arrival of Dr. Paul Niehans, the Swiss gerontologist, whose rejuvenative treatment with cells extracted from the adrenal glands of monkeys Pius had received twice before. Unbidden and unwanted, he had hastened to Rome on hearing the reports of the pope's serious illness and had pressed his way through both the crowds and the guards by telling them that he, too, was one of the pope's doctors. As soon as Galeazzi-Lisi saw Niehans, he wondered if the Swiss had come again with his cellular treatments at so inappropriate a time. When Niehans, who just wanted the publicity of being one of the physicians at the dying pope's bedside, explained that he had no intention of trying to intervene in the current treatment or to prescribe new drugs, Galeazzi-Lisi was somewhat mollified, and, with as much grace as he could muster, said that he would be grateful if Niehans would join his efforts to those of the other doctors in the effort to save the pope—an empty statement, but one which defused the situation.

As the evening passed, all the signs of the approaching end became more acute. At seven, Pius's blood pressure was 150/80, respiration 46, pulse 130. A half hour later, his pulse was 140 and his respiration was 48, but the pope's blood pressure had begun its final fall, and stood at 140/90. At eight, the weakening continued: respiration 50, pulse 120, and blood pressure 140/80. By nine, Pius's increasing tachycardia had now driven his pulse to 142, his fever had risen to 105.5, while his blood pressure had dropped to 135/90. An hour later, his vital signs remained much the same—a fever of 104 and a pulse of 140—but now the old pope's death rattles were frequent and loud enough for all those in the room to hear them. By 11:00 P.M., the full force of the cardio-respiratory collapse was evident in all of the pope's vital signs—temperature 105.8, pulse 145, respiration 52, blood pressure 135/80.

Periodically, thoughout the evening, various prelates had said Mass at the little portable altar which had been set up so that Pius could hear Mass that morning. A little after midnight, Pius's single closest assistant, Archbishop Domenico Tardini, had come for his turn to offer mass at the bedside of the dying pope. When Pius had resumed the office of secretary of state himself, in 1944 after the death of Cardinal Luigi Maglione, he assigned the daily managerial affairs of the secretariat to two monsignori, Domenico Tardini and Giovanni Battista Montini. When Montini was exiled to the office of archbishop of Milan in 1954, Tardini was left as the church's principal diplomat, after the pope himself. Now, in 1958, he was the most powerful prelate in the church who was not yet a cardinal. While Tardini was vesting, microphones were installed by the altar so that his Mass could be broadcast over Vatican Radio. Many Romans stayed awake for this service, because Tardini, like Pius, was a native Roman whose person, as well as his warm voice and local accent, were well-known in the city. At the end of the mass, Tardini turned to face his patron and began to recite the prayers for the dying. Those who listened already had heard the gravity of his tone, a voice usually light and full of good humor, and now they heard the pauses, cracks, and efforts at control while Tardini made his way through the prayers.

As soon as Tardini had finished, Galeazzi-Lisi took the pope's temperature again. It had risen to 105.8. By 1:30 A.M., the pope's vital signs were: respiration 56, pulse 140, blood pressure 130/80, and temperature 106.2. A half hour later, Pius's systolic pressure had dropped to 70 and his fever had risen to 108.1. Now the end was expected at any moment, but still Pius struggled on in his silent fight to cling to life. The death agony was so prolonged that many of those present felt themselves drawn to a point of emotional and physical exhaustion. Another hour and a half passed. At 3:30, Galeazzi-Lisi took Pius's vital signs again, but noted in his record only that his systolic pressure had dropped to 60. Still the people around him could hear his gasping little pants and his persistant death rattle. Now those kneeling around the bed were both startled and appalled as they saw Galeazzi-Lisi take a camera from his bag and begin to snap pictures of the agonized pope.

Finally, at 3:52 A.M., Dr. Gasbarrini, reponding to a particularly loud death rattle, quickly put his stethoscope to Pius's heart, and then briefly felt for a pulse in the pope's wrist. Then, standing, he said, rather loudly, "He is dead"—later, this moment would become the official time of death, although Pius still lived. Galeazzi-Lisi rounded on the people in the bedroom and said, "No, no, he has not died, he breathes." But Tardini, trusting more in the word of a renowned medical professor than in the last attempt of the oculist who had served as Pius's private physician to retain medical authority, repeated Gasbarrini's words that Pius was dead. In the following four minutes, Pius did, indeed, breathe twice, at long intervals, after which a small rivulet of blood issued from the right corner of his lips; then his head, which had been elevated a little on pillows to assist his breathing, dropped forward. Galeazzi-Lisi bent over Pius one last time, to satisfy himself that the agony really was over, and then announced, "The Holy Father has died." It was 3:57 A.M., Thursday, October 9, 1958. At that moment, Cardinal Alfredo Ottaviani stepped forward and took Gasbarrini's stethoscope. Placing it firmly over Pius's heart, he verified for himself that the last had come. The he straigthened, and nodded affirmitively to Tisserant.

For a few seconds, the quiet of the murmurs, arising from prayer and from hushed conversation, which had permeated the room for hours was silenced. An absolute stillness enveloped the bedroom while the reality that the man who had been the most autocratic pope of the century, as well as the longest-reigning one, was truly gone. In that stillness, someone near the rear of the small group of about a dozen people stepped back and opened the door which led from the bedroom to the small antecamera. Suddenly, the leading edge of the great throng outside pushed its way into the death chamber and surged toward Pius's body. Now there were more than thirty people crowded into a space that had become both cramped and chaotic. Some tried to touch his bed and the covers over his body. Among the importunate was a television camera crew. Now, with an imperious roar, Cardinal Tisserant ordered the new throng to be driven out, an order with which Sister Pasqualina and her four nuns were happy to carry out with Germanic thoroughness. After a few more minutes, to reestablish some semblance of order, Tisserant bent over the corpse and, functioning as camerlengo *ad interim*, proclaimed that Pius XII was truly dead.

Even before this, however, Vatican Radio, which had been notified by telephone that the pope was gone, broke into its broadcast at 3:56 to announce that he had died at 3:52.

Once the official ceremony of certifying the pope's death was over, the people who had gathered at his bedside for so long began to file out of the chamber in twos and threes to find places for a little rest among the offices and antecameras of the palace.

As they left, four Conventual Franciscans, the *penitentiarii*, who had the traditional duty of carrying out the initial preparations of the pope's body, entered the room. They disrobed the corpse, sponged the body with alcohol, and shaved his beard with an electric razor.

Earlier, Pius had expressed the wish that his organs should not be removed after his death, a usual procedure in the process of embalming. Using this wish as an excuse for departing from accepted procedure, Galeazzi-Lisi now initiated a bizarre embalming process with embarassing consequences. The procedure, which had been developed by Oreste Nuzzi, a surgeon and crony of the pope's doctor, consisted of spraying the corpse with a compound of resins, oils, and other chemical compounds which were supposed to produce a deoxydizing effect that would prevent decay—Nuzzi called this "aromatic osmosis." Then the body was robed in a white cotton cassock, scarlet mozetta, and scarlet camauro. After this, the remains were inserted into a transparent plastic body-bag which was supposed to keep the "volatile oils" from evaporating and to increase the effectiveness of the embalming process. This routine was completed shortly after 2:00 P.M. The whole process was a disaster, and the process of decay was very evident by the time Pius's body reached Saint Peter's for public veneration. Galeazzi-Lisi gave the body several more "treatments," including a final one on the night of October 12 while the Basilica was closed, but to no avail. All those who approached the bier on which the body rested, and especially the members of the Pontifical Noble Guard who stood watch by it, were assailed by a stupefying and permeating stench caused by a combination of the decay of the corpse accompanied by the concomitant chemical degradation of the organic "oils and resins" which were used in the process. Even though the period of each watch was reduced in consequence, members of the Noble Guard were seen with tears running down their cheeks and discharges from their noses as a result of the high levels of irritation. Those who came to venerate the pope's remains decided, or were told, that these tears were caused by the great grief many of the guards felt at the loss of the pope. Those who were permitted to come closer to the bier knew better.

Once the first application of the embalming process was complete, two of the Noble Guards were admitted and took up stations on either side of the head of the bed, then prelates and staff inside the palace were admitted to the bedroom for a brief viewing and an opportunity to pray. The same privilege was accorded to a small number of persons outside the pontifical household, including Giovanni Gronchi, the president of Italy, and

Amintore Fanfani, the prime minister. Afterwards, late in the afternoon of the ninth, the body was taken downstairs on a portable bier and placed in the great hall; then the gates of the palace were opened for a first veneration by the citizens of the little town of Castel Gandolofo and by a considerable throng who had journeyed out from Rome for the purpose.

Shortly after midnight on the morning of the tenth, Cardinal Spellman arrived. When Pius breathed his last, the *Olympia* already was in the Atlantic on its way to New York. As soon as the news of the pope's death arrived, the captain ordered his ship to change course for Lajes in the Azores, the nearest possible landfall with an airport. On the ship's arrival, Spellman hastened to shore in a launch and then to the NATO airbase where a plane awaited him for a flight to Lisbon. At the Portuguese capital, he changed planes for a further flight to Rome. Now, less than twenty-four hours after the final moments of Pius's life, he stood by the body of his friend and patron.

While the embalming of the pope's corpse, and the making of his death mask, was taking place at Castel Gandolfo, the busiest man in Rome was the dean of the Sacred College, Eugene Tisserant. After a brief rest following Pius's death, he left the summer palace for Rome at ten o'clock in the morning and proceeded immediately to the Vatican where, as camerlengo *ad interim*, he inspected the papal apartments and had the doors sealed. In a small safe in Pius's studio, he found the pope's will, which he retrieved. All the other documents were left untouched to await decisions about them by the new pope. He then ordered that an *intimatio*, an official notice, be sent to each cardinal ordering him to Rome to participate in the conclave.

His next order of business was to determine how to conduct the first phases of the new provisions of Pius XII's election constitution, *Vacantis Apostolicæ Sedis*—which had been issued on December 8, 1945, just before the Grand Consistory. No pope had died outside Rome since Pius VI in 1799, who had died while under Napoleon's house arrest at the Château of Valence. No earlier election constitution of the modern age had considered this question, but Pius, perhaps with some sense that he might, in fact, die at Castel Gandolfo, had incorporated general provisions on what was to be done if the pope were to die elsewhere. But these were only generalities, which now had to be translated into specifics. Pius had directed that, if he were to die elsewhere, his body should be returned to Saint Peter's in "a decorous and dignified manner." With only this guidance, Tisserant quickly ordered the method, the route, and the ceremonies which would bring Pius's body back to Saint Peter's for public veneration. Finally, he ordered the other fourteen cardinals in or near Rome to participate in the first general congregation, which was to meet at 10:30 on the following morning in the Consistorial Hall in the Vatican.

By the evening, Tisserant had learned that the embalmment had not gone well, and that the pope's body was not withstanding the effects of the warm October. He dropped the traditional process of exposing the pope's body in the Chapel of the Blessed Sacrament and ordered Monsignor Enrico Dante, prefect of pontifical ceremonies, personally to supervise a crew of the *sampietrini*—the workmen who take care of the well-being of Saint Peter's Basilica—as they erected a large catafalque, five feet high and with a raked surface, so that the pope's head would be significantly higher than his feet, just in front of the high altar at the west end of the nave. He also ordered a *cordon sanitaire* of barriers and guards to be placed at some distance to the east of the catafalque, to prevent the public from getting too close to the body. Later, a press release from the Vatican explained that these steps had been taken to allow larger numbers of people to see Pius's body, but avoidance of embarrassment was the principal motive.

The first general congregation, on the morning of the tenth, was filled with pressing business. The fifteen cardinals who attended first had to elect a pro-camerlengo to take charge of all of the business of the conclave and the Holy See during the vacancy. They quickly settled on Benedetto Aloisi Masella, then seventy-nine, prefect of the Congregation for the Discipline of the Sacraments. They also voted to assign to him the apartments of the cardinal-secretary of state in the Vatican—a suite of rooms that had been vacant officially for many years.

After Aloisi Masella formally accepted his new office, the cardinals chose the two other principal officials of the coming election. The papal *maestro di camera*, Monsignor Federico Callori di Vignale, was to be the governor of the conclave; and Monsignor Alberto di Jorio was to be the secretary.

The cardinals now turned to a formal consideration of the provisions of Pius XII's election constitution. Once this was completed, there was a brief open discussion on the critical question of the day, the deteriorating condition of Pius's body and how the *novemdiali*—the nine days' of funeral services for the dead pope—would be affected by it. In addition to approving the changes Tisserant had made in the arrangements in Saint Peter's, the cardinals decided to curtail the public veneration of Pius's body and to conduct the burial of the pope on Monday evening, thus shortening the usual public rites by three days. Their decision was announced on the following morning. Finally, the cardinals decided that the *novemdiali* would conclude on the nineteenth, and that the conclave would open on the twenty-fifth.

Now the congregation concluded, and the cardinals, in twos and threes, hastened by car to Castel Gandolfo to participate in the formal procession which was to bring Pius's body back to Rome.

Shortly after midday, the coffin that contained Pius's corpse was moved from the papal apartments down to the courtyard of the summer palace. Surrounded by all the cardinals in Rome, except Aloisi Masella and Tedeschini, and by a throng of both Vatican and Italian dignitaries, the body was placed into a motor-hearse provided by the government of the city of Rome. Then the procession of twenty cars got under way, down the Via Appia Nuova and through the Porta San Giovanni to its first stop at the cathedral of Rome, the Basilica of San Giovanni in Laterano. The press of the crowds along the route was so much larger than expected that the motorized procession arrived at the basilica more than an hour behind the original schedule planned by Tisserant.

At the cathedral, its archpriest, Aloisi Masella, received the coffin, which was brought into the nave for a brief liturgy. Pius's sister, now nearly prostrate from a combination of grief and the excessive invasion of her quiet and reserved life, attended this service and then returned to her home, thus avoiding the public spectacle which was to follow. Suddenly, there was a loud crack. One of the seals on the coffin had broken from the gas pressure produced by the decay of the pope's badly embalmed body. It was a harbinger of worse to come. Near the conclusion of the service, Luigi Traglia, the vice-regent of Rome and later both cardinal and dean of the Sacred College, recited the ancient prayer, "In Paradisum deducant te Angeli," whose opening lines are best remembered by English speakers in the form Shakespeare gave them to Horatio in act five of *Hamlet*—"Good night, sweet prince;/ And *flights of angels sing thee to thy rest!*"

Once the final prayers were concluded, Pius's body was placed again in the hearse, and the signal was given to begin the largest procession the city had seen since classical times. Led by a band of a hundred caribinieri, walking nine abreast, the cortege moved northwest from the Lateran, down the Via Merulana, leftward on the Via Labicana, skirting the Colosseum, and then along the Via Dei Fori Imperiali—a modern thoroughfare driven through the ancient center of the city by Mussolini—to the Piazza Venezia. The procession now turned west again, onto the Corso Vittorio Emmanuele, passing the house where Pius was born, and then crossed the Tiber on the Ponte Vittorio Emmanuele before turning down the Via della Conciliazione and into the great piazza before Saint Peter's Basilica. This route, which can be walked briskly in little more than half an hour, took the cortege two hours to cover. Indeed, the press of the crowds was so great that it took a full half hour, from 5:30 to 6:00, to move the hearse across the Piazza di San Pietro to the entrance to the Basilica. Once there, the archpriest of Saint Peter's, Cardinal Federico Tedeschini, performed the same rites of reception as Aloisi Masella had at the Lateran. The body was conveyed into the church and the doors were closed.

As the crowd of perhaps 300,000 dispersed into the Roman sunset, the body of the pope was carried forward in the dimness of the Basilica to be re-robed and placed on the high catafalque which had been built so hastily to receive it. In the midst of the process of revesting the corpse, Galeazzi-Lisi administered another one of his embalming treatments in a now-futile effort to arrest the visible signs of decay on the pope's corpse.

Meanwhile, throughout the world, the cardinals of residential sees were making as rapid a progress as they needed to answer the call to Rome for the election. The delay that Pius XI had added to the interregnal period to enable cardinals in distant places to reach Rome for the conclave had been rendered useless by the advent of reliable air travel. In 1922, Boston's Cardinal William O'Connell had been unable to reach Rome from the New World in time to participate in the election. In 1958, Norman Gilroy, the archbishop of Sydney, boarded a plane on the evening of the ninth, already late morning on the tenth in Rome, and arrived at his destination little more than forty-eight hours later, well in time to take part in the burial services for Pius on the thirteenth.

Other cardinals, however, had a more difficult time. The *intimatio* sent to Cardinal Stepinac had, of course, been intercepted by Tito's government in Belgrade, which promptly issued a communiqué that announced that the cardinal would not be permitted to leave his house arrest in his birth village of Krasic, near Zagreb, because this would violate the terms of the agreement under which he had been released from prison. This decision, probably made by Tito personally, was reached on the evening of the eighth, when it became common knowledge that the pope was dying. In Budapest, Cardinal Mindszenty received the *intimatio* in his residence at the United States legation, where he had found refuge at the collapse of Imre Nagy's Hungarian Revolution on November 4, 1956. Through American representatives, the cardinal inquired of the government whether or not he would be permitted to leave for the conclave and, if he were allowed to go, would he be allowed to return to Hungary when the election was over. The answer he received was equivocal. He might be permitted to leave, under certain unnamed circumstances and conditions; but, if he were given permission to leave, he would not be allowed to return to Hungarian soil afterwards. In light of this uncertainty, Mindszenty issued a statement that he would not be leaving the legation. Later, when John Foster Dulles, the American secretary of state, was in Rome for the final obsequies for Pius, he met with several cardinals, including Tisserant and Aloisi Masella, who asked him to intervene personally to mitigate the demands of the Hungarian boss, János Kádár, so that Mindszenty could attend. Dulles promised that he would do all that he could to reach such a rapprochement, but he held out little hope that either the Hungarian prime minister, Ferenc Münnich, or Kádár could be persuaded to change their minds.

In Warsaw, negotiations between the government and the staff of Cardinal Stefan Wyzynski, while stiff and formal, were handled in a more cooperative vein than was the case in Hungary and Yugoslavia. Władyslav Gomułka, the new leader of the Comunist Party in Poland, had risen to power in 1956 as a part of the general de-Stalinization policies begun by Nikita Khrushchev in February of that year. One of his first acts, upon assuming control of the state, was to release Wyzynski from the house arrest to which he was confined by the former party boss, Bolesłav Bierut, in 1953. The cardinal had concluded an agreement with Gomułka soon afterward which permitted the reestablishment of religious instruction in public schools in return for a party voice in the recommendations to Rome for new elevations to the Polish hierarchy. This accommodation helped to reduce tensions which were moving towards the same popular eruption of nationalism and anti-communism which engulfed Hungary and Czechoslovakia soon afterward. Now, after some delay, as a demonstration of his level of control, Gomułka's government announced, on the fourteenth, that not only would Wyzynski be permitted to go to Rome for the election, but that he would travel with a Polish diplomatic passport.

In Le Mans, Cardinal Georges Grente's difficulty was with his staff, not his government. His people thought that, at a rather feeble eighty-six, he was too weak to withstand the rigors of both the journey and the conclave, and with this conclusion his physician agreed. His chancery, without his approval, issued a statement to that effect. But Grente, who came of hardy stock and had endured much more than this in his life, ordered preparations for an immediate departure, after he excoriated those who had tried to thwart his journey. In the archdiocesan chancery in Santiago, Chile, a similar internal problem was facing José María Caro Rodriguez who, at ninety-two, was the oldest cardinal. His staff, too, thought that he was too feeble for the task at hand, and urged him to forego the election. Like Grente, he brushed aside all such opinions and ordered immediate preparations for his departure. Soon he would set a record of sorts by becoming the oldest cardinal ever to travel by air to a conclave.

For yet others, logistical difficulties imposed by poor health had to be overcome carefully. In Detroit, Cardinal Edward Mooney had suffered since 1946 from a troubling, and sometimes critical, cardiac insufficiency, but there was no question in his mind, or on the part of his staff, that the sixty-six-year-old archbishop would make the journey. All of them thought that travel by air was too risky, so he, alone of the North American cardinals, would travel by sea. In Germany, Cardinal Thomas Tien-kin-sin, the exiled archbishop of Beijing, was recovering from a horrendous collision between the car in which he had been riding and a truck. His right arm was completely encased in a cast, while other injuries had him well bandaged generally. In addition, he was still in some residual shock as a consequence of the accident. He would travel by train in a specially-fitted litter, which could be carried in and out of railway cars and ambulances with a minimum of discomfort to the patient.

The general pattern of the plans that the distant cardinals made for travelling to Rome was that almost all of them made all, or a substantial part, of their journeys by air, for the first time in history.

On Saturday morning, October 11, the doors of Saint Peter's were opened at 6:00 for the first major public viewing of Pius's remains. In the Chapel of the Choir, the first of the nine formal requiem masses was offered by Pieter Canisius van Lierde in his capacity as vicar-general of Vatican City. To the relief of the cardinals who met in the second general congregation at 10:30, the procession of mourners passing through the Basilica seemed not to notice the general deterioration of Pius's body, kept, as they were some distance away from the massive, elevated catafalque.

When the doors were closed, at 8:00 P.M., yet another of the failed embalming treatments was tried, somewhat to the disgust of the *sampietrini*, who watched the distasteful handling of the pope's body while they were erecting tribunes on either side of the nave for the witnesses to Pius's burial.

At 6:30 A.M. on Sunday, the doors of the Basilica were opened, and again thousands of mourners passed through to see the remains of Pius XII. During the morning, the second requiem was said by Primo Principi, titular bishop of Tiana and secretary of the Pontifical Commission for Vatican City.

The third general congregation, which met at 10:30, included Manuel Arteaga y Betancourt, archbishop of Havana, who had arrived on the previous evening. In this meeting, the cardinals received another report on the condition on the pope's remains. The cardinals also spent time in discussing the very revealing press conference held by Galeazzi-Lisi on Saturday, in which the physician discussed openly the most distressing and intimate details of the pope's last days, going far beyond what any of the journalists who attended had expected, and far beyond what any of the cardinals thought appropriate. It was the beginning of the scandal which erupted over the next five days, in which many newspapers purchased from Galeazzi-Lisi the rights to publish his medical diary—much of which was quoted earlier in this chapter—together with photographs of the death agony of the pope.

Meanwhile, those cardinals whose journey to Rome was a gentle one, including the seven Italian residential archbishops, began to arrive according to carefully planned itineraries. Angelo Giuseppe Roncalli of Venice, for instance, took time to hold a full requiem for Pius in Saint Mark's Cathedral on Saturday. Then he oversaw the packing of his luggage by his secretary, Monsignor Loris Capovilla, and his valet, Guido Gussi. After this, he retired for the night. On Sunday morning, he travelled from his patriarchal palace to the main railway station by launch and boarded the 9:30 A.M. train for Rome. After he had seen to the stowage of his things, he returned to the corridor of his carriage and lowered one of the windows so that he could chat for a few moments with friends who had come to see him off. Just before the train began to move, Vittorio de Rosa, the stationmaster, called out to him, "I wish you luck." Roncalli replied, "The best luck that could happen to me would be to return here in two weeks." Though he could have reached Rome by the evening of the twelfth, Roncalli chose instead a more leisurely route through the countryside and arrived in Rome on the morning of the thirteenth.

Much to his surprise, Roncalli found a substantial crowd waiting to meet him at the Stazione Termini, the great railroad station at Rome, when his train pulled in. He turned to a cleric near him and asked if this number of people greeted each of the cardinals when they arrived. "No, since you are both a cardinal and a patriarch, you drew twice as many," was the reply. In fact, the large number of curial officials who were present in the throng was the first real indication that he was rumoured to be a serious candidate for the throne.

He was driven immediately to his temporary quarters in the Domus Mariæ in the Via Aurelia, a modern building which served as the headquarters of Women's Catholic Action in Rome.

After a brief rest and a change to prelatical dress, he went to Saint Peter's for the general congregation to be followed by the ceremony of Pius XII's burial. During the meeting, Fosatti gave Roncalli another sign of his real chances for the throne. "We want you," said Turin's archbishop tersely. At about the same time, Gaetano Cicognani remarked to another prelate, "I can imagine kneeling at his [Roncalli's] feet."

The basilica had once again been opened at 6:00 A.M. and the last public viewing of Pius's remains continued until midafternoon, when the doors were closed to the people for the last time. At about 3:00, a procession moved Pius's body from the nave to the apse of the basilica, in preparation for the interment. Among the cardinals present were both Spellman and his former auxiliary, James Francis McIntyre, now the archbishop of Los Angeles.

At four o'clock, the final rites began. First, Pius's body, now in the saddest condition, was placed in its nest of three coffins. First, into the innermost coffin of cypress, then the inner coffin was placed into one of lead, and, finally, the whole was lowered into the outer coffin of elm. Before the lids were closed, Antonio Bacci, the foremost Latinist in the Chuch and soon to be a cardinal, delivered the final eulogy. When his speech was over, a parchment copy of his address was placed in a brass cylinder and deposited at the pope's feet. Then three red velvet bags, each containing nineteen coins—one of gold, one of silver, and one of copper—also were placed in the innermost coffin; one coin of each metal for each year of his reign. This was followed by a final viewing for each of the twenty-four cardinals who were present. As they passed the body, each imparted a final triple blessing. When they had been followed by the last viewing by the pope's sister and his three nephews, three prelates of the pontifical household came forward for their final ritual offices for Pius. Monsignor Federico Callori di Vignale, the pope's *maestro di camera*, placed a silk veil over Pius's face; then Monsignor Mario Nasalli di Corneliano, Pius's cupbearer, placed a similar cloth over the feet; finally, Monsignor Enrico Dante covered the entire body with a crimson silk pall. All of this was televised for the first time, but viewers detected none of the distress the participants experienced from the pope's decaying body.

As the lids of the coffins were closed, the cardinals and the members of the Pacelli family made their way to the crypt of Saint Peter's, to a niche near the bodies of Benedict XV, Pius XI, and Cardinal Raffaele Merry del Val. While they waited, the whole of the massive set of coffins was winched onto a large wheeled frame and then brought down to the crypt. With very little ceremony, and away from the television lens, the final act of burial took place.

After these last rites, the cardinals went to their various quarters to continue the *prattiche*, the informal round of visits and conversations in which they exchanged views and discussed the forthcoming election. Of course, not only cardinals were participants in all of the visits, lucheons, dinners, and telephone calls in this studied electioneering dance. On the evening of the thirteenth, Roncalli entertained Giovanni Urbani, bishop of Verona, and Giuseppe Piazza, bishop of Bergamo—Urbani would be his successor as patriarch of Venice and the second cardinal he would name in his first creation. Both prelates had a wide network of current Roman contacts, and their conversation formed a sort of briefing for Roncalli about what had happened in the Eternal City over the past few days—gossip is the life-blood of Rome and the Roman Church.

On the morning of the fourteenth, the general congregation met at 10:30. The cardinals were elated by the news from Warsaw that Wyszynski would attend the conclave. When the meeting ended, Roncalli had a brief dialogue with Monsignor Angelo Dell'Acqua, once his secretary in Istanbul and now a *sostituto* in the secretariat of state, just below Tardini. Dell'Acqua, a real Roncalli loyalist, and the leader of the *Montiniani* in the curia, provided his former master with valuable snippets of information about the activities of the curial cardinals. Later, Roncalli went to lunch with Augusto Gianfrancheschini, bishop of Cesena, to gather more information, a task that he repeated in the evening when he dined with Giuseppe Dalla Torre, the extraordinarily well-informed editor of *L'Osservatore Romano*.

Alfredo Ottaviani was maneuvering carefully in the *prattiche*. He gathered together a faction of curial cardinals who were willing to follow his lead. Ottaviani feared a successful try for the tiara by Giuseppe Siri, the youngest cardinal. Genoa's archbishop was, if anything, even more conservative than Ottaviani, but the latter believed that his election might lead to a forty-year pontificate which, of course, would exclude all the others from any chance of a future reign. The fear was genuine. Ottaviani thought that perhaps the best course for the Church was a transitional pope, and, if that were the case, Roncalli would be a good choice for the job. He was not, however, willing to give the throne to the patriarch until some better avenues had been explored.

No pope has any rôle in the choice of his successor, but he does have methods by which he can signal the College about men he considers worthy or appropriate. Often, the first cardinal named in a reign and the cardinal to whom a new pope gives his own red hat are such persons—for Pius, these men were Gregory Peter XV Agagianian, who was very *papabile* in 1958, and Frank Spellman of New York.[1] Sometimes, a pope will display such extraordinary favour to a younger cardinal of his own creation that the Vatican bureaucracy will label him the *delfino* of that pope—in analogy to the *dauphin* as the heir of the king of France. For ten years, since he was forty, Siri was known almost universally as the *delfino* of Pius XII.

The fourteenth and fifteenth of October were free of duties except for the daily meetings of the general congregation. After the end of the congregation on the fifteeenth, Roncalli talked with Archbishop Domenico Tardini, who had functioned alone as the papal secretary of state after his colleague, Giovanni Battista Montini, had been sent to Milan in 1954. The two met for about an hour, between noon and one o'clock, which gave Tardini a chance to clarify for himself his understanding of both the Venetian patriarch's views and his personality. This was the first of several meetings during the *prattiche* in which Roncalli was vetted seriously by his colleagues and their representatives. Roncalli closed the interview by suggesting that the two lunch together, once the present preliminary soundings had taken a more definite course. Tardini agreed. When that meeting took place at the Domus Mariæ, five days later, Roncalli thought his candidacy was strong enough that he could discuss the possibility that he would make Tardini both cardinal and secretary of state, without any fear of being taken for a light-headed optimist, if he did achieve the throne. Tardini was no friend to Roncalli. When the latter became nuncio to Paris, he asked Tardini if he was responsible for the appointment. The answer was an emphatic no, Roncalli was the last candidate he would have wanted. Roncalli understood his position with the archbishop very clearly indeed. When the time did come, the new pope remarked to him, "You don't have much esteem for me, and you are perfectly right, but I esteem you. You have worked at the center of the Church, while I have worked on the outskirts; you know what it wants from the center, so we will make a good team." Tardini, not yet a cardinal, would not participate in the conclave, but he was a prelate of immense influence. Just at this time, he was thought to be supporting the candidacy of Benedetto Aloisi Masella, but very, very subtly.

Of course, Roncalli was not the only *papabile* who received the attention of many callers. Gregory Peter XV Agagianian, the favorite of a number of curial cardinals, also merited considerable attention. Although a Roman prelate for many decades, he was a native of Akhaltzikhe in the Caucasus. Lazar Agagianian, his baptismal name, entered the Armenian church and rose steadily until he was rewarded with the rank of patriarch of Cilicia of the Armenians and the cardinalate by Pius XI in 1937. Now, in 1958, he seemed to have all the attributes of a successful candidate—he was just sixty-three and not only a man with years of curial experience but just the sort of non-Italian who might win substantial support from both the Italian hierarchy and the non-Italian cardinals who thought increasingly of the attractiveness of a non-Italian pope. Pius XII's plan to increase greatly the influence and power of non-Italian cardinals and, indeed, to lead the Church to a non-Italian pope might well bear fruition in the person of the stately and imposing Agagianian. But he was of an unbending conservative mind; it was this quality which had endeared him to the curial faction—*più Romano d'un Romano*, more Roman than a Roman—and alienated him from the more liberal cardinals. Agagianian's chief proponent was Celso Costantini, who received visitors in his room at the Clinica Margherita in the Via Massimo. The pro-prefect of the Congregation of Propaganda Fide and chancellor of the Church had undergone surgery three weeks before to correct some circulatory distress, but was making a remarkable recovery. Roncalli learned of Costantini's enthusiasm for the Armenian patriarch when he called on the afternoon of the fifteenth. Venice's patriarch was stunned. He could not believe that the chancellor really thought that the time had come for a non-Italian pope, let alone one from an Eastern rite.

Another conservative who gained early attention was Valerio Valeri, now the powerful prefect of the Congregation of Religious. Valeri had been chosen for the diplomatic service in the years of Gasparri's greatest successes. He had proven himself, first as Apostolic delegate to Egypt and then as nuncio to Romania. His accomplishments merited his promotion to be nuncio in France, but there his career encountered a nearly fatal crisis. He had worked well, too well, with the Vichy government and, when the war was over, Charles de Gaulle demanded his immediate recall in disgrace. In fact, it was this precipitous retreat from France which paved the way for Roncalli's spectacular career as his successor. Valeri's career seemed in final eclipse, but Pius XII gave him an opportunity to restore himself to former favor by placing him in charge of the preparations for, and conduct of, the Jubilee of 1950. Valeri, well aware that this was his last chance to return to favour, did an outstanding job. As his reward, he was raised to the cardinalate in the creation of 1953. He had all of the traditional characteristics of a good Vatican diplomat—suave, subtle, soft spoken, smilingly accommodating. When his candidacy was first broached in the course of the *prattiche*, the six French cardinals were outraged. They viewed him as a major collaborator who was only slightly less contemptible than a similarly disposed Frenchman.

On the other side of the discussions was Giacomo Lercaro, archbishop of Bologna. Bluff, hearty, and vigorous, he had a youthful attitude and stride which belied his nearly sixty-seven years. In spite of his obvious pastoral skills, his outspokenness kept him from a bishop's throne until he was fifty-five, when he finally received Ravenna—by contrast Mimmi had been forty-seven, Roncalli forty-three, and Siri only thirty-seven when they received the mitre. Lercaro's general success in his five years in Ravenna earned him elevation to Bologna in 1952 and the cardinalate a few months later. He worked tirelessly to regain ground for the Church in a city heavily dominated politically and socially by communists and socialists—indeed, Bologna had a higher percentage of registered communist voters in 1952 than any European city outside the Soviet bloc. His liberal political views and his practical Christianity had brought him great success in only a few years, and his ultimate reward now was to be considered the leading liberal *papabile*.

A few times during the *prattiche*, other liberals raised the possibility of elevating Giovanni Battista Montini, archbishop of Milan, to the throne. As one of the two *sostituti*, or acting secretaries, who had administered the secretariat of state after the death of Cardinal Maglione in 1944, he had enjoyed Pius's highest confidence until a loss of papal trust caused the pope to move him out of the Vatican to Milan. For all of his years in the Vatican, Montini had been especially close, in spirit if not in geography, to Roncalli. This was another point which made the patriarch especially attractive to the liberals.

In spite of the fact that Pius had denied him the cardinalate that traditionally went to Milan's archbishop soon after his enthronement, Montini was thought by a few wild optimists to be *papabile*. To elevate him, however, would break a tradition more than half a millennium long which forbade the elevation of anyone not a cardinal to the papal chair. On the last occasion that it had been tried, in 1378, the result had been the sudden revelation of a paranoid megalomaniac, Urban VI—formerly Bartolommeo Prignano, archbishop of Bari—whose excesses prompted his repudiation by the cardinals who had elected him, and then the beginning of the great schism.

When the cardinals awakened on the morning of the sixteenth, they found summer gone, and a biting winter wind blowing over the city. In the meeting of the general congregation, with thirty-one cardinals present, the final form of the conclave began to emerge. They appointed three committees to carry out the organization of the electoral meeting. The committee in charge of the structural preparations for the conclave, under Benedetto Aloisi Masella as pro-camerlengo, with Tisserant and Pietro Fumasoni Biondi, the senior cardinal-priest then present in Rome, was to superintend the final physical preparations for housing the cardinals.

The committee in charge of the conclave's personnel, under Pietro Ciriaci, prefect of the Congregation of the Council, with Gaetano Cicognani, the head of the Congregation of Rites, and Gregory Peter XV Agagianian, had to inspect personally the credentials of all those who would be immured with the cardinals during the conclave. The cardinals regarded this task as particularly critical because they feared that representatives of the press were preparing a whole panoply of subterfuges in order to gain access to the papal election. Finally, a committee of two, Nicola Canali, the archdeacon, and Giuseppe Pizzardo, the powerful prefect of the Congregation of Seminaries and Universities and secretary of the Congregation of the Holy Office, was named to choose officials who would represent the temporal interests of the Vatican during the conclave.

Later, after the conclusion of the general congregation, the whole body of cardinals received the members of the diplomatic corps who were accredited to the Holy See for the purpose of accepting official condolences from them; then they received the condolences of the only non-cardinal who is entitled to be addressed as "eminence," the acting general of the Order of the Knights of Saint John of Jerusalem, the Sovereign Military Order of Malta, Ernesto Carcaci, marchese of Paterno.

Of those who were absent, perhaps the most important was Celso Costantini, the chancellor of the Church, who wished to avoid many of the time-consuming and taxing ceremonies of the *sede vacante*. He had issued a statement from his room at the Margherita Clinic on the afternoon of the preceding day that he would participate in the conclave. Now, early in the afternoon of the sixteenth, he decided on a short walk as a part of his regimen for regaining his strength. He curtailed his stroll when he began to feel ill, and returned to his room to lie down. A few moments later, he was dead. His heart had failed suddenly.

As the news of Costantini's sudden death spread to the members of the College, their sense of dismay deepened, since the chancellor was not only highly influential but very popular and well-liked.

The official business of the cardinals now done for the day, they once again dispersed to their residences or to meetings in close privacy with their colleagues. By the evening, there were forty-five cardinals in or near Rome. Six of them—Caro Rodriguez, Gerlier, Gouveia, Pla y Deniel, Arriba y Castro, and Quiroga y Palacios—had arrived during the course of the day. Four more would reach Rome on Friday the seventeenth—D'Alton, Luque, Gonçalves Cerejeira, and Joseph Ernest van Roey, the primate of Belgium and archpriest of the College.

Following a brief meeting of the general congregation on the morning of Friday, October 17, which was chiefly concerned with the arrangements for Costantini's funeral, the cardinals attended the first Mass of the final group of the *novemdiali*, which was celebrated in Saint Peter's by Marcello Mimmi, archbishop of Naples. The four absolutions, which are a part of this special set of Masses for the repose of the soul of a deceased pope, were given by Mimmi, Roncalli, McIntyre, and Joseph Wendel, the junior cardinal-priest and archbishop of Munich and Freising. Only thirty-four of the cardinals attended. Many of the remainder, though in Rome, were ill or fatigued; and a few seemed too depressed to rouse themselves to the requirements of the occasion.

But there was one item of cheering news. Stefan Wyszynski finally boarded his train in Warsaw on Friday evening, accompanied by his chaplain, his secretary, and Stanislaw Stomma, the head of the Catholic deputies in the Sjem. Rome monitored his journey with careful attention, fearing that, even at the last minute, something would be done to stop the travel of the only cardinal from a communist country to be permitted to attend the election. Some relief accompanied the news that his train had passed the Czechoslovakian frontier, but real certainty came only with the news that the cardinal and his three companions had crossed into Austria and soon would be in Vienna.

Throughout the late afternoons and evenings in the now-chilly Roman fall, the cardinals continued the *prattiche*. In several cases, groups of like-minded cardinals would choose one of their own to call upon other cardinals who were thought to be candidates to sound them out on both their principles of government and their attitudes to the pressing ecclesiastical questions of the day. On the evening of the seventeenth, Giuseppe Pizzardo came to the Domus Mariæ as the representative of a small group of powerful cardinals in the curia, the *Pentagono Vaticano*, which included Nicola Canali, Clemente Micara, Alfredo Ottaviani, and Marcello Mimmi, as well as himself. His task was to question Roncalli closely to determine if this older curial bloc could support him as a transitional pope—*un papa di passagio*—were the conclave threatened with deadlock. We have no specific details of their talk together, but Pizzardo left the meeting with a very positive opinion of the patriarch of Venice. Later, Pizzardo would lead his group of five cardinals, now augmented by Ernesto Ruffini, to support Roncalli's election.

The morning of Saturday, October 18, brought more embarrassment to the College. The general congregation learned that Galeazzi-Lisi had sold his diary of the last agony of Pius XII to a number of newspapers, together with prints of the hastily-taken snapshots of the last moments. *Il Tempo* printed most of the text, although it omitted some portions that the editors regarded as too gruesome for public consumption. This was small comfort to the cardinals who feared Pius's end would now become the subject of morbid gossip. While we have become used to such excesses in the news, in 1958 such publicity was horrifying, especially because many of the cardinals were themselves very old and very conservative in their outlook. Galeazzi-Lisi thought, apparently, that he had protected himself from any professional consequences of his action by sending a letter to Tisserant, dated that same day, tendering his resignation as chief of the Vatican's medical service. The letter was particularly offensive, because his position had lapsed with Pius's death automatically—as both he and the cardinals well knew. If the physician thought he had no consequences to suffer, he was mistaken. Not only did the cardinals reprimand him severely in this meeting of the general congregation, they then banned him from the Vatican altogether, in another order dated on the following day. On the nineteenth, Italy's prime minister, Amintore Fanfani, publicly ordered an investigation into Galeazzi-Lisi's conduct and directed Guido Gonella, the minister of justice, to chair the process. In addition, the Roman medical association ordered its own inquiry into whether or not he had violated the "juridical and moral obligations" of his profession by selling his information to the press. These sudden efforts to stem the lurid stories about Pius's death were a direct reaction to Rome's development of a new style of sensational and titillating journalism in the 1950s, one which saw the emergence of the paparazzi as daily fixtures wandering Rome's streets, accompanied by hordes of reporters on special assignment and stringers who hoped for the scoop of the day. Forty years later, this journalistic style dominates news gathering throughout the developed world, and the public has become jaded about it. In 1958, however, this excess was almost exclusively Roman—documented so well in Federico Fellini's *La Dolce Vita*—and was an ever-present worry to those who sought to protect the reputation and the image of the Roman Church.

The other notable event of Saturday morning was the arrival, at 7:30, of the official American delegation to the funerary commemorations of Pius XII. The ponderous American bureaucracy had taken so long to select its members and plan the journey that the burial was missed entirely. The delegation of three, John Foster Dulles, the secretary of state; John McCone, a prominent Catholic who was then the chairman of the Atomic Energy Commission; and Claire Booth Luce, playwright and former ambassador to Italy, was met at Ciampino by the current American ambassador, James D. Zellerbach. Father Amory Dulles, a convert to Catholicism who had become a Jesuit priest and was now studying at the Jesuit College in Rome, also came to the airport to meet his parents. The welcoming party found the secretary of state in considerable pain. During the night, a strap that supported the berth in which he was sleeping had broken suddenly and had pitched Dulles onto the floor of the converted KC-135 jet tanker on which they travelled. Dulles walked off the plane and was taken by car to the Villa Taverna, Zellerbach's residence. His wrenched back was giving him so much pain by the time he arrived that he did not attend the next Mass of the *novemdiali*, which began at 10:00. The other two representatives, however, were among the congregants when Pizzardo celebrated the requiem. The four absolutions on this occasion were given by James McGuigan, cardinal-archbishop of Toronto; Antonio Caggiano de Aze-

vado, of Rosario, Argentina; Fernando Quiroga y Palacios, of Santiago de
Compostella, Spain; and Paul-Emile Lèger, of Montreal. After the Mass,
the thirty-eight cardinals in attendance again dispersed to their consultations. In the meanwhile, somewhat recovered, Dulles went to the Quirinale to lunch with Prime Minister Fanfani, together with Selwyn Lloyd,
the British foreign minister, and Maurice Couve de Murville, his French
counterpart. After this public event, Dulles was driven secretly to a meeting with several cardinals to discuss the Mindszenty affair, but with no favorable result.

The only public activity on Sunday, the nineteenth, was the Mass in
Saint Peter's at 10:00, celebrated by Tisserant, with absolutions from
Spellman of New York, Joseph Frings of Köln, Maurice Feltin of Paris, and
Giacomo Lercaro of Bologna. This was the last of the nine Masses, and
saw nearly the whole of the diplomatic corps and a large crowd of official
representatives from foreign governments. At the service, Pius received a
final eulogy from Amleto Giovanni Cicognani, the regent of the Apostolic
Chancery and former Apostolic Delegate to the United States, and brother
of Cardinal Gaetano Cicognani.

In the late afternoon, a crowd of several hundred began to gather at the
Stazione Termini to await the arrival of the Vienna-Rome Express. Their
faith in the rumor of the day was rewarded when Wyszynski and his party
detrained from a private railway car that had been attached to the train. Poland's primate was mobbed by Polish and Italian well-wishers alike, and
was escorted with some considerable difficulty to a reserved lounge, where
he was welcomed officially by the Vatican's representatives.

Meanwhile, the visits and counter-visits of the cardinals continued.
Maurilio Fossati, Gaetano Cicognani, and Pietro Ciriaci all came to see
Roncalli. Fossati already was a determined adherent to Roncalli's cause,
but the others were exploring Roncalli's positions more tentatively.

On the twentieth, it was Roncalli's turn to call. He visited both Benedetto Aloisi Masella and Alfredo Ottaviani, two powers of the curia, to
seek their views.

In the evening, the arrival of Edward Mooney of Detroit, seemingly fit
after his long surface journey, brought the number of cardinals present to
fifty.

Before they went to their communal meeting on Tuesday, the twenty-
first, most of the cardinals attended Costantini's funeral in the little church
of San Giovanni dei Fiorentini. At this service, Roncalli was reminded of
how much he liked Jacopo Sansovino's delicate construction for Leo X.
When, on March 28, 1960, he needed a new title church for cardinal-

priests for Joseph Lefebvre, the archbishop of Bourges, he raised San Giovanni to titular rank.

The chief business of this general congregation was the drawing of lots to determine which cell each cardinal would occupy during the conclave. As usual, some cardinals were very lucky in their quarters. Spellman drew cell 46, which was one half of the apartment normally occupied by Antonio Bacci, the secretary of Latin briefs to princes. The other half of the same quarters went to Pizzardo. This was, by comparison, a delightful treat, because the windows of that part of the palace faced the gardens and could not been seen from the outside. Thus, Pizzardo and Spellman had daylight, at least. In addition, Bacci had his own small kitchen and dining room. Spellman ordered his conclavist, George Schlicthe, to stock the refrigerator with extra provisions. Perhaps Spellman anticipated his own reaction to being locked up with a "bunch of foreigners," most of whom he did not know. After the second morning of the conclave, he told Schlicthe that he could take the other cardinals at lunch and supper, but not for breakfast. So, on the morning of the twenty-eighth, Schlicthe boiled the eggs.

James Francis McIntyre did not fare nearly so well. He drew number 32, three small rooms that were part of the administrative offices of the secretariat of state. The other three rooms in that part of the palace went to Roques. All these windows were sealed and the glass was painted blue. The apartment of Monsignor Carlo Grano, one of the substitute secretaries of state and secretary of the cipher, was divided between Mooney and Pietro Ciriaci. These quarters were located below the offices of the main offices of the secretariat of state and immediately above the Sale Ducale. This elongated series of rooms opened on both sides. The windows that faced Saint Peter's Square were painted, but those panes looking inward—at the Cortile dei Pappagalli, so called from its frieze of parrots, now almost obliterated—were left unpainted.

Roncalli received the office of the commander of the Pontifical Noble Guard, while the remainder of his suite in the Vatican went to seven other cardinals, Ruffini of Palermo, Fossati of Turin, Gaetano Cicognani of the congregation of Rites, Valeri of the congregation of Religious, and two Latinos, Santiago Luís Copello of Buenos Aires and Carlos María de la Torre of Quito. They formed a congenial group, all of them well disposed to Roncalli's elevation. It was, as Monsignor Capovilla put it, "a pretty family." Tisserant wound up with rooms in the gloom of the Borgia Armory.

As the final evolutions of the *prattiche* continued, Maurice Feltin also came to call on Roncalli. Feltin was chosen for the job by his colleagues because he had grown very close to Roncalli during the nunciature in

Paris. Both men came from rugged Alpine peasant stock and they shared the distinction of being the two portliest cardinals. Almost exactly contemporary—Feltin was a year and a half younger than Roncalli—their friendship became closer when Roncalli secured Feltin's rise from Bordeaux to Paris, in succession to Cardinal Emmanel Suhard, in 1949, and both had been created cardinals on the same day. Paris's archbishop informed him of the great friendliness of the French cardinals, and their strong support for his candidacy, based upon the exemplary work he had done while nuncio to France in the preceding decade. The more important question, Feltin continued, was what attitude he would take toward the dilemma over the Worker-Priest movement in France. Roncalli assured him that he would enforce a rapprochement between the curia and the new evangelism. Feltin now offered immediate support for his candidacy. Similar encouragement was given by both Georges Grente and Clément Emile Roques when Roncalli called on them at the French College in the Via di Santa Chiara, two days later. Roncalli noted in his diary that Grente seemed in good condition, in spite of his great age, and that "both of them were very friendly to me." A number of years afterwards, Tisserant would write, with only a little exaggeration, that the French cardinals were the grand electors of John XXIII, because of the sudden ease with which he agreed to resolve the most pressing pastoral problem in France.

The Italian residential archbishops, too, were interested in Roncalli as a very plausible pope. Among this group of six, excluding Roncalli himself, the most influential and respected were the saintly, but witty and energetic, Elia Dalla Costa of Florence, now eighty-six years old, and the more somber Maurilio Fossati of Turin, then eighty-two. Age, episcopal seniority, and successful church government during the difficult Fascist and war years, gave them influence and stature among their colleagues. Both of them had determined to support Roncalli. Monsignor Loris Capovilla, Roncalli's secretary, recorded an exchange between Dalla Costa and Roncalli which left no doubt about the former's electoral position:

"You could be the future pope," beamed Dalla Costa to his Venetian counterpart.

"I?" replied the startled Roncalli.

"Yes, you—why not?"

"But I am in my seventy-seventh year."

"Ten years younger than I! If you were pope for ten years, that would be sufficient."

By now, Roncalli had learned that he had strong support for a bid for the throne from at least a quarter of the College, including several of the most senior curial cardinals, from among the conservatives, and the

French delegation—with which Wyszynski eventually associated himself—from among the more liberal. In addition, he now knew that he had substantial backing from the most influential Italian archbishops. Later, after his election, John XXIII was asked how it happened that he was so well prepared for his election, when it finally was accomplished. He replied, "I knew by certain signs that I would be chosen." These brief visits and short conversations, beginning with his first talk with Tardini on the fifteenth, were those signs.

Just after the meeting of the general congregation ended on the twenty-second came the news that Lincoln White, the spokesman for the American Department of State, had announced publicly that American attempts to intervene on behalf of Mindszenty's attendance at the conclave had been fruitless. Privately, several cardinals voiced unhappiness with the announcement, not because the overtures of the United States had been rejected, which almost all the cardinals fully expected, but because White included in his statement that America's efforts had been taken at the specific request of the College of Cardinals—a connection which Rome emphatically did not want revealed.

During the spare afternoon hours, several cardinals chose to inspect the cells in which they would stay, Roncalli among them. When his escort smilingly pointed to the sign on the door which read "Commandante," Roncalli said, "Do you believe in signs like these? I don't."

In the afternoon, fifty-one cardinals received their copies of the *intimatio*, over the signature of Aloisi Masella as pro-camerlengo, which informed them that they should appear, appropriately robed, at 9:30 on the morning of Saturday, the twenty-fifth in Saint Peter's, for the Mass of the Holy Spirit and the following ceremonies which marked the opening of the conclave. By this time, the final state of the electorate was clear. Stepinac and Mindszenty would be absent, and all the remaining fifty-two would participate—Tien-kin-sin already was travelling by train, in his specially prepared litter, from Germany. When he arrived on the next day, he was presented with his copy of the *intimatio* as soon as he was settled in his quarters. Everything, at last, seemed complete.

On the twenty-fourth, the cardinals enjoyed a day of rest from all official business, to give them time to make whatever final preparations they wished before they cut themselves off from the outside world. In the conclave precincts themselves, specially trained security personnel, accompanied by a small group of cardinals, carried out Pius XII's mandate that the whole area be swept for microphones and recording devices. World War II had introduced the Vatican to the importance of electronic eavesdropping as a valuable source of intelligence, and Pius specifically incorporated this final measure in his election constitution to ensure the absolute secrecy of the deliberations.

In the evening, Roncalli invited Giulio Andreotti, a leading Christian Democrat politician, to dine with him at the Domus Mariæ. Andreotti, who already had been minister of finance earlier in the year, and would be prime minister twice (in two ministries in 1972-1973), was close to Roncalli, as the nephew by marriage of Monsignor Giulio Belvedere, an old friend of the patriarch's from seminary days. During this visit, Roncalli was expansive about the conclave, about which, of course, he should have had no conversation at all. "I received a message of good wishes from General de Gaulle, but that does not mean that the French cardinals will vote in the way he wants. I know they would like to elect Montini, and he certainly would be good; but I do not think that the custom of choosing from the cardinals can be set aside." Roncalli's confidence brimmed over so convincingly that Andreotti, who edited the influential magazine, *Concretezza*, ordered his staff to prepare the advanced layout for the new pope with the photograph of only one cardinal—Roncalli.

On Saturday morning, at last, the beginning of the formal electoral process began. The weather had recovered to one of those beautiful fall days for which the city is famous; the cold snap of the preceding week had passed away—a mercy for the older cardinals who felt the winter more keenly in their bones.

The Mass of the Holy Spirit began at 9:30, exactly on schedule, with forty-five cardinals present. It was followed by the traditional homily on the election of a pope, delivered in sonorous, almost poetic, Latin by Antonio Bacci. Like the burial rites for Pius XII, this, too, was televised and filmed, so that the pomp and ceremony of the event was seen by many hundreds of times more people than had ever witnessed it before. In spite of the great age of many of the electors, only three needed significant help during the ceremonies: Caro Rodriguez, whose great age made him almost unable to support the weight of his robes, Tien-kin-sin, who could move only with difficulty under his heavy bandages and cast, and Josef Frings, who, a few days before, had fallen backward on a staircase and fractured the base of his spine.

When it was over, the cardinals were released for a final lunch "on the outside," before reuniting in the Pauline Chapel for the formal procession into the conclave. Perhaps for the first time, there was a sense of lightness and optimism among the cardinals. They had seen almost every aspect of this *sede vacante* plagued with troubles. The sensational publicity which surrounded and followed the death of Pius, the sudden death of Costantini, and the enforced absence of Stepinac and Mindszenty—the first time since the Venetian conclave of 1800 that secular governments had interfered with cardinals as papal electors—all had imposed a gloomy air on the proceedings. Now, all that seemed to pass. The weather was almost ideal, the crowds warm and enthusiastic, and the *prattiche* had proved to be much more amicable than the wide divergence of attitudes among the cardinals suggested that it might be.

The three Americans returned to the North American College on the Janiculum to lunch with its rector, Monsignor Martin J. O'Connor. Pomp and ceremony forgotten, Frank Spellman, Ed Mooney, and Jamie McIntyre enjoyed a relaxed and convivial meal with their host, gossiping and joking about old friends and new experiences. At the end of lunch, Mooney pushed back from the table a little to enjoy his customary after-meal cigar. When the conversation slackened, and they noticed the time passing quickly away, Mooney called to his secretary, Monsignor Joseph Breitenbeck, to tell him that a short rest was in order. Mooney asked Breitenbeck to come to his room to call him for the journey back to the Vatican in twenty-five minutes. He then left the table, while Spellman and McIntyre lingered a few minutes more for a few final words with their host.

By 2:45, the cars for the short trip were waiting in the courtyard. The cardinals from New York and Los Angeles were ready. Breitenbeck knocked on Mooney's door, and, receiving no response, opened it. Mooney was lying on his bed, his death rattle clearly audible. With considerable presence of mind, the loyal secretary administered the last rites and then summoned the other cardinals and Monsignor O'Connor. When they entered the room, Mooney was dead. With a final, hasty absolution, Spellman and McIntyre almost ran down to the courtyard and were sped to the Vatican.

Meanwhile, between 3:00 and 3:30, the cardinals and their conclavists had begun to appear at the Pauline in small groups. Not long after Roncalli arrived at 3:10, the conspicuous absence of the three Americans began to excite whispered comment among the crowd of cardinals, prelates, and attendants. The procession was forming for the march through the Sale Reale to the Sistine when a rushed clamor of cardinals and conclavists signaled the arrival of two of the Americans. In a quick, hushed word with Tisserant, Spellman announced Mooney's death. Since the cardinals were to march by twos according to their rank and seniority in the College, there was another few minutes of confusion as the procession had to re-form itself. James Charles McGuigan moved to the left side, to take the position that had been Mooney's, while Clément Emile Roques moved forward to stand with him on the right.

McGuigan's feelings, as he stood in the procession, must have been disquieting. Since the Grand Consistory in 1946, he had been flanked by two powerful Americans, Mooney of Detroit, just ahead of him, and Samuel Stritch of Chicago, just behind. Stritch had died in August and now, only a few weeks later, Mooney too was gone, reducing the weight of the United States in the College by half. Spellman, too, faced a new reality. With both of his senior colleagues gone, he, and he alone, would speak for the United States in the coming days—McIntyre, Spellman's former assistant in New York, was too junior to be considered a major figure in the election.

Amid whispered asides on the latest news, the procession reformed itself and marched with solemnity into the Sistine—first the conclavists, then the Sistine Choir singing the "Veni Creator Spiritus," and finally the cardinals. Once they all had entered, Tisserant stepped to the altar and led the customary prayers that asked divine inspiration for the cardinals in their electoral duty. After this brief rite, Monsignor Enrico Dante, the prefect of pontifical ceremonies, asked that all but the cardinals themselves leave the Sistine. Now seated on their thrones, and with Mooney's seat spontaneously left vacant in homage to his memory, the cardinals heard the text of Pius XII's election constitution in its entirety; and then each cardinal, one by one, took the oath to uphold the constitution, to defend all the rights of the Church should he be elected, to maintain the secrecy of the conclave forever, and, with the experience of 1903 still in mind, to reject any attempt by any party to exclude a specific cardinal from the throne. Then Tisserant spoke again, delivering a brief homily in which he exhorted the cardinals to abide fully by the oath each had just taken.

Now the doors to the Chapel were opened, and the two persons who would be charged officially with maintaining the inviolability and secrecy of the conclave entered to take the oath to do their duty—Prince Sigismondo Chigi-Albani-Della Rovere, on the outside of the precinct as prince-marshal of the conclave, and Monsignor Federico Callori di Vignale, on the inside as governor of the conclave. This act concluded, the cardinals retired to their cells for a brief rest, while similar oaths were administered to the remainder of the conclave's staff, first to the prelates who would guard the *rota*, a half-shelved revolving door that served as the only port of communication with the outside world, and then, in small groups, to the remainder.

Soon the Sistine was vacant, except for Aloisi Masella, as pro-camerlengo; Tisserant, the dean; Joseph Ernest van Roey, the archpriest; and Nicola Canali, the archdeacon. These four now carried out a final ritual inspection of the whole conclave area, which duplicated, in an ancient ceremony, the work of the security officials on the day before.

Then the conclave bell began to ring at a signal from Tisserant. Enrico Dante called the "extra omnes," and the conclave began.

Once the doors were sealed at last, some of the cardinals gathered in small groups to continue their gossip until they went into the Borgia Apartments for supper. Here they found one large oval table with places for each of them—the conclavists and other staff dined in adjacent rooms at trestle tables. After a meager meal, the electors went to their respective cells to reflect on the events which had turned this conclave into the most disoriented in recent history.

Sunday, after Mass in the Pauline Chapel, the cardinals proceeded swiftly to the business of voting. The choice of scrutators and infirmarians went quickly, but the latter were not needed, because the only absent cardinal, Tien-kin-sin, now entered the Sistine. His arrival was greeted with a round of spontaneous applause from the cardinals, not only because of the great efforts he had made to reach the election but also because the voting would now go even more swiftly.

The results of the first scrutiny revealed the initial positions of the parties of cardinals:

Angelo Giuseppe Roncalli	20
Gregory Peter XV Agagianian	18
Valerio Valeri	4
Giacomo Lercaro	4
Ernesto Ruffini	3
Giovanni Battista Montini	2

The greatest surprise was the two votes for the archbishop of Milan. Montini now became the first person not a cardinal to receive votes for elevation to the papacy in many centuries. His candidacy, of which there was only a hint during the *prattiche*, was seen both as an anti-Pacellian statement, because Pius had not named him to the College after he was sent to Milan in 1954, and as an insistence that the questions of Church modernization be given due and important attention—in fact, some in past two or three years had begun to label the liberal adherents of modernization the *Montiniani*. Agagianian now emerged as the official curial candidate. Four cardinals voted for Valeri as a personal tribute, because they felt that he had been treated very unfairly when he was forced out of the French nunciature—one of them was Roncalli. Lercaro, young and vigorous in life, if not in age, was too radical and controversial a bishop for serious consideration, but the votes he got, too, testified to the same concerns about the Church in the modern world that had brought support to Montini. His four votes almost certainly came from the Germans, who were impressed with his local success against the Marxists in Bologna.

The cardinals now proceeded to the second ballot, but the results were identical, or nearly so, to those produced in the first round. Following its conclusion, the ballots were taken for burning to the same small stove that had been used in 1939 with success. This time, however, the result was a public catastrophe. Either because the straw was not damp enough to produce black smoke, or because of some malfunction of the stove itself, the smoke that appeared to the throng outside was white, and stayed white. The cardinals in the Sistine first became aware that something had gone wrong when they heard the roar of the crowd in the Piazza outside. As soon as the *sfumata*, first visible at 11:53, was seen to be unmistakably white, dozens of reporters made dashes for the nearest telephones as the rest of the crowd surged towards the great balcony over the main doors of the basilica to await the new pope's first blessing. The sign was so clear that the official announcer for Vatican Radio poured the words, "It's white, it's white, we have a pope" over the airwaves. This was taken up by Italian Radio and by ANSA, the official Italian news agency. Within moments, millions around the world heard the news that the conclave of 1958 had been the shortest in modern history.

Inside the conclave, Cardinal Ottaviani, who had conducted the burning as the junior cardinal-deacon, took what steps he could to correct his error. He burned more scraps of paper with wetter straw, and soon a second gout of smoke appeared—this time quite black.

The confusion outside now became so great that the prince-marshal went to the *rota* and shouted to the attendants inside that he needed to know, directly and orally, the results of the second scrutiny—a muffled voice from within assured him that no election had taken place.

While Vatican Radio and others in the Roman media raced to correct their error, the cardinals in the conclave went to a light lunch in the Borgia Apartments and then reconvened for another two ballots. The results in the afternoon were almost exactly the same as those in the morning, leading to fears that the conclave already had become hopelessly deadlocked. After the counting of the ballots in the fourth scrutiny ended, Ottaviani expended more care in setting the papers alight by adding a considerably greater volume of wet straw to them before lighting the stove. His greater care, however, meant that the sun was setting when the first wisps of the *sfumata* were seen in the Piazza, shortly after five o'clock. To make the smoke more visible, some Vatican functionary had decided to illuminate the area above the chimney with a spotlight. When the smoke appeared, the reflection of the bright light caused it to appear white. Again, there were cries from the crowd that a pope had been elected. And again, as a second and more careful look showed unmistakable signs of black, there was a surge of confusion through the crowd. The unintended consequence of greater care had produced only greater confusion.

While the cardinals dined and then rested in their cells, Prince Chigi demonstrated the millenia-old Roman blend of practicality amid pomp. He sent some of his aides to a local fireworks factory where they purchased a set of black smoke bombs which could be ignited with safety and then thrown into the stove as the ballots were burned. These were passed through the *rota* early on the following morning and, thereafter, there was no further confusion about the results of the voting.

Elsewhere in Rome, at the North American College, Monsignor O'Connor said a requiem for Cardinal Mooney at ten in the morning, after which the cardinal's body was prepared for its return to Detroit. It was placed aboard a special plane, which left Ciampino at 7:00 that evening.

The results of the fifth and sixth scrutinies, on the morning of the twenty-seventh, showed the deadlock now complete. Agagianian maintained his bloc of about eighteen votes, while Roncalli maintained his adherence of about twenty.

When the last morning ballots were counted, Tisserant addressed the cardinals before their midday meal. Since it was clear that neither the conservatives, with Agagianian, nor the liberals, with Roncalli, could break through the impasse created by the other side, why not consider elevating the seventy-nine-year-old pro-camerlengo, Benedetto Aloisi Masella?

For Tisserant, the advantages were clear. Masella was two years older than Roncalli, which seemed to make him even more "transitional." After all, for how many years can a man of that age be expected to reign? Second, although a long-standing member of the curia—he was prefect of the Congregation for the Discipline of the Sacraments—he was not as conservative, or indeed reactionary, as his powerful colleagues of the *Pentagono Vaticano*. Again, the recent popes who had been elevated after years of curial experience, Leo XIII and Pius XII especially, had enjoyed popular and successful reigns. The dean urged his colleagues to consider this possibility as a solution to the present deadlock.

After this, Ottaviani burned the morning papers and, thanks to the real utility of the smoke bomb, there was no doubt as to the black color of the smoke when it became visible at 11:07 in the bright midday sunshine. The crowd drifted away with none of the excitement that had characterized their behavior on the preceding day.

In the afternoon scrutinies on Monday, the gloom inside the Sistine continued in sharp contrast to the brightness outside. The cardinals had not yet taken Tisserant's harangue to heart, and their votes continued the

same pattern as those of the earlier tallies. At the same time, the cramped
quarters and the deepening cold at night were taking their toll on several of
the electors. Nicola Canali, now eighty-four, spent an increasingly large
amount of time in bed, trying to overcome the fatigue caused by the worsening of his heart condition. Tien-kin-sin experienced a significant increase in pain for the conclave was not the ideal setting in which to recover
from his injuries, while Frings also found that living in these circumstances increased the distress from his fractured spine. Others were having
an even worse time. Grente (86), van Roey (84), Arteaga y Betancourt
(78), and especially Caro Rodriguez (92) were in generally fragile health
and the chill in the cells at night was exacting a hard penalty for their participation. That particular condition was so bad that word was passed
through the *rota* to have the whole heating system of the Vatican turned
on. This was necessary because one plant served all the needs of Vatican
City and heat could not be provided to the conclave area without heating
every room in the papal enclave.

After supper, movement among the cells was particularly active. Several
cardinals came to Roncalli's cell to assure him of their continuing support.
Fossati, who lived next door in cell 16, came in to encourage him (*confor-
tans eum*). Later in the evening, Ottaviani, who definitely did not want
Aloisi Masella, came to tell Roncalli that he would bring his faction to
Roncalli's side, but not in the first ballot on the following day.

Meanwhile, supporters of Tisserant's plan visited the cells of their colleagues to try to persuade them to go along with the new alignment and
bring the election to a speedy close. The success of their efforts was revealed in the results of the ninth scrutiny—the first held on Tuesday, the
twenty-eighth:

Gregory Peter XV Agagianian	18
Angelo Giuseppe Roncalli	15
Benedetto Aloisi Masella	10
Giacomo Lercaro	4
Valerio Valeri	2
Giovanni Battista Montini	2

The adherents to Tisserant's compromise were surprised that they had
not detached a single vote from Agagianian's loyal following—half of them
were in Ottaviani's pocket. Instead, they had damaged Roncalli's candidacy severely while they picked up two of Valeri's supporters as well as the
votes of three very undecided cardinals who had been throwing their votes
away in earlier scrutinies, sometimes to Gonçalves Cerejeira, sometimes to
de Barros Camara of Rio de Janeiro, and sometimes even to Wyszynski.

It now was clear that there would be no more realignment. The conservatives, chiefly curialists, commanded twenty-eight votes, those cast for Agagianian and Aloisi Masella, and probably could gain no more. The liberals had a solid twenty-one supporters who would not waver from Roncalli, the furthest they would go in the way of compromise and transition, and the even more modernist candidates, Lercaro and Montini.

No matter if Valeri's hold-out adherent passed to one side or the other, it would make no difference—Valeri's second vote came from Roncalli.

In this most absolute of stalemates, Aloisi Masella made the decisive move. Since Roncalli's election was the best result for which the *Pacelliani* could hope, he publicly and dramatically withdrew his candidacy in favor of the patriarch of Venice. Personally, he commanded wide respect, which had been responsible for his choice as pro-camerlengo in the first general congregation after the death of Pius. He had no specific political or theological agenda and his views were regarded as honest and non-partisan. The effect of his announcement was electric. The cardinals rushed to the tenth ballot, which showed the dramatic shift toward the position adopted by the pro-camerlengo:

Angelo Giuseppe Roncalli	32
Gregory Peter XV Agagianian	10
Giacomo Lercaro	4
Valerio Valeri	2
Giovanni Battista Montini	2
Benedetto Aloisi Masella	1

Spurred by Aloisi Masella, the conservatives rushed to support Roncalli. Thanks to Ottaviani's switch, he had stripped Agagianian of eight votes. He also had picked up nine of the pro-camerlengo's ten supporters from the night before. There was a visible, and audible, lifting of the gloom as the ballots were prepared for burning, with the obligatory smoke bomb. All that remained was to persuade the most ardent liberals that Roncalli certainly was the best result they could get, and then the election would be over.

While the smoke from the fifth *sfumata* was as black as any that had gone before, and produced some grumbling in the crowd that the cardinals were taking far too long in doing their duty, the mood of the College was anything but dark. The cardinals went to their lunch in the Borgia Apartments with a greater feeling of hope than they had had since the opening of the *prattiche*, more than two weeks before. Significantly, Roncalli absented himself from the communal meal for the first time. Unknown to his colleagues, yet, the patriarch was in his cell, sitting on a small divan, working with great concentration on a manuscript he had begun the night before. At about one o'clock, Capovilla came in to walk with him down to lunch. Roncalli told him, "I am not coming down. Rather, a bite here. Have something brought, and we will eat together." Guido Gussi now went to the kitchen and foraged for his master. He returned at 1:20 with some soup, a slice of meat, a glass of wine, and an apple. After this picnic, Roncalli napped for about twenty minutes, and then returned to work on his manuscript.

The midday conversation at the communal table in the Appartamenti Borgia turned on the emergence of the new electoral situation. The four Germans who were thought to be Lercaro's supporters were the special targets of the discourse, although they were not addressed specifically, while Aloisi Masella's last adherent was left to meditate on the dramatic change his favorite had worked in the election.

The cardinals reassembled in the Sistine at four o'clock in an atmosphere that was almost jovial. When Roncalli joined them, he received a number of whispered encouragements, especially from those who had favored him from the beginning. The French cardinal-archbishops were all smiles, nodding and beaming to all those around them. In addition to his strong support from the Italian episcopacy, Roncalli now had half the curia and nearly all of the cardinals from the New World in his column. The only mystery that remained was to see if the Germans and one or two other liberals had been persuaded by the mood and the arguments. The eleventh scrutiny revealed the consequences of the lunchtime exhortations:

Angelo Giuseppe Roncalli	38
Gregory Peter XV Agagianian	10
Giacomo Lercaro	2
Valerio Valeri	1

At 4:50, Roncalli was now pope, in a surprising conclusion to one of the most fractious conclaves in modern times.

The patriarch had destroyed the historical tradition that no major candidate ever recovers from a loss of support during the balloting. He had picked up just what he needed to achieve the throne—two of Lercaro's Germans; both of Montini's adherents, one of whom probably was Lercaro himself, Valeri's stalwart hold out, and Aloisi Masella's last devotee. Only twelve cardinals still were unreconciled to a Roncalli pontificate—ten conservatives who did not follow the lead of Ottaviani and two very liberal Germans who continued to support Lercaro. Roncalli himself continued to vote for Valeri to the end. As the result of the last vote was announced, there was an explosion of excited chatter amid a general conviviality that could not have been imagined on the night before.

The cardinals lowered the canopies above their thrones in recognition that they were not, now, all potential pontiffs. After he had lowered the canopy above his own chair, McGuigan reached to his left and performed the same office for that which covered Mooney's vacant throne. It was the last Roman act in memory of Detroit's dead cardinal.

Tisserant approached Roncalli to ask him the question whose affirmative answer begins all reigns, "Do you accept the election, canonically made, of yourself as pontiff?" In response, Roncalli drew from his pocket the Latin text over which he had worked so long through the hours of the preceding night and during the lunch hour in his cell:

> At the sound of your voice, "I am made to tremble, and I fear."[2] For what I know well of my poverty and littleness is enough to bring me to confusion.
>
> But seeing in the votes of my brothers, the most eminent cardinals of the Holy Roman Church, the sign of the will of God, I accept the election made by them. I bend my head and my back to the chalice of bitterness and to the yoke of the cross.
>
> On the solemn feast of Christ the King, all of us have chanted: "The Lord is our judge; the Lord is our law-giver; the Lord is our king. He will save us."

The cardinals began to whisper among themselves. This was very different, indeed, from the usual short answer called for by both regulation and custom, and much more than the terse response of Pius XII in 1939. Tisserant paused briefly to allow quiet to be restored. "By what name will you be called?" Roncalli continued:

> Venerable brothers, I will be called John. This name is dear to me because it is the name of our father. It is dear because it is the title of the humble parish where we received baptism. It is the solemn name of innumerable cathedrals, spread throughout the world, and, in the first place, of the blessed and holy basilica of the Lateran, our cathedral.
>
> It is the name which in the long series of the Roman pontiffs has been used most. Indeed, there have been twenty-two unquestionably legitimate supreme pontiffs named John. Nearly all had a brief pontificate.
>
> We have preferred to shield the smallness of our own name behind this magnificent succession of Roman pontiffs.
>
> And was not Saint Mark the Evangelist, the glory and protector of our dear Venice, he whom Saint Peter, prince of the apostles and first bishop of the Roman Church, loved as his own son, also called John?
>
> But we love the name John, so dear to us and to all the Church,

particularly because it was borne by two men who were most close to Christ the Lord, the divine redeemer of all the world and founder of the Church:

John the Baptist, the precursor of our Lord. He was not, indeed, the Light; but the witness to the Light; and he truly was the unconquered witness of truth, of justice, in his preaching, in the baptism of repentance, in the blood he shed.

And the other John: the disciple and evangelist, preferred by Christ and by His most sweet mother, who ate the last supper, leaned on the breast of our Lord, and, thereby, obtained that charitable love which burned in him with a vivid and apostolic flame until great old age.

May God dispose that both these Johns shall plead in all the Church for our most humble pastoral ministry, which succeeds that so well conducted to its end by our lamented predecessor of venerable memory, Pius XII, and those of his predecessors, so glorious in the Church.

May they proclaim to the clergy and to all the people our work, by which we desire "to prepare for the Lord a perfect people, to cut straight the windings of every street, and make rough paths into smooth roads, so that all mankind shall see the saving power of God."[3]

And may John the Evangelist, who, as he himself attests, took with him Mary, the mother of Christ and our mother, sustain, together with her, this same exhortation, which concerns the life and the joy of the Catholic Church and also the peace and the prosperity of all peoples.

My children, love one another. Love one another because this is the great commandment of the Lord.

Venerable brothers, may God in His mercy grant that, bearing the name of the first of this series of supreme pontiffs, we can, with the help of divine grace, have his sanctity of life and his strength of soul unto the shedding of our blood, if God so wills.

His climactic invocation of the name of Pope John I was too subtle for some of those present, but was not lost on those who were well versed in Church history. The first John also had been elderly and in poor health when he was chosen to be the successor of the powerful and skillful Hormisdas on August 13, 523—and Hormisdas, in spite of his Persian name, sprang from an established aristocratic family, as had Pius XII. John I, too, had come to the throne in the midst of an implacable "cold war," this one between the Eastern emperor, Justin I, and the most powerful of western rulers, Theodoric, king of the Ostrogoths. Caught up in a massive theological and political conflict by virtue of his office, John was summoned to

Ravenna by Theodoric, an adherent of the Arian heresy, who ordered the new bishop of Rome to lead an embassy to Constantinople to wrest from Justin immediate concessions, including an end to the persecution of Arians, the return of churches which had been seized from them, and the free ability of Arians who had been converted forcibly to return to their old faith without penalty. John straightforwardly told Theodoric that he would undertake the embassy to secure the first two concessions, but that he would not attempt to gain the last. He departed for the imperial capital—the first pope to journey to the New Rome—and was received with a splendor and dignity which went far to easing his pain from his humiliation by Theodoric. John I was willing to bend on every matter which did not affect the essentials of the faith and his spirit of cooperation so moved the emperor that every one of Theodoric's demands was granted except, as expected, the right of newly orthodox Christians to reconvert to Arianism. When John had achieved all that he could as a negotiator between both sides, he returned to Ravenna, where Theodoric erupted in fury over the pope's failure to achieve every wish. Theodoric by this time was deeply suspicious of everyone around him—he already had executed John's close friend, the Christian philosopher, Boethius. While the Ostrogothic king meditated on whether or not to send the pope to the block, too, John died on May 18, 526, worn out by the privations of his house arrest in Ravenna. A week later, he was buried in Saint Peter's.

John XXIII's invocation of his memory was a clear signal that he, also, would compromise on all but the essentials and that he, too, would not merely talk peace and concord, both within the Church and in the world of superpower politics, but that he would move to act upon his word by negotiation. Choosing the most common of all Christian names also gave John XXIII the opportunity to use the name to forge ties with others for whom the name had varying significances. For example, to Cardinal Feltin he later said that he had chosen the name "in memory of France and in memory of John XXII who continued the history of the papacy in France." John could be as subtle and as careful as the most seasoned Vatican curialist.

Once he had finished his long address of acceptance, John was escorted to the sacristy to don his papal robes for the first time. In shedding his cardinal's robes for the last time, John first took his red zucchetto—the little skull cap which descends in tradition from the Jewish yarmulke—and placed it on the head of the secretary of the conclave, Albert di Jorio, as a sign that he would be made a cardinal in the first consistory of the new reign. This revived an age-old tradition which had lapsed since Pius X had done the same for Raffaele Merry del Val in 1903. Ottaviani now opened the doors of the Sistine and summoned in Monsignor Enrico Dante, as master of pontifical ceremonies, to witness the remaining acts of the electoral process.

The robing process was chaotic. The doors of the Sistine had been thrown open to all, which was against the established procedure, and a mob of prelates and servants pushed in to congratulate John. Tisserant had a difficult time expelling them so that the new pope would have some room and time. Capovilla pushed through the crowd to ask his master for a first blessing for Venice, Bergamo, and Sotto il Monte, the three "hometowns" of the pope. "Yes, gladly, first for those related by the Spirit, then the relatives of my blood." As Capovilla was swept away in the throng, John called out to him, "We will talk about it later, later."

The papal tailor, Annibale Giammarelli, whose firm had dressed the popes for a century and a half, provided three complete sets of robes to ensure that one would fit the new pope fairly well, no matter who was elected. The first set John tried on could not even be buttoned over his substantial girth. The second was a little better, and it was in these clothes that the rest of the day went. On the following morning, Capovilla telephoned the haberdasher to complain loudly about the bad fit. Giammarelli asked whether John had tried all three outfits, and was told that there had been time for only two robings. "Try the third," he said. It was sent for at once, and fit John perfectly, for Giammarelli, too, had anticipated that Roncalli could very well be the next pope, and had prepared one set of vestments especially for him.

Meanwhile, Ottaviani packed the stove with the ballots from the eleventh scrutiny and a mass of very dry straw so that there would be no doubt that the smoke would be white. Nicola Canali, the archdeacon, carefully expended his strength in forming up the procession that he would lead through the Hall of Benedictions to the great balcony to announce John's election to the people in the Piazza and, through television, to the world. He would become the first cardinal-archdeacon whose actual voice would, within a few hours, be heard by more than a billion people.

Outside, the white smoke was first seen at 5:08. In the fading Roman twilight, spotlights were turned on the windows which lead out from the Hall of Benedictions. At a minute after six, Canali appeared and announced the election of Angelo Giuseppe Roncalli as John XXIII and then made a quick departure. To say that he was disgruntled at the outcome is to say the least. Canali, a dedicated Fascist as well as a financial genius, had been one of the holdouts for Agagianian.

A few moments later, attendants lowered the same great tapestry with the Pacelli arms crowned by the papal tiara and keys that Pius XII had used when he blessed the throng. Soon after, all the lights in the Hall of Benedictions were turned on, the doors opened again. First, Tisserant and Micara appeared, accompanied by a prelate who carried a large golden cross. When John appeared next, there was a moment of uncertainty, for his figure seemed dwarfed by the tall and stately cardinals with him. In a second or two, the crowd had recognized the white vestments and began their swelling cheers. John quickly imparted his first blessing *urbi et orbi* and stood for a few moments to acknowledge the cheers. He then stepped into the Hall of Benedictions, the doors were closed, and the lights switched off. The new reign had begun.

Spurred on by the realization that he would have a short reign, John XXIII moved forward at once to put his stamp on the Vatican and the Church. Almost immediately, he ordered the date of his coronation moved up from November 9 to November 4, the feast of his favorite saint, Cardinal Carlo Borromeo. He also called a meeting of all the heads of the Roman congregations, many of whom had borne only an acting title for years. "There have been too many *sostituti* here, we will remedy that," he quickly announced. At the same time, he asked for a list of all those whose offices, whether curial or residential, generally merited the cardinalate. When, within a week, he was given a list of twenty-three names, from which he was expected to prune five, since the maximum size of the College had been fixed at seventy by Sixtus V in 1587, he simply said that he would create all on them in a consistory on December 15. He brushed away almost four hundred years of papal custom as if it had never existed. He also brushed away the rule that two brothers cannot be cardinals at the same time, by elevating Amleto Giovanni Cicognani, the younger brother of Cardinal Gaetano Cicognani. This last promotion was greeted with considerable satisfaction in the United States, where the younger brother had been the Apostolic Delegate for a quarter of a century.

This group of new cardinals, which included Richard James Cushing of Boston and John O'Hara of Philadelphia to fill the seats once occupied by Stritch and Mooney, did, however, reverse the long, slow course of Pius XII's internationalizing policy with regard to the College, for no fewer than fourteen of the twenty-three were Italians.

John's desire to change the direction of Church affairs rapidly was resisted by the curia, including some of those men whom he had elevated so speedily to the cardinalate. Within twelve weeks of his election, he understood that even his pontifical powers were inadequate to bring about the changes swiftly.

As early as November 2, two days before his coronation, he broached the idea of calling a general council of the Church with Cardinal Ernesto

Ruffini. By January 8, he had decided on his course of action, confiding his plans to a few whom he swore to secrecy. He scheduled a Mass at the ancient abbey of San Paolo *fuori le mura* for Thursday the twenty-ninth, to which he summoned all the cardinals who were in Rome—seventeen of them. After Mass, at about 1:10, he shocked the cardinals who had accompanied him by announcing that he would summon a general council of the whole Church to carry out his *aggiornamento*. The stunned cardinals had no reaction at all, to the pope's great disappointment. After a few moments of cold silence, John simply said, "We would have expected that the cardinals, after listening to our address, might have crowded around to express their approval and good wishes." They continued to stare at him. Tardini had released the announcement of the council to Vatican Radio for broadcast at 12:30, so, in fact, the public knew of John's plans before the College. As the pope left the abbey by car, a single voice cried out, "*Viva al concilio!*"

Later, the cardinals' vociferous objections began. John swept their views aside—the revolution had begun.

NOTES

1. When visitors to Saint Patrick's look up to see Cardinal Spellman's red hat suspended from the roof of the cathedral, they also are looking at the red hat of Eugenio Pacelli as cardinal-secretary of state.

2. "Tremens factus sum ego, et timeo." Ps. 119:120.

3. Luke 3:4-6.

IV. Preserving the Legacy

From November 2, 1958, two days before his coronation, until the last day of his life, Pope John XXIII's reign was dominated by preparations for, and then the first session of, the Second Vatican Council. The College of Cardinals, as well as other Catholic institutions, felt the weight of John's *aggiornamento*, but not, perhaps, to quite the same degree. At the outset of his reign, Roncalli had perceived the policy of Pius XII with regard to the College—to weaken the Italian contingent and withhold the red hat from curial officials. In spite of this, his first creation, of twenty-three cardinals on Monday, December 15, 1958, was in every way a traditional one, except for the number promoted:

Giovanni Battista Enrico Antonio Maria Montini: *Abp. of Milan*
Giovanni Urbani: *Patriarch of Venice*
Paolo Giobbe: *Datarius of the Holy See*
Giuseppe Fietta
Fernando Cento
Carlo Chiarlo: *Apostolic Signature*
Amleto Giovanni Cicognani
José Garribi y Rivera: *Archbishop of Guadalajara*
Antonio Maria Barbieri: *Archbishop of Montevideo*
William Godfrey: *Archbishop of Westminster*
Carlo Confalonieri: *Consistorial Congregation*
Richard James Cushing: *Archbishop of Boston*
Alfonso Castaldo: *Archbishop of Naples*
Paul Marie A. Richaud: *Archbishop of Bordeaux*
John Francis O'Hara: *Archbishop of Philadelphia*
José María Bueno y Monreal: *Archbishop of Seville*
Franz König: *Archbishop of Vienna*
Julius Döpfner: *Abp. of Munich and Freising*
Domenico Tardini: *Secretary of State*
Alberto di Jorio: *Secretary of the Conclave*
Francesco Bracci: *Dean of the Sacred Roman Rota*
Francesco Roberti: *Pref. of the Apostolic Signature*
Andre Jullien

Eleven of the new cardinals were long-standing members of the curia. As had been so often the case in the past, all four of the new cardinal-deacons, di Jorio, Bracci, Roberti, and Jullien—each of them a curial official—were not yet bishops when they received the cardinalate. Later, John XXIII decreed, in the motu proprio, *Cum gravissima*, of Monday, April 16, 1962, that all cardinals, regardless of the order to which they belonged, would henceforth also be bishops. Three days later, he personally consecrated all twelve living cardinal-deacons—Ottaviani from the reign of Pius XII and eleven of his own creations.

Ten of the other twelve were all residential archbishops from sees which traditionally were held by cardinals. Some had waited but a short time for their red hats after their archiepiscopal elevations—Urbani, who followed Roncalli at Venice, just thirty-four days; Castaldo, Mimmi's successor at Naples, ten months; and Bueno y Monreal, the successor of Segura y Saenz at Seville, twenty months. Others, ignored by Pius XII, had waited years for the distinction that had graced their predecessors: Cushing had followed O'Connell at Boston in 1944; Richaud came to Bordeaux in February, 1950, but there had been no red hat for the city since the death of Paulin Pierre Andrieu on February 15, 1935; while O'Hara had succeeded Dougherty in Philadelphia in 1951.

If anything, the situation for the new curial cardinals had been worse. Tardini should have been confirmed as secretary of state and elevated to the cardinalate in 1946, for example. Montini might well have been elevated at the same time, but, because he was nine and a half years younger than Tardini, 1953 might have been more appropriate. Once he arrived in Milan, in late 1954, a red hat should have been forthcoming almost immediately.

Perhaps the saddest case was that of Amleto Giovanni Cicognani. The early stages of his career in the Vatican had been very successful, although he had been selected for service in the curia rather late in life. He was made undersecretary of the Consistorial Congregation on December 16, 1922, seventeen years after his ordination, as a part of Pietro Gasparri's reshuffling and consolidation of the curia after the accession of Pius XI. Once he had achieved a responsible position, Cicognani demonstrated his abilities to give every satisfaction to Pius XI and Gasparri. In early 1928, he became an assessor of the Congregation for the Oriental Churches; and, less than two years later, he became the secretary, or presiding prelate, of the pontifical commission for the codification of Oriental canon law. It was in these posts that he first came to know Roncalli, since he had to deal with Bulgarian matters as well as the circumstances of the Uniate churches frequently. His reward for a job well done was his appointment to be Apostolic delegate to the United States, on March 17, 1933, and his elevation as titular archbishop of Laodicea in Phrygia on the twenty-third of the following month. Then he was forgotten. He came to Washington in the first, heady days of Franklin Roosevelt's administration and remained in place through the terms of Harry Truman and most of the Eisenhower administration. When Pius elevated his elder brother, Gaetano, to the cardinalate in 1953, the Vatican had the perfect explanation for overlooking him. Since canon law forbade brothers from being cardinals at the same time, Gaetano's red hat seemed to mark the end of Amleto's rise in the Church, at least until his brother's death. Of course, popes in the past had dispensed brothers from that legal requirement. Leo XIII did not hesitate to create the Vannutelli brothers, Serafino (b. 1834) on March 14, 1887, and Vincenzo (b. 1836) on December 30, 1889. The two brothers served in the College together for twenty-five years. But Pius XII was not minded to dispense with regulations in favor of merit, so Amleto labored on in Washington until John brought him home, after a quarter century, and made him a cardinal and prefect of the Congregation for the Oriental Churches. When John's cardinal-secretary of state, Domenico Tardini, died on July 30, 1961, there was no *sostituto* with enough experience and talent to take his office. John had to make a quick decision, because he had several current lines of diplomatic dialogue which were both delicate and potentially fruitful—not the least of which was the establishment of a sound relationship with the new Catholic president of the United States, John F. Kennedy. Cicognani, during his last decade in Washington, had established cordial ties with the junior senator from Massachusetts and his family. While reflecting on the problem at Tardini's funeral, on August 2, John decided that Cicognani, already a cardinal and a congregational prefect, was the best person to take over the Vatican's highest and most demanding job. Cicognani had to be constrained to accept the position—he already was seventy-eight. In the next twelve years, he brought both a zest for the work and a sureness in carrying out papal policy, for both John and Paul VI, that made his tenure the most successful operation of the secretariat since Pacelli's time.

Only two of the new cardinals of 1958 came from sees, and nations, which had never seen a cardinal before: José Garribi y Rivera, archbishop of Guadalajara, Mexico, since 1936, was his nation's first native cardinal;[1] as was Antonio María Barbieri, archbishop of Montevideo, Uruguay, since 1940. These two promotions were the first hints of the broadening changes to come.

In this creation, the cardinals were, on average, substantially older when they received the red hat than were the cardinals created by Pius XII. This is not surprising, since John was himself seventy-seven, and many of those he named were persons he had known, and with whom he had worked, in his own career. Many, he thought, had been passed over unfairly during the consistory of 1953 or had been slighted by Pius's failure to hold a consistory for creating cardinals in the last five and a half years of his reign. Pius's fifty-six creations had averaged 63 years, 3 months, and 29 days in age at the time of their elevation to the College. The first twenty-three of John's cardinals, by contrast, averaged 68 years, 2 months, and 24 days in age. This difference of nearly five full years meant that there was no generational change from the population from which Pius XII drew his cardinals. In fact, the average age of the new creations in 1953 had been 64 years, 7 months, and 2 days, so the new cardinals in 1958 were, collectively, only two years and three months younger than the cardinals who had been created nearly six years before.

In the light of later developments at Vatican II, John often has been faulted for this first creation. It has been argued that he hastened too quickly to fill the vacancies in the College, without considering the effect these new cardinals would have on his own plans for the renewal of the Church. In part, this is true. Several of the new curial cardinals, including Giobbe, John's old master at the Roman Seminary, as well as Cento, Confalonieri, di Jorio, and Roberti were among the leading figures who opposed the general principle of *aggiornamento*. He created them cardinals, although he knew their views very well, because he used the cardinalate to reward a long and faithful career, as many of his predecessors had done—after all, he had, himself, received the cardinalate in 1953 under that principle. He did not choose to withhold the cardinalate as a punishment for real or fancied transgressions against his own policies—they hardly had been formed yet—or as a method for controlling the curia more closely. Unlike Pius, whose relations with the College generally were dictatorial and absolute, John was neither vindictive nor fearful. Pius had said that he wanted executors, not collaborators. John preferred experienced collaborators, if he could get them.

At the same time, several of the cardinals of 1958 were significant leaders of reform already. Later, they would prove to be the council's liberal leaders. Among them were König, Döpfner, and Amleto Cicognani.

Beyond these issues, however, was a more subtle plan. John's enlargement of the College produced no resistance from the curia, because eleven of the new cardinals were drawn from its ranks. Sixtus V (1585–1590) had limited the membership of the College to seventy, and no pope before John had thought himself able to break that barrier, in spite of pressures to do so in several reigns. Roncalli, however, overrode many provisions of Sixtus's constitutions, *Postquam verus* (December 3, 1586) and *Religiosa* (April 13, 1587), without qualm. Once the Roman establishment had accepted a rise in the number of cardinals to seventy-four, there was little objection that they could make to further increases. Both John and the curia knew that a precedent had been set. By the spring of 1962, John had increased the size of the College to eighty-seven. His successors have more than doubled the Sixtine limit, which has allowed the College to incorporate representatives of many more geographies and cultures throughout the world than could ever have been accommodated under the old rules. But John's first enlargement was carried out without difficulty or rancor only because he stifled any curial opposition before it was formed. Sweetening the medicine with a dose of eleven curial cardinals is just what it took for success.

Near the end of each consistory in which the pope creates new cardinals, a few items of formal business are taken up, so that the newly invested can act, for the first time, both ceremonially and formally, as official advisors of the pope. In the consistory of December 15, 1958, John chose for this purpose the appointment of a few new bishops. In such cases, the pope reads out the names of those he is appointing, together with the sees they will occupy. When he is done, the cardinals who are present give their assent to his acts. Once, centuries ago, the cardinals often entered into vociferous debates with the popes over such appointments, but all disagreement in public disappeared in the sixteenth century. On this occasion, John's list started with the small diocese of Vittorio Veneto, in northeastern Italy, and the name of its new bishop, Albino Luciani. Don Albino, whom Roncalli had met once on a train, came to John's attention through the high recommendation of his old friend, Girolamo Bordignon, the Capuchin bishop of Belluno. Since Vittorio Veneto was in John's old province of Venice, he decided to consecrate Luciani a bishop himself; and did so on December 27, in Saint Peter's. Thus, the consistory of December 15, 1958, takes a very special place in the history of the Church. One pope, John XXIII, presents the name of a new bishop to a consistory of cardinals that includes, for his first act as cardinal, another pope, Paul VI; and the new bishop is, himself, yet another pope, John Paul I, whose name commemorated both his predecessors. When a new bishop is consecrated, the principal consecrator presents his new brother with some token as a personal remembrance and keepsake of the occasion. John gave Luciani a golden chain which Pius XII had given to him. Of such connections, from person to person, from generation to generation, is woven the massive historical continuity of the Catholic Church.

The year 1959 saw the deaths of only three cardinals, Grente (on May 4), Luque (on May 7), and Tedeschini (on November 2), so that by Advent

the number of living cardinals was still seventy-one. John decided on another substantial enlargement of the College. He had a list of fifteen men to
whom he wished to give the red hat. But a sudden, precipitous creation of
all fifteen might well have animated the opposition from the curia that he
was working to avoid. In his second consistory, December 14, 1959, he elevated only eight new cardinals, to bring the total membership in the College to seventy-nine—ease forward, ease forward slowly; push, but not too
hard.

As he had done in the year before, John placed the curial officials first,
two of them as cardinal-priests and four of them as cardinal-deacons. Only
one of the new cardinals was a residential archbishop.

Paolo Marella: *Archp. St. Peter's, Pref. of the "Fabbrica"*
Gustavo Testa: *Secy. of the Cong. for the Oriental Churches*
Albert Gregory Meyer: *Archbishop of Chicago*
Arcadio Larraona: *Prefect of the Congregation of Rites*
Francesco Morano: *Member, Congs. of Ceremonies and Sacraments*
William Theodore Heard: *Dean of the Sacred Roman Rota*
Augustin Bea, S. J.: *Confessor of Pius XII*

Again, John used the cardinalate to reward successful careers, but the
service he acknowledged was symbolic as well as careerist. Marella had
been Roncalli's successor in Paris, and was now recalled from that nunciature for the cardinalate, and to be Tedeschini's successor as archpriest of
Saint Peter's. But the symbolism lay in his term as Apostolic delegate in Japan from 1933 to 1948. He had been one of the few European diplomats to
have seen and evaluated the physical, social, and political effects of the
atom bombs which destroyed Hiroshima and Nagasaki, and he was the
only one to have post-war credibility. His term in Paris was not a happy
one; he had failed to resolve the quarrel with the French cardinals and
bishops over the worker-priest movement, and de Gaulle was, frankly, glad
to get rid of him. But his earlier work, which included service in the Apostolic delegation in Washington for ten years (1923–1933) and a term as delegate to Australia and New Zealand (1948–1953), as well as his time in
Japan, had given him a breadth of view about the Pacific rim which few
men in European diplomacy could match in 1959.

For Gustavo Testa, John had a special and fond regard. He was born
into a peasant family in Boltiere in the diocese of Bergamo on July 18,
1886. His family's farm was only a few miles away from the holdings of the
Roncallis, and the new cardinal's culture and background were almost
identical to John's. They had first met in 1905, and, almost immediately,
Roncalli, four and a half years the elder, had taken a special interest in the

clerical training and career of his fellow countryman. While Roncalli was still secretary to his first patron, Bishop Radini Tedeschi of Bergamo, Testa had been appointed professor of Hebrew at the diocesan seminary. During the war years, their friendship had moved from one of patron and acolyte to one based on shared ideas and plans. Roncalli and Testa were recruited for Vatican service at about the same time, late in 1919. As Roncalli began his work in Rome at the Congregation for the Propagation of the Faith, under Cardinal Willem van Rossum, Testa was posted to the staff of the nunciature in Vienna. Testa now began a career of many years in minor, if sensitive, posts, where he gathered a wide array of experiences and expertise. In 1923, he was sent on two delicate missions, to the Ruhr and Saar, to report on post-war conditions in these regions. Then it was off to Peru in 1924 for a quick fact-finding mission, and back to Rome for work on the staff of the Congregation of Extraordinary Ecclesiastical Affairs. He served in Munich from 1927 to 1929. In the latter year, he was appointed counselor in the newly established nunciature to Italy. His quiet and steady success in that post brought him the rank of titular archbishop of Amasea (November 1, 1934) and an assignment as Apostolic delegate to Egypt and Arabia. In 1942, he returned to Rome for another period of staff assignments, this time for the secretariat of state. In 1948, he was given his most sensitive responsibility when he was made Apostolic delegate to Palestine and regent of the Latin rite patriarchate of Jerusalem. For the next five years, he watched over the Vatican's interests in the volatile world of the newly independent Israel. He executed his tasks so well that, in the end, he was liked by nobody and respected by everybody. His general evenhandedness allowed him to steer a careful course among the shoals of ethnic, religious, and national conflict. The strain was immense and, gradually, he became less and less effective. On March 6, 1953, just after Roncalli's triumphant conclusion to his nunciature in France and enthronement as patriarch of Venice, Testa was made nuncio to Switzerland. Like Roncalli, he had returned home, albeit across a national border from the place of his birth. He could not have expected otherwise than to conclude his career in the calm backwater of the Swiss nunciature, but Roncalli's election to the papacy changed everything.

Once he had settled into firm control, John recalled Testa to Rome and the cardinalate. At first, he was given no particular curial responsibilities but rather made a member of no fewer than five major congregations and four pontifical commissions. Here, he acted as John's eyes and ears, providing the pope with information to help him guide curial affairs gently in the direction he wished them to go. Soon he became secretary of the Congregation for the Oriental Churches and pro-president of two important commissions, for the administration of the goods of the Holy See and for the special administration of the Vatican.

John was closer to Testa, and trusted him more as a lifelong friend and fellow Bergamasque, than he was to anyone else in his reign. Testa, for his part, was loyal personally to John to the exclusion of any other consideration or motive.

Every prelate, from the supernumerary papal chamberlains to the cardinals, bears a coat of arms. If he does not have the hereditary right to one of his own, the Heraldic Commission of the Pontifical Court—in John's reign, it was under the presidency of Monsignor Federico Callori di Vignale—provides one or more designs, in consultation with the grantee, from which the prelate chooses one. Testa, true to his peasant origins, had refused any design at all on his archiepiscopal arms but, as cardinal, this would not do. His arms had to be displayed above the entrance to his title church—San Girolamo degli Schiavoni—and beside his entry in the *Annuario Pontificio* every year. He rejected the designs of the Heraldic Commission and, in frustration, he was asked just what it was he wanted to appear on his shield. He said that he wished the shield to remain perfectly plain with only the words SOLA GRATIA TUA placed on it, with the motto below the shield, ET PATRIA ET COR. With this, he literally wore his heart on his sleeve, "Thanks Only to You." It might have suited the Heraldic Commission to believe its own annotation, that the "you" referred to God, but everyone knew, and Testa made no secret of it, that the "you" was John himself. The motto completed the full circle of Testa's devotion, "and country and heart." Even though Testa was much more conservative politically and socially than the pope, John knew that he could rely on his beloved don Gustavo to carry out to the letter, and more, his every instruction.

Aloisius Joseph Muench was born in Milwaukee, February 18, 1889, into a family of working-class German immigrants. He was ordained in 1913, received his master's degree from the University of Wisconsin in 1919, and his doctorate from the University of Fribourg in 1921. Fitted best for an academic career, he spent several years in a variety of posts in teaching and academic administration until he was chosen to become the third bishop of Fargo, North Dakota, in 1935. Eleven years later, his Lenten pastoral message brought him forcefully to the attention of Pius XII. In his text, he systematically criticized, and effectively destroyed, the Morganthau Plan, a comprehensive outline of the future of post-war Germany that called for the restriction of the Germans to an entirely rural economy. Muench's address was widely reprinted and read with care and attention both in the United States and in Germany. At that moment, Pius needed someone to reestablish the Vatican's diplomatic engagement in Germany, especially with the occupying powers. An unimpeachably patriotic American who spoke German like a native, Muench was a sound choice. Once his appointment as Apostolic visitor was official, Robert Patterson, Truman's secretary of war, added an American commission as liaison between the United States Military Government and the Catholic Church in Germany. This dual appointment established a framework for dealing effectively with the actual situation. Muench also established and deepened a friendship with the American commander, General Lucius Clay, which gave him a wider latitude to exert his influence than his official positions entitled him. He became, in effect, the leading administrator of the whole panoply of relief efforts for Germany, both public and private. When West Germany established its government, in 1951, Muench became the first nuncio. With the cardinalate, Muench came to Rome as a member of the Congregation of Extraordinary Ecclesiastical Affairs. The first American ever to hold a regular curial appointment, he brought with him not only extensive information about Soviet diplomatic and administrative operations in East Germany but also a wealth of experience in dealing with officials from the Eastern bloc.

Arcadio Larraona, a Spanish Claretian who had made his religious profession in 1903, when he was sixteen, had begun his rise in the Church when he was appointed professor of Roman law at the Apollinare in 1918. In December, 1943, he was made undersecretary of the Congregation of Religious, from which he was advanced to secretary of the congregation on November 11, 1950. An archconservative with Fascist leanings—he admired Francisco Franco greatly—he also had strong ties to Opus Dei. Since he was perhaps the most extreme rightist to be created a cardinal in John's pontificate, it is hard to understand today why the pope advanced him. John may have wished this appointment to act as a gesture of cooperation with the conservative Spanish church, with which he was not on particularly good terms—he elevated only three Spanish cardinals among the fifty-two he created, a noticeably smaller percentage than other recent popes had done. Later, after the death of Canali, August 3, 1961, John made Larraona the penitentiary major, but his inflexibility and harshness caused the pope to remove him the following year—an almost unprecedented step, because it had been a lifetime post for many pontificates. Later still, Paul VI made him prefect of the Congregation of Rites. In that position, he proved so much an obstacle to liturgical reform that Paul removed him from that responsibility, too, in February, 1968. His abrasive personality and his extreme views made him useless in the administration of the Church during and after Vatican II.

Francesco Morano was the oldest man whom John created a cardinal, in fact, the only one who was substantially older than John himself. Morano was born on June 8, 1872, at Calvani, and was now eighty-seven years old. He had combined his vocation to the priesthood with his lifelong love of astronomy and, after ordination and a doctorate, he was made an assistant at the Vatican Observatory, where he served from 1900 to 1903. Thus, he was the only cardinal of his time who could claim to have had a Vatican appointment from Leo XIII. In 1901, he enhanced his scholarly reputation by publishing a small volume of mathematical tables for application in astrophotography, *Tavole Matematiche pei Calcoli di Riduzione delle Fotografie Stellari per la Zona Vaticana*. On the strength of that work, and for other articles, he was made a member of the Pontifical Academy of Sciences in 1916. For many years after leaving the Observatory, he served in an assortment of staff positions in the curia, including terms at the Holy Office (1903–1912), the Apostolic Signature (1921), and as a judge of the Rota (1925). After the Lateran Treaties made the Vatican a financial power in Italy, he finally found his niche as a member of the Pontifical Commission for the Vatican Banking Office (1930–1940). A highly respected researcher in several fields, from astronomy to canon law, he was elevated by John as a mark of respect for his disinterested scholarship.

William Theodore Heard, the first Scottish cardinal since the sixteenth century, was a native of Edinburgh who had converted from the Church of Scotland at the age of twenty-six, in 1910. Eight years later, he was ordained, and served as a parish priest in Southwark from 1921 to 1927. In the latter year, his expertise in canon law caused him to be called to Rome as a judge of the Rota. After thirty-one years' service on that tribunal, he became its dean in 1958. John thought that, as the head of the Church's judiciary, he deserved the red hat.

Finally, Augustin Bea, the Jesuit who had been Pius XII's confessor for years, was rewarded for his part in rejuvenating biblical studies after World War II. Bea, whose influence on Pius XII was very great, opened the pope's eyes to the necessity of bringing Catholic biblical scholarship up to, or even beyond, the level achieved by non-Catholics in the nineteenth and twentieth centuries. Once Pius decided to act, he commissioned Bea to write an encyclical on the subject for his signature. *Divino Afflante Spiritu*, issued on September 30, 1943, provided the fundamental guidance and encouragement. Bea was the ideal man to lead the effort. He had taught the Old Testament at the Theologate at Valkenburg in the Netherlands from 1917 to 1921. After a term as the Jesuit provincial in Bavaria, and work to establish the Sophia University in Tokyo, he became a professor at the Pontifical Biblical Institute in 1928. Two years later, he was made the

Institute's rector. In his nineteen years in that office, he trained literally dozens of significant scholars in biblical exegesis and criticism. As the publication director of the Institute's journal, *Biblica*, and as the head of the pontifical commission on biblical studies, he led the way in establishing higher standards of rigourous scholarship in biblical studies, winning professional respect among Protestants as well as Catholics.

One of John's central ideas for the council was that it should act as a gateway to a closer understanding between Catholics and their "separated brethren." But how was this to be achieved? John was looking for the man whose knowledge of biblical matters and of German theology was so great that he could draw to himself a wide audience for a discussion of real ecumenism. He found Bea, six months older than himself and in partial retirement. John gave him the cardinalate to give him the unquestioned prestige and authority in the Vatican to carry forward the ecumenical plan—except there was no plan on the day Bea received the red hat. It would be up to the Jesuit to create one and then implement it. In fact, it was Lorenz Jaeger, archbishop of Paderborn and later cardinal, who elaborated the concept of a small, but effective and powerful, body to deal exclusively with ecumenical questions. Bea presented Jaeger's plan to the pope in early March, 1960. In the motu proprio, *Supremo Dei Nutu*, issued a few weeks later, John established the Secretariat for the Promotion of Christian Unity and appointed Bea its president. The old Jesuit thus began an entirely new career, the most important in his life, which occupied his ninth decade of life, and made him perhaps the most important proponent of the unity of Christians since Georg Calixt.

The smooth acceptance of these eight cardinals, some of whom, like Marella and Larraona, were favorites of the curia, allowed John to go forward with the remaining seven names on his original list. Five of these seven names would have produced the most vehement objections by the curia, if the way had not been prepared so carefully in the first two consistories. On March 28, 1960, only one hundred five days after his last creation of cardinals, John increased the College's size to eighty-five—Stepinac had died on February 10, which had diminished the previous total of seventy-nine by one.

Luigi Traglia: *Pro-Vicar for the City and Diocese of Rome*
Peter Tatsuo Doi: *Archbishop of Tokyo*
Joseph Lefebvre: *Archbishop of Bourges*
Bernard Jan Alfrink: *Archbishop of Utrecht*
Ruffino I. Santos: *Archbishop of Manila*
Laurean Rugambwa: *Bishop of Rutabo, Tanganyika*
Antonio Bacci: *Secretary of Latin Briefs to Princes*

The red hats for Traglia, for years the real governor of the local Roman Church, and Bacci, the Church's foremost Latinist, were rewards for their long and successful careers. But the others belonged to a new class of churchmen who represented a pastoral tradition that was based on the special ecclesiastical and liturgical needs of populations whose conditions were not usually the subject of much attention in Rome. They were the sort of men whom John hoped would lead the Church to a broader, more inclusive state. In Alfrink, John restored a residential cardinalate to the Netherlands, with the knowledge that the leader of the Dutch episcopate was at the forefront of the movement for social and theological, as well as political, reform in the Church. Lefebvre, while not so loud in his calls for change as Alfrink, was leading his archdiocese in central France towards a more liberal position, as well. For Japan and the Philippines, respectively, the elevation of Tatsuo Doi and Santos as the first cardinals in their countries, signaled a coming-of-age for Catholicism in their national cultures. John was determined that the Catholic population in the southern nation would have recognition for its position as the largest Christian community in the western Pacific; and that the northern nation's small, but economically and politically influential, community would be encouraged, as well.

But the stunning event which drew attention to the pope's desire to internationalize the government of the Church further, and to recognize the value of native Catholicism in non-European cultures, was the elevation of Laurean Rugambwa as Black Africa's first native cardinal.

John now had named thirty-eight of the fifty-two cardinals he would appoint in his reign. The College, pacified on the right by the inclusion of long-serving curial officials, began to take on the broader and more diverse composition that the pope had envisioned. Pius XII had greatly expanded the geographical base of the College, but he did not appoint cardinals whose views were in substantial conflict with those of the curia. With creations like Cushing, Döpfner, Meyer, Bea, Rugambwa, and, especially, Alfrink, John had done just that. He had succeeded in establishing a counterpoise to Vatican thinking that was too scattered and too diverse to be managed easily or swept away cavalierly. In the same consistory, John named three cardinals *in pectore*, whose names he never revealed. Since nothing survives to suggest who they were, any documented attempt to identify them is impossible. It seems likely, however, that all three were prelates in the Eastern bloc; and that John did not wish to name them to avoid a repetition of the Mindszenty and Stepinac crises of 1958.

During the rest of 1960, four more cardinals died, Fumasoni-Biondi (July 12), O'Hara (August 28), Fietta (October 1), and Wendel (December 31). Two of them, O'Hara and Fietta, were the first to die among his own creations. John announced a consistory for January 16, 1961, to replace these four. In this creation, he began to pull the proportions of curial to non-curial cardinals back towards the residential episcopacy. He had lost three curial cardinals and one residential archbishop; he created three residential archbishops and one curial official. He had lost three Europeans and one non-European; he replaced them with three non-Europeans and one European:

Joseph Elmer Ritter: *Archbishop of Saint Louis*
José Humberto Quintero: *Archbishop of Caracas*
Luis Concha: *Archbishop of Bogotá*
Giuseppe Ferretto: *Assessor of the Consistorial Congregation*

Ritter filled O'Hara's seat, one American for one American. Ferretto, who was the secretary of the College of Cardinals in addition to his post at the Consistorial Congregation, essentially replaced Pietro Fumasoni-Biondi, a senior curialist who had been made a cardinal by Pius XI in 1933. John used the other places to augment the representation of Latin America in the College.

As the preparations for the council increased in intensity during the remainder of 1961 and early 1962, eight more cardinals died. Among them was the archpriest of the College, Joseph Ernest van Roey, the archbishop of Malines-Brussels and the primate of Belgium (August 6, 1961). John replaced him with Leo Jozef Suenens, on December 15, 1961, and then elevated Suenens to the cardinalate three months later. Belgium now had a primate who was even more committed to the renewal of the Church than was Alfrink in the Netherlands. Two other deaths, that of Tardini (July 30, 1961) and Canali (August 3, one day after Tardini's funeral), brought the central curial establishment of Pius XII to a final close. Tardini, the master of Pian statecraft, and Canali, Pius's financial genius, were too valuable to be lost in the early, formative stages of John's reign. Their body of knowledge and the continuity they brought to daily affairs were exceptionally important. Now that they were gone, John could turn more positively to remaking the highest levels of the curia to a pattern that pleased him more. His first step was to appoint Amleto Giovanni Cicognani to be the cardinal-secretary of state. At last, John had a principal executive officer whom he liked and trusted unreservedly. James W. Spain, an American academic who lived in Rome, prepared an analytical report on the cardinal-secretary of state and other members of the College for the Central Intelligence Agency just weeks before John's death. He correctly summarized the pope's relationship to Cicognani by saying that John regarded him as "an old friend of great experience who has become one of the family, like a trusted doctor." Tardini had never enjoyed such a close relationship with either of the popes he served.

Also gone in this period were Mimmi (March 6, 1961), dalla Costa of Florence (December 22, 1961), Gaetano Cicognani (February 5, 1962), Teodosio Clemente de Gouveia of Lourenço Marques, the last White African cardinal (February 6, the day after the elder Cicognani), and Muench (February 15, 1962). The death of dalla Costa, who was less than half a year away from his ninetieth birthday, certainly was not unexpected, but he was John's old friend and ally and would be missed. Muench was a substantial loss. Although he was seventy-three, his death was surprising, and was a loss of significant expertise on Eastern Europe just when John's plans for increasing dialogue with communist leaders was progressing well. Muench was taken back to his beloved Fargo for burial—he had retained his original diocese for twenty-three years, all through his diplomatic career, until the cardinalate mandated that he resign.

To replace these men, John held his fifth and last consistory for the creation of new cardinals on March 19, 1962. On that occasion, he appointed ten, which raised the membership of the College to eighty-seven, not quite double what it had been on the day John was elected pope.

José da Costa Nuñes: *Former Abp. of Goa, Patriarch ad personam*
Ildebrando Antoniutti: *Vatican diplomat*
Efrem Forni: *Vatican diplomat*
Juan Landázuri Ricketts: *Archbishop of Lima*
Raúl Silva Henriquez: *Archbishop of Santiago de Chile*
Leo Jozef Suenens: *Archbishop of Malines-Brussels*
Giovanni Panico: *Vatican diplomat*
Gabriel Akakios Coussa: *Secretary, Oriental Churches*
Michael Browne: *Master General of the Dominicans*
Joaquín Anselmo María Albareda: *Librarian of the Vatican*

The appointments of Landázuri Ricketts, a Franciscan who had been made coadjutor of Lima in 1952 and had succeeded as archbishop later in the same year, and Silva Henriquez, who was bishop of Valparaiso from 1959 to 1961, before he was promoted to Santiago, demonstrated again John's intention to give Latin America the widest possible representation in the College—in less than four years he had advanced the leading prelates of Mexico, Uruguay, Venezuela, Colombia, Peru, and Chile. Pius XII had a distinct preference for eastern South America. Of his five Latin American creations who survived him, three were Brazilian archbishops and one was the archbishop of Buenos Aires; his remaining Hispanic creation was Carlos María de la Torre of Quito. In addition, Santiago Luís

Copello, former archbishop of Buenos Aires, was now in Rome as the chancellor of the Church. John's promotions doubled the number of Hispanics in the College and gave a significant presence to western South America and Mexico for the first time.

The new curial appointments of Antoniutti, Forni, and Panico were the usual rewards for long diplomatic service, while Coussa and Albareda were rewarded for similar successes in Rome—Albareda's appointment also was an honor to the Benedictines. The Dominican General, Father Michael Browne, was close to John personally. Although an Irish ecclesiastical conservative, he did not join with the anti-Bea forces on the Biblical Commission—especially Pizzardo, Ottaviani, and Ruffini. John's personal intervention, in May, 1962, to save Bea from the cardinals who were attacking his principles probably was based on information provided to him by Browne.

José da Costa Nuñes was the last notable Portuguese colonial prelate. Born in Candelaria in 1880, and ordained in 1903, he had been appointed bishop of Macao by Benedict XV in 1920. After twenty years' service, Pius XII had made him archbishop of Goa, primate of the East, and patriarch of the East Indies, in 1940. Da Costa Nunes was called to Rome as vice chancellor of the Church in 1953, with the rank of titular archbishop of Odesso and the title of patriarch *ad personam*. After nine years in that position, John gave him the red at the age of eighty-two to cap his career.

After this consistory, John's complete attention was taken up with the preparations for the council and he devoted no more time to selecting new cardinals. Two of his most recent creations died within four months of their appointment, Panico (July 7) and Coussa (July 29). Early in 1963, just after the end of the first session of the council, John lost his English archbishop, William Godfrey, on January 22. His death was followed by that of his Irish counterpart, John D'Alton, the archbishop of Armagh, on February 1, and by that of Manuel Arteaga y Betancourt of Havana, on March 20.

Those deaths left the membership of the College at eighty-two during the last two and a half months of John's life. Eighty of them would elect his successor.

In 1957, while still cardinal-patriarch of Venice, John had prepared a will based on the premise that he might die suddenly. Now, in the summer of 1961, he began to sense that his death might well be slow and lingering. During his stay at Castel Gandolfo, he prepared a new preamble to his will, only four short paragraphs, dated September 12, 1961.

In this revised text, he expressed his new understanding of his own end: "I await the arrival of Sister Death and will welcome her simply and joyfully in whatever circumstances it will please the Lord to send her."

By late November, 1961, with the opening of the council less than a year away, John acknowledged his gastric pain for the first time. He wrote in his diary:

> I notice in my body the beginning of some trouble that must be natural for an old man. I bear it with resignation, even if it is sometimes rather tiresome and also makes me afraid it will get worse. It is not pleasant to think too much about this; but once more, I feel prepared for anything.

Did he understand already that these were the first signs of the stomach cancer that would kill him eventually? Was death the "anything" for which he was prepared, perhaps before the council was opened? Although he said nothing to his familiars immediately, since he knew that gastric tumors were regarded as largely inoperable at that time, it seemed very likely that he did understand. Stomach cancer ran strongly in his family. Indeed, of his three elder sisters, two already had died of the condition, Ancilla (b. 1880) in 1953 and Teresa (b. 1879) in 1954—the eldest, Caterina, had died at the age of five in 1883.

By mid-September, 1962, with his workload increasing, his insistent agonies persuaded him to allow a complete medical examination. He had not left the Vatican for Castel Gandolfo that summer, but chose instead to retire for a brief spiritual retreat to the Torre San Giovanni (Saint John's Tower) in the Vatican Gardens, a ninth-century construction which John had restored and modernized. It was there, about September 15, that he had his physical examination. The written report of it was given to him on Sunday, September 23, the last day of his retreat. It confirmed his worst suspicions—he would die relatively soon.

With the opening of the council scheduled for October 11, he had no time to dwell on his condition. He was near the zenith of his pontificate, and he would let nothing interfere with its triumph. He continued to guide the final preparations as if nothing dark loomed ahead.

On October 4, he became the first pope since Pius IX to leave the environs of Rome, when he journeyed to the shrine of Loreto to pray for the success of the council. He boarded a special train at 6:30 A.M., which then stopped at the Trastevere Station so that he could be joined by Amintore Fanfani, now the prime minister of Italy. Everywhere the train stopped—Orte, Narni, Terni, Spoleto, Foligno, Fabriano, Iesi, Falconara, Ancona, and Assisi—vast throngs of cheering people turned out to see him. If he ever had doubts about how ordinary people outside Rome felt about him, these enthusiastic receptions dispelled all of them.

While he was on this brief trip, hundreds of bishops were pouring into Rome for the opening day of Vatican II. The Eternal City had not seen such sustained excitement and world interest in centuries, perhaps not since the first great jubilee, held by Boniface VIII in 1300.

The solemn opening of the council took place in Saint Peter's with a long ceremony that began at 8:00. John himself did not speak until almost noon. Until then, the succession of rites and ceremonies had been something of a Roman endurance test for the council fathers. The only thrilling action for them came when John entered the basilica, not on the *sedia gestatoria* that was expected but rather walking the full length of the nave—a bishop among other bishops.

John's thirty-seven-minute address, *Gaudet Mater Ecclesia*, revealed his broad historical vision of the Church—as the only pope to have been an historian could—and, with this as his foundation, he exhorted Catholics and other Christians alike to "expect a leap forward in doctrinal insight and the education of consciences in ever greater fidelity to authentic teaching. *But this authentic doctrine has to be studied and expounded in the light of the research methods and the language of modern thought.*" It was the whole scope of his *aggiornamento* distilled into a few words.

But the dying pope reached the fullest crescendo of his life not enthroned with his brother bishops in the splendour of Saint Peter's, but later in that same night. John, exhausted both by his preparations for the council and by the ceremonies of opening it, retired a little earlier than was his custom. As the twilight passed away, thousands and thousands of ordinary Romans gathered in the Piazza and began to call for him, ever louder and louder. By the time the crowd had reached perhaps half a million persons, John responded to the deafening clamour underneath his window. The lights in his apartment went on and the window to his study opened. John spoke to them not from the great balcony above the façade of the basilica, but rather from the intimacy of his own lodgings, just as any Italian might speak to his friends from an open window. In the moonlight, he said to them, "Dear children, dear children, I hear your voices. . . . My voice is an isolated one, but it echoes the voice of the whole world. Here, in effect, the whole world is represented. . . . Now go back home and give your little children a kiss—tell them it is from Pope John."

John did not attend the meetings of the council, but rather received extensive daily briefings of its doings—largely accounts of the disorganization of the proceedings and the rejection of the *schemata* for the council's work that had been prepared by the curia. It quickly became clear that the council was not going to be a one-session event, as John originally had hoped, but that it would need to meet again, perhaps in three or four more sessions. Ostensibly, John was not attending the daily sessions in order to permit the council fathers the widest freedom of debate, since his presence alone might have stifled some of the more vigourous reforms being advocated by the most progressive bishops. In fact, it was his rapidly deteriorating condition, which included increasing periods of exhaustion, which kept him away. He still hoped to maintain his secret while the council met.

During November, as his condition worsened, a new medical team was gathered to care for him as the cancer progressed. John himself appointed Dr. Antonio Gasbarrini, the sensible physician who had been present in Pius XII's last hours, as his personal physician, to succeed Dr. Filippo Rocchi, who had died recently. Gasbarrini, like the pope, was eighty-one years old, but fully vigourous and at the height of his profession. After Pius's death, he had accepted an appointment as professor of clinical medicine at the University of Bologna, where he now lived. Pietro Valdoni was, at sixty-three, Italy's leading scholar of the thorax and the arteries. He was given an appointment as regular medical consultant. His professional successes had elevated him to a professorship of surgery at the University of Rome and the directorship of the surgical section at the Policlinica, one of the city's foremost hospitals.

On November 16, Dr. Valdoni introduced John to the third new member of the team, Dr. Piero Mazzoni, a leading young anesthesiologist and president of the Italian Society of Anesthesiology, who moved into a suite of rooms directly adjacent to the pope's apartment—he would be available at any time the pope experienced a crisis. He was chosen because he also was an expert in the new technique of radiation therapy. He recommended an immediate course of cobalt-ray treatments for the tumor, in spite of the certainty of ænemia, the principal side effect of the procedure.

Finally, Dr. Mario Fontana, 58, became the archiater, the chief of the Vatican medical services.

In addition, the five nuns of the Sisters of the Poor from Bergamo who served the pope in daily life all had their nursing training revetted to ensure that they would be ready for any eventuality. These preparations were supervised by their leader, the pope's housekeeper, Mother Saveria Bertoli.

That these careful and methodical preparations were necessary was confirmed during the night of Tuesday, November 27. John's cries awakened Monsignor Capovilla, who slept on a cot outside the pope's door. Capovilla looked in, saw the suffering, and ran to get Dr. Mazzoni from his rooms nearby. He also ran, and found John in agony from a massive gastric hemorrhage. He immediately injected coagulants and morphine, and began a plasma drip. By the early morning, the episode was controlled and John was able to sleep for a short time.

Of course, the pope's general audience for Wednesday had to be canceled. On Thursday, November 29, *L'Osservatore Romano* disclosed that John's "symptoms of gastric disturbance were getting worse. . . ." Although the word "cancer" was not used, Romans who were accustomed to reading between the lines of the Vatican's official paper of record knew immediately, from the phrase "getting worse," that the situation was grave. John's peasant hardiness, however, brought a rally that was truly remarkable. By December 1, his condition had improved significantly. On the following day, he resumed his normal activities and held a general audience.

On Wednesday, December 5, he conducted the general audience from his window—still too weak to move much about the large and rambling Apostolic Palace. The council fathers were released early, so that they also could attend. Though his voice was weaker than it had been, his speech was not confined only to a few words. He spoke of his recent illness and his convalescence, and then went on to convey another of his clearly worded statements on the nature of the council: "What a spectacle we see here today—the whole Church in all its fullness: behold its bishops! behold its priests! behold its Christian people! A whole family here present, the family of Christ."

Three days later, he came again to Saint Peter's to address the council as it adjourned its first session. By now, most of those present knew about the reality of John's gastric cancer. They knew that probably they would not see him on the throne when they returned to Rome for the second session in September, 1962—if, indeed, there were a second session, for the bull of convocation would lapse with the death of the pope. Now, they saw for themselves—his cheeks were drawn, his skin was mottled, and the remarkable sparkle of his warm brown eyes had dimmed. Within days, word began to spread beyond Rome that John's illness probably was mortal. Still, the word "cancer" was absent from the vocabularies of those who were willing to talk publicly about the situation at all. Cardinal Léger, in mid-December, used the common discourse of the time when he confined himself to saying that the pope's illness "will remain with him until the end of his days."

The pope continued with nearly all of his full daily schedule, as he weakened little by little. By early February, his distressed appearance caused the Vatican to release a statement that he was suffering from a cold. On Sunday, February 3, the crowd which had gathered in the piazza for his blessing saw it dimly imparted from behind a curtained window, which was deemed necessary because of the pope's "cold." In fact, the ravages of his disease were now clearly visible even to the least informed.

Nevertheless, he pressed on. He opened Lent with a visit to the ancient title church of Santa Sabina, and continued in the following days with parish visits throughout Rome and its environs, going as far as Ostia, Quarto Miglio, and Borgata di San Basilio. This final round of public appearances added to his growing exhaustion. On Monday, March 18, he fell suddenly while ascending his throne for an audience. The end was nearer.

During the final weeks in which he was able to function, his great worry was to complete and issue his last encyclical, *Pacem in Terris*. John's climactic expression of his hopes for the Church and the world had to be promulgated officially before he died, or it would become an unknown dead letter—every pope's authority ceases absolutely with his death. The great document was dated Maundy Thursday, April 11. His task as teacher now seemed done.

Two days later, on Holy Saturday, John met for the last time with Giacomo Manzù, the avowedly communist sculptor who was his friend and limner. John praised the bronze bust of himself, but the words did not elevate the artist's spirit. John was a wreck of a man, a distant recollection of the hearty portrait that Manzù had begun more than a year earlier.

John held up surprisingly well during the long Easter service on April 14. By May 1, his condition had deteriorated so much that his memory and coordination were compromised seriously. He lost his place while saying Mass, the one text that a priest for more than fifty years knows more intimately than any other.

John already had taken steps to ensure the smooth conduct of the coming conclave. On September 5, 1962, just before he turned all of his attention to the opening of the council, he issued the motu proprio, *Summi Pontificis Electio*, the governing rules for the next election. John made only a few amendments to the terms of Pius XII's election constitution of 1945. Most importantly, he reduced the number of votes necessary for a valid election to two thirds of the voters, dispensing with the two-thirds-plus-one rule that Pius XII had enacted as a consequence of his momentary embarrassment in 1939. Now, John tried to obviate the problems that were caused in 1958 when Hungary and Yugoslavia forbade their cardinals to attend the conclave. Tito could not block Alojzije Stepinac this time—the Croatian archbishop died on February 10, 1960. Only Mindszenty now was in peril, still a reluctant lodger in the American legation in Budapest.

On May 7, the day on which John suffered his greatest relapse since November, Archbishop Agostino Casaroli, the under secretary of the Congregation for Extraordinary Ecclesiastical Affairs, arrived secretly in the Hungarian capital. This journey was Casaroli's part in John's carefully planned preparations for papal death. Casaroli met with József Prantner, the minister of the newly established bureau of ecclesiastical affairs, as well as with several Catholic bishops and American diplomats, to try to arrive at a *modus vivendi* to permit Hungary's primate to leave the legation for Rome on terms that Mindszenty would accept. Casaroli's negotiations bore some fruit. On May 9, Turner B. Shelton, of the American legation, and Dr. James Lynsky, the medical officer of the American embassy in Belgrade—who had been flown in to give the appearance of objectivity to discussions of the cardinal's condition—met with Hungarian officials to see if Mindszenty, who was still under a sentence of life imprisonment, could qualify for a recently enacted amnesty, under which prisoners older than sixty and in poor health could be released from further penalties. Mindszenty's own insistence that he be permitted to return to Budapest after his possible Roman visit, and his concern about the administration of the Church if some successor were to be named in his absence, caused a final rupture in the talks. Casaroli returned to Rome, unable to fulfill John's wish that Mindszenty be present for the balloting in the Sistine.

While Casaroli was shuttling back and forth to various offices and ministries in Budapest, John began to rally from his serious relapse of the seventh. He successfully struggled to receive more than ten thousand pilgrims in his regular general audience on Wednesday the eighth, but trips that he had scheduled to Montecassino and the Pompeii shrine had to be canceled. Gasbarrini, who arrived from Bologna on Wednesday evening, conducted a thorough examination of his patient on Thursday morning. His presence alerted both the Vatican and the Roman public that the pope's condition was worse. When he was pressed, in an interview later on Thursday, to admit finally that John was in the final throes of cancer, Gasbarrini again refused to comment or elaborate on his patient's condition, saying that he could "say nothing about it. I am bound by professional secrecy." By this time, of course, there was no secret.

On Friday, May 10, came the last glory of his pontificate. John received the president of Italy, Antonio Segni, in the Sala Regia. Segni presented him with a gold collar and medal, emblematic of John's being named the first recipient of the Balzan Peace Prize—which had been announced publicly on the preceding March 1. John held this ceremony in his throne room, rather than in Saint Peter's, to make the distinction that he accepted the award in his secular rôle as head of state rather than in his religious state as pontiff. Later, John went to the basilica to receive the scroll that commemorated the prize, an opportunity he used for public prayers for peace. Now all the splendor of the Tridentine papacy was employed for the occasion. John, surrounded by his court, heard the silver trumpets introduce the Sistine Choir's magnificent rendition of the *Tu es Petrus*. Following the service, the pope gave his last important address. "Peace," he said, "is the greatest treasure of life in a community, the most luminous point in the history of humanity and Christianity, the object of the trustful expectations of the Church and the people."

Because Segni was stricken with laryngitis, the second half of the ceremony saw Giovanni Gronchi, the former president, as the presenter. John used his remarks to minimize his own role and to associate his work with his predecessors—from Leo XIII to Pius XII.

The audience for these ceremonies was as politically eclectic as John's own messages about peace. In addition to his principal attendant for the day, Monsignor Federico Callori di Vignale, the crowd included thirty cardinals, among them Cardinal Wyszynski—conveniently in Rome to discuss the council; John wished him to stay in Rome so that he would not have to be extricated from Warsaw with delicacy, as he had in 1958. Also present were Sergei K. Romanovski, chairman of the Soviet committee for cultural relations with foreign countries, and Josef Kobernyckyj-Dyckowskyj Slipyj, the exiled metropolitan archbishop of Lwow in the Ukraine, who had been released from his years in the Gulag as a part of John's first friendly contacts with Nikita Khruschev.

By the time John mounted the *sedia gestatoria* to leave the basilica, he obviously was both wracked with pain and exhausted. He leaned forward on the throne with his head clasped in his hands, ignoring completely the thunderous rolls of applause that followed him down the nave.

At 5:30 P.M. on the next day, John left the Vatican for the last time when he paid an official call on President Segni at the Palazzo Quirinale. Pius XI had called on Vittorio Emmanuele III at the palace in 1929, to mark the celebration of the Lateran Treaties. Since that time, any thought that a pope would call there to visit the head of the Italian state was resisted strenuously by the Vatican's bureaucrats. It would be demeaning to do so, they argued, because the Quirinale had for centuries been the summer urban palace of the popes. As usual, John ignored such reasoning. Of course, as a sound scholar, he did have a small historical joke for the occasion. He dressed himself in a scarlet mozzetta edged with ermine over his white surplice, and he wore a red galeretto—the very costume his predecessors had worn regularly during the zenith of the Quirinale as a papal residence in the eighteenth century.

He told Capovilla during the drive from the Vatican that, although in considerable distress, he was going as "an act of deference towards my country, because I owe so much not only to Bergamo but to Italy." The journey was a triumph. Thousands lined the streets of the motorcade to cheer him and receive his blessing. On his arrival, Segni greeted him and escorted him to the Pauline Chapel in the palace, where once the popes said their daily Mass when they were in residence. Then to the audience balcony, where John acknowledged the crowd and blessed them.

By this time, John's condition was alarming. Segni quickly escorted him to the central chair, where John fixed a rigid smile on his face as he attempted to control the waves of pain. In his brief remarks, he said that he would devote the $230,000 prize to a perpetual fund in favor of peace. In his last days, he did exactly that, and the revenue still is used today to finance some of the peacemaking activities of John Paul II. Sitting with the pope were Cicognani, as cardinal-secretary of state, and the four other winners of Balzan prizes, Paul Hindemith of Germany for music, Karl von Frisch from Austria for biology, Andrej Kolmogorov of the Soviet Union for mathematics, and Samuel Eliot Morison, the American historian.

On the return trip, John exhibited all the signs of profound exhaustion. However, once back at home, he rallied again—long enough to see scenes of his day on television. John still attempted to keep his full regular schedule, but this became increasingly difficult for him. He was now in constant pain, yet he wished to minimize the number and the dosages of the analgesics and sedatives that were given to him. On the morning of Tuesday, May 14, he was almost overcome with a surge of pain while donning his amice for Mass. The color drained from his face as he experienced a sudden spasm. Capovilla, who was now never more than steps from his side, quickly asked how he felt. "Like Saint Laurence on the gridiron," John replied. But the pope continued to draw upon his hardy peasant strength to rally, again and again, from these daily attacks. By that evening, he was well enough to walk to the Sala Clementina to listen to the Bamberger Symphoniker play the *Pastoral Symphony* of Beethoven.

By Wednesday night, his pain robbed him of sleep. He refused a sedative and spent the night reading the manuscript of a journal that Giulio Arrigoni, bishop of Lucca, had kept during the First Vatican Council. The text, which lay unnoticed in the library of the seminary at Bergamo for decades, had just been rediscovered and sent to the pope because of his profound interest in church history. John's last pontifical act was to order its edition and publication. The task was undertaken by the most distinguished ecclesiastical historian of the time, Michele Maccarone, and was published by Editrice Antenore on June 3, 1966, the third anniversary of John's death. Today, thanks to John's dedication to the historical profession to the end, it is one of the most important sources for the study of Pius IX's council.

On Friday, May 17, John said Mass for the last time. His condition was now so grave that the Roman people wondered how he found the strength to continue. It is not surprising that both the Vatican and the people were amazed at the announcement by President Kennedy's press secretary, Pierre Salinger, that Kennedy would call on the pope during his forthcoming visit to Italy, probably on the twenty-first or twenty-second of June. Was America's intelligence network so poor that it did not know the reality that was so well understood by Rome's man in the street?

On the night of the eighteenth, John was wracked with vomiting and became so weakened that he was now confined to his bed. The small portable altar that was installed in the study next to the bedroom when popes were dying was set up once again. Capovilla inaugurated the altar and gave his old master communion.

John's condition remained stable through the following night and by the twentieth he was able walk to his library on the floor below to receive Wyszynski, who escorted three Polish bishops who were on their *ad limina* visits: Antoni Baraniak of Poznan, Franciszek Jop of Opole, and Bolesław Kominek of Wrocław, later a cardinal. His mood was pessimistic, now. When Poland's primate said to him, "Good-bye until September," John replied, "In September, you will find me or . . . someone else. It only takes a month, you know: the funeral of one and the elevation of another."

After this audience, a new round of hemorrhages began. During the early morning hours of the twenty-second, the loss of blood became so great that transfusions were started.

Now, any hope that he could hold his regular Wednesday general audiences was gone. The assembly for the twenty-second was canceled—although he did stagger to the window to bless the large crowd—and no other was ever held.

Later, he suffered another serious relapse with a massive loss of blood and another set of transfusions. By Thursday morning, however, he was once again strong enough to appear at his window to impart another blessing to the throng of people who had gathered in the Piazza. At 6:30 P.M., he received his old friend, Gustavo Testa, whom he had raised to the cardinalate in 1959. When he saw John's state, Testa began to cry. "Dear don Gustavo," John consoled him, "we have to take things as they are. I have had a long life, and served the Church, and left some small impression on history. By God's grace, I have not behaved poorly: so, not one day more. If the Lord wishes me to remain here one day longer, very well, otherwise we are off."

Day by day, his pain grew worse, his condition deteriorated, as he prepared for the end. On Sunday, the twenty-sixth, he again hemorrhaged badly, although he did rise from his bed for a short while. Then came another round of examinations from Valdoni and Gasbarrini, who had arrived from Bologna in answer to an urgent summons. Later that evening, John rallied again and met with Cicognani for forty-five minutes. During the night, he received another transfusion and, later, received Cicognani twice on the twenty-seventh, and again twice on Tuesday, the twenty-eighth. Through him, as cardinal-secretary of state, the pope remained actively the head of the Church.

On Tuesday, as well, *L'Osservatore Romano* finally dropped the fiction that John was suffering from "gastropathy," a general stomach distress, and admitted the cancer:

> The hemorrhages caused by the gastric heteroplasia, which has affected the Holy Father for about a year, after being arrested for several months, have had an accentuated resumption in recent days.
>
> They have now been attenuated, and the organic consequences linked to them are, through today, limited and compensated by the curative measures adopted.

Even now, although the admission that John had a "heteroplasia," a tumor of abnormal cells, made the situation very clear, the official press could not bring themselves to admit honestly that the pope had only a few days to live.

Finally, on the twenty-ninth, the hemorrhages were stopped and John showed some small signs of improvement. But, of course, this was only a fleeting event. John continued with his twice-daily meetings with Cicognani.

The night of May 29–30 proved to be John's last real repose. He awakened alert and refreshed. Suddenly, at 11:30, there was another massive hemorrhage. The pope was convulsed with pain. Mazzoni examined him swiftly and diagnosed a perforation of the tumor. At about noon, John was examined by Gasbarrini. Sedatives were given and, as John slipped into sleep, Gasbarrini was confident enough about the situation to return to Bologna. Another examination at 8:30 by Valdoni confirmed John's final, slight rally, but the medical order now came that he was to have nothing more by mouth, because eating or drinking might cause another outbreak of gastric bleeding. No news of this crisis was reported on Vatican Radio or in *L'Osservatore Romano*. The series of medical bulletins continued a somewhat optimistic tone, which deceived the press and public alike. Suddenly, at nightfall on the thirtieth, John became unconscious.

On Friday morning, May 31, John awakened to a visit by Valdoni who detected peritonitis. He knew that this grave condition heralded the end. The doctors, minus Gasbarrini who was again summoned from Bologna, agreed that there was nothing more that could be done.

It fell to loyal Monsignor Capovilla to tell John that the situation was hopeless at last. John asked his secretary to tell him precisely what the doctors's opinion was. "Their verdict, Holy Father, is that it is the end. The tumor has done its work."

John's optimism never left him, even as he remembered the fates of his two sisters a decade before. He inquired about the possibility of an operation, as had been done many decades earlier for his old mentor, Giacomo Maria Radini-Tedeschi, bishop of Bergamo, who had succumbed to cancer in August, 1914. "It is too late," Capovilla told him, "the cancer has, at last, overcome your long resistance." As the old secretary collapsed at John's bedside, the pope quietly told him to follow precisely the directions which are set forth in the *Cærimoniale Episcoporum*. "Help me to die as a bishop or a pope should," he said to Capovilla.

He was now placed in an oxygen tent, as the troop of persons who were entitled to be present for the death of a pope began to come in. At 11:00, John's confessor, Monsignor Alfredo Cavagna, gave him the viaticum, after which the papal sacristan, Bishop Pieter Canisius van Lierde, administered the sacrament of extreme unction—the final preparations for the journey home. Overcome, van Lierde forgot the order of anointing the five senses and John patiently directed him in the proper conduct of the sacrament. By this time, there were twenty people crowded into the bedroom: Cicognani; his principal assistant, Antonio Samorè; Angelo Dell'Acqua; Gustavo Testa; the doctors and nurses; other members of the pontifical household; the five old Bergamasque nuns who had cared for him; and Raimondo Manzini, the editor of *L'Osservatore Romano*. For each, he had a word and a blessing. Throughout the rest of the day, prelates and cardinals filed by the beside for final words with the dying pontiff.

Some received special instructions. He told his nephew, Monsignor Giovanni Battista Roncalli, to convey a greeting and a special blessing to the people of Sotto il Monte, his birthplace, and Bergamo, his most beloved diocese. He entrusted Capovilla with the task of watching over his family at home, but, he told his secretary, first "when this is all over, get some rest and go to see your mother."

Finally, just before six o'clock, the throng had dwindled to seven cardinals, the men who would lead the Church when he was gone: Cicognani; Tisserant, the dean of the College; Alfredo Ottaviani, the archdeacon; Santiago Luís Copello, the chancellor of the Church; Benedetto Aloisi Masella, still the camerlengo; Fernando Cento, the penitentiary major; and Alberto di Jorio, the secretary of the conclave in 1958 and now with the Congregation of the Sacraments. He refused their request for a deathbed consistory to make public the names of the three cardinals he had created *in petto* in the consistory of March 28, 1960: "out of respect for the Sacred College." John was not going to risk a repetition of the Stepinac and Mindszenty situations in 1958—for all of the secret cardinals were from communist countries. He took their names to his grave.

Just after seven, there were more waves of pain. The pope received heavy sedation and was soon unconscious. He was still asleep when Montini arrived at the Vatican with the surviving Roncallis of John's generation: his brothers, Alfredo, Zaverio, and Giuseppe, and his sister, Assunta. Montini had come from Milan in answer to John's summons to discuss the strategy for the coming conclave. Montini, like the immediate family, stayed near John until the end.

Just after midnight on Whitsunday, Capovilla said a Mass for the Roncalli family at the altar in the study. Two hours later, John awakened to find his closest family with him. At first, he was confused and seemed to believe that he was, once again, the papal nuncio in Paris. He began to speak French to one of the doctors. He quickly regained his faculties, recognized his relatives, sat up, and—now that it no longer mattered what he consumed—enjoyed his favorite morning treat, a cup of strong espresso.

Revived, he spoke in an almost bantering way to his family. "I am still here, when, yesterday, I thought I was gone . . . I could get better . . . If I get worse, what a disappointment for you." He now slept a little more and then reawakened at 3:45 to find his friend, Giuseppe Piazza, bishop of Bergamo, with a small delegation of fellow countrymen, including the mayors of Bergamo and Sotto il Monte, the pastor of Roncalli's childhood church, and Andrea Spada, the editor of *L'Eco di Bergamo*.

The presence of his family and others from the North revived John again, for the last time. Between five and eight o'clock on the morning of Saturday, June 1, he seemed almost like his old self. Even though he was in great pain, his vital signs stabilized; his pulse had returned to normal. But it was the last, supreme effort of a convivial and social man. He genuinely enjoyed this company, which acted as a tonic to his waning powers. At eight, however, he began to sink rapidly. Within a few minutes, he suffered a respiratory crisis and dropped suddenly into a state between sleep and coma. His temperature rose dramatically, but dropped back to 100.5 Fahrenheit.

Gasbarrini, Valdoni, and Mazzoni are all constantly at his side throughout the day. John sank further into unconsciousness, although, to the surprise of the doctors, his pulse remained regular and his temperature remained stable at 100.4. Although his breathing was now very labored, there were no other signs of acute suffering.

At 3:40 P.M., he awoke. As he became conscious, he resumed the prayer he had been saying when he had become comatose in the morning. Those attending him now included Cento and Cicognani; his confessor, Monsignor Cavagna; Monsignor Dell'Acqua; Bishop Piazza of Bergamo; and his relatives. By five o'clock, his temperature was gently, but steadily, rising. His three doctors conducted another examination which confirmed that the peritonitis was now far advanced. At about this time, his mind began to wander, as he mumbled prayers and invocations in disorientation and distress. Soon, he slipped into a deep sleep.

During the night between June 1 and 2, he had some short periods of wakefulness and lucidity. On one occasion, he was able to take several sips of water. At 3:00 A.M., a crucifix was placed in his hands. He grasped it with all his remaining strength and would not let it go—it stayed in his hands to the end. At 7:45, it became Cicognani's turn to say Mass at the altar in the study. John followed the service with his eyes, but without much animation. By 10:00 A.M., his temperature had risen again and his distress was even greater. At noon, he asked what time it was and, soon afterward, he told his nephew, Zaverio, who was standing at the end of the bed, to move aside a little, because he was blocking John's view of a crucifix on the opposite wall.

During the rest of June 2, the pope gradually declined, and was conscious for only brief periods. By midafternoon, his temperature was 102 and his pulse now fluctuated rapidly between 130 and 135. Later, his temperature rose to 103.1, although his pulse continued in the same narrow, elevated range.

Shortly after five, John mumbled a bit of the *Regina Coeli* and a few more invocations to saints. At eight, he had another crisis, which was controlled by drugs. It fell to Cardinal Fernando Cento, as the penitentiary major, to lead the prayers for the dying. Now he began that duty. But this was yet premature. John held on.

John was largely unconscious, his condition very grave. Valdoni issued a statement that expressed his wonder at the hardihood of the old Bergamasque peasant—though wracked with disease and pain, death was not imminent. By late in the evening of the second, John was awake again and seemed to follow the evening prayers.

And yet again, at 3:00 A.M. on the morning of the third, he rose to attention long enough to say, twice, "Lord, you know that I love you." He would never again speak clearly. In his last hours, he tried to speak again, but his words were faint and indistinct. One prelate bent his ear down almost to the pope's lips. He seemed as if he might be trying to say, "Ut unum sint"—"That all may be one." This was the cause, he had mentioned some days before, for which he was offering up his suffering.

At 5:00 A.M., Capovilla said Mass. John seemed to pay some attention to the service, but it is not clear how much he understood of what was happening. Then, his near coma returned.

All through the day, the death watch continued. The pope's bedroom filled with prelates, friends, and family. They were quiet. There was nothing of the unseemly and disordered behavior that had disfigured the death of Pius XII.

Crowded into the room were Tisserant, Aloisi Masella, and Cicognani; John's three brothers and his sister; three of his nephews, Giovanni Battista, Zaverio, and Flavio; four of his nieces, two of whom, Angela and Anna, were nuns; his two faithful valets, Guido and Giampaolo[2] Gussi; the three doctors; Cavagna and van Lierde, the sacristan; Federico Belotti, his principal nurse; the five nuns of his household; the devoted Capovilla; and, in the shadows, Montini.

Periodically, while semi-conscious, his hand feebly drew the sign of the cross—like Benedict XV and Pius XI, he knew how to die like a pope.

At 1:00 P.M., there was another crisis, but Gasbarrini and his colleagues controlled this one, too. By three, John was quiet.

Just as he wished, his life ebbed away slowly and deliberately. By 7:20, his shallow, labored breathing and falling pulse indicated that the end was but minutes away. Gasbarrini whispered to Aloisi Masella, the camerlengo, that little time remained. The latter, similarly, conveyed the news to Cento, who now began the prayers for the dying again. Everything was orderly and punctilious. In the study, Cardinal Luigi Traglia, the cardinal-vicar of Rome, said Mass for the dying pope. Just before 7:45, Traglia concluded the Mass—the "Ite, Missa est" was heard clearly in the bedroom. John now trembled slightly and his breath failed.

At 7:49, Cento stopped his prayers. He leaned over the bed, straightened, and announced formally, "Vere papa mortuus est"—"Truly, the pope is dead." One of the chamberlains stepped forward and drew a veil over John's face. Now the lights in the bedroom were turned up. Outside, in the piazza, the thousands who had gathered to watch and pray knew that the end had come. At 7:54, Vatican Radio made the formal public announcement of John's passing.

Those in the bedroom knelt and prayed the "In paradisum," then the "Magnificat," and then the "Te Deum." Within a few minutes, Giacomo Manzù, artist as well as friend to the last, came in to take a death mask and a cast of John's right hand, which had blessed so many in his fifty-eight years as a priest.

Now began the execution of the two Roncallian plans for the end of the reign. The first, a very public exercise, was his simplified funeral and burial. The second, a very private one carried out by John's most trusted allies, was to ensure the election of Giovanni Battista Montini as his successor.

John's cordial relationship with Montini, sixteen years his junior, dated from 1925, when Montini began to act as Roncalli's eyes and ears in the Roman curia. Though they were not close personally, their friendship ripened through a rich correspondence which extended from Roncalli's years as delegate in Sofia to the end of his nunciature in France. When Pius XII exiled Montini to Milan in 1954, the patriarch of Venice was shocked at the sudden loss of his closest "inside man."

In 1958, Montini became the first non-cardinal in centuries to receive votes in the conclave. That he got any at all reflected the opinion of several cardinals, and many other prelates, that Montini should have received the cardinalate shortly after his archiepiscopal appointment, as Milan's ordinaries traditionally did. John made his best expression of regret for Pius's omission by naming him as the first cardinal in the first consistory of his pontificate.

Throughout his reign, John remarked in several conversations that Montini should be his successor, and expressed the opinion that he would make a good pope—indeed, while still cardinal-patriarch, he told his visiting cousins, Giovanni and Candida Roncalli, "The only thing left for me now is to become pope, but that will not happen, because the next pope will be your archbishop (Montini)." At this time, almost everyone, Roncalli among them, believed that Pius certainly would raise Montini to the cardinalate before he died, even if that were to be a deathbed creation.

That these observations were neither casual nor personal, but rather tied closely to his vision of the council, was revealed in his conversation on February 9, 1963, with the Jesuit journalist, Roberto Tucci, editor of *Civiltà Cattolica* and Paul VI's head of Vatican Radio. He told Tucci that he wished everything to be done to prevent the next election from becoming "a conclave against me, for that would destroy all I have set out to achieve." The furthest he could go to promote Montini as the one to be trusted to continue his work was his homily on November 4, 1962, the feast of his favorite saint, Cardinal Carlo Borommeo. In this address, John dwelt on all that Rome had learned from Milan since the time of Ambrose, including the washing of the feet on Maundy Thursday—that Rome could learn anything from anyplace else was almost unthinkable for Romans, in general, and the curia, in particular. He went on to say how beloved Montini, "the first cardinal whom we created," was to him. It was as close as any modern pope had come to naming his hoped-for successor. Had he done more than this, he certainly would have defeated Montini's candidacy before it began, because the custom that no pope can have any voice in the choice of his successor is rigid and inflexible.

So, as the two popes had agreed, Montini left the deathbed of his ultimate patron and mentor and returned to Milan to watch and wait while others—the Montiniani—prepared the way to the throne for him.

Meanwhile, as soon as John had breathed his last, the camerlengo, Benedetto Aloisi Masella, ordered the death certificate to be drawn up. He did not seal the bedroom, however. Following the simplified directions of John himself, he ordered the body to be washed and then robed for a viewing by the family and invited guests in the morning. Within another hour, Tisserant dispatched the intimatio to all eighty-two members of the College of Cardinals, ordering them to gather in Rome.

If past elections were any guide, the cardinals who were residential archbishops in distant sees would take some time to order their pressing daily affairs and then set out for Rome, in time to participate in perhaps one or two general congregations before the opening of the conclave, fifteen or eighteen days after the death of the pope. While the curial cardinals could no longer rely on the complete absence of the more remote cardinals, they did assume that they had sufficient time to make their influence dominant in preparing the conclave itself, on the one hand, and establishing a strong voting bloc, on the other. Generally, they were nearly all in or near Rome when the pope died, so that they had a large majority in the early meetings of the general congregation. Since they were in close proximity to one another, it was they who set the tone and rhythm of the *prattiche*—leaving the late arrivals to take a place in the game as best they could. In this way, the curia had strongly influenced, if not dominated, conclaves for centuries.

The rise of industrial technology in the nineteenth century played a significant part in changing this. By 1878, the telegraph and steam transportation meant that most European cardinals would participate in conclaves, even if they still lacked the reliable and intimate information and contacts to enter fully into the early evolutions of the *prattiche*. As late as 1939, non-European cardinals found themselves in a breakneck race to arrive in time for the conclave itself, and never had a chance to take part in the all-important informal negotiations which established the candidates and the voting blocs for the election. The obstacles of communication and travel had begun to crumble in 1958, as the telephone and the airplane superseded the telegraph and steam transportation. Now, in 1963, the whole pre-conclave dance of the curial cardinals never even got to an opening curtain. At the same time, John's long fight against cancer gave the non-Roman cardinals a chance to begin their own *prattiche*—generally by telephone—well in advance of the pope's death. While such early negotiations were forbidden by both law and custom, John actually encouraged this new informal practice.

On Tuesday morning, June 4, most of the thirty-five cardinals in Rome joined the Roncalli family and such invited dignitaries as President Segni and Amintore Fanfani, who was now leading a caretaker government in anticipation of national elections, for the first viewing of John's body in the papal apartments. At the conclusion of this brief period, the body was placed on a portable bier and carried from the palace down to the piazza and then into Saint Peter's. The hidden passage of the papal corpse through night-darkened corridors from the apartments to the basilica gave way to John's wish that he pass, for a last time, among the people. Once inside the basilica, the bier was placed on the same high, sloping catafalque that had been used at the funerals of Pius XI and Pius XII. Unlike the circumstances in 1958, however, this was installed immediately in front of the high altar in the presence of thirty cardinals. John's body, now clothed in full pontificals, was prepared quickly for the first public viewing at 8:00 A.M. on Wednesday.

During the night, a cold front swept over the city. By the time the basilica was opened, a pouring rain, punctuated by heavy thunderstorms, soaked the crowd of one hundred fifty thousand who had gathered for the exposition of John's remains.

At 10:00, the first general congregation met in the Consistorial Hall with thirty-two cardinals. To the surprise of the Romans, one of them was Achille Liénart, bishop of Lille. He had boarded a plane for Rome within hours after learning that John was dead, a simple matter but one which startled the curia by its efficiency and purpose.

A major force on the left during the council's first session, Liénart's presence was a first warning that the curial cardinals would have little time to set their agenda—electing a pope who would bring the council to a swift conclusion without disturbing the order and structure of the Church they had dominated for so long. On seeing the bishop of Lille, Tisserant, no friend of Liénart, observed that the council had prepared the conclave rather than the other way about.

The business of the meeting went swiftly. The cardinals decided that the conclave's opening ceremonies would take place on the afternoon of Wednesday, the nineteenth. Tisserant used some small hand tools to deface and bend John's fisherman's ring, and the chancellor, Santiago Luís Copello, exhibited the shattered remains of John's papal seal, which he had crushed with a die stamp earlier on Tuesday. After these rituals, the cardinals dispersed for the remainder of the day.

The presence of Liénart in the general congregation reduced the ability of the curial faction to maneuvre. If they attempted to organize the conclave to reduce the influence of the Joannine, pro-conciliar cardinals, the Frenchman was sure to protest, and protest loudly.

At the same time, Montini had a small, but enthusiastic and loyal, cadre of prelates in the curia, led by Monsignor Angelo Dell'Acqua, John's most trusted private negotiator. Dell'Acqua and his friends were sure to keep the arriving *Montiniani* informed about who visited whom, and for how long, and perhaps even snippets of the dialogue they overheard.

Tisserant and the other leaders of the curia were not yet more than mildly worried. One Frenchman, no matter how obnoxious, was someone with whom they could deal with careful planning and execution. The remainder of Tuesday, however, caused their sense of disquiet to mount. Every international flight that came into Fiumicino seemed to bring with it another favorite cardinal of the council, another enemy of the establishment. First, it was Joseph Elmer Ritter of St. Louis, then came Paul Emile Léger of Montreal, then Julius Döpfner of Munich. This was serious, indeed.

Ritter was the cardinal who had mounted the most powerful challenge to the proposition that Latin had to be retained as the only liturgical language of the Church: "Once one has accepted the necessity and usefulness of renewal, then nothing can be, *a priori*, excluded from scrutiny, except the essence of the Mystical Body and its divine origin . . . for that reason the council cannot be indifferent to the reform and renewal of the liturgy," he had proclaimed. For Léger, a prelate whom John respected more than almost any other cardinal, the laity were not a herd to be led but a people, the Children of God, to be served and respected. Four years later, he would resign his see of Montreal to devote the rest of his life to service in an African leper colony. When John learned that the council of presidents he had formed to organize the council was attempting to pass the first session's confusion and lack of action over to the second session, scheduled for the fall of 1963, he preempted its power by creating a new coordinating commission to bring greater direction and order to the business of conciliar renewal.

He chose Cicognani to lead it, but also drafted the three most dedicated liberals as major participants, Liénart, Leo Jozef Suenens, and—Julius Döpfner. The work of the commission was energized by the driving presence of the leading cardinals from France, Belgium, and Germany. Their work, which was well under way when John died, completely undermined the plans of the conservative curialists, like Ernesto Ruffini and Alfredo

Ottaviani. Now the conclave, too, was going to reflect the liberal stamp of men like these.

Tuesday's express from Bologna added to the problem. Giacomo Lercaro, the most forthrightly liberal of all the Italian cardinals, was on it. Lercaro was especially hated in the Roman establishment, for, under Pius XII, he had limited his outspoken views and actions to a few symbolic moments, but, under John, he had moved further to the left in every way. By June, 1963, he was thought to be more anti-curial than even the most distant of residential archbishops. He was a traitor to his class.

On Thursday morning, the meeting of the second general congregation at 10:00 was short and civil, but the tension was evident and the conversation cold. One point of discussion was that Mindszenty would be absent from another conclave. Bishop Endre Hamvas had been asked to conduct a final round of negotiations with the Hungarian government and with the cardinal-primate. Like all earlier discussions, these, too, foundered on the refusal of the government to permit Mindszenty to return if he were to leave the country, and the cardinal's refusal to go, unless he were guaranteed the right to return. Suffering from an attack of high blood pressure, doubtless aggravated by anxiety, he told one questioner, "I will not leave Hungary, even if they elect me pope."

The cardinals also verified that all the preparations for John's burial were complete and in order; then they adjourned to prepare for the funeral ceremonies later in the day.

In the late afternoon, one hour before the burial rites began, John's body was lifted from the catafalque and carried through the nave to the steps of the basilica. Once outside, the *sediari* raised it aloft so that the people of Rome could see their Papa Roncalli for the last time. Then the bearers retraced their steps.

The burial ceremonies, conducted by Pericle Felici, secretary-general of the first session of the council and later a cardinal, were attended by forty cardinals, including three of the five Americans—McIntyre, Ritter, and Albert Gregory Meyer of Chicago. In addition to the Roncallis, there were about fifty members of the diplomatic corps, nearly all of the Roman nobility, and a large congregation of guests.

The act of burial was read by Monsignor Nicola Metta, after which four attendants lifted the portable bier and lowered it into the innermost of the three coffins. In a departure from 1958, the three coffins already had been nested together, so there was no need for the large winch or the time necessary to insert the caskets.

Next came the reading of the eulogy by Monsignor Amleto Tondini, the secretary of Latin briefs to princes. Its cold, formal language reflected Tondini's clear dislike of John, the council, and renewal. When he finished, a copy of the document was sealed in a metal tube and placed in the inner coffin, as were two velvet bags which contained specimens of all the coins and medals which had been minted in John's short reign—rather than the three bags of four gold, silver, and bronze coins, respectively.

Each of the cardinals came forward, at a swifter pace than had occurred at the same ceremony in 1958, and imparted a final blessing and absolution. Then John's face and hands were covered by veils and a crimson pall was drawn over the remains. Swiftly, a large, heavy brocade outer cover was drawn over the whole and the coffin, on its wheeled carriage, was pushed to the entrance of the crypt.

While the family and a small group of cardinals and prelates descended into the crypt for the burial itself, the rest of the guests, including the cardinals who did not have to be present officially, were escorted from the basilica and the outer doors were closed for the night.

Below, a large stone sarcophagus had been prepared in the little, white-washed chapel that faced the tomb of Pius XI. Beside it now gathered six cardinals—Aloisi Masella the camerlengo, Tisserant the dean, Liénart the archpriest of the College, Ottaviani the archdeacon, Cicognani, and Paolo Marella, the archpriest of Saint Peter's. With them were John's brothers and sister, the three nephews, and two nieces, Angela and Anna. In addition, Enrico Dante, the prefect of pontifical ceremonies, was there to supervise the notary who would be the official witness to the entombment, a few prelates, and the workmen who would seal the lids on the coffins, place the heavy set into the sarcophagus, and then seal its lid.

In nearly complete silence, the work progressed quickly. When it was over, one prelate looked at his watch. John, now entombed, had been dead for seventy-one hours. All had been completed in forty hours less than it had taken to place Pius XII in his final resting place.

As the family and the cardinals left the crypt, the workmen began to prepare the small chapel for a public opening in the morning. Upstairs, another crew removed the tribunes that had been erected for those who saw the burial rites. Within two hours, the basilica was ready for the first Mass of the *novemdiali* on Friday morning.

Throughout all these ceremonies, Montini was conspicuous by his absence. Among the Italian cardinals, only he and Carlo Chiarlo were absent. The latter was seriously ill and bedridden in his villa near Lucca, but Montini was healthy and strong—and, in the minds of the curial cardinals who were not privy to the electoral plans, shirking his duties and responsibilities. He had offered a well-attended public Mass in Milan's cathedral for the repose of John's soul, but he was not rushing to Rome to partici-

pate in the formalities of the general congregations or in the complex ma-
neuvreings of the *prattiche*.

The public events on Friday morning went smoothly. Near John's
tomb, the workmen had prepared a small altar. Here, as the public filed
through the crypt, a series of Masses were said for the repose of John's
soul—one of them by Giovanni Battista Roncalli. Here, too, the plain people of Rome gathered to continue to pay their respects. Above them, the
first of the nine solemn Masses of the *novemdiali* was chanted before a
more socially and politically important audience. They looked upon the
bare catafalque which had held the pope's bier on the preceding day. The
people below were close to John. Many offered prayers for his intercession
for their troubles—for them, he already was a saint.

The third general congregation received the official notice from Carlos
María de la Torre, archbishop of Quito, that he would not attend the conclave. In December, he had been brought down by a devastating thrombosis which left him largely bedridden and incapacitated. In the days
following the episode, his staff expected him to die at any time. He lived
on, but really never recovered, until the last day of July, 1968.

With this notice, the scope of the conclave was clear at last. Eighty cardinals would elect the new pope, barring more sudden death or incapacity.

In the afternoon, Aloisi Masella corrected his one technical omission.
He was driven out to Castel Gandolfo to retrieve the keys to the villa and to
seal the pope's summer study. It did not matter, in fact, because all John's
papers had come back with him to the Vatican after his last visit.

By the morning of Saturday, the eighth, fifty cardinals were in Rome,
but several were too ill or too busy to attend the fourth general congregation at 10:00. This was the first meeting devoted wholly to organizing the
coming election.

First, the cardinals chose two committees. The first, with Carlo Confalonieri as chairman, assisted by Luigi Traglia and Michael Browne, the
Irish Dominican, would examine the credentials of all those who would be
authorized to enter the conclave. Confalonieri was the obvious choice for
the job. He had attended his first conclave in 1922, when he had been
Ratti's conclavist. He had served as a prelate in the conclaves in 1939 and
1958. Now a cardinal, he was the only man in the Church who had been
inside three earlier conclaves. Now, in his fourth, he would be an elector
for the first time—forty-one years after he first heard the words, "Extra
omnes."

The second committee, chaired by Pietro Ciriaci, with Alberto di Jorio
and Gustavo Testa as his assistants, was to preside over the lottery which
would assign cells to the cardinals. Di Jorio had been the secretary of the

conclave in 1958 and Testa was closer to John personally than any other cardinal, but it was the scrupulously fair Ciriaci would preside. Pietro Ciriaci had an especially difficult cross to bear in life. He looked so much like the French comedian, Fernandel, that he frequently was mistaken for him in public, especially when dressed in clerical robes. By 1963, Fernandel had made four wildly successful films in the rôle of Don Camillo, Giovanni Guareschi's simple but clever country priest who has "hands like shovels" and converses often with God, particularly about his *bête-noire*, the communist mayor, Peppone. The books were comedic best-sellers—Americans were fond of comparing Guareschi to James Thurber—and were translated into more than a dozen languages, while the films spread knowledge of the character even more widely. Although he was seventeen years older than Fernandel, Pietro Ciriaci had to be very careful when he appeared in public in the daylight. He always attracted second looks, and it was not unknown for children to run up to him crying, "Don Camillo, Don Camillo." A native Roman, the cardinal had imbibed from infancy the spirit of a city which has seen all the world's silliness for more than two millennia, so he bore his burden of *doppelgänger* with outward good humour—although it certainly complicated his public life.

One of the first points of discussion was how to forestall any confusion about the smoke signals. The congregation decided on a small innovation. They ordered a set of two electric lights, one white and one dark, to be set up in the offices of Vatican Radio. The switches for them would be placed inside the Sistine. At the end of each voting session, the junior cardinal-deacon, the Spanish Benedictine, Joaquín Anselmo María Albareda, would turn on and off the appropriate switch just after he had prepared the ballots for burning.

More importantly, the cardinals, following the dictates of John's regulations in *Summi Pontificis Electio*, confirmed that each elector would be accompanied by only one conclavist, unless the state of his health was so poor that he required a second attendant. They then allotted a second attendant to two cardinals, one of whom was Enrique Pla y Deniel, archbishop of Toledo. All of these conclavists would be clerics, for the first time. Loyal valets, like John's devoted Guido Gussi, would no longer be housed in the conclave. The cardinals also considered other questions about the size and placement of the conclave's staff and determined the schedule of *maestri di camera*, guardians of the *rota*, physicians, dentists, carpenters, cooks, bakers, waiters, guards, and firemen.

By the end of the meeting, the number of people who had to be housed within the conclave's precincts was set: eighty electors, eighty-two conclavists, and a staff of one hundred nineteen. Even though the number of cardinal-electors was twenty-nine more that those in 1958, the reduction in the number of conclavists, from one hundred three to eighty-two, meant that the plans, and most of the equipment, from the election of John could be used again, unaltered.

The exclusion of all laymen from the conclave—everybody down to the cooks, bakers, and carpenters would be either priest, brother, or nun—was supposed to increase the probability that the actions of the electors would remain forever a secret. The only exception to this total exclusion was the fire brigade; it would consist of three firemen to be borrowed from Rome's department.

The public activities of the day consisted only of the second Mass of the nine-days requiems, chanted in the basilica by Roberto Ronca, titular archbishop of Lepanto.

In the following night, at 2:00 A.M., Spellman's plane touched down at Fiumicino after an eight-hour direct flight from New York. He was met at planeside by his old friend, Martin J. O'Connor, the rector of the North American College, who sped him away for a brief rest before the fifth general congregation on Sunday morning.

A few hours later, James McGuigan of Toronto also landed, quickly followed by Laurean Rugambwa, who had changed planes twice in his journey from his archdiocese of Bukoba in Tanganyika. Their presence brought the number of cardinals in the general congregation on Sunday to forty-two.

June 9 was Trinity Sunday, so the meeting of the cardinals was short and there was no requiem of the *novemdiali*. It was generally quiet in Rome; even the visits and calls of the *prattiche* were much diminished in honor of one of the Church's most solemn feasts.

On Monday morning, the chief excitement was watching the workmen install a shiny new aluminum chimney for the stove in the Sistine. Many hundreds in the piazza, and many of the staff who peered from convenient windows, watched the men as they clambered over the sloping roof and manhandled the new pipe into position. Inside the chapel, the old stove was brought in from storage and connected to the exhaust. It had been fitted with a new lid, on which was inscribed "1939—1958—1963," to commemorate its use in three elections.

The formal business of the sixth general congregation, with fifty-three cardinals present, was to receive the members of the diplomatic community who came to present their official condolences on John's death. After this ritual ended, the cardinals dealt with a few details and dispersed.

In the afternoon, Richard James Cushing of Boston arrived at Fiumicino. Now all five American electors were assembled together.

Spellman would be their leader in the *prattiche*. Although quite conservative, and close to the most conservative American, McIntyre, who once had been his closest aide in New York, Spellman understood the temper of change, in the Church, in the council, and in the College. His three liberal colleagues, Cushing, Meyer, and Ritter, set the political tone of the American delegation; Spellman decided with his colleagues to support Montini's candidacy for the throne. He did not, of course, communicate this decision to his old curial friends, but rather bided his time to achieve the greatest political benefit for the American Church from the new pope.

In the evening, Wyzynski left Warsaw by train. There was little difficulty on this occasion. The cardinal recently had acted as a "shuttle-diplomat," conveying messages between John and the Polish boss, Władysław Gomułka. He had, in fact, only returned to Warsaw on May 24, after two last meetings with John, and had conferred since then with Gomułka. Nevertheless, the cardinals were relieved when they learned that his train was under way, and more relieved when it crossed into free Europe.

On Tuesday, June 11, the fourth Mass of the *novemdiali* was said by Primo Principi, the principal assistant to Cardinal Paolo Marella, archpriest of Saint Peter's. The bare catafalque seemed increasingly to rivet the attention of the people who came, reminding them more and more forcefully of the man who was gone. Unlike similar occasions in 1939 and 1958, many were deeply moved by the Masses, a fact not overlooked by both the pro-conciliar and pro-curial cardinals.

In the general congregation on Tuesday morning, the electors decided to continue the practice, introduced in 1958 by the prince-marshal, Sigismondo Chigi, of adding a smoke-producing device to the ballots when they were burned. Instead of smoke bombs from a fireworks factory, they chose to use black flares, which were provided by the Italian Air Force with assurances of their reliability and safety.

After another round of solving small problems, the cardinals received a delegation from the Knights of Saint John, the Sovereign Military Order of Malta, led by their grand master, Angelo de Mojana di Cologna. Mojana, the seventy-seventh grand master of the order, and the only person not a cardinal entitled to be addressed as "Your Eminence," had been confirmed in his position by John in May, 1962. Once he had presented the official condolences of the knights, the congregation adjourned.

So far, at least for the curia cardinals, the course of the *prattiche* went smoothly. Of course, they heard Montini's name often, but largely in the context of continuing the council. That this was the chief talking point in his favor seemed to cheer the conservatives somewhat. It did not seem to reveal any real commitment to the Milanese archbishop. After all, whoever the new pope would be, the council was too firmly established to risk canceling it without at least a second session. Ciriaci pointed out that "even if Ottaviani were elected, he would not be able to do anything other than complete the council." But that was missing the agenda of the *Montiniani*. They looked towards Montini as the cardinal who was *most likely* to continue the council to fulfill *John's plans for reanimation and renewal*. They were not, by any means, in agreement about what this last proposition meant, for John had not laid out any specific set of goals for the council to achieve. Indeed, except for efforts to thwart the crippling of the assembly, John carefully had not preestablished some pattern of accomplishment. What the cardinals *did* know was that John had wished to have Montini succeed him; what they *thought they knew* was that Montini had a clear vision of John's hope for Vatican II. That the first conclusion was true is indisputable, that the second assumption was equally true is, in retrospect, highly debatable. Nevertheless, in 1963 the two elements went hand-in-hand, so that those who were most committed to the "success" of the council were drawn inevitably into the *Montiniani*.

On Wednesday, June 12, neither Wyzynski's arrival in Rome, nor the fifth Mass of the *novemdiali*, nor the formal business of the eighth general congregation occupied the principal attention of the cardinals. The excitement was that Montini's candidacy had received two major benefits from two very unlikely sources. First, Spain's Francisco Franco made a clumsy and ill-fated attempt to block Montini's ascent to the throne. It was as if he were trying to exercise the veto that had been possessed for so long by the Hapsburg and Bourbon kings of his country. Apparently, he little understood the effect of Rampolla's exclusion in the conclave of 1903, although he did know enough not to use the word "veto" or the phrase "right of exclusion." In his message, conveyed to the cardinals by one of the Spanish electors—possibly Arcadio Larraona—in the form of "advice," he kept just slightly within the prohibition of Pius X in the constitution *Commissum nobis*, of January 20, 1904. The cardinals, collectively, were outraged just the same. The language of the "advice" was strong—Montini was not a suitable pope for modern Christendom—but Franco was far too weak in the affairs of the world, and the affairs of the Church, to be heeded seriously. The heavy-footed Fascist approach to dealing with the Church was simply intolerable in the 1960s. What made the situation even worse was that the message was no longer private or secret. Many already had been informed that the nature, if not the precise text, of the "advice" would appear in the following day's edition of *Il Messagero*. More than one cardinal, especially those who wavered in their decision, were pushed closer to supporting Montini just because of Franco's opposition. There could be no question that any secular leader, no matter how ostensibly "Catholic," could have a voice in selecting the new pope. In addition, the best reason that could be advanced for Franco's opposition was that Montini had sent him a letter in the preceding October which urged him to show clemency to political prisoners. That was it? It was just too much.

While this infuriation was going on, a number of cardinals were allowed to see, or actually were given copies of, a secret report prepared by Italy's military intelligence apparatus, SIFAR (Servizio Informazioni Forze Armata). SIFAR was strongly distrusted, even by the politicians and bureaucrats it was created to serve, because it had smoothly taken up many members of Mussolini's secret police, the OVRA (Opera Vigilanza Repressione Antifascismo), when it was formed after World War II. The report claimed that Cardinal Agagianian was in touch with Soviet agents through his sister, Elisaveta Papikova, who was staying with him. SIFAR alleged that Papikova, then seventy-one years old, had met with a representative of the Soviet Embassy who was known to be a KGB agent. What had happened, in fact, was that a minor official of the embassy, an Armenian like the Agagianians, had called on her to help her with some of the endless Soviet paperwork that was necessary for her to submit, as a Soviet citizen, to allow Papikova to prolong her stay in Italy. SIFAR's efforts, code-named "Operation Conclave," backfired badly. Apparently, they were convinced that Agagianian, as not only foreign-born but "Russian" to boot, was a "liberal." They also thought he was being scouted by the cardinals as a serious *papabile*. Neither was true.

Although he had once been Roncalli's chief rival in 1958, the very conservative patriarch was no longer in contention for the throne, even in the wildest surmises. The report was, however, another irritant to the whole College. The liberals saw it as another attempt by the right to influence the election; the curialists saw the report as a misguided and clumsy effort that destroyed any possibility that they *might* advance Agagianian as a candidate, if their earlier choices faltered—after all, in 1958, his prospects had seemed quite good at one time.

In the years since 1963, a number of cardinals have continued to be privy to information provided by SID (Servizio Informazioni Difesa, which SIFAR was renamed in 1966, partly to try to efface its earlier ineptitudes). But, increasingly, they have used this information as a guide to what *not* to think about the subjects of the reports.

Friday the fourteenth was quiet. The sixth Mass of the *novemdiali* and the tenth general congregation marked the passage of the day. The *prattiche*, which should now have been at full tide, seemed almost nonexistent. Arcadio Larraona, the self-appointed spokesman for the conservatives, told one Roman gossip that the liberals, the "innovators," as he called them, were badly divided.

When pressed further to expound on whether or not this meant a fight in the conclave between the partisans of Montini and those of Lercaro, he quickly dropped the subject. It was not that he wished to say no more, it was just that he was baffled—his rhetoric had taken him beyond his information. In fact, there were more than a dozen of the *Montiniani* who would have preferred Lercaro, if Bologna's archbishop could mount a credible campaign, but they were not prepared to back him at the cost of a divided conclave that would let the conservatives slip over a "compromise" candidate with rightist views.

Angelo Dell'Acqua continued to gather up the strings that tied the pro-conciliar cardinals to a common cause. Because he did most of his informal canvassing by telephone, and since he was not a cardinal, few outside his own circle paid much attention to his comings and goings, which was all the better for the liberal cause. He also was in daily contact with Montini by telephone, to report on the evolution of events—no one, apparently, had any idea at all about when Montini would come down from Milan. One conservative wag thought that perhaps Montini wanted a real mandate by being elected *in absentia*. After all, never before in the history of the Church had a cardinal who wanted the throne been able to mount a serious campaign through surrogates.

As a diversion, most of the public speculation dwelt on Confalonieri as a possible Pius XIII—a liberal Pius more in keeping with his mentor, Pius XI, than with Ratti's successor. While a serious bid by Confalonieri was expected by no one, some of the conservatives saw this speculation as more evidence that the liberals were not dedicated entirely to either Montini or Lercaro.

Saturday's general congregation, the eleventh, saw the cardinals draft a telegram to Mindszenty, whose text was to be made public, in which they expressed solidarity with him in his lonely protest against Hungary's communist government. It was a small expression to indicate that his absence from the conclave, while regrettable and perhaps foolhardy, was acceptable.

Later came the seventh Mass of the *novemdiali*, the first of the last three, all to be celebrated by cardinals. Sixty-seven members of the College processed to the rite, in two columns led by Tisserant and Aloisi Masella. The Mass was celebrated by Giuseppe Ferretto, the cardinal-bishop of Sabina.

Sunday the sixteenth, which should have seen a heightened level of activity among both cardinals and prelates alike, passed as another apolitical day, filled with the brief business of the twelfth general congregation and the elaborate cardinalitial ceremony of the penultimate day of the *novemdiali*.

Monday's general meeting was short. The participants went immediately into Saint Peter's for the last Mass. The celebrant was Tisserant, assisted by Wyzynski, Liénart, Spellman, and Paolo Giobbe, who had been Roncalli's prefect at the Roman seminary, had gone on to be rector of the College of the Propaganda Fide, and was now the datarius of the Holy See. Seventy other cardinals witnessed the five celebrants impart the three-fold absolutions, as did delegations from eighty-four foreign governments, and four members of the Roncalli family, brother Giuseppe, nephew Giovanni Battista, and nieces, Angela and Anna. The delegations stressed the powerful, rather than the ceremonial. While the Belgians had sent Prince Albert de Liége, the heir apparent to the throne, the French and the Germans sent their foreign ministers, Maurice Couve de Murville and Gerhard Schröder. The Americans were led by Lyndon Johnson, himself only one hundred sixty-two days away from the presidency.

Outside in the piazza, the Italian army provided a full suite of military honors—Sergeant Roncalli had served willingly, as a good citizen should, in the Great War. Among the troops who participated was a company from the 73rd Lombard Infantry, the pope's old regiment.

But the whispered gossip focused not on the personalities in attendance but on the one who was not there. Seventy-five cardinals participated in these last rites, and four were too ill or too fatigued to last through the ceremony—and then there was Montini. Where was he?

After the end of the *novemdiali*, the cardinals continued with last minute preparations for entering the conclave. Before Spellman returned to the North American College to join his colleagues, he shared a little ceremony with Cicognani. As John had instructed his secretary of state on his deathbed, the cardinal of New York now received back the stole he had given to the pope for his eightieth birthday, on November 25, 1961. John had worn it for the opening ceremonies of the council, a fact which Cicognani inscribed in a note that he included with the stole.

Individually or in small groups, most of the cardinals spent the afternoon and evening packing for their short move to the Vatican. Some enjoyed quiet suppers with friends or family. During this quiet interlude, Montini arrived without excitement or notice. He continued to efface himself entirely from the *prattiche*, even at this late hour.

Instead of going immediately to the Lombard College, the usual lodgings of cardinal-archbishops of Milan when they are in Rome, he stowed his luggage, already packed and arranged for the conclave, in the convent of the Sisters of Maria Bambina—he was the cardinal-protector of their order. Then he left Rome in a closed car for the short ride to Castel Gandolfo to stay the remaining two nights before the conclave with his old friend, Emilio Bonomelli, the administrator and historian of the villa.

Here he remained, largely in seclusion, except for a brief journey on the following morning down to the Milanese church in Rome, San Carlo al Corso, where he said Mass for a small group of the Milanese community in Rome.

During the afternoon, most of the preparatory time was taken up with administering the conclave oath to the conclavists and the other members of the staff. The Pauline Chapel was used for this purpose. Aloisi Masella thought, correctly, that moving this long process out of the Sistine, and the conclave, altogether would reduce greatly both the schedule and the confusion when the actual opening ceremonies took place on the afternoon of the following day.

While he stayed at Castel Gandolfo, which brought back so many memories of the years he had served Pius XII there, Montini did receive a very small number of callers. One of them was Lercaro, who came on the evening of June 18. This was the most delicate negotiation of all. It was no secret that Bologna's archbishop wanted the throne, as well, and that he had a loyal following of perhaps two dozen cardinals who would back his campaign all the way to stalemate, if necessary. But Lercaro knew also that the curial cardinals were more opposed to his candidacy than to any other. If he were to persist in his campaign beyond some point of absolute intolerance on the part of the conservatives, he might well wreck the chances for electing any cardinal committed to the preservation of John's legacy. We have no record of the conversation between the two most powerful liberal Italians, but it seems likely that Montini welcomed a bid by Lercaro in the opening ballots. If the latter were to surge ahead to a surprising victory—which was, indeed, very unlikely—Montini would happily yield the next reign to him. After the meeting, Lercaro's spirits were buoyed up considerably. He had denied, pointedly and loudly, to everyone for weeks that he had any real ambitions to be pope. Now, after his cordial conversation with Montini, he let his watchfulness slip in a letter to the community of orphans that he housed in his palace: "I ardently hope and consider it probable that I will be returning to you, *but with a little less certainty than I thought when I left Bologna for Rome.*"

At about the same time, and not very far away, in the Franciscan house at Frascati, the council's most liberal leaders gathered together to decide on their plan of action in the conclave. Present at the meeting were Liénart, Frings, Suenens, König, Léger, and Alfrink. It was precisely the group that had met in the preparatory stages of the council to plan systematically to ensure the rejection of Ottaviani's elaborate scheme for controlling the council through a hand-picked commission of one hundred eighty. Their success was complete, and Ottaviani literally was stunned on the first working day of the council, October 14, 1962, when his plan was defeated by an overwhelming vote. The same group of men, minus Montini and Lercaro who were engaged elsewhere, met now to decide on the methods they would use to thwart Ottaviani and the curialists again, this time in the conclave itself. They did not simply agree to endorse and support Montini, however. Several hours of earnest conversation and debate covered all the possible options they had, to ensure that the new pope would be one who would continue, with full effort and commitment, the *aggiornamento* in the council. At one point, they nearly all agreed that Leo Jozef Suenens was the ideal man for that job, but further reflection also brought agreement that the time for a non-Italian pope—especially one hated so bitterly by the Roman establishment—had not yet arrived. No, it would have to be another Italian. So, Montini or Lercaro? By the time the session was over, they had made their decision. It would be Montini. When he learned what the progressives had decided, almost certainly in a telephone conversation with one of them, he expressed every satisfaction. Though eager for their support, he emphasized that his bid for the crown was still being conducted almost clandestinely, and so he would not make any public acknowledgment of their interest, or of the telephone conversation.

Meanwhile, the centerpiece of the whole campaign was quietly drawing his work to a close. Angelo Dell'Acqua exchanged visits with a few last cardinals whose support he regarded as essential but who were still uncommitted to Montini. One of them was Gustavo Testa. Dell'Acqua regarded his participation as essential, because he had been so close to John personally—for almost sixty years, since the early days in Bergamo—and because that friendship and devotion was not only recognized but greatly respected by many other cardinals. Testa's reasons for hesitation were straightforward—he just did not like Montini; he did not like him at all. In their meeting, Dell'Acqua stressed that John had wished Montini to follow him on the throne, and that the pope had considered every option carefully before settling on the Milanese archbishop. Gradually, variations on this theme wore down Testa's resistance and, in the end, he agreed to support Montini. This was a powerful commitment, as Dell'Acqua well knew. Simpler and plainer than even John himself, Testa was a bluff peasant who kept precisely to his word, when he gave it. Later, he said to another prelate, "I'll back him out of respect for Dell'Acqua, not because I am convinced."—"*aderisco—disse—per rispetto a Dell'Acqua, non perché convinto.*" That *aderisco* proved to be perhaps the essential promise on which the election would turn. Later still, Dell'Acqua received the cardinalate partly because Testa, stalwart peasant that he was, did exactly what he said he would do.

All the pieces that were necessary to solve the chess problem successfully were now in place, except the rook on the eighth. Now that, too, was placed carefully on the board. Early on the morning of Wednesday, June 19—long before the Mass of the Holy Spirit and the other ceremonies which would mark the beginning of the election—Spellman left the North American College and was driven to Castel Gandolfo. Here, two old friends from the prewar days of the secretariat of state met for the last time as equals. Although he was considerably more conservative in his political views than Montini, Spellman appreciated greatly the Italian's quiet but effective leadership of the Church's anti-Fascists, both before and during the war. He also understood that the forces that were propelling the council to greater and greater degrees of liberalism were the visible portion of a great sea of dissatisfaction which would have to be dammed and controlled by a skillful Church diplomat lest it burst, as in the early sixteenth century, and wash away much of what had been accomplished in rebuilding the Church during the past four centuries. Spellman was sure that Montini was the man for the job. He promised Montini his own vote, and implied with assurance that he would bring the other four Americans along with him. A final handshake, in the American style, and it was done.

Of course, the conservatives had a well-formed plan, as well. Because their favorite, Giuseppe Siri, Pius XII's *delfino*, was far too reactionary to win any votes from the progressives, Ottaviani, Tisserant, and Pizzardo led an effort to bring all the curial votes on which they could count to the recently created Ildebrando Antoniutti.

So, Montini's great rival would be Antoniutti, a rather colorless, but good-hearted man, who was born at Udine, near Friuli, on August 3, 1898. He sprang from the same family as the polyglot and translator, Father Pietro Antoniutti (1732–1827), whose knowledge of Latin, Greek, French, German, and, especially, English was proverbial in his time. Pietro translated thirty works from English into Italian, including two volumes of anthologies of the writings of Benjamin Franklin, *Opere Filosofiche* and *Opere Politiche*. In the next generation after the cardinal, actor Omero Antoniutti comes from the same stock.

After a laureate in theology, the future cardinal was ordained on December 5, 1920, at the slightly early age of twenty-two. Seven years later, he began his diplomatic career. He served on missions to China and Portugal between 1927 and 1936, after which he was chosen by Pacelli to be Apostolic delegate to Albania. In keeping with the dignity of his new station, he was made titular archbishop of Synnada in Phrygia on June 29, 1936. During his year in that post, 1936 to 1937, he became acquainted with Roncalli, who was conducting similar diplomatic affairs in another nearby Muslim state, Turkey. While in Tirana, he became particularly close to the Albanians on his staff and in the small Catholic population in the city. In later years, he reflected his care for the Albanian people by becoming a supporter of the Albanian American Catholic Charity, an organization devoted to resettling displaced Albanians, among other causes.

In 1937, he served briefly as *chargé d'affaires* in the nunciature in Madrid. Following this, he was appointed Apostolic delegate to Canada, where he served until 1953. In those years, he impressed his opposite number in the United States, Amleto Giovanni Cicognani, with his levelheadedness and easy cooperation. His success in Canada eventually was rewarded by his elevation to the nunciature at Madrid, one of the two or three most prestigious posts in the Vatican's diplomatic service. In Spain, Antoniutti followed Gaetano Cicognani, who had managed very well from 1938 through the difficult war years, until he was recalled to Rome for his well-deserved cardinalate in January, 1953.

After nine years in the nunciature, Antoniutti benefited from the goodwill of both John and Amleto Cicognani. He was called home and created a cardinal on March 19, 1962. Although some of the curia thought that he had been too friendly to Franco to maintain his diplomatic objectivity, and others thought that he had failed in Madrid because of his unwillingness to criticize the Fascist government with vigor, in general he had satisfied the two men whose opinion really counted, John and Cicognani. Since his cardinalate, he had served primarily on the Congregation for the Oriental Churches.

Now in his sixty-fifth year, he had amassed a fund of respect and goodwill, especially among the moderate conservatives. It was true that his conservatism was especially patriarchal. As head of the council's commission to study religious life, he refused to permit any nuns to participate. When his decision was protested vigorously, he waved it away with the remark, "Perhaps at the *fourth* Vatican Council." Later, under Paul VI, he became prefect of the Congregation of Religious, from which he retired in September, 1973. Less than a year later, on August 1, 1974, just two days short of his seventy-sixth birthday, he was killed in an automobile accident near Bologna.

Antoniutti's cheerfulness, the curialists thought, might be enough to persuade some of the less-committed liberals that he would not be bad as a candidate of compromise, if the campaigns of Montini and Lercaro failed. Ottaviani and his circle would back him fully from the opening ballot, and stick with him long enough to determine with certainty whether or not he was ultimately electable.

The *prattiche* was over. The results of the evolutions and negotiations had produced three candidates, Montini, Lercaro, and Antoniutti. There was a considerable disparity, however, in the intelligence each side had about the other. The progressives knew all about the position of Antoniutti. They had some detailed account of the work of the chief curialist managers, Ottaviani, Siri, Bacci, and Larraona. By contrast, the conservatives had little understanding of the backing Montini had received, nor did they know that Lercaro's candidacy was for the sunshine only and that he, himself, was prepared to back away if it seemed likely that the liberals would suffer defeat. This was the first conclave in history in which the animosity and fear between the two major factions was so great that it cut off any substantial dialogue between them.

Seventy-seven of the eighty cardinals in Rome gathered in Saint Peter's for the Mass of the Holy Spirit, celebrated by Tisserant. After the Mass, the cardinals listened to the traditional homily, which was delivered in this conclave by Amleto Tondini, secretary of Latin briefs to princes and the composer of John's official eulogy. If the progressive cardinals needed any reminder of the crisis that would ensue from the election of a conservative pope, Tondini provided it. His address was a vicious attack on John personally and on his pontifical program. "Doubt should be cast," he intoned, "on the enthusiastic applause received by the pope of peace, and it is to be wondered whether this enthusiasm came from people who were true believers, who accepted all of the dogmatic and moral teachings of the Church." If John had been applauded by communists, like Khruschev and Gomulka, and by notorious anti-clericals, like de Gaulle, then that applause was false for true believers, and the man who excited it was, by virtue of having generated it, false, as well. Tondini had offended the conciliarists beyond repair by going far, far away from the mood and temper of the majority of the electors. But he paid his price. Unlike all of his predecessors for several pontificates, most recently Antonio Bacci, he would never receive the cardinalate as the reward for his years of service. Indeed, several of the electors compared his address with Bacci's in 1958 in the most unfavorable terms. Not only was it graceless and in the poorest taste, but the Latin was not nearly as polished and elegant as that of his former superior.

After the address, the cardinals reunited in the Pauline, with the conclavists and the members of the staff, for the formal procession into the Sistine Chapel. In solemn files, accompanied by the Sistine Choir, the procession repeated the age-old electoral parade. First came the staff; then the conclavists; then the choir; then Enrico Dante, the prefect of pontifical ceremonies, carrying aloft a large gold cross; and then the cardinals, led by Tisserant and Aloisi Masella.

Once they were in the Sistine, Tisserant recited the traditional prayers for divine guidance. When the cardinals were seated on their thrones, he read the texts of Pius XII's constitution, *Vacantis apostolicæ sedis*, and John's amendments to it, *Summi pontificis electio*. After this, one by one, the cardinals took the oath to abide without deviation from all of the requirements of both documents.

After the oath-taking, Tisserant delivered a short address in which he urged the electors to do their duty honestly and conscientiously. At the end of these brief remarks, the cardinals witnessed the oaths of the senior officials of the conclave, including the prince-marshal, Sigismondo Chigi-Albani-della Rovere, and the governor of the conclave, Federico Callori di Vignale—both of them were repeating the rôles they had played in 1958.

Dante's cry of "extra omnes" was taken up by the other masters of ceremonies and soon the last door, the one leading to the courtyard of San Damaso, was locked from both sides. Inside the conclave, Aloisi Masella and Dante shared the custody of the keys, while Prince Chigi held the external ones. At that moment, the most elaborate official flag in the world, the banner of Chigi as hereditary prince-marshal of the conclave of the Holy Roman Church, was raised outside Saint Peter's.[3]

Once the doors were locked, the cardinals retired to their cells, except for Aloisi Masella, and the three chiefs of order, Tisserant, Liénart, and Ottaviani. These four processed through the entire conclave area with lanterns in the ancient search for interlopers and breaches of the sealed area.

At nine o'clock on Thursday, June 20, the cardinals united for Mass in the Pauline Chapel before entering the Sistine for the first ballot of the conclave. After the formalities of choosing the three scrutators, three infirmarians, and three tellers, they began to vote. What little knowledge we have of the results of this and the following five ballots is based upon hints and recollections from several participants, rather than upon written notes or memoranda. Consequently, the tallies are a composite from a number of sources.

Although the totals are in close agreement, the sources do not agree on the exact numbers for some of the ballots.

Giovanni Battista Montini	28
Ildebrando Antoniutti	24
Giacomo Lercaro	22
Francesco Roberti	5
Giuseppe Pizzardo	1

There was little surprise. The main strengths of the two voting blocs were revealed clearly. The progressives had concentrated all of their votes on Montini and Lercaro, for a total of fifty, while the conservatives demonstrated their allegiance in the votes for Antoniutti, and Roberti, for a total of twenty-nine. One side or the other would have to yield to some degree or there would be a complete stalemate. Fifty-four votes were required for a successful candidate to achieve the throne, and the twenty-nine conservatives could block forever the candidacy of any cardinal they could not stomach. Of the two leading figures, the curialists slightly preferred Montini to Lercaro, whose ultra-progressive tendencies and fiery temper they feared, but that was not an admission that they would consider Montini seriously for pope.

The cardinals moved forward without delay to the second ballot. The results were practically the same. The second voting went so swiftly that the junior cardinal-deacon, Joaquín Anselmo María Albareda, began to burn the morning's ballots only eighty minutes after the first scrutiny began. The black *sfumata*, enhanced by the military flares, was seen plainly in the piazza at 11:54 a.m.

The cardinals left the Sistine for their communal lunch in a state of great tension. For more than three-quarters of a century, the deadlocks between the two wings of the College had been broken successfully by open and frank compromises and negotiations, which had led to short conclaves of no more than five days. This time, however, the stakes were higher than they had been in earlier modern elections—much higher. In retrospect, it seemed that some of the most closely contested conclaves had hinged on questions which were, in the light of history, rather unimportant. In 1922, for example, the central issue had been what posture the papacy would adopt with the Italian national government; in 1958, it had been whether or not to continue the policies of Pius XII without much change—an impasse that was solved by electing an elderly transitional pope who was thought to be unable to make serious alteration in the few years that remained to him.

John had surprised his electors from both sides of ecclesiastical opinion. He had begun changes that would alter every aspect of the Church more than had been seen at any time since the Council of Trent, if they were allowed to evolve themselves to completion.

In 1963, the essential question was whether those changes would be allowed to progress—to what ultimate result no one from either party knew—or whether the new pope would limit the scope and effectiveness of the council by shutting it down at the earliest opportunity, and then lead the Chuch back to something that approximated Catholicism as it had been at the death of Pius XII. Each side saw itself as good fighters for the soul of the Church. And each side viewed the attitudes and policies of its opponent as absolutely unthinkable, not merely unacceptable, so there was no room at all for the political or social compromises which had resolved earlier conflicts and led to swift elections. Yet, because the conservatives controlled more than one third of the votes, there would have to be some shift in the relative positions of the two factions, or there simply would be no election.

The cardinals did not have to look back to the Middle Ages, to the three great vacancies of more than two years each.[4] In recent times, from the view of churchmen steeped in the long history of the papacy, there had been conclaves so long that they precipitated crises of one sort or another in Rome and in the Church. Every *sede vacante* from 1644 to 1800 had lasted more than a month—and five of them had lasted more than four months. As recently as 1740, the papacy had remained vacant for one hundred ninety-two days until Prospero Lambertini became Benedict XIV— and that resolution had come about because Lambertini had addressed the College openly. He told them that, unlike the major candidates who had deadlocked the election for so long, he was just a "jolly fellow" who had no particular agenda to advance. He was chosen on the ballot that followed his speech.

Just in the last century, there had been a forty-nine-day vacancy before Pius VIII was chosen in 1829, and then a sixty-four-day one before the choice of his successor, Gregory XVI, in 1831. It was only with the two-day conclave in which Giovanni Maria Mastai-Ferretti became Pius IX on June 16, 1846, that the era of short elections began. By contrast with these earlier marathons, the longest conclave in the most recent decades had been the five-day session that ended with the choice of Pius X in 1903—a total vacancy of fifteen days, shorter than the time between a papal death and the opening of the conclave, after Pius XI changed the interval from nine to fifteen days in 1922.

So, it was not thoughts of medieval elections over which the cardinals reflected during the luncheon period, nor even the long vacancies of the seventeenth and eighteenth centuries, but rather the two months and more vacancies of little more than a century ago. A session of one month and twenty-three days, like 1830–1831, would push the proclamation of a new pope well into August; one of a month and eight days, like 1829, would keep the conclave locked until late July. The conclave precincts were not air-conditioned or dehumidified, and already two cardinals, Pla y Deniel and Chiarlo, were seriously ill. Several others were so old and so fragile that a long session in Rome's notorious summer could well kill them, or force them to leave the conclave in a wretched state—Francesco Morano, the cardinal-astronomer, was eighty-nine, and thirteen others were eighty or more. The two who were most seriously ill, Pla y Deniel and Chiarlo, were eighty-six and eighty-one, respectively. In addition, the over-eighties included many of the most powerful and influential cardinals in the Church—Aloisi Masella (83), Micara (83), Cicognani (80), Feltin (80), and Bea (81); indeed, if the conclave were to last more than ten days, Bea—Pius XII's confessor and John XXIII's leading ecumenist—would mark his eighty-second birthday, on the twenty-eighth of June, and Aloisi Masella would celebrate his eighty-fourth on the next day. The loss of even one or two of the most powerful cardinals might well make the abyss between the factions more unbridgeable, because these men had the experience and prestige to make the deals that their junior colleagues could not. By contrast, only ten of the electors were under sixty—Julius Döpfner was the youngest at forty-nine.

During the lunch, Suenens openly appealed to Lercaro's supporters to switch their votes to Montini, so that the progressives could define their full complement as quickly as possible. While many on the left did not think that Montini was as completely committed to renewal and reform as Lercaro, they also knew that the latter was wholly unelectable, and that the prospects for a serious deadlock were now extraordinarily likely. It was better to put up a solid front and to negotiate from unity than to fragment the progressive vote and wait for a conservative counter-attack.

In this pessimistic mood, the cardinals returned to the Sistine for the third ballot. The two immediate questions were whether Lercaro's faction was willing to rally to Montini, and whether Antoniutti could pick up some votes from the progressives, who might think him moderate enough to allow the council to continue in the general direction it had during the first session. The tally answered both queries:

Giovanni Battista Montini	45
Ildebrando Antoniutti	22
Francesco Roberti	7
Giacomo Lercaro	5
Giuseppe Pizzardo	1

More than three-quarters of Lercaro's supporters had heeded Suenens's call, but the progressives still were not entirely a solid phalanx. Antoniutti was now seen to be completely unacceptable; he actually had lost votes to Roberti and had gained none at all from the progressives.

Without comment, the cardinals should have proceeded to the fourth ballot. The rules of the conclave forbade any conversation at all in the inter-voting period—the regulations demanded complete religious silence. Nevertheless, the College was startled when Gustavo Testa, seated between Confalonieri and di Jorio, burst out loudly, swinging his head back and forth to his companions, that the conclave was a travesty of what was expected of it. The cardinals who were refusing to elect Montini should stop their plots against him; his brother cardinals should recall that they were on oath to elect the best candidate; they should not risk throwing away the immense goodwill that John had brought to the Church on something so corrupt as partisan politics. It may have been that Testa, a very corpulent seventy-six years old, was dismayed, too, by the prospects of a long fight, but his reasons probably were just as he stated them, with especial emphasis on the wasting of John's legacy.

The reaction was as sudden and powerful. Siri leaped to his feet and left his throne, loudly protesting to Tisserant that this violation of the regulations was intolerable. Most of the other cardinals broke out into loud and rapid conversation with those near them; a few shouted protests or encouragement; a few others shouted for order. It fell to Tisserant, as dean of the College, to reimpose order on the assembly. Eventually, his authority and presence prevailed, and the cardinals, many of them now agitated and emotional, completed the fourth ballot.

Testa's sharp outburst had produced some effect:

Giovanni Battista Montini	50
Ildebrando Antoniutti	19
Francesco Roberti	8
Giacomo Lercaro	2
Giuseppe Pizzardo	1

Montini was only four votes away from the tiara, but he had won over only two of the conservatives—Antoniutti's third loss went to Roberti. Even if he were able to secure the votes of Lercaro's last, most dedicated adherents, he would never achieve the throne without at least two more of the curialists, who still presented a united opposition of twenty-seven votes.

In that light, Montini's gain of five votes did not encourage his supporters. One vote less than fifty-four would bar Milan's archbishop from the throne.

The black *sfumata* from Albareda's second fire of the day was seen in the piazza at 5:17 P.M. In contrast to the quick morning voting, which had taken eighty minutes, the afternoon balloting had lasted more than three hours. Testa had generated considerable heat; it remained to be seen if there was to be any light.

The hot and sultry day gave way to a cooler night as a small but steady breeze pushed through the city. The ventilation in the conclave, while not the best—only a few windows opened on the inside courtyards and a few doors opened onto interior galleries and loggias—was sufficient to bring some relief. During this brief coolness, a number of meetings took place in the cells of the cardinals or in secluded parts of the precincts. Some were formal, if hastily planned, gatherings.

Among the conservatives, a stalwart who had, thus far, little to say was Clemente Micara, the eighty-three-year-old and semiretired cardinal-vicar of Rome. Abrupt and dry in manner, he was not only conservative politically and theologically but also a man who had resented John's interference in his work as the prelate who governed the diocese of Rome as the pope's surrogate. John had occasion, more than once, to remind him that, although he was the cardinal-vicar, the pope was the true bishop, and that it was the latter's will that must prevail. Now Micara joined together with Fernando Cento, the major penitentiary, and Carlo Confalonieri, Pius XI's old friend and servant, in a short conversation with Testa. The cardinal-vicar openly acknowledged that the curialists had no more plausible candidates to offer. He suggested to the other two conservatives that their party should admit this as a fact and gracefully capitulate to the *Montiniani*, perhaps, thereby, winning some favor for themselves in the next reign. Testa, after all, did have a point. If the cardinals failed to elect John's successor quickly, the laity, Catholic and non-Catholic alike, might soon conceive of the College as a completely reactionary body that was committed to dispersing John's very favorable inheritance. In Testa's presence, the other two agreed. They would switch to Montini in the morning.

Elsewhere, Ottaviani was coming to a similar conclusion. He spoke to several of his colleagues, suggesting that an opportune change now would place Montini in their debt for his final achievement of the papacy. This might sway him to their side in close decisions in the coming reign—in Rome, a man does not forget his "friends." Among those with whom he spoke, Siri flatly rejected this stratagem. He acknowledged that Antoniutti's candidacy was finished. He thought that Roberti's win of a few votes from the earlier official candidate signaled the possibility that he might be electable as a compromise. Siri *really* hated Montini, as only a younger brother who vies with a successful elder for a father's affection can—such was their relationship to Pius XII throughout the late forties and early fifties. May was Siri's lucky month. He was born May 20, 1906. While he was still thirty-seven, Pius made him titular bishop of Livias and auxiliary at Genoa on May 7, 1944. Two years and one week later, on May 14, 1946, he became archbishop of Genoa. When Pius created him a cardinal on January 12, 1953, he became the youngest creation of the reign. It was no wonder that the people of Rome, as well as the staff of the curia, christened him Pius's *delfino*—his dauphin and heir. Siri rejoiced when Montini was exiled to Milan at the end of 1954, but, before that, it had been the latter who had been the pope's closest confidant and who had wielded true power in the pope's name. If Siri was close to Pius the old man, it was Montini who was closer to Pius the pope. Siri was apoplectic at the thought that Montini actually would assume the patrimony of the eldest son, the throne itself. Siri's hope that Francesco Roberti was the right man to bar Montini's ascent was ill-conceived at best.

Roberti was a quiet academic rather than an administrator or pastor. In contrast to the others who had received votes, he was mild, perhaps even colorless. Born July 7, 1889, at Pergola, he became professor of canon law at the Apollinare in 1918, only five years after his ordination. He took to the intricacies of the code with great relish and held his professorship with enthusiasm and vigor for twenty years. Afterwards, he served on the staffs of a number of curial congregations, until John made him a cardinal-deacon on December 15, 1958, and appointed him prefect of the Apostolic Signature. He left many of the duties of that office, to superintend the official issuance of all papal documents, in the hands of his juniors, however. He preferred his work as a member of the commission for the authentic interpretation of the code of canon law. His chief claim to distinction was his massive *Dizionario di Teologia Morale*, a 1503-page reference work, published in 1954, whose compilation had taken him years, although he had a very able assistant in Pietro Palazzini, later also a cardinal.[5] Though in good health, indeed robust, he was, at seventy-three, too old to be more than another transitional pope, and that certainly was not what the College wanted in 1963.

Ottaviani apparently agreed to let Siri have his way for the fifth ballot. That was as far as he was willing to go with that cause.

Montini himself met at least two of his colleagues during the evening. As in the earlier course of the campaign, he did not press either of them for support. When he encountered König in the Galleria del Lapidario, he looked both sad and worried. Montini expressed the obligatory phrases in which he hoped that he would not be elected, but, probably in reference to whether or not he should withdraw his candidacy in the face of united curial opposition, he went on, "Just now, I am in darkness and cannot see anything clearly."

At about the same hour, however, he encountered Cicognani and told him that, if he became pope, he would retain John's loyal second as cardinal-secretary of state.

As soon as the morning Mass was over, the cardinals rushed to vote, to discover if the night's reflections and conversations had made any difference at all. They could not tell where precisely the shift had come, but it was evident:

Giovanni Battista Montini	53
Ildebrando Antoniutti	13
Francesco Roberti	11
Giacomo Lercaro	2
Giuseppe Pizzardo	1

Montini was one vote away from the throne. It was obvious, as the cardinals moved to the sixth ballot, that all three of the gains had been from conservatives. Micara, Confalonieri, and Cento had made their move, just as they had told Testa. Now it was Ottaviani's turn, since Siri's espousal of Roberti's cause had produced nothing:

Giovanni Battista Montini	57
Ildebrando Antoniutti	12
Francesco Roberti	9
Giacomo Lercaro	2
Giuseppe Pizzardo	1

There was no atmosphere of elation and, surprisingly, not much sense of relief, either. Montini had reached the throne, but just barely. More than a fourth of the College remained completely opposed to his reign, and that quarter included a majority of those men on whom the new pope would have to rely daily in governing the Church. Montini himself had provided the sole vote for Pizzardo, in memory of an old patronage and friendship now dead.

Tisserant, flanked by Liénart and Ottaviani, approached Montini's throne to put the essential question. Montini's reply was as clipped as Roncalli's had been verbose. He merely said, "Accepto"—"I accept." To the question of what name he would bear, he simply said, "Paulus."

It was done. The cardinals lowered the canopies over their thrones; Albareda prepared the ballots for burning, signaled Vatican Radio that there was a new pope, and set the papers alight.

Like every conclave, this one, too, had its grand electors, but they were a disparate lot: Suenens, for having persuaded most of Lercaro's following to switch to Montini; Testa, for having galvanized some of the electors with his outburst; Micara, for realizing the futility of the conservative cause; Spellman, a conservative himself, for bringing at least the five Americans to Montini's side; and even Ottaviani, for capitulating with as much grace as he could muster. But the grandest elector of all was not even in the conclave. Paul owed his pontificate most to Angelo Dell'Acqua and his network of contacts and information.

Outside, it was 11:22 when the crowd first saw the white *sfumata*. Unlike the public impatience in 1958, when the conclave went into a third day, the people's intuition had sensed the gravity of the election, and the intransigence of the two factions. They did not expect a hasty conclusion, so the piazza was not thronged to capacity with onlookers waiting for white smoke. The election on the sixth ballot—it had happened so quickly that many newspapers, including the *New York Times*, reported that the election had occurred on the fifth scrutiny—reached many at home or office, or in their cars. Rome experienced one of its most choking traffic jams, as thousands tried to reach Bernini's colonnade before the new pope appeared.

Inside, Paul moved quickly to don his white habit. In that moment, he was both cold and unforgiving, so he set his red zucchetto aside and did not place it on the head of the secretary of the conclave, Monsignor Francesco Carpino, as John had done for Alberto di Jorio. Four years later, when his view of his own election had become somewhat more equable, Paul made Carpino both cardinal and archbishop of Palermo.

When he returned to the papal throne before the main altar of the Sistine, to receive the first obedience of the cardinals, he had recovered his equanimity. When Lercaro sank to his knees before the new pontiff, Paul said to him, with some real feeling, "So, this is how life goes, Your Eminence, you really should be sitting here now." Perhaps he realized that, whatever blunders Lercaro might have made, however offensive he might be, the Bolognese was strong enough to carry out his vision of John's plan in a way that Montini, himself, could not.

At the end of the obedience, Paul asked the cardinals to remain in the conclave's precincts until five o'clock. He would return to lunch with them before they departed.

It was almost 12:30 when the doors from the Hall of Benedictions opened and Ottaviani appeared to announce the election. He relished the moment, in spite of the defeat of his cause. He began *Annuntio vobis, gaudeam magnum, habemus papam. Eminentissimum ac Reverendissimum Dominum, Dominum Joannes*—just the beginnings of some cheers, a moment's more anticipation—was it Urbani?—was it Montini?—Ottaviani hesitated just a fraction of a moment more, he continued *Baptista*; there was a swelling roar from the mass of people below—it was Montini. Ottaviani's voice would have been drowned out were it not for the high volume of the microphones. He continued: *Montini, qui sibi nomen impo-suit Paulus Sextus.*

He then withdrew quickly. Soon, with John's arms on the tapestry below him, Paul gave his first blessing to an eager throng. He had been in Rome for so many years, he had met and encouraged so many in his time, that he seemed one of them; as Roman as Pius XII had been, in spite of his birth in the north, and in spite of his eight and a half years in Milan.

Paul then went to his lunch with the cardinals. His conversation sought to restore some sense of fraternity and good feeling among those who had been his equals. He failed. In some ways, it set the tone for the rest of his fifteen-year pontificate.

The council went on splendidly for three more annual sessions. As it drew to a close, Paul began to implement its reforms with dedication, but not as sweepingly as the council's texts gave him latitude to do. Both sides considered him a failure. The conservatives in the Church, whose extreme leadership was soon assumed by the French archbishop, Marcel Lefebvre, thought that he had betrayed all the achievements and glories of the Council of Trent and the reigns since it. The liberals thought that he did not go far enough to make the Church fully responsive to the faithful in the present age. In the developed world, priests, brothers, and nuns left their ministries in droves, convinced that they could do the work of their vocation better outside the formal structure of the Church than within it.

In the minds of most of the people, and many of the clergy, the great document of the reign was not one of the acts of the council, but Paul's encyclical, *Humanæ Vitæ*, of July 25, 1968. The question was artificial contraception. Here, in rejecting entirely the recommendations that were given to him by the study commission that John established in March, 1963, Paul returned with inflexibility to the rule of Pius XII, pronounced more than a decade before the invention of "the pill."

> The responsible exercise of parenthood implies, therefore, that husband and wife recognize fully their own duties towards God, towards themselves, towards the family and towards society, in a correct hierarchy of values. . . .
>
> In the task of transmitting life, therefore, they are not free to proceed completely at will, as if they could determine in a wholly autonomous way the honest path to follow; but they must conform their activity to the creative intention of God, expressed in the very nature of marriage of its acts, and manifested by the constant teaching of the Church. . . .
>
> God has wisely disposed natural laws and rhythms of fecundity which, of themselves, cause a separation in the succession of births. Nonetheless the Church, calling men back to the observance of the

norms of the natural law, as interpreted by their constant doctrine, teaches that each and every marriage act (*quilibet matrimonii usus*) must remain open to the transmission of life. . . .

That teaching, often set forth by the magisterium, is founded upon the inseparable connection, willed by God and unable to be broken by man on his own initiative, between the two meanings of the conjugal act: the unitive meaning and the procreative meaning.

Sadly, these are the words for which he will be best remembered in the proximate future of the Church. In the minds of many of the laity, he placed the use of artificial contraceptives on the same level of sin, or nearly the same level, as abortion.

Then, too, came the financial crisis of the later seventies, with both great losses and great embarrassment. How he needed, then, that wily old Fascist and financial genius, Nicola Canali!

His pilgrimages to places remote from Rome were great successes, but already they have been eclipsed in number and effect by the constant travels of John Paul II.

In 1975, he wrote: "What is my state of mind? Am I Hamlet? Or Don Quixote? On the left? On the right? I do not think I have been understood properly." The evolution of history will answer those questions for him, many decades from now.

NOTES

1. Francisco Antonio de Lorenzana, archbishop of Mexico from 1766 to 1772, was translated to Toledo in the latter year, and created a cardinal on March 30, 1789, by Pius VI.

2. This contraction of Giovanni Paolo (John Paul), like Giambattista for Giovanni Battista, has been common for centuries in the Italian northeast. This helps to explain why another native of the lands of the old Venetian Republic, Albino Luciani, could reply "Joannes Paulus" so readily when he was asked by what name he would be known as pope. For him, in the language of his thinking, he would be Giampaolo— one name commemorating his two predecessors, not two.

3. The standard bears an *ombrellone*, a large lawn-tentlike device, under which is displayed the full achievement of the prince-marshal's arms, which commemorates his inheritance of the honors and distinctions of three great papal families: quarterly, 1. *azure an oak-tree eradicated or, its four branches knotted-saltireways*

(for the house of Della Rovere, the family of Sixtus IV [1472–84] and Julius II [1503–13]), 2 and 3. *Gules in base a mount of six coupeux and, in chief, an estoile or* (for the house of Chigi, the family of Alexander VII [1655–67]), 4. *Azure a fess between an estoile of six rays in chief and a mount of three hillocks in base or* (for the house of Albani, the family of Clement XI [1700–1721]). Today, with the banners of the Russian, German, and Austrian empires gone, no standard actually used as a mark of sovereignty matches it in complexity and elaboration.

4. The longest vacancy in the documented history of the Church was that of 1,006 days, from the death of Clement IV on September 29, 1268, to the elevation of Gregory X on September 1, 1271. It was this crisis that caused Gregory to implement the conclave system. Almost as bad was the 840-day vacancy from the death of Clement V on April 20, 1314, to the choice of John XXII on August 7, 1316; and the 822-day period from the death of Nicholas IV on April 4,

1292, to the election of Celestine V on July 5, 1294. It is worth noting that two of these three vacancies were concluded only with the compromise choice of a prelate who was not a cardinal, Gregory X and Celestine V.

5. An English translation, *Dictionary of Moral Theology*, was published in London by Burns and Oates in 1962, this time in only 1352 pages. It has great merit and remains one of the two or three best references on the subject.

V. Paul's Revolution

For most people, the excitement and hope that was generated by the Second Vatican Council, and the efforts by Paul VI and others to implement—or not to implement—the council's pronouncements, dominate memories of his reign. The consensus about Paul and his reign today is that he was, in general, a failure. Unable to project the warmth and attractiveness of John XXIII, he seemed less a pastor and more a business manager in the American sense. However, within the government of the Church, Paul became the most powerful pope to rule, as well as to reign, in the past three centuries. To see how Montini changed the nature of papal government fundamentally, it is useful to examine his treatment of the College of Cardinals, the curia, and the residential hierarchy.

Primarily, for the purpose of understanding the two most recent conclaves and the coming election, notice must be taken of how Paul reshaped the College of Cardinals, both as an institution and as a body of electors. Of course, a large part of the alteration took place because of the personalities of the men he chose for the cardinalate, but he also constitutionally altered the College in a number of significant ways, through Apostolic constitutions and other pontifical rescripts. Before an understanding can be reached about the remarkable elections of John Paul I and John Paul II in 1978, it is necessary to step carefully through the methods by which Paul VI prepared the way for them. Without those changes, the cardinals almost certainly would never have elected a man from a background of urban poverty who was as approachable as John Paul I; nor would they then have chosen not only the first man in four hundred fifty-five years whose native language was not Italian, but also the first Slavic pope in the Church's history.

While it is facile to make these statements, their importance must be borne in mind.

No other modern pope, not even Benedict XV in 1914, began his reign with so much open conflict with the curia and its leaders. Paul found the circumstances of his election so distasteful—and the enmity of the curial cardinals who were opposed to him, and to the continuation and broadening of the council, so menacing—that he decided from the opening days of his reign to alter the College, and especially its curial membership, so profoundly that it was unlikely that another episode like that of the conclave of 1963 ever could be repeated.

The council's momentum and the necessity to secure his control of curial administration occupied the forefront of Paul's attention until the late winter of 1965, after the end of the council's third session. In the meantime, the composition of the College remained almost unaltered. Of the eighty-one cardinals alive at the moment of his election, only five had died.[1] Nevertheless, despite the fact that there still were seventy-six members of the College, Paul decided on its immediate and extensive enlargement. In addition, he undertook the first, and perhaps, historically, the greatest of his constitutional changes to the College's nature.

On February 22, 1965, he created twenty-seven new cardinals, which raised the population of the College to more than a hundred for the first time.

Throughout history, the cardinals were integral to the clergy of the diocese of Rome. Until the end of the twelfth century, all the members of the College were officially resident at the papal court, as well. Paul VI broke this association by creating a new order of cardinals, for the Eastern Rite patriarchs. They were to rank just below the cardinal-bishops, but above all of the cardinals of the other two orders. For the first time, there were papal electors who were not incardinated into the ranks of the local prelates who were immediately subject to the bishop of Rome. Into this new order, Paul first transferred Ignace Gabriel Tappouni, the Syrian Rite's patriarch of Antioch, who had been created a cardinal by Pius XI on December 16, 1935. The eighty-five-year-old Tappouni thus became the senior cardinal-patriarch of the new order, with Saigh, Meouchi, and Sidarouss as his colleagues. This was the greatest constitutional change in the nature of the College since Alexander III decreed, in 1180, that all cardinals need not be resident at the papal court, which he did when he created Konrad von Wittelsbach, archbishop of Mainz.

The following shows the beginning of the pattern he would develop and expand during the other five consistories in which he created cardinals:

Maximos IV Saigh: *Melkite Patriarch of Antioch*
Paul Pierre Meouchi: *Maronite Patriarch of Antioch*
Stephanos I Sidarouss: *Coptic Patriarch of Alexandria*
Josef Kobernyckyj-Dyckowskyj Slipyj: *Major Abp. of Lviv, Ukraine*
Lorenz Jaeger: *Archbishop of Paderborn*
Thomas Benjamin Cooray: *Archbishop of Colombo (Sri Lanka)*
Josef Beran: *Archbishop of Prague*
Maurice Roy: *Archbishop of Québec*

Joseph Marie Martin: *Archbishop of Rouen*
Owen McCann: *Archbishop of Capetown*
Léon-Etienne Duval: *Archbishop of Algiers*
Ermenegildo Florit: *Archbishop of Florence*
Franjo Seper: *Archbishop of Zagreb*
John Carmel Heenan: *Archbishop of Westminster*
Jean Villot: *Archbishop of Lyon*
Paul Zoungrana: *Archbishop of Ouagadougou, Burkina Faso*
Lawrence Joseph Shehan: *Archbishop of Baltimore*
Enrico Dante: *Prefect of Pontifical Ceremonies*
Cesare Zerba: *Congregation of Sacraments*
Agnello Rossi: *Archbishop of São Paulo*
Giovanni Colombo: *Archbishop of Milan*
William Conway: *Archbishop of Armagh*
Angel Herrera y Oria: *Bishop of Malaga*
Federico Callori di Vignale: *Vatican administration*
Joseph Cardijn: *Founder, Young Christian Workers*
Charles Journet: *Theologian*
Giulio Bevilacqua: *Pastor, La Pace (S. Antonio), Brescia*

Besides the new cardinal-patriarchs, eighteen other creations were residential ordinaries—although Slipyj was in permanent exile from his Ukrainian flock. While most of the new ordinarial cardinals were from sees whose holders traditionally were cardinals, some were elevated to extend the internationalizing policies of Pius and John. Maurice Roy of Québec and Léon-Etienne Duval of Algiers were promoted for their pastoral commitments alone. Owen McCann, South Africa's first cardinal, already was an outspoken opponent of apartheid, long before opposition to it became an international *cause celebre*. Paul Zoungrana of Ouagadougou was Black Africa's second cardinal. Angel Herrera y Oria was rewarded for his decades of service as an anti-Fascist proponent of Catholic Action in Spain. His had been a late vocation: born December 19, 1886, he did not become a priest until 1940. In the years before his ministry, he had been a lawyer and a leading Catholic journalist and publisher in Spain. His deep involvement with questions of labor equity and with Catholic Action—he once was president of Spain's Central Catholic Action Organization—stimulated his vocation, which Pius XII rewarded with elevation to the diocese of Malaga in 1947.

Lorenz Jaeger of Paderborn had anticipated John's desire to open dialogues with non-Catholics. He founded the Adam Möhler Institut precisely to train specialists in Lutheran thought and in ecumenism, to prepare them for "interdenominational conversations." In January, 1959, when John announced the coming of the council, Jaeger set to work at once on a major work on conciliar history, theory, and theology. His book, *Das Ökumenische Konzil, die Kirche und die Christenheit: Erbe und Auftrag*, was published in 1960.[2] Widely read, it became almost at once the single most important text which influenced the future council fathers as they prepared for their parts in John's *aggiornamento*. As was noted before, it was Jaeger's draft plan which John accepted as the organizing model for the Secretariat for Promoting Christian Unity.

Paul's creation of Josef Beran was a particular signal to the East that the new dialogue of cooperation was not to be seen as an easing of the Church's fundamental stand on communism. Beran, ordained in 1911, was the rector of the archdiocesan seminary in Prague at the opening of World War II. Tortured repeatedly at Dachau, he barely survived until his liberation by American troops in 1945. On November 4, 1946, Pius made him archbishop of Prague, in succession to Cardinal Karl Kaspar, who had died in the spring of 1941. A fierce national patriot, Beran opposed communism with the same zeal that he had shown against the Nazis. In 1949, he was placed under house arrest, largely incommunicado, at a remote monastery in Moravia. Again, for years he was subjected to long episodes of brutal treatment, until the circumstances of his confinement were eased somewhat in 1963 as a part of John's new initiatives in the East. Paul created him a cardinal for the express purpose of facilitating his escape—by 1965, he was in exceptionally poor health as a consequence of his decades of harsh treatment. An agreement with the Czech government allowed him to come to Rome to receive his red hat, with the proviso that he not return.[3]

Franjo Seper was Stepinac's successor as archbishop of Zagreb, and had been the old cardinal's secretary for many years, as well as rector of Zagreb's seminary from 1941 to 1951, when it was suppressed.

Paul chose two of the four new cardinal-deacons, Joseph Cardijn and Charles Journet, to began his installation of major figures of Catholic thought who were not connected in any way with the Roman curial establishment. Cardijn, a native of Brussels and a priest for almost sixty years, was the founder of the Young Christian Workers movement, which had once been labeled as a suspect organization by the Congregation of the Holy Office. His cardinalate marked his complete public rehabilitation and the refutation of those who had attacked his work. Charles Journet, a native of Geneva, had taught dogmatic theology at the diocesan seminary at Fribourg since 1924. He was a tireless and prolific writer whose works had a profound effect on many young priests for forty years, including Montini. His years of correspondence with Jacques Maritain can be said to form a backdrop for thinking about speculative theology in this century.[4]

The cardinal whom Paul created as a personal tribute was Giulio Bevilacqua. The pope had first met him when, as a young priest and recently professed Oratorian, Bevilacqua came to Brescia to serve in the parish of San Antonio (La Pace). They were introduced to one another by the pope's paternal grandmother, Francesca, who lived in Bevilacqua's new parish. Bevilacqua was brash and forthright, but also intellectually accomplished.[5] The young priest was just what the adolescent Montini needed to steer his intellectual and cultural interests, and eventually to help to inspire his vocation. Both the man and the boy were enthusiastic bicycle riders, and so their friendship deepened during long, companionable rides through the countryside of northern Italy. Their first period of friendship ended when Bevilacqua, like Roncalli, was drafted into the army in early 1917. He became a chaplain in the Fifth Alpine Regiment.

After the war, they met occasionally; but it was not until February, 1928, that they became close again. Montini was now a young priest, working his way through the labyrinths of the Vatican, when Bevilacqua was expelled from La Pace by the Fascists for his sermons against them. Called to Rome by Cardinal Camillo Laurenti, the prefect of the Congregation of Religious, the Oratorian was placed under the cardinal's protection, as much to preserve the delicate diplomatic negotiations with Mussolini as for his personal safety.

For some time, Montini had lived in a series of rooms and small apartments, often in cramped circumstances. In August, he rented a small three-story house on the Aventine and Bevilacqua came as a housemate to save costs. Their mutual anti-Fascist opinions, and their willingness to advance those ideas publicly, made their friendship closer, and more dangerous. These arrangements continued for five years—neither was at home very much—until Montini's rise earned him apartments in the Vatican. Bevilacqua continued to visit Montini from time to time—in early June, 1941, now a chaplain aboard a hospital ship, he appeared at Montini's door in the Vatican in a state of near exhaustion and stayed for several days, mostly asleep—and they corresponded regularly. After the war, Bevilacqua returned to his parish at La Pace to resume his pastoral work.

Now that "don Battista" was pope, he notified his old mentor and friend of his intention to make him a cardinal. At first, Bevilacqua thought that this was a joke. When he was told that he would be elevated in the consistory of February 22, 1965, he said that he would accept the dignity only if he were permitted to remain the simple priest of La Pace. Paul readily agreed to this proviso, and Bevilacqua was ranked twenty-seventh and last of the creations on that day—he was the only one who was not a patriarch, bishop, or curial official.

On the day set aside for the newly created cardinals to receive the congratulations of their families, friends, and associates, the pope's presence usually is not felt—it is the only private day in a series committed to ceremonies, duties, and official appointments. For Bevilacqua, however, it was a little different. In the midst of receiving congratulatory gifts and tokens, a prelate arrived with a basket swathed in gold and white ribbons, the papal colors. It was Paul's personal acknowledgment of all that the old priest had meant to him. Inside the basket was a very small kitten.[6]

The three new curial cardinals, Dante, Zerba, and Callori di Vignale, were noticeably less rightist than their older colleagues. Of the twenty-seven men who were elevated in this consistory, only five were Italians. The number of living cardinals now stood at one hundred three.

With this consistory, Paul crippled forever the ability of the old conservative wing of the curia to dominate the College. Had a new conclave been held in 1965, there could have been no recapitulation of the divisive fear and hatred that had characterized the election in 1963. The curialists were now firmly outnumbered. That Paul could hold this consistory with little resistance from the Vatican bureaucracy rests, however, on the ground that had been prepared by John XXIII in his careful breaking of the four-centuries old policies of Sixtus V.

Paul VI had every reason to be satisfied with his first efforts to remold the College. Inside the Vatican, there had been some resistance to his wholesale enlargement and to some of the men he created, notably Jaeger, Cardijn, and Journet. Paul quickly moved to neutralize curial obstinacy with the able support of Cicognani and his staff—many of those who had worked so hard to ensure Montini's election to the throne.

Of course, the principal way in which Paul VI could put his stamp on the Church was the manner in which he chose to implement the decrees of the council. It was he who had to translate the advisory or prescriptive general texts into specific actions. For residential cardinals, as for other ordinaries, the most powerful generality was embodied in the decree on the pastoral office of bishops in the Church, *Christus Dominus*, issued on October 28, 1965. Buried in the document was the text:

> As the pastoral office of bishops is so important and onerous, diocesan bishops and others whose juridical position corresponds to theirs are earnestly requested to resign from their office if on account of advanced age or from any other grave cause they become less able to carry out their duties. This they should do on their own initiative or when invited to do so by the competent authority. If the competent authority accepts the resignation it will make provision for the suit-

able support of those who have retired and for the special rights to be accorded to them. (II, i, 21).

Nothing here suggests that bishops who wish to retain their episcopal power until death are forbidden to do so. They should resign their episcopal duties and responsibilities on their own initiative or when they are asked to do so "by the competent authority," the pope. Paul decided to use that opening to bring to a close the effective episcopacy of every older bishop in the Church by setting a mandatory age for retirement, a rule which was quite unforeseen by the council fathers when they issued the decree. On August 6, 1966, Paul issued the motu proprio, *Ecclesiæ Sanctæ*, which contained a long menu of executive actions to implement parts of four of the council's decrees. It was section eleven of the new pronouncement that changed forever the principle that the effectiveness of the episcopal office was for life, barring a personal decision by a bishop to relinquish it:

> That the prescription of No. 21 of the Decree *Christus Dominus* may be put into effect, all bishops of dioceses and others who are juridically their equals are earnestly requested of their own free will to tender their resignation from office not later than at the completion of their 75th year of age to the competent authority which will make provision after examining all circumstances of individual cases. A bishop whose resignation from office has been accepted may maintain a home in his diocese if he wishes. Furthermore the diocese itself must provide the bishop who resigns with appropriate and fitting sustenance. It is the right of the territorial episcopal conferences to determine by way of a general norm the ways in which dioceses must satisfy this obligation.

At one stroke, almost twenty percent of the bishops of the Catholic Church were expected to submit resignations from their offices immediately. Because the reason for doing so was age, Paul effectively eliminated almost all the surviving bishops from the time of Pius XI as well as a very substantial number of those who had been appointed by Pius XII. Of course, the Congregation of Bishops was not prepared to supply the names of new bishops for so large a number of dioceses, so the practical rule became *nunc pro tunc*—"now for later." The bishop would resign, but remain in office temporarily while a replacement for him was found, whenever that might be; and when a successor was named, the old ordinary vanished from power almost at once. The limbo-like nature of a bishop's control of his diocese beyond his seventy-fifth birthday meant that a great deal of his effective executive control ceased when he passed the fatal age.

He *might* rule on for several more years, or he *could* be gone in a week, depending on the Vatican—no useful long-term planning can be done under such circumstances. Once he was gone, all of the basis for his practical authority disappeared, whether or not he held some higher ecclesiastical appointment, such as the cardinalate. Further, if Paul could so effectively brush away the practical power of an Apostolic office, how much more easily could he revise or abolish the power of offices, like the cardinalate, which had no biblical foundation.

The episcopal limitation of *Ecclesiæ Sanctæ* immediately placed twenty-three cardinals, most of whom were conservative and powerful ordinaries, into the limbo of authority mentioned above. Waiting to go were three of Pius XI's five surviving cardinals[7] and no fewer than thirteen of the twenty-five creations of Pius XII, including almost all of the residential archbishops.[8] By contrast, only three of John XXIII's surviving thirty-nine were affected immediately.[9] Of Paul's cardinals—twenty-six of the twenty-seven were living, only Bevilacqua had died—just four were affected.[10]

Since they were, after all, cardinals, most of these men did not think they would be treated in the same manner as less powerful and less important bishops. For them, the rule was more *tunc* than *nunc*; and *tunc* would be when they decided it was time to go, or the tomb, if they so wished. A few were eager for retirement and submitted resignations gladly, like Feltin in Paris, who was succeeded by his coadjutor, Pierre Veuillot, on December 21, 1966. Some were correct in their assumption that their resignations would never be accepted; Spellman died as archbishop of New York on December 2, 1967; but de Vasconcellos Motta continued on as archbishop of the great Brazilian shrine-city of Aparecida until his death on September 18, 1982, at the age of ninety-two! The pope did not dare to accept the *pro forma* resignations of the two Eastern rite patriarchs for fear of the reaction he could expect from their churches, if he had. Beran was far too valuable as the exiled archbishop of Prague to lose that symbolism. But Paul's power over the older cardinals was now substantially greater than it ever had been, and could be exercised at any time. Ruffini, archbishop of Palermo and one of the most reactionary members of the College, was outraged when he found himself replaced on June 26, 1967, by Francesco Carpino, a curial official who received Palermo and the red hat on the same day.

Lercaro was more baffled and sorry by the way he was treated. He opened his copy of *L'Osservatore Romano* on Monday morning, February 12, 1968, to find that Paul VI had "kindly accepted his resignation for reasons of advanced age and ill health," and that the archdiocese's coadjutor, Antonio Poma, was now archbishop. Accompanying the official acceptance was a letter from Cicognani praising Bologna's archbishop for his "spontaneous decision." In retrospect, it is clear that Lercaro was punished for taking the spirit, as well as the letter, of Vatican II much too seriously. He already had established several mixed commissions, of clergy, religious, and laity, to examine the most pressing ecclesiastical questions— the rôle of women in the Church, and the place of the laity in choosing pastors and bishops, for example. He also made no secret of his intention to appoint a pastoral council to superintend and facilitate all of the decisions of Vatican II throughout the archdiocese. That had to be stopped. The warning shot across the bow came with the sudden, and unwelcome, appointment of Poma to be coadjutor with right of succession on July 16, 1967. Poma, a Pavian and archbishop of Mantua since September 8, 1954, was much more conservative in his views than Lercaro, especially in liturgical matters. Lercaro recognized the event for what it was. He wrote to one friend to say that Poma had been sent in "to stop a moving train." Lercaro thought he was safe, however. Not only was he a cardinal who had been a major leader at the council, he was the man who had bowed aside to permit Montini to receive the full backing of the liberal cardinals in the conclave. Surely, Paul would not forget that he owed the papal throne itself in large part to Bologna's archbishop. He miscalculated seriously.[11] Lercaro lived on until October 18, 1976, a dutifully quiet witness as all his plans for the renewal of his archdiocese were shelved. The train was stopped, after all. He was, like several others, a victim of the bitterness of the conclave.

Once Paul had established the principle that bishops could be superannuated, he turned again to the text of *Christus Dominus*. The decree not only applied to diocesan bishops but also to "others whose juridical position corresponds to theirs." By 1967, Paul would move in force to apply the requirements of *Ecclesiæ Sanctæ* to the senior members of the curia, as well.

Symbolically significant, but of less real importance, were the changes Paul made to the ceremonies and signs of the cardinalate. After 1967, the pope no longer presented the great red hat with fifteen tassels, the *galerum rubrum*, to the new cardinals in a semi-public consistory.[12] Beginning with his second set of creations, the pope officiated at a concelebrated Mass in the Piazza di San Pietro after which the new cardinals were given scarlet birettas. The cardinal's ring, which for centuries had been set with a sapphire, was reduced to a simple band of gold. Within three years, much of the rest of the pomp that belonged to the cardinalate was abolished. They lost their great *cappa magna* with its thirty-two-foot-long train, and their coats of arms were no longer printed in the *Annuario Pontificio*.

Before Paul conducted even more revolutionary changes to the curia—he had promised them in his first address to the council on September 29, 1963—he decided to swell the number of cardinals still further. The success of the first cardinalitial consistory moved the pope to use precisely the same plan again—with roughly the same demographics of representation.

On June 26, 1967, he again created twenty-seven new cardinals. In the period between the two consistories, only twelve cardinals had died.[13] Their deaths reduced the number of cardinals to ninety-one. Of the losses, the two most unexpected were the deaths of John's American conciliarists, Meyer (age 62) and Ritter (age 74). Meyer, in particular, was a particularly severe loss—he did not live to see the fourth, final session of the council. Almost the spirit of the *aggiornamento* in the United States, he had adopted two areas of reform: the absolute need for a conciliar declaration on religious liberty; and a complete reform of the Church's theological and social position on Judaism. Without them, he often stated, the holding of the council was a waste of time.

The addition of the new cardinals raised the number to one hundred eighteen, more than twice the number of fifty-three who had been alive on the morning that Roncalli became John XXIII, less than nine years before:

Nicolás Fasolino: *Archbishop of Santa Fe, Argentina*
Giuseppe Beltrami: *Vatican diplomat*
Gabriel Marie Garrone: *Prefect, Cong. for Catholic Education*
Patrick Aloysius O'Boyle: *Archbishop of Washington*
Maximilian de Furstenberg: *Prefect, Cong. for Oriental Churches*
Antonio Samorè: *President, Pont. Commission for Latin America*
Francesco Carpino: *Archbishop of Palermo*
José Clemente Maurer: *Archbishop of Sucre*
Pietro Parente: *Assessor, Cong. of the Holy Office*
Carlo Grano: *Vatican diplomat*
Angelo Dell'Acqua: *Cardinal-Vicar of Rome*
Dino Staffa: *Pro-prefect of the Apostolic Signature*
John Joseph Krol: *Archbishop of Philadelphia*
John Patrick Cody: *Archbishop of Chicago*
Corrado Ursi: *Archbishop of Naples*
Alfred Bengsch: *Archbishop-Bishop of Berlin*
Justinus Darmajuwono: *Archbishop of Semarang, Indonesia*
Karol Wojtyła: *Archbishop of Kraków*
Michele Pellegrino: *Archbishop of Turin*
Alexandre Charles Renard: *Archbishop of Lyon*
Pierre Veuillot: *Archbishop of Paris*
Alfredo Pacini: *Vatican diplomat*

Antonio Riberi: *Vatican diplomat*
Egidio Vagnozzi: *Vatican diplomat*
Pericle Felici: *President, Comm. for Revision of Code of Canon Law*
Francis James Brennan: *Dean of the Rota*
Benno Walter Gut: *Abbot Primate, Benedictine Confederation*

The appointment of Fasolino as the senior creation of the consistory was not so much a reward for his participation in the council as it was the installation of an Argentinean in the College after the recent death of Copello. Indeed, Paul already had his resignation from the archdiocese of Santa Fe in hand, but he was the most highly respected churchman in his country and a popular choice for the cardinalate. The elevation of the Polish-American archbishop of Philadelphia, John Krol, and the promotion of Pericle Felici in Rome, were both rewards for major contributions to the success of the council. The latter had been the secretary of the council, while the former had served as under-secretary in addition to his archiepiscopal duties.

O'Boyle in Washington was a pastoral appointment. Paul's views on social justice were strong, and he had noted with approval how O'Boyle had steered a positive course through the difficult problems generated by the sudden desegregation of the public school system in the capital of the United States, when Dwight Eisenhower ordered that the Supreme Court's decision in *Brown vs. Board of Education of Topeka* must be implemented at once in all jurisdictions under immediate federal control. A confusing plan for carrying out that order led to near chaos and the beginning of rapid "white flight" from the city to the suburbs in Maryland and Virginia. Many white parents tried to enroll their children in the Catholic school system, regardless of their own religious beliefs. O'Boyle ordered that his schools not be used as a means of thwarting the decisions of both national and local authority, in spite of the great increase in revenue that might have been generated had he decided to acquiesce silently to an enlarged enrollment. With the school crisis in the city itself largely dissipated by the later '60s, O'Boyle's cardinalate was a reward for his commitment to social and racial justice in a practical forum.

The red hats for Angelo Dell'Acqua, most loyal of loyal supporters, and Antonio Samorè were anticipatory promotions for the reworking of the secretariat of state that Paul would enact later in the year. Veuillot in Paris and Carpino for Palermo received the cardinalate not just as holders of important archdioceses but as reflections of just how fast the provisions of *Ecclesiæ Sanctæ* could be made to work.[14]

Because Indonesia is the country in the world with the largest Muslim population, Paul wanted to extend the cardinalate there as a symbol of his willingness to have a more open dialogue with the people of the Koran. As a part of that effort, he was in the formative stages of exploring a possible papal visit. Justinus Darmajuwono was the most eligible prelate in the nation, although he had been archbishop only since December 10, 1963. To match firsts, Maurer became Bolivia's first cardinal, which completed the cycle, begun by John XXIII, of having every South American nation with a red hat.

No fewer than five of the new cardinals were career papal diplomats who were being recalled to the curia with the cardinalate. All of them were men who had begun their diplomatic work during the years when Montini controlled the secretariat of state for Pius XII, but it was for their recent successes that they were rewarded—Beltrami in Lebanon (1950–1959) and the Netherlands (1959–1967); Grano, John's choice as nuncio to Italy (1958–1967); Pacini in Haiti and the Dominican Republic (1946–1949), Uruguay (1949–1960), and Switzerland (1960–1967); Riberi, a close papal friend, in Spain (1959–1967); and Vagnozzi for his able work as the first nuncio to the Philippines (1951–1958) and then as Cicognani's successor in the United States (1958–1967).

John Patrick Cody had begun his ecclesiastical career as one of those bright young seminarians who are singled out for study in Rome, where he was ordained on December 8, 1931. He stayed in Rome in a number of minor Vatican staff appointments until 1938. This service marked him out as a young star of the American church. When the newly installed archbishop of Saint Louis, Joseph Elmer Ritter,[15] asked for an auxiliary, he received Cody, who was made titular bishop of Apollonia and auxiliary bishop on July 2, 1947. Ritter soon became unhappy with Cody, so he was appointed coadjutor bishop of Saint Joseph, Missouri, on January 27, 1954, and became bishop there on May 9, 1955.[16] Again, Cody was not quite what was expected, but he was appointed coadjutor to the combined diocese of Kansas City–Saint Joseph on August 29, 1956, and became bishop of that see, too, on the following October 11. Soon, it was necessary to move him along again, this time as titular archbishop of Bostra and coadjutor of New Orleans, on August 10, 1961. On June 1, 1962, he became apostolic administrator of that city, and then archbishop two years later. In spite of his failings, and the fact that he was not well liked in the American hierarchy, the pope appointed him to Chicago on June 16, 1965, in succession to the much-admired Albert Meyer. The cardinalate came in due course, as it had to his three immediate predecessors, Mundelein, Stritch, and Meyer. His tenure was a disaster, but there was no other position to which he could be moved. The investigation of his finances and conduct by a federal grand jury was closed when he died.

Francis Joseph Brennan, a native of Shenandoah, Pennsylvania, and for twenty years a professor at Saint Charles Seminary at Overbrook, had come to Rome in 1940 to serve as a judge of the Rota. Now its dean, he received the cardinalate as his predecessor, William Theodore Heard, had as a mark of distinction for his distinguished legal career. Only once before, in 1946, had four Americans received the cardinalate at the same time.

The primatial abbot of the Benedictines, Benno Gut, received the red hat more for his scholarship than for his position in his order, to which he was elected on September 24, 1959. He had been deeply involved in editing the works of biblical scholar Hildebrand Hopfl,[17] and had been one of the four scholars nominated to serve on the pontifical body that Paul set up under Lercaro in early 1964 to implement the council's constitution on the liturgy, *Sacrosanctum Concilium*. When Lercaro was removed as archbishop of Bologna in 1968, he also lost his position as head of the pontifical council on the liturgy. Paul tried to sweeten the punishment somewhat by also removing, on the same day, the reactionary Cardinal Arcadio Larraona, Lercaro's chief curial enemy, as prefect of the Congregation of Rites. Cardinal Gut then assumed both the prefecture and the chair of the pontifical council.

Alexandre Charles Renard, appointed bishop of Versailles on August 19, 1953, was elevated to the rank of archbishop of Lyon, the primatial see of France, on the same day he received the cardinalate. The incumbent at Lyon, Jean Villot, created a cardinal in 1965, was transferred to the curia, as prefect of the Congregation of Rites. Soon, however, he would take on a much higher office, as secretary of state.

Later events, however, have shown that the most important new cardinal of 1967 was the archbishop of Kraków, Karol Wojtyła, who became Poland's second living residential cardinal. For several years, Cardinal Wyzynski had planned a major national celebration in 1966 on the millennium of the Christianization of Poland, symbolized by the baptism of Mieszko I, Duke of the Polonie, in 966. The event was not only to be an example of the devotion of the Polish people to Catholicism but also a warning to the government of the latent power of the Church. Paul, fresh from triumphant visits to Jerusalem, Bombay, and New York, wished very much to participate in the culminating ceremonies of the celebration, which were to take place in May at the monastery of Jasna Gora, where the icon of the Polish people, Our Lady of Czestochowa, is enshrined. Wyzynski was not happy with the pope's intention to insert himself into what he regarded as a Polish national celebration. Paul's continuing dialogue with the communist leaders of the Eastern bloc dismayed the Polish primate, who was a master of confrontational politics. Moreover, the cardinal was not an avid supporter of many of the council's decisions, which Paul endorsed and implemented. To Wyzynski, they seemed to weaken or narrow the stark contrast between Catholicism and Marxism. The cardinal had perfected a rhythm of confrontation which served him well for years, first negotiating some ease in the posture of the Church to the government and then escalating tensions again with one of his "thunderstorms." When he learned that Monsignor Achille Silvestrini of the secretariat of state had entered into serious negotiations with Warsaw to facilitate the papal visit, he decided to act decisively to thwart the plan altogether. In the last days of 1965, the Polish bishops, following the direction of the cardinal, released a statement in which they called for a reconciliation with the German Church. Wyzynski knew very well that this document, which had not been cleared, or even discussed, with the government, would provoke an instant hardening of relations with the Church. He was right. In January, 1966, the cardinal was refused a visa to visit Rome, and then all negotiations with the Vatican about the pope's visit were canceled. Wyzynski's actions were perfectly obvious to Paul and Cicognani, and both were enraged by the ploy. Although Poland had never had two residential cardinals at one time, the pope thought that it was time to put at least a small check on Wyzynski's power—he was not only archbishop of Warsaw and Gniezno, primate of Poland, and cardinal, but also papal legate. Wojtyła, no particular friend of the primate, although he always supported his leader in the name of ecclesiastical solidarity, would serve the pope's purpose very well.

Once the second cardinalitial consistory was brought to a successful conclusion, Paul turned his attention to the final steps of promulgating a new constitution for the complete reform of the curia. The constitution *Regimini Ecclesiæ Universæ*, which had been expected, and dreaded, in Rome for four years, was dated August 15, 1967, with its provisions to come into effect on January 1, 1968. Nominally, the document was the work of a special pontifical commission of cardinals, under the presidency of Francesco Roberti.[18] In fact, not just the principles but even the text of the document sprang largely from the mind of the pope. The final text was written mainly by the pope's new protegé, Giovanni Benelli.

The fundamental organization with which the pope had to contend was established by Sixtus V (1585-1590) in the constitution *Immensa Æterni Dei* of January 22, 1588. It was meant to streamline the Vatican's control over the reforms of the Council of Trent, and probably was not intended to remain the structure of Vatican administration for four centuries. Over time, its provisions had been altered and expanded—notably by Pius X in the constitution *Sapienti Consilio* of June 29, 1908, later incorporated into the code of canon law by Benedict XV—but no fundamental reform of the curia had been undertaken since Sixtus's time. *Regimini* was an uneven document which did little to remedy some serious problems of Church government, but it did increase greatly the pope's control over the curia.[19] The most important aspects of the reform were that the secretariat of state was elevated to be the immediate executive arm of the pope, and its cardinal-secretary became, in effect, the papal prime minister. Cicognani, the incumbent, now had overriding authority to take initiatives with regard to the business of the other congregations, commissions, and councils, whose prefects and presidents were now, in fact, subordinate to him. The secretariat itself, in keeping with its new responsibilities, was enlarged substantially. First, the diplomatic service was reorganized and placed under the newly founded Sacred Council for the Public Affairs of the Church, under the presidency of Cardinal Antonio Samorè. He was, in turn, assisted in the daily operations of the Council by its secretary, Agostino Casaroli, who received the rank of titular archbishop of Cartagina on July 16, 1967. The executive functions of the secrertariat were expanded to include the prefecture of Vatican City, which conducts all of the governmental functions of the papal state, as well as the offices of the Secretariat of Briefs to Princes, the Secretariat of Latin Letters, and the Commission for the Instruments of Social Communication—the three offices which control all of the Vatican's documentation. To this collection was added a Central Statistics Office, which assumed control of most of the flow of information within the curia. All of these were placed under Samorè's colleague, Cardinal Angelo Dell'Acqua. He was supported by a new *sostituto*, chosen by Paul VI as the brightest and most able young curial official, Giovanni Benelli. This was the first prominent position given to the forty-six-year-old Florentine. But Paul had monitored his career closely since the day that he entered the offices of the secretariat of state, under Montini's immediate eye, in August, 1947. During the next two decades, he had been shuffled through a variety of diplomatic staff positions to give him the widest possible exposure to the diplomacy of the Church. He was sent to work in the nunciatures in Ireland (1950–1953), France (1953–1960), Brazil (1960–1962), and Spain (1962–1965). After this, he spent a year as the Vatican's observer at UNESCO before he was made titular archbishop of Tusurus (September 11, 1966), pro-nuncio in Senegal, and apostolic delegate to western Africa. After only three months, Paul recalled him to Rome and entrusted him, in early 1967, with much of the work of drafting *Regimini*. Already, Paul had determined to make Benelli his *delfino*, his chosen political heir. Benelli's years in the executive of the secretariat of state (1966–1977), where he gradually assumed more and more control, saw him rise higher and higher in the pope's estimation until, for Paul, he had even more of the closeness that the pope had once had with Pius XII as well as much of the affection which Giuseppe Siri had enjoyed from the former pontiff.

The secretariat of state alone now had three cardinals, instead of one. They were assisted by two powerful archbishops who relieved their superiors of much of the daily control of Vatican admnisitration. At the moment these reforms were effected, all five of the powerful prelates were Italian, but Cicognani wanted to relinquish his office as soon as possible. Now eighty-four, he felt himself unable to sustain the increased work his office demanded of him. Paul asked him to continue through a brief period of transition until he could find a suitable successor. Privately, the pope had decided that the new prime minister should not be an Italian. His choice was the archbishop of Lyon, Jean Villot, who was called away from France to become the prefect of the Congregation of the Clergy in June, just two months before *Regimini* was issued. Villot's prefecture, however, was something of a ruse to insert him into the curia—he already was a cardinal—until he had mastered enough of the intricacies of Vatican business to be appointed cardinal-secretary of state. By early 1969, he was ready, and Cicognani gratefully retired.

According to the provisions of the new constitution, all curial officials, including the cardinal-prefects, were limited to five-year terms in office; their renewal for another term in office was entirely at the personal discretion of the pope.

Beyond this provison, Paul isssued a complete new set of regulations for the curia to implement the finer points in *Regimini*. The *Regolamento Generale della Curia Romana*, issued on February 22, 1968, ordered that all but the highest ranking officials were to retire at seventy, while all the rest were to vacate their offices at seventy-five, just as bishops were required to do—this was the interpretation Paul gave to the passage in *Christus Dominus* that applied not only to bishops but also to "others whose juridical position corresponds to theirs." In this way, the lifetime fiefdoms of great power which the prefects had enjoyed for centuries were shattered forever. No future pope is likely to regrant to the cardinals of the curia the vast powers which had accumulated from the sixteenth century to the twentieth, and which it had taken three reigns for the popes to recover.

Moreover, *Regimini* required that the various curial congregations and commissions incorporate into their membership representative diocesan bishops, whose votes were equal to those of the members who were cardinals—the congregations, in particular, were to have seven bishops each.[20] Laypersons could now be appointed as consultors, or full members of the staffs, of the curial offices, and languages other than Latin could now be used in both official and working documents. Finally, the curial offices were told explicitly, in an appendix to the constitution, that no serious or unusual business of any kind could be undertaken until the pope was notified, and all decisions in every office had to have express papal approval before they could take effect, unless the pope had granted a specific exception.

Within months, most of Paul's old curial adversaries were driven from power—Ottaviani was among the first to go, replaced in early 1968 by Cardinal Franjo Seper, a Croatian conservative who never quite mastered the intricacies of his job, but who was somewhat less rigid in his interpretation of the council's intentions than his predecessor.

The intention of Vatican II, that the pope should share power in a collegial way with bishops and others in the community of Catholics, had been remolded by Paul VI brilliantly, primarily through *Ecclesiæ Sanctæ* and *Regimini Ecclesiæ Universæ*, to make him the most absolute ruler the Church had seen since the seventeenth century. John XXIII once described Montini as "a little like Hamlet," and this proved to be the difficulty for the Church. Having gathered nearly all immediate executive power into his own hands, Paul wielded it in ways which often vacillated so much from decision to decision and policy to policy that it often was unclear to what degree the council's "collegiality" and "consultancy" meant anything at all. This so dismayed, and sometimes frightened, Catholics in developed and sophisticated cultures that they began to leave the Church in droves, clergy, religious, and laity alike. With them, they took much of the money which had flowed with regularity into the coffers of earlier popes, just at the time that Vatican expenses grew substantially in order to fund the various collegial and consultative bodies that the council had wanted—bodies which now were often window dressing to give the appearance of broad agreement with the pope's own initiatives. Even as Paul became more and more powerful in the Vatican and in the hierarchy, he became less and less so among the general Catholic community. As his public demonstrations of engagement increased, his ability to pay for them waned.

It is not clear what schedule Paul may have had in mind for the further enlargement of the College after the publication of *Ecclesiæ Sanctæ* and *Regimini Ecclesiæ Universæ*. Certainly the replacements for those cardinal-archbishops whose resignations Paul had accepted expected themselves to be named to the College within a short time. Between the consistory in 1967 and the end of 1968, sixteen cardinals died, five of them in July, 1968, alone.[21] The death of John XXIII's old friend, Gustavo

Testa, on February 28, 1969, reduced the number of living cardinals to one hundred one. By that time, Paul already had decided to enlarge the College substantially once again.

With his third creation—April 28, 1969—Paul finally drew almost entirely on the twentieth century for the men who were elevated. In 1965, fourteen of the twenty-seven creations were men born in the last century; in 1967, nine of the twenty-seven were. In 1969, however, only three of the thirty-three were born in the nineteenth century, and only one, Miguel Darío Miranda y Gómez, could even remember Leo XIII:

Paul Yü Pin: *Archbishop of Nanking*
Alfredo Vicente Scherer: *Archbishop of Pôrto Alegre, Brazil*
Julio Rosales: *Archbishop of Cebú, Philippines*
Gordon Joseph Gray: *Archbishop of Saint Andrews and Edinburgh*
Thomas Peter McKeefry: *Archbishop of Wellington*
Miguel Darío Miranda y Gómez: *Archbishop of México [City]*
Joseph Parecattil: *Archbishop of Ernakulam*
John Francis Dearden: *Archbishop of Detroit*
François Marty: *Archbishop of Paris*
Jérôme Rakotomalala: *Archbishop of Tananarive, Madagascar*
George Bernard Flahiff: *Archbishop of Winnipeg*
Paul Gouyon: *Archbishop of Rennes*
Mario Casariego: *Archbishop of Guatemala [City]*
Vicente Enrique y Tarancón: *Archbishop of Toledo*
Joseph Malula: *Archbishop of Kinshasa*
Pablo Muñoz Vega: *Archbishop of Quito*
Antonio Poma: *Archbishop of Bologna*
John Joseph Carberry: *Archbishop of Saint Louis*
Terence James Cooke: *Archbishop of New York*
Stephan Sou Hwan Kim: *Archbishop of Seoul*
Arturo Tabera Araoz: *Archbishop of Pamplona*
Eugenio de Araújo Sales: *Archbishop of São Salvador do Bahia*
Joseph Höffner: *Archbishop of Köln*
John Joseph Wright: *Prefect, Congregation of the Clergy*
Paolo Bertoli: *Prefect, Cong. for the Causes of Saints*
Sebastiano Baggio: *Archbishop of Cagliari*
Silvio Oddi: *Pres., Comm. for Sancs. of Pompeii and Loreto*
Giuseppe Paupini: *Vatican diplomat*
Giacomo Violardo: *Secy., Cong. for the Disc. of the Sacraments*
Jan Willebrands: *Pres., Secretariat for Christian Unity*
Mario Nasalli-Rocca di Corneliano: *Vatican administration*

Sergio Guerri: *Pro-pres., Pont. Comm. for Vatican City*
Jean Daniélou: *Jesuit Theologian*

In addition, Paul created another cardinal *in pectore*, whose name he would reveal in 1973.

These new cardinals were the first to fall under the simplified rules of ceremony and dress, some of which the pope announced at this consistory. As he had ruled earlier, these cardinals did not receive the centuries-old *galerum rubrum*, the traditional red hat of the office of cardinal; they received a red biretta instead. Moreover, Paul exhorted them, and their colleagues, to reduced the use of scarlet in their dress and to retain more of the plain black attire that generally distinguished clerics from others in normal life.

As expected, eleven of the new cardinals filled archiepiscopal seats that had been vacated by cardinal-predecessors in the recent past.[22] Five more cardinals were their nations's first occupants of seats in the College,[23] while five others were from archdioceses that had not been occupied by a cardinal before.[24] Still another three occupied sees that had not seen a cardinal in many generations.[25] Altogether, it was another extension of the policy of internationalizing the College which had been begun by Pius XII, extended by John XXIII, and broadened greatly by Paul VI in his earlier consistories. No fewer than twenty-four of the new cardinals were residential archbishops, of whom only two were Italians. Of the eight curial officials who were given the red hat, most were "new men" who were advanced to posts which had been redefined in *Regimini*, and thus were loyal exclusively to Paul VI himself.

The outstanding new curial cardinal was Jan Willebrands, who had assisted Augustin Bea at the Secretariat for Christian Unity almost since its foundation. Bea's death, on November 16, 1968, advanced Willebrands into his old mentor's position.

Finally, Paul continued the policy of elevating distingushed modern theologians to the cardinalate which he had begun with the creation of Journet in 1965, by elevating Jean Daniélou, a French Jesuit. In fact, his elevation came as a complete surprise. The expectation in Rome was that the pope would elevate the much more famous Jesuit theologian, Henri de Lubac, whose works he read and admired greatly. But when de Lubac was notified that his creation was imminent, he peremptorily refused the honor, on the grounds that John XXIII's requirement that all cardinals also be bishops was an abuse of an apostolic office.[26] Daniélou was substituted quickly, to give the creation the composition that Paul desired. His hasty choice came to haunt Paul after Daniélou's sudden death, on May 20, 1974, from a heart attack, late at night, in lay costume, in a quarter of

Paris where it was most unlikely ever to find a cardinal.

One appointment that surprised many in the Vatican was the elevation of the bishop of Pittsburgh, John Joseph Wright, who also was transferred to Rome to become the new prefect of the Congregation of the Clergy, in succession to Jean Villot, who was elevated to the office of cardinal-secretary of state. Wright became the first American to reach one of the powerful Vatican prefectures. Known at home as the "egg-head," he first attracted Paul's attention by his spirited defense of the necessity for the council to address, and approve, the idea of religious liberty.

Wright took his elevation with great *gravitas*, as did most of the others—but not all. Carberry, accompanied by a planeload of friends and family, had a jolly ride from Saint Louis to Rome, during much of which he entertained his guests with extemporaneous performances on his harmonica.

One issue associated with the great enlargement of the College under John XXIII and Paul VI was their need to find suitable Roman titles for all these new cardinals. Essentially, the three orders of cardinals represent the episcopal structure of the diocese of Rome, of which the pope is bishop. Thus, the cardinal-bishops are the historical ordinaries of the dioceses which are directly suffragan to Rome; the cardinal-priests are the pastors of the major Roman parishes—originally twenty-five in number and called "tituli," hence the use of the term "title" for the church given to each new cardinal-priest; and the cardinal-deacons are the successors of the classical Roman administrators of the fourteen civic regions.

With the geat increase in the number of cardinals, new titles and diaconates had to be erected for them. This was not difficult, since Rome—like all other large, post-industrial metropolitan areas—has expanded greatly in population and geography since the later nineteenth century. Consequently, many new parishes were created, both in the city and in the surrounding suburbs. Many of these were made titles for cardinal-priests or diaconates for cardinal-deacons by John XXIII, Paul VI, and John Paul II.

Paul VI rarely exhibited his sense of humour in public. When he did, the point of his joke often was missed, because of its subtlety.

Mario Nasalli-Rocca di Corneliano was named near the end of the list of those who were created on April 28, 1969. He was born August 12, 1903, in Piacenza, into a local noble family of great antiquity. His father's brother, Giovanni Battista Nasalli-Rocca di Corneliano, became archbishop of Bologna and then, on May 23, 1923, a cardinal. The young Mario decided to follow his uncle into an ecclesiastical career. He obtained a degree in canon law, and then studied at the Vatican Diplomatic

Academy. After he was ordained in 1927, he took advantage of his uncle's connections to secure a place in the secretariat of state. By 1959, after decades in minor posts, he became the principal pontifical scheduler. It is he whom you see in the background in so many photographs of both John XXIII and Paul VI when they received important visitors at the Vatican.

Nasalli Rocca's post was not of great ecclesiastical or political importance, and he was certain, as the years passed, that he would never advance in the hierarchy, as his uncle had done. Besides, the times of John and Paul were not particularly favorable for the careers of aristocrats, as former pontificates had been. For years, he said to friends and colleagues, "I will cut off my head if I am made a cardinal." He certainly was surprised to be named titular archbishop of Antium on April 11, 1969, and then a cardinal-deacon seventeen days later, when Paul gave him the newly created diaconate of San Giovanni Battista decollato—Saint John the Baptist *beheaded*. This little joke was not lost on either the new cardinal or his friends, but, of course, attracted no notice at all outside of the small papal circle.

Paul used the setting of this consistory to make three important announcements of new papal policy. The first was the publication of the motu proprio *Mysterii Paschali*, which promulgated the new ordo and its associated calendar. The second was a further fine-tuning of his curial reforms in which he divided the Congregation of Rites into two distinct bodies, the Congregation of Divine Worship, to control all liturgical matters, and the Congregation for the Causes of Saints, which would rule all matters concerning canonization and beatification. The third, and most alarming to the remaining conservatives in the curia, was the establishment of a new International Theological Commission, whose thirty members would be coequal with the consultors of the Congregation for the Doctrine of the Faith.

At a stroke, Paul provided a body to rival, and possibly eclipse, Ottaviani and his staff in the matters that were most sensitive to the council, and to the Church as a whole.

The additions of 1969 raised the number of living cardinals to one hundred thirty-four. Soon, Paul VI would limit the number of cardinals who could be papal electors to those under the age of eighty, so the membership of the College from this consistory to the death of Josef Beran on May 17, constituted the greatest number of papal electors thus far—a record that probably will stand for several decades to come.

In 1970, before he made any other rearrangement of the curia or the cardinalate, he appointed Jean Villot to the office of camerlengo. Villot's office of secretary of state would lapse on Paul's death, but the pope wished to ensure that he would remain officially in charge of all of the active business of the Church during the *sede vacante*. In a rare display of personal consideration for a conservative cardinal, he did not make his intentions known until after the death of Benedetto Aloisi Masella on September 30, 1970, at the age of ninety-one. Aloisi Masella had done well in supervising the conclaves of 1958 and 1963, so perhaps Paul, still in reasonably good health, thought it suitable that he retain his powerful office, in spite of his great age. Paul made Villot's formal appointment on October 16, 1970.

With the College of Cardinals packed with his own creations, with the episcopacy substantially stripped of its older conservative members, and with the curia humbled and subordinated as it had been to no other modern pope, Paul was now ready to extinguish the last fragments of power that were still possessed by his old reactionary enemies in the College.

On November 21, 1970, Paul issued the motu proprio *Ingravescentem Ætatem*, which was to become effective on January 1, 1971. In its provisions, he again used the reason of age to remove from cardinals who were eighty years old or more, any rights in the choice of a new pope. Like the pounding of a revengeful drum, he reminded the members of the College of all the earlier provisions that he had enacted, and then went forward with his new blows to the power and prestige of the cardinalate:

> The natural relationship between the increasing burden of age and the ability to perform certain major offices, such as those of diocesan bishop and parish priest, was dealt with by the Second Vatican Ecumenical Council in the Decree *Christus Dominus* (21 and 31). Implementing the wishes of the Council Fathers, we, by our Apostolic Letter *Ecclesiæ Sanctæ* of 6 August 1966, called on bishops and parish priests voluntarily to submit their resignation not later than their seventy-fifth birthday (11 and 20, paragraph 3).
>
> The same question of age was touched on by the general regulations of the Roman Curia, issued under the title *Regolamento Generale della Curia Romana*, which we approved and ordered to be published on 22 February 1968. It is laid down therein that major and minor officials should retire from office on the completion of their seventieth year, and higher prelates at the beginning of their seventy-fifth year of age (article 101, paragraph 1).
>
> It seems to us now that the good of the Church demands that the increasing burden of age should be taken into consideration also for the illustrious office of the cardinalate, to which we have on several occasions given special attention. It is in fact a particularly important office which demands great prudence, both for its quite unique connection with our supreme office at the service of the whole Church and because of the high importance it has for all the Church when the Apostolic See falls vacant.

Accordingly, after long and mature consideration of the whole question, and continuing to trust for the future in the unceasing counsel and prayers of all the cardinals without distinction, we decree:

I. Cardinals in charge of departments of the Roman Curia (listed in article 1 of the *Regolamento Generale*) or to the other permanent institutions of the Apostolic See and Vatican City are requested to submit their resignation voluntarily to the Pope on the completion of their seventy-fifth year of age. After due consideration of all the circumstances of each case, he will judge whether it is fitting to accept the resignation immediately.

II. On the completion of eighty years of age, cardinals:

1. cease to be members of the departments of the Roman Curia and of the other institutions mentioned in the above article;

2. lose the right to elect the Pope and consequently also that of entering the conclave. If, however, a cardinal completes his eightieth year after the beginning of the conclave, he continues to enjoy the right of electing the Pope on that occasion.

III. The arrangements in articles I and II take effect even when the five-year term dealt with in article 2, paragraph 5, of the Apostolic Constitution *Regimini Ecclesiæ Universæ* is not yet completed.

IV. What is laid down in article II above applies no less to cardinals who, by exception, continue in charge of a diocese, or keep its title without the function of governing it, after their eightieth year.

The remaining four articles ensured to the aged cardinals all the ceremonial privileges of their office, including the right to attend the meetings of the general congregations during the vacancy of the papacy. But all of what was important, including most especially the right to have an active vote in choosing a new pope, was taken away. Of the one hundred twenty-six cardinals alive on January 1, 1971, no fewer than twenty-five immediately lost their status as papal electors—almost a fifth of the whole College. All three of Pius XI's surviving creations were dismissed,[27] including the still powerful and influential Tisserant, as were seven of the remaining eighteen cardinals of Pius XII.[28] John XXIII's surviving group of thirty lost twelve of their number, including most of the old curial cardinals whom Roncalli had elevated to placate the Vatican establishment when he began to enlarge the College's membership.[29] By contrast, only three of Paul VI's seventy-five living creations lost their vote.[30] The number of papal electors was reduced suddenly to one hundred one, fewer than there had been when Paul completed his first enlargement of the College in 1965.

Half the list of names looked very much like a litany of the men who had opposed the elevation of Montini to the papal throne vehemently in 1963—especially Tisserant and Ottaviani, but also Giobbe, Forni, Heard, Roberti, Larraona, Browne, Cento, Bacci, and di Jorio.

For Ottaviani, a true Roman of the Romans of the old school—his father had been a baker in the Trastevere—the degradation was very great. He had celebrated his eightieth birthday on October 29, 1970, when he already knew of the coming pronouncement. Less than a month later, it became official, and five weeks after that he was no longer an elector. Tisserant, the dean of the College and a cardinal for almost thirty-five years, had even stronger feelings. He had been a major figure in Church government when Montini was still a simple priest; indeed he had been a cardinal for almost twenty years when Montini was made an archbishop. Both of these cardinals gave open and angry interviews on Italian television to publicize their anger and distress, but, of course, to no avail. Ottaviani went to his grave convinced that Paul VI had chosen the age of eighty as the fatal mark just because that was precisely the cardinal's age. Perhaps he was right, after all. None of the twenty-five showed any signs of senility or intellectual feebleness, although some, like Cicognani, Bacci, Browne, and Callori di Vignale, were now physically impaired or ill. Indeed, Cicognani had shouldered the burden of cardinal-secretary of state until he was well into his eighties—Paul could not have thought it possible that the end of the eighth decade of life automatically rendered any particular person incompetent.

At the same time, several of the cardinals who lost their votes were old allies and supporters who were shabbily treated for their loyalty and long service—including Liénart, Feltin, and Frings, who all had helped Montini to the throne; and, of course, Cicognani, who had pressed on strongly for years carrying out Paul's wishes.

Was *Ingravescentem Ætatem* the last step in a seven-year-long plan of papal revenge? Many in Rome, both inside and outside the Vatican, thought so. Paul's systematic program to remove older bishops and archbishops from authority, to pack the College of Cardinals quickly with a majority of his own creations, and to deprive older cardinals of their most cherished privileges, when combined with the natural attrition of the College and the episcopacy through death, produced a College and a hierarchy that was absolutely subservient to his will. Every major opponent of his view of Vatican II and of papal goverment was rendered powerless and, officially at least, silent.

Paul VI deferred any further actions with the College for more than two years, and almost four years after his third creation of cardinals. In the interval between the consistory of April 28, 1969, and the next appointments to the College, on March 5, 1973, twenty cardinals had died. There were now eighty-six electors among the one hundred fourteen living cardinals. The three cardinals who died in 1969, after the consistory of April 30, and the five others who died in 1970, were all electors.[31] Of the twelve cardinals who died after January 1, 1971, and before the consistory of March 5, 1973, only four had been electors.[32] In addition, eleven other cardinals passed their eightieth birthdays and were no longer electors.[33] The result of this attrition was that the number of papal electors now stood at eighty-six. Twenty-eight of the superannuated cardinals were still alive. The influence of Paul's predecessors, through the cardinals they had created, now was reduced substantially. Among those who were gone were three of Pius XI's last four cardinals; four more creations of Pius XII; eight of John XXIII's creations; but only five cardinals of the total of eighty-seven who had been elevated by Paul VI.

Since all thirty of the newly-created cardinals, as well as the cardinal who had been created in 1969 but whose name was published now, were within the prescribed age to be electors, the number of those elegible to vote rose to one hundred seventeen, while the total number of living cardinals rose to one hundred forty-five.

Stepan Trochta: *Bishop of Litomerice, Czechoslavakia*
Albino Luciani: *Patriarch of Venice*
Antonio Ribeiro: *Patriarch of Lisbon*
James Robert Knox: *Archbishop of Melbourne*
Avelar Brandão Vilela: *Archbishop of São Salvador da Bahia*
Joseph Cordeiro: *Archbishop of Karachi*
Anibal Muñoz Duque: *Archbishop of Bogotá*
Bolesław Kominek: *Archbishop of Wroclaw*
Luís Aponte Martinez: *Archbishop of San Juan de Puerto Rico*
Raúl Francisco Primatesta: *Archbishop of Cordoba, Argentina*
Salvatore Pappalardo: *Archbishop of Palermo*
Marcelo González Martín: *Archbishop of Toledo*
Louis Jean Guyot: *Archbishop of Toulouse*
Ugo Poletti: *Cardinal-Vicar of Rome*
Timothy Manning: *Archbishop of Los Angeles*
Paul Yoshigoro Taguchi: *Archbishop of Osaka*
Maurice Otunga: *Archbishop of Nairobi*
José Salazar López: *Archbishop of Guadalajara*
Emile Biayenda: *Archbishop of Brazzaville*
Humberto Sousa Medeiros: *Archbishop of Boston*
Paulo Evaristo Arns: *Archbishop of São Paulo*
James Darcy Freeman: *Archbishop of Sydney*

Narciso Jubany Arnau: *Archbishop of Barcelona*
Hermann Volk: *Bishop of Mainz*
Pio Taofinu'u: *Bishop of Apia, Western Samoa*
Sergio Pignedoli: *Pres., Secretariat for Non-Christians*
Luigi Raimondi: *Pref., Cong. for Causes of Saints*
Umberto Mozzoni: *Vatican administration*
Paul Philippe: *Pref., Cong. for the Oriental Churches*
Pietro Palazzini: *Vatican administration*
Ferdinando Giuseppe Antonelli: *Secy., Cong. for the Causes of Saints*

The demographic pattern that Paul had begun to develop in 1965 and 1967, and had further refined in 1969, continued. Twelve of the thirty-one names were those of archbishops of major sees who had replaced earlier cardinals.[34] Eight other cardinals represented sees that were included in the College for the first time or whose bishops had not been cardinals for at least several generations. These cardinals, with one exception, were national gains in the College for their countries.[35] The remaining four residential ordinaries were the first representation of their peoples—two Africans, one Asian, and one from Oceania.[36] Since several of the cardinals whom these archbishops replaced were still electors, though no longer serving as archbishops, and two others replaced cardinals whom Paul transferred to the curia, there was a gain in the national representation in several countries, notably in South America, where Brazil gained two new cardinals, and Argentina, one, and Australia, which now had three cardinals instead of one.

The seven new curial cardinals, six of whom were Italians, included the usual rewards for long diplomatic service, in the case of three,[37] and exemplary service in careers in the curia, in the case of the others.[38]

The fact that the number of cardinal-electors now stood at one hundred seventeen was not without significance. Paul had been meditating for some time on a new election constitution to replace the documents of Pius XII and John XXIII. One clause upon which he reflected was that which would stipulate the maximum number of cardinals who could be papal electors. In addition, he considered incorporating the elected presidents of the various national councils of bishops into the conclave—a truly revolutionary step which would diminish the cardinalate further, since the members of the College would no longer be the sole electors of the pope.

This radical step was, itself, prelude to the idea that the College eventually could be abolished altogether. Vatican II had stressed the collegiality of the bishops in governing the Church by divine institution, since the office was recognized and well established in the New Testament canon. The cardinalate, by contrast, was a strictly man-made body which had evolved from the local government of the diocese of Rome, and in no sense could be found before the later years of the third century. Moreover, the cardinal-bishops did not become involved in choosing a new pope until Nicholas II's constitution, *In nomine Domini*, of April 13, 1059; the other two orders of cardinals were not licit electors until Alexander III made them so in the constitution *Licet de vitanda discordia* in 1179. Was a biblical model of the government of the Christian community not to be preferred over a medieval introduction—one which had been implemented largely as a method to limit the power of the German emperors to interfere in choosing new popes and to forestall riots by the Roman people during a vacancy? Many council fathers regarded it as a scandal and a theological error that the bishops had so little power in the government of the Church, though their order was apostolic in nature (after all, the pope himself was first the bishop of Rome), while the cardinals wielded tremendous power, privilege, and tenure in their stead.

When the conservatives heard that Paul's new constitution might well contain a phrase which stripped the cardinals of their centuries-old right, they mounted a strong campaign to stop the innovation. Giuseppe Siri hastened to see Paul VI to discuss the matter. In a ninety-minute meeting, the Genoese archbishop pressed home his theme:

> It was like a game of ping-pong; he [Paul] listened to my arguments and countered with his own dialectic. I held back till the end one last objection: it was a mistake to put on the same level cardinals who are named by the pope and bishops who are appointed in a different way. Cardinals are answerable to no one, while bishops have to account for their decisions. So they can be easily "conditioned." This term alarmed Paul VI. "Very well," he said, "it will be the sacred college and it alone that will elect the pope." Then I took his hand, kissed his ring, and fled. If I had gone on any more, he would have flung an ashtray at my head.

Siri may be exaggerating the importance of this particular meeting—many others who had the pope's ear were similarly opposed—but he does capture the essence of Paul's reason for finally retaining the cardinals as the sole papal electors. Every candidate for the cardinalate was vetted personally by the pope, and he alone drew up the final list of creations for each consistory in which he named new cardinals. Bishops, on the other had, were decided upon in various stages of examination, with the ultimate selection in the hands of the Congregation of Bishops; although, of course, it was the pope's official appointment that elevated a man to the episcopal office. In reality, most popes did little more than grant an assent to choices that had been made by others. So the new constituton would preserve the cardinalate as the higest office in the Church after the papacy.

Romano Pontifici Eligendo finally was signed by Paul on October 1, 1975, and pubished on the following November 13. While it did not depart from precedent as much as liberals had hoped and conservatives had feared, it did codify a number of steps which Paul had been implementing slowly for some time. For example, it made official the greatly enlarged numbers of papal electors, setting the total at one hundred twenty—three more than the number of electors that had been reached in the consistory of March 5, 1973:

> The right to elect the Roman Pontiff belongs exclusively to the cardi-
> nals of the Holy Roman Church, except for those of them who, in
> accordance with the norm previously established (in *Ingravescentem
> Ætatem*, II, 2), shall have completed their eightieth year when the
> time comes for entering into the conclave; **the number of cardinal
> electors shall not, however, exceed one hundred twenty.** Excluded
> from among the electors, therefore, is any person of any other ecclesi-
> astical rank and any layperson of whatever rank and order. (II, i, 33).

Paul also reemphasized that all curial offices became vacant when the pope died, so as to leave the new pontiff utterly unfettered in the chioce of a new staff. This had been embodied in *Regimini*, eight years before, but was restated as a part of the electoral rules to give it added force:

> In accordance with the Apostolic Constitution *Regimini Ecclesiæ
> Universæ*, **all cardinals who are prefects of the agencies of the
> Roman Curia, including the Cardinal Secretary of State, are to
> resign their offices at the death of the pontiff.** Exceptions are the
> Camerlengo of the Holy Roman Church, the Major Penitentiary and
> the Vicar General of the Diocese of Rome; these are to handle ordi-
> nary business and bring before the Sacred College of Cardinals mat-
> ters requiring referral to the Supreme Pontiff. (III, 14).

These were restatements, in a somewhat stronger language, of what al-
ready was the norm. When it came to provisions that were new, or greatly enhanced from those of earlier reigns, Paul was even more decisive. In or-
der to prevent the breach of secrecy which had allowed the outside world to know something of the bitterness that had pervaded the election of 1963, Paul imposed the strongest oath thus far on the electors and others who would be inside the conclave. In the first general congregation following his death, the cardinals were required to swear that their every action would be hidden at all times—those who arrived later also had to swear the oath:

"We, the Cardinal Bishops, Priests and Deacons of the Holy Roman Church, promise and swear on oath that we will, each and all of us, observe exactly all that is set down in the Apostolic Constitution *Romano Pontifici Eligendo* of the Supreme Pontiff Paul VI, and that we will maintain a scrupulous secrecy concerning everything discussed in the meetings of the cardinals whether before or during the conclave, and concerning everything that in any way relates to the election of the Roman Pontiff."

Then each Cardinal is to say: "And I, . . . Cardinal . . . , solemnly promise and swear on oath." Laying his hand on the Gospel, each is to add: "So help me God and these holy Gospels of God which I touch with my hand." (II, 12).

As if this were not strong enough, Paul also strengthened the normal oath taken by the cardinals at the beginning of the conclave:

Immediately after morning Mass, or in the afternoon of that day if it seems preferable, the electors enter the conclave. . . . after which the cardinal electors take an oath according to the following formula which the dean or the cardinal who is senior in rank and age is to recite in a loud voice:

"Each and all of us, the cardinal electors present in this conclave, promise and swear on oath that we will observe faithfully and to the letter all the prescriptions contained in the Apostolic Constitution *Romano Pontifici Eligendo* of the Supreme Pontiff Paul VI, dated October 1, 1975. We also promise and swear on oath that whoever of us in God's providence is elected Roman Pontiff will fully and zealously assert and defend the spiritual and temporal rights and freedom of the Holy See, and, if need arises, will lay unyielding claim to them. Above all, we promise and swear on oath that all of us, and even our conclavists if there be any, will preserve a scrupulous secrecy regarding everything that relates in any way to the election of the Roman Pontiff and everything that goes on in the conclave and relates directly or indirectly to the voting. Moreover, we will never in any way break that secrecy whether during the conclave or after the election of the new pontiff, unless that same pontiff gives us special permission and explicit authorization. In addition, we will under no conditions accept from any civil power, under any pretext, a commission to propose a veto or 'exclusion,' even in the form of a simple wish; nor will we manifest such a desired veto, should we in any way come to know of one, or give aid or favor to any interference, protest or other form of intervention, by which secular authorities of any order or rank or any groups of persons or any individuals try to take a hand in the election of the pontiff."

Then each cardinal elector is to say: "And I, . . . Cardinal . . . , promise and swear on oath"; whereupon he is to place his hand on the Gospel and add: "So help me God and these holy Gospels of God which I touch with my hand." (II, iii, 49).

The conclave staff was required to take another oath which provided heavy spiritual penalties in case of violations:

All the officials and staff, clerical or lay, of the conclave, as well as all the conclavists, if there are any, are to take an oath, in Latin or some other language; it is to be administered by the Camerlengo of the Holy Roman Church, once he has made sure that each of them clearly understands the importance of the oath and the meaning of the formula. One or two days before entering into the conclave, in the presence of the secretary of the conclave and the master of pontifical ceremonies, who have been delegated for the purpose by the Camerlengo (in whose presence they themselves had earlier taken the oath [above]), the officials and others are to pronounce the following formula in the national language suitable for them:

"I, . . . , promise and swear that I will preserve an inviolate secrecy concerning each and every action taken and decree passed in the meetings of the cardinals with regard to the election of the new pontiff, and concerning everything done in the conclave or place of election that directly or indirectly has to do with the balloting, and concerning everything that I shall in any way come to know. Neither directly nor indirectly, by gesture or word or writing or in any other way, shall I violate this secrecy. I also promise and swear that in the conclave I shall not use any kind of transmitter or receiver or any photographic equipment this under pain of automatic excommunication reserved in a very special way to the Apostolic See, if I violate this precept. I shall preserve this secrecy with scrupulous care even after the election of the new pontiff, unless he grants me special permission and explicit authorization.

"I likewise promise and swear that I shall in no way aid in or favor any interference, protest or other action by which civil authorities of any order or rank or any groups of persons or any individuals try to take a hand in the election of the pontiff.

"So help me God and these holy Gospels of God which I touch with my hand."

In spite of these spiritual promises, Paul thought that worldly measures had to be introduced, as well, to ensure secrecy. He added to the permanent staff of the conclave both the architect who set up the area and two technicians who were to sweep the precincts for electronic equipment of any kind:

Also to be present are to be some priests from the religious orders, so that there may be a sufficient number of confessors in the various lan-

guages; two doctors, one of them a surgeon, the other a general practitioner, and one or two male nurses; **the architect of the conclave
with two experts in technological matters** (*cf.* numbers 55 and 61).
All of these are to be nominated by the Camerlengo of the Holy
Roman Church and his cardinal assistants, and approved by a majority of the cardinals. To these are to be added others in suitable numbers who will minister to the needs of the conclave; they are
appointed by the committee . . . of cardinals established for the purpose. (II, i, 44).

These two technicians were to carry out precisely prescribed inspec-
tions which largely superseded the ancient, traditional tour of the conclave
area by the senior cardinals of the three orders and the camerlengo:

The Cardinal Camerlengo and the three cardinals who are his assistants at any given time are bound to keep careful watch and to visit
the entire premises frequently, in person or through delegates, in
order to see that the conclave enclosure is in no way breached. **At
these visitations, the two technicians are always to be present and,
if necessary, to use the apt means our age provides for detecting the
possible presence of the instruments mentioned below in II, i, 61.**
If any such instruments be found, those responsible for them are to
be expelled from the conclave and be subject to serious penalties as
the future pontiff shall judge fit. (II, i, 55).

Finally, in order to protect the cardinal electors against the indiscretion of others and against insidious attempts to limit their independence of judgment and freedom of decision, We entirely forbid
the introduction into the conclave, under any pretext, or the use,
should these already be there, of any equipment for recording, playing back or transmitting voices or pictures. (II, i, 61).

Because of the large number of electors who had to be housed in the traditional area in the Vatican, and also to increase the secrecy he cherished,
Paul abolished altogether the office of conclavist. No cardinal, unless
gravely ill and in need of constant attention, would be permitted to bring a
servant into the conclave:

**The cardinal electors may not bring with them conclavists, or pri-
vate servants, clerical or lay.** This can be permitted only by way of
exception in the special case of serious ill health. The cardinal in
question shall submit an express request, with his reasons, to the
Cardinal Camerlengo who in turn will propose it to the committee or
commission of cardinals appointed for the purpose. The latter are to
decide and, if they think the request should be granted, they are to
investigate very carefully the character of the person admitted as a
servant. (II, i, 45).

There was another traditional symbol gone, one which dated from the first conclaves in the thirteenth century.

With regard to the balloting itself, perhaps the most surprising regulation was Paul's reinstatement of the two-thirds-plus-one rule that Pius XII had established in *Vacantis Apostolica Sedis,* but which John had abolished later in *Summi Pontificis Electio:*

> We fully confirm the rule determined long ago and subsequently observed with scrupulous care, that a two-thirds majority is required for the valid election of a Roman Pontiff. We also wish to keep in force the norm established by Our predecessor Pius XII, that the majority must always be two-thirds plus one. (V, 65).

With *Romano Pontifici Eligendo*, Paul VI completed the cycle of regulatory documents by which he reshaped the hierarchy, the curia, and the cardinalate. He had alternated consistories for the creation of new cardinals with these new regulations to achieve a step-by-step radical change without any real revolt by any of the prelates affected by them. The creation of 1965 had been followed by *Ecclesiæ Sanctæ* (1966), which called for the resignation of ordinaries at the age of seventy-five. This gave him the opportunity to create new cardinals who were archbishops of major sees not because their predecessors had died but because they had been forced from office. The creation of June, 1967, was followed by *Regimini Ecclesiæ Universæ*, in August, which forced from power many of the established figures of the curia. This, in turn, presented another opportunity to create new cardinals by promoting the officials who occupied the offices from which the old prelates had been retired. It is not surprising that the consistory of April 30, 1969, saw the elevation of more new curial cardinals than any other in the reign—nine of the thirty-three names announced for that day. The creation of 1969 was followed by *Ingravescentem Ætatem* (1970), which deprived cardinals who had become eighty of their vote in the conclave. This immediately turned the cardinalate into an honorary office for the older members of the College and gave Paul a plausibe reason to create new cardinals to fill the active spaces they had occupied. The creation of March 5, 1973, saw six men elevated who warranted promotion only because fellow-countrymen had lost their right to vote. Several others reached the cardinalate only because of the earlier requirements of resignation and curial replacement.

Finally, the election constitution in 1975 codified specifically all of the earlier changes. It restated several clauses of both *Regimini* and *Ingravescentem Ætatem* to emphasize further that much of it was a codification in final form of earlier, separate pronouncements.

For the first time, Paul was constrained by his own regulations in the number of new cardinals he could appoint, if all of them were to be valid electors, because the number of the latter could not exceed one hundred twenty.

Between the consistory of 1973 and May, 1976, an unprecedented twenty-eight cardinals died. Of them, twelve were still electors when they died;[39] while sixteen others were among the superannuated cardinals.[40] In addition, five other still-living cardinals had passed their eightieth birthdays, and had lost their right to vote.[41] These reductions left the College with ninety-nine electors of a total of one hundred seventeen.

In his fifth promotion, of May 24, 1976, Paul published the names of twenty new cardinals, raising the electorate to one hundred nineteen:

Octavio Antonio Beras Rojas: *Archbishop of Santo Domingo*
Juan Carlos Aramburu: *Archbishop of Buenos Aires*
Corrado Bafile: *Pref., Cong. for Causes of Saints*
Hyacinthe Thiandoum: *Archbishop of Dakar, Senegal*
Emmanuel Kiwanuka Nsubuga: *Archbishop of Kampala, Uganda*
Lawrence Trevor Picachy: *Archbishop of Calcutta*
Jaime L. Sin: *Archbishop of Manila*
William Wakefield Baum: *Archbishop of Washington*
Aloisio Lorscheider: *Archbishop of Fortaleza, Brazil*
Reginald John Delargey: *Archbishop of Wellington*
László Lékai: *Archbishop of Esztergom, Hungary*
George Basil Hume: *Archbishop of Westminster*
Victor Razafimahatratra: *Abp. of Antananarivo (Tananarive)*
Dominic Ignatius Ekandem: *Bishop of Ikot Ekpene, Nigeria*
Joseph Marie Trin-nhu-Khuê: *Archbishop of Hanoi*
Opilio Rossi: *Vatican diplomat*
Giuseppe Maria Sensi: *Vatican diplomat*
Joseph Schröffer: *Secy., Cong. for Catholic Education*
Eduardo Francisco Pironio: *Pref., Religious and Secular Insts.*
Bolesław Filipiak: *Dean of the Rota*

The addition of the cardinal whose name was reserved *in petto* by the pope, but which could be published at any time, made the whole body of electors a potential one hundred twenty, precisely the number that Paul had specified in the election constitution.

In general, the cardinals who were created in 1976 were drawn from the same backgrounds as those Paul created in earlier promotions. Seven of the fourteen ordinaries were the successors of cardinals in their sees.[42] The elevation of the seventh living Brazilian cardinal signalled Paul's continued recognition of the importance of the Church in that country, especially in the face of a growing tyrannical government under which the Church, much like the case in Eastern Europe, offered the only real counterpoise for the people. This consistory saw another cardinal for India, the first for Calcutta, as well as the Dominican Republic's first papal elector. Paul celebrated the end of the war in Vietnam by creating the archbishop of Hanoi as southeast Asia's first cardinal. But the surprise of the occasion was the great broadening of Black Africa's representation in the College, signalling that Paul was now beginning to recognize that continent as he and John XXIII already had established a strong representation for Latin America. In addition to Razafimahatratra in Antananarivo, there were three other Black cardinals, all of whom were the first in their people's history—Thiandoum for Senegal, Nsubuga for Uganda, and Ekandem for Nigeria.

Several of the new cardinals were more surprised at their elevations than was the Vatican establishment. Victor Razafimahatratra, a fifty-four-year-old Jesuit, had been bishop of the poor and small diocese of Farafangana in the south of Madagascar only since April 18, 1971. After the death of Cardinal Rakotomalala, on November 1, 1975, the see of Tananarive remained vacant for several months, while the nuncio to the Malagassy Republic gathered information on suitable succesors and forwarded it to the Congregation of Bishops for consideration. In this process, Razafimahatratra had no idea that he was under any consideration for the office. Suddenly, in early April, 1976, he received a call from the nuncio to inform him that he had been named the new archbishop. He asked for time to make a retreat to consider whether he was worthy enough to accept the appointment. "You can have fifteen minutes," was the envoy's reply. The appointment was announced on April 10. Four days later, the nuncio called again. The new archbishop thought that perhaps Rome was having second thoughts about his suitability for the new post—he certainly hoped so. But the nuncio's first words to him were, "And you also have been made a cardinal." The shock was compounded by the fact that Razafimahatratra was too poor to afford the trip to Rome, so the Congregation for the Evangelization of Peoples had to send him an advance payment to make his journey possible. The same condition affected another Jesuit cardinal, Lawrence Picachy of Calcutta. Much less distinguished in his own diocese than its most famous nun, he was used to being defined as "Mother Teresa's bishop." He also needed sudden financial aid to cover the costs of being made a cardinal.

There was less surprise in Hungary at the elevation of Lékai; the feelings among the people were more those of distaste. Paul appointed Lékai to be Mindszenty's successor, with the title of administrator of the see, on

March 16, 1972, after the old cardinal finally was persuaded to vacate the American legation and come to Rome. After Mindszenty's death, on May 6, 1975, Lékai was appointed officially to fill the primacy as soon as the minimum period of mourning had passed. The new primate had earned his national credibility by imprisonment and torture by the Nazis during World War II, but he seemed too much an appeaser of the communist government by comparison with his predecessor—he spoke frequently of "peaceful coexistence," and "realities" and often recalled Lot's wife, who was punished for looking back. So the Hungarians did not respond with uninhibited joy to their new cardinal.

In Manila, the elevation of Jaime Sin was greeted with real joy, extending the happiness that greeted his appointment as archbishop on January 21, 1974. Sin was a relief after the years of Ruffino Santos, an autocratic and proud prelate who was a close friend of President Ferdinand Marcos. Santos reputedly had amassed a personal fortune of more than a million dollars before his death. The alienation he engendered was so great that Manila almost seemed an obvious site for the most serious attempt on the life of the pope, when he arrived at the city's airport on November 27, 1970. Though the attempt was made by a Bolivian, it was the Philippine atmosphere that made the site particularly plausible. As Paul journeyed to Manila's cathedral, he could not miss the signs that were held up by people in the crowd. Some proclaimed "Explain the Unexplained Wealth of the Church," others bluntly said, "Santos Retire." The new archbishop went about the hard task of restoring the credibility of the Church and the archdiocese with great fervor, and the cardinalate was a reward for his early and substantial successes. He was at a dinner when he was informed publicly that he was to be created a cardinal. Turning to a fellow diner, he simply remarked, in English, that he had never expected that there would be a Cardinal Sin in the Church.

Among the new curial cardinals, Bafile now became prefect of the Congregation for the Causes of Saints in succession to Luigi Raimondi;[43] while Filipiak had been Brennan's successor as dean of the Rota, a promotion which continued the custom restored in modern times by John XXIII when he promoted William Theodore Heard. The creations of Rossi and Sensi were the usual rewards for a successful diplomatic career.[44]

The remaining two curial promotions were drawn from the new managers and diplomats whom Paul had recruited internationally as a part of his effort to destroy the Italian control of the Vatican's administrative apparatus. Eduardo Francisco Pironio was a native of Nueve de Julio, Argentina, and the twenty-second and youngest child of his parents, who were immigrants from Friuli. After several years as a teacher of theology in the seminary of the diocese of Mercede, he was brought to Rome as the peritus, or special advisor, to the Argentinean bishops at Vatican II. Later, he became secretary (1967–1970) and then president (1970–1975) of CELAM, the conference of Latin American bishops. At the famous meeting of CELAM in Medellin, Colombia, he was the leading figure who shaped the declaration of the conference's aims, which moved the Church in Latin America away from its traditional position of alliance with the established social classes and committed it to a closer and deeper support of deprived people. Later still, he became a vocal critic of the repressive actions of the Argentinean government. His considerable successes caused Paul to appoint him pro-prefect of the Congregation of Religious and Secular Institutes on September 30, 1975, although there is some evidence to show that Paul also called him away from his homeland to prevent possible violent acts against him. With his cardinalate came the rank of prefect of the congregation. Later, in 1984, John Paul II made him president of the Pontifical Council for the Laity. In this post, he was credited with the idea of holding the World Youth Days, which have proven to be some of the most popular of John Paul II's events. Pironio could be recognized easily from the jaunty beret he wore in preference to more traditional ecclesiastical headgear.

Joseph Schröffer, a native of Ingolstadt, completed nine years of theological studies in Rome at the Gregorianum before returning to Germany in 1931. Ten years later, Pius XII made him administrator of the diocese of Eichstätt, since the pope refused to appoint new members of the hierarchy during World War II. In 1948, he became bishop and went on to serve as president of the German chapters of the Pax Christi movement. When Paul reorganized the curia in 1967, he summoned Schröffer to become secretary of the Congregation of Catholic Education, where he provided effective leadership for many years.

In the thirteen months between the creation of May 24, 1976, and Paul's final elevation of four new cardinals, together with the publication of the creation held *in petto*, on June 27, 1977, five cardinals had died, of whom three were electors.[45] The tragedy among them was the death of Emile Biayenda, still only fifty years old, who was taken from his home in Brazzaville and shot during the early hours of March 23 by partisans of a former president, Alphonse Massamba-Debat. The latter's forces had attempted a coup d'etat in Brazzaville on March 19 in which the man who had overthrown his goverment in 1968, President Marien Ngouabi, was killed. Cardinal Biayenda had improved relations significantly with Ngouabi's Marxist government, and had met with the president earlier on the day of the coup. Biayenda was the second cardinal of this century to meet a violent death.[46] The coup failed and Massamba-Debat was himself executed a short time later.

In addition, two other cardinals had joined the College's non-voting population.[47] This reduction of the number of published electors to one hundred fourteen was now augmented by five:

Frantisek Tomásek: *Administrator of Prague*
Giovanni Benelli: *Archbishop of Florence*
Bernardin Gantin: *President, Pont. Comm. "Justitia et Pax"*
Joseph Ratzinger: *Archbishop of Munich and Freising*
Mario Luigi Ciappi: *Theologian of the Pontifical Household*

The date of the consistory was set to accommodate Benelli's immediate elevation to the cardinalate following his promotion to Florence earlier in the month.

The whole number of cardinals now stood at one hundred thirty-seven, of whom one hundred nineteen were valid electors and eighteen were retired.

Paul had made Frantisek Tomásek the administrator of Prague on February 18, 1965, to act as vicar for Josef Beran. When the latter died in 1969, Paul continued Tomásek in the post during a period of hard dealing with the Czech government. The situation by May, 1976, showed signs of easing, so Paul secretly elevated the administrator to the College in the expectation that he would be able to publish his name soon. The consistory of 1977 gave him that opportunity, although the earlier creation *in petto* could have been published at any time. In conjunction with the publication of his name, Tomásek was made archbishop of Prague in name as well as in function. His contribution to the success of the Velvet Revolution in 1989 proved that Paul's evolution of policy towards Czechoslovakia in the 1960s and 1970s had been a wise one.

Bernardin Gantin was the first Black African curial cardinal in the history of the Church. A native of Dahomey (now Benin), born in 1922 and ordained in 1951, Pius XII had made him titular bishop of Tipasa in Mauretania and auxiliary for the archdiocese of Cotonou on February 3, 1957. From 1960 to 1971, he was archbishop of Cotonou and then was brought to Rome thanks to the favorable impression he made at the council. Paul attached him to the Congregation for the Evangelization of Peoples—the former Propaganda Fide—first as an assistant secretary (1971–1973) and then as secretary (1973–1975). In 1975, he was made vice president of the Pontifical Commission for Justice and Peace, and then elevated to the presidency of the commission in the following year.

His later career has been nothing less than spectacular. In the consistory of 1977, he was made a cardinal-deacon and assigned, as the second incumbent, to the diaconate of Sacro Cuore di Gesu Cristo Re. In 1984, John Paul II appointed him prefect of the Congregation of Bishops and raised him to the rank of cardinal-priest, in the consistory of June 25 of that year, in which he retained his diaconate as a presbyterial title. Two years later, on September 29, 1986, he was made cardinal-bishop of Palestrina in succession to Carlo Confalonieri, who had died on August 1. Gantin vacated the office of prefect of the Congregation of Bishops in June, 1998.

In 1993, following new guidelines set by John Paul II, Agnello Rossi retired from the rank of dean of the College.[48] The six cardinal-bishops then met to elect the new dean of the College on June 4, 1993, and chose Gantin. On the following day, John Paul II confirmed him as dean and made him Rossi's successor as cardinal-bishop of Ostia. At the close of the twentieth century, he is the highest ranking and most powerful Black prelate in the history of the modern Church. In the next sede vacante, he can be expected to preside over the meetings of the general congregation of cardinals who will prepare the conclave. And, considering the vast respect in which he is held in Rome, he will be a major figure in the next papal election.

Another creation in 1977 whose later career brought him power and influence far beyond the heights he had achieved when he was made cardinal was Joseph Ratzinger, archbishop of Munich and Freising. Born on April 16, 1927, and ordained in 1951, he served as professor of dogmatic theology at the University of Regensburg from 1969 to 1977. Paul also appointed him a member of the International Theological Commission. Ironically, in the light of later events, the pope was attracted to him because of his liberal views on a number of theological questions. His performance merited his elevation to the archdiocese of Munich on March 25, 1977, and the cardinalate three months later.

As the years passed, Ratzinger became steadily more conservative in his views, and closer in thought to the theological positions of John Paul II. In 1981, he was brought to Rome as prefect of the Congregation for the Doctrine of the Faith and resigned as archbishop of Munich on February 15, 1982. His new office and power soon brought him additional ecclesiastical tasks and distinctions. On April 5, 1993, John Paul elevated him to the ranks of the cardinal bishops, as cardinal-bishop of Velletri, in succession to the equally powerful and influential Sebastiano Baggio, who had died on March 21. During the reign of John Paul II, his authority over doctrinal matters has become absolute, eclipsing the power held by any of his predecessors since Ottaviani in the years before the Second Vatican Council.

Not only his prefecture but also his leadership of both the Biblical and Theological commissions and his active role in the second section of the secretariat of state have contributed to his position as perhaps the most powerful of all the curial cardinals at the end of the century. In the year 2000, he still will be only seventy-three.

Mario Luigi Ciappi, a Dominican theologian who was brought into the papal household by Pius XII, served five popes as Master of the Sacred Palace, the theologian of the pontifical household. A Florentine, he was born October 6, 1909. While still in his doctoral studies at the Angelicum, he was ordained on March 26, 1932, by Cardinal Francesco Marchetti-Selvaggiani, then the cardinal-vicar of Rome. After he received his doctorate, he continued his studies at the University of Fribourg and then the University of Louvain. Then he returned to the Angelicum as a professor of dogmatic and moral theology. One of his students in this period was Karol Wojtyła. In May, 1955, Pius XII appointed him to his pontifical theological post, where he was continued in office by John XXIII and Paul VI. While the cardinalate is not a usual accompaniment to the office, a number of important and influential Dominicans have been elevated to the College for their theological services to the pope. Among them were Annibale Annibaldeschi della Molara, created a cardinal on May 22, 1262, one of the most influential Dominicans of the thirteenth century to whom Thomas Aquinas dedicated part two of his *Catena Aurea*; and Vincenzo Maculano da Firenzuola, perhaps the most distinguished civil and military engineer of the first half of the seventeenth century. A Dominican, too, Maculano was made Master of the Sacred Palace by Urban VIII in 1639, and then created a cardinal by the same pope on December 16, 1641. Interestingly, his closeness to Urban was won by his stout theological defense of Galileo, not for his amazing feats of design and construction, which included a reconstruction of the defenses of Malta for the Knights of Saint John. Mario Luigi Ciappi was in very distinguished company.

But, in 1977, the most important creation was that of Paul's principal curial confidant, Giovanni Benelli. His closeness to the pope had made him both feared and cultivated among all of the curial officials, even though, like Montini himself under Pius XII, he was not a cardinal and held no rank higher than that of *sostituto* in the secretariat of state. It is clear that Paul realized that he was coming to the end of his reign, and he wished to place Benelli in a position to be a major figure in the coming conclave. To do that, he had to move him out of the curia and into some pastoral office where he could develop and exercise his own network in a way quite distinct from the operations of the Vatican. When Cardinal Ermenegildo Florit submitted his resignation as archbishop of Florence in

July, 1976, on reaching his seventy-fifth birthday, the stage was set. Within a few days, Benelli and the pope agreed that Florence was the right setting for Benelli in the coming *sede vacante*. It was extremely difficult for Paul to part with his right hand, but he knew that he must, if Benelli were to retain a larger sphere of influence in the Church, and perhaps rise to the papacy himself one day. Benelli himself described the difficulty of this decision:

> The pope called me one evening to his private apartment. Tears streamed down his cheeks. He looked very old. His heart was weak. He knew that he could die at any moment. The tears were so abundant that they marked his blotter. Then he said that I should go to Florence, because it was a post that my service merited and because he did not know how much longer he would live.
>
> He added that he still wished me to work with him, and that he would telephone me whenever it was necessary. In his tears, he begged me to accept. So I accepted.
>
> It was painful to go. Pope Paul and I had such a symbiosis that it was enough for him to begin a sentence for me to complete it. A half-word was all I needed to understand his thought. We were two parts of a unity. The determining factor was his thought that his death was imminent. But he lived on for nearly two years. It was a very hard time for him.

Benelli does not allude at all to the tremendous antipathy he had accumulated over the years in the secretariat of state. Even Villot, who had been his friend and who had been advanced to the position of cardinal-secretary of state on Benelli's strong recommendation, had come to resent his overt power—it was Benelli, not Villot, who customarily received ambassadors to the Vatican, for example. When Villot called a meeting of the entire staff of the secretariat to announce that Benelli shortly would be going to Florence, there was a thunderous roll of applause. When he went on to announce that the new archbishop also would be made a cardinal within a few days, the applause was much, much less.

Benelli's appointment to Florence was made official on June 3, and the cardinalate came only twenty-four days later.

By the time Paul breathed his last, little more than a year later, the College of Cardinals had lost four electors from the total of one hundred nineteen that Paul had established in 1977; three by death and another from forced retirement.[49] Four other retired cardinals also died.[50] Villot, therefore, sent the *intimatio* to one hundred thirty cardinals, since the fifteen who were retired still retained their right to a non-voting seat in the general congregations, where at least their voices still could be heard.

NOTES

1. Valeri (July 22, 1963), Jullien (January 11, 1964), Chiarlo (January 21), Roques (September 4), and Gerlier (January 17, 1965).

2. Paderborn: Verlag Bonifacius-Druckerei, 1960. Translated as *The Ecumenical Council, the Church and Christendom* (London: Geoffrey Chapman, 1961; New York: P. J. Kenedy, 1962).

3. Beran died in Rome on May 17, 1969. As the thirtieth anniversary of his death approaches, Rome announced on April 2, 1998, that the official cause for his beatification had been opened.

4. His influential articles and books are so many and varied that one can mention only the most important. The beginnings of his elaboration of thought appear in *L'Esprit du Protestantisme en Suisse* (Paris: Nouvelle Librairie Nationale, 1925), and are extended in *De la Bible Catholique a la Bible Protestante*. (Paris: A. Blot, 1930). Perhaps the work which most influenced Paul VI was *La Juridiction de l'Eglise sur la Cité* (Paris: Desclee, de Brouwer et cie., 1931); but his magnum opus was the widely acclaimed *L'Eglise du Verbe Incarné: Essai de Theologie Speculative*, (3 vols., Bruges: Desclee, de Brouwer, 1941; translated as *The Church of the Word Incarnate; an Essay in Speculative Theology*, London and New York: Sheed and Ward, 1955). At the time he was given the cardinalate, he was at work on a major interpretation of the council's understanding of the nature of the Church, *Le Mystere de l'Eglise selon le Deuxieme Concile Vatican*. Paul himself would encourage its speedy translation into Italian, as *Il Mistero della Chiesa secondo il Concilio Vaticano II* and its publication in the pope's native Brescia (Queriniana, 1967).

5. He received his doctorate in 1905 from the School of Political and Social Sciences of the University of Louvain, with a formidable dissertation on labor laws and legislation in Italy. That work, *Saggio su la Legislazione Operaia in Italia,* was published in the following year (Torino: Fratelli Bocca, 1906) and later reprinted (Brescia: Sintesi, 1973).

6. Giulio Bevilacqua was to enjoy his cardinalate for only seventy-three days. He died on May 6, 1965, and was buried in his beloved parish church in Brescia. He was the first creation of Paul VI to die.

7. Goncalves Cerejeira at Lisbon (born November 29, 1888), Liénart at Lille (born February 7, 1884), and Tappouni, the Syrian patriarch of Antioch (born November 3, 1879).

8. De Vasconcellos Motta of Aparecida, Brazil (born July 16, 1890), Spellman of New York (born May 4, 1889), Pla y Deniel of Toledo (born December 19, 1876), Frings of Köln (born February 6, 1887), Ruffini of Palermo (born January 19, 1888), Caggiano of Buenos Aires (born January 30, 1889), Tien-kin-sin of Beijing, but now administrator of Taipei (born October 24, 1890), da Silva of Sao Salvador do Bahia, Brazil (born April 8, 1876), Feltin of Paris (born May 15, 1883), de la Torre of Quito (born November 15, 1873), McIntyre of Los Angeles (born June 25, 1886), Lercaro of Bologna (born October 28, 1891), and de Arriba y Castro of Tarragona (born April 8, 1886).

9. Garribi y Rivera of Guadalajara (born January 30, 1889, the same day as Caggiano), Richaud of Bordeaux (born April 16, 1887), and Concha (born November 7, 1891).

10. Maximos IV Saigh, Melkite patriarch of Antioch (born April 10, 1878), Beran of Prague (born December 12, 1888), Martin of Rouen (born August 9, 1891), and Herrera y Oria of Malaga (born December 12, 1886).

11. He should have noticed that Poma was transferred from Mantua to be titular archbishop of Gerpiniana *pro illa vice* when he was sent to Bologna. A titular diocese which is elevated to archiepiscopal status temporarily is usually not conferred on a prelate who can be expected to remain very long with that title. Moreover, Poma was ambitious and already fifty-seven. He would not have accepted the new appointment unless he expected a swift rise to the cardinalate—he had been archbishop of a major see for almost thirteen years.

12. The cardinals who were created in 1967 were the last to receive red hats from the hands of the pope. Cardinals, however, can still have one, if they pay for it themselves or have it given to them by friends. The old tradition of suspending the hat by a wire from the roof of the cathedral, as a sign that the see had once been held by a cardinal, thus can be preserved. A recent example is the case of Joseph Bernardin, archbishop of Chicago. A group of his friends bought him his cardinal's hat from the Roman haberdasher who still makes them—it cost about $400.00 in 1983—and, after his death on November 14, 1996, it was hoisted to the ceiling

to hang with those of the four other dead cardinal-archbishops of Chicago, Mundelein, Stritch, Meyer, and Cody. The traditional expression in English, and in several other European languages, "to get the red hat," when a prelate is elevated to the cardinalate almost certainly will not disappear.

13. Four in 1965 (Micara, March 11; Fossati, March 30; Meyer, April 7; and Bevilacqua, August 6); three in 1966 (Castaldo, March 3; Albareda, July 19; and Ciriaci, December 30); and five more in 1967, before the consistory (Copello, February 9; Bracci, March 24; Dante, April 24; Ritter, June 10; and Ruffini, June 11).

14. Veuillot had been professor of philosophy in minor seminary of the archdiocese of Paris from 1942 to 1949, and then served the next decade in Rome on the staff of the secretariat of state. It was in the latter position that he first came to know Montini, who regarded him highly. It was during the Roman years that he wrote a text which became one of the anticipatory readings for the council fathers, *Notre Sacerdoce: Documents Pontificaux de Pie X a nos jours* (Paris: Fleurus, 1954), translated as *The Catholic Priesthood According to the Teaching of the Church: Papal Documents from Pius X to Pius XII* (Westminster, Maryland: Newman Press, 1958; Dublin: Gill, 1957). His reward for his Roman service was appointment as bishop of Angers on July 1, 1959. He was made coadjutor with right of succession at Paris on June 12, 1961, and followed Feltin as archbishop on December 21, 1966.

15. He was appointed archbishop of Saint Louis on July 20, 1946, in succession to Pius XII's shortest-lived cardinal, John Glennon. Ritter had been an auxiliary bishop himself, at Indianapolis, in 1933–1934, and then had become bishop of that city on March 24, 1934. Ten years later, on November 11, 1944, he was made the first archbishop of that see. Glennon was a hard act to follow in Saint Louis, where he was the admired and beloved ordinary for more than forty years. Early in his tenure as archbishop, Glennon's devoted supporters hoped that he would soon receive the cardinalate. The Catholic owners of the local baseball and football teams expressed their wish by naming both teams the *Cardinals*. Decades later, their wish came true; Glennon received the red hat from Pius XII in the Grand Consistory of February 18, 1946. Exhausted from his journey to Rome and the rigours of the ceremonies, the eighty-

three-year-old Glennon died at Dublin on March 9, 1946. He had stopped in Ireland to visit his birthplace, on his return journey to Saint Louis.

16. Perhaps he already had begun his long association with his "cousin by marriage," Helen Dolan Wilson. Within a few years, he had channeled a fortune that was thought to exceed a million dollars to her.

17. His most important contribution was: Hildebrand Hopfl (1872-1934), *Introductio in Sacros utriusque Testamenti Libros Compendium*, 5th ed., rev. by Benno Gut (3 vols., Roma: A. Arnodo, 1960).

18. Its other members were Andre Jullien, Anselmo Albareda, William Theodore Heard, and Efrem Forni.

19. Some powerful congregations simply had their names changed to something that was supposed to be more palatable to bishops and laity alike. The Supreme Sacred Congregation of the Holy Office of the Inquisition became the Sacred Congregation for the Doctrine of the Faith, but its absolute power over all matters concerned with theology, faith, and belief remained unchanged, so dissent could be stifled as easily after the reform as before it.

20. This elaborated and extended an earlier decree, *Pro comperto sane*, of August 6, 1967.

21. Tien-kin-sin (July 24, 1967); Cardijn (July 25); Saigh (November 5); Spellman (December 2); Riberi (December 16); Pacini (December 23); Tappouni (January 29, 1968); Richaud (February 5); Veuillot (February 14); Brennan (July 2); Pla y Deniel (July 5); Morano (July 12); Herrera y Oria (July 28); de la Torre (July 31); da Silva (August 14); and Bea (November 16, 1968).

22. Yü Pin, the exiled archbishop of Nanking, to replace Tien-kin-sin, the exiled archbishop of Beijing; Dearden to replace Mooney (died October 25, 1958); Marty to replace Veuillot; Gouyon to replace Roques (died September 4, 1964); Enrique y Tarancón to replace Pla y Deniel; Muñoz Vega to replace de la Torre; Poma to replace Lercaro; Carberry to replace Ritter; Cooke to replace Spellman; Araújo Sales to replace da Silva; and Höffner to replace Frings (resigned January 24, 1969, died December 16, 1978).

23. New Zealand, with McKeefry in Wellington; the Malagassy Republic (Madagascar) with Rakotomalala in Antananarivo; Guatemala, with Casariego; Zaire, with Malula in Kinshasa; and

Korea, with Sou Hwan Kim in Seoul.

24. Scherer in Pôrto Alegre, Brazil; Rosales in Cebú, the Philippines; Miranda y Gómez in Mexico City; Parecattil in Ernakulam, India; and Flahiff in Winnipeg, Canada.

25. Gordon Joseph Gray, archbishop of Saint Andrews and Edinburgh, was the first residential Scottish cardinal since David Beaton, before the Reformation; Baggio was only the second cardinal in the history of the diocese of Cagliari, the first having been Diego Gregorio Cadello (archbishop, May 27, 1798; cardinal, January 17, 1803; died, June 5, 1807); and Tabera Araoz was the first cardinal in Pamplona since the sixteenth century, although several cardinals had been administrators of the diocese, or had held it *in commendam*, in the Renaissance, notably Cesare Borgia, from 1491 to 1493.

26. *Cum gravissima*, motu proprio of April 16, 1962. Once John Paul II dispensed de Lubac from the requirement of episcopal consecration, he was created a cardinal on February 2, 1983.

27. Liénart (born February 7, 1884); Tisserant (born March 24, 1884); and Gonçalves Cerejeira (born November 29, 1888).

28. Feltin (born May 15, 1883); de Arriba y Castro (born April 8, 1886); McIntyre (born June 25, 1886); Frings (born February 6, 1887); Caggiano (born January 30, 1889); de Vasconcellos Motta (born July 16, 1890); and Ottaviani (born October 29, 1890).

29. Giobbe (born January 10, 1880); da Costa Nuñes (born March 15, 1880); Cicognani (born February 24, 1883); Cento (born August 10, 1883); Heard (born February 24, 1884); di Jorio (born July 18, 1884); Bacci (born September 4, 1885); Browne (born May 6, 1887); Larraona (born November 13, 1887); Forni (born January 10, 1889); Garribi y Rivera (born June 30, 1889); and Roberti (born July 7, 1889).

30. Grano (born October 14, 1887); Beltrami (born January 17, 1889); and Callori di Vignale (born December 15, 1890).

31. Beran (May 17, 1969); Fasolino (August 13, 1969); Urbani (September 18, 1969); Tatsuo Doi (February 21, 1970); Pizzardo (August 1, 1970); Aloisi Masella (Sepetmber 30, 1970); Cushing (November 2, 1970); and Gut (December 8, 1970).

32. The electors who died were de Barros Camara (February 18, 1971, the 25th anniversary of his cardinalate); Agagianian (May 16, 1971); Quiroga y Palacios (December 7, 1971); and Angelo Dell'Acqua (August 27, 1972). The

superannuated cardinals were Bacci (January 20, 1971); Browne (March 31, 1971); Callori di Vignale (August 10, 1971); Tisserant (February 21, 1972); Garribi y Rivera (May 27, 1972); Paolo Giobbe (August 14, 1972); Cento (January 13, 1973); and Liénart (February 15, 1973).

33. Those who became superannuated in this period were Journet (born January 26, 1891); Parente (born February 16, 1891); Martin (born August 9, 1891); Lercaro (born October 26, 1891); Concha (born November 7, 1891); Slipyj (born February 17, 1892); Mindszenty (born March 29, 1892); Lefèbvre and Zerba (both born April 15, 1892); Jaeger (born September 23, 1892); and Barbieri (born October 12, 1892).

34. Luciani at Venice, after Urbani who died December 18, 1969; Ribeiro at Lisbon, after Gonçalves Cerejeira, who had resigned in 1971; Brandão Vilela at São Salvador do Bahia, to replace Araújo Sales, who was transferred to Rio de Janeiro in 1971; Muñoz Duque at Bogotá, after Concha, who resigned July 29, 1972; Pappalardo at Palermo, following Carpino, who resigned on October 17, 1970, to retrun to the curia as referencary of the Congregation of Bishops; González Martín at Toledo, succeeding Enrique y Tarancón, who was transferred to Madrid on December 4, 1971; Gouyot at Toulouse, the second successor of Saliège, who had died November 5, 1956; Manning at Los Angeles, following McIntyre, whose resignation became effective January 21, 1970; Salazar Lopez at Guadalajara, after Garribi y Rivera, who had resigned in 1969 and died May 27, 1972; Medeiros at Boston, succeeding Cushing, whose resignation was accepted on Sepetmber 8, 1970, and who had died on the following November 2; Arns at São Paulo, following Agnello Rossi, who was transferred to Rome as the prefect of the Congregaton for the Evalgelization of Peoples (the old Propaganda Fide, before *Regimini*) on October 22, 1970; and Freeman at Sydney, succeeding Gilroy, who resigned July 9, 1971.

35. The primier cardinals were Knox at Melbourne, whose creation gave Australia three cardinals; Aponte Martinez at San Juan, whose appointment was calculated to be an increase in the representation from the United States; Primatesta at Cordoba, Argentina; Yoshigoro Taguchi at Osaka was appointed to fill the place of Tatsuo Doi of Tokyo, who had died on February 21, 1970; and, finally, Trochta at Litomerice, whose name had been held *in petto*

since 1969, filled the place of Beran for Czecholslovakia (died May 17, 1969). Barcelona had not had a cardinal-archbishop since the death of Salvador Casanas y Pagés in 1908; Wroclaw had not had a cardinal since, in the days when it was Breslau, the death of Melchior von Diepenbrock in 1853; and Mainz, whose holder for centuries was an archbishop-prince-elector of the Holy Roman Empire, had seen no cardinals since the Renaissance.

36. Otunga of Nairobi, Kemya; Biayenda of Brazzaville, Republic of the Congo; Cordeiro of Karachi, Pakistan; and Taofinu'u of the diocese of Apia in Western Samoa.

37.Pignedoli had been nuncio in Bolivia (1950-1954), Venezuela (1954-1955), delegate to Central and West Africa (1960-1964) and, finally, to Canada (1964-1977). He also had been Montini's auxiliary at Milan (1955-1960). Between 1967 and 1973, he served in the curia as the secretary of the Congregation for the Evangelization of Peoples. Raimondi had served as secretary of the nunciature in Guatemala (1938-1942); auditor of the Apostolic delegation in Washington (1942-1949), where he became a confidant of Cicognani; first consultor and chargé d'affaires at the internunciature in India (1949-1953); nuncio to Haiti (1954-1967); and the Apostolic delegate to the United States, in succession to Vagnozzi, from 1967 to 1973. Mozoni, after early service in Ottawa, London, and Lisbon, became nuncio to Bolivia (1954-1958), Argentina (1958-1969), and Brazil (1969-1973).

38. Poletti had been auxiliary bishop of Novaro (1958-1967) and then archbishop of Spoleto (1967-1969) before being summoned to Rome as Dell'Acqua's deputy. When the latter died, August 27, 1972, Poletti began to discharge the duties of the cardinal-vicar of Rome; now he bore the title as well as the responsibilities. Philippe, a Dominican theologian, became a professor at the Angelicum in 1935, and, after several minor curial staff appointments, secretary of the Congregation for the Doctrine of the Faith in 1967. Palazzini was placed in a number of positions in academic administration in his early career; became professor of moral theology at the Lateran University; and then secretary of the Congregation of the Clergy (formerly the Congregation of the Council) from 1958 to 1973. Antonelli, a Franciscan, originally was an historian who taught church history (1928-1932) and then Christian archaeology (1932-

1965) at the Antonianum, where he also served as rector from 1937 to 1943, and again from 1953 to 1959. In 1965, he was made secretary of the Congregation of Rites, and then transferred to the same rank in the Congregation for the Causes of Saints four years later.

39. The dead electors included one more creation of Pius XII, McGuigan (died April 9, 1974); and three creations of John XXIII: Ferretto (died March 17, 1973); Santos (died September 3, 1973); and Antoniutti, the conservative candidate in the conclave of 1963 (died August 1, 1974). By contrast, eight of the electors who died were creations of Paul VI: McKeefry (died November 18, 1973); Kominek (died March 10, 1974); Trochta (died April 6, 1974); Daniélou (died May 20, 1974); Tabera Araoz (died June 13, 1975); Raimondi (died June 24, 1975); Rakotomalala (died November 1, 1975); and Heenan (died November 7, 1975).

40. They included three of Pius XII's cardinals: de Arriba y Castro (died March 8, 1973); Mindszenty (died May 6, 1975); and Feltin (died September 27, 1975). Six were creations of John XXIII: Lefèbvre (died April 2, 1973); Larraona (died May 7, 1973); Heard (died September 16, 1973); Cicognani (died December 17, 1973); Concha (died September 18, 1975); and Forni (died February 27, 1976). Seven were cardinals created by Paul VI: Zerba (died July 11, 1973); Beltrami (died December 13, 1973); Meouchi (became superannuated April 1, 1974; and died January 11, 1975); Jaeger (died April 1, 1975); Journet (died April 15, 1975); Martin (died January 24, 1976); and Grano (died April 2, 1976).

41. One more of Pius XII's cardinals, Gilroy (born January 22, 1896); three of John XXIII's cardinals: Confalonieri (born July 25, 1893); Marella (born January 25, 1895); and Traglia (born April 3, 1895). Only one of Paul VI's creations had become superannuated, Miranda y Gómez (born December 19, 1895).

42. Aramburu became archbishop of Buenos Aires on April 22, 1975, after Caggiano finally relinquished his see. His local power and influence had made him too valuable to remove until he was eighty-six. Sin in Manila replaced Santos (died September 3, 1973); Delargey in Wellington, after McKeefry (died November 18, 1973); Lékai as archbishop of Esztergom and primate of Hungary after the death of Mindszenty (died May 6, 1975), who also was too important a symbol to remove from his official see; Hume at Westminster, after Heenan (died November 7,

1975); Razafimahatratra at Tananrive, following Rakotomalala (died November 1, 1975); and Baum at Washington, after O'Boyle had resigned—Baum was appointed to the see on March 5, 1973, as a part of the official business of the consistory for creating cardinals on that date.

43. Died June 24, 1975.

44. Opilio Rossi, a native of New York City, although an Italian citizen, had been nuncio to Ecuador (1953–1959), Chile (1959–1961), and Austria (1961–1976). Sensi was nuncio to Costa Rica (1955), apostolic delegate to Jerusalem (1956–1962), nuncio to Ireland (1962–1967), and nuncio to Portugal (1967–1976).

45. The three electors were Döpfner (died July 24, 1976), a creation of John XXIII, and Biayenda (died March 23, 1977) and Conway (died April 17, 1977), both of whom were elevated by Paul VI. The two nonvoting cardinals who died were Lercaro (died October 18, 1976), a creation of Pius XII, and da Costa Nuñes (died November 30, 1976), a creation of John XXIII.

46. The first was Juan Soldevilla y Romero, archbishop of Saragossa, who was ambushed and shot by Spanish anarchists on June 24, 1923. He, in turn, was the first cardinal to die with great violence since the execution of Cardinal Carrlo Carafa in 1561.

47. Antonelli (born July 14, 1896) and O'Boyle (born July 18, 1896), both of whom were elevated by Paul VI.

48. He died May 21, 1995. He became the first dean of the College to resign that office, although one other had been suspended. In 1517, following the discovery of the conspiracy to murder Leo X, the dean of the time, Raffaele Riario, great-nephew of Pope Sixtus IV (1472–1484) was deprived of his active cardinalate after it was revealed that he was deeply involved in the plot. After paying an enormous fine, he was reinstated and died July 9, 1521.

49. The three who had died were Staffa (died August 7, 1977); Yoshigoro Taguchi (died February 23, 1978); and Violardo (died March 17, 1978). The cardinal who had passed his eightieth birthday was Lawrence Joseph Shehan of Baltimore, who was born on March 18, 1898, and not on the following December 18, as is often stated.

50. Gonçalves Cerejeira, the last creation of Pius XI, died on August 2, 1977. Two creations of John XXIII died, Roberti on July 16, 1977, and Traglia on November 22, 1977; and one of Pius XII, Gilroy, on October 21, 1977.

VI. The Pauline Elections

I. John Paul I

The consistory of June 27, 1977, was the last step Paul took in his complex and difficult plan to restructure the curia, the hierarchy, and the cardinalate. He had achieved nearly all of his program for curial and hierarchial reform without generating widespread effective opposition from either the curia or the hierarchy. Like so many other successful policies of his reign, achieving these reforms had been rather like, as one commentator put it, "giving a haircut to a drowsy lion."

From that time forward, increasingly weakened from the infirmities of age, Paul slowed the pace of his government. So few initiatives continued that rumors began to circulate that he also would resign his see on his eightieth birthday to allow another to assume control of the absolute monarchy he had created. There was no truth to these tales, although they received wide coverage in the press. When his eighty-first year began, on September 26, without sudden change, the rumors died away, overtaken by events.

In fact, it was a surprise that Paul lived to be eighty. The middle child of three brothers, he was endowed from infancy with the weakest constitution, both physically and emotionally. As sometimes happens in families, it was the brightest and most intellectually active child who had the poorest health—both his elder brother, Ludovico (born May 8, 1896), and his younger, Francesco (born September 22, 1900), were seldom really ill. Battista, by contrast, was constantly at risk, especially from colds, influenzas, and other respiratory infections. From the first decade of his life, he had an annual winter bout with one or more of these conditions in almost every year until his death. At the same time, although he was comfortable with sixteen-hour workdays, he often stretched his physical capacities to their limits and paid the price for doing so in periodic bouts of depression and exhaustion. The worst of these came in 1935, when he collapsed from extreme overstrain in February. Ottaviani, then his immediate superior in the curia, sent him to the seaside resort of Nettuno, thirty miles south of Rome, for complete rest and restoration.[1] With his salary fully paid—a rare favor then among minor curial officials of the time—Montini remained in the first real quietude he had known in years until the following July. He would never again suffer so great a collapse, since he now knew the warning signs well enough, when they appeared, to restrict his pace slightly to prevent a total breakdown.

His first real challenge from the advancing years came in early 1967, when he began to show signs of an alarming enlargement of his prostate. The demands on his time, particularly from the work of the Synod of Bishops, caused him to postpone the necessary surgery again and again. In the late summer, he was catheterized as a consequence of his deteriorating condition, but still he insisted that he could not spare the time for the necessary surgery. The visit by Patriarch Athenagoras on October 26–28 finally pushed him to the edge of collapse. His condition so worsened that he had to cancel the address he was to have given to the closing session of the Synod on October 29. There was no thought of making Paul's condition public—*the pope is not sick until dead* is the Roman traditional truism—that vision of papal strength would not be shattered until John Paul II had to be rushed to the Gemelli when he was shot. Paul's principal physician, Dr. Mario Fontana, ordered a room in the palace to be readied as an operating theater. There, Dr. Pietro Valdoni, the urologist who had been a major medical figure in the last days of John XXIII, operated on the pope on November 4. Although the preparations for the operation and its performance had been conducted quietly, everybody in the Vatican knew the true state of affairs. The degree to which Paul was hated in the curia was revealed when the rumor began, and was amplified quickly, that the surgery had been a failure, that inoperable cancer had been discovered, and that the pope was only weeks, if not days, from death. In fact, Paul made a swift and remarkable recovery, his condition completely corrected, under the devoted care of Dr. Ugo Piazzi, a friend of forty years, whom Paul had called to care for him in the post-operative period. Paul began to renew his familiar pace at once. When he awoke from the anesthetic, he insisted on rising to walk six-and-a-half times around his library, precisely the distance and time it took him to say the rosary.

Paul, in spite of his surprising recuperative powers, remained largely bedridden until the end of the year. That incapacity did not prevent him from resuming his daily schedule of work within a few days, however. By December 23, he was well enough not only to meet for the second time with Lyndon Johnson but to have a stormy exchange with him over the conduct of the war in Vietnam. Johnson's visit left one particular lasting impression on the pope and his household, alike. He arrived by helicopter, landing in the Vatican gardens. This display of imperial power at first angered the pontifical court—the disturbance damaged a number of the arrangements in the garden severely, even though it was winter—but the practicality of arriving and leaving the Vatican with no need to consider Rome's proverbially bad traffic impressed itself at once. Soon, Paul himself began to travel near the city by the same means, especially when he went on his summer vacations to Castel Gandolfo.

Not long after he had recovered, Paul began to experience more and more pain from degenerative osteoarthritis, especially in his right knee. Over the next decade, this condition worsened. Eventually, he was substantially impaired in his movement, especially in his right knee. Although arthroplasty was now a well-established medical discipline, and a prosthesis was an option to cure the condition, Paul was considered too old and too delicate to withstand such surgery. By 1977, when he arose each day, it took him several minutes of concentrated effort to rest any weight on his right leg, and he was ordered by Dr. Fontana always to walk slowly and with deliberation. Nevertheless, the pope's condition was not critical. He had a daily regimen of medication for the condition, although some of the capsules provided by Fontana were homeopathic, which were perhaps not as effective as other, more standard, drugs might have been.

Twice in 1977, once in April and again in August, Paul had comparatively mild episodes of circulatory distress. Fontana regarded these with enough seriousness to add Digoxin to Paul's medications.

In 1978, his annual attack of influenza came in mid-March. By the evening of Tuesday, the fourteenth, he was so ill that his usual general audience on Wednesday had to be canceled. On Thursday, while he was still suffering greatly, came the news that his close friend, former prime minister Aldo Moro, had been kidnapped as he left his house in Rome by members of Italy's major terrorist group, the Red Brigade. Although Paul had himself barely escaped assassination on more than one occasion, and although he had lost others who were close to him to violence in the Fascist years, this event affected him deeply. He had first met Moro, and had become his friend, in the years of anti-Fascist activity when the future politician had become active in the Federazione Universitaria Cattolica (FUCI), Montini's principal cause in the years before the war. In those years, Montini also knew Eleonora Chiavarelli. When Moro married her, Montini became perhaps their closest family friend, on the same footing as a beloved uncle. He followed, and quietly supported, Moro's rise to greater and greater prominence in Italian politics. On December 5, 1963, Moro became prime minister, just five and a half months after Paul was elected pope. Juggling a difficult coalition, Moro led three successive ministries until June 5, 1968, giving Italy one of its longest periods of political stability since World War II. The Vatican's relations with Italy warmed to greater cordiality, of course.

All through the fifty-five day captivity of Moro, the pope was increasingly anxious. This period reached an apex on the evening of April 20, when Paul received a letter from his friend, forwarded to him by the Moro family. Couched in formal, stiff language, Moro's letter begged Paul for his personal intercession to secure his release. The pope's response was to move swiftly to intervene, but Villot, who had discussed the matter at length with the sitting prime minister, Giulio Andreotti, John XXIII's old friend, had learned that the position of the Italian government was that the pope should remain altogether outside the crisis. Were he to become involved, it would be an interference into the internal affairs of the Italian state. Paul was thwarted by the burden of being an independent monarch of a separate state, as codified in the Lateran treaties of 1929.

In the overnight hours between the twenty-first and twenty-second, Paul composed an open letter to the Red Brigade in which he appealed personally for Moro's release. The pope's letter was reproduced in hundreds of photocopies and widely distributed to the press. It was impossible for the kidnappers not to see it. But Paul's touching appeal was to no avail. Moro's body was discovered on May 9 in the trunk of a car that had been left in the paved connection between the Piazza del Gesu and the Via delle Botteghe Oscure. He had been shot more than a dozen times.

Now recovered from the flu, Paul himself conducted Moro's requiem on May 13 in Saint John Lateran, the pope's cathedral as bishop of Rome. The depth of Paul's feeling can be judged by his homily, in which he upbraided God for not protecting his old friend. It was the pope's last significant appearance on the world's stage.

The Moro affair left the pope both depressed and debilitated. Paul's two private secretaries, Pasquale Macchi, his man for years, and John Magee, who came in 1976, joined with Mario Fontana to urge the pope to begin his summer vacation at Castel Gandolfo a little earlier than usual, in order to give him more time for recuperation. Paul refused. The summer schedule would proceed exactly according to plan.

Promptly as scheduled, on the morning of Friday, July 14, the pope left the palace for the summer. When he came out into the Cortile di San Damaso for the short car ride to the helipad, he was surrounded briefly both by well-wishers from the curial staff and by the members of his household who would be making the journey to Castel Gandolfo by car. As Paul got into his car, Archbishop Giuseppe Caprio, Benelli's successor as the *sostituto* in the secretariat of state, bent over to wish him a fine vacation. Paul replied, "We go, but we do not know whether we will return—or how we will return." He already had persuaded himself that the end was near.

At Castel Gandolfo, Dr. Fontana visited Paul twice each day, once when he arose in the morning and again in the evening after dinner. His daily medications were augmented by periodic injections of vitamins, but otherwise his medical regimen was unaltered. Villot and his deputy, Caprio, mindful of the need for rest and quiet, minimized the number of papers he was brought to read or sign.

The gardeners at the villa had erected a set of awnings over some of the paths and, when the weather was not exceptionally hot or humid, Paul would take a short walk, leaning on the arm of either Monsignor Macchi or Father Magee, to relieve the pain in his right knee.

He was not isolated. He continued his smaller summer audiences on Wednesdays, holding the last one on August 2. And he received a number of callers who had been invited to meet with him in brief sessions—Lillian Carter, the mother of the American president, was among them.

During the last two weeks of July, Paul stayed entirely within the precincts of the villa, but on Tuesday, August 1, he suddenly decided to be driven to the nearby village of San Giuseppe di Frattocchie, so that he could pray at the tomb of his first patron and mentor, Cardinal Giuseppe Pizzardo, on the occasion of the eighth anniversary of the cardinal's death. Frattocchie stood for the whole history of Latium; it was the Latin Bovillæ, just at the sixth milestone of the ancient Via Appia, and it was the home of the Togliati Institute, a leading communist intellectual center in modern Italy. Why he chose that time and that circumstance to do this is conjectural; after all he and the cardinal had vehemently opposed each other many times in the years before Pizzardo's death in 1970 at the age of ninety-three. When he emerged from the memorial Mass, he told the small crowd of surprised villagers who had gathered quickly to see him that his own death could not be far away—in fact it would be less than a week.

Paul was driven back to Castel Gandolfo in an open car late in the afternoon. He had been seen to perspire freely during the memorial for Pizzardo, and now, as the temperature became cooler while he rode, he began to catch a chill. Following a physically exhausting day for him, it proved to be a turning point in his health.

On the morning of Thursday, August 3, the pope, even in his last days, continued to break tradition and precedent, by receiving, at 11:15, the newly installed president of Italy, Sandro Pertini. A blunt-spoken Socialist, Pertini had been elected Italy's head of state on July 8 and had taken his oath of office on the following day. One of the items of greatest importance on his agenda was to complete the renegotiation of the concordat of 1929. He asked for the audience to persuade Paul to intervene in the talks to move them forward with greater speed. It was meant to be a short official visit, but it turned into a long and rambling conversation of more than two and a half hours, much of which was about mutual friends. Pertini knew, and admired, Paul's brother, Senator Ludovico Montini, in spite of their opposing sides on almost every political question. Paul's old student associate from the 1930s, Franco Costa, was Pertini's cousin. Though obviously tired and strained, Paul relished this visit, and brushed Monsignor Macchi away several times when he entered the study to conclude the visit.

When he awakened on the fourth, he already had a fever. In his morning examination, Fontana concluded that this was caused by a bacterial infection of the bladder. He immediately began a course of antibiotics and ordered the pope to rest in bed for the remainder of the day. As the day wore on, Paul began to feel somewhat better. He insisted on getting up to take his evening meal in the usual way.

Paul never was a heavy eater, and in the last years of his life his meals often were very small. By late 1977, he was eating even less, possibly as a side effect of the Digoxin he was now taking for his heart. So, when he ate almost nothing on the evening of the fourth, that circumstance, in itself, caused no alarm. After eating, he watched a western on television with Father Magee, after which he said the rosary with his junior secretary and went to bed. Monsignor Macchi sat in a chair beside the bed and read to him passages from catechetical works by the French theologian, Jean Guitton, whose work he admired. Soon, he was asleep. It was the end of his last peaceful day.

At three o'clock in the morning of Saturday the fifth, the bell that connected Paul's bedroom with the other quarters in the papal apartments rang three times—it was Paul's signal that he needed help. When Macchi and Magee rushed into his bedroom, they found him sitting on the side of his bed, overcome with labored breathing. The two secretaries helped him into a chair and gave him oxygen that was on hand for just such an emergency. While Magee administered the oxygen, Macchi went to awaken Mario Fontana and bring him quickly to the pope. The pope told Fontana that his arthritis was exceptionally painful—it was a secondary effect of the pope's high fever, which had risen substantially since the doctor had seen him in the previous evening. The cystitis was worse. After a hurried examination, Paul returned to bed; there did not seem to be any immediate danger. The dosage of the antibiotics was increased, and Fontana telephoned Professor Fabio Prosperi, a leading urologist in Rome who had succeeded Pietro Valdoni as a consultant in this specialty. Prosperi agreed with the course of treatment Fontana had undertaken, and made himself available should there be later complications. Fontana also telephoned his chief subordinate in the Vatican Health Service, Dr. Renato Buzzonetti, and had him come to Castel Gandolfo for a round-the-clock medical watch.

There was no question that Paul would be unable to appear on Sunday for the recitation of the noon Angelus, so it was necessary to prepare some public statement about his condition. Fontana's first bulletin made no mention of either the cystitits or the resulting fever, and the text released by the Vatican was short:

> We have been advised that for some days the Holy Father has suf-fered from an acute worsening of his arthritis from which he has been suffering for some time. His personal physician, Mario Fontana, has advised him to take a few days of complete rest. Thus the pope will be unable to pray with the faithful on Sunday at Castel Gandolfo.

The pope rested quietly through most of Saturday. Although his condition seemed to stabilize, there was no real improvement. He finally drifted into sleep at about 11:30 P.M., after which those around him retired for the night. There was no watch with him in his bedroom; his condition still did not seem serious enough for that. The level of anxiety was high enough, however, that his immediate staff—Sister Giacomina, his housekeeper, Monsignor Macchi, Father Magee, and Dr. Fontana—were all clustered outside the bedroom door at 6:30 on the following morning, waiting to hear the ring of the pope's old alarm clock. A few moments after it sounded, they entered the room to find Paul awake and alert, but lying almost immobile in bed. His condition clearly had deteriorated during the night. Fontana's first examination of the morning revealed that the pope's temperature was now over 100° Fahrenheit, that his blood pressure was somewhat elevated, and that his pulse was weaker. In a shallow voice, Paul told Fontana that his knee was especially painful. Fontana decided to inject a heart stimulant and to begin an intravenous drip of antibiotics in a stronger effort to control the bladder infection that was sapping the pope's strength.

Macchi and Magee helped Paul to rise from his bed briefly, in order to allow Sister Giacomina and another nun on the housekeeping staff to change the sheets. During this brief interlude, Macchi mentioned that this day is the thirty-third anniversary of the bombing of Hiroshima. Paul replied that he intended to discuss the event in his remarks at the Angelus—he had forgotten that his public appearance had been canceled.

After he was returned to his bed, he fell again into a restless sleep, from which he awoke at about eleven o'clock. The shutters of his bedroom were closed against the midday heat and the curtains were drawn. He asked Macchi what time it was. When his secretary told him it was eleven, he glanced at his clock, saw that it said only 10:45, and remarked, "Look, my old clock is as tired as I am."

Soon afterward, Sister Giacomina brought him a small bowl of soup and a glass of fresh lemonade. Fontana helped the nun to sit Paul up in bed for this refreshment. While he sipped the lemonade, he was quite lucid and conversational, thanking all those around him for their care and concern for him.

A few moments later, he insisted on being helped to a chair, so that he could pray the Angelus at noon, even if it was in private and not shared with the pilgrims, as it usually was. As he was placed in the chair, he said: "On this great feast of the Transfiguration, I want to recite the Angelus for all the faithful of the Church." Though he had not used the papal "We," it was his pontifical voice that spoke; still the pope doing his spiritual duty.

After the prayers, he was again returned to bed, and again fell asleep. Although the pope had not worsened significantly since the morning, Pasquale Macchi thought, at last, that it was time to inform the necessary Vatican officials that the pope's condition was, in fact, grave. He did not make the calls himself, but rather followed the precise protocol of the situation by going downstairs in the villa to see Monsignor Jacques Martin, the prefect of the apostolic palace. Martin, later a cardinal himself, then telephoned Jean Villot, the cardinal-secretary of state, to pass on the latest information on the pope's circumstances. It was Villot who made similar calls to Caprio, his deputy; to Carlo Confalonieri, the dean of the College; Ugo Poletti, the cardinal-vicar of Rome; Ludovico Montini, the pope's brother; and Marco, the pope's nephew.

Finally, he telephoned the communist mayor of Rome, Giulio Carlo Argan, to ask him to provide police escorts at short notice for the cars that would take these men to Castel Gandolfo, if that should become necessary. The mayor wasted no time in sending the motorcycle police to the Piazza di San Pietro and to the homes of Ludovico and Marco Montini. Villot, no stranger to sudden death among his friends and family, ordered a car to wait for him, ready for the fastest possible trip to the papal villa.

In midafternoon, Paul awoke again. Fontana had returned to the bedroom at 2:00 P.M. and had watched the pope carefully during his most recent sleep. Now, he bent over the bed to take the pope's blood pressure, pulse, and temperature. For the first time, Fontana really was alarmed. Paul's pulse fluctuated wildly and his blood pressure was greatly elevated. He immediately administered an injection to try to reduce Paul's pulse to normal. He then used the bedside electric bell to call Sister Giacomina. Together, they helped the pope to sit up in bed, and then placed wet towels on his head and face to lower his temperature and gave him glasses of water to rehydrate him. All these traditional remedies, together with the injection, had a sudden and beneficial effect. Paul's heartbeat became regular, although weak; and his temperature dropped.

Mario Fontana hoped that the final crisis had now been passed, and he left the bedroom for a methodical conference about the next steps to take. Joining him were Macchi, Magee, and the prefect of the palace, Jacques Martin.

While still in the midst of their discussions, the electric bell sounded again, pressed this time by Sister Giacomina who had just seen the pope suddenly enter another crisis. The four men rushed to the bedroom, where they found Paul highly flushed, his hair matted with perspiration. Again, Paul responded well to sudden treatment and within a few moments he was calm and lucid. He asked that Macchi say Mass for him at six o'clock in the little chapel adjacent to the bedroom. He then told Martin to telephone his brother and nephew to ask them to come to him. He then settled back on his pillows quietly. After a few minutes, he again spoke, almost inaudibly now. Magee bent over him to catch the words. "What do you want, Holiness." "*Caro*, a little patience," was the reply.

But it was Villot whom Martin called first, and then the relatives. Villot's plan was activated, and, a few minutes after 5:30, the escorted cars were on their way to Castel Gandolfo. Sunday evening's light traffic made the journeys easier. Ludovico Montini entered the gates of the villa at 5:55.

Within a few minutes, all of those who had been summoned were outside the bedroom door. Macchi briefed them quickly on the two crises that had taken place earlier in the day and then asked them to take only a moment or two with the pope before going into the adjacent chapel for Macchi's Mass.

While the others were in the chapel, with its door opened to the bedroom, Magee remained at Paul's side, holding his hand. The pope followed the Mass alertly and with great care, receiving communion in both kinds. Just as Macchi ended the Mass, Paul suddenly gripped Magee's hand and was convulsed so powerfully that the secretary thought he might fall out of his bed. Fontana performed a quick examination and diagnosis, and then told those in the apartments that Paul had suffered a massive heart attack.

Cardinal Villot then bent over the pope to ask him if he would like to be anointed now. "Yes, quickly, quickly," Paul said faintly. When the cardinal had completed the sacrament, the pope murmured *grazie*, tried to trace a blessing with his right hand, and then closed his eyes. Villot stepped back to allow Fontana to perform another rapid examination. When Fontana had finished, he told those in the room that the pope was still alive, but just barely.

At about 7:35, Paul opened his eyes briefly. They were glazed and un-seeing. Then he closed them again, and slipped into unconsciousness. Monsignor Martin realized suddenly that there had been no bulletin for the public for many hours. He left the bedroom to telephone Father Romeo Panciroli, the secretary of the Pontifical Commission for Social Communications, the only prelate even remotely connected with the press whom he could reach on a Sunday evening in August. It was Panciroli who released the short announcement that the pope had suffered a heart attack and was semi-conscious.

A little after nine o'clock, Paul awakened again. He began to speak, but his voice was so faint and disconnected that no one could understand him. Macchi signaled everyone present for absolute silence as he bent over his dying master. Paul was reciting, again and again, the opening phrase of the Lord's Prayer.

By 9:30, Paul was unconscious again. While the others knelt in the bed-room and recited the prayers for the dying, Fontana monitored Paul's wan-ing life closely. At 9:41, he turned away from his patient and said, "The pope is dead."

Every account given later by those who were present in the room fo-cused on the next event. As soon as Fontana finished speaking, the little Polish alarm clock that Paul had bought in Warsaw, more than a half cen-tury before, suddenly began to ring.

Villot, as camerlengo of the Church, now assumed immediate control. Paul had prepared him well for the office. As secretary of state under the new rules proclaimed in *Regimini*, Villot knew every nuance and detail of Paul's government; as camerlengo, he would use his knowledge and exper-tise to rule the Church until a successor could be elected. This was pre-cisely the arrangement that Pius XI had made for Pacelli in 1939; the difference was that Villot himself was not a candidate for the throne.

Villot had noticed earlier that the pope was not wearing his Fisherman's Ring when he died. That ring had to be found at once, for a later ceremo-nial destruction in the general congregation of cardinals—together with the official papal seals for documents. Recovering the ring was not just a preparation for a medieval ceremony of no real significance. It was the de-vice with which popes authenticated documents they themselves issued directly. In the hands of another, it could be used to create back-dated doc-uments in the late pope's name. In fact, it had been used in just that way on a number of occasions centuries before, which was the reason for securing and destroying it publicly. Villot peremptorily told Macchi to find the ring at once.

The camerlengo's first decisions had to be about the disposition of

Paul's body and the first stages of planning for the funeral. For this, he had only two short texts to guide him. The first, in the election constitution *Romano Pontifici Eligendo*, was as vague as Pius XII's similar specification in 1945:

> If the Roman Pontiff dies outside the city, the Sacred College of Cardinals shall take all the measures necessary to assure that the corpse is transferred in a worthy and fitting manner to the Vatican Basilica. (I, v, 29).

The second was a short codicil that Paul had added to his will on July 14, 1973: "I want my funeral to be as simple as possible and I want neither tomb nor special monument. A few offerings (prayers and good works)."

Villot tried to keep to these brief prescriptions as closely as possible. He ordered Paul's body to be suitably robed and placed in the apartments of the Swiss Guards for a brief public viewing, first by the usual invited dignitaries and then by the crowd that was sure to gather.

He then returned to the Vatican to seal the pope's apartments and to dispatch the *intimatio* to the members of the College. Later, he would issue an order for the first general congregation to meet on the evening of Monday, August 7. This delay of half a day in holding the congregation was caused by the fact that all of Italy was just at the beginning of the *ferragosto*, that long vacation which is nearly inviolable. Only four of the one hundred thirty cardinals were in the vicinity of Rome when the pope died, three of whom had been at his bedside. Villot scheduled the evening meeting to allow cardinals who were vacationing in villas and towns outside the city to have time to reach the Vatican.

On Monday morning, just before ten o'clock, the official representatives of the governments of Italy and Rome gathered at the villa. Escorted to the pope's bier by Dino Monduzzi, the regent of the pontifical household and Martin's principal subordinate, were Sandro Pertini, Italy's president and Paul's last official caller; Amintore Fanfani, president of the senate; Giulio Andreotti, the prime minister; Virginio Rognoni, minister of the interior; and Giulio Carlo Argan, the mayor of Rome. Perhaps it was especially fitting that these men should begin the ceremonies of Paul's departure, since they were nearly all on the left of Italian politics—Argan was a communist—and it was the opening to the left which had formed the basis for Paul's foreign policy throughout his reign. Ludovico and Marco Montini also were present. After the invited guests had left, the doors to the villa were opened to the public at ten o'clock. During the day, about thirty thousand people came to the first viewing.

When the first meeting of the general congregation finally convened in the Sala Bologna, Villot found himself trumped by Carlo Confalonieri, the eighty-five-year-old cardinal-bishop of Ostia and dean of the College. Paul's rules had taken away his vote in the conclave, but his right to preside at the general congregations had not been addressed in any of Paul's prescriptions for the College of Cardinals. Moreover, the dean was not only as intellectually sharp as he had ever been, he also was the most knowledgeable and experienced man in the world on the subject of conclaves—his first involvement with the institution coming in 1922, when he had been Ratti's secretary and conclavist. He was the only man alive who had been inside four conclaves, two of them as an elector. And Confalonieri had his candidate, whose fortunes he wanted to improve. Villot was not sure how to proceed in these circumstances, but he gave way with good grace to the presidency of the dean. Fifteen cardinals had been able to reach the Vatican from places outside Rome by Monday evening, so the first meeting had nineteen participants.

In a firm voice, Confalonieri read to them the first part of Paul's election constitution, as he was required to do, and then he administered the oath of secrecy to the cardinals, again according to Paul's order. The cardinals decided to hold Paul's funeral and burial at 6:00 P.M. on Saturday, August 12. This was, perhaps, an unwise decision, since it required Paul's body to be above ground for almost six full days after his death. The date was chosen to allow the greatest possible time for remote cardinals to arrive for it. In addition, they hoped that the abbreviated embalming process that Paul's body would receive on Monday night would prevent any of the embarrassment that had ensued in 1958, when Pius XII's corpse had begun to decay so quickly after his death. The weather was hot, but not so oppressive as it usually was in August, so the general congregation risked the long delay. The rest of the schedule fell into place from the original decision. Paul body's would remain at Castel Gandolfo until Wednesday evening, when it would be moved to Saint Peter's. Thursday and Friday would be the times of public viewing, with the funeral to take place on Saturday evening, beginning at 6:00. The funeral itself would be unique in the history of the modern Church. With the pope's closed coffin before them on the steps of the basilica, the cardinals, with Confalonieri presiding, would hold the ceremonies in the piazza, to accommodate the largest possible crowd. The nine days of funeral commemorations would begin on Sunday, the thirteenth, and continue through the twentieth.

After this decision, the cardinals deferred other business until the next meeting. When they again met on Tuesday morning, the congregation chose to open the conclave on the evening of Friday, August 25—the last possible day permitted under the rules of *Romano Pontifici Eligendo*. Villot, who was not well-liked by the Vatican's staff or by the Romans, simply because he was a Frenchman, now became the subject of a cascade of nasty gossip. It was said that he delayed the opening of the conclave for as long as possible in order to enjoy his powers for as much time as he could. Many of the bitterest comments came from the minor ranks of the Vatican staff who were charged with the arrangement for the conclave. They resented having to stay throughout almost all of the month of August—Rome's worst summer month—without any chance of even a part of their traditional vacations. Their complaints were taken up eagerly by many in the press, who had similar thought of being trapped for most of a month inside the sweltering confines of the city.

The reality was much plainer. Most of the cardinals really did not know each other and were unfamiliar with the evolution of the *prattiche*. The early general congregations, attended almost entirely by experienced curial cardinals and Italian ordinaries, thought that the newer cardinals, especially those from the Third World, most of whom were completely unfamiliar with Rome and the Vatican, needed time to adjust to Rome and to get acquainted with one another before they were plunged into the actual business of electing a new pope. Of course, they were not unmindful that the greater the time allotted for the *prattiche*, the more time they would have to influence the less experienced electors.

By this time, the number of electors who would participate in the conclave was becoming clear. In Boston, at the Tufts Medical Center, Cardinal John Joseph Wright released the notice he already had sent to Villot. He would be unable to attend. He was recovering from an operation on his leg muscles and would remain in the hospital for cataract surgery as soon as he had recovered sufficiently from the first operation. Bolesław Filipiak, the former dean of the Rota, also was too ill to participate. He would be absent from the second conclave of 1978, as well, and died in Poznan on October 12. Villot assumed that Valerian Gracias, the cardinal of Bombay and one of the four cardinals created by Pius XII who was still eligible to vote, would not attend. He was known to be in the last stages of terminal cancer. The message which confirmed this expectation was received on Friday, the eleventh. On Monday, September 11, he died. It seemed that one hundred twelve electors, the greatest number in history, would choose Paul's successor. There would be three cardinals created by Pius XII, for whom this would be the third election, and eight others created by John XXIII. The remaining one hundred one would be electing their first pope. These figures show, again, the great effect Paul's reforms had on the College in only fifteen years.

Among the visitors who came to Castel Gandolfo on Tuesday were two men who had played leading parts in the life and pontificate of Paul VI. Cardinal Sergio Pignedoli had been at Paul's side for decades, first in the secretariat of state, then as his auxiliary in Milan, and finally again in the curia, as the president of the Secretariat for Non-Christians—a Vatican office near to Paul's heart. While the *prattiche* had not yet started, Pignedoli already was planning a major campaign to secure the throne for himself. It was not merely personal ambition that drove him, but rather a desire to see Paul succeeded by someone who would maintain and expand the initiative the pope had begun. Pignedoli regarded himself as the one candidate who could ensure that Paul's pontificate would be a beginning and not a conclusion to the wide-ranging reforms he had conducted.

By contrast, Paul's *delfino*, Giovanni Benelli, had no intention of trying to secure the crown for himself. Brash and overbearing at times, he was still widely respected as the man who had been closest personally to Paul for most of the years of the reign. He also was preparing a campaign for the conclave, but not for himself. Paul had sent him to Florence with the cardinalate to make him a deliberate outsider, a man of pastoral experience— even though small and recent—who could influence the majority of the other electors who belonged to the same group of cardinals that he now did. In fact, many of Paul's creations knew Rome and Paul VI through the eyes of Benelli, who had met or conversed with dozens of them in his capacity as Paul VI's facilitator. However little many of the new cardinals knew about the procedures and pattern of conclaves, they knew that Benelli, in both a political and a filial way, could speak for the dead pope. This general attitude gave Benelli a degree of influence that no other cardinal had possessed in decades—not even Montini in 1963. Moreover, in the rivalry between the curial cardinals and their ordinarial brothers, the fact that no one in Rome had thought to inform Benelli of the seriousness of Paul's condition in the last two days of his life, was regarded by some cardinals as a deliberate insult, which brought even more interest to what Benelli would have to say about the coming election.

At Wednesday's meeting, Paul's ring and seals were defaced, after which the cardinals adjourned early to prepare themselves for the ceremony of receiving Paul's body at Saint Peter's later in the day.

Meanwhile, at Castel Gandolfo, the pope's body was made available for viewing again on Tuesday and Wednesday, after which it was readied for the journey back to Saint Peter's on Wednesday evening. The plan that Villot had chosen, and which had been approved by the general congregation, was a modification of that which had been used for Pius XII in 1968—he had been the only other pope to die there, in spite of the fact that the villa had been a papal summer retreat since the time of Urban VIII

(1623–1644). On Wednesday evening, a closed coffin containing Paul's body was placed in a motor-hearse for the fifteen-mile trip to Rome. After a brief stop at the cathedral of Saint John Lateran for a recitation of the prayers for the dead, the corpse arrived at the Vatican just as the last sunlight faded from the piazza. The crowds who have turned out to see the pope's body pass were much smaller than those in 1958, thinned on this occasion by the combination of the *ferragosto* and the unhappiness many Italians felt at the way Paul had remolded the Church.

On Thursday and Friday, the doors of Saint Peter's were opened to the public at 7:00 A.M., and closed at 8:00 P.M. On each day, about a hundred thousand people passed through the great church for the public viewing, a much smaller number than had come to see the last of John XXIII. The most notable departure from the custom at such former events was that the great catafalque which had elevated the bodies of Pius XII and John XXIII had been discarded in favor of a much smaller and lower one, in keeping with Paul's desire for modesty. The exposure of the body had brought ravages, in spite of the injections of embalming fluid on Monday night. By Friday, the people could see some deformity of the face. Fontana told Villot that the coffin would have to be closed early, simply as a matter of decorum if for no other reason.

While these public ceremonies continued, more and more planes landed bearing cardinals coming to Rome for the election. On Thursday, August 10, the number of cardinals who attended the fourth general congregation rose to forty-three. Two days later, in the meeting of the congregation before the pope's funeral, there were more than a hundred present. A typical arrival was Albino Luciani, the patriarch of Venice. He left his see at six o'clock in the morning of the tenth and, by that evening, was installed with the Augustinians at their convent of Santa Monica, at 25 Via del Sant'Uffizio, near the *bracchio Costantino* of Bernini's colonnade.[3] Also staying there was Cardinal James Darcy Freeman, archbishop of Sydney.

Perhaps the most harrowing journey was that of Samoa's cardinal, Pio Taofinu'u. On Sunday, August 6, just as Paul was in his last hours, the cardinal was travelling by canoe to one of the outlying islands of his diocese to say Mass. On landing, a wave tossed the canoe and upset the cardinal. As he gathered his footing, he was stabbed in the foot by a jagged piece of coral. With his foot hastily bandaged, and limping painfully, he learned by radio telephone that Paul had died. He returned to Apia, again by canoe, and then by plane to New Zealand, and then onward with connecting flights to Rome. During the thirty-hour trip, his foot became badly infected, so that he arrived for the election feverish and in real anguish. He was taken immediately to the hospital, where relieving surgery was performed on his foot. Two weeks later, when the conclave began, he was still limping painfully along, but he declined to make an application to be attended by a conclavist during the election.

On Friday evening, the Vatican announced that the hours for public viewing would be extended to Saturday. On that morning, for six more hours, the doors were opened again.

Each day after the normal business, the cardinals in the general congregation received the traditional delegations which came to express their condolences. On Saturday morning, there was another departure from the custom of papal funerals. The cardinals received representatives from other Christian churches. After their presentation, Confalonieri returned an address of thanks for their presence. His short, quite ecumenical, speech signaled the completion of another cycle in the history of the Catholic church in this century. When Ratti was elected Pope Pius XI in 1922, Confalonieri had been present during the wrangling over whether or not to open the doors to the balcony that faced outward into the piazza for the pope's first blessing. Now, fifty-six years later, he spoke to a varied collection of men who represented nearly all of the major non-Catholic churches in the world. The doors had been opened fully in a way that not even John XXIII could have dreamed. The outlook for reintegration of all Christians in one community was not rosy, but, at least, Christians were talking to one another, however formally and stiffly. And Rome was at the center of the conversation.

Shortly after noon on Saturday, the doors of the basilica were closed. At 2:00, the plain inner coffin was closed. At 5:00, twelve *sediari*, the men who traditionally bore the pope on the *sedia gestatoria*, carried the coffin out of Saint Peter's and placed in on a large oriental carpet which covered the front steps. Promptly at six, one hundred three cardinals concelebrated the requiem with Confalonieri at an altar that had been set up in the piazza. The whole ceremony was televised to every part of the world—and the commentators drew attention to invited guests of special significance, not just state representatives, like the delegation from the United States that included Senator Edward Kennedy and Mrs. Rosalynn Carter, but also to men such as Nikodim, the metropolitan of Leningrad, who represented the Russian Orthodox Church. The main liturgy was in Latin, but special prayers for the dead were offered in other ancient and exotic languages as well. Antoine Pierre Khoraiche, the Maronite patriarch of Antioch, in his Eastern vestments, offered prayers in both Arabic and Aramaic.

During the ceremony, Cardinal Paul Yü Pin, the exiled archbishop of Nanking, suddenly became ill and had to withdraw. He was taken back to the convent that was his temporary residence in Rome and put to bed.

At the conclusion of the requiem, Paul's coffin was carried back into the basilica. A small group of guests, including the Montinis, watched while the nesting of the two other coffins was completed and then they descended into the crypt where Paul was entombed in an excavated grave only about a hundred feet from the resting place of John XXIII. Following the schedule used in 1963, the *sampietrini* worked all night to prepare the tomb for public viewing on the following morning. At 7:00 A.M., the public was admitted to the crypt.

Later on Sunday morning, the seventh general congregation received the foreign dignitaries who had come to Rome for the funeral, including Rosalynn Carter, after which it adjourned for the day.

During these days, the first phases of the *prattiche* finally were under way. Most of these meetings and telephone conversations were undocumented and their precise exchanges will never be known. A few have been reported, but not enough of the Roman activity was observed to make a complete reconstruction possible.

As early as the evening of the ninth, after Paul's body had been brought to Saint Peter's, Agnello Rossi, the Brazilian cardinal who had been Paul VI's last prefect of the Congregation for the Evangelization of Peoples, came to the Via della Conciliazione to call on Pericle Felici, the archdeacon of the College and the prefect of the Apostolic Signature. Rossi was, in effect, an emissary from Pignedoli, sent to inquire whether Felici would support the latter's candidacy as a means of prolonging the policies of Paul VI. Felici, who had been the secretary of the Second Vatican Council, and also was close to Paul, is said to have rejected the proposal out of hand.

Some European cardinals did not even remain in Rome in the days after the funeral. Many went home for a few more days of pastoral work, others retreated to healthful country places in Italy to conduct their further negotiations by telephone. One of the latter was Leo Josef Suenens, the archbishop of Malines-Brussels. The leading figure on the left in the council, he also was exceptionally friendly with Giovanni Benelli, who had acted so often as a conduit of information for him from the pope, and from him to the papal ear. Together, by telephone, they began to form their campaign for the conclave.

In Rome from the eighth to the evening of the sixteenth, and then in Florence until shortly before the conclave, Benelli did not have to reach far to find cardinals who were eager to have his opinion and, indeed, to be swayed by his views. The telephone calls began almost as soon as Paul had died, and increased in number and duration almost every day. Giovanni

Benelli was going to be the grand elector of the conclave of 1978, whether he wished to be or not—and he did wish to be.

Benelli's search for a candidate began with the question of whether there was to be another Italian pope. The demographics of the College were now such that almost any European who became a favorite, and most Latin Americans, too, might be able to reach the throne. Benelli determined, however, that the time for a break from tradition of such magnitude had not yet arrived. He would support an Italian cardinal. The next issue became: for which cardinal would he campaign? It could not be a curial official, not even one Paul relied upon fully, like Pignedoli or Sebastiano Baggio. The residential archbishops who made up the vast majority of the College would insist on a pope who had, to some degree, experiences which paralleled their own.

That basic assurance had to be there for any cardinal to achieve two-thirds-plus-one of the votes for the papal chair. The population from which the next pope must come was, therefore, nine, or rather eight, since Benelli himself would not be a candidate. This was not because he did not desire the papacy—he did hope that he might one day ascend the throne—but he was too pragmatic to flatter himself. He was only fifty-seven years old and, if elected, he might have a reign of more than twenty years—not a pleasing prospect, since his election would mean both that most of the cardinals would never vote in another conclave and that the essentials of Paul's policies, no matter how much admired, would remain in place for years to come.

Then, if not Benelli himself, who among the remaining eight? Siri, the archconservative, was out of the question. Poma was despised by several vocal cardinals for his too-eager willingness to unseat Lercaro at Bologna, so he could not be made to seem a reformer in the "true spirit" of Vatican II. Unless a deadlock in the conclave forced a turn to a compromise candidate, Ermenegildo Florit, Benelli's predecessor at Florence, probably was too old at seventy-seven; age also struck against Giovanni Colombo at Milan (75) and Michele Pellegrino (74) who had already resigned as archbishop of Turin.[4] The same questions about youth probably also made Salvatore Pappalardo (59), archbishop of Palermo, not an easy candidate to elect. So that left two: Corrado Ursi (70), archbishop of Naples, and Albino Luciani (65), the patriarch of Venice.

Benelli considered his two possibilities carefully. Both were simple pastors in the best model of John XXIII—indeed, John had consecrated Luciani a bishop and Paul had appointed him to Roncalli's old chair at Venice. Ursi was, perhaps, the more forceful and outgoing personality, but he also was older and too "southern" for many of the other Italians—he was a native of Andria, near Bari; it had been centuries since there had been a Pugliese on the throne.

So, after some careful deliberation about the chances of each of them, Benelli chose Luciani as his candidate, by a process of elimination. Benelli's choice of Luciani was the result of reasoning from a strictly political basis. He hardly knew the patriarch, except by reputation, and he knew nothing about Luciani's private personality or about his health. Had he known even a little, he almost certainly would never have chosen him as the man who would be pope—Luciani was shy and retiring in the presence of the powerful, although he often was friendly and open with people of common backgrounds, like himself; and he was in very, very poor health.

How much Benelli discussed his thinking with the dean of the College, Carlo Confalonieri, is unknown. Perhaps they did not speak of specific candidates at all. If so, the dean seems to have followed almost precisely the same path of reasoning to determine that Luciani would be his candidate, too. The dean's familiarity with the patriarch of Venice was likewise professional and not personal, but it extended over a much longer period of time than Benelli's. Confalonieri had been the prefect of the Congregation of Bishops when Luciani had been vetted for the office of bishop of Vittorio Veneto in 1958.

Later, he was aware that Luciani had not been Paul VI's first choice for a successor to Giovanni Urbani as patriarch. Indeed, Paul was about to name another prelate when his attention was drawn to a complaint that the people of Venice were being offered too small a rôle in the choice of their new patriarch, which contravened the intention of Vatican II that the people of a diocese, both clerical and lay, should have a voice in the choice of their bishop. The document which asserted the conciliar claim also mentioned Luciani prominently as a native of the region who had demonstrated extraordinary pastoral skills in the nearby diocese of Vittorio Veneto. Paul stayed his pen, and then made Luciani patriarch.[5] But Confalonieri also knew nothing about the general state of Luciani's health. Neither he nor Benelli was much concerned; most Italian cardinal-archbishops lived well into their seventies, and there was no overt reason to think that Luciani would be an exception.

Benelli also learned a great lesson from Dell'Acqua's successful lobbying on behalf of Montini in 1963. The telephone was the instrument for a successful *prattiche*. It was no longer necessary to gather together with a few other cardinals for a semi-secret meeting in an evening before the conclave began. The telephone made it possible to reach any cardinal swiftly and to discuss any situation precisely, without any need for social niceties or complex, clandestine arrangements. Moreover, aides and secretaries, too, could be kept out of the discussions altogether, because there was no need for messengers and go-betweens. And, perhaps most beneficial at all, there was no reason to stay in Rome for the negotiations—in fact, Benelli went back to Florence on the evening of the sixteenth and remained there for more than a week.

In Rome, Confalonieri conducted a more old-fashioned form of the *prattiche*. Like Benelli, the dean lauded Luciani to the conservatives as a forceful opponent of communism, because he had publicly and forcefully opposed the communists in the national election of 1975; to the liberals, he was put forward as a man wholly devoted to the pastoral life of his diocese, and, especially, to the care of the poor.[6] He could be all things to all men.

He could, indeed, because he was not well-travelled and was hardly known at all to most of the members of the College—but, then, with only a few exceptions, almost all of them curial officials, none of the cardinals knew much about other cardinals. A majority of them were meeting their colleagues for the first time during the *prattiche*. Cardinals like Taofinu'u of Western Samoa and Trin-nhu-Khuê of Hanoi had seldom left their native lands; others, like Thiandoum of Senegal and Otunga of Kenya, had studied in Rome as young men, but had little other exposure to the highest reaches of Church government and life outside their homelands. Men like these were disposed to follow the lead of more knowledgeable and experienced cardinals who were well-known to them by reputation, like Benelli and Confalonieri.

Instead of urging cardinals to support Luciani from the first ballot, Benelli told them to vote for whomever they wished on the first scrutiny. Then, once they saw the confusion caused by an election in which practically no one knew anyone else, he asked them to switch their support to Luciani as the candidate he regarded as the best possibility for carrying forward the spirit of John XXIII and Paul VI. Confalonieri offered similar suggestions in the informal conversations he had with newly arrived cardinals after the sessions of the general congregation. Both powerful prelates skillfully offered the patriarch not as the official candidate of a party but as someone to be "discovered" once a pattern of disorganization was revealed.

Of course, Luciani soon heard of Benelli's, and the dean's, plans. Later, he revealed, again and again, that he thought himself unsuited to be pope, so it is surprising that he offered no objection to Benelli's plans in the days before the conclave opened; nor did they consult him about their program. Perhaps, in an odd way, he thought the whole scheme to be something of a joke, with no real chance of success. This view is plausible when one considers his humble opinion of himself—his motto as cardinal was

Humilitas. It may have seemed inconceivable to him that the College actually would choose him in preference to better-known and more powerful cardinals, men who were well-known to Paul VI, like Pignedoli, Baggio, and Benelli himself; or over men he regarded as more holy and spiritual than he, like Ursi.

The daily business of the *sede vacante* progressed in the midst of these negotiations. On Wednesday, August 16, one hundred three cardinals attended the general congregation. Paul Yü Pin was conspicuous by his absence. Suddenly, word came that he was dead of heart failure at the age of seventy-seven. There was no real depth of emotion associated with the news. He was unknown to most of the other electors, so the situation was not quite comparable to the shock that followed the news of Mooney's death in 1958, just minutes before the conclave began. Nevertheless, Villot and Confalonieri now had another set of tasks to perform, arranging for the funeral and burial of their Chinese colleague. His death also changed the arithmetic of the election slightly. Under Paul's two-thirds-plus-one rule, it would have taken seventy-six votes to elect a new pope, if there were one hundred twelve electors. Now, with one hundred and eleven expected to participate, the successful candidate would need only seventy-five votes.

For several meetings, the general congregation had put off dealing with the protests of the cardinals who were over eighty about their exclusion from the conclave. Finally, it became impossible to turn them aside any longer. In the acrimonious and bitter meeting of August 17, Ottaviani and several others put forth their best arguments for having the provisions of *Ingravescentem Ætatem* and *Romano Pontifici Eligendo* set aside on historical and theological grounds. They were not standing alone. Several cardinals in their seventies, facing the loss of their active cardinalate soon, joined their older colleagues in the vocal protest.

Their attempt was doomed to fail, because the congregation did not have the power to set aside any of the regulations issued by Paul VI. Nevertheless, the arguments were long and heavy, as the older cardinals insisted on a full hearing for their complaints. Four electors who had been present on Wednesday, anticipating the trouble and desiring to avoid it, absented themselves from the meeting—Benelli, for example, conveniently had returned to Florence on the preceding evening. They wished to avoid any involvement in the dispute. When it was over, the *esclusi* were still excluded.

The lunch at the Collegio Pio Latino Americano on the Via Aurelia, after the general congregation met on Thursday, was one of the larger and better-known gatherings in the *prattiche.* The eighteen Latin American cardinals met together in the college's reception hall to receive Luciani. He arrived with his secretary, don Diego Lorenzi, in the same plain and slightly dented Lancia 2000 car in which they had driven to Rome. Luciani brought with him copies of his book, *Illustrissimi*, and gave one to each of the cardinals.

The moderator of the meeting, Juan Carlos Aramburu, archbishop of Buenos Aires, urged Luciani to describe how he had come to write the book, a series of conversational vignettes with both historical and fictional figures, which the patriarch did in an open and engaging way. Later, the leading Argentinean cardinal commented, "this fine and wonderful man could be a good pope." Several days later, after another collegial dinner of Latin American cardinals, Aramburu announced publicly that he would not vote for Luciani, after all. He gave no reason.

The cardinal who had worked the hardest to get the Latin Americans to consider Luciani seriously was Alosio Lorscheider, archbishop of Fortaleza, Brazil. He had met Luciani in 1975 when the patriarch had made one of his rare trips away from Italy. He had come to Brazil to visit working families who had emigrated from the Veneto in search of a new and prosperous life. The invitation from the cardinals at the Collegio Pio Latino Americano also was a direct consequence of Benelli's many telephone calls and Confalonieri's conversations and asides, but Luciani himself still did not seem to realize that he was being vetted very seriously for the throne. Of course, other cardinals, including Sebastiano Baggio and Paolo Bertoli, were vetted at similar receptions and luncheons, so perhaps Luciani had convinced himself that these rounds of discussions and meetings were just a part of the usual trappings of pre-conclave activities.

Friday, August 18, was a busier day for both the cardinals and the people in Rome. The morning meeting of the general congregation took up a suggestion that the time of the conclave's opening be moved back from 5:00 P.M. on the twenty-fifth to 4:30. The primary reason for adding the half hour was the realization that, since there were no conclavists, the cardinals would have to get other members of the staff in the conclave to manhandle their baggage into their cells, if they were not able to do this themselves. A secondary excuse relied on a decision they had not yet taken, but a topic already under discussion—whether or not to allow the procession into the conclave to be televised. If it were, the extra half hour would allow more time for a video feed to the eastern United States and Canada, while sacrificing the same time for broadcast to the Islamic populations of eastern Asia, who were much less likely to watch the Christian ceremonial event.

In addition to this session of the general congregation, ninety-five cardinals attended the requiem for Cardinal Yü Pin in Saint Peter's. Few among the public, which included large throngs of tourists who often eclipsed the number of Romans themselves who gathered at the Vatican to watch for any exciting events, bothered to attend the service. It had received little notice in the press, and, besides, the funerals of cardinals, even in Saint Peter's, were ordinary occurrences for Romans. Instead, the popular attractions of the day began with the testing of the stove in the Sistine. After the people were treated to a few gouts of smoke from the chimney above the chapel, and, after a good lunch taken out of the glare of the sun, many rushed off to the shadow of the Pantheon, at 34 Via Santa Chiara, to look at the three sets of vestments in the window of Gammarelli's, in one of which the new pope would be robed. Annibale Gammarelli, the fifth generation of his family to be the principal clerical tailor in Rome, had decided to place his work on public display briefly, in a rare departure from the traditional reticence of the firm.[7]

A few who were interested more in the Italian government than in the Church's administration went off to Santa Maria *degli Angeli*, the Renaissance church that Michelangelo constructed in the midst of the central hall of the Baths of Diocletian. Here, archbishop Romolo Carboni said a special commemorative Mass for Paul VI that was attended by the leading members of Italy's political life, including President Sandro Pertini and Prime Minister Giulio Andreotti.

The general congregation on Saturday the nineteenth was short. The main topic of discussion was how to respond to the large number of requests by journalists to visit the conclave precincts before the election began. With almost a thousand accredited members of the press in Rome for the conclave, the cardinals knew that all of them could not be accommodated without seriously compromising the security of the area—no number of staff could be expected to keep all of these outsiders under observation as they milled around. Finally, the members of the congregation voted to permit sixty visitors, all of whom would have to submit their credentials for additional scrutiny before they would be admitted to the tour on Wednesday, August 23. In addition to this business, the official notice from Filipiak in Poznan, confirming that he was too ill to attend the conclave, was received; as was a short communication from Cardinal Trinh-nhu-Khuê that he was in transit and would arrive as soon as possible. The cardinals soon adjourned to allow themselves time to prepare for the final Mass of the *novemdiali* on Sunday.

On this occasion, the Mass, which usually was chanted by a cardinal, was celebrated by Hemaiagh Pierre XVII Ghedighian, Cardinal Agagianian's second successor as patriarch of Cilicia of the Armenians.

On Sunday evening, Cardinal Trin-nhu-Khuê arrived in Rome, which brought the number of cardinal-electors almost to their full complement.

At Monday's meeting of the general congregation, the cardinals first considered a long letter of complaint addressed to them and signed by dozens of members of the press. The sixty spaces allotted to them on the one day that tours of the conclave precincts would be permitted was, in their opinion, completely inadequate. The letter asked the cardinals to raise the number of journalists who would be permitted on the tour. In the meantime, the press office had received more than seven hundred requests for permission to tour the conclave. The cardinals deferred a final decision on the matter until the following day, but, unless they were to have something of a revolt on their hands, they knew that they would have to be more forthcoming with the necessary passes. They did decide, finally, to permit the whole set of ceremonies for the opening of the conclave to be televised. In general, however, it should be noted that the members of the press were on very good terms with the cardinals. Each nation's journalists paid close attention to the comings and goings of "their" cardinals, and many reporters developed easy exchanges, and even freindly ties, with the electors whom they trailed from site to site. While crossing the Piazza di San Pietro to go into the general congregation on the twenty-first, Medeiros of Boston spotted one of the American journalists who often covered him. He broke from a small group of cardinals, sidled over to the reporter, and whispered, "How are the Red Sox doing." He learned that they led in the American League East by eight and a half games. "Deo gratias," he replied, and rejoined his companions.

When they met again on Tuesday, the cardinals voted to raise the number of press representatives who would be admitted to the tour to one hundred; further than this they were not willing to go. They also responded to a point of discussion that medical emergencies might require more than the attention that could be offered by the limited medical staff which was to be immured with them. After some discussion, they voted to permit one telephone line to be connected to the conclave, to be monitored at all times both inside the precincts and at its outside connection at the Vatican exchange. An additional motion that an internal telephone system be set up so that the electors could talk privately with one another from their cells was voted down quickly. Most importantly, they voted a resolution to restrict the procedure of voting in the conclave to the ballot only; and to reject either of the other two possible methods for choosing the new pope, by acclamation or by compromise. These were alternative methods which had been incorporated into every papal document on conclaves since the Middle Ages, but they had never been used.

One hundred nine cardinals attended the general congregation on the twenty-third, where they discussed the last details of the conclave's organization. They made no more decisions on matters of importance and Confalonieri released no statement about their deliberations after they adjourned.

The public tours of the conclave also took place on Wednesday. First, ambassadors and other diplomats accredited to the Vatican, together with a few invited guests; and then the hundred-member delegation from the press. What they saw was a blend of the old and the new, according to plans approved by Villot. The general areas of the conclave were much as they had been in former elections. The Borgia Apartments once again had been fitted up as a refectory, with cooking facilities provided for the Sisters of the Hospice of Saint Martha, who traditionally catered the conclaves.[8] But the one hundred twelve cells to accommodate the large number of electors were hastily fabricated and very small. Each had a small camp-bed, night table, writing desk, *prie-dieu*, and crucifix. All of these were squeezed into an area about eight by ten feet.

It was a great change from earlier elections in the century, when cardinals of the curia often kept their own apartments, if they happened to fall within the conclave, as Pacelli had done in 1939. The eight Americans had none of the luxury experienced by William O'Connell in 1939, when he had been allotted most of the pope's own apartment as his cell.[9]

The rest of the staff who would be locked in the conclave with the electors were afforded even more spartan quarters. Most of them received the same camp-bed as the electors, but not the other items provided to the cardinals, and their quarters were laid out as cramped dormitories.

In the Sistine, the workmen had found more space by raising the level by a little more than three feet and extending a wooden floor over the benches on both sides of the chapel which normally were used by visitors to get a better view of Michelangelo's incomparable ceiling. On each side of the temporary surface, the *sampietrini* placed two rows of chairs with small desks—no thrones, no canopies.

On the twenty-fourth, an organization announced that it had sponsored a computerized analysis of all of the variables in the election. Its conclusion was that Sebastiano Baggio would be elected. So much for computerized analyses.

The morning of Friday, August 25, saw an excited rise in activity and interest throughout Rome. Everyone from the cardinals to the cab drivers was relieved that the opening of the election was now at hand. Villot's decision to postpone the opening day of the conclave to the last possible date after the death of Paul VI had produced a sort of suspension with impatience during the last week. This effect was heightened by the weather, which remained sultry and hot, interspersed with a few afternoon thunderstorms and occasional showers. Of course, the tourist business in Rome had boomed. Americans, in particular, were fond of coming to Italy in the summer, and the added excitement of the coming conclave swelled the usual throng.

Within the Vatican itself, there was more interest and involvement than usually was the case with papal elections. Paul's revolution had brought into the government so many new members of the staff that a very large percentage of the whole curial estabishment had never seen a conclave before, a circumstance which differed from most past elections. Of course, no fewer than one hundred of the one hundred eleven electors, the creations of Paul VI, also were participating for the first time. For some of them, the vitality of the occasion was almost too great. The youngest cardinal, Sin of Manila, with his fiftieth birthday just six days away, was bathed and dressed for the day even before the first light of dawn reached the city. He later said that he felt "like a new boy going to a new school, just very excited." Other cardinals revealed similar feelings by their actions. Timothy Manning of Los Angeles also was among those who had readied himself excitedly in the early hours of the morning.

All through the city, everyone who had a rôle to play in the great event was readying himself for a moment on the stage. At 10:00, Annibale Gammarelli carried out three boxes, each with a complete set of papal vestments, and drove them to the Vatican so that they could be placed in the sacristy of the Sistine.

By eleven o'clock, more than six thousand persons had gathered in Saint Peter's to attend the concelebrated Mass of the cardinals, with Carlo Confalonieri as the principal celebrant. Villot delivered the closing homily for the Mass of the Holy Spirit. He chose for his text the ninth verse of the fifteenth chapter of John, where Jesus said: "As the Father hath loved me, so have I loved you; continue ye in my love." When the Mass was over, the cardinals were shepherded from the basilica by Monsignor Virgilo Noè, the master of ceremonies, to disperse for their last five hours of freedom.

For most of the cardinals, the afternoon was one for relaxation and visits with friends. Benelli had completed the campaign he had mapped so carefully, and Confalonieri had no more meetings of the general congregation in which to buttonhole new cardinals to talk about Luciani. Giuseppe Siri, who had put himself forward quietly as the official conservative candidate, also had no more politicking to engage him. Everything that the most influential cardinals could do before the conclave to make their wishes known had been done.

Promptly at 4:40, the procession into the conclave, from the Pauline Chapel to the Sistine, began. The master of ceremonies, Monsignor Virgilio Noè, had organized everything so carefully that the procession seemed like a quick march. Television cameras followed the cardinals as they formed up in the Pauline for the procession. Smiles predominated, as if the cardinals were going on a collegial holiday rather than into the conclave.

When a reporter from New Zealand saw Reginald John Delargey, the archbishop of Wellington, he called out, "How long you going to be, Reggie?"

"I'll see you Monday," was the reply.[10]

By 4:46, all of the members of the conclave, from the cardinals to the cooks, were within the precincts. With only minor confusion, the cardinals took their seats in the Sistine for the first business of the conclave. The last sights that the television audience saw were of Noè, wearing a broad smile, as he turned directly towards the camera, clapped his hands, and called out "Extra omnes"—"Everybody out." It was 4:59 P.M.

Once inside the conclave, Villot assumed control through another office. He became acting dean of the College.[11] Of the six cardinal-bishops, the two who were senior to him, Carlo Confalonieri and Paolo Marella, were not in the conclave.[12] The other three, Antonio Samorè, Sebastiano Baggio, and Francesco Carpino, were below him in seniority.[13]

The first order of business was Villot's public reading of part two of *Romano Pontifici Eligendo*, just as that constitution required him to do. Then he recited carefully the general oath of secrecy, after which each of the cardinals in seniority, beginning with the other cardinal-bishops, left their chairs and repeated their portion of the oath with their hands on the Gospels, which were opened on the central table of the scrutators just in front of the altar.

At the end of the rotation, when the oath had been taken by the junior cardinal-deacon, Mario Luigi Ciappi, the senior members of the conclave staff were admitted to the Sistine to take a similar oath—beginning with the prefect of the pontifical household, Jacques Martin; followed by the special delegate of the pontifical commission for Vatican City, Marchese Giulio Sacchetti; and then the prefect of the Swiss Guard, Franz Pfyffer von Altishoffen, the eleventh member of his family to have been the Guard's commander.[14] Paul's constitution had abolished the centuries-old office of prince-marshal of the conclave, and the duties of that office had been transferred to this triumvirate of officials. Officially, they were responsible for the security and secrecy of the conclave.

After these rites were concluded, the cardinals left the Sistine for their cells, and then for dinner in the Borgia Apartments. The doors to the conclave precincts were now locked. Then Villot, accompanied by three other cardinals, went about the traditional full inspection of the area. This time, however, the ceremonial aspect of their tour, with lanterns, was abandoned, as Paul had ordered. Instead, they were accompanied by the two security technicians whom Paul had specified in his constitution. This was no mere ceremony upgraded from past traditions. The chief of Vatican security, Camillo Cibin, had requested special training for his elite corps of electronic specialists from the American government, which quietly provided it under a special presidential authorization. The inspection was meticulous and thorough, assisted by the lastest counterintelligence equipment.

In the meantime, the sisters in the kitchen prepared the evening meal of pasta, bread, and fruit, and drink—a choice of red or white wine, beer, or mineral water. Because so many of the cardinals knew only a few of their colleagues, the diners grouped together in national or regional parties, with very little of the table-hopping that had been common in 1958 and many earlier elections. No matter how profound the rivalries and disagreements had been in past elections, the cardinals knew, or knew about, one another. For this reason, electoral meetings had some of the flavor of a professional convention. That social aspect had disappeared entirely in 1978.

With a hundred eleven votes to be cast, tallied, and announced, the cardinals started to vote in the Sistine immediately after Saturday morning's Mass. If they were going to conduct four scrutinies each day, there was no time to waste. First, the electors chose by lot the three scrutators, three informarians, and three tellers for the day. The first three, who would collect, count, and announce the votes, were Karol Wojtyła, Aloisio Lorscheider, and Bernardin Gantin.

Since Benelli, in particular, had urged the cardinals to vote for their own favorites on the first ballot, and since so many of them were strangers to one another, the results of the first round of voting surprised no one. At first, it seemed as if the conservative cardinals, backing their candidate, Giuseppe Siri, were the most organized bloc:

Giuseppe Siri	25
Albino Luciani	23
Sergio Pignedoli	18
Sebastiano Baggio	9
Franz König	8
Paolo Bertoli	5
Eduardo Pironio	4

| Pericle Felici | 2 |
| Aloisio Lorscheider | 2 |

In addition, fifteen other cardinals got just one vote each. The total of sixty-six votes collected by the three leading candidates indicated the main course of development in the election. The remaining conservatives—who were not very conservative by the standards of 1958 and 1963—were solidly behind Siri. Those who desired a continuation of, or even an expansion of, the broadening polices of Paul VI generally were gathered behind Luciani, as the candidate of Benelli and Confalonieri, or Pignedoli. Now that the outlines of the candidacies were translated into actual votes, the cardinals went on to the second ballot with a clearer view of the persons and the parties:

Albino Luciani	53
Giuseppe Siri	24
Sergio Pignedoli	15
Aloisio Lorscheider	4
Sebastiano Baggio	4
Joseph Cordeiro	4
Karol Wojtyła	4
Pericle Felici	3

Without any consultation among themselves, the electors had achieved a major realignment. Siri had lost only one vote, and Pignedoli only three, but the generally nonaligned cardinals, who had been the major focus of Benelli's campaign, now followed his suggestion and had voted for Luciani. Luciani's other gains, which almost certainly included Pignedoli's losses, probably came from cardinals who followed Benelli's lead now, only because the patriarch's election would at least prolong Italian control of the papacy for one more reign. Lorscheider's votes indicated that he remained the official candidate of a small group of Latin Americans. Joseph Cordeiro, Gracias's successor as archbishop of Bombay, picked up three more than the one vote he had received on the first ballot—three votes almost certainly cast by Asians, who were almost the only electors who knew him. Finally, there was a new name, put forward by four cardinals who hoped that Karol Wojtyła would appear as a plausible non-Italian alternative to Benelli's push to elect Luciani.

John Paul I, in remarks before the Angelus on the twenty-seventh, recalled his feelings as the results of the second ballot became official:

> Yesterday morning, I went to the Sistine Chapel to vote peacefully. I
> never imagined what was about to take place. When things became

dangerous for me, two of my colleagues whispered words of encouragement. One of them said, "Courage, if the Lord gives a burden, he also gives the strength to carry it." And the other said. "Do not be afraid, the whole world is praying for the new pope." Then, when the moment came, I accepted.[15]

At last, Luciani realized that Benelli and Confalonieri really did intend to have him elected pope. It was not a joke, or an event that would pass when the cardinals moved on to some more exciting or better-prepared candidate. He was only nineteen votes from reaching the throne. The unspoken question during the lunch—the sisters offered chicken or pork over rice, a rare treat—was how the curial establishment, represented by the ten votes for Baggio and the eight for Felici, would go in the next ballot. If they swallowed their dislike for Pignedoli as a mere copier of Paul in policy and government and decided to support him as a curial colleague, they might be able to bring others to their side to defeat Benelli, whom they liked even less that Pignedoli. If, on the other hand, they would not support Pignedoli, no matter what other outcome might ensue, the curialists might move to Luciani, just because he clearly was not at all like Paul, however fervently he might believe in the good aims of Vatican II.

Following Paul's instructions to the letter, not only the ballots and tally sheets but also all the notes and jottings of the cardnals now were collected and burned in the stove by Mario Luigi Ciappi. Then the cardinals left the Sistine for lunch.

During the conversations over the midday meal, both Felici and Baggio withdrew their candidacies and urged their supporters to vote for Luciani. Other cardinals who respected the opinions of these two—especially Felici, who had won great respect as secretary of Vatican II—were moved to rethink their positions in the light of the withdrawal of two respected curial officials. The sudden disappearance of the names of Cordeiro and Wojtyła on the next ballot, and a dramatic shift in the population of cardinals who supported Pignedoli, suggests strongly that this was the case.

The reunion of the cardinals in the Sistine for the afternoon voting was pervaded with another burst of excitement and vitality. As in the morning, the procedure was conducted swiftly. The results, and the consequences, were both startling and revealing:

Albino Luciani	92
Sergio Pignedoli	17
Aloisio Lorscheider	2

Luciani had been elected pope in the shortest conclave in the history of the Church, far surpassing the seventy-five he had needed to win! The largest surprise was the shift in Pignedoli's support. He had lost almost all of the cardinals who had voted for him in the morning—their votes had gone to Luciani; first, because he obviously could win, and also because Benelli presumably had vetted him thoroughly to determine if he would govern the Church in the best spirit of Paul VI. But, at the same time, many of the votes of the conservatives had moved to Pignedoli, because he seemed preferable to some in the curia than any cardinal chosen by Benelli.

What happened next was an even greater surprise. Before he could respond to Villot's formal question of whether he accepted the election, Luciani stood by his chair and gave a short speech, the tenor of which was that, while he was willing to accept the decision of the College, he was, in fact, not suited for the papacy. He wished his colleagues to consider their reasons for voting for him carefully, and he wished for another ballot, so that they might have a chance to choose another, if they wished to do so. This was an unprecedented moment in the history of papal elections—a candidate who refused, and yet did not refuse. Since so many procedures were new, Luciani's request, entirely without historical precedent, produced no demonstrations of either outrage at the spontaneous modification of the normal procedures for election or of urgings and remonstrations to accept the result of the third ballot. The cardinals simply proceeded to hold another vote. These results of the fourth ballot are conjectural, but are in accord with all the fragmentary descriptions of it:

Albino Luciani	102
Aloisio Lorscheider	1
Nemini (for no one)	8

The die-hard conservatives, almost certanly led by Siri, revealed themselves as a party of no more than eight.[16] They knew that confirmation of Luciani's election was certain, but they still were unwilling to vote for any candidate supported by Benelli. Having no wish to injure any one of their number politically by singling out a specific candidate, they turned in blank ballots. It was, in effect, an abstention. All of the remaining votes had gone to the third patriarch of Venice to be elected to the papacy in this century, except Luciani's own vote, which went to Lorscheider.

When Villot, as acting dean, accompanied by Giuseppe Siri, the senior cardinal-priest in the conclave, and Pericle Felici, the archdeacon, asked Luciani now if he accepted the election, he dutifully replied that he did. Then, when he was asked by what name he would be called, he replied, "John Paul." It was another thousand-year-old custom swept away. A pope had taken a double name for the first time.

After he had chosen his name, he was overheard to say his first Italian words as sovereign pontiff, "May God forgive you for what you have done to me."

In his allocution for the Angelus on the day after his election, he explained to the audience, without the use of the pontifical "We," but certainly with easy colloquial Italian:

> As for the choice of a name, when they asked me, I had to stop and think; and my thoughts went in this way. Pope John wanted to consecrate me a bishop with his own hands here in the basilica of Saint Peter's. Then though I was unworthy, I succeeded him in the see of Saint Mark—in that Venice that still is filled with the spirit of Pope John. The gondoliers remember him, the sisters, everybody. On the other side, Pope Paul not only made me a cardinal, but, some months before that, in the piazza of Saint Mark's, he made me blush in front of twenty thousand people, because he took off his stole and placed it on my shoulders. I never was so red-faced. Also, in the fifteen years of his pontificate, this pope showed not only me but the whole world how he loved the Church, how he served it, worked for it, and suffered for this Church of Christ. So I took the name John Paul.
>
> Be sure of this. I do not have the wisdom of heart of Pope John. I do not have the preparation and culture of Pope Paul. But now I stand in their place. I will try to serve the Church, and hope that you will help me with your prayers.

While John Paul I went to the sacristy to don one set of Gammarelli's robes, several cardinals approached Benelli to offer their congratulations on the quick success of his own campaign. In the meantime, Cardinal Ciappi gathered together all of the papers from the afternoon scrutinies and set them alight in the stove. He also tossed in all of the remaining supply of white flares he had received. The result of this was not what the junior cardinal-deacon expected. The smoke that people in the piazza saw at 6:24 P.M. was not bright white but rather more a muddy gray color. The combination of paper, straw, the flares, and their residue failed to give a clear signal. Within a minute or two, however, the hue of the smoke began to lighten and it became very clear that the smoke was white. The seasoned observers in the crowd were shocked. No other conclave had produced a result on the first day, and, because there were so many electors in this one, it was almost inconceivable that there should be a new pope so soon. It was one of those decisions—like Churchill's defeat in 1945 or Truman's victory in 1948—that leaves pollsters and pundits profoundly embarrassed at their own *hubris*.

In the Sistine, the cardinals now came forward, one by one, to offer a first homage to the new pope, who was seated on a chair in front of the altar. When Suenens knelt before him, the cardinal said, "Thank you for saying yes." John Paul I smiled his reply, "Perhaps it would have been better if I had said no."

The traditional unfolding of the news continued. It still was broad daylight when Pericle Felici came out onto the balcony at 7:32. After he announced the election of the patriarch of Venice, and surprised the people with John Paul's choice of his papal name, he withdrew.[17] Five minues later, John Paul I appeared to impart his first blessing.

The whole election had passed so quickly that Carberry had enjoyed only two of the ten chocolate bars he had brought with him into the conclave as extra fuel for the deliberations.

In the evening, the members of the press and the broadcast media rushed to catch up with a story that had gotten away from them. Luciani's name had appeared on few lists of *papabili* before the election; and in the few tallies on which it did appear, it usually was to be found near the bottom. No election since the choice of Ratti in 1922 had come so unexpectedly. Every person in Rome who was thought to have some explanation for the speedy conclave and the unexpected pope was interviewed. Those whom the press wanted to interview most, the cardinal electors, were unavailable, because the new pope had asked them to remain together in the conclave so that he could concelebrate Mass with them in the Sistine chapel in the morning. So it was the small group of older cardinals who attracted the greatest amount of attention from the press on the evening after the election. Most of them, at least, had attended the meetings of the general congregation before the conclave began, so their observations and comments might be of real interest. Most revealing of all were the comments made by Confalonieri, when he appeared on RAI, the Italian national television network:

> [John Paul's election] certainly was not a surprise for me or for the other cardinals. The name of Patriarch Luciani was one which had attracted the attention of the cardinal electors in the last days of the pre-conclave period. The press missed this altogether, perhaps because it was misled by the modest and reserved attitude of the patriarch of Venice. I have to admit that, at the start, a number of cardinals were not well-acquainted with him, but this could no longer be said after the daily meetings that were held under my presidency.

Benelli did not solicit any public praise or comment because he was one of the two grand electors of August, 1978. Confalonieri, at eighty-five, was beyond false modesty or contriving a historical position, so he was perfectly willing for others to know that he was the other grand elector, even though he had not voted. Most of those who heard the words of the smiling and jovial dean did not notice, as many Italian journalists did, the reproof of the press for missing Luciani's candidacy altogether. They simply had not done their jobs well.

In fact, the rapid end of the conclave and the near-unanimity of choice was a consequence of Paul VI's carefully evolved reconstruction of the College. His reforms had all but eliminated the power of the unmovable pre-conciliar conservatives—in 1963, there had been about twenty-four of them among the eighty electors; in 1978, no more than eight of the one hundred eleven voters. He also had destroyed, or crippled, the bases of independent power that many cardinals once had enjoyed. In their place he had created offices and ordinariates filled with obedient executors. A large number of them were so far outside the normal daily flow of Vatican information that they could be said to be operating in the dark. Cardinals from Latin America, Asia, and Africa, in particular, had to choose a leader quickly and then follow him, unless the election were to be prolonged through an extensive period for learning more about possible *papabili*. While Paul VI had not tried to influence the choice of a specific successor directly, as Pius XI had in singling out Pacelli, or as John XXIII had in designing the outline of a campaign to ensure the success of Montini, he did place his most trusted confidant, Giovanni Benelli, in a position to become the leader to whom many cardinals would have to turn in their strange circumstances and environment. Every aspect of the Pauline revolution seemed designed to make certain that the hatreds and conflicts that had manifested themselves so clearly in 1963 would forever become a thing of the past. The speed and smoothness of the August conclave, and the rapid choice of so dedicated a pastoral figure as John Paul I, were the fruits of Paul's meticulous work. The great symbol of John Paul's pastoral, rather than papal, approach to government occurred when he declined a coronation altogether. At 6:00 P.M. on September 3, Pericle Felici instead placed the pallium of his new episcopal office on his shoulders to mark "the inauguration of his ministry as supreme pastor."

But neither Paul nor anyone else could have forseen the consequences of this success. In thirty-four days, John Paul I was dead.

II. John Paul II

Every account agrees that, from the outset of his reign, John Paul regarded himself as having been the wrong choice. Within days, he was praying for a speedy death to relieve him of an office which he thought himself too unworthy to hold. He knew, but to what degree is uncertain, that he was in very bad health from a worsening circulatory condition, so he was not overly emotional or illogical in expecting his reign to be shorter rather than longer—a few months or years, perhaps, rather than more than a decade.

We will never understand fully the precise circumstances of his death, or perhaps even its cause, because the people around him, from his own secretaries to Villot, the camerlengo, were unprepared to deal with a sudden papal death. There seemed to be no precedent for handling the news in a way that was most flattering to the Vatican, to the staff, and to the memory of John Paul himself. The last pope to die so quickly had been Leo XI, who had succumbed on April 27, 1605, after occupying the throne for only twenty-six days.

In the months and years after John Paul I's death, many who were involved to some degree refused to talk about it at all; others talked only in half-stories or elliptical accounts; still others talked too much. Journalists had no real difficulty in finding inconsistencies and lies in the first official account of the pope's death and the finding of his body, and these discoveries made them even more sceptical about later accounts that sought to rectify the disparities in the various versions of the story. When this was combined with the sea of gossip which flows through and around the Vatican at all times, conspiricists emerged by the dozen to assert that he had been murdered, either by a clique of a few insiders who feared the changes he was expected to make or by a population of involvement which extended from the Vatican, through Italian freemasonry, to international financial circles, and even the Mafia. If any modern pope were to have been murdered by a Vatican establishment that was almost entirely opposed to his policies, and who feared his every action, it would have been Paul VI, not John Paul I.

John Cornwell, in his retrospective of the event, *A Thief in the Night*, has done the best job of marshalling all the evidence that is likely ever to be revealed, and subjecting the information to the requirements of Occam's Razor:

> The simplest explanation that accounts for all of the variables is the one explanation which is most likely to be true. This, of course, does not state that the simplest explanation is the true one; it does state a principle of not multiplying accidentals beyond necessity.

In that light, it seems probable that John Paul I died in his bed at some time not far removed from midnight on Friday, September 29, 1978. The cause of death probably was a pulmonary embolism caused by the sudden release of a blood clot in a vein in his badly swollen legs. His body was discovered by his housekeeper, Sister Vincenza, after he failed to open his door to retrieve his early morning coffee, which she habitually prepared and placed on a tray outside his bedroom. Soon afterwards, both don Diego Lorenzo, John Paul's secretary as patriarch of Venice and now his principal papal secretary, and John Magee, Paul VI's Irish retainer whom John Paul had reappointed as his second secretary, were in the presence of the dead pope. By 5:40, Magee was on the telephone to Villot with the critical information, and, by six, Villot was in the apartments of the pope verifying the event for himself. Within a few more minues, Dr. Renato Buzzonetti, who received a call from Magee at 5:42, arrived to give a formal medical opinion. At 6:20, Lorenzi telephoned the pope's neice, Pia, to inform her and the Luciani family. At seven, Vatican Radio announced that the pope was dead.

For Villot, the event was staggering. It was not the news which had to be handled with care, or the public shock that had to be managed, it was that the entire process of a papal election had to be repeated at once. His was the reaction of the experienced and dedicated administrator. For him, the conclave, perhaps the most dramatic and consequential moment in the government of the Church, was more a task and an expense than a great event. The workmen had only recently finished taking down and removing all of the partitions, furnishings, and equipment for the last conclave; now, at even more expense, they would have to put it all back together again. Villot was not well, himself. A nervous chain-smoker by habit, he was, at almost seventy-three, in poor health as a consequence of overwork and pressure. The death of John Paul I, and the sudden gyrations and duties attendant on it, hastened his own end. He dropped dead in the street outside the Vatican on February 9, 1979, only a few days more than four months after he had first stood over the body of John Paul I.

For the second time in two months, Villot acted not as secretary of state but as camerlengo. He sealed the pope's apartments and office, ordered his staff to the telephones to inform the cardinals in Rome of the event, and dispatched the intimatio to every member of the College. Villot could be thankful for only two things. First, the plans for the funeral and burial of Paul VI could be used again, largely unaltered; then the small flaws that had appeared in the execution of the plans and schedules for the last conclave could be corrected by reason of past experience and also used again. He could afford to treat the election of John Paul I as a dress rehearsal for the next conclave, from a logistical point of view.

The members of the College were, in general, fortunate. Because so many of them were so seldom in Rome, many of the electors had remained in the city or its vicinity to conduct business of various kinds with the members of the curia while they were in Italy. Consequently, a large number were spared the expense and trouble they would have had if they had gone home after John Paul I's ceremony of inauguration. For that reason, more than half the College was present at the first general congregation on Satuday morning.

Once again, the assembly was chaired by Carlo Confalonieri, who hastened through the required reading of part one of Paul's election constitution so that the business at hand could be dealth with quickly. Already, a number of journalists had detected serious flaws and inconsistencies in the stories that were released about the pope's death. Rome and the Vatican, always awash in gossip and populated by tipsters and informers, generated a whole industry of conspiritorial theories. Who had really discovered the pope's body? How did he really die? What was he reading when he died? Where were his glasses? And on and on, through every variation that carried sensational details with it.

The cardinals' main order of the day was to determine whether there should be an autopsy of some sort to try to circumscribe the rumors with some scientific account of the pope's end. After a lengthy discusion, twenty-nine of them voted to support a compromise suggestion by Pericle Felici that a board of three competent medical authorities, two physicians and one pathologist, should view the corpse and inquire swiftly into the accounts of those who had seen the pope's body on Friday morning. The three examiners's names would be kept secret, to prevent them from being hounded by the press and the broadcast media; they would present their preliminary conclusions on whether there should be a full autopsy at the next meeting of the general congregation on Monday—there would be no meeting of the cardinals on Sunday, to give the examiners time to do their work.

Unfortunately, by the time the three were named and told what they were to do, the time of John Paul's death was more than thirty-six hours past, and his body already had received one embalming treatment similar to that given to the corpse of Paul VI. The fact that the evolving schedule for the medical inquiry was running behind the normal schedule that follows the death of a pope would produce a division of professional opinion. The medical commission would raise more suspicions than it quelled.

The cardinals also voted to conduct the pope's funeral on Wednesday, October 4, rather than the day before. John Paul's public audiences in his short reign were far larger than those of Paul VI at almost any time in his pontificate, revealing a degree of popularity that the former pontiff had never enjoyed. The "smiling pope," as the Romans frequently called him, won the affection of the people with his easy-going, colloquial style in a way that no other modern pope had, except John XXIII—and many in the Church already regarded Roncalli as a saint. In addition, the early funeral was thought to be in keeping with John Paul's sentiments, because it was the feast of Saint Francis of Assisi, the pope's favorite. The cardinals foretold correctly that the throngs who would turn out for the public viewing would be much larger than those which had come to see Paul VI, both because John Paul I was inherently more sympathetic and because the *ferragosto* now was over and Rome's thousands of vacationers had returned to the city. In addition, if there were to be an autopsy, it would be better to have the corpse in the basilica for a night retrieval than to have it already buried in the crypt.

During the long discussion about the growing tide of scandal surrounding the death of John Paul, several cardinals raised the question of whether there ever had been a post-mortem examination of a pope, or even an opening of his body for embalmment. Many of the curial cardinals were quite familiar with many such events in the past history of the papacy. Santi Vincenzo ed Anastasio, facing the Trevi Fountain, is the parish church of the Quirinal Palace. In its crypt are urns which contain the heart, lungs, and other viscera of twenty-six of the twenty-seven popes from Sixtus V (1585–1590) to Pius VIII (1829–1830)—only Pius VI (1775–1799) has no urn, because he died at the château of Valence in France; all the rest died in the Quirinal. But evisceration and even autopsy go back far before the time of Sixtus V in the history of the popes.[18] Indeed, the earliest documented autopsy of the body of a pope was performed in the sixteenth century.

From the time of the Hildebrandine reform of the papacy in the mid-eleventh century, the youngest man elected to the papal throne was Giovanni de' Medici, who became Leo X on March 9, 1513, at the age of thirty-seven. When he died, eight and a half years later, on December 1, 1521, he still was only forty-five. Since he already had weathered one complex and serious plot against his life, in May and June, 1517—in which several cardinals were involved and for which one of them, Alfonso Petrucci, was executed—there were suspicions about his sudden demise at so young an age. These were heightened when the master of ceremonies, Paris de Grassis, reported to the general congregation that the pope's body suddenly had become very swollen, even though it was December.[19] The cardinals asked the Paduan anatomist, Bernardino Speroni, to lead a team of other physicians in an autopsy of Leo.[20] Speroni and his assistants concluded that the pope had died of poison, but they had no data on which to base their conclusion—which was the safe one given the suspicions of the time. Leo's remains then were buried quickly and without much ceremony.

In spite of these and other well-documented historical details, the cardinals wanted specific information from official records to buttress their deliberations on Monday.

Cardinal Pericle Felici, the archdeacon of the College and archivist of the Second Vatican Council, took up the task of searching for more details. Late on Saturday, he joined with Cardinal Antonio Samorè, now the librarian and archivist of the Church, and the latter's two principal assistants, Martino Giusti, prefect of the archives, and Charles Lamb, the senior archivist, in a thorough search of the archives of the Vatican for precedents, preferably modern, for a post-mortem examination of a dead pope. It was perhaps the most exciting historical detective work any of them had ever done—and all four were fascinated by this type of historical inquiry.

At first, they began on the wrong trail, because Felici thought he remembered that the corpse of Pius VII (died August 20, 1823) had been autopsied, and it was for details of this autopsy that they searched in vain. Eventually, they stumbled across a handwritten account by Prince Agostino Chigi—prince marshal of the conclaves of 1829, 1830, and 1831—which described a post-mortem examination of the body of Pius VIII (died November 30, 1830). It was carried out because of the suddenness of the pope's end and because he was convulsed several times in his last hours. So, in the end, they did find their modern example to present to the general congregation at Monday's meeting.

In the evening, after the commission had completed their examination of John Paul's body, the corpse was placed on a bier and carried out of the apostolic palace, across the piazza, and into Saint Peter's. Here, it would be prepared for the public viewing, which would last all day Sunday, Monday, and Tuesday. More than a hundred thousand people gathered under a colorful and brilliant sunset to watch the procession. It was a remarkable setting during the rainiest season of Rome's year.

Later still, habitual diners at L'Eau Vive, a little restaurant in the Via Monterone, were slightly startled to notice three of the most powerful and influential cardinals in the Church, Giovanni Benelli, Leo Jozef Suenens, and Jan Willebrands, dining together at an out-of-the-way table. The conciliar liberals were organizing. The *prattiche* had begun.

On Sunday, the whole public activitiy centered on the opening of the basilica and the long lines of thousands of viewers who came to see John Paul. The cardinals in Rome, more than eighty of them, began to visit each other and to ply the telephone in an effort to develop some approach to the next election. Once again, considerable attention was paid to Benelli's ideas, but he had not yet determined which candidate to support now. His triumph in August had turned out to be mixed. On the positive side, and many cardinals agreed it was the most important accomplishment, Benelli had succeeded in choosing a candidate who instantly brought an era of good feeling into the Church. But this was counterbalanced by the winner's poor health—reliable word of his long-standing condition of swollen legs and difficulty in walking, which suggested serious circulatory problems, had now spread through the College. The next pope would have to be a man in very good health, the stronger the better.

Benelli still did not want Ursi, the Italian cardinal most like John Paul I. He had vetted him thoroughly as a possible pope in August and had rejected him for a gamut of reasons that ran from his attrocious accent to his personal devotion and holiness, which argued against a man who would be able to seize control of the huge absolute monarchy that Paul VI had created. Luciani had seemed a more likely person for that task in August, and he had proven to be quite timid and uncertain of how to wield the absolute power he was required to exercise in Paul's new Vatican. Yet Benelli still was wedded to the idea that the next pope should speak Italian as his native language, as every pope had since 1524. The archbishop of Florence certainly was seeking a consensus that would allow the new pope to be elevated with something of the speed and sureness with which the College had chosen John Paul I. Increasingly, the cardinals with whom he consulted suggested that he stand as a candidate himself. He was only fifty-seven, it was true, but his relative youth presupposed a long, stable reign.

Moreover, he was highly respected by most of the cardinals flung throughout the world as residential ordinaries. Only one wing of the curia, albeit a large one, would oppose him vehemently because he had wielded so much power inside the administration as Paul's most trusted executor. It was flattering and so easy to agree with these opinions, that Benelli decided that he might as well be the next pope. This decision, at which he arrived only with substantial encouragement, nevertheless was his greatest political error.

For the archconservative of the College, Giuseppe Siri, archbishop of Genoa, it was now or not ever. He was one of just three valid electors who survived from the reign of Pius XII, since Valerian Gracias lost his battle against cancer on September 11.[21] At seventy-two, it was just possible to achieve the throne, if he were to mount a campaign that made him seem sympathetic to the work of John XXIII and Paul VI and, obviously, less reactionary than he truly was. He was in remarkably good health, still in full control of his diocese, and well-liked still by a large population in the curia. If he could attract the initial support of even forty cardinals, it might provide him with enough momentum to reach the throne. For Siri, it was worth the effort.

Unlike the case in August, when many cardinals did not even have the telephone numbers of their colleagues, the electors of October had the experience of a recent conclave. They now understood something of the maneuvering and politicking that characterized the *prattiche*, so some ventured to explore other candidacies seriously on their own.

Eighty-five cardinals were present when the second general congregation convened in the Sala Bologna at 11:00 A.M. on Monday, October 2. By that time, Confalonieri had two reports from the team which had examined the corpse of John Paul I. The first, from the two physicians, concluded that they found no reason to doubt Dr. Renato Buzzonetti's pronouncement that John Paul had died from an acute myocardial infarction. Consequently, they found no reason to recommend an autopsy, especially since the embalming injections that the corpse had received and the length of time that had passed would, in their opinion, make any results of an autopsy now questionable. The pathologist, in keeping with his own training and experience, thought that the cardinals should order an autopsy. In spite of the conditions described by his other two colleagues, he concluded that there were sufficient reasons for conducting the examination—including the fact that Buzzonetti had never examined John Paul while he was alive.

After the two reports were presented, the cardinals entered into a contentious and often loud discussion on the course to be followed. Felici, who had seemd to incline toward the view that an autopsy was in order, now changed his mind and no longer supported that course of action. Two of the most influential liberal cardinals, König and Enrique y Tarancón, argued vehemently that there should be no autopsy, because of the additional sensationalism such an event would add to the already wild speculations that were starting to appear generally in the press and on television. Their views were important, because, in general, they stood squarely on the side of a more open Church. If they regarded the certain publicity as too dangerous, and even scandalous, then the views of the more conservative cardinals, of which we have no direct report, must have been even stronger. Eventually, Confalonieri, who pointed out that both physicians had rejected the idea of a post-mortem examination, also voiced opposition to the idea. When a vote finally was taken, the cardinals rejected the proposal by an overwhelming majority.

Once this decision had been made, the cardinals voted swiftly to set the date for the opening of the conclave as Saturday, October 14. This was the earliest permissible day under the constitution of Paul VI—fifteen days after the death of the former pope. Many of the reasons that had seemed so cogent for postponing the conclave in August to the last possible day now no longer applied. The cardinals knew each other much better than before, and so many of them already were in Rome, or could reach the city in a few hours by air, that a great delay in waiting for late arrivals did not seem necessary.

By late Tuesday afternoon, there were more than a hundred cardinals in the city of the one hundred twenty-seven living members of the College. Moveover, of the one hundred twelve potential electors, fewer than a dozen were still absent. The speculation in the press about the *papabili* was even more feverish than had been the case in August. The shortness of John Paul I's reign, the conflicting details about his death, and the presence of so many electors in the city so soon after the death of the pope, when combined with the journalistic failure to even speculate about the election of Luciani in August, made every morsel of gossip and every sighting of a cardinal worth persuing as a potential source of news. In 1939, most journalists, like almost all other close observers of the world situation at the death of Pius XI, were perfectly correct in predicting the elevation of Pacelli to the throne. Since that time, the mania for gossip had overtaken the historical principles of news gathering in Rome—treating every easily obtainable tidbit of gossip with distrust and applying a long historical view to the process of papal election—so that the public speculation about various candidacies, or possible candidacies, was of at least as great a value as the material which appeared in print.

Typical of this sort of non-news was the wide publicity given to the computerized prediction, using the "complex decision-making model," of the National Opinion Research Center in Chicago—an effort far removed from the actual evolution of the *prattiche*. The model used for the August conclave had been dead wrong, but newer techniques and methods had changed all that. The new pope would be Corrado Ursi, archbishop of Naples. The Romans, shaking their heads at this exhibition of American chutzpah, merely smiled. Popes who had espoused a particularly holy way of life had been disasters in the past—like Benedict XIII (1723-1730)—and the experiment was not likely to be tried again in 1978. Moreover, there was that Pugliese accent. Of course, some observers detected the new techniques and methods easily. The software had given weight to all of the obvious characteristics of John Paul I—his age, his commitment to the pastoral life, his approachability, his personal humility, and so forth. The Italian cardinal who came closest to John Paul I in these regards was, indeed, Ursi. It was the reason that Benelli had considered him, too, in his final reasoning about *papabili* in August. But Benelli had rejected him as a candidate for serious political and adminstrative reasons already, and was not about to adopt Ursi as his candidate now.

Because its reporter was more concerned with groups and trends than with picking specific names, it was the Spanish journal, *Blanco y Negro*, which came closest to an accurate and sober profile of the situation in Rome. Its issue of October 10, which represented ten days of solid research, separated the members of the College into four distinct electoral groups:

The moderate *Montiniani*, a cohesive bloc of forty-two, formed the largest party. Its members followed Benelli's leadership and were determined to secure a pope who would continue Paul VI's program, whether their candidate had a personality like Luciani's or not.

The more "reforming" *Montiniani* might have been described better as the conciliar liberals. A group of twenty-seven, led by Willebrands, Marty, Renard, and Enrique y Tarancón, they were determined to have a pope who would press forward, even more than Paul VI had done, to implement their vision of the full intent of Vatican II. Almost all of them were non-Italian Europeans.

Near them, but not of them, was a bloc of fourteen cardinals from the Third World who followed the ideas and spirit, if not the direct leadership, of Paul Zoungrana. *Blanco y Negro* called them the "radical evangelicals."

Finally were the conservatives, twenty-eight in number, under whose banner could be found many of the curialists, a few older Latin Americans, and two or three cardinals from Eastern Europe. Among the latter, the journal presciently idetified two, Laszlo Lékai, the Hungarian primate, and Karol Wojtyła, the archbishop of Krakow.

Other, better known and more widely circulated, magazines and newspapers spent most of their space for the papal election in rehashing the information they thought they possessed from the August election. *Time*, for example, gave prominence to the possibilities of Baggio, Bertoli, and Pignedoli, without realizing that even the most prominent of them, Pignedoli, had been advanced seriously in the August election, and then soundly rejected. It also gave some attention to other possibilities from outside the curia, including Aloisio Lorscheider. If there was one cardinal among all the electors who had no chance whatever of being elected pope, it was he. At almost the very moment that John Paul I had died in Rome, Lorscheider had suffered his own massive heart attack in Fortaleza. Quick stabilizing treatment, followed by appropriate surgery—which included implanting a pacemaker—saved his life and left him without serious disability. Lorscheider's crisis was well publicized, but *Time* and other popular journals seem to have missed the news. In the early days of October, many other members of the College thought it almost certain that he would be unable to attend the election at all. In the end, he did participate in the conclave, but without any chance of ascending to the throne.

Lorscheider's heart attack and John Paul's sudden death made every candidate's health a major qualification. Even cardinals who thought they had only a small opportunity to become pope took steps to reassure their colleagues on that matter. Karol Wojtyła, for example, had an electrocardiogram taken before he left Krakow for the second conclave, and made certain that its favorable results were part of the information about him for anyone who inquired.

The speed with which the members of the College gathered to choose another pope was visible at John Paul's funeral on Wednesday, October 4, the feast of Saint Francis of Assisi. Ninety-four other cardinals joined Confalonieri in the concelebration of the Mass, which was in every way a recapitulation of the rite for Paul VI. Even the text used by the dean in his homily was the same passage from the Gospel of John.

The day was the fourth consecutive one of rain and damp, so the crowd was less that had attended Paul's funeral. Yet it was a much larger one than had been expected because of the weather and the fact that it was a Wednesday in a workweek. By four o'clock, the invited guests were seated on puddled green plastic chairs. The guests formed a much less stellar assemblage than had been the case for Paul VI, because Villot had informed each of the governments who were to send delelgations that he did not expect them to interupt the schedules of their highest dignitaries for a second time within five weeks.

By 5:50 P.M., it was over. Twelve *sediari* carried the closed coffin back into the basilica for the final acts of burial, just as they had done for Paul. Pope John Paul I, whom the Romans had called the "smiling pope," was laid to rest in the crypt beneath a marble slab which was surmounted by two fifteenth-century bas-reliefs of flying angels.

On the morning of the fifth, the crypt was opened to the public so that mourners and sightseers alike could file past the burial place of John Paul I. Upstairs, in the basilica, the first Mass of the *novemdiali* was said by Giuseppe Siri. Normally, this Mass was not one of those celebrated by a cardinal, but Siri seems to have asked that he be permitted to be the celebrant on the first day, and this request was granted. Confalonieri, Villot, Benelli, and the rest of the astute observers knew that Siri would take the occasion to make his love for John Paul clear, and thus further his own aims as a candidate. They do not seem to have been alarmed at this, since they regarded the conservative party as too weak to give Siri enough support to become pope. Siri's homily was a masterful effort at retrospective regard, while saying nothing concrete about the dead pope:

> With his style so close to the Gospel, it can be said that Pope John Paul I opened an era. He opened it, and then quietly went away. In all simplicity, he spoke on the firmness of Catholic doctrine, on ecclesiastical discipline, on spirituality which is the basis of the value of human existence. He affirmed that there is a hierarchy in these things—and then he was silent. The people understood and loved him.

It was a masterful perfomance in the old tradition of Roman ecclesiastical oratory. But neither his listeners nor the other electors who saw copies of his text were deceived by his rhetoric. He had disliked John Paul I almost as much as he had loathed Paul VI. Siri might have hated him more, had he lived longer. Nevertheless, Siri had used the occasion to offer a softening of his former archconservative positions in every area, from the legacy of Vatican II to the reforms of Paul VI. His praise was meant to suggest that he, too, could compromise with the left and reach an accommodation with them, were he to be elected pope.

Pericle Felici, who was the celebrant at the second Mass of the *novemdiali*, on Friday, October 6, also used the occasion to make clear how much of a friend he had been to Luciani, from years past. He elaborated on the story of how he had presented the future pope with a small reproduction of the Stations of the Cross to memorialize a retreat that the cardinal-patriarch had conducted for the clergy of northeastern Italy, and on how appreciative Luciani had been to receive the gift. It was more of the traditional, almost bathetic, oratory of ecclesiastical Rome. But Felici was not an aspiring candidate for the papal chair.

In the sixth general congregation on the same day, Confalonieri asked the assembled cardinals to take up the issue of the latest round of fighting in Lebanon. On this occasion, it was the Maronite Christians who seemed to be suffering the most from the Syrian attack. The dean thought it prudent to make some sort of gesture of intervention on behalf of the Christian population. The cardinals voted to authorize Confalonieri to dispatch telegrams to both Hafez al-Assad, president of Syria, and to Kurt Waldheim, secretary general of the United Nations. Of course, neither wire had any effect on the situation, but the cardinals looked grieved and concerned at the current round of bloodshed, and the Christians in communion with Rome could take heart that their spiritual capital had not forgotten them in the midst of the preparations for the conclave.

This public business was no real distraction from the conduct of the *prattiche*, which had to move swiftly because of the shortened schedule for the next conclave. Even though the telephone was now the principal medium for negotiations, there still were discussions which needed to take place in person, either among cardinals themselves or through trusted confidants and advisors. Occasionally, the latter were noticed by the Romans as they carried on with their daily lives. Sometimes, too, they became the general subject of gossip in the city and were recorded in the press or in diaries and notes which later became public. One such exchange took place at midday on Sunday, October 8, when Benelli's secretary came to the little church of San Stanislao, the Polish church in Rome, to have lunch with the cardinal-archbishop of Krakow, Karol Wojtyła, and his two most trusted friends, Bishop Andrzej Maria Deskur, president of the Pontifical Commission for Social Communications, and Bishop Władisław Rubin, secretary general of the Synod of Bishops.[22] It is almost certain that the exchange of views over lunch concerned whether Wojtyła, a leading conservative among the Eastern Europeans, would be willing to add his support to Benelli's candidacy for the throne. The lunch is memorable only because one of the participants was the future pope, but it is representative of many other meetings in Rome in the days before the conclave.

The important event on Monday morning, October 9, was not the formal meeting of the general congregation, but rather an informal gathering of staff, including the master of ceremonies, Virgilio Noé, in Villot's office to complete the physical arrangements for the conclave and to answer specific requests for special arrangements submitted by several cardinals. For Villot, the one criterion for responding favorably to these requests was cost. The operating budget for the whole curia had been exceeded greatly by the expenses of the conclave in August. Now the deficit would escalate further with the added expenses of another conclave in the same fiscal year. As data released in the next reign would reveal, Vatican finances were in remarkably poor condition both because of mismanagement by Paul's financial advisors and because of the great strain placed on the apostolic fisc by the many new offices, programs, and initiatives undertaken by Paul VI without regard to their expense.

One by one, Villot considered the special requests. A group of French cardinals wished to know if the conclave could be stocked with Vichy water, instead of, or in addition to, the Italian mineral water that had been supplied in August. Even though the cost for it will be a little great, Villot approved the request. Corrado Ursi's desire that the chairs in the Sistine be placed farther apart to afford the cardinals more privacy as they filled out their ballots had to be refused—the Chapel was again to be crowded with more than a hundred electors, and the fifteenth-century room was already packed to accommodate the electors. Timothy Manning of Los Angeles asked for a small coffee bar with a refrigerator, an easy request to grant. Aramburu wanted a selection of dishes from South American cuisine added to the daily menu. That was impossible. The good sisters who did the cooking had a repertoire that was essentially limited to pasta, salad, and fruit. There certainly was no time to train them in preparing new dishes or money for supplies to enhance the menu. The list of requests was long, and reviewing it was tedious. While some were easy to grant, like the memorandum from one cardinal who asked that the conclave staff ensure that he had an ashtray in his cell, others had to be refused for sheer impossibility, and the refusal couched in the most polite terms, like Cody's complaint that the lighting system throughout the conclave in August was so inadequate that, for October, it should be replaced entirely by more modern fixtures.

By the time the general congregation met later in the morning, the whole arragement of committees and staff was settled. The senior staff was the same as that in the August election: the prefect of the pontifical household, Jacques Martin; the secretary of the conclave, Ernesto Civardi; the sacristan, Pieter Canisius van Lierde, who was performing that office in his fourth conclave; and the master of ceremonies, Virgilio Noè. On this occasion, the first of the three cardinalitial commissions consisted of Samorè, Arns, and Oddi, to conduct the daily administration of the Church under the authority of Villot. The second, König, Krol, and Cordeiro, would designate, and examine the credentials of, those who were to enter the conclave. The third—Guerri, Wojtyła, and Thiandoum—was in charge of the building and enclosing of the conclave, and the arrangement of the cells.

At this time in the *prattiche*, one important meeting occurred on the afternoon of the tenth, when six of the leading liberals met together to see if they could devise a common approach to the election. Suenens, Jubany Arnau, Alfrink, and König, representing the European conciliarists, and Arns and Lorscheider—who was still very weak from his recent heart surgery—representing liberal South America, discussed the various known candidacies for several hours. Other cardinals who were named as having attended the meeting are less certain to have done so, including Enrique y Tarancón of Madrid, Marty of Paris, and Willebrands of Utrecht. In the end, most of the electors who were present agreed to support Benelli, who was, after all, Paul VI's man. If his bid were to fail, they agreed that they probably would support Ugo Poletti, even though a member of the curia as cardinal-vicar of Rome, as a suitable substitute. Poletti might be regarded as having the necessary pastoral experience from his years as administrator of the diocese of Rome for Paul VI. If an Italian did not win the throne speedily, the leaders agreed to switch their support to a popular non-Italian European who might be able to gather enough support to win quickly.

If the latter course seemed best, then the ancient principle that no pope should come from a politically powerful country should be applied. The last time the cardinals had ignored the dictum also was the last time they had elected a non-Italian pope. They had hastened to choose Adrian Dedel as Adrian VI in 1522, because they thought that Dedel, the former tutor of the Emperor Charles V, and later one of his chief counsellors, would bring his master's aid more quickly to Rome's needs in the opening round of the Reformation. It was all the more surprising because Dedel was not even present in the conclave. Adrian VI had proved himself to be a frosty reformer himself, and a pope too easily swayed by the wishes of his former master. The cardinals would not again recapitulate the error, which was the same one that had made John XXII (1316–1334) too willing to accede to the wishes of successive kings of France in his time, and had made popes in the mid-eleventh century too pliable in the hands of the Emperor Henry IV who had elevated them to the papal chair.

If non-Italian and European, the new pope would have to come from a nation which did not strut its power on the world's stage. This criterion immediately eliminated Hume of Westminster, a highly respected Benedictine, as well as the cardinals from France and Germany. Eliminating others, like König himself, who had developed too many enemies to be a serious candidate, and others because of age and qualifications, two possibilities emerged—the newly appointed archbishop of Utrecht, Jan Willebrands, and the experienced Polish pastor, Karol Wojtyła. It is almost certain that the latter's name was first introduced into the discussion by the cardinal-archbishop of Barcelona, Narciso Jubany Arnau. The Spanish prelate's interest had produced immediate support from König, who respected his Polish colleague, in spite of Wojtyła's strongly conservative views. Of all those known to have been present at the meeting, he was, by far, the most theologically conservative. That should have been a signal that his candidate would not hold to the policy of openness and conciliarism that had characterized Paul VI, and would likely have been extended and elaborated by John Paul I.

One product of raising Wojtyła's name as a potential pope was a sudden interest in his recent views. By the afternoon of the eleventh, the library of the Collegio Pio Latino Americano was seeing more cardinals than it had at any time in its history, because the collection included several copies of the text of the Lenten retreat that Wojtyła had preached in 1976 for Paul VI and the curia, which had been published under the title *Segno di Contrad-*

dizione. The cardinals who read the text were, in the main, impressed favorably. His thinking on Christian apologetics and devotional practice, while quite different from those of the Brazilian activist, dom Helder Camara, whose work with a similar title seems to have inspired Wojtyła, were neither too conservatively extreme nor too far from the apparent mainstream of Catholic liberal thought. The little book, almost ignored by Catholic readers and thinkers when it appeared, proved to contain the words which ushered Wojtyła to the throne as John Paul II.[23]

Another of the important moments in the *prattiche* occurred on the evening of Thursday, October 11, at the French College. Fifteen of the cardinal archbishops joined together to determine how they would be able to counter the candidacy of Siri and ensure the election of a pope dedicated to conciliar reforms. It was an eclectic and multinational gathering where the chief commonality was that all the cardinals were francophones. The French were represented by Gouyon and Marty, the Canadians were Roy and Flahiff, the Brazilians were Arns and Lorscheider, the French-speaking Africans were Gantin and Thiandoum, the Italians were Colombo and Pappalardo, while Belgium had Suenens, Korea had Kim, and Britain had Hume.

After a lengthy discussion on the dangers to liturgical reform, the position on religious liberty, and episcopal collegiality if Siri were enthroned, they decided generally to support either Ursi or Colombo in the first phase of the election, and then Poletti, if it proved to be impossible to elect one of the two candidates they really favoured.

In the last week before the conclave opened, the speed of the *prattiche* rose to levels never seen before during the preparation for a conclave. Three factors contributed to the almost feverish nature of the negotiations: the shortened schedule for the *sede vacante*, the large number of cardinals involved in these meetings and telephone calls, and the efforts by Benelli's supporters to put together a coalition which would raise him to the throne.

The large and active networks of Benelli's contacts and supporters was far larger and more influential than anything the conservatives could muster. Siri and his partisans had to devise another way to persuade the electors that their view was the one which should predominate in the conclave. Since many of them were disliked and distrusted by the non-European cardinals, who now held the balance of power in the College with fifty-six votes, another way had to be found to reach and persuade these men. Unlike a large number of the non-Italian Europeans, only a few of these more remote cardinals were really influential, but all of them had votes that were as important as the vote of Benelli himself.[24]

To accomplish their electoral aims, the curial conservatives decided on a public campaign in the press and on television, designed to impress the uncommitted or wavering cardinals of the huge public desire for a more theologically and socially rigid government after the vacillating years of Paul VI. Almost every Italian newspaper "revealed" that Siri was to enter the conclave with more than fifty votes committed to his election, which gave the impression that a bandwagon for the Genoese already was under way. RAI, Italian national television, ran a lauditory ten-minute biographical sketch of him, almost as if he already were pope. He also gave interviews that were designed to portray him as a senior cardinal who was above all of the disputes that had emerged during and after Vatican II. But all this publicity began to backfire on his cause almost as soon as it appeared. Even the least well-informed cardinals perceived that some attempt was being made to sway them in a way that was not quite proper.

Any hope that Siri had of mounting a successful campaign he dashed himself in a long and wide-ranging interview that he gave on the thirteenth to a reporter from one of northern Italy's two most influential papers, the *Gazzetta del Popolo*. By arrangement with the editors, the interview was not to be published until Sunday, October 15, but either the paper decided to ignore their bargain with the cardinal—their anger at the way Siri had abused their man in Rome might have provided enough of a reason to do that—or the people at the copy desk did not know of it. Consequently, the whole text appeared on Saturday morning, instead—just before the cardinals united for the Mass of the Holy Spirit. Not only had Siri made the fatal mistake of revealing his true feelings—he is reputed to have said that the Church would need fifty years (or a hundred, or four hundred, depending upon who tells the story) to recover from the reign of John XXIII—but he had allowed the entire session to be taped, which permitted the paper to prove the truthfulness of Siri's comments. Siri unabashedly revealed his intention, if elected, to reverse most of the new initiatives undertaken as a consequence of the council. And he made those revelations in his habitual voice imperial. He was at his nasty best. To one question, he replied to the reporter, "I do not understand how you could ask such a stupid question. If you really want an answer, you will have to sit down and be quiet for three hours." To another, he replied, "That is a question I would answer only for my confessor." If he were pope, there would be no continuation of the uncertainties of Paul VI, to be sure, but also there would be no continuation of the quiet humility and human feeling of John Paul I.

On Saturday morning, a dozen cardinals were seen to have the latest issue of the *Gazzetta del Popolo* with them; doubtless many dozens more knew of the contents of Siri's interview before the procession into the conclave. Siri had ruined himself.

Benelli, however, got no last-minute boost in his candidacy by Siri's collapse. The dedicated conservatives, instead, began to search for another candidate who might be acceptable to the two-thirds-plus-one of the electorate they needed to win to their side.

Late on Thursday, October 12, the final composition of the conclave became clear. Although Villot had been notified that Filipiak was near death in Poznan and, as in August, would certainly not attend the conclave, word now came that he had died of an embolism earlier on Thursday. But John Joseph Wright, who had missed the earlier election because of his surgeries in Boston, was present for the October meeting. He was confined to a wheelchair while he continued to recover from the surgery on his leg muscles, and he now peered at the world through his new post-cataract glasses. Although in a deplorable state, he would be one of the electors. Because of his condition, he merited a conclavist under the provisions of the consitution of Paul VI. He solicited, and received, permisson for his secretary, Father Donald W. Wuerl, to minister to his needs.[25] The October election would have all one hundred eleven eligible electors in attendance.

Following precisely the schedule for the opening of the conclave that had been used in August, the cardinals assembled for the Mass of the Holy Spirit in Saint Peter's on Saturday morning, October 14. Everything went as before, even the text for the homily was the same one that had been used in the previous meeting, but this time with the preferatory words, *Ancora, una volta* ("Again, once more"). This time, however, the crowd in the basilica was much larger than it had been in August.

Following the Mass, the cardinals dispersed to gather their luggage and to have a little respite from public events before the afternoon reunion for the procession into the conclave. Then, as before, the electors processed to the Sistine Chapel, the customary oaths were taken, the doors were sealed, and then Villot, his three cardinal assistants, and the two security technicians inspected the precincts, all according to the rules and procedures established in Paul's consitution. Once again, the public moments of the day were televised. This time, however, the viewers saw a distinctly older-looking group of men. Wright in his wheelchair, Lorscheider moving carefully as he recovered from his heart surgery, and Gouyon, who also had endured surgery since the last election, were the obvious physical demonstrations of this, but the other cardinals, too, had grimmer expressions and fewer smiles for the watchers on either side of the procession.

Almost every event was marked at a slightly earlier time than had been the case in August, however. Familiarity with the rules and procedures was one reason, but another was the eagerness of all the participants to get to the business at hand. In the former election, the cardinals comported themselves almost as if they were going on a brief, cheerful holiday. This time, there was a greater degree of tension and seriousness about the election. The electors had been sobered by the brief pontificate and sudden end of John Paul I, and they were concerned that the evolution of the *prattiche* had produced no clear and obvious course for the election.

Benelli had a large number of supporters, but their support was less firm for his candidacy now than it had been for his choice of Luciani in August. Siri had embarrassed himself, and the College, by his intemperate interview, and no one, not even the conservatives themselves, knew how to respond or which new candidate to advance.

The first evening meal was the usual fare of pasta followed by fruit, all washed down with wine, beer, or mineral water—including the optional Vichy water asked for by the French cardinals. After this, the cardinals retired to their cells, some to receive visitors, some to continue with the duties from which they were taken by the necessity of the election. Wojtyła, in cell ninety-six, for example, seems to have spent the evening poring over an official statement from the Polish minister in charge of ecclesiastical matters.

As soon as the electors had heard Mass on Sunday morning, they proceeded to the Sistine for the first ballot. The eagerness now was to determine the general outline of parties and candidates now that the *prattiche* was over. The results produced few surprises:

Giuseppe Siri	23
Giovanni Benelli	22
Corrado Ursi	18
Pericle Felici	17
Salvatore Pappalardo	15
Karol Wojtyła	5
Ugo Poletti	4
Bernardin Gantin	3
Jan Willebrands	2
Basil Hume	1
Jaime Sin	1

It was certainly no surprise that six of the seven cardinals who received the largest number of votes were Italian, with a total of ninety-nine of the one hundred and eleven votes. Perhaps it was a little unusual that Siri should have retained the support of as many as twenty-three electors after his gaffe in the newspaper interview, but he was the overwhelming favorite among the curialists of a more conservative stamp and of a few residential ordinaries who longed for the Church of Pius XII. The European liberals, for the most part, had split their vote among Benelli, the avowed and public candidate, Ursi, and Pappalardo. Moderate conservatives, not wedded to Siri as the indespensible man, as well as a few conciliarists who remembered his useful days at Vatican II, had chosen to support Felici, perhaps in the hope of starting a boomlet for a compromise candidate. Of the twelve votes that had gone to non-Italians, Gantin's three probably were from fellow Africans, since he was only recently a cardinal and not well known outside the work of the Pontifical Commission on Justice and Peace. The votes for Hume and Sin obviously had come from personal convictions that these men would be excellent popes. Willebrands's two came from similar personal convictions, combined with respect for his ecumenical work as president of the Secretariat for Christian Unity since 1969.

The five votes for Wojtyła sprang from a more considered and political motive. There certainly was not going to be a Black African pope in 1978, like Gantin; or a pope from a nation that still enjoyed the reputation for power and influence, like Britain's Hume; or a Filipino pope, like Sin; or a pope with only limited pastoral experience, like Willebrands, who had been made archbishop of Utrecht in 1975, but still served actively in the curia. But there might be a chance for a non-Italian European from a powerless country who had considerable respect as a pastor—like Wojtyła. That clearly was the view of one of the two cardinals who are known to have voted for him on the first ballot, Franz König of Vienna. Wojtyła's other known vote came from John Joseph Krol of Philadelphia, a Polish-American who would have supported any plausible Polish candidate even if he had not been a close friend of the archbishop of Krakow.

The tallies of the first ballot did clarify the politcal groups in this conclave. The liberals, perhaps better termed the progressive *Montiniani*, commanded fifty-nine votes, those that had been cast for Benelli, Ursi, Pappalardo, and Poletti. These were cardinals who were committed to electing a pope who would continue, and even expand, the policies and initiatives of Paul VI based upon the work of Vatican II. It was from this community that John Paul I had come. The moderate *Montiniani* were close to the same view, but perhaps with a little rightward correction in general policy. They were the seventeen cardinals who had supported Felici. The conservatives, twenty-three in number, had stood by Siri. By contrast, the "radical evangelicals" from the Third World seemed to command only four votes, the three for Gantin—one of which almost certainly was Zoungrana's—and the vote for Sin of Manila. The remaining eight votes belonged to independents who were not willing to ally themselves with any of these four recognized groups.

As soon as the last teller, or reviser, had finished checking the validity of the last vote, the cardinals continued with the second ballot. The results showed a further clarification of candidates rather than any realignment of political position:

Giovanni Benelli	40
Pericle Felici	30
Corrado Ursi	18
Giuseppe Siri	11
Karol Wojtyła	9
Ugo Poletti	3

Benelli now had two thirds of the progressive *Montiniani* behind him, since he had picked up almost all the votes that had gone to Pappalardo on the first ballot. Siri was finished as a credible candidate, and most of his votes seem to have migrated to Felici, only because the archdeacon seemed to be the only alternative to Benelli's election. Ursi had retained the votes of the eighteen cardinals who thought that the Church needed another pope as much like John Paul I as possible, regardless of his ability to grasp and hold Paul VI's autocratic power. But the subtlest shift was the additional four votes that had come to Wojtyła. They seem to have come from conservatives who, perceiving the end of Siri, looked for a candidate who would give a distinct turn to the right in Church government—no more laicized priests, no more tinkering with the liturgy, and no more debate on the orthodoxy of established Thomism. All four of these cardinals probably were not Italian, and Aramburu of Buenos Aires—the cardinal who said with pride that he had never voted for Luciani in August—almost certainly was one of them.

The last few minutes of the session were devoted, as always, to the collection and burning of ballots, tally sheets, and notes. Once Mario Luigi Ciappi had added the requisite amount of moistened straw and a black flare to the papers in the stove, and then set it alight, the doors of the Sistine were opened and the cardinals went to another of the good sisters's monochromatic meals. The black smoke was seen in the piazza at 11:26.

The discussions among the members of the various parties during the day's intermission continued on the question of whether Benelli was the right man for pope. He clearly was the leader now, but he was strong, almost too strong, for the taste of many. True, he would continue forward with the policies and initiatives of Paul VI, but certainly with none of that pope's hesitation and doubt. He was brusque, loud, and imperious to start with, and what he would do with the combination of Paul's new-made papal power and Pius XII's autocratic rigidity, frightened a few—especially those conservatives who thought their views, and perhaps they themselves, would be swept completely out of Rome.

After lunch, the cardinals had about an hour for the ancient Roman custom of the *pennichella*. Not a leisurely siesta, nor yet the brief, post-lunch one-cigarette relaxation of the British, but rather something more than a half hour for renewal before continuing with the work of the day.[26]

The fourth ballot was begun as soon as the cardinals were seated once more in the Sistine. Was Benelli now going to surge forward to election?

Giovanni Benelli	45
Pericle Felici	27
Corrado Ursi	18
Karol Wojtyła	9
Giuseppe Siri	5
Others	7

The tide continued to move slowly in Benelli's favor. He had gained five more votes, three of them at the expense of Felici. But Ursi's followers, who knew quite well that the Florentine archbishop was incapable of a papacy that resembled that of John Paul I, remained steadfast behind their open and saintly candidate. Siri's adherents now began to scatter to temporizing votes, since they had no clear view of whom to support as their leader's candidacy foundered.

At this juncture, quite outside the old rules and Paul's consitution alike, Villot proposed a thirty-minute intermission before the next ballot. The last results of the morning and the first in the afternoon were so close that it was obvious that none of the luncheon conversation had produced any change in alignment at all. During this brief pause, Ursi's faction decided that it was time to give up. Their candidate was never going to raise his total beyond the number of his most loyal support. At the same time, Felici's voters came to the same conclusion about their candidate, that is was time to move on. For some of them, Benelli was better than any of the alternatives, although others thought that it was time to advance the possibility of an older, compromise candidate, in the way that the electors had found John XXIII in 1958. These men pitched on Giovanni Colombo, the seventy-five-year-old cardinal who had been Paul VI's choice to succeed him as archbishop of Milan.

Finally, Siri's conservatives came to the conclusion that there was one candidate who still stood who was infinitely preferable to Benelli, Felici, or Ursi, and that was the archbishop of Krakow. They would reunite behind him, at least for the purposes of stopping Benelli. These sudden realignments, agreed to in quick, whispered conversations, showed themselves in the last results of the day:

Giovanni Benelli	65
Karol Wojtyła	24
Giovanni Colombo	14
Corrado Ursi	4
Others	4

Benelli had profitted most by the collapse of both Ursi and Felici. He probably got about ten votes from each faction. The first ballot in the morning might well see him collect the ten more votes he needed to become pope. Some of the conversation in the evening was devoted to guessing whether he would be Paul VII, as Pius XII had paid homage to his predecessor, Pius XI.

The opposition to his papacy was now reduced to only a few: some moderate *Montiniani*, who were advancing Colombo as a compromise to stop Benelli; and the conservatives, who now came to the side of Wojtyła for the same purpose, and in greater number.

Outside, at 5:30 P.M., a large spotlight had been turned on the chimney to make the signal clearer to the crowd. When the smoke began to appear at 6:40 it was at first indistinct in the glare of the light, but soon its blackness was unmistakable.

After dinner, the rounds of visits and conversation pushed forward. Wojtyła had, by this time, gained another major adherent to his cause, Madrid's archbishop, Enrique y Tarancón. Now he had three men to act as grand electors for his candidacy. König wanted him, in spite of his tendency to conservative views, because he was exceptionally personable, healthy, a friend, and, most especially, non-Italian. Krol wanted his friend because he was Polish.

Enrique y Tarancón came to Wojtyła's side because the Spaniard thought that he was just the right combination of social liberal and theological conservative to lead the Church during an immediate future in which his country would have to pass from the hard and socially rigid government of Franco to something else, an uncertain "something else" that could be a democracy, perhaps under the heir to the throne, Juan Carlos, or almost anything that might come from a social explosion once Franco was gone.

These three men decided to try to persuade as many wavering cardinals as they could to support Wojtyła on the first ballot of the morning, in the hope that a surprising rise in his count would make him the obvious choice to stop Benelli's accession. One of them, probably not Krol, used the good offices of the prefect of the Congregation of Bishops, Sebastiano Baggio, as a gateway to the remaining strong conservatives. Baggio, now reconciled to the possibility of a non-Italian pope, seems to have agreed to bring with him as many of his friends—and he had many in the curia—as he could. Other possible supporters who needed gentle handling were the moderates who were voting for Colombo. Clearly, they did not want Benelli, but they also were unlikely to support a conservative candidate simply because he seemed to be the only standing alternative. They needed to be shown that Wojtyła would govern largely in the spirit of Paul VI, if not exactly in keeping with the main thrust of his policies. Although not an enthusiastic supporter of all of the decisions of the council, Wojtyła had taken a leading part in some of its greater pronouncements, notably in the drafting of *Lumen Gentium*, the council's declaration on the dogmatic constitution of the Church.

Benelli's supporters, quite cheerful in their expectation that Monday would see their man as pope, also urged those who had not voted for Benelli to come to his aid now. The objects of their persuasion were the moderate Montiniani who had voted for Colombo on the last ballot. The principal argument was that only Benelli could be expected to continue the policies of Paul VI and the council. He should not fail to have that opportunity. Among those who worked in this cause were McCann of Capetown, Picachy of Calcutta, Ribeiro of Lisbon, and Patriarch Sidarouss, who had been elated by the many steps Paul had taken to recognize the unique experience and value of the Eastern Churches.

In the morning, the final lines were drawn when Colombo passed the word that he wished to have his name withdrawn from any further consideration. He already had submitted his resignation from the see of Milan to Paul VI in the preceding December, and he was known to agree with the principle that retirement because of age was sound ecclesiastical government. In this light, he was unwilling to have his name put forward for the papal chair at his advanced age, in spite of the fact that he was almost two years younger than Roncalli had been when the patriarch of Venice had become John XXIII. Moreover, the activities of the preceding evening had eroded his small support, both on the left, for Benelli, and on the right, for Wojtyła.

The results of the fifth ballot of the conclave showed how the previous evenings persuasions had gone:

Giovanni Benelli	70
Karol Wojtyła	40
Giovanni Colombo	1

Was Villot one of the cardinals who were opposed to Benelli at any price? It may have been so, because he had suffered greatly during the last years of Benelli's stay in the Vatican as Paul's right hand. Though he held the highest offices in the curia, secretary of state and camerlengo, he had been eclipsed again and again by his younger assistant, acting in the name of the pope. There is hardly any other explanation for the fact that the Frenchman now ordered another fifteen-minute break in the schedule of the balloting. If the sixth ballot had been taken immediately after the fifth, and with no consultation or conversation, as the rules required, surely Benelli, only five votes away from the throne, would have achieved his goal. But those fifteen minutes were just enough time for Benelli's weakest supporters to respond to the question of whether they really wanted a man who could be expected to exercise absolute and autocratic rule over the Church for perhaps two decades or more. Benelli was only fifty-seven and, given the age reached by most of the recent Italian popes, he might well have a reign that would exceed that of Leo XIII and become the second-longest reigning pope in history. Of course, Wojtyła was only fifty-eight, but longevity was not a part of his family's history, although his present health was good, through his long dedication to physical fitness. The asides in those critical minutes began to make a difference, as the sixth ballot showed:

Giovanni Benelli	59
Karol Wojtyła	52

Wojtyła had taken eleven votes from Benelli in the most surprising shift in the history of modern conclaves, and he had picked up Colombo's last adherent. The forces now were almost equal. Perhaps the principle that no candidate recovers after the tide begins to recede would now assert itself. Was Benelli really finished, even though he still led in the voting?

In the piazza, the crowd was much smaller than it had been on Sunday. It was a workday and no one really thought there was much chance that the election would come to the same sort of speedy conclusion that had been achieved in August. The smoke from Ciappi's fire was first seen as a mixed gray signal at 11:15. Soon, it began to change for the darker and, in a few minutes, it became clearly black.

Lunch in the Borgia Apartments was so filled with conversation and negotiation that it lasted far longer than its alloted time, and with very little attention to the food. The sisters, somewhat peeved, eventually began to point to the tables to indicate to the cardinals that it was time to clear them. The main thrust of Wojtyła's adherents as they spoke especially to those who were not Italian was not that the Polish cardinal would continue in the manner of Paul VI and John Paul I but rather that it was, after all, time to think of the stunning possibility of a non-Italian pope for the first time in four hundred fifty years. If that triumph, which would undoubtedly please millions of Catholics, were to be achieved in this election, it would have to be Wojtyła. Policy and politics were pushed aside to draw attention to this historical novelty.

During the *pennichella*, König, who had supported the Polish archbishop from the beginning, and Wyzynski, who came late to the side of a fellow countryman he did not like but who was about to bring glory to beloved Poland, both came to Wojtyła's cell. The Polish primate argued that his colleague had to accept the results of the luncheon persuasions, which were going to bring the papacy to the archbishop of Krakow. His election would do more for the Church in Poland in one minute than all the efforts of the past forty years; it would be so great a triumph that the government itself might totter, if not fall. For Wyzynski, that was all that mattered. König took a much wider view. To Wojtyła's comment that the latest results were a mistake, he replied that the results indicated the trend of the cardinals and that there was no mistake at all. Briefly, the question of a name for the new pope passed through the conversation. Wojtyła suggested that he would like to be called Stanislas. That revealed more than anything else his still narrow view of his papacy. It was too much. "You will be called John Paul II," said König, in absolute tones. Wojtyła's answer was, "Let us see what happens in the afternoon."

The sole idea of actually electing a non-Italian pope had swept through a College of Cardinals that included fifty-six non-Europeans as well as many from the Continent who hoped that the centuries of Italian rule could be brought to an end now. This was made clear in the seventh ballot:

| Karol Wojtyła | 73 |
| Giovanni Benelli | 38 |

Every other consideration—continuing the policies of Paul VI, advancing the principles of the council, the humble and winning style of John Paul I, Benelli's own reputation as Paul VI's *delfino*—was being swept aside in the interest of a sensational novelty that would surely bring a burst of goodwill to the new pope, and to the cardinals who had elected him.

Benelli himself, understanding that the high tide was over, smiled and gestured a release from promises to the cardinals generally. In defeat, it was his finest moment.

With no pause at all, which brought the day's schedule back to expectations, in spite of the long lunch, the cardinals voted for the eighth time. By 5:20, the tally of the votes was complete:

| Karol Wojtyła | 97 |
| Giovanni Benelli | 14 |

It was over. It was the culmination of a third of a century of a major papal initiative. When Pius XII was asked what the consequences would be of his appointment of so many non-Italians and so few from the curia among the cardinals he elevated in his Grand Consistory of February 18, 1946, he had said that perhaps there would be a "foreign" pope. Generally, he had continued to expand on that purpose in the creation of 1953. John XXIII, while he did not perceive Pius's direction at first, also extended the College into lands which had never had representation, notably in Latin America. And he had signalled the beginning of a new breadth to the cardinalate by his appointment of Laurean Rugambwa, who was here voting in 1978. Paul had carried the principles of broadened membership still further—Rugambwa had eleven Black African colleagues in the conclave that had just elected Karol Wojtyła, and there were nineteen Spanish-speaking or Portuguese-speaking cardinals from the new world in this conclave, compared to the two in 1939 or the nine in 1958. There were nine Asians here, compared with one in 1958, and none in the conclaves before that. The College of Cardinals had fulfilled one revolution; not one of the council or one of Paul VI, but rather the plan of Pius XII.

Villot now formally approached Wojtyła and asked him if he accepted his election as pontiff. The Polish cardinal replied, "With obedience in faith to Christ, my Lord, and with trust in the mother of Christ and the Church, in spite of great difficulties, I accept." To Villot's next question, by what name he would be known, Wojtyła, mindful of König's admonition, simply said, "John Paul II."

As Ciappi conducted the gathering of all the ballots and other papers and burned them, the pope went the the sacristy, chose one of the three sets of vestments, and robed himself—commenting, "I do not need anyone to vest me."

During the first obedience of the cardinals, with John Paul II standing before the altar, he asked the electors to remain in the conclave on Monday night so that he could dine with them, and then celebrate Mass with them on Tuesday morning. As with the election of John Paul I, one of the masters of ceremonies had placed an armchair for the pope before the altar. When Virgilio Noè gestured for the new pope to be seated, John Paul II said to him, "No, I receive my brothers standing up."

Outside, at 6:19 P.M., a clear signal of white smoke was seen. At 6:43, floodlights were switched on to illuminate the balcony, and, a minute later, Felici appeared to make the formal announcement of the election. He could not resist playing the moment for its full sensational value. Over the microphones, his voice was unmistakably clear: *Annuntio vobis, gaudeam magnum, habemus papam. Eminentissimum ac Reverendissimum Dominum, Dominum Carolum.* . . . He came to a full stop, smiling broadly. In many parts of the piazza, there were audible gasps. The only Charles of whom most of them had heard was Carlo Confalonieri, the aged dean of the College, who was not even in the conclave. Yet, it seemed that he had been chosen pope. There were no other Italian cardinals with his baptismal name. Felici relished the moment, . . . *Sanctæ Romanæ Ecclesiæ Cardinalem,* he raised his voice and, very carefully and clearly correctly pronounced the surname of the new pope . . . Wojtyła (Voy-TI-wa). He continued, *Qui sibi nomen imposuit Joanni Pauli Secundi.* There still was considerable confusion. Who was Wojtyła? One woman, who can stand for many in the throng that evening, was overheard to ask a neighbor in the crowd who the pope was. "Di Polonia," he replied. "Ah, di Bologna," she said, with a tone of satisfied recognition. "No, Signora, di Polonia. Un Polacco."

At 7:22, John Paul II finally appeared on the balcony to give his first papal blessing, *Urbi et Orbi.* After he gave the opening invocation for the blessing, and had received the reply from the crowd, he paused. Before imparting the sign of the cross over the crowd, he seized the historical moment:

> Dear Brothers and Sisters, we still are grieved after the death of our most beloved Pope John Paul I. And now the most eminent cardinals have called a new bishop of Rome. They have called him from a distant land, distant but always close through our communion in the Christian faith and tradition. I was afraid to accept that responsibility, but I did so in a spirit of obedience to the Lord and total faithfulness to Mary, our most holy mother.
>
> I do not know whether I can explain myself well in your—no, our—Italian language. If I make a mistake you will correct me. And so I present myself to all of you to confess our common faith, our hope, and our fidelity to Mary, the mother of Christ and of the Church; and also to begin anew on this road of history and of the Church. I begin with the help of God and the help of men.

It was a winning and sympathetic moment, with all the right touches, from the recollection of John Paul I to the allusion to "our" Italian language. The pope completed his blessing, and then withdrew. Almost immediately, he went to his dinner with the cardinals.

John Paul II's inaugural remarks were his alone, and composed in the space of only a few minutes. It was an unplanned revelation of himself, and the import of his remarks was not lost on many observers. Twice he had invoked the name of Mary, but there had been no mention of the Christ of the Gospels, the central theological theme of Vatican II. He already had begun the long, slow turn to the right, moving toward the nostalgic Catholicism of Pius XII and his Tridentine predecessors. Almost two decades later, as an ultraconservative movement to have Mary declared to be the co-redemptrix of mankind attracted favorable papal attention, the opening remarks of his reign began to assume more weight than they had on that cool October evening.

Of course, no pope can foretell with certainty who his successor will be; and no pope creates cardinals for an exclusive set of narrow reasons, so every population of the College of Cardinals has men who espouse a wide variety of theological, political, and social views, no matter how carefully the pope has chosen his men to reflect his own opinions. In the interest of a sensational historical development, the cardinals had elected a man who had been elevated to the cardinalate in the first place not because of his dedication to, or admiration of, the aims of Vatican II, but because Paul VI had needed a counterpoise in Poland to the autocratic authority of the primate, Wyzynski. Wojtyła's appointment in 1967 had been political. He was chosen because he was there, not because he was close in spirit to either John XXIII or Paul VI. It is probable that no cardinal who cast a vote for the Polish archbishop even knew of the audience that Paul VI had given to Wyzynski and thirty-eight other Polish bishops on November 13, 1965, just as the council's fourth session was ending. With Wojtyła right behind him, the Polish primate had told the pope bluntly that it would not be possible to implement the decisions of the council in Poland for some time to come, because of the political situation. He asked Paul to leave the conduct of some later introduction of conciliar reform into Poland entirely in the hands of the Polish episcopacy. Paul was stunned and angered, but not alarmed. After all, Wyzynski would never be his successor, of that he could be sure.

Now, in 1978, the College had given the Church the most conservative pope since Pius X (1903–1914).

At the final dinner in the conclave, John Paul II took the same seat he had used on Saturday and Sunday, rather than a presiding chair or throne. During the meal, he walked around the room, chatting with, and embracing, the cardinals in a free and comfortable manner. All of them still were enjoying the euphoria of the occasion. When he reached Villot, he asked the camerlengo if there were any champagne in the conclave. Villot replied that three cases had been brought in as a part of the extraordinary supplies. John Paul told him to bring them out. Villot, in turn, passed the order to the master of ceremonies, Virgilio Noè. Soon, the sisters of the hospice of Saint Martha came in bearing trays of bottles and glasses—a rôle quite different from their usual plain service of pasta and table wine. John Paul gestured to them to bring the bottles to him, and he began uncorking them with a practiced hand. As he handed a glass to Krol, he said to him, "I must return to your Philadelphia soon, so that you and I can sing together again."

Krol replied, "At any time, on any day, Holiness." Cooke of New York, who was next to Krol, commented "Why don't you sing now." After more encouragement, Krol stood and sang the old Latin wish for many years of life, *Plurimos annos, plurimos.* As he continued, other cardinals began to stand and join in. It was music with which most of them were familiar. When Krol was finished, there was a round of applause, and another cardinal called out, "Why not sing 'The Highlander'?"—a favorite song of the new pope. To this, Wyzynski added, "In Polish." With another gesture of encouragement, Krol began one of Poland's most famous lieder:[27]

> Góralu czy ci nie żal
> Odchodzić od stron ojczystych
> Świerkowych lasów i hal
> I tych potoków przejrzystych.
> Góralu czy ci nie żal
> Góralu wracaj do hal.

> A góral na góry spoziera
> I łzy rękawem ociera
> I góry porzucić trzeba
> Dla chleba panie dla chleba.

> Góralu wróć się do hal
> W chatach zostali ojcowie,
> Gdy pójdziesz od nich hen w dal,
> Cóż z nimi będzie, och kto wie?

> A góral jak dziecko płacze,
> Może ich już nie obaczę
> I starych porzucić trzeba
> Dla chleba panie dla chleba.

> Góralu, nie odchodż nie
> Na wzgórku u Męki Boskiej
> Tam matka twa płacze cię
> Uschnie z tęsknoty i troski.

Now some of the cardinals began to lose their euphoria for confusion. Here was expression they did not understand in a language they did not understand to music they did not understand. This time, Krol was a soloist. When he completed his rendition, John Paul said to him, "Sing it once again, and I will join you." Together, they recapitulated the song.

By this time, only the singers and Wyzynski had any idea at all about what was occurring. The two dozen Italian cardinals, in particular, realized with some shock just what a change was to come over the Church.

The non-Polish silence was first broken when the prefect of the pontifical household, Jacques Martin, a culturally sophisticated Frenchman, whispered an aside to the principal master of ceremonies, Virgilio Noè, also a man of considerable culture, "It must be the way they do things in Poland."

After the pope and Krol had finished, the tension eased somewhat, amid some applause and laughter, and the dinner went on.

The official commencement of the reign came at 10:00 A.M. on Sunday, October 22, when the archdeacon imposed the pallium on John Paul II before a crowd of two hundred thousand who had gathered in the piazza. But the real signal that John Paul II would mold the Church to his own view came with "Góralu czy ci nie żal."

NOTES

1. The house where he stayed is only a few dozen yards from the beach stormed by American troops on January 22, 1944, on the first day of the Anzio campaign. It took three months to secure the immediate locality completely.

2. Later, Fontana and his assistant, Buzzonetti, released their official diagnosis. The pope, they said, had first experienced an unexpected, serious, and progressive rise in arterial pressure; which was followed rapidly by the typical symptoms of an insufficiency of the left ventricle, together with clinical symptoms of acute pulmonary edema.

3. Santa Monica may seem an odd name for a religious house for men, but she has a special significance for the Augustinians, since she was the great theologian's mother.

4. Colombo also had submitted his resignation on reaching his seventy-fifth birthday, December 6, 1977, but its effect was pending while the search for a new archbishop of Milan continued. This task was being conducted with great care. Not only was Milan the largest diocese in Italy other than Rome itself, it was Montini's own former see, and Paul took great interest in the question of who would fill his former chair.

5. Luciani's name had appeared on at least one short list of possible patriarchs, but it was soon removed, because it was thought that he did not want to leave Vittorio Veneto. A later list included the names of Cardinal Antonio Samorè and Monsignor Franco Costa, the deputy director of Catholic Action in Italy. After the letter of complaint, which was signed by more than a hundred representatives of the Venetian laity, many of them prominent, Luciani's name was replaced on the list of serious candidates to be considered. The official appointment to the patriarchate was made on December 15, 1969. Luciani was installed as patriarch on February 8, 1970.

6. In a pastoral letter to the people of Venice, in February, 1976, he told them: "I have urged . . . parish priests to rid themselves of the gold, pearls, and rings that have been offered by the

faithful as *ex votos*. I myself [offer] the gold chain which once belonged to Pope Pius XII and which was given to me by Pope John XXIII when he consecrated me a bishop. It is small in view of the immensity of the needs. Perhaps, however, it will help people to understand that the real treasures of the Church are the poor, the disinherited, and the weak. They should be helped, not by the occasional gift of alms, but rather in a way that will allow them to rise to the standard of living and the level of education to which they have a right." For this chain and two other items, he received about sixteen thousand dollars, all of which went directly to charities. No bishop inspired by the tone and discourse of Vatican II could fail to respond.

7. The shop, founded in 1792, has provided nearly every cleric and religious in Rome with vestments, habits, and ordinary clothing since that time. Every pope since Pius VII (1800–1823) has been outfitted by Gammarelli, except Pius XII, a native Roman, who preferred clothing from his family tailor.

8. A traditional anecdote, trotted out at every modern conclave, is that recent conclaves are short because the Sisters's cooking is so dreadful. Before 1878, the cardinals's meals were made in their own kitchens and then delivered to them through the rota by the stewards of their households, the *dapiferi*. The twice-daily processions of the *dapiferi* and their subordinates through the streets from the residences to the conclave was one of the chief public spectacles in Rome in conclave-time.

9. The eight electors from the United States were John Joseph Krol (archbishop of Philadelphia, created 1967), John Patrick Cody (Chicago, 1967), John Francis Dearden (Detroit, 1969), John Joseph Carberry (St. Louis, 1969), Terence James Cooke (New York, 1969), Timothy Manning (Los Angeles, 1973), Humberto Sousa Medeiros (Boston, 1973), and William Wakefield Baum (Washington, 1976). John Joseph Wright, prefect of the Congregation of the Clergy (1969) was eligible, but did not attend. Three other American cardinals were over eighty and were barred from the conclave—James Francis McIntyre (emeritus of Los Angeles, 1953), Lawrence Joseph Shehan (emeritus of Baltimore, 1965), and Patrick Aloysius O'Boyle (emeritus of Washington, 1967).

10. Delargey kept his lifelong cheerfulness and sense of camaraderie, even though he knew that he was dying of cancer. He did survive past his sixty-fourth birthday, on December 10, and died in Wellington on January 29, 1979.

11. In fact, he was third in seniority among the six cardinal-bishops, the leading prelates in the College. Paul created him a cardinal on February 22, 1965, and advanced him to the rank of cardinal-bishop of Frascati on December 12, 1974—when he already was cardinal-secretary of state and camerlengo—in succession to Amleto Giovanni Cicognani, who had died a year before, on December 17, 1973.

12. Carlo Confalonieri was created a cardinal by John XXIII on December 15, 1958. He became a cardinal-bishop on March 14, 1972, when Paul advanced him to the suburbicarian diocese of Palestrina. He became dean of the College and cardinal-bishop of Ostia on December 13, 1977, after the death of Cardinal Luigi Traglia on the preceding November 22. Paolo Marella was created a cardnial on December 14, 1959, also by John XXIII. Paul made him cardinal-bishop of Porto and Santa Ruffina on March 14, 1972, in succession to Eugene Tisserant, who died on the preceding February 21.

13. Antonio Samorè was created on June 26, 1967, and advanced to the rank of cardinal-bishop of Sabina on December 12, 1974, as was Villot. He was junior to the camerlengo, however, because the date of his creation as a cardinal was later that Villot's advancement to the cardinalate. He succeeded Giuseppe Ferretto, who died March 17, 1973. Sebastiano Baggio was created April 30, 1969, and became cardinal-bishop of Velletri on December 12, 1974, in succession to Ildebrando Antoniutti (died August 1, 1974). Finally, Francesco Carpino was created June 26, 1967, and made cardinal-bishop of Albano on January 27, 1978, after the death of Luigi Traglia.

14. Sacchetti was the inheritor of the largest part of the old office of prince-marshal, including the right to keep the outside set of keys to the conclave. The importance of his family in papal affairs began with the career of Cardinal Giulio Sacchetti, the friend and confidant of Pope Urban VIII (1623-1644). Before Urban created him a cardinal on January 19, 1626, he had served as secretary of the Congregation of the Council and then as nuncio in Spain. As cardinal, the Florentine was prefect of the apostolic signature for many years. He died June 28, 1663, after a cardinalate of thirty-seven years. His nephew, Urbano, also was a cardinal.

15. The first cardinal, possibly either Jan

Willebrands of the Secretariat for Christian Unity or Antonio Rebeiro, patriarch of Lisbon, whose chairs flanked Luciani's, merely was abbreviating or paraphrasing Paul's exhortation to his successor in part two of his constitution, which the electors had heard read aloud to them on the previous evening: "We ask him who shall be elected not to be frightened by the seriousness of the office into refusing it when he is called to it but to bow humbly to the divine will and plan. For God who lays the burden on him also supports him so that he can carry the burden. He who is the source of the burden also helps a man to cope with it. He who bestows the dignity gives the weak man strength lest he falter before the magnitude of the task." (ii, vi, 86).

16. While we can speculate on the identities of these eight—Siri almost certainly was among them—we do know the name of one. Juan Carlos Aramburu of Buenos Aires said later that he was one cardinal who did not vote for Luciani.

17. Felici committed one solecism in his announcement, however. He announced the name with a number—"qui sibi nomen imposuit Joanni Pauli Primi"—which, in Latin as in Italian or English, violated the logic of the language. He was John Paul, and could not be John Paul I until there was a John Paul II. Unique identifiers do not require numbers, as in the case of earlier popes whose names were never used again, Simmachus, Hormisdas, Severinus, and so forth. But a unique name had not occurred in more than a thousand years. The last "numberless" pope had been Lando, who reigned from July, 913, to February, 914.

18. Though it was an act of preservation rather than a post-mortem examination, some medical historians incorrectly point to the opening of the body of Alexander V in Bologna in May, 1410, as the first "modern" post-mortem—i.e., the opening of the body in a search for the cause of death. The physician and surgeon who performed the procedure, Pietro di Argelata, was the most distinguished professor of medicine of the time in the oldest medical school in Europe, the University of Bologna. The temptation to describe the exenteration of Alexander V as an autopsy, post-mortem, or forensic examination was understandable, since Argelata's procedure included evisceration, and his description resembled the exact protocol of an autopsy.

19. Paris de Grassis was the man who had invented the rota for the second conclave of 1503 in order to prevent any oral communication between the people sealed in the conclave and those on the outside. Still used today—modern conclaves usually have two of them—it consists of a rotating vertical panel of wood encased in an open drum with two apertures, one facing inward to the conclave and the other outward to the external guardians of the election, with shelves built on at least one side so that objects can be passed into and out of the conclave, once they have been inspected to ensure that they are free of messages and other prohibited items. Formerly, their chief use was to pass food to the cardinals. Americans, in particular, need not wait for a conclave in Rome to see one. Thomas Jefferson heard about it while he was serving as ambassador to France (1783–1789), perhaps from descriptions of the conclave that elected Pius VI in the fall and winter of 1774–1775. When he returned to Monticello, he had one built into the wall between his dining room and the outside corridor into which food was brought from the kitchen. In this way, he and his guests could dine in complete privacy, well away from the ears of servants and others in the house who might reveal sensitive comments or opinions. In that way, it promoted a free, open, and uninhibited exchange of ideas over a good dinner. Besides, Jefferson liked the immediate hospitality of serving his guests himself. Later, other architects and builders copied what they thought to be Jefferson's inspired design in other houses. This is the contribution of the Roman conclave to American domestic architecture.

20. The whole question of autopsies of popes excited such interest in 1978, and has been discussed without sound information so many times since, that it is worth reprinting the precise details from the account of Paolo Giovio, who had first-hand knowledge of the autopsy on Leo: "Sed ea febris, quod ex intervallis lacesserat, a medicis adulantibus, aut iudicio deceptis aliquandiu neglecta, adeo vehementer demum incubuit, ut pene priusquam morbus dignosci posset, & fatalis hora sentiretur, turbata ratione fit ereptus: paucis tamen ante horas quam e vita migaret, supplex, iunctus elatisque manibus, atque oculis in coepie coniectis. . . . Fuêre qui existimarent eum indito poculis veneno fuisse sublatum: nam cor eius atri livoris maculas ostendit, & lien prodigiosæ tenuitatis est repertus, quasi peculiaris & oculta veneni potestas totum id visceris exedisset. . . . Adauxit

quoque patrati sceleris suspicionem, quod ipse sub auroram, quum septima noctis hora pontifex expirasset, specie venandi cum canib. Vaticanam portam exiuisset, adeo ut a prætorianis uti fugitiuus carperentur." [Pauli Iovii Novocomensis episcopi Nucerini, *De Vita Leonis Decimi Pont. Max. libri quatuor: his ordine temporum accesserunt Hadriani Sexti Pont. Max. et Pompeii Columnæ Cardinalis vitæ*, ab eodem Paulo Iovio conscriptæ (Florentiæ: Officina Laurentii Torrentini, 1549), lib. IV, 107–108].

21. Gracias was the only cardinal to die in the short reign of John Paul I, and no cardinal passed over his eightieth birthday in that brief span. The other two creations of Pius XII who were still electors were Stefan Wyzynski and Paul Emile Léger.

22. Both men would be created cardinals by John Paul II, Rubin in 1979 and Deskur in 1985.

23. Since this volume was so important in bringing the papacy to the first Polish pope, it deserves some additional attention. The retreat's text was, indeed, a conservative response to the *Signo di Contradiccion* of dom Helder Camara, the archbishop of Olina and Recife. After the retreat, the text was published as *Segno di Contraddizione: Meditazioni* (Milano: Vita e pensiero, 1977, volume 2 of the series *Fede e Mondo Moderno*, vi, 224 pp.). After becoming Pope John Paul II, the text was translated into many languages quickly. The standard English translation, by Mary Smith, was published as *Sign of Contradiction* (Middlegreen, Slough: St Paul Publications, 1979, xii, 206 pp., ISBNs 0854391428 and 0854391584). That edition was reprinted several times, notably London: Hodder and Stoughton, 1979 and 1980; and, as a paperback only, London: G. Chapman, 1979, ISBN 0225662639. The American edition, a reprint of the English edition, is *Sign of Contradiction* (New York: Seabury Press, a Crossroad Book, 1979, xiv, 206 pp.) The most useful commentary on the pope's views is Filippo Gentiloni, "Karol Wojtyla: nel Segno della Contraddizione" (Milano: Baldini & Castoldi, 1996, number 53 in the series I Saggi, 108 pp.)

24. These fifty-six electors included nine Asians, twelve Africans, fourteen North Americans (including nine from the United States, the second largest national contingent after Italy), four from Oceania, and seventeen from countries in Central and South America and the Caribbean.

25. Cardinal Wright never fully recovered from his muscular problems or his surgeries, and died on August 10, 1979. Donald Wuerl was born in the Mount Washington neighborhood of Pittsburgh on November 12, 1940. He first came to Cardinal Wright's attention during the latter's decade as bishop of Pittsburgh (1959–1969). After an undergraduate education at the Catholic University of American in Washington, Wuerl went on to study at the North American College in Rome, and then at the Angelicum. Here, under the direction of the pastoral scholar, Gundisalvus M. Grech, he completed his doctoral dissertation, *The Priesthood: the Doctrine of the Third Synod of Bishops and Recent Theological Conclusions*, in 1973. By that time, Wright was in the curia and a cardinal and had appointed Father Wuerl to be his secretary. Wuerl's graduate research led to his first major book, *The Catholic Priesthood Today* (Chicago: Franciscan Herald Press, 1976), which has been widely read and influential. The early patronage of Cardinal Wright prepared Wuerl for a remarkable and successful career. Ordained on December 17, 1966, in Rome, he was made titular bishop of Rosemarkie and auxiliary bishop of Seattle on January 6, 1986. Two years later, on February 11, 1988, he became Wright's third successor as bishop of Pittsburgh, after Anthony Joseph Bevilacqua was elevated to archbishop of Philadelphia. A tireless writer on catechetical and pastoral matters, Wuerl today is one of the most influential and respected members of the American hierarchy. It seems quite likely that he, like Justin Rigali in Saint Louis, will be a cardinal in the next reign.

26. The word usually is translated "nap," but that is inadequate to describe how the time is used by many Romans.

27. The song is not, as is often said, a folk song or ballad. The text is by Maria Konopnicka (1842–1910). A wide-ranging nationalistic poet, novelist, translator, essayist, and children's writer, her poetry in particular reflected Polish patriotic aspirations for independence in the nineteenth century. Today, perhaps her most highly admired work is her long poem about Polish peasant emigrants to the New World, *Mr Balcer in Brasil*. The musical setting is by Michal Swiezynski.

VII. John Paul II and the College: The Early Years

Broadly speaking, the terms "liberal" and "conservative" have lost much of their old meaning in the College of Cardinals during the pontificate of John Paul II. Before John XXIII and the Second Vatican Council, cardinals who held strongly conservative theological views—admirers of Pius IX and Pius X—carried this outlook over to the social and political sphere, as well. The converse also held true. Cardinals with a more open and modern approach to theology—disciples of Leo XIII and Benedict XV—tended to have more modern and progressive views on social and political questions.

The overwhelming triumph of liberal prelates at Vatican II, led by advanced social and political thinkers like Leo Suenens and Achille Liénart, eventually pushed John XXIII's *aggiornamento* far beyond what he envisioned. In most cases, Paul VI tried to carry out the intentions of the council faithfully, which meant both a more open, non-Roman approach to theology, on the one hand, and a transformation of the hierarchy, in general, to a population which supported liberal, even "leftist," political and social views. But factional triumph always brings reaction. In the case of the College of Cardinals, as with episcopal and archiepiscopal appointments, John Paul II has advanced men whom he regards as absolutely faithful to the magisterium—rigid adherence to orthodoxy, as the pope sees it—but who also are committed to a "pastoral" ministry—a concerned care for the people and their well-being. This bifurcation has produced a large number of cardinals—like Roger Mahony in Los Angeles, William Keeler in Baltimore, and Anthony Bevilacqua in Philadelphia, in the United States—who cannot be placed into the categories of "liberal" or "conservative" with any confidence.

Richard Cushing of Boston can stand as a symbol of the traditional liberal. He spoke openly of the possibility of a married priesthood while, at the same time, he greatly increased the social outreach programs of the archdiocese of Boston—so much so that his successor, Humberto Medeiros, found a deficit of twenty-five million dollars when he first examined Boston's ledgers. By contrast, John Cody of Chicago is the symbolic conservative. His theology held very close to the narrow interpretation of Trent to be found in the *Baltimore Catechism*.

At the same time, he ruled Chicago as an autocrat—some of his priests called him "Nero" quite openly in conversation—and took little effective notice of the great increase in urban poverty and the growth of foreign-language populations who needed the special care of the Church in a time of alienation, transition, and dislocation.

These two men, of course, were more complex in their views and their government than the foregoing paragraph suggests, but as symbols they can serve to illustrate the point that none of the American cardinals who will vote in the next conclave can be placed into a category with either Cushing or Cody.

The observer can make a similar case for the European and Commonwealth cardinals, and national hierarchies, as well.

In this and the two succeeding chapters, the terms "liberal" and "conservative" refer more to theological positions, especially with regard to the more advanced ideas of Vatican II, than to social attitudes and policies.

Because the cardinals named by John Paul II will constitute the overwhelming majority of the electors who will choose the next pope, and because current information on many of the cardinals is not easy to obtain, it is valuable to take notice of their lives and careers in somewhat greater detail than was the case with earlier members of the College. This information, and the brief collection of biographical details on the current electors—which are to be found largely in notes—may prove valuable for understanding a little more about them.

On Monday, October 16, 1978, at the moment of his elevation, John Paul II inherited a College of Cardinals of one hundred twenty-five members, of whom one hundred ten were valid papal electors.

John Paul II's original ideas on the College and its future are unclear, including his private schedule for creating new members. What is clear is that, from the beginning of his reign, John Paul II chose to deal with the College as a whole in a much more conservative manner than his predecessors had. John XXIII and then Paul VI had transformed the College boldly, first by increasing the size of the College to unprecedented levels, and then by seeking a much broader international representation in the enlarged College they created. Until 1998, John Paul returned to an adherence to the limits on the College's size that had been established by his predecessors, in this case to the limit of no more than one hundred twenty electors at one time. There was no particular reason for doing this, since the number one hundred twenty seems to have been chosen, in part, because of the limitations on the number of seats that could be fitted into the

Sistine Chapel. Of course, no unchangeable rule states that conclaves must be held there. In fact, conclaves have been held in a number of places in Rome, and in other cities, as well. Pius VII was elected in Venice in 1800. Following the precedent of both of his immediate predecessors, John Paul II could have increased the number of voting members of the College quickly, to place his stamp on the electorate in the same manner that Paul VI had used. But he did not.

Under the rules of Paul VI, he had ten immediate vacancies that he could fill at any time. This number grew over the next five months by two, with the deaths of Joseph Marie Trin-nhu-Khuê of Hanoi, on November 27, 1978, and Reginald John Delargey of Wellington, on January 29, 1980.[1] Any earlier plans that he might have made, however, were superseded on March 9, 1979, when Jean Villot, the cardinal-secretary of state, whom he had reappointed on his election, suddenly dropped dead on a street near the Vatican.[2]

It was necessary for the pope to appoint a new secretary of state as soon as possible, since the office carries with it so much responsibility and power. And the holder of the office always is a cardinal. Because Villot's death was so unexpected, John Paul made the first and obvious choice of a successor, Agostino Casaroli. He was born in Castel San Giovanni on November 24, 1914, and came to the Vatican as a member of the staff of the secretariat of state in 1940. In 1961, John XXIII made him *sostituto* in the Congregation of Extraordinary Ecclesiastical Affairs. He served there until the reorganization of the curia in 1967 under *Regimini* abolished it and created the Council for the Public Affairs of the Church instead, of which Casaroli was made the first secretary. He served Paul VI well as the principal Church negotiator for Eastern Europe. In that rôle, he made many visits to Hungary, Yugoslavia, Czechoslovakia, Bulgaria, and Poland. John Paul II knew perfectly well of his failed negotiations in 1966 with the Polish government for the putative visit of Paul VI. These particular negotiations were frustrated by the activities of Cardinal Wyzynski. When Paul made Villot secretary of state on the retirement of Cicognani, Casaroli stepped forward to be the principal executive of the secretariat, handling the daily office affairs while Paul's right hand, Giovanni Benelli, carried out the private actions and initiatives of the pope. For the Vatican, the speed of Casaroli's elevation to be pro-secretary of state was remarkable. He was appointed officially on April 28, only fifty days after Villot died.[3] At the same time, Giuseppe Caprio, who had followed Benelli as *sostituto* in the secretariat of state, was made president of the Administration of the Patrimony of the Holy See (which became the prefecture of Economic Affairs in 1981), becoming Casaroli's principal deputy. Almost immediately afterward, John Paul needed to hold a consistory for the creation of new cardinals in order to raise Casaroli to that dignity, and to confirm him as cardinal-secretary of state; and also to reward Caprio, who deserved the cardinalate also because of his enlarged responsibilities.

By that time, the pope already had a list of thirteen other names of men he wished to elevate to the College. With only only thirteen vacancies for electors, however, there was no way he could accomodate all fifteen of his choices. He decided to hold the first cardinalitial consistory of his reign on June 30, 1979, because it was the eightieth birthday of Cardinal Frantisek Tomásek, archbishop of Prague. His loss of suffrage meant that John Paul could name fourteen cardinals in the consistory, and reserve one name *in pectore*.

Agostino Casaroli: *Secretary of State*

Giuseppe Caprio: *Pres., Admin. of Patrimony of Holy See*

Marco Cé: *Patriarch of Venice*

Egano Righi-Lambertini: *Vatican administration*

Joseph-Marie Trinh van-Can: *Archbishop of Hanoi*

Ernesto Civardi: *Secretary, Conclaves, 1978*

Ernesto Corripio Ahumada: *Archbishop of Mexico City*

Joseph Asajiro Satowaki: *Archbishop of Nagasaki*

Roger Etchegaray: *Archbishop of Marseilles*

Anastasio Alberto Ballestrero: *Archbishop of Turin*

Tomàs Ó Fiaich (Thomas Fee): *Archbishop of Armagh*

Gerald Emmet Carter: *Archbishop of Toronto*

Franciszek Macharski: *Archbishop of Kraków*

Władisław Rubin: *Secretary General, Synod of Bishops*

Once again, Poland had three cardinals, as it had done once before under Paul VI during the cardinalate of Bolesław Filipiak. John Paul II took great delight in elevating his old friend, Władisław Rubin, who had been his chief contact in Rome for years. He also was particularly happy to advance Franciszek Macharski, a native of Kraków who was born two days after the pope's seventh birthday. Ordained a priest on April 2, 1950, he went on to further academic study at the University of Fribourg, from 1956 to 1960. He then returned to Kraków to teach pastoral theology in the archdiocesan seminary, now detached from its ancient home as a part of the University. His views and teachings brought him close to Karol Wojtyła, whose friend he became. Wojtyła appointed him rector of the seminary in 1970. John Paul's election opened the see of Kraków for a new archbishop, and the pope appointed Macharski to the office on December 30, 1978, and consecrated him personally on the following January 6. At the end of the century, Macharski remains the pope's principal friend and ally in the Polish episcopacy, and certainly will be one of the two leading Polish cardinals in the next conclave.

The elevation of Marco Cé followed his appointment as patriarch of Venice, in succession to Luciani, on December 7, 1978—John Paul I had not lived to appoint his successor at Venice.[4]

Other appointments of residential ordinaries followed the principles established by Paul VI. Some were ordinaries who had succeeded cardinals in archdioceses that had been ruled by cardinal-archbishops for generations past, like Anastasio Alberto Ballestrero at Turin[5] and Tomás Ó Fiaich at Armagh,[6] others were the successors of archbishops whom Paul VI had made cardinals with the expectation that future holders of the sees also would be cardinals in the new internationalized College, like Trinh van-Can at Hanoi[7] and Ernesto Corripio Ahumada at Mexico City.[8]

John Paul II also followed precedent in naming Japan's new cardinal. Paul VI did not identify the archdiocese of Tokyo as cardinalitial, in the manner that he treated other capital cities whose archbishops both he and John XXIII had made cardinals. Rather, he determined to choose another senior Japanese prelate to follow Peter Tatsuo Doi, who died on February 21, 1970. So it was Paul Yoshigoro Taguchi, archbishop of Osaka, not Tokyo, who was named on March 5, 1973. After he died, on February 23, 1978, the question became which archbishop would fill his seat. John Paul II decided on the symbolic choice of Joseph Asajiro Satowaki, archbishop of Nagasaki. The new cardinal had distinguished himself as apostolic administrator of Taiwan during the years of Japanese occupation. He tried his best to mitigate the worst offenses of the Japanese military authorities against the local population, with some minor successes. At the end of the war, he returned to Japan as both director of the minor seminary at Nagasaki and administrator of the devastated archdiocese. On May 3, 1955, he became the first bishop of Kagashima; then, on December 19, 1968, Paul VI brought him back to Nagasaki as archbishop. Ten years later, he assumed the presidency of the Episcopal Conference of Japan. The cardinalate was both a reward for his new position in the Japanese hierarchy and a specific distinction to the city of which he was archbishop.

Canada, with its relatively small Catholic population, would now be represented by four cardinals, with the creation of Gerald Emmet Carter of Toronto. All of them were electors. Léger, archbishop of Montreal from 1950 to 1968, when he resigned to become a missionary to lepers, was still active as a cardinal, although he had submitted an additional resignation from archiepiscopal status to take effect on his seventy-fifth birthday, on April 26, 1979.

At the same time, Roy in Quebec (born January 25, 1905) and Flahiff in

Winnipeg (born October 26, 1905) both had more than a half decade of eligibility as electors to run. Carter, born March 1, 1912, had been president of the Canadian Conference of Catholic Bishops from 1975 to 1977, while he was bishop of London, Ontario. On April 27, 1978, he became James Charles McGuigan's second successor at Toronto. His elevation to the College in 1979 was just a continuation of Paul VI's policy of often elevating presidents or former presidents of national conferences of bishops. It seems, again, as if the new pope was simply following the guidelines of his predecessor and had not yet evolved his own criteria for membership in the College.

A similar pattern seems to have governed the elevation of Roger Etchegaray, archbishop of Marseilles since December 22, 1970. He was elected head of the French Episcopal Conference in 1975 and was still serving in that office in 1979.[9]

The curial equivalent of national administrative service, like that of Satowaki, Etchegaray, and Carter, was the condition of Egano Righi-Lambertini, who had been the Vatican's special envoy at the Council of Europe after 1974, combining this duty with his service as nuncio to France, from 1969.[10]

Finally, Ernesto Civardi, who had not received the red *zucchetto* from the hands of either John Paul I or John Paul II, was the secretary of the conclaves that had elected both popes. Like most other prelates who had served in that office, the cardinalate came to him—in this reign sooner rather than later.[11] The final evidence that this creation bore more of the stamp of his predecessor, and the Vatican bureaucracy that Paul had installed, is that four of the fourteen cardinals created in 1979 were Italian. That substantial a percentage of Italian representation would not be reached again until 1998, because John Paul II has gone further than any modern pope to reduce Italian influence in the College.

After John Paul II was shot, at 5:00 P.M. on Wednesday, May 13, 1981, all extraordinary administrative business in the Vatican ceased for a time. First came more than five hours of surgery to save his life and then a long convalescense at the Policlinica Agostino Gemelli. During the first operation, the pope was given a temporary colostomy, in order to give the perforations he had suffered a chance to heal. He returned to the Vatican on June 3, after twenty-two days of hospitalization, but with instructions to moderate his usual heavy schedule. While in this convalescense, he was attacked by an infection of cytomegalovirus, a condition similar to mononucleosis.[12] On June 20, he was admitted to the Gemelli again in order to monitor the progress of the viral infection and to treat his symptoms speedily. Once recovered, he underwent another abdominal operation on

August 5 to reconnect his colon. After a brief stay at the Vatican, he went to Castel Gandolfo on August 16 to continue his convalescence.

During this period, the daily business of the Church continued under the leadership of Casaroli, who held almost daily conferences with the pope. Indeed, some extraordinary initiatives that began before the attempted assassination also continued, especially the first meeting on July 13 of the council of cardinals that John Paul II had appointed in the light of the horrendous financial condition of the Church that he inherited from Paul VI.

By late winter, 1982, John Paul was fully recovered. On February 12, he resumed his itinerary of international trips with a four-stop journey to West Africa.

The pope's brush with death was followed by another attempt to kill him, at Fatima on the first annivesary of Agça's shooting. Camillo Cibin, the chief of Vatican security, bore the knife-wielding assailant to the ground. These episodes hastened the pope's plan to realign both the College and the curia to bring Church administration more in line with his own views, and to speed the work to promulgate the new code of canon law.

The first major effort of 1983 was the apostolic constitution *Sacræ disciplinæ leges*, issued on January 25, which established the new code. This was followed immediately by his second creation of cardinals on February 2, 1983. Since 1979, the College had undergone a relatively small but significant shift. Of the one hundred twenty electors in the College at the end of his first creation in 1979, nine had died, while another seven had passed their eightieth birthdays.[13] In addition, six of the cardinals who had become superannuated before the first creation also had died.[14] This reduced the College to a membership of one hundred twenty, of whom one hundred four were electors. To fill the College again, John Paul created eighteen new cardinals. Among them were two prelates who already were over eighty, an innovation which turned the cardinalate into an honorary office for the first time in history. John Paul II would extend and amplify this custom in subsequent consistories, so that today there are a number of members of the College who have never been papal electors. The creations of 1983 were:

Antoine Pierre Khoraiche: *Patriarch of Antioch (Maronites)*
Bernard Yago: *Archbishop of Abidjan, Ivory Coast*
Aurelio Sabattani: *Prefect of the Apostolic Signature*
Franjo Kuharic: *Archbishop of Zagreb*
Giuseppe Casoria: *Prefect, Congregation of Sacraments*
José Alí Lebrún Moratinos: *Archbishop of Caracas*

Joseph Louis Bernardin: *Archbishop of Chicago*
Michael Michai Kitbunchu: *Archbishop of Bangkok*
Alexandre do Nascimento: *Archbishop of Lubango, Angola*
Alfonso López Trujillo: *Archbishop of Medellin, Colombia*
Godfried Danneels: *Archbishop of Malines-Brussels*
Thomas Stafford Williams: *Archbishop of Wellington*
Carlo Maria Martini: *Archbishop of Milan*
Jean-Marie Lustiger: *Archbishop of Paris*
Józef Glemp: *Archbishop of Warsaw and Gniezno*
Julijans Vaivods: *Administrator of Riga and Liepaja*
Joachim Meisner: *Bishop of Berlin*
Henri de Lubac, S.J.: *Theologian*

The creation of 1983 was the first of three promotions which may be described as transitional, because some new members of the College were men who had become locally prominent during Paul VI's government and were now continuing their rise by achieving the cardinalate. Others, by contrast, were newly appointed archbishops who often were elevated unexpectedly by John Paul II without reference to the criteria which had been established in the time of his predecessor.

The two non-voting creations were exceptions to both these principles. Henri de Lubac, the most distinguished French theologian of his age after Teilhard de Chardin, had been selected for the cardinalate by Paul VI, but had refused the honor because he did not think it appropriate for cardinal-deacons necessarily also to be bishops. John Paul II dispensed him from the need for episcopal consecration, so that he could accept the cardinal's dignity without violating his principles.[15] De Lubac, a native of Cambrai, born February 20, 1896, entered the Jesuit order in October, 1913, and was ordained on August 22, 1927. Two years later, he joined the theological faculty at Lyons, where he taught both fundamental theology and religious history. Deeply influenced by the thought of Pierre Teilhard de Chardin, de Lubac published a major theological work on free will and determinism, *Surnaturel: Études Historiques*, in 1946. Almost immediately, his work was reported to the Congregation of the Holy Office as theologically suspect. The ensuing attacks on him and his work, both offically from Rome and unofficially from some corners of French Catholic thinking, eventually drove him from his teaching position. John XXIII rehabilitated him entirely and he was reinstated in his academic position. He then served as the chief consultor for the preparator theological commission for the Second Vatican Council and became one of the *periti* at the council when it opened. Later, in 1969, Paul VI made him a member of the International Theological Commission. His creation as cardinal in 1983 was an experiment by John Paul II to mask his reversal of many of the main directions of conciliar thinking. It was the pope's special adaptation of a ploy used by many princes in the past. Once your rival has been defeated decisively, load him with honors and distinctions to sweeten the sting of loss and to obligate him even further. The success of the experiment in the case of de Lubac was so great that John Paul II has used the method repeatedly by elevating elderly figures who played important parts in the direction of the council to the cardinalate as a meaningless distinction in their old age. In some cases, discussed later, he has waited so long that his cardinal designate has died while waiting for the red hat or has enjoyed the cardinalate for only a few days.

The other non-elector was Julijans Vaivods, Latvia's Catholic hero, who was eighty-seven years old when he achieved the cardinalate. Ordained on April 7, 1918, he was primarily a teacher and writer in the years before World War II. In 1944, he became vicar general of Liepaja. The heroism he displayed in combatting both national socialism and communism through his writing was all the more remarkable because he was almost fifty when he began his fight. Repeatedly detained, questioned, and imprisoned, he was released from one term of exile in time to attend the council. During the third session of Vatican II, on November 18, 1964, he was quietly consecrated titular bishop of Macriana Major and appointed apostolic administrator of both the archdiocese of Riga and the diocese of Liepaja. Still serving actively, in spite of his age and considerable political constraint, his cardinalate was meant to serve as a possible shield to protect him from additional persecution. He continued as cardinal-administrator until his death on May 23, 1990, at eighty-nine.[16]

Vaivods's red hat also defused any resentment on the part of Latvian Catholics that might have been engendered by an increase in the number of Polish cardinals, which rose to the unprecedented number of four in this consistory. Another Slavic red hat went to Franjo Kuharic, Seper's successor as archbishop of Zagreb.[17]

The new cardinal-patriarch on this occasion was Antoine Pierre Khoraiche, patriarch of Antioch of the Maronites, successor of Paul Pierre Meouchi.[18] As patriarch and as cardinal, he worked to reconcile the many factions, both ethinic and religious, which had shattered Lebanon in the 1970s and 1980s. He also tried to promote the withdrawal of foreign troops from Lebanese soil.

Only two new curial cardinals were created in this consistory, both of whom had made their curial reputations as jurists. Further creations awaited John Paul's partial reorganization of the curia, announced on April 9, 1984, and a further, and more radical, restructuring of the Vatican bureaucracy, which the pope enacted in the apostolic constitution, *Pastor Bonus*. This consitution was dated June 28, 1988, and published on the occasion of the fourth consistory for the creation of new cardinals, but its provisions did not take effect until March 1, 1989.

Aurelio Sabattani had been placed in the charge of the Apostolic Signature as pro-prefect in 1982. Now, with the cardinalate, he began a five-year term as prefect.[19] Giuseppe Casoria had been made pro-prefect of the Congregation for Sacraments and Divine Worship in 1981. He became prefect on his creation as cardinal, but served only a one-year term in office.[20]

Three of the new archiepiscopal electors were created as an extension of Paul VI's efforts to transform the College into a body of national representatives from the community of nations, no matter how small the resident Catholic population in those nations might be. This policy brought the cardinalate to the Ivory Coast's Bernard Yago,[21] Angola's Alexandre do Nascimento,[22] and Thailand's Michael Michai Kitbunchu.[23]

The two new Latin American cardinals, Alfonso López Trujillo of Medellin and José Alí Lebrún Moratinos of Caracas, were chosen less as national representatives than as counterpoises to the liberal body of cardinals in Central and South America who had been elevated by Paul VI. Their appointments were the beginning of John Paul II's decided shift towards conservatism in the College.

López Trujillo had led the archconservative reaction to the new, socially conscious movement which emerged from the Medellin Conference in 1965, and rallied enough support to become secretary general of CELAM on November 22, 1972.[24] After considerable resistance, he was confirmed in office for a second term on November 1, 1974, and then voted president in March, 1979, serving until 1983. He became archbishop of Medellin on June 2, 1979. His espousal of what has been termed a theology of submission rather than a theology of liberation appealed strongly to the conservative instincts of John Paul II, who gave him the cardinalate for his efforts. Now Colombia had two cardinals. But his controversial stand in favor of pre-conciliar norms in the Latin American Church eventually made his tenure in office difficult. On November 8, 1990, John Paul II transferred him to Rome as president of the Pontifical Council for the Family. López Trujillo resigned Medellin on January 9, 1991. José Alí Lebrún Moratinos was perhaps less extreme in his views, but he, too, favored the abandonment of Liberation Theology as a cure for the social and economic ills of Latin America.[25]

Perhaps the most purely pastoral creation in this consistory was that of Thomas Stafford Williams, archbishop of Wellington.[26] Although his views and outlook had been formed by Vatican II and although he had held no prelatical office before beccomming archbishop, he was regarded as suitable and uncontroversial when he was made archbishop. Since that time, however, he has revealed himself to be a man of strong liberalizing tendencies. An example of his work, which certainly did not please the pope, can be seen in his part in the declaration on gender inclusiveness in language that was issued by the New Zealand Catholic Bishops' Conference in April, 1984.

It was easy to find a succesor to Reginald Delargey at Wellington, because he left behind him a happy and prosperous archdiocese. But it was very difficult to find someone to assume control of Chicago following the death of John Patrick Cody on April 25, 1982. The spiritual and economic affairs of the see were nearly in ruins. When Cody died, he was in the nineteenth month of a federal grand jury investigation into charges that he had misappropriated as much as one million dollars of the tax exempt funds of the archdiocese for his own personal use, including real estate, insurance, and other business dealings that included Helen Dolan Wilson, widely believed to be his mistress, and her son. In addition, rebellion among both clergy and laity was almost open. Both Paul VI and John Paul I knew of some of Cody's problems in the last days of their lives, but John Paul II had chosen not to press the issue of a possible retirement. By 1981, the situation was so grave that replacing Cody became a matter of real importance in the Vatican. His death changed the nature of the needed solution but not the general state of affairs. Without regard for political or theological inclinations, John Paul needed a new archbishop with a personality that could win back respect and regard for the Catholic Church in Chicago and a manager who could put the affairs of the archdiocese in order as quickly as possible. Moreover, that man had to be found quickly, before the see suffered any further damage from a lack of leadership. Rome's choice was inspired. On July 8, 1982, John Paul transferred Joseph Louis Bernardin from Cincinnati.[27] In his fourteen years as archbishop, Bernardin recovered almost all the goodwill that Cody had lost, beginning with the decision by the United States Attorney, Daniel Webb, to close the investigation by the grand jury with no indictments. By the time the cardinal died, on November 14, 1996, he had become perhaps the most respected and beloved ordinary in the history of Chicago in the estimation of the people—even eclipsing Albert Gregory Meyer.[28]

Bernardin's appointment to the cardinalate in 1983 was a special moment in the evolution of Catholicism in America. Largely an immigrant creation in the century following the Irish potato famine, the American Church had been dominated, for almost all of its rise to maturity, by Irish-

American clergymen. To a lesser extent, German-American Catholics also came to wield considerable influence in the American Church. Of the twenty-six residential American archbishops who became cardinals before 1983, no fewer than twenty were entirely or largely of Irish ancestry, while another four were German-Americans.[29] However, the second largest Catholic population in the United States after the major period of Catholic emigration to America closed were people of Italian ancestry. They were, in spite of their heritage, highly under-represented in the hierarchy for many decades. Bernardin, as late as 1983, was the first American cardinal to come from that background.[30]

Somewhat more diplomatic delicacy was needed to find a successor to Alfred Bengsch in Berlin, following his death on December 13, 1979. Here the criteria included an ability to work skillfully with the East German government as well as to maintain a certain degree of ecumenical openness with other German churches. Joachim Meisner, the auxiliary administrator of Erfurt-Meiningen, met those requirements.[31] His appointment as bishop of Berlin was made official on April 22, 1980. Though not well-known in Berlin, he quickly established himself through his willingness to discuss every question in an engaging yet straightforward manner. On December 20, 1988, Cardinal Meisner was elevated to archiepiscopal rank and transferred to Köln to succeed Joseph Höffner.

The same principles, with even more delicacy, had been required in 1981 to find a successor for Stefan Wyszynski in Warsaw. The old primate had died of cancer on May 28, just as the pope was beginning to recover from the attempt on his life. Indeed, in the last days of May, the two had spoken together by telephone for the last time from their respective hospital beds. Now, while John Paul was still unable to grasp the reins of daily business fully, speed was necessary to find a new primate for Poland.

The first slight stirrings toward toppling the Polish communist government and ending the Soviet domination of Polish affairs had begun with John Paul II's election in 1978, when the wild popular outpouring of enthusiasm over the event had produced demonstrations throughout Poland which the government had been unable to curb. The rumblings became more palpable with the pope's first visit to Poland, June 2–10, 1979. Again, the government was unable to control the situation at all. In the days before the pope arrived, a series of conversations between Edward Gierek, first secretary of the Polish Communist Party, and Leonid Brezhnev were devoted exclusively to the problem of stopping John Paul from coming to Poland. Gierek's conclusion was that it was impossible. Within a year, the strikes at Gdansk had given birth to *Solidarity*, which had been granted its first official recognition on August 30, 1980. The ensuing fall and winter saw an increase in popular pressure against the government which eventually precipitated the crisis of December 12–13, in which martial law was declared. It was just as the tension was becomming critical that the old primate died, and while the pope was hospitalized and unable to function with his normal speed and dedication.

The nature of the situation meant that a new primate had to be found with no delay. It was clear that the man had to be a skilled negotiator, not prone to the "thunderstorms" with which Wyszynski had destabilized church-state relations in Poland so frequently over the years. The new primate's personality also had to be strong enough to assume not only the leadership of the Polish Church but also, with the certain cardinalate to follow, the leadership of a large part of the Eastern bloc of cardinals. In addition, he had to know the intricacies of Poland's secret, as well as public, relationships with the Vatican, for there would be no time for training on the job. From a very short list of candidates, John Paul chose Józef Glemp, a canon lawyer of considerable intellectual subtlety who had been Wyszynski's secretary for many years, and bishop of Warmia since March 4, 1979.[32] Glemp was not a man of much social understanding, as his later difficulties with the Jewish community would show, but he was the right man in 1981 to hold the Church in Poland on a steady, careful course during the crises which followed his official appointment on July 7, 1981. The cardinalate was expected for him in the next consistory of John Paul II, and he was duly elevated in 1983.

The red hat for Jean-Marie Lustiger marked the highest distinction but one in the Catholic Church for the first Jewish cardinal since those of the Pierleoni family in the twelfth century. He was born in Paris on September 16, 1926. His parents were Jewish immigrants from Poland. Both of them, who had come to France to escape the traditional anti-Semitism of Eastern European culture, were captured and deported to death camps by the Germans—his mother died at Auschwitz in 1943. He escaped a similar fate because his parents had sent him to a boarding school in Orleans where his origins, they hoped, would be more difficult to trace. Later, he was hidden by a French Catholic family in that city, whose influence on him was profound and whose great kindness he repaid by becoming a Catholic himself. He was baptized on August 25, 1940, just before his fourteenth birthday. The circumstances of his life in the War moved him spiritually and he had discovered his vocation by the end of the conflict. His intellectual brilliance shone in his work at the Institut Catholique, where he obtained a licentiate in theology, and at the Sorbonne, where he took degrees in both the humanities and philosophy. After he completed his early academic studies, he was ordained on April 17, 1954. From the outset of his

Catholic life, in a remarkable display of personal distinction, he never abjured or fled from his Jewish heritage. This steadfastness did not hinder his rise in the Church and, thanks not only to the brilliance of his mind but also to his Polish ancestry, John Paul II made him bishop of Orleans on November 10, 1979. He was consecrated for the office on the following December 8. By the time Lustiger became a bishop, François Marty had submitted his resignation as archbishop of Paris on reaching his seventy-fifth brithday, May 18, 1979. The process of choosing a successor for him, which took almost two years, was a matter of considerable consultation and analysis. To the amazement of Paris's citizens, John Paul II responded to growing evidence of anti-Semitism in France by raising Lustiger to the archiepiscopal see of the nation's capital on January 31, 1981. Now, in the consistory of 1983, he was made cardinal-priest of the title of Santi Marcellino e Pietro, one of the twenty-five original titles—Roman parishes headed by cardinals. Although he is the fifth cardinal of French antecessors to hold the title in this century, the church is better known for its original and nonconforming cardinals over the centuries, ranging from Francisco Ximenés y Cisneros (1507–1517), the great Spanish reformer, administrator, and intellectual, to Pasquale d'Acquaviva d'Aragona (1661–1677), who wore his biretta always cocked to one side to indiate that he took neither himself nor his cardinalate too seriously.

In the years since his creation as cardinal, Lustiger has added to his considerable fame as a politically astute intellectual and a pastor of deep personal involvement. He has, of course, continued to be a Jew, leaving the theological conundrum of his dual citizenship for others to worry about:

> For me to say that I am no longer a Jew would be to deny my father
> and mother, my grandfathers and grandmothers. I am a Jew in the
> same measure as all my other relatives. . . [who were] butchered in
> Auschwitz or in other camps . . .

Finally, John Paul continued his penchant for seeking out prelates of unusual academic and scholarly attainment by elevating one of the Church's foremost biblical scholars, the Jesuit exegete and commentator, Carlo Maria Martini, to be Giovanni Colombo's successor at Milan, two days before New Year's, 1979, and then cardinal, in 1983. Martini, perhaps the most important and advanced scholar and thinker in the College today, was born in Turin on February 15, 1927. He joined the Society of Jesus at the close of World War II in Italy, September 25, 1944, and was ordained on July 13, 1952, at the age of twenty-five, an unusually young age for a Jesuit. In 1958, he joined the faculty of the seminary at Chieti, but his career there lasted only three years before he was called to Rome as a professor at the Pontifical Biblical Institute. From 1969 to 1978, he was rector of the Institute, before he was made rector of the Gregorianum. During the years in Rome, he acquired the respect and then the friendship of Cardinal Sebastiano Baggio, Paul VI's last prefect of the Congregation of Bishops, who recommended him strongly to John Paul II as a successor to Colombo, who had submitted his resignation from Milan in December, 1977. Although Martini had no immediate curial experience, nor had he ever been an ordinary, nor had he much exposure to pastoral duties, John Paul eventually appointed him to Milan on the sheer weight of his impressive, almost magisterial, biblical scholarship. He already had published a dozen significant monographs and editions, as well as many articles of real scholarly merit, the number of which has trebled during his years as archbishop and cardinal—although his more recent works have been more personal and pastoral in nature. Among his earlier works of importance are *Il Problema della Recensionalita del Codice B alla Luce del Papiro Bodmer XIV*, a meticulous textual examination and criticism of the earliest surviving texts of the Gospel of Luke,[33] his modern edition with commentary of the Acts of the Apostles,[34] his discussion of some of the most significant of the Dead Sea Scrolls, *Notes on the Papyri of Qumran Cave 7*,[35] and his comprehensive review of modern scholarship on the subject of resurrection, *Il Problema Storico della Risurrezione negli Studi Recenti*.[36]

In more recent years, he has been a leader in espousing a stronger course of ecumenism, which has included his approval for a world council of all Christian churches. He also has led in establishing a greater breadth of discussion and rapprochement with Judaism and in acknowledging publicly the grave difficulties of the current teachings on birth control. Many of his views have made him less and less popular in Rome, but at the same time, have brought him considerable respect and attention elsewhere.

Since only sixteen of the eighteen new cardinals were electors at the time of their creations, the College's membership at the conclusion of the consistory of 1983 saw a full complement of one hundred twenty electors of a total of one hundred thirty-eight.

Between February 2, 1983, and the next consistory for the creation of new cardinals, May 25, 1985, the superannuation of eighteen of the membership certainly was anticipated,[37] but the deaths of no fewer than nine electors was not.[38] The additional deaths of four of the aged cardinals, and that of Joseph Schröffer, who had become eighty on February 20, 1983, reduced the whole membership of the College to one hundred twenty-four, of whom ninety-three were electors.[39] Of the cardinals created by Pius XII, only two still lived, Siri and Léger, of whom only the former was still an elector. Of the eight surviving creations of John XXIII,[40] only König, Rugambwa, Landázuri Ricketts, and Silva Henriquez were still electors. Of the eighty-two surviving creations of Paul VI, fifty-nine were still electors.

The third consistory of the reign saw the elevation of twenty-eight new cardinals, but one of them, Pietro Pavan, already was beyond the age of eighty when he was named.[41] Consequently, there were twenty-seven new electors, which again brought the College to its full electoral complement of one hundred twenty. The whole number of cardinals, as of May 25, was one hundred fifty-two.

No fewer than twelve of the new cardinals were curial officials who had risen with John Paul's reorganization of the bureaucracy in April, 1984; while fifteen others were residential ordinaries:

Luigi Dadaglio: *Penetentiary Major*
D. Simon Lourdusamy: *Prefect, Oriental Churches*
Francis A. Arinze: *Pres., Secretariat for Non-Christians*
Juan Francisco Fresno Larrain: *Archbishop of Santiago, Chile*
Antonio Innocenti: *Vatican diplomat*
Miguel Obando Bravo: *Archbishop of Managua*
Angel Suquía Goicoechea: *Archbishop of Madrid*
Jean Jerôme Hamer: *Pref., Cong. Rel. and Secular Insts.*
Ricardo J. Vidal: *Archbishop of Cebú, Philippines*
Henryk Roman Gulbinowicz: *Archbishop of Wroclaw*
Paulos Tzadua: *Archbishop of Addis Ababa*
Jozef Tomko: *Pref., Cong. for Evangelization of Peoples*
Myroslav Ivan Lubachivsky: *Archbishop of Lwow*
Andrzej Maria Deskur: *Vatican administration*
Paul Poupard: *Pres., Secretariat for Non-Believers*
Louis-Albert Vachon: *Archbishop of Québec*
Albert Decourtray: *Archbishop of Lyon*
Rosalio José Castillo Lara: *Pres., Authentic Interp. Canon Law*
Friedrich Wetter: *Archbishop of Munich and Freising*
Silvano Piovanelli: *Archbishop of Florence*
Adrianus Johannes Simonis: *Archbishop of Utrecht*
Edouard Gagnon: *Pres., Pontifical Council for the Family*
Alfons Maria Stickler: *Librarian and Archivist*
Bernard Francis Law: *Archbishop of Boston*
John Joseph O'Connor: *Archbishop of New York*
Giacomo Biffi: *Archbishop of Bologna*
Pietro Pavan

No pope can remold the Vatican and the Church to his own views of faith and government very quickly, unless he is prepared to circumvent the normal governmental apparatus, as John XXIII did by calling the council, or to explode the existing order in the name of some higher mandate, as Paul VI did in expanding the College and the hierarchy and in restructuring and enlarging the curia. John Paul II, a much more conservative pope than his immediate predecessors, was unwilling to embark on any such dramatic action. Rather, he contented himself with letting attrition—retirement and death—make room for him to place men of his own choosing in positions of power. The criteria he used in deciding whom he would promote have been, first, a rigid adherence to the magisterium in every sense of teaching, from doctrine, to social teaching, to political behavior, and to liturgical matters, and then a commitment to social action, even if that meant distorting traditional Catholic norms.

The creations of 1985 form a body of men who, for the first time, were all drawn from the population that met those criteria. No fewer than a third of them were prelates with a strong exposure to traditional Spanish and Latin American Catholicism, with its rigidity and intolerance for dissent, on the one hand, and its relative comfort with ecclesiastical secrecy and mystery, exemplified in a strong devotion to Marian cults, like Fatima, and in institutions like Opus Dei.

More than in any other of John Paul II's seven consistories for creating new cardinals, it was the curial appointments in 1985 who drew the most attention. Among these new cardinals were two former nuncios to Spain, Luigi Dadaglio,[42] who was now the penetentiary major, and Antonio Innocenti,[43] who would soon become the prefect of the Congregation of the Clergy. Though Dadaglio is now dead and Innocenti now retired, in the 1980s they put a distinctly conservative stamp on their work in the curia. The same can be said of the new prefect of the Congregation for Sacraments and Divine Worship, Paul Augustin Mayer.[44] The pope, and these new cardinals, knew that their age precluded them from long cardinalitial careers, but they would last long enough to move the bureaucracy away from the openness, which had begun to emerge under Paul VI, towards a more rigid, doctrinal conservatism.

It was from the younger curial cardinals, none of whom were Italian, that John Paul expected the greatest effort to close the windows in the Vatican that John XXIII and Paul VI had thrown open so vigorously. Of them, perhaps the most distinguished has proved to be Francis A. Arinze.[45]

Long before inculturation,[46] and its allied movements, indigenization and contextualization, became Rome's norms for evangelizing non-Christian peoples, with its elements of drum ritual and liturgical dance, Arinze attracted surprised and favorable notice with his doctoral dissertation at the University of Rome in 1960, *Ibo Sacrifice as an Introduction to the Cat-*

echesis of Holy Mass.[47] In his narrative, he anticipates most of the principles of inculturation that began to appear in Asian books and tracts nearly twenty years later. Once he had returned to Nigeria, he became a leading figure in educational policy and reform in his homeland, and continued to publish widely. One work, in particular, *Partnership in Education between Church and State in Eastern Nigeria*, attracted so much favorable comment that Paul VI made him a bishop partly on the strength of it.[48]

Once John Paul had decided on a course of action for the Secretariat for Non-Christians, he summoned Arinze to Rome to take charge of the effort. Arinze's cardinalate in 1985 was a further recognition of the success of his work. Widely seen on television, by the end of the century Arinze had become the best-known African cardinal.

Arinze, soon to be the star of the Vatican's efforts in the Third World, had to have an opposite as prefect of the Congregation for the Evangelization of Peoples who would join him in steering the process of inculturation to become the official Roman policy for all missionary work in traditionally non-Christian regions. John Paul chose the first Slovak prelate to achieve the cardinalate in modern times, Jozef Tomko.[49] He has proven to be more of a follower than a leader, and has allowed more public, and perhaps ambitious, prelates, like Arinze, to make general policy in matters of evangelization.

John Paul also needed a new prefect of the Congregation for the Oriental Churches who would be absolutely rigid in suppressing any dissent that might arise from Eastern theologians who objected to his new policies and procedures. He found that man in the person of the Indian archbishop, D. Simon Lourdusamy, who knew little about the rites of the ancient Levantine and Slavic Churches, but did know how to project Rome's will to non-Latin populations.[50] Paul VI had brought him to Rome in 1971 and, after fourteen years, he had become the consummate curial official. John Paul now gave him the cardinalate and the prefecture. As the present reign comes to a close, he has become one of the most influential prelates in the curia, whose views on the Third World in particular are widely sought.

When the massive revision of the code of canon law was nearing its close in 1982, John Paul II brought Rosalio José Castillo Lara, then just an auxiliary bishop in Venezuela although a well-regarded former professor of canon law, to Rome to oversee the final stages of preparation.[51] After the new code was promulgated in the following year, the pope created a new curial body to ensure that it was given strict observance, the Pontifical Commission for the Authentic Interpretation of the Code of Canon Law, and made Castillo Lara its head. Later, after his cardinalate, his reputation for probity and careful administration made him an outstanding candidate to manage many of the Vatican's fiscal affairs. John Paul moved him into several such tasks early in this decade, where he remains as a pivotal official in the operation of the Vatican state.

Even more conservative than these prelates was John Paul's choice of Edouard Gagnon to fill the position of president of the Pontifical Council for the Family, which was created to be the Vatican's primary organization for enforcing recent doctrine on the laity, including the provisions of *Humanæ Vitæ*.[52] Edouard Gagnon, whose cardinalate firmly established him as a leading figure in the curia, is so conservative in his views that when he was appointed as an envoy to the schismatic archbishop Marcel Lefebvre in 1987, the archbishop's supporters hailed the move because Gagnon, they proclaimed, was the one cardinal in the College who was closest to their own views.

In his years in the curia, Gagnon has adopted an authoritarian style that often imitates the old ways of the curia before John XXIII. This has led to a number of signal failures, one of which was the negotiation with the Lefebvrists, which have won him little regard or respect from the members of the College who are residential archbishops.

An example of his work emerged recently when a member of a conservative Catholic organization, Catholics United for the Faith, then resident in the archdiocese of Milwaukee, wrote to the cardinal to complain about the content of a series of publications on sex education and ethics called *The New Creation*.[53] These teaching materials are used in the schools of about eighty dioceses and had been in print, without much controversy, since the mid-1980s. Gagnon responded to the complaint by writing a reply in which he stated that the work was "a travesty of sex education." In a subsequent letter, he also stated that he "expressed the judgment of the Holy Father." The series had received the imprimatur from two successive archbishops of Dubuque, James J. Byrne (1962–1983) and Daniel W. Kucera, OSB (1984–1995). Archbishop Kucera learned about the whole controversy when copies of the correspondence were sent to him by a third party.

Later, he wrote, "At no time had Cardinal Gagnon contacted me about the material contained in his letters." And he noted further that catechetical books, such as those in *The New Creation* series, were under the jurisdiction of the Congregation of Clergy, not the Pontifical Council for the Family. Beyond that, no one from the Vatican has ever discussed the moral or ethical content of the materials with the publisher. Whatever Paul VI meant precisely by the policy of episcopal consultation, it is certainly over for Gagnon. These, and other peremptory actions, have dimished him significantly, although he continues to enjoy the trust and favor of the pope.

Two much less controversial curial officials were the new Dominican cardinal, Jean Jerôme Hamer, the new prefect of the Congregation for Religious and Secular Institutes,[54] and the new Salesian in the College, Alfons Maria Stickler, an entirely apolitical scholar who was made Librarian and Archivist of the Holy Roman Church.[55] Stickler later became something of a thorn in the curia's paw, because he has espoused the cause of a wider restoration of the Tridentine Mass. As one commentator put it, Cardinal Stickler does not understand why inculturation and contextualization should not apply to Europeans, too.

Another respected member of the curia who received the red hat in 1985—not so vehemently doctrinal as some of his colleagues—was Paul Poupard, the new president of both the Secretariat for Non-Believers and the Council of Culture.[56] The new curial representatives were rounded out with a red hat for the pope's old friend and close confidant, Andrzej Maria Deskur, the retired president of the Pontifical Council for Social Communications.[57]

Of the fifteen residential archbishops who became cardinals in 1985, two were more than new national representations; they were personal tributes to men who had defended the Church in times of great trial. Miguel Obando Bravo of Nicaragua had spent all of his decade and a half as archbishop of Managua defending his people, first against the Somozas, then from the excesses of civil war, and finally against the Sandinistas.[58] At least he was able to count on the prestige of his archiepiscopal office to help him in his efforts, because more than eighty-five percent of Nicaragua's population of about four and a half million is Catholic. For Paulos Tzadua of Addis Ababa there could be no such reliance on his standing as a Catholic archbishop.[59] His flock consisted of a mere three hundred thousand in a national population of almost fifty million. Yet he, too, had opposed, as strongly as he could, the tyrannical Mengistu regime while also dealing with the famine that swept his country for years.

By contrast, most of the new European archbishops were carefully chosen conservative replacements for liberal cardinals of Paul VI who had retired or died. For the most part, these men did not have the stature of their predecessors, but that was a small consideration when balanced against their more pliable obedience to the magisterium. The Dutch Church, generally the most rebellious population in modern European Catholicism, saw Jan Willebrands replaced by Adrianus Johannes Simonis.[60] Munich and Freising received Friedrich Wetter to fill the place vacated by Joseph Ratzinger, who now was a leading figure of the curia.[61] Madrid saw Angel Suquía Goicoechea take the place of Vicente Enrique y Tarancón.[62] And, at Lyon, the new primate of the Gauls was Albert Decourtray, replacing Alexandre Charles Renard.[63]

All these men now received the cardinalate as the usual distinction of their archiepiscopal office. Of them, only Decourtray matched or exceeded the ability and distinction of his predecessor.

The new red hats for Florence and Bologna were given for the same reason, and to men of much the same stamp. Silvano Piovanelli was no match for Benelli,[64] and Giacomo Biffi was a sudden and unexpected replacement for Enrico Manfredini at Bologna.[65] As one Bolognese put it: "I am on a ladder called Lercaro—Poma—Manfredini—Biffi. Can you guess which way I am going?"

Biffi, overjoyed to be cardinal and archbishop after his unsatisfactory years as auxiliary in Milan under Colombo, has become the leading rightist ecclesiastic in Italy in gratitude to John Paul II for his advancement. His attacks against every deviation from Rome's norms have been particularly harsh and abrasive. Among his special targets have been not only homosexuals, pro-choice activists, and feminists—hardly favorites of the pope—but also unwed mothers and the victims of AIDS. He has campaigned vigorously to banish the music of Mozart and Schubert from liturgical celebrations, and has said that thoughts of ordaining women are like thoughts of celebrating the Eucharist by consecrating Coca-Cola. Siri revived. Of course, Biffi, a standing joke among much of the Italian press, is not helped in his image or reputation in recent years by the fact that his name also has become, thanks to a transfer from English and Canadian slang, the noun for a child's training toilet.

The Slavic Church was rewarded with another cardinalate for Poland, in the person of Henryk Roman Gulbinowicz, archbishop of Wroclaw,[66] and for the Ukraine, where Miroslav Ivan Lubachivsky had replaced Slipyj as the metropolitan archbishop of Lwow and was now made a cardinal.[67] While, in Asia, a second cardinalate for the Philippines was granted to the archbishop of Cebú, Ricardo J. Vidal.[68]

In the New World, two more conservative replacements for liberal predecessors occurred with the cardinalates for Juan Francisco Fresno Larrain in Santiago, Chile,[69] and Louis-Albert Vachon in Quebec.[70]

The two new American cardinals also are emblematic of John Paul II's steady transition of the College to a more conservative composition. The deaths of Humberto Sousa Medeiros of Boston, on September 17, 1983, and Terence James Cooke of New York just nineteen days later, on October 6, left vacant two of the most important ordinariates in the United States. Pio Laghi, the former nuncio in Argentina, had been posted to Washington as apostolic delegate in 1980 to succeed Jean Jadot, who was

recalled to Rome. The measure of Jadot's Pauline liberalism and its distasteful effect on John Paul is seen by the fact that he was the only delegate
to Washington since the post was created in 1893 who was not created a
cardinal eventually. During his ten years in Washington, Laghi's recommendations to Rome on episcopal appointments were much more conservative than those of any of his three predecessors. A reflection of this new
style, in which there was to be no toleration for dissent and no constructive
dialogue with dissenters, was apparent immediately in the men chosen to
fill the sees of the dead cardinals. Both Bernard Francis Law, who received
Boston, and John Joseph O'Connor, who received New York, were men
who sprang from a military background and always had found themselves
comfortable in combative atmosphere and rigid adherence to authority.

Law was born in Torreon, Mexico, on November 4, 1931, the son of a
career officer in the United States Army Air Corps who had been posted
there as a part of the American efforts to restrain the political situation in
Mexico which would lead to revolution a few years later. He grew up in the
segregated South and became a priest in Jackson, Mississippi, in 1961, before the real emergence of the Civil Rights movement in the Gulf states.[71]
When he was given episcopal rank, he was sent to Springfield-Cape Girardeau, Missouri, as the successor to William Wakefield Baum, who had
been transferred to succeed Patrick O'Boyle as archbishop of Washington.
Thanks to Laghi's strong recommendation, Law was given Boston on January 11, 1984. The political and doctrinal conservatism which is in keeping
with his background is, perhaps, nowhere more apparent than in his reaction to Cardinal Bernardin's "Catholic Common Project," an effort begun
in Chicago to bring Catholics of differing opinions and attitudes together
in the interests of harmony. Law responded to the original statement of intentions, "Called to be Catholic: Church in a Time of Peril,"[72] by de-
nouncing its principles of open discussion in language that precisely
reflects the policy of John Paul II:

> It is unfortunate that the Cardinal's [Bernardin's] initiative has tied
> itself to this statement. . . . Throughout [this text] there are gratu-
> itous assumptions, and at significant points it breathes an ideological
> bias which it elsewhere decries in others . . . the fundamental flaw in
> this document is its appeal for "dialogue" as a path to "common
> ground." The church already has "common ground." It is found in
> Sacred Scripture and Tradition, and it is mediated to us through the
> authoritative and binding teaching of the Magisterium.

The proposal by one cardinal-archbishop, Bernardin, who had come to
archiepiscopal rank under Jadot and had been created a cardinal in the
earlier phases of John Paul II's transition to rigid doctrinal conservatism,

and the reaction of another, Law, who had risen to Boston under Laghi and was created later in John Paul's transition, shows, broadly speaking, the change in the Church's direction, not only in the United States. The tension exhibited in the differing attitudes towards a movement like "Common Ground" illuminates one fundamental differnce in approach to the problems of the modern Church which will be fought out, perhaps bitterly, in the next conclave.

O'Connor was not the son of a military officer; rather he became an officer himself.[73] Following his ordination in Philadelphia, he spent seven years in various teaching and pastoral tasks before he found his calling as a chaplain in the United States Navy. For twenty-seven years, from 1952 to 1979, he served both naval and Marine units, with combat service in both Korea and Vietnam. He first attracted wide public notice in 1967, when he published a spirited defense of the War in Vietnam on the basis of moral authority, just as the anti-war movement was gaining force. His 250-page tract, *A Chaplain Looks at Vietnam*,[74] cheered the hawks, both in and out of government. It paved the way for his rise to the rank of rear admiral and the post of chief of chaplains, given by President Gerald Ford in 1975. When O'Connor retired from active military service in 1979, John Paul II made him titular bishop of Curzola and auxiliary bishop of the American military vicariate on April 18.[75] Four years later, on May 6, 1983, he was transferred to be bishop of Scranton, Pennsylvania, in succession to J. Carroll McCormick, another Philadelphian. Cooke's sudden death provided the opportunity to fill New York with another strong conservative, and O'Connor was transferred there on January 26, 1984. During his years in Scranton and New York, O'Connor has kept strong ties with military life, including many old friends, both active and retired. He remains a close and careful student of military policy and the evolution of the military aspects of modern technology. This is not particularly well known, but one speech from an early time in his episcopate which reveals his interests and concerns was "The Technologies of Warfare in the Next Decade," which he gave as the keynote address of the meeting of the Institute for Theological Encounter with Science and Technology in October, 1981.[76]

Since he came to New York, and especially since the death of Bernardin in November, 1996, O'Connor has become the preeminent American cardinal. At the end of the century, his power is reflected in the fact that, although he submitted his resignation, *nunc pro tunc*, as archbishop of New York in January, 1995, he has not been replaced. If the next conclave convenes before January, 2000, when he becomes eighty and will lose his vote, O'Connor will be the leader of the Americans in the election.

During the thirty-seven months between John Paul II's third and fourth cardinalitial consistories, the population of the College finally shifted from a dominance by the creations of Paul VI to a majority of members created by John Paul II. In this period, only five electors died,[77] but eighteen others passed their eightieth birthdays and lost right to vote in the conclave.[78] Among those was the last of Pius XII's cardinals to do so, Siri, now the retired archbishop of Genoa. Of John XXIII's creations, Suenens already had been superannuated, and now, in this period, two of the remaining four lost their suffrage, König and Silva Henriquez. Only two could still vote in a conclave, Rugambwa and Landázuri Ricketts. In addition, all five of the dead electors and thirteen of those who became eighty were creations of Paul VI. Only three of the superannuated cardinals—Righi-Lambertini, Civardi, and Khoraiche—were creations of John Paul II. The number of electors, consequently, had fallen to ninety-seven. Eleven other retired cardinals died in this period, including one, Höffner, who had just passed his eightieth birthday when he died.[79] These additional losses reduced the whole membership in the College to one hundred thirty-six, but the new creations brought the number up to one hundred sixty. Since all the new cardinals were electors, the number of those who were eligible to vote rose to one hundred twenty-one, which exceeded Paul VI's rules, in the period between June 28 and July 26—when Corrado Ursi, the retired archbishop of Naples, reached his eightieth birthday.

This consistory marked the first occasion on which John Paul II exceeded the number of electors that had been prescribed in Paul's constitution, *Romano Pontifici Eligendo*; he would do this again in all of his future consistories. John Paul's breaking of the rules of his predecessor seems almost timid when compared with the sweeping changes wrought by John XXIII and Paul VI.

As has been mentioned, popes often use a consistory in which they create new cardinals to publish ceremonially some important enactment or to make major episcopal or archiepiscopal appointments. John Paul II used the consistory of June 28, 1988, to release the new apostolic constitution, *Pastor Bonus*, which superseded Paul VI's provisions in *Regimini* and gave a whole new structure to the Curia Romana. Its provisions, which continue today, became effective on March 1, 1989.

In this consistory, John Paul II again emphasized the elevation of residential archbishops by giving the red hat to no fewer than nineteen of them, and promoting, by contrast, only five curial officials. He wished to wait until the results of his reforms in *Pastor Bonus* could be assessed before creating a larger number of new curial cardinals. The new members of the College were:

Eduardo Martinez Somalo: *Pref., Cong. Divine Worship & Sacraments*

Achille Silvestrini: *Prefect, Apostolic Signature*
Angelo Felici: *Prefect, Cong. for the Causes of Saints*
Paul Grégoire: *Archbishop of Montréal*
Anthony Padiyara: *Archbishop of Ernakulam (Syro-Malabar Rite)*
José Freire Falcão: *Archbishop of Brasilia*
Michele Giordano: *Archbishop of Naples*
Alexandre José Maria dos Santos: *Abp. of Maputo (Lourenço Marques)*
Giovanni Canestri: *Archbishop of Genoa*
Antonio Maria Javierre Ortas: *Librarian and Archivist*
Simon Ignatius Pimenta: *Archbishop of Bombay*
Mario Revollo Bravo: *Archbishop of Bogotá*
Edward Bede Clancy: *Archbishop of Sydney*
Lucas Moreira Neves: *Archbishop of São Salvador da Bahia*
James Aloysius Hickey: *Archbishop of Washington*
Edmund Casimir Szoka: *Archbishop of Detroit*
László Paskai: *Archbishop of Esztergom*
Christian Wiyghan Tumi: *Archbishop of Garoua, Cameroon*
Hans Hermann Groër: *Archbishop of Vienna*
Jacques Martin: *Prefect, Pontifical Household (retired 1986)*
Franz Hengsbach: *Bishop of Essen*
Vincentas Sladkevicius: *Administrator of Kaisiadorys, Lithuania*
Jean Margéot: *Bishop of Port-Louis, Mauritius*
John Baptist Wu Cheng-chung: *Bishop of Hong Kong*

On the original list of names of those to be created, the name of the aged Swiss theologian, Hans Urs von Balthasar, also appeared. He was another of those men of Vatican II who were to be honored with a meaningless distinction, since he was long past the age of eighty. He died, however, on June 26, two days before the consistory.

The list of those elevated in 1988 began with two curial officials whose careers would evolve over the next decade to make them among the most influential and powerful of the cardinals.

Eduardo Martinez Somalo, the newly designated prefect of the Congregation of Divine Worship and Sacraments, a dry, humorless Spaniard, is an ultraconservative with close ties to Opus Dei who had worked for decades in the Secretariat of State in a series of minor positions.[80] In the time of Paul VI, his views certainly were unfashionable and his opportunities for advancement were few. The arrival of John Paul II opened doors for him, beginning with his promotion to be *sostituto* in the Secretariat of State in 1979, where he remained, with increasing authority, until his cardinalate. After his cardinalate, his rise to even higher positions was swift. From 1988 to 1992, he was prefect of the Congregation for Divine Worship and Sacraments. After that term in office, John Paul II, on January 21, 1992, made him prefect of the Congregation for Institutes of Consecrated Life and Societies of Apostolic Life. After Sebastiano Baggio died, on March 21, 1993, the pope made him camerlengo on the following April 5.[81] When D. Simon Lourdusamy left the order of cardinal-deacons on January 29, 1996, Martinez Somalo became archdeacon.

In the next *sede vacante*, Martinez Somalo, as both camerlengo and archdeacon, will be in the unique position of governing the daily affairs of the Church until the next pope is elected, and having the privilege of announcing the name of the new pope.[82]

Almost as powerful, but much more friendly and moderate, was Achille Silvestrini, who is now regarded as the only curial cardinal who is genuinely *papabile*.[83] He joined the curia as a member of the staff of the Secretariat of State in 1953. After twenty years in minor staff positions, he was made *sostituto* in the Council for the Public Affairs of the Church in 1973. John Paul VI lifted him from obscurity after twenty-five years of curial work and made him titular bishop of Novaliciana, with the personal title of archbishop, on May 4, 1979, and secretary of the Council in which he worked, which later became the second section of the Secretariat of State.[84] With his cardinalate in 1988, he was transferred to be prefect of the Apostolic Signature (1988–1991). On May 24, 1991, John Paul II made him prefect of the Congregation for the Oriental Churches. Today, Silvestrini still retains an influential seat in the second section of the Secretariat of State. Silvestrini's career is exceptional because he achieved the cardinalate through work in the Secretariat of State without the long trail of overseas diplomatic posts which constitute the backgrounds of most of the men who have risen to the cardinalate from the Secretariat. Less doctrinaire in the matter of absolute adherence to the ordinary magisterium than most of his curial colleagues, Silvestrini is widely liked and has accumulated a large following both among curial cardinals and among residential cardinal-archbishops whom he has befriended over the years. Whether he achieves the throne or not, he will be a major figure in the *prattiche* that will precede the election of John Paul's successor.

The third important cardinal with a curial background to be elevated in 1988 was Lucas Moreira Neves, archbishop of São Salvador da Bahia.[85] Paul VI had made him titular bishop of Feradi Major and auxiliary bishop of São Paulo on June 9, 1967 (consecrated August 26). In 1974, he was called to Rome and made vice president of the Pontifical Commission for the Laity, where he served for five years. On October 15, 1979, John Paul II raised him to the rank of archbishop and made him secretary for the Congregation of Bishops, where he remained until 1987. Near the conclusion of this term in office, he was transferred to the rank of titular archbishop of Vescovio, on January 3, 1987; and, after the death of Avelar Brandão Vilela, on December 19, 1986, John Paul II then appointed Neves to be archbishop of São Salvador da Bahia, on July 9, 1987. It is no secret that Neves is one of the cardinals whom John Paul would like to have as a successor, and his appointment to a major archdiocese in Brazil, followed by the cardinalate, duplicates the method Paul VI had used to make Benelli a major figure in the conclaves of 1978—a man of both curial and pastoral experience. John Paul II later reconsidered this manoeuvre and recalled him to Rome, where he would be closer to the pope. In June, 1998, he became cardinal-bishop of Sabina, in succession to Eduardo Pironio, and also prefect of the Congregation of Bishops. Neves, however, is severely diabetic, with growing problems caused by the disease; and he will be seventy-three years old in September, 1998, which almost certainly will make him too old for serious consideration as a candidate in the next conclave, although he almost certainly will be advanced as a candidate by the strongly conservative cardinals.

The other active curial official in the consistory of 1988 was Angelo Felici.[86] When he was recalled to Rome for the cardinalate, he also was made prefect of the Congregation for the Causes of Saints. He retired from his prefecture in 1995 and was then made president of the Pontifical Commission "Ecclesia Dei" on December 16, 1995, in succession to Innocenti, who had retired. His influence generally has been small, and that which he had has waned during his cardinalate, because he is regarded as the most extreme conservative in the College, eclipsing even Edouard Gagnon. His opinions echo the views of the integrists of the earlier years of this century, and his attitudes on collegiality and ecumenism have made him the very model of the style of curial cardinal who is most distrusted by residential ordinaries who must govern the Church locally.

A second Spanish curial official who was promoted was Antonio Maria Javierre Ortas.[87] His new position as Librarian and Archivist of the Holy Roman Church in succession to Alfons Maria Stickler would normally have been the zenith of his career. Unlike other recent Librarians, however, he went on, after three and a half years in that position, to be prefect of the Congregation of Divine Worship and the Sacraments on January 24, 1992. He retired in 1996.

Finally, among prelates with a long Roman background, the red hat went to Jacques Martin, almost as an afterthought, since his active cardinalate could last but fifty-nine days.[88]

Most of the archbishops who were made cardinals in this consistory were the successors to other cardinals who had died or retired from ordinariates which had residential cardinals. Italy was represented by two of them, Giovanni Canestri of Genoa[89] and Michele Giordano of Naples.[90] India also was represented by two, Simon Ignatius Pimenta of Bombay[91] and Anthony Padiyara of Ernakulam of the Syro-Malabar rite.[92] Other cardinals who were national representatives in traditional cardinalitial sees were Mario Revollo Bravo of Bogotá, Colombia;[93] Edward Bede Clancy of Sydney, Australia;[94] and László Paskai of Esztergom, soon to be transformed into Esztergom–Budapest.[95] In addition, Canada received a new cardinal in a traditional archdiocese, Paul Grégoire,[96] and Brazil a second cardinal in this creation for its capital city, Brasilia, in the person of José Freire Falcão.[97]

There were five new additions to national representations from Europe, Africa, and East Asia. Lithuania was honored with Vincentas Sladkevicius,[98] Mozambique with Alexandre José Maria dos Santos,[99] Cameroon with Christian Wiyghan Tumi,[100] Mauritius with Jean Margéot,[101] and Hong Kong with John Baptist Wu Cheng-chung.[102] These appointments continued the international expansion of the College which was made a policy by Pius XII and was continued in subsequent reigns. But the elevation of Margéot to represent Mauritius, a nation of little more than one million inhabitants, of whom only about a quarter are Catholics; or Tumi of Cameroon and dos Santos of Mozambique, who represent little, underdeveloped nations with small populations, of which only a small percentage are Catholic, has extended the process of internationalization to the point where the College looks increasingly less like the Senate of the Church and more like a disproportional House of Representatives.

The two new German-speaking cardinals were the aged conciliarist Franz Hengsbach, bishop of Essen for thirty-five years, whose appointment almost was as meaningless as that of Pavan,[103] and Hans Hermann Groër, König's successor as archbishop of Vienna.[104]

Later events would prove Groër's elevation, both to the episcopacy and to the cardinalate, to be the most disastrous of John Paul II's reign. In March, 1995, a number of men came forward who had been under his care in the mid-1970s, when he had been at Roggendorf. They accused him of having sexually molested them. Within weeks, Groër first resigned as president of the Austrian Episcopal Conference (April 6, 1995) and then as archbishop of Vienna (September 14, 1995). His resignation as archbishop occurred coincidentally with his seventy-fifth birthday, but it was accepted on the day following its submission, a rare event in the modern hierarchy. Subsequent investigations by the Austrian government, the Vatican, and representatives of the national episcopal conference confirmed the truth of the allegations. The whole evolution of the scandal persists in Austria today, and was a major subject for discussion when John Paul II visited the country in mid-1998. From the position of the College of Cardinals, the conclusion of the scandal came soon after Groër's audience with the pope at the Vatican on February 20, 1998. By April, Groër had resigned all his cardinalitial rights but did not, as had been the case with earlier resignations—notably that of Louis Billot in 1927—renounce the title of cardinal. He will not be an elector in the coming conclave.

Of the two Americans named to the College—both natives of Michigan—the senior was James Aloysius Hickey, archbishop of Washington,[105] and the junior was Edmund Casimir Szoka, archbishop of Detroit.[106] Hickey is a competent if unimaginative administrator whose rise during Laghi's delegation in Washington was assured by his past career, including a term as rector of the North American College, and his conservative doctrinal views. Szoka, by contrast, is something of a financial and administrative wizard. When the search began for a successor to John Francis Dearden in Detroit, who resigned on July 15, 1980, one of the principal criteria for deciding upon the new archbishop was skill in financial management, because the old cardinal's pastoral projects, combined with the social and economic decline of the city itself, had left the economy of the see in shambles.[107] Szoka, who had built the diocese of Gaylord on a sound financial basis, was the obvious choice, and was transferred to Detroit on March 21, 1981. Within a few years, using modern techniques of fund-raising and relying on the goodwill engendered by open books and public accountability, he reestablished the archdiocese on a firm footing.

While Szoka was lifting Detroit from a state not far from bankruptcy, the Vatican's own finances continued on the downward spiral which had begun early in the reign of Paul VI through a combination of overextension and corrupt management. John Paul II had spent more than a decade with committees and advisors trying to devise a method for restoring complete solvency to the collection of financial institutions operated by the Holy See. Finally, almost in desperation, the pope called Szoka to Rome and made him president of the newly established Prefecture of the Economic Affairs of the Holy See on January 22, 1990.[108] By the end of 1992, the Vatican's finances were in the black for the first time in twenty-three years, a task accomplished by Szoka with a skillful amalgam of modern managerial and accounting techniques with a comparatively open approach to sharing knowledge about Rome's needs with major donors in the developed world. By the end of 1997, Szoka had produced a modest, but real, surplus for the year of eleven million dollars, marking the fifth consecutive year in which he has closed the Vatican's books in the black. Since most curial officials spend no more than one five-year period in office, Szoka was replaced officially in his presidency in 1997 by Archbishop Sergio Sebastiani, who was made pro-president. But Szoka continues to watch the Vatican's accounts carefully from his new position, from October, 1997, as president of the Pontifical Commission for Vatican City, which makes him the chief daily administrator of the Vatican's physical establishment. The surpluses Szoka has developed will fund the large and expensive plans that have been envisioned for the celebration of the jubilee in 2000.

After the creation of 1988, and before the next cardinalitial consistory, on June 28, 1991, exactly three years later, twenty-one cardinals died, of whom seven were electors at the time of their deaths.[109] These losses reduced the whole membership of the College to one hundred thirty-nine. In addition, thirteen cardinals passed their eightieth birthdays in this three-year span, of whom one, Franz Hengsbach, also died in the interim.[110] This change reduced the number of electors to one hundred one. The loss of twenty electors in so short a period was reason enough to hold a consistory for the creation of new cardinals, but there were other pressing reasons. First was the retirement of Agostino Casaroli as cardinal-secretary of state in December, 1990. John Paul chose Angelo Sodano as his successor, with the title of pro-secretary, but the holder of the Vatican's highest administrative position was entitled to the cardinalate at the earliest possible date. Then there were the prelates who had been advanced to the important curial councils and congregations that had been reorganized or established under the constitution *Pastor Bonus* in 1989. If they were to enjoy the same rank and privileges as their more senior colleagues, they, too, would have to be elevated to the cardinalate, as much for the prestige of their curial offices as for personal merit. Finally, a number of important archdioceses that were traditionally held by cardinals had changed ordinaries in this period, and the new incumbents also were entitled to early membership in the College, including the archbishops of Philadelphia, Los Angeles, Buenos Aires, Turin, and Armagh.

The list of the new cardinals, released on May 29, fulfilled all of these needs. It contained twenty-two names, twenty new electors and two of the aged churchmen of Vatican II, who now received personal, but otherwise meaningless, distinction. But before them stood the name of Ignatius Gong Pin-mei, the creation whom John Paul had made *in pectore* in 1979 and whose name was now published.[111] The remaining names of 1991 were:

Angelo Sodano: *Secretary of State*
Alexandru Todea: *Archbishop of Fagaras and Alba Julia*
Robert Coffy: *Archbishop of Marseilles*

Frédéric Etsou-Nzabi-Bamungwabi: *Archbishop of Kinshasa*
Nicolás de Jesús López Rodríguez: *Archbishop of Santo Domingo*
Antonio Quarracino: *Archbishop of Buenos Aires*
Roger Michael Mahony: *Archbishop of Los Angeles*
Juan Jesús Posadas Ocampo: *Archbishop of Guadalajara*
Anthony Joseph Bevilacqua: *Archbishop of Philadelphia*
Giovanni Saldarini: *Archbishop of Turin*
Cahal Brendan Daly: *Archbishop of Armagh*
Camillo Ruini: *Cardinal Vicar of Rome*
Ján Chryzostom Korec: *Bishop of Nitra*
Henri Schwery: *Bishop of Sion*
Georg Maximilian Sterzinsky: *Archbishop of Berlin*
Guido del Mestri: *Vatican diplomat (retired)*
Pio Laghi: *Prefect, Cong. for Catholic Education*
Edward Idris Cassidy: *President, Counc. for Christian Unity*
José T. Sánchez: *Prefect, Congregation of the Clergy*
Virgilio Noè: *Vicar General for Vatican City*
Fiorenzo Angelini: *Pres., P.C. for Health Care Workers*
Paolo Dezza: *Former Administrator, Society of Jesus*

As expected, the name of Angelo Sodano appeared first on the list.[112] The other active curial cardinals included the new cardinal-vicar of Rome, Camillo Ruini,[113] and his colleague in the same position for Vatican City, Virgilio Noè,[114] together with four new heads of councils or congregations—Edward Idris Cassidy,[115] José T. Sánchez,[116] Fiorenzo Angelini,[117] and the important and successful diplomat, Pio Laghi.[118]

The creation of Laghi, in particular, was significant for the Italian curial establishment. Ever since his appointment to Washington in 1980 as apostolic delegate, his eventual cardinalate was assumed as a certainty. Once he had achieved it, he became, almost immediately, the leading candidate of the Vatican bureaucracy to follow John Paul II as pope. Indeed, his name began to be seen more and more in the press as a significant candidate in the next conclave—carefully leaked to improve the recognition of his name and to give publicity to some of his diplomatic accomplishments, which included securing formal relations with the United States in 1984. In addition to his friends in the curia, several American cardinals who owed their rise to his recommendations to the pope were thought to be considering him favorably.

Any hope by his friends that he eventually might be pope was exploded in May, 1997, when it was revealed that he had considerable knowledge about the excesses of the military government in Argentina during the period of his nunciature there, from 1974 to 1980. His involvement with those who tortured and killed thousands of people secretly had been revealed in the late 1980's in the writings of Argentina's formost newspaper columnist, Horacio Verbitsky, but the writer's work had attracted little notice, in spite of its explosive content. It was only when his name appeared on a long published list of those who knew about the *desaparecidos* that real attention came to be paid: "Monseñor Pío Laghi—Imputado como visto en CCD Ingenio Nueva Baviera, Legajo de CONADEP 1276/0440." It soon became clear that Laghi at one time had a list of those who had disappeared, but that he had never revealed that he had it, and that he may have ordered it destroyed. Finally, as the substance of the evidence grew more impressive, the Argentinean organization which has led the fight for accountability for the atrocities, the Mothers of the Plaza of May, forwarded a petition to the Italian government in which they requested a formal investigation and, if it was warranted, a trial. Under the provisions of the Lateran Treaties of 1929 and their successors, Laghi is immune from the Italian justice system, but the evidence against him is strong and his candidacy for the throne is impossible.

Of course, Laghi has denied all of the charges levelled against him—they are entirely "defamatory and without foundation," according to the cardinal—and every measure has been taken to support him officially. On May 21, 1997, *L'Osservatore Romano* expressed its "full solidarity" with Laghi and said there was no real basis for any of the accusations. The government of Argentina, mindful of the importance of maintaining good relations with a very conservative pope, issued a statement in which it expressed its official "regrets" over the "unjust" charges. The statement, issued over the signature of the minister for cultural affairs, Angel Centeno, said that Argentina "wishes to offer a witness of justice and recognition to someone who accomplished a mission that was difficult under the circumstances, and whose actions showed an energetic example of true Christian charity." The Argentinean bishops' conference also came to Laghi's side, by praising him for his work "for welfare, freedom, and life, in difficult times." Nevertheless, the Mothers and their leader, Hebe de Bonafini, have compiled an impressive dossier of evidence that Laghi had some real knowledge of the fate of many of the minimum of nine thousand people who disppeared during the worst years of the military regime.[119]

The remaining two curial prelates were Guido del Mestri, a retired diplomat, and the Jesuit administrator and confessor, Paolo Dezza. Del Mestri received the red hat because he was the highest ranking Bosnian in the recent history of the Vatican, and John Paul wished to express by some sign his concern for the carnage that already was occurring across the Adriatic.[120] Dezza was rewarded for his service to John Paul in taming and subordinating the Jesuits earlier in the 1980s.[121] Now approaching a century in age, and the College's second oldest cardinal in 1998, Dezza continues to be active intellectually and physically. His revelations about both Pius XII and Paul VI—he was an intellectual companion of the former and the confessor of the latter—are still newsworthy, such as his story about Paul VI contemplating abdication and his tales of Pius XII's dilemmas about how to manage relations with Germany during World War II. Since he revealed none of these details when he was an active curial official, their veracity has been questioned. In the end, it really does not matter, since the stories reinforce Dezza's current reputation as the "old, odd character" in the College of Cardinals. Some have lamented that he will not have a vote in the next conclave, or play a part in the *prattiche* that leads to the election, because his outspoken directness would be refreshing at the time.

The European ordinaries who received the red hat in 1991 belonged, for the most part, to archdioceses that had been headed by cardinals in the past. On the list were Robert Coffy, who had followed Roger Etchegaray at Marseilles;[122] Cahal Brendan Daly, who succeded Tómas Ó Fiaich at Armagh;[123] Giovanni Saldarini, who followed A. A. Ballestrero at Turin;[124] and Georg Maximilian Sterzinsky at Berlin, as the successor of Joachim Meisner.[125] Among these men, the surprise had been the elevation of a prelate with Polish antecessors to Berlin and then a speedy cardinalate for him. But this was in keeping with the pope's intention not only to enlarge the Polish contingent in the College but also to promote prelates of Polish ancestry from other parts of the world.

Two other Europeans who received the red hat were national representatives who reflected the new political geography of the continent after the end of the Cold War. Switzerland received its first residential cardinal in centuries in the person of Henri Schwery,[126] and the Slovaks were accorded a residential cardinal to place them in ecclesiastical parity with the Czechs with the elevation of Ján Korec, bishop of Nitra.[127] Korec, a Catholic hero of the resistance to Marxism, was a popular figure whose elevation particularly pleased Slovak nationalists, who were preparing to enforce the dissolution of Czechoslovakia into two nations.

Farther to the east, and in a much less Catholic environment, Romania received its first red hat for a residential ordinary in the person of another figure from the long decades of resistance, Alexandru Todea.[128]

Africa, on this occasion, was represented by only one new cardinal, Frédéric Etsou-Nzabi-Bamungwabi, the successor of Joseph Malula at Kinshasa.[129] But Latin America received three honors. In Argentina, Antonio Quarracino at Buenos Aires;[130] in Santo Domingo, Nicolàs de Jesùs

López Rodríguez, the archbishop of the oldest see in the New World;[131] and in Mexico, Juan Jesús Posadas Ocampo, archbishop of Guadalajara.[132]

The tragic figure among these cardinals was Posadas Ocampo. Within two years, on May 24, 1993, he was cut down in a furious burst of gunfire while sitting in his car at the airport at Guadalajara. Six others died, as well. The results of the official investigation were that a hit squad of the Tiajuana drug organization, then headed by the Arellano Felix brothers, Benjamin, Francisco and Ramon, mistook the cardinal's car for that of another drug lord, Joaquin Guzman Loera, and opened fire. This conclusion, however, is widely distrusted throughout northern Mexico, and conflicting theories abound about the reason for the cardinal's death. The early stages of the inquiry certainly were managed badly, and not all the evidence supports the Mexican government's official conclusions.

Finally, this consistory saw the elevation of two more Italian-Americans, very different from one another in personality and background yet strikingly similar to each other, and to Law of Boston and O'Connor of New York, in their intolerance of dissent. Roger Michael Mahony of Los Angeles, a social engineer with strong opinions in favor of multiculturalism in the Church, is the first native of southern California to lead Los Angeles, now the largest archdiocese in the United States.[133] His East Coast counterpart, Anthony Joseph Bevilacqua, is, by contrast, a skilled canon and civil lawyer who is characterized by his meticulous attention to the minutiæ of ecclesiastical administration without any desire to alter the social mores of the Catholics under his care.[134] Both new cardinals, however, had met the test of Pio Laghi, the former pro-nuncio, for unswerving adherence to the magisterium and loyalty to the social teachings of John Paul II.

In the formal consistory of 1991, John Paul II introduced a new and simplified rite for the creation of new cardinals. Following a liturgical greeting, the pope reads the formula of creation, and solemnly proclaims the names of the new cardinals. The first of the new cardinals then addresses the Holy Father, on behalf of everyone. This is followed by the Liturgy of the Word, the pope's homily, the Profession of Faith, and the taking of the oath by each cardinal. Each new cardinal then kneels before the pope to receive the cardinal's biretta and to be assigned a title or diaconate. After the pope places the biretta on the head of the new cardinal, he says, in part: "(This is) red as a sign of the dignity of the office of a cardinal, signifying that you are ready to act with fortitude, even to the point of spilling your blood for the increase of the Christian faith, for peace and harmony among the people of God, for freedom and the spread of the Holy Roman Catholic Church." The rite ends when the pope hands over the bull of the creation of Cardinals, assigns a title or diaconate to each one, and exchanges a kiss of peace with the new members of the College. The cardinals also exchange the kiss of peace with each other.

The consistory of June 28, 1991, brought to an end the transitional period in John Paul II's evolution of the College of Cardinals. The number of electors again stood at one hundred twenty-one of a full membership of one hundred sixty-two. A substantial majority of the cardinal-electors were now men who not only had been made cardinals by him but also had been appointed to hierarchial or curial positions based upon their adherence to his policies and ideas, rather than loyalty to the more liberal ways of John XXIII and Paul VI.

Time has shown that John Paul's haste to fill vacancies in the College during the transitional years on only an ideological basis has produced great mistakes, like the elevation of Groër, now identified by his fellow Austrian bishops as a pedophile, and Laghi, who was at least a silent witness to torture and murder. But these lessons, as they emerged, were not ignored. The cardinals elevated in 1998 were vetted much more carefully than the men elevated in earlier consistories.

Nevertheless, John Paul has compromised the historical reputation of the College more than any other pope in modern history. Paul VI, it is true, had elevated one cardinal, Cody of Chicago, who is supposed by many to have kept a mistress, but one has to return to at least the eighteenth century to find other cardinals with such unsavory and hidden pasts. One thing, at least, can be said in favor of the rigidity of form, administration, and government which grew from the reforms of the Council of Trent in the sixteenth century; the prelates who rose to positions of great power had been subjected to years of intense, inquisitorial observation that was so close as to make the rise of completely dishonorable men almost impossible.

In addition, the bestowal of the cardinalate on aged men whose ideas largely have been rejected, and who can never participate in the chief duty of cardinals by voting for a new pope, has further diminished the College by making the cardinalate, for the first time in history, something which can be given as an honorary distinction, rather like the traditional American gold watch presented on the occasion of retirement. Paul VI clearly never envisioned that his provisions under *Ingravescentem Ætatem* would be used in this way.

The cardinalate during the later years of John Paul II has been handled somewhat differently, though still with a strong ideological requirement. Part of the change may be caused by the pope's increasingly bad health; part may be caused by the pope's confidence that he already has molded the College to choose a successor who will govern much like himself. If the latter is the case, history has its usual surprise in store, since the College almost never elects a pope who is much in the mold of the pontiff who has made most of the electors cardinals—as John XXIII differed greatly from Pius XII, Paul VI from John XXIII, and, certainly, John Paul II from Paul VI.

NOTES

1. One of the fifteen superannuated cardinals also died in this period; Joseph Frings, one of the few surviving creations of Pius XII in 1946, died on December 17, 1978, at the age of ninety-one.

2. He was taken immediately to the hospital and pronounced dead. Vatican officials soon appeared to claim his body, which they then took back to his apartments in the apostolic palace. The official notice of his death said that he had died in his residence. Thus Rome was spared another possible embrassment so soon after the death of John Paul I. In the case of Villot, the revised statement of fact worked.

3. Casaroli will be remembered as the principal of the three secretaries of state in the reign of John Paul II. He became a cardinal-bishop, with the see of Porto e Santa Ruffina, on May 25, 1985, and sub-dean of the College on June 5, 1993. He retired as secretary of state at the end of November, 1990, and was succeeded by Angelo Sodano. He died June 9, 1998.

4. Cé was born at Izano, near Crema, on July 8, 1925, and was ordained on March 27, 1948. Soon after his ordination, he began to teach both scripture and dogmatic theology in the diocesan seminary at Crema, and then served as rector of the seminary from 1955 to 1970. While rector, he presided over the liturgical commission of the diocese of Crema, in addition to preaching at a large number of retreats for youth. On April 22, 1970, Paul VI appointed him titular bishop of Vulturia (Volturia) and auxiliary bishop of Bologna for Antonio Poma. He was consecrated in Crema by its bishop, Carlo Manzania, on May 17, 1970. He began his work as auxiliary of Bologna and vicar general of the diocese on the following June 29. On May 1, 1976, he was appointed general ecclesiastical assistant for Catholic Action in Italy, and held that office until he became patriarch. When

Albino Luciani vacated the patriarchate of Venice on becoming John Paul I, he undertook the task of finding a new patriarch for his old see as quickly as possible. His candidate, however, repeatedly refused the promotion. At this juncture, John Paul died, and the Venetian post was filled by the promotion of Cé by John Paul II on December 7, 1978. He took possession of the patriarchate on January 1, 1979, and made his formal entry into the city on the following January 7.

5. Ballestrero had been archbishop of Bari from December 21, 1973. Just a year before he died, Paul appointed him to Turin on August 1, 1977, to succeed Cardinal Michele Pellegrino, whose resignation because of age was accepted on July 27. Ballestrero resigned Turin, again because of age, on January 31, 1989; lost his active vote as an elector on reaching his eightieth birthday, October 3, 1993; and died June 21, 1998.

6. Appointed on August 18, 1977, to succeed William Conway, who had died on April 17. Every archbishop of Armagh has been a cardinal since Pius IX elevated Paul Cullen to the College on June 22, 1866. Ó Fiaich is unusual among modern residential cardinals because he comes from an exclusively academic background. Born November 3, 1923, and ordained July 6, 1948, he spent almost all of his priestly life as a teacher and administrator at Maynooth—lecturer in modern history (1953), professor (1959), vice president (1970), and president (1974–1977). In those years, he published widely, especially in Irish Catholic history in the age of Elizabeth. He died May 8, 1990.

7. Trinh van-Can was born March 19, 1921, in Trac But, and ordained a priest of the archdiocese of Hanoi on December 8, 1949. After serving his whole career there, he became coadjutor archbishop with the right of succession to Arch-

bishop, later Cardinal, Trin-nhu-Khuê, on June 2, 1963. He became archbishop of Hanoi immediately on his predecessor's death, November 27, 1978. Trin-nhu-Khuê was the first cardinal to die in the pontificate of John Paul II.

8. The career of Ernesto Corripio Ahumada demonstrates a rare advancement in measured stages to increased levels of responsibility. He was born June 29, 1919, in Tampico, and was ordained in Rome on October 25, 1942. After the war, he returned to his native diocese and taught at the local seminary until 1950. His first position in the hierarchy came on December 27, 1952, when he was made titular bishop of Zapara and auxiliary of Tampico. A little more than three years later, on February 25, 1956, he became bishop of Tampico. After almost a dozen years of successful service there, he was made archbishop of Antequera on July 25, 1967. Again, after a decade of demonstrated success, he was advanced to the larger and more complex archdiocese of Puebla de los Angeles on March 11, 1976. Soon after arriving in that post, however, he began to be considered seriously as a successor to Cardinal Miguel Darío Miranda y Gómez, the archbishop of Mexico. Although Miranda had submitted his official resignation at the end of 1970, when he reached seventy-five, there was a real reluctance to replace him, since he had handled the myriad problems in Mexico City with such skill. By 1977, at eighty-one, he was no longer able to function with the effectiveness he once did. The need to find a successor for him became a pressing and serious question. After long deliberation, the Congregation of Bishops finally recommended to Paul VI that Corripio Ahumada take the post. The appointment was made on July 19, 1977, on the same day that the resignation of Miranda y Gómez was accepted officially.

9. Etchegaray was born in Espelette, near Bayonne, on September 25, 1922, and was ordained on July 13, 1947. In 1961, he founded the National Office for Pastoral Activities in Paris. From 1961 to 1966, he was deputy director of the French Episcopal Conference, and then went on to be general secretary of it, from 1966 to 1970. On March 29, 1969, Paul VI made him titular bishop of Gemelle di Numidia and auxiliary archbishop of Paris (consecrated May 27). On December 22, 1970, Paul promoted him to be archbishop of Marseilles, and, on November 25, 1975, prelate of the Mission de France. From 1979 to 1981, he was the president of the

French Episcopal Conference. He was called to Rome in 1984 and made president of the Pontifical Council "Cor Unum." He retained that office until 1995. On April 8, 1984, he also became president of the Pontifical Council "Justitia et Pax," from which he retired in 1998. On November 15, 1994, John Paul II placed him in charge of all of the preparations for the jubilee in 2000 by appointing him president of the newly-created Central Committee for the Jubilee of the Holy Year 2000. This position he retains today. On June 24, 1998, he was raised to the order of cardinal-bishops, as cardinal-bishop of Porto and Santa Ruffina, in succession to Agostino Casaroli, who had died on June 9. Marseilles, in spite of its importance in the history of modern France, was not a see that traditionally was cardinalitial.

10. These duties were the capstones of another long and successful diplomatic career. Born February 22, 1906, and ordained on May 25, 1929, he entered the secretariat of state ten years later. He completed his apprenticeship with service in France (1949-1954) under Roncalli, Costa Rica (1955), Britain (1955-1957), and then as the first apostolic delegate to Korea (1957-1960). On October 28, 1960, John XXIII, who knew him well from the days in Paris, appointed him titular archbishop of Doclea and nuncio to Lebanon, where he served until 1963. This was followed by nunciatures in Chile (1963-1967) and Italy (1967-1969) before his posting to Paris.

11. Before that, Civardi had worked in a number of responsible curial offices, notably as *sostituto* for the Congregation of Bishops (1953-1967) and then as secretary of the same congregation (1967-1979). While in the latter office, he also was secretary of the College of Cardinals.

12. In fact, this may have been a recurrence of an earlier infection, stimulated by the blows to his system caused by the attempted assassination. He was diagnosed as having mononucleosis in the late summer of 1963 and his recuperation caused him to miss the opening day of the second session of Vatican II on September 29. He finally arrived in Rome on October 7. The bout with cytomegalovirus in 1981 suggests that the earlier diagnosis in 1963 had been erroneous. Conventional infectious mononucleosis is most often caused by the Epstein-Barr virus (HHV-4), but cytomegalovirus (HHV-5) is genetically quite similar and infections of it exhibit very similar symptoms.

13. The nine electors who died were John Joseph Wright (August 10, 1979); Alfred Bengsch (December 13, 1979); Sergio Pignedoli (June 15, 1980); Egidio Vagnozzi (December 26, 1980); Stefan Wyzynski (May 28, 1981); Franjo Seper (December 30, 1981); Pericle Felici (March 22, 1982); John Patrick Cody (April 25, 1982); and Giovanni Benelli (October 26, 1982). The seven who became superannuated in this period were José Clemente Maurer (March 13, 1980); Bernard Jan Alfrink (July 5, 1980); Ermenegildo Florit (July 5, 1981); Gabriel-Marie Garrone (October 12, 1981); Thomas B. Cooray (December 28, 1981); José Humberto Quintero (September 22, 1982); and Giovanni Colombo (December 6, 1982).

14. Four creations of Pius XII: James Francis McIntyre (July 16, 1979); Alfredo Ottaviani (August 3, 1979); Antonio Caggiano (October 23, 1979); and Carlos Carmelo de Vasconcellos Motta (September 18, 1982). Two creations of John XXIII: Antonio Maria Barbieri (July 6, 1979) and Alberto di Jorio (September 5, 1979).

15. For this reason, his name came last on the list of those promoted in this consistory.

16. His position in Latvia's modern history was not dimmed by his death. On August 18, 1995, the centenary of his birth, Latvia issued an eight sentims postage stamp to commemorate him.

17. Kuharic was born on April 15, 1919, in Pribic, Croatia, as the youngest in a family of thirteen children. He entered the minor seminary of the archdiocese of Zagreb in 1931, where he remained until 1939. He was ordained on July 15, 1945, and was appointed immediately to a parish in a region under communist control. In 1946, he added another parish, that of Rakov Potok, whose previous pastor had been executed. On February 22, 1947, he also was almost murdered. Paul VI named him titular bishop of Meta and auxiliary bishop of Zagreb on February 15, 1964 (consecrated May 3). In 1968, he was made administrator of Zagreb when the archbishop, Cardinal Franjo Seper, was called to Rome to become prefect of the Congregation for the Doctrine of the Faith. In September, 1969, he was elected president of the Yugoslav Episcopal Conference for the first of his four terms. On June 16, 1970, Kuharic was promoted to the rank of archbishop of Zagreb. He submitted his resignation as archbishop in April, 1994, but continues in office.

18. Khoraiche was born in Ain Ebel, near Tyre, Lebanon, on Sepetmber 20, 1907, and was ordained on April 12, 1930. Pius XII made him titular bishop of Tarsus of the Maronites and auxiliary bishop of Sidon (Saïda) on April 25, 1950 (consecrated October 15, 1950). On November 25, 1957, he became bishop of Sidon of the Maronites. On February 3, 1975, twenty-three days after the death of his predecessor, he was elected patriarch of Antioch. Twelve days later, on February 15, Paul VI extended ecclesial communion to him as a fellow patriarch. Khoraiche resigned his patriarchal office on April 3, 1986, and died August 19, 1994.

19. Sabattani was born October 18, 1912, in Castel Fiumanese, and was ordained July 26, 1935. He won early distinction as a canonist and jurist in the diocese of Imola, and later became a functionary of the tribunal of Bologna. He entered the curia in 1955 as an auditor of the Rota. On June 24, 1965, Paul VI made him titular archbishop of Justiniana Prima (consecrated July 25) and prelate of Loreto (resigned September 30, 1971). In 1971, he became both secretary of the Apostolic Signature and a consultor to the secretariat of state. His appointment as prefect was published on February 3, the day after his cardinalitial creation. From 1983 to 1991, he was archpriest of Saint Peter's.

20. He was born in Acerra on October 1, 1908, and was ordained on December 21, 1930. He entered the curia in 1937. His first important distinction was as undersecretary of what is now the Congregation for Sacraments and Divine Worship (1959–1969). After serving as secretary of the same congregation (1969–1973), he transferred, also as secretary, to the Congregation for the Causes of Saints (1973–1981). Paul VI made him titular bishop of Vescovia, with the title ad personam of archbishop, on January 6, 1972 (consecrated February 13). His appointment as prefect of the Congregation of Sacraments and Divine Worship became official on February 3, 1983.

21. Bernard Yago was born in Pass, in the French colony of the Ivory Coast, probably in July, 1916, although the day is uncertain. He completed his theological and philosophical studies in Africa and was ordained on May 1, 1947, becoming only the second native priest in the Ivory Coast. Between 1948 and 1956, Yago taught at the Minor Seminary of Bingerville, and then served as pastor of the church of Sainte Jeanne d'Arc in Treichville. In 1958, he went to Europe for futher study in the Social

Sciences. When he returned, he was made president of Catholic Action for Abidjan in 1959. When the Ivory Coast was detached from the authority of the Congregation for the Propagation of the Faith by John XXIII, Yago was named Archbishop of Abidjan on April 5, 1960. John consecrated him personally in Saint Peter's on the following May 8.

22. Alexandre do Nascimento was born in Malanje, Angola, on March 1, 1925, and ordained on December 20, 1952. He received his degree in theology from the Gregorianum and then taught dogmatic theology at the major seminary in Luanda. He served on the staff of the cathedral of Luanda from 1956 to 1961, when he fled to Lisbon, on the outbreak of the long civil war. Ten years later, he returned to Angola. In 1971 he became professor at the Pius XII Institute of Social Sciences and secretary of Caritas in Angola. On August 10, 1975, Paul VI made him bishop of Malanje and he was elected vice president of the Angolan Episcopal Conference. He was promoted to the rank of Archbishop of Lubango on February 3, 1977. In 1982, he was taken hostage by guerrillas, and held from October 15 to November 16. After his release, he was created a cardinal primarily as a shield for him against further danger, as was the case with Vaivods. He was appointed Archbishop of Luanda on February 16, 1986.

23. He was born in Samphran, near Bangkok, on January 25, 1929, and was ordained on December 20, 1959. When the Catholic Church in Thailand was made an independent entity with a native hierarchy on December 18, 1965, two archdioceses were created by Paul VI: Bangkok and Thare-Nongseng. From 1965 to 1972, Kitbunchu was rector of the major seminary in Bangkok. On December 18, 1972, Kitbunchu became the second archbishop of Bangkok.

24. Alfonso López Trujillo was born in Villa Hermosa, Tolima, Colombia, on November 8, 1935, into an aristocratic family, closer in antecedent to the backgrounds of the Latin American cardinals of an earlier age than to the more plebean origins of the Latin American cardinals created by John XXIII and Paul VI. His father, for example, was a major governmental figure with the State General Accounting Office, while his brother has been a minister of state. A cousin, José Rivera Mejìa, was bishop of Socorro y San Gil until 1975. López Trujillo was ordained on November 13, 1960, and then stud-

ied in Rome at both the Angelicum and the Teresianum. Paul VI named him titular bishop of Boseta and auxiliary in Bogota to Cardinal Aníbal Muñoz Duque on February 25, 1971. On May 22, 1978, he became coadjutor archbishop of Medellin, and succeeded to that see on June 2, 1979.

25. José Alí Lebrún Moratinos was born in Puerto Cabello, Carabobo, Venezuela, on March 19, 1919. After studies in the Caracas Seminary, he went to the Collegio Pio Latino Americano in Rome and completed his studies at the Gregorianum. He was ordained in Rome on December 19, 1943. Pius XII made him titular bishop of Arado de Fenicia and auxiliary of Maracaibo on August 2, 1956. On October 23, 1957, he was made apostolic administrator of Maracaibo and served until a new ordinary was appointed. His reward for that service was his appointment to be bishop of Maracay on June 21, 1958, with a further transfer to the more important diocese of Valencia en Venezuela on March 19, 1962. On September 16, 1972, he was made titular archbishop of Voncaria and, five days later, coadjutor of Caracas and apostolic administrator of the archdiocese for Cardinal José Humberto Quintero. When the latter's resignation was accepted on May 24, 1980, Lebrún Moratinos acceded to the see. On May 27, 1995, he resigned Caracas because of age.

26. Williams was born in Wellington, March 20, 1930, and was educated successively at Holy Cross Primary School, Seatoun; Saints Peter and Paul, Lower Hutt; St. Patrick's College, Wellington; St. Kevin's College, Oamaru; Holy Cross Seminary, Mosgiel; and then at the Collegium De Propaganda Fide in Rome, where he studied theology. He was ordained in Rome on December 20, 1959. After he completed his studies in Rome, he went to Dublin and took a degree in social sciences from University College in 1962. Returning to New Zealand, he served in St. Patrick's parish, Palmerston North (1963-1965) and then became director of the Catholic Enquiry Centre, Wellington (1966-1970). He followed this with missionary work at Leolomoega, Western Samoa (1971-1975), and then returned as pastor at Holy Family Parish, Porirua East, in 1976. He was consecrated archbishop in Wellington on December 20, 1979.

27. Joseph Louis Bernardin was born in Columbia, South Carolina, on April 22, 1928, the son of immigrants from the village of Tonadico, near Trent in the Dolomites. His

father, a stonemason, died when he was six, and he, his mother, and his sister were taken in by two uncles. He was a brilliant student who already had been accepted into medical school when he decided to become a priest, instead. After being graduated from the University of South Carolina in Columbia, he was accepted as a seminarian by John J. Russell, then Bishop of Charleston. He studied at St. Mary's College, St. Mary, Kentucky; at St. Mary's Seminary, Baltimore (B.A., Philosophy); and at the Catholic University of America, Washington, D.C. (M.A., Education, 1952). He was ordained by Bishop Russell on April 26, 1952, in St. Joseph Church, Columbia. In the following fourteen years, in the diocese of Charleston, he served four bishops as chancellor, vicar general, diocesan consultor, and administrator of the diocese during a vacancy. John XXIII named him both papal chamberlain (1959) and domestic prelate (1962). On March 4, 1966, he was appointed titular bishop of Lugara and, five days later, auxiliary bishop of Atlanta. Whe he was consecrated, on April 26, 1966, he became the youngest bishop in the United States. Again, after the death of Archbishop Paul J. Hallinan, he was administrator of a major diocese. On April 10, 1968, Bernardin was elected general secretary of the National Conference of Catholic Bishops and the United States Catholic Conference by the administrations of both those conferences. His services, especially in conducting reorganizations to bring both bodies into conformity with the new policies of Vatican II, were well rewarded. On November 21, 1972, Paul VI elevated him to be archbishop of Cincinnati and he was installed by Luigi Raimondi, the apostolic delegate and later cardinal, on December 19, 1972. From November, 1974, to November, 1977, he served as president of both of the national American conferences.

28. An opinion supported by the fact that more than ten times as many people came to the public viewing of his coffin than had come to similar viewings for any of his predecessors. Bernardin also was a man of rare good humor and wit. He learned that he was terminally ill with liver cancer early in 1996. Soon afterward, he visited the mausoleum of the archbishops of Chicago in Mount Carmel Cemetery to choose a crypt for himself. Pointing to the one next to that which contains the remains of his predecessor, he remarked with a dry smile, "I've always been a little left of Cody."

29. The Irish-Americans were McCloskey, Gibbons, Farley, O'Connell, Dougherty, Hayes, Glennon, Mooney, Spellman, Stritch, McIntyre, O'Hara, Cushing, Shehan, Cody, O'Boyle, Carberry, Cooke, Dearden, and Manning. The German-Americans were Mundelein, Meyer, Ritter, and Baum. One, Krol, was a Polish-American and one, Medeiros, was Portuguese in ethnicity.

30. Since 1983, John Paul II has created two other Italian-American cardinals, Anthony Joseph Bevilacqua and Roger Michael Mahony, both in 1991.

31. Meisner was born on December 25, 1933, in Breslau (now Wroclaw, Poland), and ordained on December 22, 1962. In 1966, he became director of Caritas in the diocese of Erfurt-Meiningen, where he remained for nine years. On March 17, 1975, Paul VI named him titular bishop of Vina and auxiliary to the apostolic administrator of Erfurt-Meiningen. In December, 1976, the bishops of the German Episcopal Conference chose him to represent them at the fourth Synod of Bishops.

32. Józef Glemp was born on December 18, 1929, in Inowroclaw in Kujawia, where his father, Kazimierz, worked in the salt mines. During the German occupation, he was sent as forced labor to a German farm. In March, 1945, he entered the state academic secondary school "Jan Kasprowicz" in Inowroclaw, from which he was graduated on May 25, 1950. He first entered the University of Warsaw, but soon transferred to the Nicolaj Kopernik University in Torun where his course of studies prepared him to enter the primatial major seminary in Gniezno. Two years later, he went on to the archiepiscopal seminary in Poznan. He was ordained in Gniezno on May 25, 1956. Because of a governmental prohibition, he could not take up his assignment at the parish of the Annunciation in Inowroclaw, so he was first posted as an assistant at Saint James in Mogilno. On December 7, 1956, he became chaplain to the Dominican Sisters in Mielzyn near Gniezno, in an institution for incurably ill children. At the same time, he taught religion in the school of Ruchocinek and in a home for youthful offenders in Witkowo, near Gniezno. After several other short pastoral assignments, he was sent to Rome in 1958 for studies in both canon and civil law at the Pontifical Lateran University, which he completed in 1962. He received his licentiate of both laws on June 20, 1960, and his doctorate on

June 23, 1964, with a thesis on the evolution of the concept of legal fiction, *De evolutione conceptus fictionis iuris*. He then spent another year at the Gregorianum studying Latin stylistics, to complement a three-year course in the academy of the Rota. In 1964, Glemp returned to Gniezno, to become secretary of the primatial major seminary and notary in the metropolitan curia and the metropolitan tribunal. On December 1, 1967, he joined the secretariat of the primate of Poland, and soon became Wyzynski's chaplain and private secretary. On January 15, 1975, he was appointed secretary of the Commission of the Polish Episcopate for matters concerning Polish institutions in Rome, and, later in the same year he became a member of the Commission of the Episcopate for the Revision of Canon Law. Paul VI named him a chaplain of honor (monsignor) on November 29, 1972, and four years later, on March 19, 1976, he was created gremial canon of the primatial chapter of Gniezno. In one of his earliest appointments to the Polish hierarchy, John Paul II made him bishop of Warmia on March 4, 1979.

33. Roma: Pontificio Istituto Biblico, 1966, *Analecta Biblica*, 26. Papyrus Bodmer XIV, which was copied between 175 and 200 A.D., contains Luke 3–8, and is the oldest surviving version of that text.

34. *Atti degli Apostoli* (Roma: Edizioni Paoline, 1970, *Nuovissima Versione della Bibbia dai Testi Originali*, v. 37).

35. Supplement to the *Journal of Biblical Literature*, v. 91, no. 2, 1972.

36. Roma: Libreria Editrice dell'Universita Gregoriana, 1959, 174 pp., in the series *Analecta Gregoriana, cura Pontificiæ Universitatis Gregorianæ Edita* (v. 104), *Facultatis Theologicæ, sectio B*, v. 32.

37. Scherer (born February 3, 1903); Schröffer (born February 20, 1903, died September 7, 1983); Pellegrino (born April 25, 1903); Muñoz Vega (born May 23, 1903); Bafile (born July 4, 1903); Nasalli-Rocca di Corneliano (born August 12, 1903); Duval (born November 9, 1903); Volk (born December 27, 1903); Satowaki (born February 1, 1904); Sidarouss (born February 22, 1904); Léger (born April 26, 1904); Marty (born May 18, 1904); Suenens (born July 16, 1904); Carberry (born July 31, 1904); Bueno y Monreal (born September 11, 1904); De Furstenberg (born October 23, 1904); Roy (born January 25, 1905); and Carpino (born May 18, 1905).

38. Samorè (February 3, 1983); Rosales (June 2, 1983); Casariego (June 15, 1983); Knox (June 26, 1983); Medeiros (September 17, 1983); Cooke (October 6, 1983); Renard (October 8, 1983); Mozzoni (archdeacon, November 7, 1983); and Philippe (archdeacon, April 9, 1984).

39. Quintero (July 8, 1984); Shehan (August 26, 1984); Slipyj (September 7, 1984); Marella (October 15, 1984); and Schröffer, mentioned above (September 7, 1983).

40. Confalonieri, Bueno y Monreal, König, Alfrink, Rugambwa, Landázuri Ricketts, Silva Henriquez, and Suenens.

41. Pavan was born in Povegliano on August 30, 1903, and was ordained on July 18, 1928. Like de Lubac before him, John Paul dispensed him from the necessity of episcopal consecration, so his name appeared last on the list of those elevated. A close collaborator of John XXIII, he was largely responsible for the text of John's two most famous encyclicals, *Mater et Magistra* and *Pacem in Terris*. At Vatican II, he was one of the principal periti. From 1969 to 1974, he was the rector of the Pontifical Lateran University. He died December 26, 1994.

42. Dadaglio was born at Sezzadio, near Acqui, on September 28, 1914, and was ordained on May 22, 1937. He then entered the diplomatic service and was posted to successive staff positions in Haiti, the United States, Canada, Australia, New Zealand, and Colombia. John XXIII made him titular bishop of Lero, with the personal title of archbishop, on October 28, 1961 (consecrated December 8), and sent him as nuncio to Venezuela, where he served until 1967. He was nuncio to Spain (1967–1980), where he proved able to deal with Franco's regime. When the time for Spain's polical change came, Dadaglio was quietly recalled to Rome by John Paul II and made secretary of the Congregation of Sacraments and Divine Worship in 1980. He remained in that post until 1984, when he was made pro-major penetentiary. On May 27, 1985, after his elevation to the cardinalate, he became major penetentiary. He died August 22, 1990.

43. Innocenti was born in Poppi, near Fiesole, on August 23, 1915, and was ordained on July 17, 1938. After years on the staffs of various curial offices, he was chosen to be nuncio to Paraguay in 1967 and was made titular bishop of Eclano, with the personal title of archbishop, on December 15, 1967 (consecrated February 18,

1968). In 1973, he returned to Rome to be the secretary of the Congregation for the Causes of Saints. Two years later, he began a five-year term as secretary of the Congregation for Sacraments and Divine Worship. In 1980, he was made nuncio to Spain during the period of transition to the post-Franco era. In that office, he succeeded Luigi Dadaglio. He was recalled by John Paul II for the cardinalate. From 1986 to 1991, he was prefect of the Congregation of the Clergy, and, from 1988 to 1991, also president of the Pontifical Commission for the Preservation of the Artistic Patrimony of the Church. In 1991, he was made president of the Pontifical Commission "Ecclesia Dei," in succession to Paul Augustin Mayer, from which he retired in December, 1995.

44. Mayer was born in Altötting, near Passau, on May 23, 1911, and, having become a Benedictine, was ordained August 25, 1935. In 1949, he began a seventeen-year period as rector of the Pontifical Atehnæum of San Anselmo, the Benedictine university in Rome. Paul VI made him titular bishop of Satriano, with the personal title of archbishop, on January 6, 1972 (consecrated February 13), and secretary of the Congregation for Religious and Secular Institutes. He served in that position until 1984, when John Paul II made him pro-prefect of the Congregation for the Sacraments and Divine Worship. He became prefect of the Congregation on receiving the cardinalate. In 1988, he vacated the prefecture and was made president of the Pontifical Commission "Ecclesia Dei," from which he retired in 1991.

45. Arinze was born in Eziowelle, Nigeria, on November 1, 1932, and was ordained on November 23, 1958. He taught at the Bigard Memorial Seminary, and later was regional secretary for Catholic Education for Eastern Nigeria. Paul VI made him titular bishop of Fissiana and auxiliary bishop of the archdiocese of Onitsha on July 6, 1965 (consecrated August 29). Two years later, on June 26, 1967, he became archbishop of Onitsha. In 1979, Arinze was elected to a term as president of the Nigerian Bishops' Conference, but, on April 8, John Paul II summoned him to Rome as pro-president of the Secretariat for Non-Christians. His appointment as president became effective on May 27, 1985, immediately after he was created a cardinal. On June 28, 1988, in the apostolic constitution, *Pastor Bonus*, the Secretariat for Non-Christians became the Pontifical Council for Inter-Religious Dialogue, with Arinze remaining as president.

46. Perhaps the definition provided by the 1997 Synod of Bishops will serve here: "Jesus's message and the Gospel as originally preached by the apostles had many features of the Jewish culture of the day. At the same time, their teaching was different from that culture because, with its new values and priorities, it challenged customary practices and beliefs. Wherever the Word of God is preached and welcomed, this dual dynamic is at work. The existing culture with its positive aspects, its 'seeds of the Word', its germs of truth and justice, is fostered, becoming, as it were, a new language into which God's Word is translated. At the same time, the existing culture is challenged by the Gospel and is gradually converted. The positive elements of that culture then provide assistance in further preaching God's message to the people of that same culture."

47. The first part was later published in Nigeria with the title *Sacrifice in Ibo Religion* ([Ibadan, Nigeria]: Ibadan University Press, 1970).

48. *Partnership in Education between Church and State in Eastern Nigeria* (Onitsha, Nigeria: Ude's Printing & Publishing Company, 1965), 44 pp.

49. Tomko was born in Udavske, near Kosice, in what is now the Slovak Republic, on March 11, 1924, and was ordained on March 12, 1949. He studied at the Pontifical Lateran University and then at the Gregorianum, where he took degrees in theology, canon law, and the social sciences. In 1966, Paul VI appointed him head of the doctrinal office of the Congregation for the Doctrine of the Faith. Later, Tomko worked in the Secretariat of State and in other staff positions in the curia. John Paul II named him titular archbishop of Doclea on July 12, 1979 (consecrated September 15). He then became secretary general of the Synod of Bishops and served in that task until 1985. His appointment as prefect of the Congregation for the Evangelization of Peoples and Grand Chancellor of the Pontifical Urban University became effective a few days after his creation as cardinal.

50. Lourdusamy was born at Kalleri, India, on February 5, 1924, and was ordained December 21, 1951. He was among the new population of local priests in traditionally non-Catholic parts of the world who were discovered by the Congregation of Bishops as a part of John

XXIII's efforts to create independent national episcopacies. John made him titular bishop of Sozusa in Libya and auxiliary bishop of Bangalore for the aging archbishop, Thomas Pothacamury, on July 2, 1962 (consecrated August 22). Two years later, he was made titular archbishop of Philippi and coadjutor archbishop of Bangalore, with the right of succession, on November 9, 1964, when just forty years of age. He became archbishop of Bangalore on January 11, 1968. After only three years in that office, however, Paul VI called him to Rome as *sostituto* for the Congregation for the Evangelization of Peoples, of which he became secretary in 1973. He is one of the few liberal curial officials—Gantin is another—retained and advanced by John Paul II. After his cardinalate, he was made prefect of the Congregation for the Oriental Churches, where he served until 1991. On the death of Aurelio Sabattani, on April 5, 1993, he became archdeacon of the College, but he relinquished the privilege of announcing the election of the next pope when he joined the ranks of the cardinal-priests in 1996.

51. Castillo Lara was born in San Casimiro, near Maracay, Venezuela, on September 4, 1922, the third son of seven children. He became a Salesian and was ordained on September 4, 1949, by his uncle, Castillo Hernandez, archbishop of Caracas. In 1950, he went to the Salesian University in Turin to study canon law. In September, 1954, he became professor of canon law there, and then occupied a similar position at the Salesianum in Rome from 1957 to 1965. Paul VI made him titular bishop of Precausa and auxiliary bishop of Trujillo on March 26, 1973 (consecrated May 24). John Paul II promoted him to the rank of archbishop on May 26, 1982, and brought him to Rome as the pro-president of the Pontifical Commission for the Revision of the Code of Canon Law. After the new code was promulgated, in the apostolic constitution, *Sacræ disciplinæ leges*, on January 25, 1983, much of the bureaucracy of the commission was transformed into the Pontifical Commission for the Authentic Interpretation of the Code of Canon Law, again with Castillo Lara as pro-president. He became president of the Administration of the Patrimony of the Holy See on receiving the cardinalate, and then was made president of its curial successor, the Pontifical Commission for the State of Vatican City, on October 31, 1990. He also serves as a member of the Cardinals' Supervisory Commission

for the Institute for Religious Works (IOR).

52. Gagnon was born in Port-Daniel, near Gaspe, Canada, on January 15, 1918, and was ordained on August 15, 1940. Paul VI made him bishop of Saint Paul in Alberta on February 19, 1969 (consecrated March 25), but he resigned that diocese on May 3, 1972, when he became rector of the Canadian College in Rome, where he served until 1977. In that period, he also was vice president and secretary of the Pontifical Committee for the Family (1973–1980), which became the Pontifical Council for the Family. Gagnon was made titular archbishop of Justiniana Prima and pro-president of the Council on July 7, 1983, and then became president on the occasion of his cardinalate. In 1990, he vacated that office, and, on June 3, 1991, John Paul II made him president of the Pontifical Committee for International Eucharistic Congresses.

53. Dubuque, Iowa: William C. Brown, year varies with volumes in the series.

54. Hamer was born in Brussels on June 1, 1916, and entered the Dominican Order in 1934 with the name Jerôme. In 1940, he was drafted, but his military service ended after three months of combat and prison. He was ordained on August 3, 1941, and, three years later, received his doctorate in theology. He then taught dogmatic theology, ecclesiology, and fundamental theology at the Studium of La Sartre at Louvain. In 1952–1953, he taught at the Angelicum in Rome, and from 1962 to 1964 served as Secretary General of Studies for the Dominican Order. At Vatican II, he was a consultor for the Secretariat for Christian Unity, of which he served as secretary from 1969 to 1973. In the latter year, he was transferred to the same office with the Congregation for the Doctrine of the Faith. At that time, Paul VI made him titular bishop of Lorium with the personal title of archbishop on June 14, 1973 (consecrated June 29). In 1984, John Paul II made him pro-prefect of the Congregation for Religious and Secular Institutes, of which he became prefect at the time he was made a cardinal. He died on December 2, 1976.

55. Stickler, the second of twelve children, was born in Neunkirchen, near Vienna, on August 23, 1910. He entered the Salesians, and professed his first vows on August 15, 1928. After further study in Rome, he was ordained on March 27, 1937. He took his degree in canon law in 1940 and and then taught in two Salesian universities, Turin (1940–1957) and Rome

(1957–1958). From 1958 to 1966, he was rector of the Salesianum. In 1971, Paul VI made him prefect of the Vatican Library, where he undertook the construction of the subterranean depository where the most ancient manuscripts are now stored. He served as an expert at Vatican II. On September 8, 1983, John Paul II made him titular bishop of Bolsena, with personal title of archbishop (consecrated November 1). In 1984, he was made pro-librarian and pro-archivist of the Church. His appointment as Librarian and Archivist of the Holy Roman Church became effective on May 27, 1985, two days after his cardinalate. He retired from that position on July 1, 1988.

56. Poupard was born in Bouzille, near Angers, on August 30, 1930, and was ordained on December 18, 1954. He ended a teaching career in 1959, when he joined the staff of the Secretariat of State. Later, he returned to France and served for ten years as rector of the Institut Catholique in Paris. John Paul II appointed him titular bishop of Usula on February 2, 1979, and then made him a titular archbishop on June 28, 1980, when he became pro-president of the Secretariat for Non-Believers, and, two years later, president of the executive committee of the newly created Pontifical Council of Culture. On March 25, 1993, the pope merged both bureaus under the leadership of Poupard.

57. Deskur was born in Sancygnio, near Kielce, on February 29, 1924, into a family of French heritage. He studied law at the Jagellonian University in Kraków, where he was secretary of the Bratniak, an important student association. After later study in the seminary of Kraków, he was ordained on August 20, 1950. After further study of moral theology at the University of Freiburg, he joined the staff of the Secretariat of State in 1952. From 1973 to 1984, he was president of the Pontifical Council for Social Communications, where he established the Vatican Press Office. Deskur was named titular bishop of Tene by Paul VI on June 17, 1974 (consecrated June 30), and then promoted to archbishop by John Paul II on February, 15, 1980.

58. Obando Bravo was born in La Libertad (Chontales), near Juigalpa, Nicaragua, on February 2, 1926, and was ordained on August 10, 1958. He became a Salesian and rose steadily in his order. After a period as a professor of mathematics and physics in a number of Salesian institutions, he was appointed prefect of discipline and rector at the Salesian seminary in San Salvador (1961–1968). Paul VI made him titular bishop of Puzia di Bizaena and auxiliary bishop of Matagalpa on January 18, 1968 (consecrated March 31), and then made him archbishop of Managua on February 16, 1970.

59. Tzadua was born in Addifini, near Asmara, Ethiopia, on August 25, 1921. He began his studies at the seminary of Cherer, but was prevented from finishing because of the Italian attack in 1936. Finally, on March 12, 1944, he was ordained. He immediately became vice parish priest of the cathedral of Asmara and director of the cathedral school, which he soon made the finest school in the city. In 1953, he received a certificate in Classics from the Academia Ferdinando Martini, the Italian high school in Asmara. This gave him the credentials that he needed to apply for opportunities for higher education in Europe. He received a scholarship to the University of Milan, from which he was graduated in 1957 with a degree in political and social sciences, and, in 1958, in law. Paul VI made him titular bishop of Abila in Palestina and auxiliary bishop of Addis Ababa on March 1, 1973 (consecrated May 20). He became archbishop of Addis Ababa on February 24, 1977.

60. Simonis was born in Lisse, near Rotterdam, on November 26, 1931, and was ordained on June 15, 1957. He studied biblical exegestics in Rome between 1959 and 1966. Paul VI named him bishop of Rotterdam on December 29, 1970 (consecrated March 20, 1971). He was made coadjutor of Utrecht for Jan Willebrands on June 27, 1983, and then became archbishop of Utrecht on December 3, 1983, when Willebrands resignation became effective. He later served as the president of the Netherlands Bishops' Conference.

61. Wetter, the son of a railroad executive, was born in Landau, near Speyer, on February 20, 1928. He studied theology at the Gregorianum and was ordained on October 10, 1953. In 1962, he became professor of fundamental theology at the Higher Institute of Philosophy and Theology at Eichstätt. In 1967, he transferred to a professorship in dogmatic theology at the University of Mainz. On May 28, 1968, Paul VI appointed him bishop of Speyer (consecrated June 29). When Joseph Ratzinger was appointed prefect of the Congregation for the Doctrine of the Faith in 1982, his former archiepiscopal office of Munich and Freising became

vacant, and Wetter was chosen to take his place on October 28, 1982.

62. Suquía Goicoechea was born in Zaldivia, near San Sebastián, on October 2, 1916, and was ordained on July 7, 1940. Paul VI made him bishop of Almeria on May 17, 1966 (consecrated July 16). On November 28, 1969, he was transferred to be bishop of Malaga, and then was made archbishop of Santiago de Compostella on April 13, 1973. Ten years later, on April 12, 1983, he again was transferred, this time to Madrid as the successor of Vicente Enrique y Tarancón, whose resignation became effective on that date. He retired from Madrid on July 28, 1994, and was succeeded by Antonio Maria Rouco Varela.

63. Decourtray was born in Wattignies, near Lille in the north of France on April 9, 1923, and was ordained on June 29, 1947, after studies in Rome and at the Ecole Biblique in Jerusalem. On May 27, 1971, Paul VI made him titular bishop of Ippona Zarito and auxiliary bishop of Dijon (consecrated July 3). On April 22, 1974, he became bishop of Dijon. In 1979, he was diagnosed with cancer of the larynx for which he had immediate surgery. Although he recovered, he lost his voice for three months. In June, 1981, when Alexandre Charles Renard submitted his resignation as archbishop of Lyon, John Paul II chose Decourtray to be his successor, with his appointment to take effect on October 29, 1981. He also was named prelate of the "Mission de France," on April 23, 1982. During his archiepiscopacy, he made special efforts to reach both the Jewish and Islamic communities in the city and region, but, in spite of his close ties to the latter, he was a vigorous supporter of the Gulf War, in one of the last important public pronouncements of his tenure, claiming that "War is better than dishonor." After Cardinal Glemp had seriously mishandled the problem of the Carmelite monastery at Auschwitz, he stepped in and resolved the issue through his close cooperation with the international Jewish community. He served as president of the French Episcopal Conference from 1987 to 1990. On September 12, 1994, he suddenly suffered a massive stroke, from which he died four days later. At his funeral, representatives of both the Jewish and Muslim confessions prayed at his coffin in the forecourt of the cathedral—an unprecedented event in the history of the Church.

64. Piovanelli was born at Ronta di Mugello, in Tuscany, on February 21, 1924, and was ordained on July 13, 1947. He was made titular bishop of Tubune di Mauretania and auxiliary bishop of Florence, for Giovanni Benelli, on May 28, 1982 (consecrated June 24). After Benelli's death, October 26, 1982, Piovanelli became the leading candidate to succeed him, even though he had been auxiliary bishop for only a few months. On March 18, 1983, after an unusually long process of selection, Piovanelli was made archbishop of Florence on March 18, 1983.

65. Biffi was born in Milan, June 13, 1928, and was ordained on December 23, 1950. In his early service, he was pastor of Santi Martiri Anauniani at Legnano (1960-69), and at Sant'Andrea in Milan (1969-75). On February 11, 1975, he was made a canon of the cathedral chapter of Milan. On December 7, 1975, Paul VI made him titular bishop of Fidene and auxiliary to Giovanni Colombo, archbishop of Milan. Colombo consecrated him in his parish of Sant'Andrea on January 11, 1976. When Colombo retired, Biffi was passed over for appointment as archbishop in favor of Carlo Maria Martini, which might have signalled the end of, or a long pause in, his ecclesiastical career. But the succession in Bologna changed that. When Antonio Poma submitted his resignation from that see on reaching his seventy-fifth birthday, John Paul II chose Enrico Manfredini for the office and accepted Poma's resignation on February 11, 1983. Manfredini, who was on the list for promotion to the cardinalate in the next consistory, died only ten months after his appointment as archbishop. The result was Biffi's elevation to Bologna on April 19, 1984. He took possession of his new see on the following June 1, and made his solemn entry into office on the following day. On July 7, 1984, he was elected president of the Episcopal Conference of Emilia-Romagna.

66. Gulbinowicz was born in Szukiszki, near Vilnius, on October 17, 1928, and entered the seminary at Vilnius when he was sixteen years old. After he was ordained on June 18, 1950, he entered the University of Lublin for further theological study. He received his doctorate in moral theology in 1955, and, in 1959, became a professor at the seminary of the diocese of Warmia. Paul VI made him titular bishop of Acci on January 12, 1970 (consecrated February 8), and apostolic administrator of the Polish territory within the Lithuanian archdiocese of

Vilnius. His success there, particularly in fostering new parishes against considerable state opposition, caused Paul to promote him to be archbishop of Wroclaw (Breslau), on January 3, 1976. As archbishop, he founded the influential newspaper, *Nowe Zycie* (New Life).

67. Lubachivsky was born in Dolyna, in the Ukraine, on June 24, 1914. He began his studies in Lwow (Leopoli) in 1933, and then went to Innsbruck, Austria, and Sion, Switzerland, for further academic work. He was ordained on September 21, 1938, and later received a degree in scriptural studies from the Gregorianum, in 1942. In 1947, Lubachivsky moved to the United States, where he remained with only one interruption for thirty years. He became an American citizen in 1952. In 1967, he returned to Rome to teach for a year at the Ukrainian College. When he returned to the United States, he became the spiritual director of the Ukrainian seminaries at Washington, D.C., and Stanford, California. John Paul II made him bishop of Philadelphia (Pennsylvania) of the Ukrainians on September 13, 1979 (consecrated November 13). On March 27, 1980, after only a few weeks as ordinary in Philadelphia, he was made coadjutor with right of succession of Lwow (Leopoli) for Cardinal Josef Kobernyckyj-Dyckowskyj Slipyj, the exiled metropolitan archbishop, who died September 7, 1984. On that date, Lubachivsky became major archbishop of Lwow. For a number of years after his cardinalate, he resided in Rome, but in March, 1991, he was able to return to the Ukraine to take up the administration of his metropolia. On March 30, 1991, he accepted the administration from archbishop Volodymir Sterniuk, the eighty-four-year-old leader of the Ukrainian Eastern-Rite Catholics during the absences of Slipyj and Lubachivsky—the years of the "Catacomb Church."

68. Vidal was born in Mogpoc, near Boac, in the Philippines, on February 6, 1931, and was ordained on March 17, 1956. Paul VI made him titular bishop of Claterna and coadjutor bishop of Melalos on September 10, 1971 (consecrated November 30). On August 22, 1973, he became archbishop of Lipa. John Paul II, on April 13, 1981, made him coadjutor archbishop with the right of succession at Cebú, of which he became archbishop on August 24, 1982.

69. Fresno Larrain, the fourth of five children, was born in Santiago de Chile on July 26, 1914. After studies at the seminary of Santiago, he attended the Gregorianum, from which he received a degree in canon law. He was ordained on December 18, 1937, after which he became the spiritual director and vice rector of the minor seminary of the archdiocese of Santiago. Pius XII named him bishop of Copiapò on June 15, 1958 (consecrated August 15). After Vatican II, he was president of the vocations department of the Latin American Episcopal Conference (CELAM). He also served a term as president of episcopal committee for the Collegio Pio Latino Americano. Paul VI promoted him to bishop of La Serena on July 28, 1967, and John Paul II transferred him to Santiago de Chile on May 3, 1983. He retired as archbishop of Santiago on March 30, 1990.

70. Vachon was born at Saint-Frédéric de Beauce, Québec, on February 4, 1912, and was ordained June 11, 1938. He received his Ph.D. from the Université Laval in 1947 and his doctorate in theology from the Angelicum in 1949. From 1941 to 1947, he was professor of philosophy at the Université Laval, and then successively professor of theology (1949–1955), superior of the Grand Séminaire de Québec (1955–1959), vice rector of the Université Laval (1959–1960), and rector (1960–1972). While in the last position, he conducted the transfer of the university to the management of a public corporation. He also was superior general of the Séminaire de Québec from 1960 to 1977. He was made a companion of the Order of Canada in 1969 for his writings on educational policy. On April 4, 1977, Paul VI made him titular bishop of Mesarfelta (consecrated May 14) and auxiliary to Maurice Roy, archbishop of Québec. On March 20, 1981, he became archbishop of Québec and primate of Canada when Roy's resignation was accepted. He, in turn, resigned on March 17, 1990.

71. Law was born in Torreon, Mexico, on November 4, 1931, and was ordained for the clergy of the diocese of Jackson, Mississippi, on May 21, 1961. From 1963 to 1968, he was the editor of the diocesan newspaper, *Mississippi Today*. In 1968, he began a three-year term as director of the Committee on Ecumenical and Interreligious Affairs of the National Conference of Catholic Bishops. His reward for a job well done was his appointment by Paul VI as bishop of Springfield-Cape Girardeau, Missouri, on October 22, 1973. He was consecrated and installed as bishop on the following December 5. He was installed in Boston on March 23,

1984.

72. Reprinted in full in *America*, August 31, 1996.

73. O'Connor was born in Philadelphia on January 15, 1920, and was ordained on December 15, 1945.

74. Cleveland: World Publishing Company, 1968.

75. Consecrated bishop on May 27, 1979.

76. *ITEST Proceedings*, January 29, 1982.

77. Poma (died September 25, 1985); Lekai (died June 30, 1986); Brandão Vilela (died December 19, 1986); Muñoz Duque (died January 15, 1987); and Parecattil (died February 20, 1987).

78. Guyot (born July 7, 1905); König (born August 3, 1905); Flahiff (born October 26, 1905); Guerri (born December 25, 1905); Righi-Lambertini (born February 22, 1906); Siri (born May 20, 1906); Civardi (born October 21, 1906); Beras Rojas (born November 16, 1906); Höffner (born December 24, 1906); Paupini (born February 25, 1907); Enrique y Tarancón (born May 14, 1907); Sensi (born May 27, 1907); McCann (born June 29, 1907); Khoraiche (born September 20, 1907); Silva Henriquez (born September 27, 1907); Dearden (born October 15, 1907); Freeman (born November 19, 1907); and Bertoli (born February 1, 1908).

79. Roy (died October 24, 1985); Florit (died December 8, 1985); Miranda y Gómez (March 15, 1986); Confalonieri (August 1, 1986); Pellegrino (died October 10, 1986); Parente (died December 29, 1986); O'Boyle (August 10, 1987); Bueno y Monreal (August 20, 1987); Sidarouss (died August 23, 1987); Höffner [see note above] (died October 16, 1987); and Alfrink (died December 17, 1987).

80. Martinez Somalo was born in Baños de Rio Tobia, near Calahorra, Spain, on March 31, 1927, and was ordained on March 19, 1950. He joined the staff of the Secretariat of State in 1956 and served in a variety of curial positions until 1979. Paul VI made him titular bishop of Tagora, with the personal title of archbishop, on November 12, 1975 (consecrated December 13).

81. Jean Villot was the first non-Italian camerlengo since the fourteenth century, and Martinez Somalo is the second; although Friedrich von Schwarenberg did serve briefly as pro-camerlengo for a few days after the election of Leo XIII in 1878. Martinez Somalo is the first Spaniard to hold the office.

82. If he does not opt for the rank of cardinal-priest, which is his right by seniority.

83. Silvestrini was born at Brisighella, near Faenza, on October 25, 1923, and was ordained on July 13, 1946.

84. He was consecrated on May 27, 1979.

85. Neves was born at São João del Rei, Brazil, on September 16, 1925. He joined the Dominicans and was ordained on July 9, 1950.

86. Felici was born in Segni, near Rome, on July 26, 1919, and was ordained on April 4, 1942. He entered the Vatican diplomatic service in 1945 and served in a number of staff positions until Paul VI made him titular bishop of Cesariana, with the personal title of archbishop, on July 22, 1967 (consecrated September 24) and sent him to be nuncio to the Netherlands. He remained in that position until 1976, when he became nuncio to Portugal. He capped his diplomatic career as nuncio to France from 1979 to 1988.

87. Javierre Ortas was born at Siétamo, near Huesca, on February 21, 1921. He joined the Salesians and was ordained on April 24, 1949. His works on ecumenism brought him to the attention of Paul VI, who made him titular bishop of Meta, with the personal title of archbishop, on May 20, 1976 (consecrated June 29), and secretary of the Congregation for Catholic Education. He relinquished that position at the time of his cardinalate.

88. Martin was born at Amiens on August 26, 1908, and was ordained October 14, 1934. He was soon attached to the curia, where he served in a number of staff positions. Paul VI made him titular bishop of Neapolis in Palestina on January 5, 1964 (consecrated February 11), and attached him to the staff of the pontifical household. In 1969, he was made prefect of the Pontifical Household and, in that position, played an important part in the events of 1978. On his retirement in 1986, he was promoted to be archbishop, with the same titular see, on December 18. He passed his eightieth birthday on August 26, 1988, only fifty-nine days after his achievement of the cardinalate. He died September 27, 1992.

89. Canestri was born at Castelspina, near Alessandria, in the north of Italy, on September 30, 1918, and was ordained on April 12, 1941. In 1959, he was made spiritual director of the seminary of the diocese of Rome. Two years later, on July 8, 1961, John XXIII made him titular bishop of Tenedo and auxiliary bishop for the cardinal-vicar of Rome, Clemente Micara.

Canestri was consecrated on the following July 30. Paul VI rewarded his long and difficult work as the principal Roman auxiliary by making him bishop of Tortona on January 7, 1971. Four years later, Paul called him back to the curia and made him vice regent of Rome and titular bishop of Monterano, with the personal title of archbishop, on February 8, 1975. John Paul II transferred him yet again, to be archbishop of Cagliari, on March 22, 1984. Finally, he was made archbishop of Genoa on July 6, 1987. He resigned his last archiepiscopal office on April 20, 1995.

90. Giordano was born at Sant'Arcangelo, near Tursi, on September 26, 1930, and was ordained July 5, 1953. Paul VI named him titular bishop of Lari Castello and auxiliary bishop of Matera on December 23, 1971 (consecrated February 5, 1972). He succeeded to the combined dioceses of Matera and Irsina on June 12, 1974. On May 9, 1987, John Paul II made him archbishop of Naples in succession to Corrado Ursi. At the time of his creation, Giordano was the youngest cardinal in the College.

91. Pimenta was born at Marol, near Bombay, on March 1, 1920, and was ordained on December 21, 1949. Paul VI made him titular bishop of Bocconia and auxiliary bishop of Bombay on June 5 1971 (consecrated June 29). As Valerian Gracias became weaker in his fight against cancer, it was clear that the archdiocese needed a stronger administrative hand. Paul VI chose to make Pimenta coadjutor archbishop with the right of succession on February 26, 1977. He succeeded to the archiepiscopal office on the death of Gracias, September 11, 1978, in one of the few major changes in the hierarchy to take place during the brief reign of John Paul I.

92. Padiyara was born at Manimala, near Changanacherry, India, on February 11, 1921, into a family of the Syro-Malabar rite. He was ordained for the Latin rite diocese of Coimbatore on December 19, 1945. Pius XII appointed him the first Latin rite bishop of Ootacamund on July 3, 1955 (consecrated October 16). Paul VI named him archbishop of Changanacherry of the Syro-Malabar rite on June 14, 1970, at which time he reentered the rite that was traditional in his family. On April 23, 1985, John Paul II promoted him to be archbishop of Ernakulam of the Syro-Malabar rite. John Paul II elevated his ordinariate to be the major archdiocese of Ernakulam-Angamaly on December 16, 1992. Padiyara resigned as major archbishop

on December 18, 1996, after struggling for years to bring harmony to the two Catholic communities under his jurisdiction, those who follow the ancient Syrian Christian liturgy and those who follow the local Indian-Christian customs.

93. Revollo Bravo was born in Genoa on June 15, 1919, and was ordained a priest in the clergy of the archdiocese of Bogotá on October 31, 1943. On November 13, 1973, Paul VI made him titular bishop of Tinisa in Numidia and auxiliary bishop of Bogotá (consecrated in Bogotá on December 2). Paul VI also promoted him to be archbishop of Nueva Pamplona on February 28, 1978. On July 25, 1984, John Paul II transferred him to the office of archbishop of Bogotá, in succession to Aníbal Muñoz Duque. Revollo Bravo resigned Bogotá on June 15, 1994, and died, at the age of seventy-six, on November 3, 1995.

94. Clancy was born in Lithgow, near Bathurst, New South Wales, on December 13, 1923, and was ordained July 23, 1949. Paul VI made him titular bishop of Ard Carna and auxiliary bishop of Sydney on October 25, 1973 (consecrated January 19, 1974). In one of his earliest pontifical acts, John Paul II made him archbishop of Canberra on November 24, 1978. A little more than four years later, on February 12, 1983, he returned to Sydney as its archbishop, in succession to James Darcy Freeman, who had submitted his resignation in November, 1982, on reaching seventy-five, but which became effective with Clancy's appointment. Recently, Clancy has faced problems in his see because of the growing popularity of communal confessions, which he had tried to suppress. For the third time in eighteen months, he collapsed from an attack of low blood pressure on April 9, 1978, and canceled his program for Easter. While his condition always is reported as not serious, it is clear that he is not in good health.

95. Paskai was born on May 8, 1927, in Szeged, in southeast Hungary. He entered the Franciscans and was ordained on March 3, 1951. Between 1955 and 1962, he was professor of philosophy at the seminary of Szeged, and then transferred to the seminary of Budapest as spiritual director. In 1967, he was given the chair of philosophy at the Budapest Theological Academy, and, in 1973, he became rector. Paul VI appointed him titular bishop of Bavagaliana and apostolic administrator of Veszprem on March 2, 1978 (consecrated April 5). On

March 31 of the following year, relations with the Hungarian government had improved to the point where he could be named bishop of Veszprem in his own right. On April 5, 1982, John Paul II made him coadjutor archbishop of Kalocsa. Four years later, on July 8, 1986, he became president of the Hungarian Episcopal Conference. He was promoted to the primatial see of Esztergom on March 3, 1987, in succession to László Lekai, who had died on June 30, 1986. The archdiocese was renamed Esztergom-Budapest in 1993.

96. Grégoire was born at Verdun, near Montréal, on October 24, 1911, and was ordained on May 22, 1937. After several more years of university study, he became director of the Séminaire de Sainte-Thérèse, and then almoner of students at the Université de Montréal. John XXIII made him titular bishop of Curubi and auxiliary bishop of Montréal, for Leger, on October 26, 1961 (consecrated December 27). Léger appointed him both vicar general of the archdiocese and director of the office of the clergy. He became Léger's successor as archbishop of Montréal on April 20, 1968. Inspired by his predecessor, he made strong, and generally successful, attempts to introduce the reforms of Vatican II, especially in creating semi-independent pastoral sectors, a council of priests, and a pastoral council. As the independence movement grew in Québec during his tenure, he became a leader in reforming education based on the French language, and created a wide variety of new archdiocesan organizations to the new social and pastoral needs. His resignation as archbishop was accepted on March 17, 1990. He died on October 30, 1993.

97. Falcão was born in Erere, near Limoeiro do Norte, Brazil, on October 23, 1925, and was ordained on June 19, 1949. Paul VI named him titular bishop of Vardimissa and coadjutor of the diocese Limoeiro do Norte on April 24, 1967 (consecrated June 17). On the following August 19, after only a few weeks as coadjutor, he became bishop of Limoeiro do Norte. Only a little more than four years later, on November 25, 1971, he was made archbishop of Teresina. John Paul II transferred him to the archdiocese of Brasilia, on February 15, 1984. During his episcopacy, he has held several positions of importance in the Brazilian Episcopal Conference. He is one of the best known prelates in Brazil, thanks to his many articles for two widely circulated newspapers, *Jornal do Brasil* and *Correiro Braziliense*.

98. Sladkevicius was born on August 20, 1920, in Guroniai, near Zasliai, Lithuania. He began his studies in a Jesuit high school, and later entered the seminary and was ordained on March 25, 1944. In 1952, he became professor of dogmatic theology at the seminary of Kaunas. Pius XII made him titular bishop of Abora and auxiliary bishop of Kaisiadorys on November 14, 1957 (consecrated December 25), but he was not permitted by the government to assume his episcopal functions. Additional troubles with the regime caused him to be placed under house arrest in 1959, and he remained a prisoner until 1982. A thawing in the relationship between the Vatican and the Lithuanian government allowed John Paul II to appoint Sladkevicius to the post of apostolic administrator of the diocese of Kaisiadorys on July 15, 1982. He remained in that office until 1988. In April, 1988, he became president of the Lithuanian Episcopal Conference, and, on March 10, 1989, he was appointed archbishop of Kaunas and primate of Lithuania. His resignation became effective May 4, 1996.

99. Dos Santos was born in Zavala, Mozambique, on March 18, 1924. He began his formal studies with Franciscan missionaries but later, after attendance at Mozambique's minor seminary, he was sent to Portugal to enroll in a course in philosophy offered by the White Fathers. In 1947, he became a Franciscan novice of the Portuguese province of Varatojo near Lisbon, and took his final vows in 1951. He was ordained on June 25, 1953, as Mozambique's first native priest. After Mozambique became independent from Portugal, Paul VI named dos Santos archbishop of Maputo on December 23, 1974 (consecrated March 9, 1975). As archbishop, he founded the Caritas of Mozambique and served as its first president. On August 22, 1981, he also created the Women's Union of Piety.

100. Tumi was born on October 15, 1930, in Kikaikelaki, near Kumbo, Cameroon. After completing studies at Nigerian seminaries, he went on to Lyon, to study theology, and to Freiburg to study philosophy. He was ordained on April 17, 1966, and then returned to his native diocese. In 1973, he was made rector of the Regional Seminary of Bambui in Nigeria. On December 6, 1979, John Paul II made him the first bishop of Yagoua (consecrated January 6, 1980). He became vice president of the Cameroon Episcopal Conference on April 23, 1982.

On the following November 19, he was appointed coadjutor with right of succession in the archdiocese of Garoua, to which he succeeded on March 17, 1984. Tumi was named president of the Cameroon Episcopal Conference in 1985. As cardinal, on August 31, 1991, he was transferred to be archbishop of Douala.

101. Margéot was born on February 3, 1916 in Quatre-Bornes, near Port-Louis, Mauritius. He received his secondary school certificate in philosophy and his university degree in theology at the Gregorianum, and was ordained on December 17, 1938. He then returned to Mauritius, where he was a pastor for many years. In 1956, his was made vicar general of the diocese of Port-Louis. Paul VI appointed him bishop of Port-Louis on February 6, 1969 (consecrated May 4). In 1985, he became the first president of the Indian Ocean Episcopal Conference. He resigned Port-Louis on February 15, 1993, immediately after his seventy-fifth birthday.

102. Wu Cheng-chung was born in Shui-tsai, near Kaying, China, on March 26, 1925. He was ordained on July 6, 1952, for the clergy of the diocese of Hsinchu, Taiwan. Paul VI appointed him bishop of Hong Kong on April 5, 1975 (consecrated July 25). In recent years, he has spent most of his time facing the problem of Hong Kong's reunification with China, because of the fear that Chinese restrictions on religious rights eventually will come into force in Hong Kong—Wu has become the only functioning, legitimate ordinary in China, since the reunion. The same possibilities have caused many Catholics, especially the wealthier supporters of the Church, to flee the former colony, which has somewhat destabilized the Church in Hong Kong financially. This, in turn, has caused a curtailment of social and pastoral services just when increased tension has increased the need for them.

103. Hengsbach was born at Velmede, near Paderborn, on September 10, 1910, and was ordained on March 13, 1937. Pius XII, as a part of his efforts to restore Catholicism in Germany, made Hengsbach titular bishop of Cantano and auxiliary bishop of Paderborn on August 20, 1953 (consecrated September 29). At Paderborn, he became close to his superior, Lorenz Jaeger, later cardinal, one of the most influential bishops at Vatican II. On November 18, 1957, Pius XII erected the diocese of Essen and appointed Hengsbach as the first bishop. He was enthroned in his new cathedral on January

1, 1958. He already had submitted his resignation from Essen on reaching his seventy-fifth birthday in 1985, but he was too well regarded to be replaced easily. After his creation as cardinal, he continued in his episcopal position until his death, in the Elizabeth-Krankenhaus in Essen, on June 24, 1991, at the age of eighty.

104. Groër was born to Sudetan German parents in Vienna, on October 13, 1919, but retained his Czechoslovakian citizenship until 1939. He was ordained on April 12, 1942. He became prefect at the minor seminary of Hollabrunn in 1946 and remained in that office until 1952. Between 1952 and 1974, he labored to restore the pilgrimages to the shrine of Our Lady of Roggendorf, which had been abolished in the eighteenth century by the Emperor Joseph II. In 1970, he became spiritual director of the Legion of Mary in Austria. In 1974, Groër joined the Benedictine community of Roggendorf, entered the novitiate in 1976, and took his solemn vows as a Benedictine in 1980. On July 15, 1986, John Paul II named him archbishop of Vienna in succession to König. His resignation from Vienna became effective on September 14, 1995.

105. Hickey was born October 11, 1920, in Midland, Michigan. After elementary school at Saint Brigid's in Midland, he went to the minor seminary at Saint Joseph Seminary, in Grand Rapids, from which he was graduated in 1938. He then attended Sacred Heart Seminary College in Detroit, from which he was graduated in 1942 with a bachelor of arts degree in philosophy. He then went on for four more years of study in Washington at the Theological College and received his licentiate in sacred theology from the Catholic University of America in 1946. He was ordained for the diocese of Saginaw, Michigan, on June 15, 1946. His academic successes marked him as one of the bright young American priests who would benefit from further study in Rome, to which he was sent after a brief period as associate pastor of Saint Joseph's parish. In 1950, he received his doctorate in canon law from the Pontifical Lateran University, and in the following year he received a doctorate in moral theology from the Angelicum. When he returned to Saginaw, he was appointed secretary to the bishop, Stephen S. Woznicki, and served in that position from 1951 to 1960. Paul VI made him titular bishop of Taraqua and auxiliary bishop of Saginaw on February 18, 1967 (consecrated April 14), but,

after only two years in that position, he went to Rome as the rector of the North American College. At the end of his term there, Paul VI made him bishop of Cleveland on May 31, 1974, and John Paul II transferred him to be archbishop of Washington on June 17, 1980, when the former incumbent there, Cardinal William Wakefield Baum, was called to Rome to join the curia.

106. Szoka was born in Grand Rapids on September 14, 1927, and received his higher education at Sacred Heart Seminary in Detroit; Saint John's Provincial Seminary in Plymouth, Michigan; and the Pontifical Lateran University. He was ordained for the diocese of Marquette on June 5, 1954. He quickly proved himself to be an active administrator and builder with a real flair for finanacial management. When Paul VI erected the diocese of Gaylord, Michigan, he appointed Szoka its first bishop on June 11, 1971 (consecrated July 20).

107. Readers of American detective fiction may recognize a partial portrait of Cardinal Dearden as "Archbishop Mark Boyle" in the series of murder mysteries by William X. Kienzle, beginning with The Rosary Murders in 1979.

108. Szoka's resignation as archbishop of Detroit was accepted on April 28, 1990, when Adam Joseph Maida became his successor.

109. The seven electors were Malula (died June 14, 1989); Manning (died June 23, 1989); Ó Fiaich (died May 8, 1990); Trinh Van-Can (died May 18, 1990); Dadaglio (died August 22, 1990); Rubin (died November 28, 1990); and Nsubuga (died April 20, 1991). The fourteen cardinals who already were superannuated and then died in this period were Volk (died July 1, 1988); Dearden and Guyot (both died August 1, 1988); de Furstenberg (died September 22, 1988); Cooray (died October 29, 1988); Nasalli-Rocca di Corneliano (died November 9, 1988); Siri (died May 2, 1989); Flahiff (died August 22, 1989); Civardi (died November 28, 1989); Vaivods (died May 23, 1990); Maurer (died June 27, 1990); Beras Rojas (died November 30, 1990); Hengsbach (superannuated on September 10, 1990, died January 24, 1991); and Freeman (died March 16, 1991).

110. The remaining twelve who became superannuated were Ursi (born July 26, 1908); Martin (born August 26, 1908); Willebrands (born September 4, 1909); Ciappi (born October 6, 1909); López Salazar (born January 12, 1910); Opilio Rossi (born May 14, 1910); Gray (born August 10, 1910); Stickler (born August 23, 1910); Gouyon (born October 24, 1910); Krol (born October 26, 1910); Oddi (born November 14, 1910); and Mayer (born May 23, 1911)

111. Gong, or Kung as it is more usually transliterated, was born in P'ou-tong, near Shanghai, on August 2, 1901, and was ordained May 28, 1930. After some years as a schoolteacher and a period as an evangelist and missionary, Pius XII made him bishop of Soochow on October 7, 1949, already a period of great danger for Catholic priests in China. He was consecrated on June 9, 1949. On July 15, 1950, he was promoted to be bishop of Shanghai. In 1955, the repressions of Mao Tse-tung finally caught him and he was imprisoned. Finally tried in 1960, he was sentenced to life in prison. In 1985, he was released after thrity years in various camps and jails. His political rights were restored officially on January 5, 1988, but they were canceled again in 1998, when the government refused to renew his passport when he submitted an application to do so from his residence in the United States. John Paul II had named Gong a cardinal, in pectore, in his first consistory in 1979, but published his name only in the consistory of 1991, after he had been removed safely from China to the United States in 1988. He continues to hold the now-titular offices of bishop of Shanghai and apostolic administrator of Soochow. By 1998, he had become the oldest living cardinal. He lives in nearly complete retirement at Our Lady Queen of the Clergy Home in Stamford, Connecticut.

112. Sodano was born at Isola d'Asti on November 23, 1927, and was ordained on September 23, 1950. He entered the diplomatic service in 1959, and subsequently served in staff positions in Ecuador and Uruguay. Paul VI made him titular bishop of Nova di Cesare, with the personal title of archbishop, on November 30, 1977 (consecrated January 15, 1978) and sent him to Chile as nuncio. After ten years in Santiago, during the Pinochet regime, he was recalled to Rome as secretary of the Pontifical Council for Relations with States. On December 1, 1990, he became pro-secretary of state on the retirement of Casaroli. His appointment as cardinal-secretary of state became official on June 29, 1991, the day after his cardinalate. On January 10, 1994, he was made cardinal-bishop of Albano in succession to Francesco Carpino, who had died on the previous October 5. As

cardinal-bishop, he retained his former title as cardinal-priest, Santa Maria Nuova, *in commendam*.

113. Ruini was born at Sassuolo, in the diocese of Reggio Emilia-Guastalla, February 19, 1931, and was ordained December 8, 1954. After a career in teaching in a number of seminaries in central Italy, John Paul II made him titular bishop of Nepte and auxiliary bishop of Reggio Emilia-Guastalla on May 16, 1983 (consecrated June 29). From 1986 to 1991, he served as secretary of the Italian Episcopal Conference, and then served a term as its president in 1991. On January 17, 1991, he was raised to the rank of archbishop and made pro-vicar of Rome, in anticipation of his cardinalate. On the following July 1, he was appointed formally as cardinal-vicar of Rome and archpriest of the archbasilica of Saint John Lateran. Subsequently, he became grand chancellor of the Pontifical Lateran University and, on December 29, 1992, he was made president of the *Peregrinatio ad Petri Sedem*, in preparation for the Jubilee in 2000, a position which he vacated in 1996.

114. Noè was born at Zelata di Bereguardo, near Pavia, of March 30, 1922, and was ordained on October 1, 1944. From 1970 to 1982, he was master of pontifical ceremonies and *sostituto* in the Congregation for Sacraments and Divine Worship. John Paul II made him titular bishop of Voncaria, with the personal title of archbishop, on January 30, 1982 (consecrated March 6). In 1989, he was made coadjutor archpriest of Saint Peter's. On January 14, 1991, he was made pro-vicar general of Vatican City. On July 1, 1991, three days after his cardinalate, he was formally appointed to the positions of cardinal-vicar of the Vatican, archpriest of Saint Peter's, and president of the Fabric of Saint Peter's. In addition, the pope made him president on the Cardinalitial Commission for the Pontifical Sanctuaries of Pompeii, Loreto, and Bari, on September 12, 1993.

115. Cassidy was born in Sydney on July 5, 1924, and was ordained on July 23, 1949, a few days after his twenty-fifth birthday. He entered the diplomatic service in 1955, and then was posted to staff positions in India, Ireland, El Salvador, and Argentina. Paul VI made him titular bishop of Amanzia, with the personal title of archbishop, on October 27, 1970 (consecrated November 15) and sent him as pro-nuncio to the Republic of China on Taiwan, where he remained until 1979. To his duties in Taiwan

was added the task of pro-nuncio to Bangladesh and apostolic delegate to Burma, from 1973 to 1979. He then was sent to be pro-nuncio to Lesotho and apostolic delegate to southern Africa, from 1979 to 1984. Finally, he was given a major European post as pro-nuncio to the Netherlands, where he served from 1984 to 1988. He was recalled to Rome as *sostituto* for general affairs in the Secretariat of State in 1988. Cassidy was made president of the Pontifical Council for the Promotion of Christian Unity on December 12, 1989, and continues in that position at the end of the century.

116. Sánchez was born in Pandan, near Virac, on March 17, 1920, and was ordained on May 12, 1946. Paul VI made him titular bishop of Lesvi and coadjutor bishop of Lucena on February 5, 1968 (consecrated May 12). He succeeded to Lucena on September 25, 1976. He was made archbishop of Nueva Segovia by John Paul II on January 12, 1982, but was called to Rome to become secretary of the Congregation for the Evangelization of Peoples in 1985. His resignation from Nueva Segovia became effective in 1986. After serving in his first curial position until 1991, he was made prefect of the Congregation of the Clergy immediately after his cardinalate. He also was the president of the Pontifical Commission for the Preservation of the Artistic and Historic Patrimony of the Holy See from 1991 to 1993. Sánchez retired in 1996.

117. Angelini, a native Roman, was born on August 1, 1916, and ordained on February 3, 1940. From 1947 to 1954, he served Pius XII as master of pontifical ceremonies, an office in which his colleague in 1991, Virgilio Noè, would be his remote successor. On June 27, 1956, Pius XII made him titular bishop of Messene (consecrated July 29) and head of the apostolate to workers in health care under the office of the cardinal-vicar of Rome. As a part of John Paul II's initial reforms of the curia, Angelini was made president of the new Pontifical Commission for Pastoral Assistance to Health Care Workers, when that organization was established in the motu proprio, *Dolentium Hominum*, of February 11, 1985. On the same day, Angelini was raised to the rank of archbishop, with the titular see he had held as bishop. When the further reforms ordered in the apostolic constituion, *Pastor Bonus*, went into effect on March 1, 1989, Angelini became president of the new Pontifical Council for Pastoral Assistance to Health Care Workers. His elevation to the

cardinalate signified the growing importance of the Council's work in the estimation of the pope. He retired in 1997, and was replaced by Archbishop Javier Lozano Barragan.

118. Laghi was born at Castiglione, near Forli, on May 21, 1922, and was ordained on April 20, 1946. He entered the diplomatic service in 1952, and spent the early years of his career in Nicaragua. He was made secretary of the apostolic delegation in Washington, under Amleto Cicognani, in 1954, and remained there until 1961. In the latter year, he was posted to India. He returned to Rome for a term on the Pontifical Council for the Public Affairs of the Church. On May 24, 1969, Paul VI made him titular archbishop of Mauriana, an old title for titular bishops which had been raised to archiepiscopal status on this occasion. Laghi was consecrated on June 22, and then sent to be apostolic delegate to Jerusalem and to the Palestinians. In 1974, he was promoted to be nuncio to Argentina. In 1980, he became the last apostolic delegate to the United States and then the first pro-nuncio, when diplomatic relations with the Vatican were established in 1984. In 1990, he was recalled to Rome, and became pro-prefect of the Congregation for Catholic Education (formerly the Congregation of Seminaries and Institutes of Study) on April 6. His appointment as prefect was made formally on July 1, 1991, three days after his cardinalate. Subsequently, he was made grand chancellor of the Gregorianum and, on May 8, 1993, cardinal-patron of the Sovereign Military Order of Malta (the Knights of Saint John). In 1998, he retains his prefecture.

119. Amazingly, after all the revelations, uninformed journalists, as recently as May, 1998, continue to believe that he remains *papabile*, and his picture is still printed in newspapers and magazines over the caption that he will be a major figure in the next conclave.

120. Del Mestri was born in Banja Luka, Bosnia, on January 13, 1911, and was ordained in the basilica of Saint John Lateran on April 11, 1936. In 1940, he entered the diplomatic service for assignment in Yugoslavia during the worst of the German occupation. Subsequently, he was posted to positions in Lebanon, Romania, Syria, and Indonesia. John XXIII made him titular archbishop of the diocese of Tuscamia, which had been raised to archiepiscopal status for him, on October 28, 1961 (consecrated December 31). With his new rank, he was sent

to East Africa as apostolic delegate. In 1965, he became the first pro-nuncio in Kenya, when that nation achieved independence and established diplomatic relations with the Vatican. After two years, he was transferred to be apostolic delegate in Mexico, where he remained until 1970. He then spent five years, 1970 to 1975, as the apostolic delegate in Canada, followed by a nine-year term as pro-nuncio in West Germany, He retired from active service in 1984. He died on Agust 2, 1993.

121. Dezza was born in Parma on December 13, 1901. He entered the Jesuits in 1918, and was ordained on March 25, 1928. He made his solemn profession as a member of the Society of Jesus in 1935. During the war years. he was rector of the Gregorianum, and later became Paul VI's confessor. In October, 1981, when Dezza was eighty, John Paul II named him as governing delegate of the Society of Jesus, to supersede the superior general, Pedro Arrupe, who had fallen victim to a stroke. It was a difficult time for Dezza and the Jesuits, because the pope's interference in the government of the Society was seen, correctly, as a preemption of the order's traditional rights because of its theological liberalism and its recent political involvement, notably in Latin America. On September 14, 1983, Peter-Hans Kolvenbach was elected superior general of the Society of Jesus to replace Pedro Arrupe. This brought Dezza's role as papal delegate to the Society to an end. Like de Lubac before him, Dezza had objections to the requirement that he receive episcopal consecration as a prerequisite for the cardinalate, so John Paul II dispensed him from that before his creation as cardinal.

122. Coffy was born at Le Biot, near Annecy, on October 24, 1920, and was ordained four days after his twenty-fourth birthday, on October 28, 1944. For many years, he held the chair of dogmatic theology at the major seminary of Annecy. Paul VI appointed him bishop of Gap on February 11, 1967 (consecrated April 23), and then promoted him to be archbishop of Albi on June 15, 1974. John Paul advanced him to be archbishop of Marseilles on April 13, 1985, five days after his predecessor there, Roger Etchegaray, was made president of the Pontifical Council "Justitia et Pax." Coffy died July 15, 1995.

123. Daly, the third of seven children, was born in Loughguile, Northern Ireland, on October 1, 1917. After his university education

in philosophy and theology, he entered Saint Patrick College, the national seminary of Ireland. Later, he undertook additional study in philosophy at the Institut Catholique in Paris. He was ordained on June 22, 1941. Daly then embarked on a scholarly and academic life, during which he was the theological *peritus* for the Irish hierarchy at Vatican II. Paul VI made him bishop of Ardagh on May 26, 1967 (consecrated July 16), and, in 1974, made him a member of the staff of the Secretariat for Christian Unity. Daly achieved some renown for his pastoral letter to Protestants in 1979, in which he begged for Christian unity and an end to violence in Northern Ireland. John Paul II transferred him to the ancient see of Down and Connor on August 24, 1982, and then made him archbishop of Armagh on November 6, 1990, in succession to Tomas Ó Fiaich, who retired. Daly retired on October 1, 1996, at the age of seventy-nine.

124. Saldarini was born at Cantù, near Milan, on December 11, 1924, and was ordained on May 31, 1947. He taught biblical exegesis and commentary at the seminary of the archdiocese of Milan from 1952 to 1967. John Paul II made him titular bishop of Gaudiaba and auxiliary bishop of Milan on November 10, 1984 (consecrated December 7) and then archbishop of Turin, in succession to Anastasio Alberto Ballestrero, on January 31, 1989. He also bears the title of Pontifical Custodian of the Holy Shroud.

125. Sterzinsky was born on February 9, 1936, in Warlack, near Warmia (now in Poland). He lost his mother when very young, and fled with his family to Thuringia at the end of World War II. Later, he studied philosophy and theology at the Regional Seminary of Erfurt, and, on June 29, 1960, was ordained. After a period as a teacher of theology at Erfurt, he served from 1966 to 1981 as parish priest of the church of St. John the Baptist in Jena. In the milieu of the university in Jena, he became a dedicated ecumenist, which, in part, contributed to his later rise in the hierarchy. From 1981 to 1989, he served as vicar general for the apostolic administrator of the diocese of Erfurt-Meiningen. On May 28, 1989, John Paul II appointed him archbishop of Berlin in succession to Joachim Meisner, who had been transferred to Köln. He was consecrated on the following September 9.

126. Schwery was born on June 14, 1932, in Saint-Leonard, near Sion, as the youngest child in a large family, and was ordained on July 7,

1957. In 1961, he began to teach in Sion, and eventually he became director of the minor seminary there. Later, he was made rector of the college. From 1958 to 1966, he was the diocesan chaplain for the Jeunesse Étudiante Catholique (JEC), the international catholic student movement; and he also was a military chaplain from 1958 to 1977. On July 22, 1977, Paul VI named him bishop of Sion (consecrated September 17). From 1978 to 1983, he was a member of the Congregation for Catholic Education, and, for two consecutive terms, he was president of the Conference of Swiss Bishops. He retired as bishop of Sion on April 1, 1995.

127. Korec was born in Bosany, Slovakia, on January 22, 1924, and entered the Society of Jesus on September 15, 1939. He was forced to interrupt his studies in 1950 on the suppression of religious orders in East Germany. He finally was ordained on October 1, 1950. On August 24, 1951, he was secretly consecrated a bishop. He then worked for nine years in a factory, while conducting his ministry in secret. In 1960, he was arrested and sentenced to sixteen years in prison for "betraying the nation" by helping seminarians with their studies and for ordaining priests. He was released in 1968 in a general amnesty. On his release, he had to be hospitalized because of illnesses and general debilitation brought on by his treatment in prison. In 1969, he was officially "rehabilitated." After he left the hospital, he worked first as a garbage collector, and then once again in a factory. In 1974, his "rehabilitation" was canceled and he was reincarcerated to serve the remainder of his previous sentence. He was later released, because of his poor health. His continued as a "bishopworker" until 1984. After the success of the "Velvet Revolution," John Paul II, on February 6, 1990, made him bishop of Nitra, so that, at last, he became a residential ordinary.

128. Todea was born on June 5, 1912, in Teleac, Romania, and was ordained on March 25, 1939, for the Byzantine Romanian rite. He was assigned to a succession of small parishes until the suppression of the Byzantine-Rite Church in Romania in 1948. Pius XII made him titular bishop of Cesaropolis on July 4, 1950, and he was consecrated secretly on the following November 19 by Archbishop Gerald P. O'Hara, the Vatican's representative in Romania. In 1951, on the discovery of his episcopacy by the government, he was arrested and condemned to life imprisonment. In 1964, an

amnesty brought his release. Almost immediately afterward, he began a semi-secret reorganization of the Greek-rite community. On March 14, 1990, John Paul II made him archbishop of Fagaras and Alba Julia of the Romanians, in anticipation of his cardinalate. He retired from his archiepiscopacy on July 20, 1994.

129. Etsou-Nzabi-Bamungwabi was born on December 3, 1930, in Mazalonga, near Lisala, in the Belgian Congo (subsequently Zaire, and Republic of Congo). He was ordained on July 13, 1958. He received a degree in sociology from the Institut Catholique in Paris and another in pastoral theology from "Lumen Vitæ," the Institut International de Catéchèse et de Pastorale, in Brussels. He was president of the Kinshasha Province, and then vice-president of the Zaire Assembly of Major Seminary Superiors. Paul VI named him titular archbishop of Menefessi and coadjutor archbishop of Mbandaka-Bikoro on July 8, 1976. He was consecrated by Joseph Malula on the following November 7. On November 11, 1977, he succeeded as archbishop of Mbandaka-Bikoro. He was transferred to Kinshasa, as Malula's successor, on July 7, 1990, and then almost immediately elected as vice-president of the Zaire Episcopal Conference. He is the second cardinal from the Republic of Congo.

130. Quarracino was born in Pollica, near Salerno in southern Italy, on August 8, 1923. His family moved to Argentina when he was a child. He studied at the seminary of San José at La Plata, and was ordained for the clergy of the diocese of Mercedes-Lujan on December 22, 1945. After years in pastoral work, John XXIII named him bishop of Nueve de Julio, in the province of Buenos Aires, on February 3, 1962 (consecrated April 8). Six years later, on August 3, 1968, Pope Paul VI transferred him to Avellaneda, where he served until December 18, 1985, when John Paul II transferred him to be archbishop of La Plata. He was active for many years in the Latin American Episcopal Conference, of which he became president in 1978. On July 10, 1990, he was made archbishop of Buenos Aires, in succession to Juan Carlos Aramburu, who retired. He was also made ordinary for those Eastern rite Catholics in Argentina with no regular bishop. He died February 28, 1998.

131. López Rodríguez was born in Barranca, near La Vega in the Dominican Republic, on October 31, 1936. He was sent to Rome for study at both the Angelicum and the Gregorianum, after which he returned and was ordained in La Vega on March 18, 1961. On January 16, 1978, Paul VI erected the new diocese of San Francisco de Marcoris and appointed López Rodríguez to be the first bishop (consecrated February 25). On November 15, 1981, John Paul II made him archbishop of Santo Domingo, the oldest diocese in the New World. In 1984, he became president of the Episcopal Conference of the Dominican Republic. He worked for the Latin American Episcopal Council for many years, and served as counselor of the Pontifical Committee for Latin America from 1989 to 1994.

132. Posadas Ocampo was born on November 10, 1926, at Salvatierra, near Morelia, Mexico, and was ordained on September 23, 1950. For many years, he was a professor and later the vice rector of the seminary in Morelia. Paul VI made him bishop of Tijuana on March 21, 1970 (consecrated June 14). Twelve years later, on December 28, 1982, John Paul II transferred him to Cuernavaca. On May 15, 1987, he was made archbishop of Guadalajara, as the second successor to Mexico's first cardinal, José Garibi y Rivera.

133. Mahony, and his twin brother, Louis, were born in Hollywood on February 27, 1936. The cardinal owes his Gaelic name to the Irish-American family which adopted his Canadian-Italian father. His mother, Loretta Marie Baron Mahony, is of German-American stock. Mahony was educated at Saint John's Seminary in Camarillo, California, and at the National Catholic School of Social Service at the Catholic University of America in Washington, D.C. He was ordained for the diocese of Fresno, California, on May 1, 1962. Paul VI made him titular bishop of Tamascani and auxiliary bishop of Fresno on January 2, 1975 (consecrated March 19), at the age of thirty-eight. John Paul II appointed him bishop of Stockton, California, on February 15, 1980, and then promoted him to be archbishop of Los Angeles, in succession to Timothy Manning, on July 12, 1985. He was installed as archbishop on the following September 5.

134. Bevilacqua was born in Brooklyn, New York, on June 17, 1923, one of eleven children in the family of Luigi and Maria Bevilacqua. After he was graduated from Cathedral College in 1943, he entered Immaculate Conception Seminary in Huntington, New York, where he stud-

ied for six years, completing the philosophical and theological requirements for the priesthood. He was ordained on June 11, 1949, in Saint James Cathedral, Brooklyn. In 1956, he received his doctorate in canon law from the Gregorianum, and then returned to the United States. Later, he attended Columbia University, where he received his master's degree in political science in 1962. Ten years later still, he began his studies in civil law, and received his law degree from Saint John's University Law School in Queens, New York, in 1975. In 1971, he established Brooklyn's Catholic Migration and Refugee Office, and, in 1976, he was named chancellor of the diocese of Brooklyn. Bevilacqua retained both offices until 1983. From 1968 to 1980, he was visiting professor of canon law at the Seminary of the Immaculate Conception in Huntington, New York. From 1977 to 1980, he also taught immigration law as an adjunct professor of law at Saint John's University Law

School. On November 24, 1980, John Paul II made him titular bishop of Aquæ Albæ in Byzacena and auxiliary bishop of Brooklyn (consecrated November 24). His titular diocese was assigned apparently as an allusion to his name— "white water," because of its swift flow, was thought to be safe to drink in classical times. His success as auxiliary bishop and chancellor led to his transfer to be bishop of Pittsburgh on October 10, 1983. On December 8, 1987, he was made archbishop of Philadelphia in succession to John Krol, who had retired. Bevilacqua was installed on February 11, 1988. Bevilacqua previously had served as a member of the Congregation for Religious and Secular Institutes. It is interesting that Bevilacqua still maintains his credentials as a member of several civil bars, and is licensed to practice law in New York State, in Pennsylvania, and before the United States Supreme Court.

VIII. John Paul II and the College:
The Later Years

From the outset of his pontificate, John Paul II seems to have viewed his time in the papal chair as a commitment to a mission rather than a requirement to administer the Church. In this attitude, he follows the thought and style of Pius X more closely than that of any of the intervening popes. As he has grown older, this sense of mission has intensified to the point that specific goals have eclipsed broader, more general aspirations for the Church. Early in his reign, for example, he expressed his intention to be the pope who would lead the Church into the next millennium. By May 29, 1994, the intention had become a mission. In his first public appearance after the replacement of his hip, John Paul revealed his innermost understanding of his pontificate: "I understand that I must lead Christ's Church into the third millennium by prayer, by various programs, but I saw that this is not enough: she must be led by suffering, by the attack thirteen years ago and now by this new sacrifice." More recently, as on his trip to Poland in 1998, he asked for prayers and intercessions to achieve this ambition, as if reaching a certain length of reign were more important for the Church than pressing social or theological considerations. At the same time, he has concentrated more and more of his attention on external ecclesiastical symbols rather than on the simple Christian message that was emphasized by Vatican II. Cardinal Silvio Oddi, no revolutionary or agitator against the curial establishment, has criticized the pope for forcing the Congregation for the Causes of Saints to press cases forward at a far faster rate than the work can be done with diligence. Oddi has said that John Paul has turned the Vatican into a "factory of saints." Indeed, this pope has canonized or beatified more men and women than all of his predecessors for two hundred years combined—in his twenty-five-year reign, Leo XIII canonized eighteen saints; in fewer than twenty years, John Paul II has canonized more than two hundred fifty; the exact number is unknown, because many of these saints are subsumed into categories, like the "Martryrs of Japan" and the "Jesuit Martyrs of Paraguay." As he has become more reactionary over the years, he has encouraged the development and enhancement of Marian cults, for example, which, in practical terms, move Catholicism further

away from points of agreement about Christian unity. At the same time he
has projected an image in which achieving that unity seems to have a high
priority—most notably in the encyclical, *Ut Unum sint*, issued on May 25,
1995, in which he invited further dialogue with non-Catholics on the nature
of papal primacy and the way in which popes exercise that authority. Paul
VI was more correct than he knew when he said that one of the chief obstacles to the eventual reintegration of all Christians in one Church was the
pope himself. As the century draws to a close, one of the leading questions
in Rome is whether the pope will or will not declare, perhaps infallibly, that
Mary is co-redemptrix with Christ! This is a measure of the degree of retreat from the intentions of Vatican II that John Paul II has achieved in
twenty years.

At the same time, the leading policy of his reign has been to stifle the
dissent which appeared in so many forms in the time of Paul VI. At first,
John Paul II imposed only the traditional punishment of silence which had
been used so effectively in the time of Pius XII. In 1979, for example, he
suspended the license of the distinguished thinker, Hans Küng, to teach as
a Catholic theologian. As the years have passed, his punishments for even
the slightest question of his teachings or policies have become stricter and
more condign. On January 4, 1997, he excommunicated the Sri Lankan
theologian and writer, Tissa Balasuriya, for pointing out the historical development of a number of theological excesses in Marian cults and for refusing to acknowledge that women would never receive ordination—John
Paul's personal devotion to Mary is well known, and, in the encyclical, *Ordinatio sacerdotalis*, in 1994, the pope emphatically denied that women
would ever be priests. But those who hope for the future need not despair,
because the teachings of popes, in equally strong language, are often revised or overturned by their successors. For example, in the encyclical,
Mirari vos, of August 15, 1832, Gregory XVI used comparably strong and
absolute language to condemn freedom of conscience, freedom of the
press, and the concept of the separation of Church and State. Today, those
views are dead.

For the College of Cardinals, this steady shift towards a pre-conciliar,
integrist Catholicsm has meant the regular appointment of theological and
doctrinally conservative members who support the pope's position that
the chief attribute of the loyal Catholic is absolute adherence to the magisterium and a total intolerance for any dissent from it. One measure of this
change is shown by the great number of theologically conservative Hispanic prelates the pope has brought into the curia and the numbers of
them whom he has created cardinals. The consistories of 1994 and 1998
intensified this trend. At the same time, the later years of John Paul's reign

have been characterized by a heightened degree of concern by the pope that his successor not weaken or alter the fortress of authority he has constructed. Both consistories were arranged and conducted against a backdrop of increasing papal physical distress and decline, in which an approaching end—John Paul has never lost his pragmatic Polish fatalism—has pressed him further and further to the right in his seach for men to elect the next pope.

Throughout the late spring and early summer of 1992, the pope had been suffering more and more from acute stomach pain. It was the first condition which could be ascribed to his advancing old age, for he was now seventy-two. Finally, he acceded to the advice that he reenter the hospital for a precise diagnosis of his distress.

On July 12, 1992, at the Angelus, John Paul II announced that he would go to the Policlinica Gemelli later in the evening for diagnostic tests. The situation proved to be grave. In a four-hour procedure on July 15, Dr. Francesco Crucitti, who had saved John Paul's life in 1981, and his surgical team removed a tumor, approximately the size of a baseball, from the sigmoid flexure of his colon. To remove this tumour, Crucitti entered the abdomen through the scar tissue from the surgeries a decade earlier—a narrow panel of tissue that ran from just below the pope's sternum almost to the groin.

This was done to spare the pope a fresh set of incisions and the growth of more post-operative scar tissue. After the excision of the tumor, it was biopsied and revealed "proliferating cells which were losing the benignity to assume those of a malignant degeneration, without, however, displaying invasive behavior." In other words, a clearly pre-cancerous growth which was just about to flourish as a malignancy. At the same time, an intra-surgical examinaton of John Paul's gallbladder revealed the presence of gallstones. The gall bladder also was removed to prevent the necessity for further surgery for that condition in the future. There is no doubt that modern surgical techniques, and the increased understanding of various cancers, saved the pope's life. After all, the excised tumor was not far removed in nature or in placement from the gastric hyperplasia of John XXIII, which had been declared inoperable almost immediately after its discovery, and from which the pope had died not long afterwards. John Paul II was released from the Gemelli on July 26, having made a swift, early recovery from conventional, not laparoscopic, surgery. His recovery on this occasion was remarkably good; by October 9, he was able to embark on his fifty-sixth pastoral journey—a five-day jaunt to Santo Domingo for the quincentennial of the European discovery of America. As a demonstration of his hardihood, he took a short skiing vacation during the following Christmas season, which served to inform the curia that he was fundamentally well.

He was, however, beginning to suffer from the unsteadiness of an extra-pyramidal syndrome that afflicted that part of his motor system which controls involuntary movement. Although this condition was not revealed until September, 1996, the pope has suffered from its increasing intensity for several years. It has become more noticeable recently, because its symptoms—trembling, slurred speech, and unsteady gait—resemble those of Parkinson's disease, which is closely related to it. The Vatican has discussed this condition minimally, just enough to make it clear that it is not Parkinson's from which he suffers. Were the latter to be the case, it might raise questions about his ability to continue to lead the Church, something both John Paul himself and his closest advisors wish to avoid. Whether as an effect of the syndrome, or from pure accident, the pope tripped on the hem of his cassock and fell sharply on the steps of the Hall of Benedictions on November 11, 1993, just after he had received representatives of the United Nations Food and Agriculture Organization. He was taken immediately to the Gemelli and remained there overnight. Under a general anaesthetic, his right arm and shoulder were immobilized with a sling. He kept the sling and bandages for four weeks, after which he began rather slowly to use his right arm again. As a demonstration of recovery, he went skiing in January, 1994, in spite of the strong recommendations of his medical team that he avoid such stress.

Less than three months later, and again perhaps because of a new lack of control in his legs, he fell amid the hard fixtures of the bathroom in the papal apartment, at about eleven o'clock on the evening of April 28, 1994. The consequences of this fall were more serious. He now had a complete trans-cervical fracture just below the top of his right femur. Once more, he was rushed to the Gemelli, early on the morning of the twenty-ninth, and underwent a complete replacement of his right hip. This approach was considered more likely to bring about a recovery with full mobility than a more conventional pinning of the fracture. However, John Paul has never recovered fully from the fall, and his convalescence was much slower than his consitutional rebound from the surgeries in 1981. Indeed, his recovery was so slow that he could not appear in public until May 29. His subsequent physical degeneration was startling, since his usual vigor seemed conspicuously absent. Throughout the rest of 1994, he often was visibly in distress. When he visited Zagreb, on September 10 and 11, he was almost unable to walk. Immediately afterward, his scheduled trip to the United States in October was canceled.

It was in this state that he reviewed the list of the names proposed for the cardinalate, and in which he conducted the consistory of November 26.

His troubles were not yet over, for on the day following the creation of the new cardinals, he crushed the small finger of his right hand in the door of his car as he was leaving the vehicle to enter Saint Peter's for a Mass with the new members of the College.

In the period from John Paul II's fifth and sixth creations of cardinals—from June 28, 1991, to November 26, 1994—only seven cardinal-electors died,[1] but no fewer than seventeen others passed their eightieth birthdays and lost their rights to vote in papal elections.[2] Five of the seven who died were creations of Paul VI—only Posadas Ocampo and Decourtray were from the cardinals of John Paul II. Among those who lost their voting rights were two more of the creations of John XXIII, Rugambwa and Landázuri Ricketts, and five of those elevated by Paul VI—Aramburu, Palazzini, Agnello Rossi, Jubany Arnau, and Poletti. In addition, eighteen superannuated cardinals died in this period, including Paul Grégoire, who was still an elector at the time of the consistory of 1991.[3] These changes reduced the membership in the College to one hundred thirty-seven, of whom ninety-seven were electors.

John Paul II created thirty cardinals in 1994, more than in any other of his seven cardinalitial consistories. Only twenty-four of the new members of the College were electors, however, which raised the number who were eligible to vote to one hundred twenty-one for the third time in this reign. The whole number of thirty meant that, for just two days, from November 26 to November 28, 1994, the membership in the College reached one hundred sixty-seven, the highest number in history.[4]

The new cardinals were:

Nasrallah Pierre Sfeir: *Pat. of Antioch of the Maronites*
Miloslav Vlk: *Archbishop of Prague*
Luigi Poggi: *Librarian and Archivist*
Peter Seiichi Shirayanagi: *Archbishop of Tokyo*
Vincenzo Fagiolo: *Pres., Discip. Comm. of the Curia*
Carlo Furno: *G.M., Order of the Holy Sepulchre*
Carlos Oviedo Cavada: *Archbishop of Santiago de Chile*
Thomas Joseph Winning: *Archbishop of Glasgow*
Adolfo Antonio Suárez Rivera: *Archbishop of Monterrey, Mexico*
Julius Riyadi Darmaatmadja: *Archbishop of Jakarta*
Jaime Ortega y Alamino: *Archbishop of Havana*
Jan Pieter Schotte: *Secretary General, Synod of Bishops*
Pierre Eyt: *Archbishop of Bordeaux*

Gilberto Agustoni: *Prefect, Apostolic Signature*
Emmanuel Wamala: *Archbishop of Kampala*
William Henry Keeler: *Archbishop of Baltimore*
Augusto Vargas Alzamora: *Archbishop of Lima*
Jean-Claude Turcotte: *Archbishop of Montreal*
Ricardo Maria Carles Gordó: *Archbishop of Barcelona*
Adam Joseph Maida: *Archbishop of Detroit*
Vinko Puljic: *Archbishop of Sarajevo*
Armand Gaétan Razafindratandra: *Archbishop of Antananarivo*
Paul Joseph Pham Dinh Tung: *Archbishop of Hanoi*
Juan Sandoval Íñiguez: *Archbishop of Guadalajara*
Bernardino Echeverria Ruiz: *Archbishop Emeritus of Guayaquil*
Kazimierz Swiatek: *Archbishop of Minsk-Mohilev*
Ersilio Tonini: *Archbishop Emeritus of Ravenna-Cervia*
Mikel Koliqi: *Albanian Resistance Leader*
Yves Congar: *Dominican theologian*
Alois Grillmeier: *Jesuit theologian*

No fewer than six of the new cardinals were Hispanic residential archbishops. One, however, Echeverria Ruiz, the former archbishop of Guayaquil, already had passed the age of eighty.[5] Two others were Mexican, Adolfo Antonio Suárez Rivera, archbishop of Monterey,[6] and Juan Sandoval Íñiguez, archbishop of Guadalajara.[7]

The latter was appointed both archbishop and cardinal swiftly to fill the place vacated by the murder of Juan Jesús Posadas Ocampo on May 24, 1993. Indeed, John Paul II gave the new cardinal the same title church as cardinal-priest that Posadas Ocampo had held.[8] As expected, Carlos Oviedo Cavada,[9] the new archbishop of Santiago de Chile, and Augusto Vargas Alzamora,[10] the new incumbent in Lima, received the red hat. There was more than the usual amount of local celebration in both cities, because both of these new cardinals were natives of the cities whose archdioceses they led. Finally, John Paul elevated the archbishop of Havana, Jaime Lucas Ortega y Alamino, in recognition of the beginnings of successful movement towards restoring some more normal ecclesiastical relations with Fidel Castro. The Cuban leader's visit to the Vatican in 1997, and the pope's return call to Havana in 1998, were further marks of this slow evolution.[11]

The College also received a seventh Spanish-speaking cardinal in the person of Ricardo Maria Carles Gordó, archbishop of Barcelona.[12]

The remaining new non-European residential cardinals were drawn from archdioceses which were broadly representative of the remote regions of the Church that had become symbols of global Catholicism: three from East Asia, Peter Seiichi Shirayanagi of Tokyo;[13] Julius Riyadi Darmaatmadja of Semarang, Indonesia;[14] and Paul Joseph Pham Dinh Tung of Hanoi;[15] and two from Africa, Emmanuel Wamala of Kampala, Uganda;[16] and Armand Gaétan Razafindratandra of Antananarivo in the Malagasy Republic.[17]

The new voting representation from Eastern Europe consisted of one archdiocese whose holder almost always was a member of the College, Prague, with Miloslav Vlk (pronounced "Filk"),[18] and one new see which had never been represented in the College before, Vrhbosna (Sarajevo), in the person of Vinko Puljic.[19] John Paul gave the red hat to him in the midst of the disintegration and catastrophe of the Bosnian civil war in the expectation that the cardinalate would serve as an additional personal shield for him and also lend prestige to the Catholics in Bosnia who were struggling for national and cultural survival. Puljic, who was born in 1945, was nine years younger than any other member of the College at that time, and is younger than any of those created in 1998, so that he remains today the junior member of the College by birth. That the pope broke with his long-standing custom of naming older cardinals in Puljic's case is some indication of the strength of his feelings about the situation in Bosnia in 1994. A third Eastern European cardinal created on this occasion, Kasimierz Swiatek, archbishop of Minsk-Mohilev in Belarus, was, like Echeverria Ruiz in Ecuador, past the age of eighty, although he still exercised episcopal functions.[20]

For the rest of Europe, Bordeaux's Pierre Eyt became a cardinal,[21] as did Thomas Joseph Winning of Glasgow, the national representative of Scotland, with its small but growing Catholic population.[22] Like the elevation of Gordon Gray of Edinburgh before him, Winning's creation places Scotland on an equal footing in the College with England and Ireland, represented by Hume and Daly, respectively.

The cardinal-patriarch elevated on this occasion was Nasrallah Pierre Sfeir, the patriarch of Antioch for the Maronites, who normally was resident in Beirut.[23] Sfeir was only the second of the Oriental patriarchs whom John Paul named to the College—the other was Sfeir's predecessor, Antoine Pierre Khoraiche, elevated in 1979. Unlike Paul VI, John Paul II has not maintained the custom of having the heads of the Eastern rite Churches in the College, with the exception of the Maronites. Sfeir became patriarch in 1986, but the punctilious delicacy with which Rome deals with the Oriental Churches caused John Paul to withhold the cardinalate until after the death of Khoraiche, on August 19, 1994.

Finally, there were three new cardinals, all doctrinal conservatives, from

North America, Turcotte of Montréal for Canada,[24] and, for the United States, William Henry Keeler of Baltimore[25] and Adam Joseph Maida of Detroit.[26] Each of the two Americans owed his rise to the friendly patronage of earlier American cardinals who had discovered and advanced them in the early significant stages of their careers. John Krol of Philadelphia had protected and supported Keeler, especially in the years in Harrisburg, and John Dearden had done the same for Maida, both as a young priest in Pittsburgh and, later, when Maida was bishop of Green Bay and Dearden was cardinal-archbishop of Detroit.

The curia was given five new places in the College, three to Italians, one to an Italian Swiss, and one to a Belgian. The three Italians were Luigi Poggi, the Librarian and Archivist of the Church;[27] Vincenzo Fagiolo, the president of the Disciplinary Commission of the Roman Curia and the vacating president of the Pontifical Council for the Interpretation of Legislative Texts;[28] and Carlo Furno, an experienced diplomat who was made Grand Master of the Equestrian Order of the Holy Sepulchre of Jerusalem and was to function as a roving diplomat for delicate negotiations—it was he who conducted a large part of the new official cordiality between the Vatican and Cuba.[29] Red hats also went to Jan Pieter Schotte, the secretary general of the Synod of Bishops,[30] and to Gilberto Agustoni, the prefect of the Apostolic Signature.[31]

Of the six new cardinals who were past the electoral age, two, Echeverria Ruiz and Swiatek, were still pastorally active. Two others received the cardinalate as personal tributes that were quite different in nature. Ersilio Tonini was given the red hat for the sake of his friendship with the now-retired Casaroli,[32] and Mikel Koliqi for his years of suffering under Albanian communist repression.[33]

Finally, there were two red hats for two more of the aged intellects whose thought had informed the Second Vatican Council: the German-Jesuit historical scholar, Alois Grillmeier,[34] and the French-Dominican theologian, Yves Congar, who was confined to his bed, awaiting death in a Paris hospital.

Congar's thought made him the great intellectual father of the Second Vatican Council. His formidably detailed research in Church history illuminated the understanding that the Church is a group of communions, not a monolith of formal faith. As one commentator has put it, borrowing from Congar's own imagery in French, it is a beehive rather than a fortress. Congar advanced the position that all Christian churches are within the unified group, cells in the body of Christ. When he began to think and write, the word *ecumenism* itself was so little used or understood that he, himself, had to put it in quotation marks in his titles and texts, and then define it in the clearest terms for thousands of readers who had never conceived the idea before. More strongly put, modern ecumenism for all Christians begins with Yves Congar.

Congar was thirty-three, and already a finished and thorough scholar, when he made his first major contribution to the "new theology" in France in the 1930s, *Chretiens Desunis: Principes d'un "Œcumenism" Catholique*.[35] Four years later, he continued his exploration of the question of Church unity in *Esquisses du Mystere de l'Eglise*.[36]

The war interrupted his course of publication, but, at its end, he produced perhaps his most seminal work, the first extensive exploration by a modern Catholic theologian of the laity and the concept of a universal priesthood, *Sacerdoce et Laicat dans l'Eglise*.[37]

A good French patriot as well as a great French theologian, he next wrote a collection of biographical descriptions of the French officers whom the Nazis had deemed dangerous enough to warrant imprisonment in the most secure fortresses of the Reich, Colditz and Lubeck. Congar's war writing, *Leur Resistance: memorial des officiers evades anciens de Colditz et de Lubeck, morts pour la France*,[38] was as firmly rooted in sound scholarship as any of his other great treatises. In 1950 came *Vraie et Fausse Reforme dans l'Eglise*, the first of eight projected volumes on the problems of reformation and Church renewal.[39] This was followed by one of the first clear and unequivocal explorations of racism, with a universal application beyond its frame of reference, *L'Eglise Catholique devant la Question Raciale*.[40] He then continued his work on Christian unity with a major reevaluation of the causes and the course of the schism between the Eastern and Western Churches, that had taken its most definitive form in 1054, *Neuf Cents Ans Apres: Notes sur le "Schisme Oriental."*[41] Then there was another major exposition of the theme of the universal priesthood in *Jalons pour une Theologie du Laicat*.[42]

In the midst of this fruitful outpouring of scholarship, Congar was silenced in the famous "Raid on the Dominicans," the curia's attempt to smash the worker-priest movement in France following the departure of Roncalli as nuncio.[43] The "Raid" began the dark years of the repression of exploratory theology and pastoral innovation that continued until John XXIII put an end to it by rehabilitating its chief victims and calling the Second Vatican Council. Restored by Pope John, Congar became perhaps the leading figure of the council after the pontiff himself. Almost every major document issued by the council fathers bears the stamp of Congar's mind.[44]

Congar, through his intellect and sympathetic understanding for all Christians, changed Catholicism dramatically. He returned to the Bible, to the writings of the early Church fathers, and to the living spirit of the thought and writing of Thomas Aquinas to propose a truly universal Church. His work went on for years after Vatican II had ended. Finally, in the early 1990s, his physical, though not his intellectual, powers began to fail. Once John Paul II was sure that he was dying, he added his name to the list of those elevated in 1994.

A few days after the consistory, Congar was presented with his scarlet biretta in his hospital room. The great thinker was not fooled by this symbolic glorification when he was so near the grave, but he expressed his joy and satisfaction for the honor; it was a triumph of image over substance, as the old Dominican well knew. Yves Congar died at last, on June 22, 1995, after a cardinalate of just two hundred eight days. He was the last of the great thinkers of the "new theology" to pass. Later, in 1996, John Paul II is said to have included as a part of an answer to an indirect comment about his fidelity to the message of Vatican II, ". . . and I even made Father Congar a cardinal." Ironically, after all of the human passions and fears of this age have passed, John Paul II may well have his historical memory enhanced because he did elevate Congar to the College, just as one of the chief accomplishments remembered of Gregory X (1271–1276) is that he elevated Bonaventura Fidanza, the great Franciscan theologian and saint, to the cardinalate, as cardinal-bishop of Albano, in the consistory of June 3, 1273.

After the consistory of 1994, a number of journalists and commentators rushed to assume that the event marked the end of John Paul II's actions with regard to the College. The most important of several clues that this was not the case was that the pope had not yet modified the electoral process. All of the recent popes, except John Paul I, have issued new election consitutions at some point near the ends of their reigns, to correct what they believe to be the deficiencies in their predecessor's rules and to elaborate procedures that they hope will improve the process of choosing a new pope.

By 1994, John Paul II had not done that, and it was almost inconceivable that a pope of his strong personality and views would fail to make his ideas on the nature of the conclave palpable. Moreover, the domestic political and governmental crisis in Italy would soon mark so many of the Italian cardinals, both residential and curial alike, that further changes would have to be made to the membership in the College.

For most of 1995, the pope's health continued to be good. There were no more sudden events that required treatment or surgery at the Policlinica Gemelli. But, at the very end of the year, he was struck down by a severe case of influenza, which is always dangerous in a man of his age. On

Christmas Day, he was forced to cut short his participation in the usual celebrations. A night of complete and uninterrrupted rest did much to restore him, however. On the morning of the twenty-sixth, after he had said Mass and enjoyed a light breakfast, he was examined thoroughly by the principal Vatican physician, Doctor Renato Buzzonetti, who found him much improved, although still with a slight fever. At noon, the pope conducted the traditional Angelus blessing from the window of his private study. Later in the day, Doctor Joaquín Navarro-Valls, a physician himself as well as the pope's friend and public spokesman, announced that John Paul would not go to Castel Gandolfo as planned, but would stay in his apartments in the Vatican for two more days of rest.

Whether this latest bout of ill health hastened the promulgation of the new election consitution is unclear, but on February 22, 1996, the feast of the Chair of Saint Peter, John Paul subscribed to the document. It was released on the following day by the secretary of the College, Archbishop Jorge Mejia, at the press office of the Holy See. Mejia made special notice that the Pope's physical condition had no effect on his decision to regulate how the next conclave will work—which, in the way of the Vatican, is almost a certain indication that it did.

Universi Dominici Gregis—which is reprinted in full in an appendix, since it will govern rigidly the whole process for electing the next pope— enacted more fundamental changes to the conduct of the conclave than any other modern papal document. In its introduction, John Paul explains why he took up the matter of revising the conclave system once more:

> If I too now turn to this matter, it is certainly not because of any lack of esteem for those norms [of my predecessors], for which I have great respect and which I intend for the most part to confirm, at least with regard to their substance and the basic principles which inspired them. What leads me to take this step is awareness of the Church's changed situation today and the need to take into consideration the general revision of Canon Law which took place, to the satisfaction of the whole Episcopate, with the publication and promulgation first of the *Code of Canon Law* and subsequently of the *Code of Canons of the Eastern Churches*. (Introduction, para. 3)

The single most important change was the abolition altogether of the two old forms of election—election by acclamation and election by compromise.[45] Only election by scrutiny, or secret ballot, remains. As a further modification of this method, John Paul has introduced a procedure by which the new pope can be chosen, as a means of avoiding exhaustion or stalemate, by a simple majority of the electors. This sweeps away, for the next conclave at least, the custom that the new pope must be chosen by at least two-thirds of the cardinals present, first codified by Alexander III in the constitution, *Licet de vitanda*, in 1179. *Universi Dominici Gregis* spells out exactly under what circumstancs this may occur:

> In the event that the Cardinal electors find it difficult to agree on the person to be elected, after balloting has been carried out for three days in the form described above (in Section Numbers 62ff) without result, voting is to be suspended for a maximum of one day in order to allow a pause for prayer, informal discussion among the voters, and a brief spiritual exhortation given by the senior Cardinal in the Order of Deacons. Voting is then resumed in the usual manner, and after seven ballots, if the election has not taken place, there is another pause for prayer, discussion and an exhortation given by the senior Cardinal in the Order of Priests. Another series of seven ballots is then held and, if there has still been no election, this is followed by a further pause for prayer, discussion and an exhortation given by the senior Cardinal in the Order of Bishops. Voting is then resumed in the usual manner and, unless the election occurs, it is to continue for seven ballots (II, v, 74).
>
> If the balloting does not result in an election, even after the provisions of Section Number 74 have been fulfilled, the Cardinal electors shall be invited by the Camerlengo to express an opinion about the manner of proceeding. The election will then proceed in accordance with what the absolute majority of the electors decides.
>
> Nevertheless, there can be no waiving of the requirement that a valid election takes place only by an absolute majority of the votes or else by voting only on the two names which in the ballot immediately preceding have received the greatest number of votes; also in this second case only an absolute majority is required (II, v, 75)

The wording is careful and precise. There are to be twelve ballots, or thirteen, if the cardinals decide to hold one on the evening the conclave opens, for which there also is provision in the constitution. Then, if a deadlock persists, there are to be three periods of seven ballots each, followed by a decision by a majority of the cardinals on how the proceed further. At that point, a simple majority of the cardinals can decide that the new pope will be chosen by a simple majority of the cardinals. Thus, if a committed bloc, like the original supporters of Benelli in the second conclave of 1978, decides to hold out for their candidate for a maximum of thirty-four ballots, they can ensure that he will achieve the throne. The incentive for tough compromise and negotiation is now gone. Would any simple majority of the cardinals be willing to hold out for as long as twelve days to ensure the enthronement of their candidate? The deep-seated hatred and fear displayed in earlier modern elections, particulalrly those in

1922 and 1963, suggests that this is not impossible.

John Paul also has made it easier physically for the cardinals to endure a longer conclave. Instead of the spartan conditions of cots and slop pots in which the cardinals had to live in earlier conclaves, the electors will now be housed in the comparative comfort of the Vatican's new hospice, the Domus Sanctæ Marthæ, with its small suites of rooms with private baths, much like the standard furnishings of an American motel:

> By the time fixed for the beginning of the election of the Supreme Pontiff, all the Cardinal electors must have been assigned and must have taken up suitable lodging in the Domus Sanctæ Marthæ, recently built in Vatican City (II, ii, 42).

The Hospice of Saint Martha can be configured with somewhat more than a hundred duplex suites and a few more single rooms, which is hardly the same set of conditions under which earlier conclaves were held. Since the electors will have to be in the open as they walk from their lodgings to the Sistine Chapel, still the required site for balloting, the constitution also calls for strict monitoring so that they remain isolated during their short exposed period: "In particular, provision shall be made to ensure that no one approaches the Cardinal electors while they are being transported from the Domus Sanctæ Marthæ to the Apostolic Vatican Palace (II, ii, 43)."

John Paul also has done away with the two-thirds-plus-one rule for election by ballot which was first imposed by Pius XII in 1945, canceled by John XXIII in 1962, and reimposed by Paul VI in 1975. Finally, John Paul II codified what John Paul I had done from a sense of simplicity and modesty, and which he had followed by example, not by inclination—the constitution did away with the papal coronation in favor of "the solemn ceremony of the inauguration of the Pontificate (II, vii, 92)."

Universi Dominici Gregis reinforces the rules for secrecy which have been so much a part of all election consitutions in modern times, with specific reference to audiovisual equipment, a new technology not readily available in miniturized form when *Romano Pontifici Eligendo* was issued in 1975. The constitution also limits the number of electors to one hundred twenty, just as Paul VI's document had; but John Paul II abrogated that provision himself in 1998, by increasing the number of electors to one hundred twenty-three. Within a few weeks after that announcement, which came on January 18 when he announced the names of the nineteen new electors who were to be installed on February 21, 1998, death reduced the number of electors beneath the constitutional limit again. Whether the pope will make another exception in the closing phase of his reign is, of course, unknown. If he does, it seems certain that it will be only to the extent of a few more electors.

Within a few weeks of issuing the constitution, the pope's health began to cause worry again. On three occasions over the late spring and summer, he had been afflicted with abdominal pain and fever which was treated with brief rests and an antibiotic regimen. Finally, in August, the condition merited a full diagnostic examination. Its results suggested that the problems were caused by a recurrent inflammation of the pope's appendix. At first, the medical staff, led by Buzzonetti, hoped that a stronger regimen of antibiotics would suppress the condition and spare John Paul the need for yet another round of surgery.

By mid-September, however, it was clear that the condition was far too advanced for such a cure, and that the pope would have to enter the Gemelli again, for an appendectomy.

On September 14, Doctor Giorgio Ribotta, an outside specialist who is a professor at the University of Rome, conducted another examination which confirmed the diagnosis of appendicitis. Later on the same day, Joaquín Navarro-Valls announced that John Paul had been suffering, for nearly a year, from "recurring episodes of inflammation of the appendix." Since the condition had not responded to drug treatment, there would now be an operation "in the course of the current year." In fact, the pope's condition was deteriorating faster than Navarro-Valls's announcement indicated.

He was admitted to the Gemelli late on the evening of October 6 and taken immediately to the tenth-floor secure suite that had been prepared for him. On the morning of the eighth, he arose at three o'clock, and concelebrated Mass with his private secretary, Monsignor Stanislaw Dziwisz, at five, in the little chapel adjacent to his bedroom. Members of the surgical team arrived shortly before 7 A.M. in the operating room at the Gemelli, while members of the Vatican's security staff sealed off the surgical ward.

Shortly afterward, John Paul was taken to the operating room for the fifty-minute procedure that was done conventionally rather than laparoscopically because of the presence of so much adhesive tissue, which had developed after his earlier operations. He was back in his room by 9:30. The medical bulletin which followed was much more complete and informative than earlier discussions of the pope's condition:

> According to the schedule previously communicated on September 14, this morning, October 8, 1996, the Holy Father underwent—under a general anaesthesia—the surgical procedure of an appendectomy, previous to which there was a lysis (dissolving) of localized adhesions. The operation confirmed the clinical diagnosis of "recur-

ring episodes of inflammation of the appendix," as previously stated. Exploration of the area allowed for the exclusion, once again, of the presence of other pathologies. The extemporaneous histological examination showed a transmural appendicitis with evidence of fibrosis established from preceding inflammatory episodes. The morphological finding is indicative of recidivist appendicitis. The examination will be completed with the usual definitive histopathological research. The operation began at 7:50 a.m. and ended at 8:40 a.m. and was undergone well by the patient. The vital signs: cardio-circulatory, respiratory, hematological and metabolical stayed within the norm for the entire duration of the operation. Consciousness was rapidly recovered. Immediately following the surgery, the Holy Father was taken back to his room. The surgery was performed by Professor Francesco Crucitti, assisted by Professors G. B. Doglietto and R. Bellantone and by Doctor L. Sofo. The anaesthesia was administered by Professors Corrado Manni and Rodolfo Proietti, with the collaboration of Doctor (Signora) R. Ranieri. Cardiological assistance was administered by Professor Attilio Maseri. The histological examination was done by Professor A. Capelli, director of the Institute of Pathological Anatomy, and by Professor J. Prat, director of the Service of Pathological Anatomy of the "Sant. Creu y San Pau" hospital of Barcelona. Assisting were Doctor Renato Buzzonetti and Professor Luigi Ortona, to whom was entrusted the consultation for the anti-infection prophylaxis relative to the preceding cytomegalovirus infection. The next updating on the post-operative period of the Holy Father will be given through press communiques, the first of which will be made public Wednesday, October 9, at 12 noon.

Professors Francesco Crucitti, director of the Institute of Clinical Surgery; Corrado Manni, director of the Institute of Anaesthesiology and Reanimation; Rodolfo Proietti, chief of service of anaesthesia and reanimation, Gemelli Polyclinic; Luigi Ortona, director of the Institute of the Clinic of Infectious Illnesses; Attilio Maseri, director of the Cardiology Institute; and Doctor Renato Buzzonetti, personal physician of the Holy Father.

In a post-surgical press conference, Crucitti was pressed repreatedly to comment more on the pope's extra-pyramidal syndrome, to which Navarro-Valls had alluded in September. Since the Vatican had not yet denied reports that John Paul's trembling, together with his facial rigidity and stooped gait, could be signs of Parkinson's disease, the reporters had this, rather than the appendectomy, on their minds. "There are specialists who are following him. This is not my field," was all that Crucitti would say—but it was enough to confirm that the pope's deterioration had been identified with some specific neurological cause, and that he was receiving treatment for it. Crucitti then returned to the subject that he wanted to discuss by adding that the surgical incision had required about ten stitches to close and that doctors had also separated some of the adhesions. Crucitti also said the pope could leave his bed for the first time on Wednesday, October 10, and might leave the hospital in less than seven days.

On the following Sunday, the pope made a brief appearance at the window of his hospital room to greet well-wishers who had gathered below. He conspicuouly kept his left arm at his side, so that his hand was below the level of the window sill and could not be seen.

In fact, the pope did remain in the hospital for just seven days. His stitches were removed one week after the operation, on Tuesday, October 15, and he was discharged later in the afternoon.

By the end of October, John Paul II had resumed his regular working schedule, after two additional weeks of convalescence in his apartments. He had made his first public appearance on October 20, when he presided at services in St. Peter's Basilica to celebrate the 350th anniversary of the Union of Uzhorod. In spite of the new round of vigorous activity, which was designed to quell rumors about his general health, almost everyone who saw him now noticed his drawn face, stiff gait, and the shaking in his left arm which he apparently could not control.

Unlike the preceding year, 1997 was a comparatively good one for the pope physically. There were no major events that required prolonged treatment or surgery, and his prosthetic hip, which has given him trouble since it was implanted, became, year by year, more manageable. While skiing was now out of the question, he could still enjoy walks during his vacations in the Alps or at Castel Gandolfo. On April 12 and 13, he was able to accomplish his long-postponed trip to Sarajevo, his seventy-fifth journey outside Italy. For ten days, beginning on July 9, he enjoyed an Alpine vacation—this year at Les Combes. The highlight of his public year was his four-day visit to Paris for World Youth Day, August 21 to 25—he always has enjoyed the enthusiasm and the adulation of Catholic youth; while the zenith of his regnal year was the publication, on September 8, of the apostolic constitution, *Lætamur Magnopere*, in which he approved and promulgated the official version in Latin of the new Catechism of the Catholic Church.

For the College, however, the year was disastrous. In Austria, the problems raised by the public's knowledge that the former cardinal-archbishop of Vienna was a confirmed pedophile still grew. While in the Vatican itself, the revelation that Pio Laghi had been embroiled to some degree in the tyranny in Argentina during his time as nuncio there was all the more shocking because he had been identified as a leading candidate for the throne in the coming election. Then there was the collapse of conventional partisan politics in Italy, beginning in 1992 with the Mani Pulite (Clean Hands) campaign to unearth and prosecute corruption. At first, when the Christian Democrats were swept away, the Church seemed relatively unscathed, but, as more and more elements of the vast system of graft came to light, the names of cardinals began to appear, at least around the fringes, with greater frequency. Fortunately, there was no direct evidence that high ranking prelates had benefitted personally from the decades-long institutionalized corruption, but there was much to indicate that many prominent cardinals and archbishops knew about it and tacitly condoned it. Only Carlo Maria Martini of Milan, among the residential cardinal-archbishops, and Achille Silvestrini, among the major figures of the curia, seemed to be untouched by the scandals. Since John Paul II could not ignore the strong feeling, not just in Italy or the curia but in many parts of the global hierarchy, that the next reign should be that of another Italian, he came under more and more pressure to create new Italian cardinals who had been vetted thoroughly to ensure that they were free entirely of any involvement, however peripheral, in the systemic corruption that had been revealed by the work of the judges in the Mani Pulite. The very conservatism that the pope had supported since the opening of his reign made the campaign to return the papacy to Italian hands almost inevitable.

By the end of the year, when there were one hundred five living electors, the pope already had a working list of twenty eligible prelates to whom he intended to give the red hat. This necessitated raising the voting membership in the College to one hundred twenty-five, not just five more than the figure established by Paul VI in *Romano Pontifici Eligendo* but also beyond the figure recognized in *Universi Dominici Gregis* in 1996.

By mid-January, the pope had decided that Groër would have to give up his cardinalitial rights and privileges, which would lower the number of supernumerary electors to four. On January 15, he sent word to the curial officials whom he intended to elevate that he would publish the list of new names on Sunday, January 18, in Saint Peter's, and that the formal consistory for creating them would be held on February 21, after he had returned from Cuba.

Between the consistory of November 26, 1994, and January 18, 1998, the membership in the College fell from its historical zenith of one hundred sixty-seven to one hundred forty-six. Of the twenty-two cardinals who died, only four were electors.[46] The remaining seventeen deceased members were cardinals who had passed their eightieth birthdays.[47] In addition, twelve cardinals would have reached the age of eighty before the consistory on February 21 and were thus ineligible to vote, although two of them, Hamer and Yago, also died in this period.[48] As has been said, the number of electors by the time of the consistory would stand at one hundred five, officially—but was intended to be reduced by one as soon as the formal resignation by Groër could be arranged without undue attention. Of the four electors who died, one of them, Ekandem, was a creation of Paul VI, while only two of those who became superannuated also were from among Paul's cardinals—Zoungrana and González Martín. It also may be mentioned that three of the aged cardinals who died—Rugambwa, Landázuri Ricketts, and Suenens—were among the last five creations of John XXIII; in 1998, only two of his cardinals remain, König, the archpriest of the College, and Silva Henriquez.

Suddenly, on the morning of the eighteenth, John Paul was brought word that one of the men who appeared on his list, Giuseppe Uhac, the secretary of the Congregation for the Evangelization of Peoples, had died, at the age of seventy-three. The loss of his name meant that the number of electors above the pope's constitutional limits now would be three. While he had not envisioned the death of Uhac, of course, he already had prepared for some sudden change in the cardinalate by adding two more men to his list, whose names he kept *in pectore*. The publication of their names could take place at any time.

John Paul duly read the names of the nineteen new electors, as well as that of one aged Polish prelate who was to be honored, much as he had planned:

Salvatore De Giorgi: *Archbishop of Palermo*
Serafim Fernandes de Araújo: *Archbishop of Belo Horizonte*
Antonio María Rouco Varela: *Archbishop of Madrid*
Aloysius Matthew Ambrozic: *Archbishop of Toronto*
Jean Balland: *Archbishop of Lyon*
Dionigi Tettamanzi: *Archbishop of Genoa*
Polycarp Pengo: *Archbishop of Dar-es-Salaam*
Christoph Schönborn: *Archbishop of Vienna*
Norberto Rivera Carerra: *Archbishop of Mexico City*
Francis Eugene George: *Archbishop of Chicago*
Paul Shan Kuo-Hsi: *Bishop of Kaohsiung, Taiwan*
Adam Kozłowiecki: *Archbishop Emeritus of Lusaka*
Jorge Arturo Medina Estévez: *Prefect, Cong. for Divine Worship*
Alberto Bovone: *Prefect, Cong. for Causes of Saints*
Darío Castrillón Hoyos: *Prefect, Congregation for the Clergy*
Lorenzo Antonetti: *Admin., Patrimony of the Holy See*
James Francis Stafford: *Pres., Pont. Counc. for the Laity*
Giovanni Cheli: *Pres, P. C. for Past. Care of Migrants*

Francesco Colasuonno: *Nuncio to Italy*
Dino Monduzzi: *Pref. of the Pontifical Household*

In reading the list, the pope specifically identified Cheli, Colasuonno, and Monduzzi as the men who were being elevated in spite of breaking the Pauline limits. Finally, John Paul did mention the presence of the dead archbishop's name on the original list: "Also on my list was Archbishop Giuseppe Uhac, secretary of the Congregation for the Evangelization of Peoples, who had been informed of this three days ago, but whom the Lord called home this morning."

By the time of the formal consistory on February 21, another elector had died—Eduardo Pironio, one of the last advanced liberals of the time of Paul VI, on February 5. On the day before, John Paul had a long private audience in the Vatican with Groër. In their conversation, the details of his resignation were established, although they would not be carried out for some weeks.

After the consistory, the whole membership of the College increased to one hundred sixty-five. The number of electors became one hundred twenty-three, because one of the new cardinals, Adam Kozłowiecki, the re-tired archbishop of Lusaka, Zambia, already was eighty-six.[49]

The pope also continued his policy of augmenting the College with conservative pastors of major archdioceses—in this case, Aloysius Mat-thew Ambrozic, archbishop of Toronto;[50] Serafim Fernandes de Araújo, archbishop of Belo Horizonte, Brazil;[51] Norberto Rivera Carrera, arch-bishop of Mexico City;[52] Antonio Rouco Varela, archbishop of Madrid;[53] Jean Balland, archbishop of Lyon;[54] and Polycarp Pengo, archbishop of Dar-es-Salaam.[55] All these new cardinals were drawn from the standard mold from which John Paul had created new cardinal-archbishops in the past. Four other new cardinals, however, were not.

Salvatore De Giorgi, archbishop of Palermo,[56] and Dionigi Tettamanzi, archbishop of Genoa,[57] are both slightly more moderate in their doctrinal and political views than other Italian archbishops whom John Paul has made cardinals—De Giorgi somewhat so, and Tettamanzi, by an extraor-dinary margin. Both owed their rise to major Italian sees and the cardi-nalate to the pope's need to have major figures of the Italian church who were utterly free of any association with the scandals uncovered in the Mani Pulite investigations. In the case of Tettamanzi, in particular, the pope acknowledged a strong movement in the College to explore the pos-sibility of electing another Italian as the next pontiff. Since Carlo Maria Martini of Milan is not well regarded by John Paul II, and he is the Italian cardinal who is discussed most, both privately and publicly, as papabile, the pope needed to appoint at least one Italian pastor who can become the alternative to the candidacy of the archbishop of Milan—to be the focus of any movement in the next conclave to stop Martini from the possibility of reaching the throne. In order to be viable as a candidate in the coming election, Martini's Italian opponent must be sufficiently unreactionary to draw interest and support from cardinals who wish to move the Church away from the rightist position from which John Paul has sought to govern it. Tettamanzi is the papal choice for that rôle.

The situation in Chicago following the death of Cardinal Bernardin in November, 1996, also was sufficiently delicate to require very careful attention to the naming of his successor. The new archbishop would not, of course, be as liberal in his views as Bernardin, nor was it likely that he would have the sympathetic understanding which people had detected so easily in the former pastor, but he would have to be someone who was liberal enough to represent continuity, someone who would not alienate Chicago's large and loyal Catholic population, who had come genuinely to love and respect Bernardin. It also would be helpful if the new archbishop had personal attributes which, although different from those of his predecessor, would bring him an instant basis of goodwill and, indeed, sympathy. John Paul found that man in Francis Eugene George, archbishop of Portland, Oregon, before his transfer to Chicago.[58] George, the first native Chicagoan to be archbishop there, has a warm personality that was molded, in part, by his patience and fortitude in his long recovery from childhood polio. His cardinalate in 1998 ensures that he will have a voice in the election of the next pope, which the people of Chicago have expected in their archbishop for decades.

In the mid-1990s, John Paul had another pastoral crisis in a major archdiocese which was far more grave than finding a successor for a good archbishop, and where the potential for immediate and destructive damage was far greater than was the case in Chicago. Like the situation in Chicago which had led to Bernardin's rise after the death of Cody, and like the earlier crisis of confidence in the Church which had caused Paul VI to appoint Sin as archbishop of Manila after the death of Santos, the situation in Vienna in early 1995 was almost explosive. As Hans Hermann Groër came close to the age of mandatory retirement, he was embroiled more and more in the consequences of the revelation of his pedophilia. Vienna needed a new archbishop swiftly, one who would begin his tenure with a reservoir of popular respect and confidence to make it possible for him to calm the turmoil, accentuated by a growing popular anger, and perhaps win back a degree of respect for the Church in Austria. John Paul already had appointed an auxiliary bishop in Vienna in 1991 who seemed to meet the need. In

April, 1995, that man was made coadjutor archbishop with right of succession and, as soon as Groër's resignation for age could be accepted without seeming too hasty or overreactive, he stepped into the see of Vienna. Now, in the first consistory after that appointment, he was given the cardinalate, even though he was only fifty-two years old—an age which, given John Paul's penchant for appointing older cardinals, might well have indicated a wait for a later creation.

He was Christoph Maria Michael Hugo Damian Peter Adalbert, Graf von Schönborn. He has family connections that make him one of the most nobly born figures in modern Austria, which still has a lingering sympathy for the old imperial aristocracy in much the same way that it has a lingering love for the music of Johann Strauss, *sohn*.[59] In addition to two other cardinals in his immediate family, one in the eighteenth century and one in the nineteenth, he is related directly to at least twenty other cardinals and literally dozens of other bishops and archbishops. Among his ancestors are Choteks, the family of Sophie, wife of Archduke Franz Ferdinand, whose murder at Sarajevo, together with that of her husband, inaugurated World War I; as well as members of the house of Savoy—the royal family of Italy—and the Colonna, one of the two oldest Roman noble families. He is the cousin of nearly every crowned head, or pretender, in Europe, through his family's connections with the houses of Hohenzollern-Hechingen and Nassau. Several of his immediate ancestors enjoyed the distinction of having works dedicated to them by Beethoven, including members of the houses of Lobkowicz, Erdödy, and Waldstein. His ties to the old Hungarian nobility are evident in his descent from the houses of Szechenyi and Batthyany. Among his dozens of other noble connections are those to the families of Schwarzenberg, Auersperg, Dalberg, Althann, Kinsky, Anguisola, and Schenk von Stauffenberg.

This background makes him, for the Viennese, *appropriate* for the office he has filled. A professed Dominican, his academic and pastoral credentials, too, are superb. Symbolic of his view of himself in the modern Church was the fact that he dropped the particle "von" from his name when he became a priest, a gesture that has pleased many without causing them to forget what his background is.

On the day of his creation as cardinal, his appearance—a wide, friendly, open face, which strikes many as particularly sympathetic, especially when he smiles—the prestige of his family, his ecumenical commitments, and his academic brilliance all caused him to be cited as distinctly *papabile*. Of course, he is not. The cardinals are not going to elect the second youngest cardinal in the College to the papal chair, which suggests another reign of twenty years and more; nor are they likely, given the present state of the

Church in the non-European world, to advance a nobly born descendant of princes of the Holy Roman Empire. But Schönborn's tenure at Vienna, although still in its early stages, looks as if it will accomplish exactly what is necessary—he is restoring the traditional popular confidence in the Church and its hierarchy.

The East Asian ordinary elevated in 1998, another representative of Jesuits in the College, was Paul Shan Kuo-hsi, bishop of Kaohsiung, Taiwan.[60]

Also in the creation of 1998 were several of the next generation of curial officials to reach high rank. Their number was about equally divided between non-Italians who had been imported into the curia as a part of John Paul's continuing efforts to internationalize it, and Italians who had followed the traditional curial pathways to the cardinalate. Among the former were Dario Castrillón Hoyos, the new prefect of the Congregation for the Clergy, a protégé of Alfonso López Trujillo;[61] Jorge Arturo Medina Estévez, prefect of the Congregation for Divine Worship;[62] and, especially, the former archbishop of Denver, James Francis Stafford, president of the Pontifical Council for the Laity, who first came to John Paul's immediate attention in 1993 when he managed the World Youth Day for that year with great success, employing modern American publicity and managerial techniques to make the gathering a superb backdrop for a papal triumph.[63]

The new Italian curial cardinals were Lorenzo Antonetti, president of the Administration of the Patrimony of the Holy See;[64] Alberto Bovone, prefect of the Congregation for the Causes of Saints, already mortally ill;[65] Giovanni Cheli, president of Pontifical Council for the Pastoral Care of Migrants and Itinerant People, already seventy-nine and soon to lose his vote;[66] Dino Monduzzi, the retiring prefect of the Pontifical Household;[67] and, finally, the nuncio to Italy, Francesco Colasuonno.[68]

As has been mentioned, the pope also named two other cardinals *in pectore*, whose names may be published at any time. In addition, now that John Paul realizes fully that Paul VI's limits on the number of electors are not absolute, he may hold another consistory for the creation of yet more electors before his pontificate ends. Nevertheless, the consensus among observers is that the present pope has completed the general shaping of the College in the way he wishes to leave it, and that, with perhaps the exception of the publication of the last two creations *in pectore*, the College as it appears at the close of 1998 is the one which will elect his successor.

On Saturday, August 22, 1998, the latest scandal to shock the College exploded in Naples, when dozens of police descended on the offices of Michele Giordano, archbishop of Naples. While Giordano himself had no immediate statement about his predicament, he invited reporters, photographers, and television crews to watch the police go through his documents and records. His lawyer, Enrico Tuccillo, confirmed that the cardinal was being investigated for loan sharking, extortion, and associating with criminals—the same crimes for which the cardinal's brother, Mario Lucio Giordano, was jailed on the preceding Thursday. ANSA reported that prosecutors had asked the tax police to start examining Giordano's banking records in February after evidence that linked the cardinal to financial irregularities came to their attention. Immediately after the raid, the pope's spokesman, Dr. Joaquín Navarro-Valls, said that the Vatican was following the case closely, and the president of the Italian Episcopal Conference, Camillo Ruini, said that he was certain that Giordano would be found innocent.

The case is similar to the scandal which began on November 1, 1995, in which Ricardo Maria Carles Gordó, archbishop of Barcelona, was accused of being involved in a money laundering operation in which one hundred billion lire—about sixty-three million dollars at the rate of exchange at the time—was passed through the Institute for Religious Works, the principal financial institution of the Vatican. In that case, the investigation was conducted by government prosecutors in Torre Annunziata, near Naples. The accusations, which came from a shady Milanese financier, Riccardo Marocco, led to no evidence of a crime on Carles Gordó's part.

The Giordano affair, however, is more serious because the source of the allegations appears to be more credible. In any case, it is another blow to the reputation of the College of Cardinals which already has been so damaged in the later years of the reign of John Paul II.

Between the consistory of February 21, 1998, and the end of 1998, no fewer than five electors died—Antonio Quarracino, archbishop of Buenos Aires, on February 28; Jean Balland, archbishop of Lyon, on March 1; Antonio Ribeiro, patriarch of Lisbon, on March 24; Alberto Bovone, the prefect of the Congregation for the Causes of Saints, on April 17; and Carlos Oviedo Cavada, on December 7. Two of these five, Balland and Bovone, had extraordinarily short cardinalates, since both received the red hat only in the consistory of February 21. In addition, four of the superannuated cardinals also died—Agostino Casaroli, the retired secretary of state, on June 9; John Joseph Carberry, archbishop emeritus of Saint Louis, on June 17; Anastasio Alberto Ballestrero, archbishop emeritus of Turin, on June 21; and Alois Grillmeier, the Jesuit scholar, on September 13—and one of the remaining two creations of John XXIII, Raul Silva Henriquez, who died April 9, 1999. These changes reduced the number of living cardinals to one hundred fifty-six in May, 1999. The number of electors, however, was reduced by eight, to one hundred fifteen, because on Tuesday,

April 14, 1998, Groër finally announced publicly that he had relinquished all ecclesiastical duties and would leave Austria at the request of Pope John Paul II. He agreed to forfeit all his privileges and rights as both bishop and cardinal for life, including the right to participate in the conclave. In addition, three other cardinals passed their eightieth birthdays and lost their rights to vote in a conclave—Salvatore Pappalardo, born September 23, 1918; Giovanni Canestri, born September 30, 1918; and Giovanni Cheli, born October 4, 1918, the first of the electors who were created on February 21, 1998, to lose his vote. One of these cardinals, Pappalardo, was elevated by Paul VI, the other two by John Paul II.

During 1999, six electors will pass their eightieth birthdays and will lose their actives votes: José Lebrun Martinos on March 19; Raúl Primatesta on April 14; Franjo Kuharic on the following day, April 15; Paul Pham Dinh Tung on June 15; Ernesto Corripio Ahumada on June 29; and Angelo Felici on July 26. Thus, by midsummer, the number of electors will have fallen on one hundred nine. It also must be assumed that one or two electors will die in this period, which will leave the number of cardinal electors at a slightly smaller number than the College that elected John Paul II in 1978.

Of all the cardinals, only twenty-seven survive from among the creations of Paul VI, and, of these, only fourteen are still electors. These fourteen are, however, among the most powerful and influential members of the College, men of enormous prestige for a variety of reasons. First, unlike the others, they are veterans of two conclaves and understand quite well how the *prattiche* evolves and how the practical procedures for choosing a new pope operate. The creations of John Paul II are in much the same position as the cardinals of Paul VI were in the first election of 1978—they do not know many of their colleagues well, some are relative strangers to Rome itself, and they have a certain degree of uncertainty about how the mechanism of the election actually works.

Consequently, the surviving electors of Paul VI's time have a reservoir of knowledge and experience upon which other cardinals will want to draw, so their opinions and suggestions will carry some weight, even if many of them were not the regional leaders they are.

For the Latin American cardinals, three influential members are the senior Brazilians in the College, even though John Paul's policies have marginalized their direct influence for years. All three are respected supporters of Vatican II with a strong dedication to dealing with their flocks as the "children of God," as the council identified them. The two Franciscans, Paulo Evaristo Arns[69] and Aloisio Lorscheider,[70] are particularly esteemed, even by many of the conservatives who have combatted them in

CELAM and other fora over the years. It is not forgotten that Albino Luciani voted for Lorscheider on every ballot of the first conclave of 1978, even as he was being raised to the throne himself as John Paul I. Not much behind them in regard is Eugenio De Araújo Sales, who still serves as archbishop of Rio de Janeiro, even though he is three years past the age of mandatory retirement.[71] The other two Latin American creations of Paul VI, Raúl Francisco Primatesta, archbishop of Córdoba, Argentina,[72] and Luís Aponte Martinez, archbishop of San Juan de Puerto Rico,[73] are somewhat less influential but are still prelates whose opinion will be heeded.

Black Africa has two cardinals of similar regional regard, Maurice Michael Otunga, emeritus archbishop of Nairobi,[74] and Hyacinthe Thiandoum, archbishop of Dakar,[75] while a third, Bernardin Gantin, the dean of the College, is internationally respected and has a large influence to wield in the coming election.[76]

In the Pacific Basin, neither Stephen Sou Hwan Kim, emeritus archbishop of Seoul,[77] nor Pio Taofinu'u, archbishop of Samoa-Apia,[78] will assume much leadership among other East Asian or Oceanian electors; but Jaime L. Sin, archbishop of Manila, revered and respected worldwide for his opposition to Ferdinand Marcos and for his leadership in defending constitutional government in the Philippines in the 1990s, will command a considerable audience for his opinions.[79] Sin is the only living cardinal whose local political power rivals that of cardinals of the past. He was thrust into the forefront of Philippine political life when Ferdinand Marcos's rigged triumph over Corazon Aquino in the presidential election of 1986 was not generally accepted by the people. When it became clear that Marcos was about to launch another round of mass arrests, the newly resigned defense secretary, Juan Ponce Enrile, gathered about four hundred supporters outside Camp Aguinaldo. He begged for help from the cardinal. Sin then appealed for mass popular support against Marcos and for democracy. For four days, almost two million people blocked tanks and soldiers with linked arms, and with peace offerings of flowers and food. The EDSA revolution, as it is called today, restored democracy. On February 25, 1986, Aquino was proclaimed president by Claudio Teehankee, a justice of the Supreme Court, and Marcos fled. From that moment forward, Sin has been at the center of his nation's political life. More recently, Sin led the opposition to the efforts by supporters of President Fidel Ramos to amend the constitution so as to maintain that president in office. On August 21, 1997, Sin's pastoral letter on the occasion of the fourteenth anniversary of the murder of Benigno Aquino was read in every church in the archdiocese of Manila: "I call on the people now to disassociate themselves from supporting an administration [Ramos's] that has lost their trust and respect." Sin went on to compare the efforts to keep Ramos in power to the methods that allowed Ferdinand Marcos to rule the Philippines for more than twenty years and to crush his opponents, including Aquino: "We recall the untold thousands of our countrymen and women who were arrested, imprisoned, and tortured under the arrogated military power of a despot who, cheered on by his army of sycophants and parasites, was deluded to think that he and he alone could lead his country." He then thanked the Filipino senators who were resisting amendments to the constitution and urged them to "stand fast in their resolve to serve the highest interest of our people." This address to the people led to the abandonment of Ramos's struggle to remain in power, and to the constitutional and peaceful transition of presidential power to José Estrada in the national elections in May, 1998. As the millennium closes, Sin's prestige among the Philippine people has never been higher, and no decision of great national importance can be taken by the government without at least consulting his views. His stature in the Philippines already has been translated into added stature and prestige in the College of Cardinals. He will speak not only for the ecclesiastical, economic, and social interests in his region, but for those interests throughout the world. His importance in the coming election will be great.

The electors from Northern and Western Europe also will give weight to the direction taken by the Benedictine archbishop of Westminster, George Basil Hume, who commands wide respect for his pastoral life and ministry and for his devotion to the principles of Vatican II.[80]

In Rome, at century's end, two of the most powerful members of the curia are survivors from the College of Paul VI. Both are conservative, and both will have positions of leadership in the conclave that is based on the national loyalties of conservative cardinals as well as on the power they have exercised in the Vatican for years. The American penitentiary major, William Wakefield Baum, former archbishop of Washington, has had a voice in the archiepiscopal and, consequently, cardinalitial appointments of nearly all of his American colleagues.[81] In addition, he is the senior living American in the College. It is likely that he will cede the official leadership of the American electors—second greatest in number after the Italians, with eleven—to O'Connor of New York, but the views he expresses in the *prattiche* may well determine the candidate who will receive American support, at least during the early ballots.

Of course, the most powerful, and most conservative, of Paul VI's cardinal-electors is Joseph Ratzinger, prefect of the Congregation for the Doctrine of the Faith.[82] Often regarded as the most powerful man in Rome after the pope, Ratzinger will be the unquestioned leader of the non-Italian curial conservatives during the coming election, and will command a significant following from cardinals who are outside that constituency, as well. The only major rival to his influence is Angelo Sodano, the cardinal-secretary of state. But the latter is widely regarded as distinctly less able and less effective than his immediate predecessor, Agostino Casaroli, and does not hold the degree of great professional respect usually accorded to the men who have held his office, like Gasparri, Pacelli, Cicognani, and Villot. It is more likely, therefore, that cardinals who are looking to follow a curial leader who will stand for the positions of John Paul II will seek out Ratzinger rather than Sodano.

It also is worth considering the influence of the superannuated cardinals created by Paul VI. They will have, both privately in the *prattiche* and publicly in the daily general congregations before the conclave begins, a significant effect on the evolution of the pre-conclave negotiations. After all, Carlo Confalonieri played a major part in the election of John Paul I, even though he was not an elector and was absent from the conclave itself.

In the fall of 1998, there are thirteen of these older prelates. Some of them, retired archbishops from sees remote from Rome, certainly will not come to the general congregations, and indeed may not come even for the funeral of the pope. Ill health will restrain some, and the superannuation that leaves them without official power will restrain others. Paul Gouyon (born October 24, 1910),[83] Juan Carlos Aramburu (born February 11, 1912),[84] and Marcelo González Martín (born January 16, 1918)[85] are three who almost certainly will play no part in choosing the next pope. Other retired ordinaries, however, still possess real leadership in their regions and, in the age of *prattiche* by telephone, their positions with regard to candidates for the throne will be solicited by, at least, the electors from their areas. Many of the African cardinals, for example, will certainly consult Paul Zoungrana, the retired archbishop of Ouagadougou.[86] He is, in 1998, the most senior surviving cardinal created by Paul VI, and was the principal leader of the African cardinals in both conclaves in 1978. Similarly, Johannes Willebrands (born September 4, 1909), the retired archbishop of Utrecht and the former leader of the Vatican's ecumenical efforts, will influence a number of his colleagues who have Church unity and conciliar return among their priorities.[87]

Still more important, however, are the views of two retired Italian archbishops, Salvatore Pappalardo of Turin[88] and Corrado Ursi of Naples.[89] Pappalardo lost his right to vote only in September, 1998, and can be expected to air his opinions, which are not without weight, among his Italian colleagues at least. Ursi will be sought out as a pastoral figure quite close to John Paul I in his ecclesiology. It is not forgotten that those cardinal-electors in the second conclave of 1978 who wanted another pope who would be as close to Luciani as possible chose Ursi as their candidate. Indeed, had Benelli been willing to support his candidacy in the October *prattiche*, he might well have been elected. Both Pappalardo and Ursi will be in Rome for John Paul II's funeral and, if their health permits, almost certainly will stay for the meetings of the general congregation and for the excitement of the *prattiche*.

Most important of all, however, are the six surviving but retired curial cardinals of Paul VI. All of them live in Rome, some only a few hundred steps from the site of the general congregation in the Vatican, and all were powerful men at the center of affairs not only in the time of Paul VI but often well into the reign of John Paul II. Silvio Oddi, for example, still expresses his disapproving views of many of John Paul II's policies, especially with regard to beatifications and canonizations, both publicly and, even more vehemently, in private.[90] He will not abandon an opportunity to ensure that his ideas are heard by the electors. The others are equally strong-willed, and only death or grave illness will prevent them from having their say: Giuseppe Maria Sensi (born May 27, 1907);[91] Paolo Bertoli (born February 1, 1908), the retired camerlengo;[92] Opilio Rossi (born May 17, 1910), a tough prelate who seems to have acquired the outlook and the manner of the stereotypical New Yorker that he is by birth;[93] and Pietro Palazzini (born May 19, 1912).[94] Of these aged Romans, only Corrado Bafile probably is too old and too feeble to play at least a secondary rôle.[95]

Finally, we must notice the most venerable member of the College, the one surviving creation of John XXIII. The archpriest of the College, Franz König, certainly will play a significant role in choosing the next pope.[97]

König is the one grand elector from the second conclave of 1978 to survive. A friend and vigorous supporter of John XXIII and of the council, he is known to regret that he was carried away by the attractive sensation of electing a non-Italian pope in the last election, and has voiced his bitter disappointment with the direction the Church has taken under John Paul II. The former archbishop of Vienna views John Paul's actions and policies as a distinct betrayal of the spirit and intentions of Vatican II and is certain to express those views in the telephone *prattiche*, even if he, himself, is not in Rome. His telephone conversations will be among the most illuminating and interesting in the next *sede vacante*.

NOTES

1. Picachy (died November 29, 1992); Baggio (died March 21, 1993); Posadas Ocampo (murdered May 24, 1993); Razafimahatratra (died October 6, 1993); Darmajuwono (died February 3, 1994); Cordeiro (died February 11, 1994); and Decourtray (died September 16, 1994).

2. Grégoire (born October 24, 1911); Vachon (born February 4, 1912); Aramburu (born February 11, 1912); Carter (born March 1, 1912); Palazzini (born May 19, 1912); Todea (born June 5, 1912); Rugambwa (born July 12, 1912); Sabattani (born October 18, 1912); Agnello Rossi (born May 8, 1913); Jubany Arnau (born August 12, 1913); Ballestrero (born October 3, 1913); Landázuri Ricketts (born December 19, 1913); Poletti (born April 19, 1914); Lubachivsky (born June 24, 1914); Fresno Larraín (born July 26, 1914); Caprio (born November 15, 1914); and Casaroli (born November 24, 1914).

3. López Salazar (died July 9, 1991); de Lubac (died September 4, 1991); Léger (died November 13, 1991); Guerri (died March 15, 1992); Colombo (died May 20, 1992); Paupini (died July 18, 1992); Tomasek (died August 4, 1992); Martin (died September 27, 1992); Antonelli (died July 12, 1993); Gray (died July 19, 1993); del Mestri (died August 2, 1993); Carpino (died October 5, 1993); Grégoire (superannuated October 24, 1991, and died October 30, 1993); Garrone (died January 15, 1994); Marty (died February 16, 1994); McCann (died March 26, 1994); Muñoz Vega (died June 3, 1994); and Khoraiche (died August 19, 1994).

4. The death of Enrique y Tarancón on the twenty-eighth lowered the total to 166.

5. Echeverria Ruiz was born in Cotacachi, near Ibarra, Ecuador, on November 12, 1912. He entered the Franciscans in September, 1928, and was ordained on July 4, 1937. In 1941, he received his bachelor's degree in philosophy from the Antonianum. He then returned to Ecuador to pastoral work. He founded the Communion of the Sick, the publishing company of Jodoko Ricke and the magazine *Paz y Bien*. He also has served as secretary of the Equadorian Institute for Studies of the Amazon Region, as a member of the International Academy of Franciscan History, as rector of the Brotherhood of Quito, and as provincial secretary and minister of the Franciscans. Pius XII named him bishop of Ambato on October 23, 1949 (consecrated December 4). Paul VI pro-

moted him to be archbishop of Guayaquil on April 10, 1969. He retired from that office on December 7, 1989, and immediately was appointed apostolic administrator of the diocese of Ibarra, his native see. He served there until 1995.

6. Suárez Rivera was born on January 9, 1927, in San Cristóbal de Las Casa, Chiapas, Mexico. He was ordained on March 8, 1952, in the chapel of the Collegio Pio Latino Americano in Rome. Among other pastoral duties, he was diocesan director of the catechetical office for six years. Paul VI appointed him bishop of Tepic on May 14, 1971 (consecrated August 15). John Paul II made him bishop of Tlalnepantla on May 8, 1980, and then promoted him to be archbishop of Monterrey on November 8, 1983. He served as an assistant member of the Congregation of Bishops from 1979 to 1983, and was a pontifical delegate to the sixth Synod of Bishops (September-October 1983).

7. Juan Sandoval Íñiguez was born on March 28, 1933 in Yahualica, near San Juan de los Lagos, Mexico. He entered the minor seminary of the archdiocese of Guadalajara when he was twelve. Later, he studied in Rome at the Gregorianum where he received a degree in philosophy and, later, a doctorate in dogmatic theology. He was ordained October 27, 1957. In 1961, he was made spiritual director of the diocesan seminary, and then, within a year, became the prefect of discipline there. On August 22, 1980, he became rector of the seminary of Guadalajara. On March 3, 1988, John Paul II made him coadjutor bishop of Ciudad Juàrez (consecrated April 30). On April 21, 1994, he was appointed archbishop of Guadalajara, in succession to the murdered Juan Jesús Posadas Ocampo.

8. That of Nostra Signora di Guadalupe e San Filippo Martire in Via Aurelia.

9. Oviedo Cavada was born in Santiago del Chile on January 19, 1927. He entered the Mercedarians in 1944, made his solemn profession of vows on March 19, 1948, and was ordained on September 24, 1949. In January, 1953, he received his degree in canon law from the Gregorianum. In Chile, he was first a professor, then the director of the theology faculty of the Pontifical Catholic University. From 1958 to 1961, he was a member of the staff of the general curia of the Mercedarians. Paul VI made him titular bishop of Benevento and auxiliary bishop

of the archdiocese of Concepciòn on March 21, 1964 (consecrated June 7). Now a bishop, Oviedo Cavada participated in both the third and fourth sessions of Vatican II. In 1970, he was elected secretary general of the Chilean Episcopal Conference. On March 25, 1974, Paul VI promoted him to be archbishop of Antofagasta; and, on March 30, 1990, he was made archbishop of Santiago del Chile, in succession to Juan Francisco Fresno Larrain, whose resignation became effective on the same date. Oviedo Cavada also has been grand chancellor of the Pontifical Catholic University of Chile. His declining health caused him to resign as archbishop early in 1998. He died December 7, 1998.

10. Augusto Vargas Alzamora was born in Lima on November 9, 1922; entered the Society of Jesus on March 9, 1940; and was ordained in Spain on July 15, 1955. His tasks in the Society of Jesus have included being a master of novices, rector of the School of the Immaculate Conception, and provincial delegate for education. Paul VI, in one of his last pontifical acts, made him titular bishop of Cissi on June 8, 1978 (consecrated August 15), and vicar apostolic for the diocese of San Francisco Javier de Jaen en Peru. He served as vicar apostolic until 1985. In 1982, he became secretary general of the Peruvian Conference of Bishops. On December 30, 1989, John Paul II made him archbishop of Lima, in succession to Juan Landázuri Ricketts, who retired after thirty-four years as archbishop.

11. Ortega y Alamino was born in Jaguey Grande, province of Matanzas, on October 18, 1936. He became a diplomate in arts and sciences in 1955, and then entered the diocesan seminary of San Alberto Magno, which was directed by the Foreign Mission Fathers of Québec. This connection allowed him to do some of his preparatory work in Canada. He was ordained in the catheral of Matanzas on August 2, 1964. In 1966, Castro's government arrested him and sent him to the Unidades Militares de Apoyo a la Producciòn, a forced labor camp. In 1967, after a year in the camp, he was released and became a parish priest in the church of Jaguey Grande. In 1969, he was attached to the parish of the cathedral of Matanzas. For many years, together with his pastoral work, Ortega taught moral theology at the interdiocesan seminary in Havana. On December 4, 1978, John Paul II made him bishop of Pinar del Rìo (con-

secrated January 14, 1979). On November 20, 1981, he was promoted to be archbishop of San Cristobal de La Habana, as the second successor of Cuba's first cardinal, Manuel Arteaga y Bentancourt. He is now president of the Cuban Episcopal Conference.

12. Carles Gordó was born in Valencia, in Aragon, on September 24, 1926, and was ordained June 29, 1951. Paul VI made him bishop of Tortosa on June 6, 1969 (consecrated August 3). His conservative views made him an unlikely candidate for advancement in the post-Franco years, but John Paul II chose him to be archbishop of Barcelona on March 23, 1990.

13. Shirayanagi was born in Hachioji City, near Tokyo, on June 17, 1928, and was ordained on December 21, 1954. When he was only thirty-seven, Paul VI made him titular bishop of Atenia and auxiliary bishop of Tokyo for Pietro Tatsuo Doi on March 15, 1966 (consecrated May 8). Paul VI also advanced him to be titular archbishop of Castro and coadjutor archbishop of Tokyo, with right of succession, on November 15, 1969. He became archbishop of Tokyo upon the death of Doi, February 21, 1970.

14. Darmaatmadja was born in Muntilan, Mageland, Central Java, in the archdiocese of Semarang, on December 20, 1934. He entered the Society of Jesus in 1957, and was ordained on December 18, 1969. John Paul II appointed him archbishop of Semarang on February 19, 1983, (consecrated June 29), in succession to Indonesia's first cardinal, Justinus Darmajuwono, who resigned on July 3, 1981. In 1996, Darmaatmadja was transferred to be archbishop of Jakarta. In January, 1998, Darmaatmadja began a project in parishes throughout his archdiocese to organize public kitchens to feed the needy during the Asian economic crisis. The cardinal said he wanted parish priests and local social action groups to "collaborate with local communities to open public kitchens to provide meals for the hungry." He went on to say, "It should be well organized, because the crisis will perhaps last long," and made clear that his program was not exclusively Catholic.

15. Pham Dinh Tung was born at Binh Hoa, near Phat Diem, Vietnam, on June 15, 1919, and was ordained June 6, 1949. In one of his last pontifical act, John XXIII appointed him bishop of Bac Ninh on April 5, 1963, although he was not consecrated until August 15. Following the death of Joseph Marie Trinh van-Can on May 18, 1990, John Paul II appointed Pham

Dinh Tung to be apostolic administrator of Hanoi on June 18. Negotiations with the Vietnamese government for a permanent archbishop proceeded slowly, but Pham Dinh Tung finally was made archbishop of Hanoi on March 23, 1994.

16. Wamala was born on December 15, 1926, in Kamaggwa, Uganda. Of his four brothers, one became a priest and another a religious. Wamala entered the minor seminary of Bukaslasa at sixteen. In September, 1956, he was sent to Rome, where he earned his degree in theology at the Pontifical Urban University. He was ordained in Rome on December 21, 1957. After he returned to Uganda in 1960, he embarked on a career as an educator. In 1977, Paul VI conferred the title of Chaplain of His Holiness (monsignor) on Wamala. On July 17, 1981, John Paul II named Wamala bishop of Kiyinda-Mityana (consecrated November 22). On June 21, 1988, he was made coadjutor archbishop of Kampala with right of succession for Emmanuel Kiwanuka Nsubuga, whose resignation became effective on February 8, 1990, when Wamala became archbishop of Kampala. In 1990 and again in 1994, he was president of the Ugandan Episcopal Conference.

17. Razafindratandra comes from a wealthy noble family which converted to Christianity several generations ago. He was born on August 7, 1925, in Ambohimalaza, Madagascar, and was ordained on July 27, 1954. Razafindratandra completed his studies in Paris, and, soon afterwards, returned to Madagascar, first as a parish priest and later as director of the National Catechist Center. He rose to be rector of Madagascar's minor seminary, and then director of the major seminary. On April 27, 1978, Paul VI named him bishop of Mahajanga (consecrated July 2). Razafindratandra founded the Ecumenical Commission of Theology, which drafted the statute for the Council of the Madagascar Christian Churches. With its beginning in 1989, the council has played an important role in the democratic evolution of Madagascar. Razafindratandra was promoted to be archbishop of Antananarivo on February 3, 1994, in succession to Victor Razafimahatratra, who had died on the previous October 6.

18. Vlk was born on May 17, 1932, in Lisnice-Sepakov, in the diocese of Ceska Budejovice, Czechoslovakia. Since formal theological study was forbidden by the government during his youth, he studied to be an archivist at the Univerzity Karlovy (Charles University) in Prague. He then worked for several years in a number of archives in Bohemia. He studied to be a priest secretly and, during the Prague Spring, he was able to be ordained, on June 23, 1968, at the age of thirty-six. In 1971, because of his growing popularity, the government relegated him to obscure parishes in the Bohemian Forest region, and then suspended altogether his license to practice as a priest in 1978. From then until 1986, he worked as a window-washer in Prague while he carried out his priestly ministry in secret. In 1989, he was relicensed as a priest for a probationary year, but the Velvet Revolution swept away all the disabilities of the Church in Czechoslovakia in 1990. John Paul II made him bishop of his native diocese of Ceske Budejovice on February 14, 1990 (consecrated March 31). On March 27, 1991, just a year later, he was advanced to be archbishop of Prague, in succession to Frantisek Tomasek, whose resignation became effective on that date. In 1993, John Paul appointed Vlk to be president of the Council of European Episcopal Conferences, effectively ousting the former elected president, Carlo Maria Martini of Milan.

19. Puljic was born on September 8, 1945, in Prijecani, near Banja Luka, Bosnia, and was ordained on June 29, 1970. From 1978 to 1987, he served as rector of the minor seminary of Zadar. Following a brief period as a parish priest, he was appointed vice rector of the major seminary of the archdiocese of Sarajevo in 1990. John Paul II appointed him archbishop of Vrhbosna (Sarajevo) on November 19, 1990, and consecrated him personally on January 6, 1991, during the ceremonies for Epiphany at St. Peter's tomb. Puljic became the sixth archbishop of his see since the reconstitution of the Catholic hierarchy in 1881, after four hundred years of Turkish occupation. In April, 1992, the siege of Sarajevo began, and, on November 12 of the same year, John Paul II, in a letter addressed to all the bishops of Bosnia, wrote: "When I laid my hands on you on January 6, 1991, to consecrate the pastoral office of the Church of Sarajevo, I never imagined your cross would so soon become so heavy and your chalice so bitter."

20. Swiatek was born on October 21, 1914, in Walga, Estonia, and was ordained on April 8, 1939, for the clergy of the diocese of Pinsk. Immediately afterward, he was arrested by the NKVD and consigned to a cell on death row in Brest prison. He remained there until June 22,

1941, when, taking advantage of the confusion created by the German invasion, he managed to escape. On December 18, 1944, he was once again arrested by KGB agents and returned to jail, in Minsk, where he remained until July 21, 1945. At that time, Swiatek was condemned to ten years of forced labor in the Gulag and worked both in the mines and in the Siberian forest. When he finally was freed, on June 16, 1954, he returned to Pinsk and immediately resumed his pastoral activities. He was named Chaplain of His Holiness (monsignor) on February 11, 1988, and, on April 11, 1989, was made vicar general of the diocese of Pinsk. On April 13, 1991, John Paul II appointed Swiatek archbishop of Minsk-Mohilev and apostolic administrator, *ad nutum Sanctæ Sedis*, of Pinsk (consecrated May 21).

21. Eyt was born in Laruns, France, on June 4, 1934; entered the seminary of the diocese of Bayonne in 1954; and was ordained on June 29, 1961. Subsequently, he received a doctorate in theology from the Gregorianum. He then served successively as a lecturer, professor, vice rector, and rector (1967–1972) at the Catholic Institute of Toulouse. In 1980, he became a member of the International Theological Commission, and, in 1982, he was elected president of the Catholic Institutes for Higher Education in France. John Paul II named him coadjutor archbisop of Bordeaux with right of succession on June 7, 1986 (consecrated September 28). In 1987, he served as special secretary of the Seventh General Assembly of the Synod of Bishops. He succeeded as archbishop of Bordeaux on May 31, 1989.

22. Winning was born at Wishaw, Scotland, June 3, 1925, the only son of Thomas Winning and Agnes Canning Winning. He has a sister, Margaret Winning McCarron. He was educated at Saint Patrick's Primary School, Shieldmuir, and at Our Lady's High School, Motherwell. He was accepted as a student for the archdiocese of Glasgow, and completed his studies in philosophy at Saint Mary's College, Blairs (1941–1943). He then began his theological study at Saint Peter's College, Glasgow and, at the end of the Second World War, was one of the first group of students to return to Rome to the newly reopened Pontifical Scots College, where he studied from 1946 to 1949. In 1948, two new suffragan sees were created from the territory of the archdiocese of Glasgow and, in this reorganization, Winning became a student

of the newly erected diocese of Motherwell. He was ordained in Rome on December 18, 1948, for the diocese of Motherwell. In 1949, he received his licentiate in sacred theology from the Gregorianum. Returning to Scotland, he was appointed assistant priest at Saint Aloysius, Chapelhall, where he remained only until 1950. Then he returned to the Scots College, Rome, to study canon law at the Gregorianum, from which he received his doctorate in that subject in 1953. Again, he returned to Scotland, and served as assistant priest, at Saint Mary's, Hamilton, from 1953 to 1957, and at the cathedral of Our Lady of Good Aid, Motherwell, from 1957 to 1958. From 1956 to 1961, he was secretary of the diocese of Motherwell, and, from 1958 to 1961, he was chaplain to the Francisans of the Immaculate Conception at Bothwell. For the third time, he was sent to Rome, to become the spiritual director of the Pontifical Scots College, from 1961 to 1966. In 1965, he became an advocate of the Sacred Roman Rota. Another return to his homeland had him serve as parish priest at Saint Luke's, Motherwell, and as officialis of the tribunal of the diocese of Motherwell and vicar episcopal for marriage in the diocese, from 1966 until 1970. He then became first president and officialis of the newly established Scottish National Tribunal at Glasgow, from 1970 to 1972. On October, 22, 1971, Paul VI made him titular bishop of Louth (Lugmadensis) and auxiliary bishop of the archdiocese of Glasgow. He was consecrated by Archbishop James Donald Scanlan in Glasgow on November 30, 1971. He served as vicar general of the archdiocese of Glasgow from 1971 to 1974, and parish priest of Our Holy Redeemer Parish, Clydebank, from 1972 to 1974. On Scanlan's retirement, Winning was made archbishop of Glasgow on April 23, 1974. He was president of the Justice and Peace Commission of Bishops' Conference of Scotland (1973–1977); president of the National Commission for Social Welfare of the Bishops' Conference (1974–1984); president of the Catholic Education Commission of the Bishops' Conference (1977–). Since 1985, he has been president of the Bishops' Conference of Scotland. He was a delegate from the Bishops' Conference of Scotland to the Bishops' Conferences of the European Union (COMECE) from 1990 to 1996. He is a member of the Bishops' Conferences of Europe (CCEE). In 1986, he became a fellow of the Educational Institute of Scotland. He was made a Knight Commander of the Holy Sepulchre and Grand Prior of the Scottish Lieutenancy of the Equestrian Order of the Holy Sepulchre of Jerusalem in 1989; and was promoted to Knight Grand Cross in 1995. On March 17, 1997, he was appointed special papal envoy to the Saint Columba Celebrations in the dioceses of Derry and Raphoe, Ireland, which took place in the following June.

23. Sfeir was born on May 15, 1920 in the Maronite town of Raifoune in Kesserwan, Lebanon, in the diocese of Sarba of the Maronites. He was educated first in Beirut, then at the Mar abda School in Harharaya, where he completed his primary schooling. He then went to Ghazir, where he finished his secondary studies at Saint Maron Seminary. Finally, he studied philosophy and theology in 1950 at Saint Joseph's University. He was ordained May 7, 1950, and, in 1951, he was posted as resident priest of Rayfoune, where he remained until 1955. In 1956, he was appointed secretary of the Maronite patriarchate in Bkerke, and also made professor of translation in literature and philosophy at the Fréres Maronite School in Jounieh. On June 19, 1961, he was elected to be titular bishop of Tarsus of the Maronites and patriarchal vicar. On the following June 23, he was confirmed in that rank, and was consecrated on July 16, 1961. From 1961 to 1986, he remained patriarchal vicar and secretary of the Maronite patriarchate. After the resignation of Antoine Pierre Khoraiche from the patriarchate on April 3, 1986, Sfeir was elected as his successor on April 19, and his election was confirmed on April 27, 1986. John Paul II extended ecclesial communion to him as a fellow patriarch on the following May 7. Since he was vicar for his two predecessors, Sfeir was well experienced in the role of the patriarch in both the ecclesiastical and civil matters. He became a strong voice for reason and sanity in the latter years of the Lebanese conflict. At the present time, he has become the conscience of the country, pointing to the injustices that exist in the social and political spheres, and speaking up for the poor and disenfranchised. In his writings and sermons he has been presenting an agenda of how Lebanon is to achieve a future based on freedom and human rights. In the civil war in 1975–1976, the Maronites lost a considerable amount of their former political influence under the challenge of Palestinian and allied Islamic factions. All pretense at national stability collapsed after the 1982 Israeli invasion and

was recovered only to some degree with the Taif Accord of 1989, under which the Maronites ceded their primary political position to the prime minister, traditionally a Sunni Muslim. This accord, backed by Syria, has produced a Lebanese state that is dependent heavily on Damascus, and in which there remain approximately forty thousand Syrian troops in Beirut, the Beqaa Valley, and in the north. Because of the collapse of traditional politics in Lebanon, Sfeir, unlike his colleagues in the College, has become a real political leader. His position of authority among his followers is substantial, and he remains, at the end of the century, the principal leader for Lebanese who are dissatisfied with the present situation.

24. Turcotte was born June 26, 1936, at Ville de Laval, in the parish of St-Vincent-de-Paul, Montréal. After early studies at the Collège Grasset and further theological study at the Grand Séminaire de Montréal, he was ordained on May 24, 1959. He then went for further study in the social sciences to Lille. After his return to Montréal, he was entrusted with a number of responsible duties, including a term as almoner of Catholic Action in the archdiocese, diocesan moderator for seminarians at the Grand Séminaire de Montréal, director of the Maison Pie XII, and procurator of the archbishop. John Paul II made him titular bishop of Suas and auxiliary bishop of Montréal on April 14, 1982 (consecrated June 29). He acted as special coordinator for the pope's visit to Canada from September 9 to September 20, 1984. He was promoted to be archbishop of Montréal on March 17, 1990, in succession to Paul Grégoire, whose resignation was accepted on that date.

25. Keeler was born March 4, 1931 in San Antonio, Texas, the son of Thomas L. Keeler and Margaret T. Conway Keeler. He was raised in Lebanon, Pennsylvania, where he attended Saint Mary School and Lebanon Catholic High School. He received a bachelor of arts degree from Saint Charles Seminary, Overbrook, Philadelphia, in 1952, and then was sent to the Gregorianum, from which he received a licentiate in sacred theology in 1956. He was ordained for the diocese of Harrisburg, Pennsylvania, on July 17, 1955, in the cardinalitial title church of Santi Dodici Apostoli by Luigi Traglia. Returning to Harrisburg, Keeler became assistant pastor at Our Lady of Good Counsel Church, Marysville, and secretary of the diocesan tribunal (1956–1958). Then, he was again sent to Rome,

this time to study canon law at the Gregorianum, from which he received his doctorate in 1961. His bishop, George L. Leech, then reappointed him assistant pastor of Our Lady of Good Counsel Church and made him defender of the bond of the diocesan tribunal. In 1964, Leech made him pastor of the Marysville parish. He served as a *peritus* at Vatican II (1962–1965) while continuing to act as secretary to his bishop. During the council, he also served on the staff of the *Council Digest*, a daily communication service sponsored by the American bishops. In 1965, he became vice chancellor of the diocese of Harrisburg, and, in 1969, chancellor. Keeler was serving as vicar general of the diocese for Bishop Joseph T. Daley, who had succeeded Leech when the latter retired in 1971, when he was made titular bishop of Ulcinium (Dulcigno) and auxiliary bishop of Harrisburg by John Paul II on July 24, 1979. He was consecrated on September 21, 1979, in Saint Patrick's Cathedral, Harrisburg. When Daley died in 1983, the College of Consultors of the diocese elected Keeler administrator of the see on September 3, 1983. John Paul II named him bishop of Harrisburg on November 10, 1983, and he was installed on January 4, 1984, by his metropolitan, John Krol of Philadelphia. Keeler was advanced to be archbishop of Baltimore, in succession to William D. Borders, on April 11, 1989. He was installed as the fourteenth ordinary of America's primatial see on the following May 23 at the Cathedral of Mary Our Queen. In November, 1992, he became president of the National Conference of Catholic Bishops (NCCB) and the United States Catholic Conference, after having served as vice president for a three-year term that began in November, 1989. Before that, he had been chairman of the National Conference's Committee for Ecumenical and Interreligious Affairs, from 1984 to November, 1987. In that position, he helped to arrange John Paul's meetings with Jewish leaders in Miami and with Protestant leaders in Columbia, South Carolina, during the papal visit to the United States in 1987.

26. Maida was born in East Vandergrift, near Greensburg, Pennsylvania, on March 18, 1930. He was ordained for the diocese of Pittsburgh, Pennsylvania, on May 26, 1956, by Bishop John Dearden (later cardinal and archbishop of Detroit). A canon lawyer, Maida eventually rose to be vice chancellor and general counsel of the diocese. On November 7, 1983, thanks to the interest and recommendation of Dearden, Maida was appointed to be the ninth bishop of Green Bay (consecrated January 25, 1984). Maida later was appointed to several papal commissions concerning legal matters and served as a member of several national church committees and organizations dealing with canon law. When Dearden's successor at Detroit, Edmund Casimir Szoka, was called to head the Prefecture for the Economic Affairs of the Holy See, Maida was advanced to be archbishop of Detroit on April 28, 1990, the day Szoka's resignation became effective. Maida was installed as archbishop of Detroit on June 12, 1990.

27. Poggi was born on November 25, 1917, at Piacenza, and was ordained July 28, 1940. From 1944 to 1946, he studied diplomacy at the Pontifical Academy of Noble Ecclesiastics. He then began a career in the secretariat of state. On April 3, 1965, Paul VI made him titular bishop of Forontoniana (Forum Antonii), with the personal title of archbishop (consecrated May 9), and sent him as apostolic delegate to Central Africa. After a term as nuncio to Peru, he was recalled to Rome for service in the curia in 1973. Under the leadership of Casaroli, he worked on the project to improve relations with the communist nations of Eastern Europe. In 1974, Paul VI made him head of the special Delegation for Permanent Contacts with the People's Republic of Poland. John Paul II appointed him nuncio to Italy in 1986, where he remained until 1992. In the latter year, he was appointed pro-Librarian and Archivist of the Holy Roman Church, which became a full appointment on the day of his cardinalate. He retired from that position early in 1998, and was succeeded by Archbishop Jorge María Mejía.

28. Fagiolo was born in Segni, near Rome, on February 5, 1918. He is a fellow townsman of Angelo Felici, although a year and a half older. Fagiolo was ordained on March 6, 1943. He has worked closely with Achille Silvestrini on a number of curial tasks. From 1967 to 1971, he was a prelate auditor of the Rota. Paul VI made him bishop of Chieti and Vasto on November 20, 1971 (consecrated December 19), where he served until July 15, 1984, when he was recalled to curial service. In that period, he served a term as vice president of the Conference of Italian Bishops. From 1984 to 1990, he was secretary of the Congregation for Institutes of Consecrated Life and Societies of Apostolic Life. On December 29, 1990, he was made president of the Dis-

ciplinary Commission of the Roman Curia. He resigned this office in 1997 and was succeeded as president by Archbishop Mario Francesco Pompedda, who also is dean of the Rota. From 1991 to 1994, Fagiolo was president of the Pontifical Council for the Interpretation of Legislative Texts.

29. Furno was born at Bairo Canavese, near Ivrea, on December 2, 1921, and was ordained on June 25, 1944. He is a former fellow student of Achille Silvestrini at the Appollinare in Rome. In the early 1950s, he entered the diplomatic corps and saw service in Colombia and Ecuador, before a term in Jerusalem. On August 1, 1973, Paul VI made him titular bishop of Abari, with the personal title of archbishop (consecrated September 16), and sent him as nuncio to Peru. In that position, he was unable to stop the rapid spread of "liberation theology," and, after five years, he was transferred to Lebanon, where he served from 1978 to 1982. He then spent ten years as nuncio to Brazil, from 1982 to 1992, and then a two-year term as nuncio to Italy, as the successor to Luigi Poggi. On February 1, 1996, the Equestrian Order of the Holy Sepulchre of Jerusalem, already "a Juridical Person under Canon Law," received the status of "a Juridical Person in the Vatican" with its legal seat in the Vatican City State and with Carlo Furno as its grand master. On February 12, 1996, John Paul II sent a special message to the meeting that commemorated the tenth anniversary of the Cuban National Ecclesial Encounter, which was delived by Furno as the pope's personal envoy. This message for the February 21-25 meeting in Havana was the beginning of the detente which resulted in Fidel Castro being received at the Vatican on the following November 19, and then in the pope's trip to Cuba in 1998.

30. Schotte was born on April 29, 1928 in Beveren-Leie, near Brugge, Belgium. He entered the Congregation of the Immaculate Heart of Mary, the Missionaries of Scheut, in 1946, and was ordained on August 3, 1952. At first, he studied to be a missionary in China and learned Chinese, but the evolving political situation prevented him from realizing that wish. From 1956 to 1962, he was vice rector of the Congregation's theological seminary at Louvain, and, from 1963 to 1966, he served as the rector of the Immaculate Heart Mission Seminary in Washington, D.C. He came to Rome in 1967 as secretary general of the Immaculate Heart Congregation, a position he held until 1972, when he entered curial service. In 1980, John Paul II appointed him secretary of the Pontifical Congregation "Justitia et Pax," of which he became vice president in 1983. On December 20, 1983, the pope made him titular bishop of Silli (consecrated January 6, 1984). On April 24, 1985, he was raised to the rank of archbishop, with the same titular diocese, and made secretary general of the Synod of Bishops. In 1989, he also was appointed president of the Labor Office of the Holy See.

31. Agustoni was born in Schaffhausen, near Basel, Switzerland, on July 26, 1922, into a family in which two of his elder brothers were priests. He entered the seminary at a very young age and was ordained on April 20, 1946. He entered the curia on July 1, 1950, as the special protégé of Alfredo Ottaviani and went to work for his mentor in the Congregation of the Holy Office (Now, for the Doctrine of the Faith). Ottaviani, then the assessor for the Congregation, had to request Pius XII's special permission to take on a priest under the age of thirty, which, because of the theological delicacy of the work, was seldom done. In May, 1970, Agustoni passed to the Ecclesiastical Magistrature as a prelate auditor of the Rota. He remained in this position until December 18, 1986, when John Paul II named him secretary of the Congregation for the Clergy and titular bishop of Caorle, with the personal title of archbishop (consecrated January 6, 1987). He left that curial position in 1992, when John Paul II made him pro-prefect of the Supreme Tribunal of the Apostolic Signature. On the same day as his formal creation as cardinal, he was elevated to the prefecture of the Tribunal.

32. Tonini was born at Centovera di San Giorgio Piacentino, near Piacenza, on July 20, 1914. He is just a few months older than his friend and fellow seminarian, Agostino Casaroli. Tonini was ordained on April 18, 1937. He eventually rose to be vice rector and then rector of the diocesan seminary of Piacenza. For many years, he taught Italian, Latin, and Greek, and was the editor of the diocesan weekly newspaper. Paul VI, perhaps as a gesture of friendship to Casaroli, who was becoming indespensible to the pope in the negotiations with Eastern bloc countries, made Tonini bishop of Macerata-Tolentino on April 28, 1969 (consecrated June 2). Paul VI also promoted him to be archbishop of Ravenna–Cervia on November 22, 1975, an

office he occupied until his retirement on October 27, 1990. While he was archbishop, Tonini refused to reside at the archiepiscopal palace, which was in a state of collapse with no funds for restoration. Instead, he resided in a small apartment in the house of the Sisters of the Institute of Saint Theresa in Ravenna. When John Paul II came to Ravenna, Tonini simply had the sisters prepare two more apartments, one for the pope and the other for his old friends, Achille Silvestrini and Dino Monduzzi, who accompanied the pope. Tonini is well-known to Italian television viewers, among whom he has developed quite a following through his short homilies. His cardinalate, however, probably was less a tribute to his televangelism, Italian style, than to his friendship with Casaroli.

33. Koliqi was born at Shkodre (Scutari), Albania, on September 29, 1902, and was ordained on May 30, 1931. In 1936, he was appointed parish priest of the cathedral of Shkodre and vicar general of the archdiocese, nominally retaining those titles until 1991. In fact, he served three long terms of imprisonment during his life, having been sentenced to a total of forty-four years of confinement, twenty-one of them at hard labor, and another twenty-three of internment. Eventually, six years of the latter term was commuted because of his age. His crimes included listening to foreign radio broadcasts and organizing youth. Finally released altogether after the fall of communism, he became Albania's first cardinal.

34. Grillmeier was born at Pechbrunn, near Regensburg, on January 1, 1910. He entered the Society of Jesus in 1929, and was ordained on June 24, 1937. He spent his career as a teacher of dogmatic theology and theological history in various institutions. Before his cardinalate, his highest position was as a member of the theological commission at the Second Vatican Council. His fame rests on a number of significant works of theological history. Among them are a three-volume history of the Council of Chalcedon, which he wrote jointly with Heinrich Bacht, *Das Konzil von Chalkedon: Geschichte und Gegenwart* (Wurzburg: Echter-Verlag, 1951-1954). The work for which he is best known today is *Jesus der Christus im Glauben der Kirche*, which appeared in English translation as a two-volume work with the title *Christ in Christian Tradition*. The whole work is a detailed and thorough survey of Christology

from the Apostolic Age to the death of Gregory the Great (604 A.D.), with the first volume ending with Chalcedon (451 A.D.). It is the standard text today on the "ways in which the Christian community has affirmed the presence of God in Jesus of Nazareth." He died on September 13, 1998.

35. Paris: Editions du Cerf, 1937, volume 1 of the series *Unam sanctum*. Translated by M. A. Bousfield as *Divided Christendom: a Catholic Study of the Problem of Reunion* (London: G. Bles, The Centenary Press, 1939).

36. Paris: Editions du Cerf, 1941, volume 8 of the series *Unam sanctam*.

37. Paris: Editions du Vitrail, 1947, volume 2 of the series *Problemes du Clerge Diocesain*.

38. Paris: A. Renault, 1948.

39. Paris: Editions du Cerf, 1950 volume 20 of the series *Unam sanctam*, and volume 4 of Congar's *Essais sur la Communion Catholique*.

40. Paris: UNESCO, 1953, part of the series *La question Raciale et la Pensees Moderne*. Immediately issued in an English edition, *The Catholic Church and the Race Question* (Paris: UNESCO, 1953).

41. Chevetogne: Editions de Chevetogne, 1954, part of the series *Collection Irenikon*.

42. 2d ed., Paris: Editions du Cerf, 1954, volume 23 of the series *Unam sanctam*.

43. For a valuable review of this deplorable excess, see Thomas F. O'Meara, "'Raid on the Dominicans': the Repression of 1954," in *America*, v. 170 (February 5, 1994) 8-16.

44. For a good discussion of the essence of Congar's preparation for, and participation in, Vatican II, see Joseph A. Komonchak, "A Hero of Vatican II," in *Commonweal*, v. 122 (December 1, 1995) 15-17.

45. For the last modern forms of these procedures, see the text of Paul VI's consitution, *Romano Pontifici Eligendo*, in the appendix.

46. The five were: Coffy (died July 15, 1995); Revollo Bravo (died November 3, 1995); Ekandem (died November 24, 1995); and Bernardin (died November 14, 1996).

47. Enrique y Tarancón (died November 28, 1994); Pavan (died December 26, 1994); Agnello Rossi (May 21, 1995); Congar (died June 22, 1995); Krol (died March 3, 1996); Scherer (died March 8, 1996); Ciappi (died April 23, 1996); Suenens (died May 6, 1996); Duval (died May 30, 1996); Satowaki (died August 8, 1996); Hamer (superannuated on June 1, 1996, and died December 2, 1996);

Jubany Arnau (died December 26, 1996); Landázuri Ricketts (died January 16, 1997); Koliqi (died January 28, 1997); Poletti (died February 25, 1997); Yago (superannuated in July, 1996, and died October 5, 1997); and Rugambwa (died December 8, 1997).

48. The remaining ten were: Innocenti (born August 23, 1915); Margéot (born February 3, 1916); Angelini (born August 1, 1916); Suquía Goicoechea (born October 2, 1916); Zoungrana (born September 3, 1917); Daly (born October 1, 1917); Poggi (born November 25, 1917); Gagnon (born January 15, 1918); González Martín (born January 16, 1918); and Fagiolo (born February 5, 1918).

49. Kozłowiecki was born on April 1, 1911, at Huta Komorowska, near Sandomierz. He joined the Society of Jesus and was ordained on June 24, 1937. In the fall of 1939, he and twenty-four other religious were arrested in Krakow by the Gestapo and then sent to Auschwitz. In 1940, he was transferred to Dachau, where he was held to the end of the war. His condition at the time of his release was so reduced that the Jesuit vicar general proposed that he go to a warmer and more salubrious climate, and proposed his transfer to the Jesuit mission in Northern Rhodesia (now Zambia). After several years of teaching there, he was appointed apostolic administrator of the newly established prefecture of Lusaka in 1950. Pius XII made him titular bishop of Diospolis Inferior on June 4, 1955. He was consecrated bishop and appointed vicar apostolic of Lusaka on September 11, 1955. As the Catholic community continued to grow, the vicariate apostolic was raised directly to the status of a metropolitan archdiocese and Kozłowiecki was made archbishop of Lusaka on April 25, 1959. Ten years later, on May 29, 1969, he resigned Lusaka so that a native African archbishop could be appointed in his place. At that time, he was made titular bishop of Potenza Picena, with the personal title of archbishop, by Paul VI. From 1970 to 1991, he was a member of the Congregation for the Evangelization of Peoples. In 1998, he continues as a missionary in Ridgeway, Zambia.

50. Ambrozic was born at Gabrje, near Ljublana, Slovenia, on January 27, 1930. His parents took him to Austria in 1945, and then to Canada in 1948. He was ordained for the clergy of the archdiocese of Toronto on June 4, 1955. After two years' service as a curate, he was sent to Rome for further study. He earned a degree in

theology from the Angelicum and another in scripture from the Pontifical Biblical Institute. From 1960 to 1967, he taught scripture at Saint Augustine's Seminary, and then went to the University of Würzburg, where he received a doctorate in theology. From 1970 to 1976, he taught the exegesis of the New Testament at the Toronto School of Theology and also served as the dean of studies at Saint Augustine's. On March 26, 1976, Paul VI made him titular bishop of Valabria and auxiliary bishop of Toronto (consecrated May 27). John Paul II made him coadjutor of Toronto for Gerald Emmett Carter on May 22, 1986. Ambrozic became archbishop of Toronto on March 17, 1990—the same day on which Carter's resignation became effective.

51. Fernandes de Araújo was born in Minas Novas, near Aracuai, on August 13, 1924, and was ordained on March 12, 1949, for the clergy of the archdiocese of Diamantina. He has received doctorates in both theology and canon law from the Gregorianum. Early in his career, he served as a parish priest in Gouveia and taught canon law at the provincial seminary of Diamantina. He also headed the catechetical office of the archdiocese and taught religion at the local teachers' college. John XXIII appointed him titular bishop of Verinopolis and auxiliary bishop of Belo Horizonte on January 19, 1959 (consecrated May 7). He was made coadjutor archbishop with right of succession to Belo Horizonte on November 22, 1982, and succeeded to the archiepiscopal see on February 5, 1986. In October, 1992, he was one of three co-presidents whom John Paul II appointed for the Fourth General Conference of the Latin American Episcopate in Santo Domingo.

52. Rivera Carrera was born in La Purisima (Tepehuanes), near Durango, Mexico, on June 6, 1942. He was sent to Rome for study and received a doctorate in theology from the Gregorianum. He was ordained for the clergy of the archdiocese of Durango by Paul VI on July 3, 1966. After service as a curate in Rio Grande, he taught dogmatic theology for eighteen years at the archdiocesan major seminary, where he also was prefect of discipline. In 1982, he was appointed professor of ecclesiology at the Pontifical University of Mexico. On November 5, 1985, John Paul II made him the second bishop of Tehuacan (consecrated December 21). From 1989 to 1995, he was chairman of the Commis-

sion for the Family of the Mexican Episcopal Conference, and, from 1993 to 1995, he was the head of the Family Section of the Latin American Episcopal Council (CELAM). Rivera Carerra was promoted to be archbishop of Mexico City on June 13, 1995, in succession to Ernesto Corripio Ahumada, who had resigned on September 29, 1994.

53. Rouco Varela was born on August 20, 1936, in Villalba, near Lugo. Between the years 1946 and 1954, he studied at the Seminario de Mondonedo, and, in 1958, he received his licentiate in theology from the Universidad Pontificia de Salamanca. On March 28, 1969, he was ordained for the clergy of the diocese of Mondonedo-Ferrol in the old cathedral of Salamanca, and on April 1, he celebrated his first Mass in the church of his native parish, Santa María de Villalba. He then went to Munich for further study in law and theology. On July 25, 1964, he received his doctorate in canon law with the dissertation, "Iglesia y Estado en la España del siglo XVI." After his return to Spain, he became professor of fundamental theology and canon law at the Seminario de Mondonedo. In 1966, he again went to Germany, where he remained until 1969 at the Institute of Canon Law of the University of Munich as an adjunct professor. Once again in Spain, he taught public ecclesiastical canon law at the Universidad Pontificia de Salamanca, and, in 1971, he was given the chair of fundamental canon law at the University. In 1972, he became vice rector of the University. In 1973, he was made consultor to the Congregation of the Clergy. On September 17, 1976, Paul VI made him titular bishop of Gergi and auxiliary bishop of Santiago de Compostela for Angel Suquía Goicoechea, subsequently archbishop of Madrid and cardinal. Rouco Varela was consecrated on October 31, 1976. On June 30, 1984, he became archbishop of Santiago de Compostella, and received the pallium from the hands of Antonio Innocenti, then the papal nuncio to Spain. In August, 1989, he was the hosting prelate for the fourth World Youth Day. On July 28, 1994, John Paul II named him archbishop of Madrid in succession to Angel Suquía Goicoechea.

54. Balland was born in Bué, near Bourges, in Sancerre, on July 26, 1934, into a winemaking family. He was ordained for the clergy of the archdiocese of Bourges on September 3, 1961, following his theological studies at the Gregori-

anum, from which he received degrees in literature, philosophy, and theology. In addition, he later received a doctorate in philosophy from the Sorbonne. For ten years, he taught philosophy in the seminaries of Bourges, Tours, and Poitiers, successively. He then embarked on a new career in the pastoral care of rural populations. He became chaplain to the Chrétiens dans le Monde Rural (Christians in the Rural World) and vicar general of Bourges. John Paul II made him bishop of Dijon, in succession to Albert Decourtray, on November 6, 1982 (consecrated December 12). After a long and elaborate search, he was promoted to be archbishop of Reims on August 8, 1988, and then to be archbishop of Lyon, in succession to Albert Decourtray, who had died on September 16, 1994. Between 1992 and 1994, he was the papal inspector of seminaries in France, and, from 1995 to 1998, was a member of the Committee of Bishops. Unlike Decourtray, Balland was quiet and reserved, and enjoyed neither ceremonies nor television appearances. Consequently, the tone of archdiocesan government became much quieter in his time. Balland's last journey outside his diocese was his trip to Rome to receive his red biretta on February 21, 1998. On his return, he died suddenly on March 1, after a cardinalate of only eight days— the shortest in modern history.

55. Pengo was born at Mwayze, in the diocese of Sumbawanga, Tanzania, on August 5, 1944, and was ordained for the clergy of Sumbawanga on June 20, 1971, following his studies in philosophy and theology at the major seminary of Kipalapala. For two years, he served as episcopal secretary and then was sent to Rome for study at the Academy of Saint Alphonsus. Again in Tanzania, he taught moral theology at the major seminary at Kipalapala before he was named rector of the major seminary in Segerea, where he served from 1978 to 1983. On November 11, 1983, John Paul II appointed him bishop of Nachingwea (consecrated January 6, 1984). On October 17, 1986, he was made first bishop of Tunduru-Masasi. On January 22, 1990, he was made coadjutor archbishop of Dar-es-Salaam for Laurean Rugambwa, and succeeded the latter as archbishop on July 22, 1992.

56. De Giorgi was born at Vernole, near Lecce, on September 6, 1930. He was ordained for the clergy of the diocese of Lecce on June 28, 1953, by Bishop Francesco Minerva, whom he then served as secretary until 1958. On October

12, 1958, he became a parish priest at Nostra Signora delle Grazie in Santa Rosa. While there, he also was diocesan chaplain to the Teacher's Movement of Catholic Action and was the director of the diocesan pastoral office. On November 21, 1973, Paul VI made him titular bishop of Tulana and auxiliary bishop of Oria (consecrated December 27). He succeeded to Oria as coadjutor on March 17, 1978. John Paul II named him archbishop of Foggia and administrator of Bovino and Troia on April 4, 1981. He resigned Troia on September 30, 1986. On October 10, 1987, he was promoted to be archbishop of Taranto. In 1990, he became general chaplain of Catholic Action in Italy, and resigned Taranto on May 11 of that year. On April 4, 1996, he was appointed archbishop of Palermo, in succession to Salvatore Pappalardo, whose resignation became effective on that date. In 1996, he became president of the Sicilian Episcopal Conference.

57. Tettamanzi was born March 14, 1934, in Renate, near Milan, and was ordained on June 28, 1957. He received his licentiate in theology from the Gregorianum, and, in 1959, his doctorate in sacred theology from the same institution. On his return to Milan, he began a teaching career of more than twenty years. For most of this time he taught fundamental theology at the major seminary at Sotto Venegono and pastoral theology at the Priestly Institute of Mary Immaculate and at the Lombard Regional Institute of Pastoral Ministry in Milan. His academic career culminated in 1987, when he became rector of the Pontifical Lombard Seminary in Rome. In 1989, John Paul II named him to the staff of the Congregation for the Doctrine of the Faith. Later in the same year, on July 1, he was appointed archbishop of Ancona-Osimo (consecrated September 23). In this period, he served a term as chairman of the Commission for the Family of the Italian Episcopal Conference. In 1991, he became secretary general of the Italian Episcopal Conference, and resigned the see of Ancona-Osimo on April 6. On April 20, 1995, he succeeded Giovanni Canestri as archbishop of Genoa; and on May 25, he became vice president of the Italian Episcopal Conference.

58. George was born in Chicago on January 13, 1937. He overcame polio as a child, and went on to study theology at the University of Ottawa. He also earned doctorates in philosophy from Tulane University and in theology

from the Pontifical Urbanian University in Rome. He joined the Missionary Oblates of Mary Immaculate and was ordained on December 21, 1963. After he became a priest, he taught philosophy at the Oblates' seminary at Pass Christian, Texas, and at Creighton University in Omaha, Nebraska. After serving a term as provincial of the Midwestern Conference of the Oblates, he served from 1974 to 1986 as vicar general of his order. Later, he coordinated the Cambridge Center for the Study of Faith and Culture in Cambridge, Massachusetts. John Paul II appointed him bishop of Yakima, Washington, on July 10, 1990 (consecrated September 21), and then promoted him to be archbishop of Portland, Oregon, on April 30, 1996, in succession to William J. Lavada, who had gone onward to be coadjutor at San Francisco (August 17, 1995) and then archbishop of San Francisco (December 27, 1995). George was transferred to be archbishop of Chicago on April 8, 1997, in succession to Joseph Louis Bernardin, who had died on the previous November 14.

59. Schönborn, the son of Hugo Damian, Graf von Schönborn and his wife Eleonore, Freiin von Doblhoff, was born at his family's estate at Skalken (now Skalsko, in the Czech Republic), near Litomerice, on January 22, 1945, entered the Dominicans, and was ordained December 27, 1970. He studied theology at Le Salchoir; philosophy and psychology at the University of Vienna; Slavic and Byzantine Christianity at the Sorbonne; and theology at the Institut Catholique in Paris. He taught both dogmatic and Eastern Christian theology at the University of Freiburg. Since 1980, he has been a member of the International Theological Commission, and, from 1987 to 1992, he was secretary of the commission that drafted the new Catechism of the Catholic Church. He also has been a member of various commissions of the Swiss Bishops' Conference. On July 11, 1991, John Paul II made him titular bishop of Sutri and auxiliary to Groër at Vienna (consecrated September 29). On April 13, 1995, he was made coadjutor archbishop of Vienna with right of succession, and became archbishop of Vienna on September 14, 1995, when Groër vacated the see. In 1996, he preached the Lenten spiritual exercises for the pope and the curia.

60. Paul Shan Kuo-hsi was born in Puyang, near Taming, China, on December 2, 1923. He

entered the Society of Jesus in Beijing, and took his first vows there, but was forced into exile and completed his studies in philosophy and theology in the Philippines. He was ordained in Baguio on March 18, 1955. Later, he received the degree of doctor of spiritual theology from the Gregorianum. In the Philippines, he served as director of the Chinese section of Sacred Heart School in Cebu, and then went to Vietnam, where he was the *socius* of the novice master at Thu-duc. Later, he was novice master and rector of Manresa House in Changhua, Taiwan, and was rector of Saint Ignatius High School in Taipei. On November 15, 1979, John Paul II made him bishop of Hwalien (consecrated February 14, 1980). On March 4, 1991, he was transferred to be bishop of Kaohsiung. He has served as president of the Chinese Regional Bishops' Conference for three terms. Today, he is a member of the pre-synodal council for the Synod of Asia.

61. Castrillón Hoyos was born at Medellin, Colombia, on July 4, 1929, and was ordained on October 26, 1952, after his studies in theology and canon law at the Gregorianum, from which he received his doctorate in the latter subject. During his early career, he was curate in two parishes, served as director of the Cursillo movement, and was a delegate for Catholic Action. He taught canon law at the Free Civil University and was general secretary of the Colombian Bishops' Conference. Paul VI made him titular bishop of Villa del Re and coadjutor bishop of Pereira with right of succession on June 2, 1971 (consecrated July 17). He succeeded to Pereira on July 1, 1976. From 1983 to 1987, he was the general secretary of CELAM, of which he was president from 1987 to 1991. His reward for that service was his promotion to be archbishop of Bucaramanga, the center of Colombia's coffee region, on December 16, 1992. He was called to Rome, resigned Bucaramanga, and was appointed pro-prefect of the Congregation of the Clergy on June 15, 1996. He became prefect of the Congregation officially on February 23, 1998, two days after his cardinalate.

62. Medina Estévez was born in Santiago de Chile on December 23, 1926, and was ordained on June 12, 1964. After receiving a doctorate in theology, he taught both philosophy in the archdiocesan seminary and theology at the Catholic University of Chile. After serving as the dean of the University, he was pro-grand chancellor of it

from 1974 to 1985. He was a peritus at Vatican II, and later a member of the International Theological Commission; he also worked on the drafting commission for the new Catechism of the Catholic Church, which was promulgated in 1997. John Paul II named him titular bishop of Tibili and auxiliary bishop of Rancagua on December 18, 1984 (consecrated January 6, 1985). On November 25, 1987, he became bishop of Rancagua, and on April 16, 1993, he was promoted to be bishop of Valparaiso. In 1993, he preached the pope's Lenten retreat. He was made pro-prefect of the Congregation for Divine Worship and the Discipline of the Sacraments, with the personal title of archbishop, on June 21, 1996. His resignation as bishop of Valparaiso became effective on the same day.

63. Stafford was born in Baltimore on July 26, 1932. After studies at the North American College, he was ordained for the clergy of the archdiocese of Baltimore on December 15, 1957. After service as a curate in two parishes, Paul VI named him titular bishop of Respetta and auxiliary bishop of Baltimore on January 19, 1976 (consecrated February 29). John Paul II made him bishop of Memphis, Tennessee, on November 17, 1982, and promoted him again, to be archbishop of Denver on May 30, 1986. He served as chairman of the Bishops' Committee on Ecumenical and Interreligious Affairs and of the Committee on Marriage and Family Life, and was co-chairman of the Consultation between Catholics and Eastern Orthodox communicants. He also was a member of the Bishops' Committee on Doctrine. He was called to Rome as president of the Pontifical Council for the Laity on August 20, 1996, and, on the same date, his resignation as archbishop of Denver became effective.

64. Antonetti was born at Romagnano Sesia, near Novara, on July 31, 1922, and was ordained on May 26, 1945. He received his licentiate in theology from the Angelicum and his doctorate in canon law from the Gregorianum. After study at the Pontifical Ecclesiastical Academy, he entered the diplomatic service and saw his first service in Lebanon and Venezuela. After a term in Rome on the staff of the First Section for Extraordinary Affairs of the Secretariat of State, he was sent on staff appointments to France and then the United States. On February 23, 1968, Paul VI made him titular bishop of Roselle with the personal title of archbishop (consecrated May 12) and sent him as nuncio to Nicaragua

and Honduras. In 1973, he was transferred to be nuncio in Zaire, where he remained until 1977. In the latter year, he was recalled to Rome and made secretary of the Administration of the Patrimony of the Apostolic See (1977-1988). He then served as nuncio to France (1988-1995). On June 24, 1995, he was made pro-president of the Administration of the Patrimony of the Apostolic See. He became president on February 23, 1998, two days after his cardinalate.

65. Bovone was born in Frugarolo, near Alessandria in the Piedmont, on June 11, 1922, and was ordained for the clergy of the diocese of Alessandria on May 26, 1945. He then was sent to Rome for further study and received his doctorate in canon law from the Angelicum. After he also became an advocate of the Rota, he joined the curia in 1951 on the staff of the Congregation of the Council (now, Congregation of the Clergy). He was a special secretary at the Synod of Bishops in 1971, where the principal topic was the question of the priestly ministry. In 1973, he was sostituto in the Congregation for the Doctrine of the Faith. On April 5, 1984, he became secretary of that congregation, under Joseph Ratzinger, and was made titular bishop of Cæsarea in Numidia with the personal title of archbishop He was consecrated by Ratzinger on May 12. In June, 1995, he was made pro-prefect of the Congregation for the Causes of Saints, and prefect of that Congregation on February 23, 1998, two days after his cardinalate. Hospitalized, he was unable to attend the ceremony of his creation on February 21, and he died on April 17, 1998, after a cardinalate of only fifty-five days.

66. Cheli was born in Turin on October 4, 1918, and was ordained for the clergy of the diocese of Asti on June 21, 1942. After an early career as a teacher in the diocesan seminary and as chaplain to the youth section of Catholic Action, he went to Rome for further study. After he had received his licentiate in theology and his doctorate in canon law, he joined the diplomatic service and was posted successively to the nunciatures in Guatemala, Spain, and Italy. In 1967, he was recalled to Rome and attached to the staff of the Pontifical Council for the Public Affairs of the Church. In 1973, Paul VI sent him as the Vatican's permanent observer at the United Nations. In one of the few hierarchial actions of his brief reign, John Paul I made him titular bishop of Santa Giusta, with the personal title of archbishop, on September 8, 1978 (con-

secrated September 16). In 1976, John Paul II recalled him from New York and appointed him pro-president of the Pontifical Commission for Migration and Tourism, which became the Pontifical Council for the Pastoral Care of Migrants and Itinerant People on March 1, 1989, under the reorganization mandated by the constitution, *Pastor Bonus.*

67. Monduzzi was born in Brisighella, near Faenza, on April 2, 1922, and was ordained for the clergy of the diocese of Faenza on July 22, 1945, after he had completed his studies in the diocesan seminary. After he earned a doctorate *in utroque iure* (of both laws, canon and civil) from the Pontifical Lateran University, he joined the staff of Catholic Action and directed that organization's social missions in Calabria and Sardinia. He later worked for the Agrarian Reform Agency in the Fucino. In May, 1959, he became secretary in the office of the *maestro di camera* of the pope. When Paul VI's reorganization of the curia, under the provisions of the constitution *Regimini Ecclesiæ Universæ*, went into effect on January 1, 1968, Colasuonno became Secretary and Regent of the Apostolic Palace. On December 18, 1986, John Paul II made him titular bishop of Capri and prefect of the papal household. He was consecrated personally by the pope on January 6, 1987. He retired from his prefecture on his elevation to the cardinalate.

68. Colasuonno was born in Grumo Appula, near Bari, on January 2, 1925, and was ordained for the clergy of the archdiocese of Bari on September 28, 1947. He received doctorates in both theology and canon law and then taught in the archdiocesan seminary of Bari before he entered the diplomatic service in 1958. After serving in the Section for Extraordinary Ecclesiastical Affairs of the Secretariat of State, he was posted successively to the United States, India, and Taiwan. On December 6, 1974, Paul VI made him titular bishop of Truentum with the personal title of archbishop (consecrated February 9, 1975) and sent him to be the first apostolic delegate in Mozambique. In 1981, John Paul II made him pro-nuncio in Zimbabwe, and, in 1985, pro-nuncio in Yugoslavia. In 1986, the pope gave him the delicate diplomatic position of head of the delegation for permanent working contacts with Poland. From 1990 to 1994, he was the Vatican's representative to the Soviet Union and its successor states. In 1994, he was recalled to Rome and appointed nuncio to Italy.

69. Arns, the fifth of thirteen children, was born in Forquilhinha, near Tubarao, Brazil, on September 14, 1921. Three of his sisters are nuns and one of his brothers also is a Franciscan. Arns entered the Order of Friars Minor on December 10, 1943, and was ordained on November 30, 1945. In 1946, he was graduated from the Sorbonne with an honors degree in classical languages. By 1961, he already was vice provincial of his order. Arns has been editor-in-chief of the weekly magazine for religious, *Sponsa Christi*, and also has headed the Franciscan publishing center Vozes in Petropolis. Arns has taught at the minor seminary of Sgudos; on the faculties of philosophy, science, and literature at Bauru; and at the Franciscan Theological Institute and the Catholic University in Petropolis. Paul VI appointed him titular bishop of Respetta and auxiliary of São Paulo on May 2, 1966 (consecrated July 3), and advanced him to be archbishop of São Paulo on October 22, 1970. He was made a cardinal in the consistory of March 5, 1973. He resigned as archbishop in 1998.

70. Lorscheider was born in Estrela, near Porto Alegre, Brazil, on October 8, 1924. Both his parents, Joseph and Veronica, were of German stock. Lorscheider entered the Franciscan minor seminary of Taquari at the age of nine. He began his novitiate on December 1, 1942; took his solemn vows on August 22, 1946; and was ordained on August 22, 1948. After some years as a teacher of Latin, German, and mathematics at the minor seminary of Taquari, he went to Rome to study dogmatic theology at the Antonianum, from which he was graduated in 1952. He then returned to Brazil to teach dogmatic theology at the Franciscan seminary of Divinopolis. In 1958, he was appointed to a professorship in theology at the Antonianum, where he remained until 1962. In the same period, he also served as director of the Franciscan international house of studies in Rome. John XXIII named him bishop of Santo Angelo on February 3, 1962 (consecrated May 20). Paul VI named him archbishop of Fortaleza on March 26, 1973, and elevated him to cardinalate in the consistory of May 24, 1976. He has been both secretary and president of the Episcopal Conference of Brazil, and president of Caritas International. From 1975 to 1979, he was the president of CELAM, and led that organization through its most liberal and productive years. On July 12, 1995, he was transferred to be archbishop of Aparecida, site of Brazil's national Marian shrine.

71. Sales was born in Acari, near Caicó, Brazil, on November 8, 1920, and was ordained on November 21, 1943. On June 1, 1954, at the age of thirty-three, Pius XII appointed him titular bishop of Tibica and auxiliary bishop of Natal (consecrated August 15). Paul VI promoted him to the archdiocese of Sao Salvador da Bahia on October 29, 1968. He is especially well regarded for his social initiatives, including assistance for farmers and rural workers, and lessons over the radio for students who cannot attend school. He also is a major supporter of UNESCO's literacy campaign. At Vatican II, he served on the Committee for the Apostolate of the Laity. Paul VI elevated him to the cardinalate on April 28, 1969. On March 13, 1971, Paul VI also translated him to the office of archbishop of Sao Sebastiao do Rio de Janeiro.

72. Primatesta was born in Capilla del Senor, in the Diocese of Zárate-Campana, Argentina, on April 14, 1919. After attending the seminary in La Plata, he was sent to Rome in 1937, where he was graduated from the Gregorianum with degrees in theology and sacred scripture. On October 25, 1942, he was ordained in the Church of Il Gesu in Rome. In 1943, once more in Argentina, he taught Greek and Latin in the minor seminary of Zárate-Campana. In 1945, he became professor of dogmatic theology and sacred scripture at the major seminary of San José de La Plata. He has been president of the Society of Professors of Sacred Scripture in Argentina, and vice rector, general prefect, and rector of the seminary of La Plata. During the years of his professorship, he contributed a number of articles to theological reviews. On June 14, 1957, Pius XII made him titular bishop of Tanais and auxiliary bishop of La Plata (consecrated August 15). John XXIII made him bishop of San Rafael on June 12, 1961; and Paul VI made him archbishop of Córdoba on February 16, 1965. Paul VI made him a cardinal in the consistory of March 5, 1973.

73. Aponte Martinez, the first native-born Puerto Rican bishop and cardinal, was born in Lajas, near Mayaguez, on August 4, 1922, and began his studies at the major seminary of Boston, where he obtained his bachelor of arts degree in humanities. He was ordained on April 10, 1950. During his first three years as a priest, he was secretary to the bishop of Ponce, and later became a parish priest. John XXIII made

him titular bishop of Lares, and auxiliary bishop and coadjutor with right of succession to Ponce, on July 23, 1960 (consecrated October 12). He succeeded to Ponce on November 18, 1963. On November 4, 1964, Paul VI made him archbishop of San Juan. Paul VI made him a cardinal in the consistory of March 5, 1973. He is a former president of the Episcopal Conference of Puerto Rico.

74. Otunga was born in January, 1923, in Chebukwa, near Kakamega, Kenya, the son of a non-Christian tribal chief. Otunga was baptized in 1935, at the age of twelve, and went on to be graduated from Mangu High School. He entered the seminary of Kakamega, but was then sent to Rome to study theology at the College of Propaganda Fide. He was ordained in Rome on October 3, 1950, while still a student. On his return to Kenya, Otunga taught theology at Kisumu Major Seminary for three years, and was named chancellor of the diocesan curia. From 1953 to 1956, he was an attaché in the apostolic delegation in Mombassa. Pius XII named him titular bishop of Tacape and auxiliary bishop of Kisumu on November 17, 1956 (consecrated February 25, 1957). On May 21, 1960, John XXIII named him bishop of Kisii, where he served until November 15, 1969. On that date, Paul VI made him titular archbishop of Bomarzo and coadjutor with right of succession to Nairobi. He succeeded to Nairobi on October 24, 1971, and was created a cardinal in the consistory of March 5, 1973. In 1981, he also became the military ordinary of Kenya. Otunga has served as president of the national episcopate and is a member of the Permanent Commission of the Symposium of Episcopal Conferences of Africa and Madagascar. He resigned as archbishop on April 21, 1997.

75. Thiandoum, the son of a catechist, was born in Poponguine, near Dakar, Senegal, on February 2, 1921. He studied at the regional seminary in Dakar, and was ordained on April 18, 1949. From 1949 to 1951, he was a parish pastor, then went to Rome for further study. He received degrees in both philosophy and sociology from the Gregorianum in 1953. By 1955, again in Senegal, he was the representative for Catholic Action and the parish priest for the cathedral of Dakar. John XXIII named Thiandoum archbishop of Dakar on February 24, 1962 (consecrated May 20). He participated in the Second Vatican Council, particularly in discussions on liturgical reform. Paul VI created

him a cardinal in the consistory of May 24, 1976. In 1998, Thiandoum is a member of the Congregations for the Evangelization of Peoples, for the Clergy, and for the Institutes of Consecrated Life and the Societies of Apostolic Life.

76. Gantin, the son of a railway official, was born in Toffo, near Cotonou, Dahomey, now Benin, Benin, on May 8, 1922. He entered Benin's minor seminary in 1936 and was ordained on January 14, 1951. After he completed his studies, Gantin remained at the seminary as a language instructor until he went to Rome to study at the College of Saint Peter in 1953. In Rome, he first attended the Pontifical Urban University and then the Lateran University, from which he received degrees in theology and canon law. Pius XII appointed him titular bishop of Tipasa and auxiliary bishop of Cotonou on December 11, 1956, when Gantin was only thirty-four. He was consecrated on February 3, 1957. He succeeded to the archdiocese of Cotonou on January 3, 1960. He was president of the Regional Episcopal Conference (Togo, Dahomey, the Ivory Coast, Upper Volta, Senegal, Nigeria, and Guinea), when, in 1971, Paul VI called him to Rome to become associate secretary of the Congregation for the Evangelization of Peoples. From 1973 to 1975, he was the secretary of the Congregation. In the latter year, he was made vice president of the Pontifical Commission "Justitia et Pax," of which he served as president from 1976 to 1984. Paul VI created him a cardinal-deacon in the consistory of June 27, 1977, with the diaconate of Sacro Cuore del Gesu Cristo Re. On April 8, 1984, he was made prefect of the Congregation of Bishops and president of the Pontifical Commission for Latin America. He was raised to the rank of cardinal-priest by John Paul II on June 25, 1984, and his diaconate was, on the same date, raised to presbyterial status *pro hac vice* for him. On September 29, 1986, he was made cardinal-bishop of Palestrina, in succession to Carlo Confalonieri, who had died August 1. John Paul II conceded to the cardinal-bishops the right to elect the dean of the College, rather than have him rise to the position through seniority among the cardinal-bishops. These and other reforms enacted for the cardinal-bishops in 1993, permitted Agnello Rossi to retire as dean and as cardinal-bishop of Ostia. On June 4, 1993, the six cardinal bishops met and elected Gantin as dean. On the following day, John Paul II gave his papal approval, and Gantin became

cardinal-bishop of Ostia and Palestrina. In June, 1998, Gantin retired as prefect, and was succeeded by Lucas Moreira Neves. Cardinal Gantin's cardinalitial arms are *armes parlantes* on the phrase, "tree of iron" (*gan*, tree, *tin*, iron).

77. Kim was born in Tae Gu, Korea, on May 8, 1922, and was ordained on September 15, 1951. Paul VI made him bishop of Masan on February 15, 1966 (consecrated May 31); promoted him to be archbishop of Seoul on April 9, 1958; and made him a cardinal on April 28, 1969. On June 10, 1975, he also was made apostolic administrator of Pyeong Yang. He resigned as archbishop in 1998.

78. Taofinu'u was born at Falealupo, Western Samoa, on December 9, 1923, and was ordained on December 8, 1954, one day before his thirty-first birthday. He joined the Society of Mary in 1955. Paul VI appointed him bishop of Apia, for Samoa and Tokelau, on January 11, 1968 (consecrated May 29), when he became the first Polynesian bishop. He was created a cardinal in the consistory of March 5, 1973. On September 10, 1982, his see was raised to an archdiocese and he became archbishop of Samoa-Apia and Tokelau. A separation on June 26, 1992, left him with the reduced territory of the archdiocese of Samoa–Apia.

79. Sin was born on August 31, 1928, in New Washington, near Kalibo, Aklan, Republic of the Philippines, to Juan Sin and Maxima Reyes Lachinca Sin. He received his elementary education at the New Washington Elementary School; his bachelor of science degree in education from the Immaculate Conception College, Roxas City, in 1959; and his preparatory studies for the priesthood at the Saint Vincent Ferrer Archdiocesan Seminary in Jaro, Iloilo City. He was ordained on April 3, 1954. From 1954 to 1957, he was a diocesan missionary in Capiz, and then became the first rector of the Saint Pius X Seminary in Roxas City. On February 10, 1967, Paul VI made him titular bishop of Obba and auxiliary bishop of Jaro (consecrated March 18). On June 20, 1970, he was appointed apostolic administrator of the archdiocese of Jaro. On January 15, 1972, he was raised to the rank of titular archbishop of Massa Lubrense and coadjutor archbishop of Jaro with right of succession. He succeeded as archbishop on October 8, 1972. Paul VI appointed him archbishop of Manila on January 21, 1974, in succession to Ruffino I. Santos, who had died on September

3, 1973. Sin was created a cardinal in the consistory of May 24, 1976.

80. Hume was born on March 2, 1923, in Newcastle-on-Tyne, and was baptized George; he chose the name Basil when he became a Benedictine. His father, a cardiac surgeon, was an Anglican, but his French mother was Catholic—a combination that he shares with John Henry Newman. At eighteen, Hume began his studies in the Abbey of Saint Lawrence at Ampleforth, and then studied history at Oxford and took a degree in theology at the University of Fribourg. He professed his final vows as a Benedictine in 1945, and, on July 23, 1950, was ordained. After a long teaching career, be became abbot of Ampleforth in 1963. On February 9, 1976, Paul VI named him archbishop of Westminster, in succession to John Carmel Heenan, which made him the first member of a monastic order to hold the Catholic primacy of England in modern times. He was consecrated on the following March 25. He was made a cardinal in the consistory of May 24, 1976.

81. Baum was born in Dallas, Texas, on November 21, 1926. At an early age, he moved with his family to Kansas City, Missouri, where he was ordained for the clergy of the diocese of Kansas City-Saint Joseph on May 12, 1951. From 1964 to 1969, he was the executive director of the commission of the American bishops for ecumenical and interreligious affairs, and he attended Vatican II as a peritus. Paul VI appointed him bishop of Springfield-Cape Girardeau, Missouri, on February 18, 1970 (consecrated April 6). On March 5, 1973, he was appointed archbishop of Washington, in succession to Patrick Aloysius O'Boyle, but resigned that see on March 18, 1980, when he was called to Rome to become prefect of the Congregation for Catholic Education (formerly, of Seminaries and Institutes of Study). He was followed in Washington by James Aloysius Hickey. He vacated his prefecture in 1990, and was appointed penitentiary major on April 6.

82. Ratzinger was born in Marktl am Inn, near Passau, Germany, on April 16, 1927, and was ordained on June 29, 1951. He received his doctorate in 1953 with a remarkable thesis on Augustinian doctrine, *Volk und Haus Gottes in Augustins Lehre von der Kirche* (Munchen: K. Zink, 1954, a part of the series *Munchener Theologische Studien*, II. *Systematische Abteilung*). Doctrinally liberal in the early years of his career, he served as advisor to Cardinal Joseph

Frings at the Second Vatican Council, a position he received at the age of only thirty-five. He reached the apex of his teaching career as professor of dogmatic theology at the University of Regensburg. Paul VI made him archbishop of Munich and Freising on March 24, 1977, in succession to Julius Döpfner, who had died on July 24, 1976. On June 27, 1977, Paul VI made him a cardinal. John Paul II called him to Rome on November 25, 1981, to be prefect of the Congregation for the Doctrine of the Faith, president of the Pontifical Biblical Commission, and president of the International Theological Commission. He resigned the archdiocese of Munich formally on February 15, 1982. On April 5, 1993, John Paul II made him cardinal-bishop of Velletri in succession to Sebastiano Baggio, who had died on March 21.

83. Gouyon was born in Bordeaux on October 24, 1910, and was ordained on March 13, 1937. Pius XII appointed him bishop of Bayonne on August 6, 1957 (consecrated October 7). In one of his earliest pontifical acts, Paul VI made him titular archbishop of Pessinonte and coadjutor archbishop of Rennes, to Clement Emile Rocques, on September 6, 1963. When Cardinal Rocques died on September 4, 1964, Gouyon became archbishop of Rennes. Paul VI created him a cardinal in the consistory of April 28, 1969. He resigned as archbishop of Rennes on October 15, 1985.

84. Aramburu was born in Reducción, near Villa de la Concepción del Río Cuarto, Argentina, on February 11, 1912. He began his ecclesiastical studies at the seminary of Córdoba, but soon was sent to Rome for further study. He was ordained in Rome on October 28, 1934, and later received Roman degrees in canon law and moral theology. He returned to Argentina and began to teach at the seminary of Córdoba, where he was chosen vice rector. He also served on the literature and philosophy faculties of the national University. Pius XII appointed him titular bishop of Paltea and auxiliary bishop of Tucumán on October 7, 1946 (consecrated December 15). He became bishop of Tucumán on August 28, 1953, of which he was the first archbishop, when the see was raised to metropolitan status on March 13, 1957. On June 14, 1967, Paul VI transferred him to the titular diocese of Torri di Bizacena, with the title of archbishop *pro illa vice*, and named him coadjutor archbishop of Buenos Aires, with right of succession, for Antonio Caggiano. On the latter's

retirement, Aramburu became archbishop of Buenos Aires on April 22, 1975. He retired as archbishop on July 10, 1990. He also was ordinary for the members of Oriental rites in Argentina. He was made a cardinal by Paul VI in the consistory of May 24, 1976.

85. González Martín was born at Villanubla, near Valladolid, on January 16, 1918, and was ordained on June 29, 1941. For many years, he taught theology and sociology at the diocesan seminary of Valladolid, where he also founded an organization, anticipating Habitat for Humanity, which constructed houses for the poor. John XXIII made him bishop of Astorga on December 31, 1960 (consecrated March 5, 1961). On February 21, 1966, Paul VI gave him the titular diocese of Case Mediane, which was raised *pro illa vice* to an archdiocese, and made him coadjutor archbishop with right of succession to Barcelona. He succeeded to Barcelona on January 7, 1967. On December 3, 1971, he was transferred to be archbishop of Toledo, on the same day that Enrique y Tacancón vacated Toledo for Madrid. González Martín was created a cardinal in the consistory of March 5, 1973. He resigned as archbishop of Toledo on June 23, 1995, and lost his active vote in the conclave on January 16, 1998.

86. Zoungrana was born on September 3, 1917 in Ouagadougou, Burkina Faso, and received his first schooling from the White Sisters in Ouagadougou. He entered the minor seminary of Pabre in 1925, and, in 1935, went on to the major seminary at Koumi. He was ordained there on May 2, 1942, as one of his country's first three priests. He applied for admission to the novitiate of the White Fathers of Maison Carree in Algeria, and entered the order on September 24, 1948. He took his final vows in Rome in 1952, and, at the same time, received his degree in canon law from the Gregorianum. Zoungrana completed his studies with a degree in sociology from the Institut Catholique in Paris. In 1954, he became an instructor of canon law at his alma mater, the major seminary at Koumi. On April 5, 1960, John XXIII named him archbishop of Ouagadougou, and consecrated him personally in Saint Peter's on the following May 8. He resigned as archbishop on June 10, 1995. He was created a cardinal by Paul VI in the consistory of February 22, 1965. Today, he is the senior surviving cardinal of Paul VI.

87. Willebrands was born in Bovenkarspel,

near Haarlem, the Netherlands, on September 4, 1909. He studied philosophy at the Angelicum, and was ordained on May 26, 1934. From 1937 to 1940, he taught philosophy at Warmond, and, in 1945, he became the director of the major seminary there. On June 24, 1960, he was elected president of the Saint Willebrord Association, an organization that promotes ecumenical activities in Holland. To assist Augustin Bea in his pre-conciliar work, John XXIII made Willebrands secretary of the newly created Secretariat for Christian Unity, in 1960. Paul VI made him titular bishop of Mauriana on June 4, 1964 (consecrated June 28). From April 12, 1968, until his retirement in 1989, he served as president of the Secretariat for the Christian Unity. He was created a cardinal on April 28, 1969. On December 6, 1975, he was made archbishop of Utrecht, a position from which he retired on December 3, 1983. He also has served as camerlengo of the College of Cardinals.

88. Pappalardo was born at Villafranca Sicula, near Agrigento (Girgenti) in Sicily, on September 23, 1918, and was ordained on April 12, 1941. He entered the curia in the secretariat of state in 1947. Paul VI named him titular archbishop of Miletus on December 7, 1965 (consecrated January 16, 1966), and sent him to be pro-nuncio in Indonesia, where he remained until 1969. In that year, he returned to Rome for a one-year term as president of the Pontifical Ecclesiastical Academy (formerly the Pontifical Academy of Noble Ecclesiastics). On October 17, 1970, Paul VI made him archbishop of Palermo, and made him a cardinal in the consistory of March 5, 1973. He resigned as archbishop on April 4, 1996. He is the most recent creation of Paul VI to lose his vote in the conclave, on his eightieth birthday, September 23, 1998.

89. Ursi was born in Andria on July 26, 1908, and was ordained on July 25, 1931, one day before his twenty-third birthday. From 1931 to 1951, he served successively as vice rector and rector of the Pontifical Regional Seminary at Molfetta. Pius XII made him bishop of Nardo on July 31, 1951 (consecrated September 30). John XXIII advanced him to be archbishop of Acerenza on November 30, 1961; Paul VI made him archbishop of Naples on May 23, 1966, in succession to Alfonso Castaldo, who had died on the previous March 3. Ursi resigned his see on May 9, 1987, and was followed at Naples by Michele Giordano.

90. Oddi was born on November 14, 1910, in

Morfasso, near Piacenza, and was ordained May 21, 1933. He joined the staff of the curia and, on July 30, 1953, Pius XII made him titular archbishop of Messembria (consecrated September 27). From 1953 to 1969, he was, successively, apostolic delegate to Jerusalem, Palestine, Jordan, and Cyprus; internuncio to the United Arab Republic; and nuncio to Belgium and Luxembourg. Paul VI made him a cardinal in the consistory of April 28, 1969, and, on the following June 13, also appointed him pontifical legate for the patriarchal basilica of Saint Francis at Assisi. He served a term as prefect of the Congregation of the Clergy from 1979 to 1986.

91. Sensi was born in Cosenza on May 27, 1907, and was ordained December 21, 1929. He entered the diplomatic service and served in staff positions in the nunciatures in Hungary, Switzerland, Belgium, and Czechoslovakia, in the period between 1934 and 1949. Pius XII made him titular archbishop of Sardes on May 21, 1955 (consecrated July 24), and sent him to be nuncio to Costa Rica. In the following year, he became apostolic delegate to Jerusalem, where he remained until 1962. From 1962 to 1967, he was nuncio in Ireland, and from 1967 to 1976, he served in the same capacity in Portugal. Paul VI created him cardinal-deacon of Santi Biagio e Carlo ai Catinari in the consistory of May 24, 1976, and John Paul II made him cardinal-priest of the title of Regina Apostolorum on June 22, 1987.

92. Bertoli was born in Poggio Garfagnana, near Lucca, on February 1, 1908, and was ordained on August 15, 1930. He entered the diplomatic service and served terms on the staff of nunciatures in Yugoslavia, France, Haiti, and Switzerland. Pius XII named him titular archbishop of Nicomedia on March 24, 1952 (consecrated May 11) and sent him as apostolic delegate to Turkey, where he remained only a year. From 1953 to 1959, he was nuncio in Colombia; from 1959 to 1960, in Lebanon; and, from 1960 to 1969, in France. Paul VI made him cardinal-deacon of San Girolamo della Carita in Via Giulia on April 28, 1969. From 1969 to 1973, he was prefect of the Congregation for the Causes of Saints. John Paul II advanced him directly from the rank of cardinal-deacon to be cardinal-bishop of Frascati, on June 30, 1979, in succession to Jean Villot, who had died suddenly on March 9. Bertoli also followed Villot as camerlengo, an office from which he retired in 1985, when he was succeeded, on March 25, by

Sebastiano Baggio.

93. Opilio Rossi was born in New York, New York, on May 14, 1910, although he subsequently became a citizen of Italy. He was ordained for the clergy of the diocese of Piacenza (now Piacenza-Bobbio) on March 11, 1933. From 1938 to 1953, he served successively in the nunciatures in Belgium, the Netherlands, and Germany. On November 21, 1953, Pius XII made him titular archbishop of Ancyra (consecrated December 27) and sent him to be nuncio in Ecuador. In 1959, he was transferred to Chile, and, from 1961 to 1976, he was nuncio to Austria. In the consistory of May 24, 1976, Paul VI made him cardinal-deacon of Santa Maria Liberatrice al Monte Testaccio. From 1983 to 1990, he was president of the Pontifical Committee for International Eucharistic Congresses. On June 22, 1987, John Paul II advanced him to the ranks of the cardinal-priests with the title of San Lorenzo in Lucina. He also served as president of the Cardinalitial Commission for the Pontifical Sanctuaries of Pompeii, Loreto, and Bari, from 1984 to 1993.

94. Palazzini was born in Piobbico, near Pesaro, on May 19, 1912, and was ordained on December 6, 1934. In his early career, he was an academic administrator, serving as assistant vice rector of the Pontifical Major Seminary of Rome and as bursar and vice rector of the Pontifical Roman Seminary for Juridical Studies. He also was professor of moral theology at the Pontifical Lateran University. After holding staff positions in several offices of the curia, he was made secretary of the Congregation of the Council (now, of the Clergy) in 1958, where he served until 1973. John XXIII made him titular archbishop of Cæsarea in Cappadocia on August 28, 1962 (consecrated September 21). Paul VI elevated him to the cardinalate in the consistory of March 5, 1973, as cardinal-deacon of San Pier Damiano ai Monti, a newly created diaconate. After Paolo Bertoli was made cardinal-bishop of Frascati, on June 30, 1979, Palazzini was made cardinal-priest with Bertoli's old presbyterial title, San Girolamo della Carita in Via Giulia. From 1980 to 1988, he served as prefect of the Congregation for the Causes of Saints.

95. Bafile was born in L'Aquila on July 4, 1903. He practiced law in Rome for six years before he began study for the priesthood. He was ordained on April 11, 1936, at the age of thirty-two. He entered the curia on the staff of the secretariat of state in 1939, where he

remained for twenty years. John XXIII made him titular archbishop of Antiochia in Pisidia on February 11, 1960 (consecrated March 19) and sent him to West Germany as Muench's successor in the nunciature. He remained in that post for fifteen years. Paul VI recalled him to Rome and made him pro-prefect of the Congregation for the Causes of Saints on July 18, 1975. He became prefect when he was made cardinal-deacon of Santa Maria in Porticu a Campitelli on May 24, 1976. His term as prefect ended in 1980. John Paul II advanced him to the rank of cardinal-priest and elevated his diaconate to a presbyterial title, *pro hac vice*, on June 22, 1987.

96. Silva Henríquez, the sixteenth of nineteen children, was born in Talca, Chile, on September 27, 1907. His father, a farmer and industrialist, came from an old Chilean family with Portuguese origins. His mother also descended from an old Chilean family which had founded the city of Talca. By the age of twenty-two, Silva Henríquez had become a lawyer, and only later found his vocation. On January 28, 1930, he entered the Salesian novitiate at Macal (Santiago), and was then sent to the Pontifical Salesian University of Turin, Italy, to study theology. On July 3, 1938, he was ordained. For many years, he was an administrator at a number of schools and colleges in Italy. He also built a national shrine to St. John Bosco, the founder of the Salesians. When he returned to Chile, he was named president of the Federation of Catholic Colleges. In 1953, he was entrusted with organizing Caritas in Chile, and later he became the Chilean president of Caritas. He kept that office after John XXIII named him bishop of Valparaíso, on October 24, 1959 (consecrated November 29). After being chosen vice president of Caritas International, John XXIII also advanced him to be archbishop of Santiago del Chile on May 14, 1961. John XXIII also created him a cardinal in the consistory of March 19, 1962. On May 3, 1983, he retired as archbishop of Santiago.

97. König was born on August 3, 1905, in Rabenstein, near Sankt Pölten, Austria. After attending the Benedictine high school at Melk, he studied philosophy and theology from 1927 to 1933 at the Gregorianum and biblical studies under Messina at the Pontifical Biblical Institute, where König concentrated his studies on Iranian religious issues. He was ordained on October 29, 1933. In 1945, he was professor of

religion at Krems on the Danube, and, in 1948, he was appointed to the theological faculty at Salzburg to teach moral philosophy. Pius XII appointed him titular bishop of Livias and auxiliary bishop of Sankt Pölten on July 3, 1952 (consecrated August 31). Pius XII also promoted him to be archbishop of Vienna on May 10, 1956, in succession to Theodor Innitzer, who had died on the previous October 9. In Vienna, he was also ordinary for Greek-rite Catholics living in Austria. John XXIII made him president of the Pontifical Council for Dialogue with Non-Believers, and then created him a cardinal in the consistory of December 15, 1958. He retired as archbishop of Vienna on September 16, 1985, and was succeeded by Hans Hermann Groër.

IX. The Coming Election

I. The Pope's Health

The gradual decline in the pope's health continued in 1998. There were no major crises to be overcome, but small increments of increased weakening were noticeable, almost from month to month. On Sunday, January 11, during a ceremony in the Vatican, he lost his balance and began to pitch forward. A priest at his side supported him briefly, and he went on with the rite. Of course, the papal spokesman, Dr. Joaquín Navarro-Valls, denied that the pope had suffered from any dizziness and said that John Paul had merely stumbled.

Dr. Corrado Manni, who administered the anesthesia to the pope during all of his six operations, gave an interview, just before John Paul left on his trip to Cuba, in which he tried, in a rather passive way, to reassure the public about the pope's health: "When he was elected pope in 1978, he was in good physical shape. He was very athletic. He was an avid hiker and skier and continued doing these activities until recently." Manni went on to add that the pope's good health as a younger man had helped him to recover from his medical setbacks. He added, though, as an acknowledgment of the obvious, that aging and the pope's daily workload contributed to his recent frailty.

John Paul II reached a special papal milestone on May 26, 1998, when his reign became the longest in the twentieth century, passing Pius XII's tenure of nineteen years, seven months, and seven days on the throne.

In addition to his increasing debilitation, John Paul continues to exhibit markedly the effects of his extra-pyramidal syndrome. He takes a daily regimen of medication for this, but it is clear that the more pronounced symptoms recently indicate either an increased tolerance for the medication and a weakening of its effectiveness or an actual physiological advance in the progress of the disease.

In the meantime, John Paul has devoted much time recently to putting his personal affairs in order, both in Poland and in Rome, which has included making provisions for those who have been close to him. And few men are as close to the pope as Stanislaw Dziwisz, who has been John Paul's personal secretary since 1966, three years after Dziwisz was ordained. As the pontificate draws to a close, John Paul has wanted to make some ecclesiastical provision for his old friend, remembering how shabbily former papal secretaries often have been treated at the beginnings of new reigns. On February 7, 1998, in an unprecedented step in modern times, John Paul made him titular archbishop of Saint Leon and adjunct prefect of the Pontifical Household, a new position contrived for the occasion to support his archiepiscopal elevation. Of course, in reality, Dziwisz, born in 1939, continues as John Paul's secretary. The opportunity to promote Dziwisz was made possible because Dino Monduzzi vacated the office of prefect on February 21, on the occasion of his elevation to the cardinalate. To replace him, the pope named James Michael Harvey, a native of Milwaukee and a member of the staff of the Secretariat of State, and also made him a titular bishop, a title which traditionally goes with the prefecture. John Paul also appointed Piero Marini, the master of liturgical ceremonies, to episcopal rank and announced that he would conduct all three consecrations himself in Saint Peter's on Thursday, March 19, 1998— which he did.

Dr. Joaquín Navarro-Valls, the pope's press spokesman, put the best face on the new title in the public announcement of the promotion:

> Monsignor Dziwisz, as the particular secretary of the Holy Father, was already involved closely in the organization of audiences and in running the prefecture of the Papal Household. Therefore, this nomination makes formal a role and a reality already under way for some time, and which are also destined to increase in view of the great Jubilee of the year 2000.

John Paul II, however, made his affection for Dziwisz, and the scope of his duties, clear in a shaking voice at the consecration:

> The Spirit of the Lord consecrates you, my dear friend Stanislaw, from my own archdiocese of Kraków. . . . Thirty-five years ago, I myself ordained you priest in the cathedral of Wawel, and, three years later, named you my chaplain. From the beginning of my Petrine ministry, you have been at my side as a faithful secretary, sharing with me the exhaustion and the joy, the hopes and the emotions. . . . As adjunct prefect, you will put your great experience to work for the pontifical household, to the benefit of all those who approach the successor of Peter for their ministry or as pilgrims.

Whatever happens now, Archbishop Dziwisz, who now ecclesiastically outranks his official superior, Bishop Harvey, will be cared for in a manner commensurate with his new stature.

For the curia, as well as many of the non-Roman cardinals, acts like this signal that John Paul himself is preparing for the reign's closure, much as the elevation of Benelli to the cardinalate in 1977 was a signal from Paul VI that his reign was almost over.

The pope's confidence in the future of his own health and the care for it was dealt another blow on August 26, 1998, when Dr. Francesco Crucitti, who had saved his life in 1981 and had performed the other surgeries on him since that time, died in Rome at the age of sixty-seven. Crucitti, although a surgeon, was the medical figure in John Paul's life who understood his general medical condition best. In addition, he had become a close friend over the years, and was the one man John Paul II most trusted in all medical matters.

Will 1999 be the year of the conclave? Many close observers of this reign believe that it will. The principal evidence that a large number of cardinals think so is the heightened activity of the *prattiche* in the months that have followed the consistory of February 21, 1998—months that have seen Dionigi Tettamanzi emerge as a leading *papabile*. This sense of expectation is present within the curia, as well. Since the trend of curial gossip conveys the signals that the press and the broadcast media use to try to anticipate major events in the papacy and the Vatican, it is not surprising that there also has been a recent increase in speculation about the pope's end and the next conclave. The first sign of activity was the preparation of new briefings about the cardinals and the rules and policies of papal elections by a number of news organizations. ABC News led the way, perhaps a bit prematurely, with a revision of its *Papal Handbook* in the spring of 1996. By late 1998, a number of speculative articles had appeared in leading European and American publications. For example, in the United States, current presidential problems and major foreign policy issues were pushed aside for the cover story, "The Next Pope," in the May 11, 1998, issue of *U.S. News & World Report*.[1] But none of these published reports conveys the sense of tiredness and lethargy which has pervaded curial offices in 1998. Generated by a sense of *waiting*, this atmosphere is quite similar to that which could be felt in 1957 and 1958 under Pius XII, and again in late 1977 and in 1978 under Paul VI. Part of this can be seen in the mechanical way that the staffs of many of the congregations and pontifical councils go about their daily work, without much of the verve and enthusiasm that often pervades the offices that are at the center of the government of the world's largest Christian denomination. After a twenty-year pontificate, it may even be said that this stagnation, this quality of *waiting*, is deeper and more profound than at earlier similar periods in modern times.

II. Parties and Views

Because John Paul II has conducted his government of the Church from the right of the ecclesial spectrum, he has pushed the cardinalate, as well as the rest of the hierarchy, much further towards the conservative side than might have been expected in a reign that came so soon after the close of the Second Vatican Council. The number of electors who may be described as right-of-center is now a larger percentage of the College than at any time since the close of the pontificate of Pius X in 1914—although only a few of today's cardinals may be described legitimately as more conservative than the centrist position of eighty-five years ago.

In that light, we can identify four general points of view which may serve to categorize the cardinals in the coming election.

STRONG CONSERVATIVES

These cardinals, like John Paul II, refuse to see Vatican II as an innovation which altered the way in which the Church sees, and governs, itself. Instead, for them it was a complete affirmation and confirmation of traditional views. This way of looking at the council first appeared during the conciliar period among a large number of Eastern European bishops, including both Wyzynski and Wojtyła, who rejected altogether John XXIII's idea of *aggiornamento*, and saw the council simply as an intense personal spiritual experience for the bishops who participated in it. This perception caused them to oppose Paul VI's methods for putting into operation the council's decisions. Paul VI's view of the council's accomplishments and aims were, for the most part, shared widely in the developed world, and the rejection of many of his plans and programs—especially after the Extraordinary Synod of 1985—was both dismaying to many people whose spirits were raised by the energy and direction of the council and heartening to conservatives who see Paul VI as a weak and vacillating pope, and completely wrong about such fundamental concepts as episcopal collegiality, ecumenism, open dissent in theology, and the nature of the religious life. Today, there are about forty cardinals who hold these views. They are, for the most part, the younger Latin American creations of John Paul II, some Italian and other curial cardinals, and a number of cardinal-archbishops in Eastern Europe. Many of them are strong supporters of *Opus Dei*, and believe that its work is one of the best means for combating the trends of "liberalism" and "humanism" unleashed by the council. And many are leaders in the movement to have Mary declared co-redemptrix with Christ, a theological reversal of the council so profound in nature that it certainly would retard, if not stop, most ecumenical dialogue for years to come. Ritually and liturgically, all of them reject the idea that there is a place for women in holy orders, and all of them oppose disconnecting the theological position on contraception from that on abortion. Having also rejected the idea that the Church is composed of the whole body of "the people of God," as the council put it, they see no place in Church government for the laity nor do they see a collegiality of bishops as embodying any teaching authority whatever. The strong conservatives regard themselves as the heirs of John Paul II, and view the next election as an opportunity to ensure that the policies of the present reign are preserved and, perhaps, extended. Their leaders include two powerful curial cardinals from Latin America, Alfonso López Trujillo of Colombia, the president of the Pontifical Council for the Family, and Lucas Moreira Neves of Brazil, a Dominican who is now cardinal-bishop of Sabina and prefect of the Congregation of Bishops. For purposes of preliminary discussion, Neves is the cardinal of whom most of them speak as an official candidate, but there is a general understanding that the advancing course of his severe late-onset or type-II diabetes as he grows older—he was seventy-three on September 16, 1998—make him an unlikely John Paul III.

MODERATE CONSERVATIVES

A group of about thirty cardinals, mostly drawn from the creations in the consistories of the 1980s, join with their rightist colleagues in believing that Paul VI misinterpreted the intentions of Vatican II and caused, through his actions based on those misinterpretations, a destabilization of the Church which must be corrected. Nevertheless, they do not altogether reject the fundamental work of the council and also believe that many of the changes wrought in the Church during the 1960s and 1970s are now too firmly established to be undone. This group includes most of the American residential cardinals and some of the Italian ordinaries, as well as a few Latin Americans and Eastern Europeans. Although they form a less cohesive group than the strong conservatives, they do agree that the next pope cannot be positioned so far to the right in the Catholic spectrum as John Paul II has been.

Until recently, many of these moderate conservatives were considering Pio Laghi, the prefect of the Congregation for Catholic Education, as a potential candidate; but the recent revelation that he had some inside knowledge of the reign of terror in Argentina in the 1970s has all but destroyed the possibility that he can ascend the throne. As John Paul's reign closes, the name of Dionigi Tettamanzi, the recently created archbishop of

Genoa, has been heard more and more in the preliminary conversations of the moderate conservatives, although he has not yet been advanced as the major candidate of the group. The reluctance of the moderate conservatives to embrace Tettamanzi as their official candidate stems from the newness of his cardinalate—he is still a comparative stranger to many—and, more importantly, his complete and unwavering support for *Humanæ Vitæ*—which alone will attract a strong opposition from both pragmatists and conciliarists, perhaps enough to stall his candidacy entirely.

PRAGMATISTS

This is a group of about twenty-five cardinals who consider that John Paul II's inflexibility in matters where legitimate divergence of opinion exists has done much to harm the Church, which had expected so much in the years following the council. They point to the anger of the laity, especially in the United States and northern and western Europe, about the failure of the pope to address the rôle of women in the modern Church; the continuing decline in vocations, especially to the priesthood, just at a time when more and more dedication is needed to meet the expanding need for social and economic help in the Third World; and, perhaps most important of all, the failure of the pope to consider divorcing the theological views on birth control from those on abortion. They believe that John Paul I was moving in the right direction when he began to take up this last question as one of the priorities of his pontificate. The pragmatists also realize that for ecumenical dialogue to continue significantly, towards a reintegration of a unified Christian Church, it will be necessary to reduce the huge efforts made in the present reign to strengthen popular Marian devotions. These certainly have alienated even moderate Catholics who saw the council as the gateway to a return by Catholicism to the simple message of the Gospels with regard to salvation and redemption. Historically, the pragmatists know that an emphasis on a monarchical primacy in Rome and a strong commitment to Marian devotions have played the greatest part in engendering mistrust of Catholics in biblically-based creeds elsewhere in Western civilization. In this regard, they also are dismayed by the fact that the two bullets that were removed from John Paul II have been sent to Marian shrines, one to Fatima and one to the Polish national shrine at Czestochowa, where they are now venerated as holy relics. Of course, they do not favor the abandonment of centuries of Catholic tradition in favor of a new evangelism or a new Pentecostalism, with its overemphasis on the Old Testament at the expense of the New. The pragmatists believe that there are practical steps that can be taken now to give added force to the ecumenical movement and to assuage the difficulties that the faithful have in dealing with social and economic forces in the modern world in a manner that is in keeping with Catholic faith. The leadership of this group is diffuse but much of its guidance in recent years has come from Achille Silvestrini, the prefect of the Congregation for the Oriental Churches. Silvestrini, an Emiliano by background, spent all of the early and middle years of his rise in the Church working in the Congregation of Extraordinary Ecclesiastical Affairs and its successor organizations, first under Domenico Tardini, John XXIII's cardinal-secretary of state, and then under Antonio Samoré and Agostino Casaroli. When Casaroli retired as cardinal-secretary of state, in December, 1990, many observers expected Silvestrini to be appointed his successor, but John Paul II chose Angelo Sodano instead, a much more conservative if much less gifted prelate. If a pragmatic cardinal does achieve the throne, Silvestrini may have a chance at a term as secretary of state, even though he became seventy-five on October 25, 1998.

In the early evolutions of the *prattiche*, the strongest candidate of the pragmatists is Carlo Maria Martini, the Jesuit archbishop of Milan. A biblical scholar of international renown, Martini clearly is the candidate that most secular leaders in northern and western Europe would prefer on the throne. His candidacy, however, is crippled by two major conditions: his age, since he became seventy-two on February 15, 1999; and the fact that the College always has considered a Jesuit ineligible to ascend to the papal chair. Another view that is discussed among the pragmatists is that they can join with the moderate conservatives to elect an older pope for a transitional reign—if Martini is rejected, then another candidate in his seventies—with the possibility of advancing Christoph Schönborn, the Dominican archbishop of Vienna, in the conclave after the next. Schönborn is thought to be too young to be seriously *papabile* in the coming election; he was only fifty-four on January 22, 1999, and is the second youngest cardinal today.

CONCILIARISTS

A group of about twenty cardinals wishes to see a firm, committed return to the principles of the Second Vatican Council and the vision of John XXIII for the future of the Church. Although they are the fewest in number, the group includes some of the most powerful and influential members of the College—senior prelates who were raised to the cardinalate by Paul VI and have retained and expanded their power during the current reign, in spite of significant opposition to their views. The leadership of this group unofficially is in the hands of two Brazilian Franciscans, Paulo Evaristo Arns, emeritus archbishop of São Paulo, and Aloisio Lorscheider, archbishop of Aparecida; but it includes such influential cardinals as the Benedictine cardinal of England, George Basil Hume, archbishop of Westminster; Jaime L. Sin, archbishop of Manila; and Hyacinthe Thiandoum, archbishop of Dakar, Senegal.

The great weakness of the conciliarists as a party is advancing age. If they are to wield great influence in the coming election, the conclave must take place within the next two or three years, because, in general, they are among the older cardinals and the advancing years will thin their number both through death and superannuation. For example, a search already is under way to find a successor to Hume at Westminster, since he submitted his resignation from archiepiscopal office on reaching seventy-five on March 2, 1998. But replacing him hastily with a strong conservative in England is dangerous, since such an archbishop might derail the spirit of cooperation with Anglicans that Hume has done so much to foster.

The great strength of the conciliarists lies in the overwhelming desire of great numbers of Catholics to have "another John XXIII" as pope, a desire which nearly all the cardinal-electors who are residential ordinaries hear from their communicants almost daily. Another strength lies in the support they receive from a large number of the retired cardinals who still have both prestige and a voice in the affairs of the Church in their regions— among them are Corrado Ursi, the emeritus archbishop of Naples; Johannes Willebrands, the emeritus archbishop of Utrecht; Paul Zoungrana, the emeritus archbishop of Ouagadougou, Burkina Faso; and, especially, Franz König, the emeritus archbishop of Vienna, a surviving grand elector of 1978, and one of two surviving cardinals named to the College by John XXIII. These older cardinals already are active in the preliminary stages of the *prattiche*, giving strong support to the traditional concept of alternation in the papacy—that the Church does best when a conclave elects a pope whose policies diverge sharply from those of his predecessor.[2] Some of the conciliarists believe that they can join with the pragmatists to advance the cause of Martini in the next conclave. Martini, they hope, is sufficiently dedicated to the teachings of Vatican II to pull the Church back in the general direction envisioned by the council, especially towards the biblical roots of essential faith. Moreover, the conciliarists know that John Paul II's punishment of the Jesuits in 1981 does not sit well with many cardinals from religious orders, not just the Jesuits, since the major orders have a long tradition of self-government free of direct papal interference. They also hope that Martini will appoint new cardinals whose views of the council will be more in keeping with the ideas of Paul VI than those of John Paul II.

Of course, the membership of each of these groups is fluid to some degree. Many pragmatists are rather conservative in their doctrinal views, but realize that too strong an adherence to these views may not be in the best interests of the Church or the papacy in the opening years of the new millennium. Many conciliarists realize that some of the actions that Paul VI took to further the program of the council have proven to be destabilizing to the community of the "people of God," and should not be undertaken in their original form again.

Finally, members in all the groups face an issue which cuts across all party interests—namely, whether the Church is best served by electing another Italian pope, rather than to continue with the breaking of centuries of precedent which began with the election of John Paul II. In general, all the cardinals realize that Wojtyła was finally chosen because the October conclave in 1978 was swept away by the thought that they were shattering that precedent in choosing a Pole for Peter's chair. In retrospect, it seems to many of them a poor basis on which to choose a pope.

III. Issues

In the preliminaries of the *prattiche*, several major—often global—issues are under discussion, with a view to determining the opinions of major *papabili* about them, and how each of them may address the pressing problems in the next pontificate.

VOCATIONS

Of course, like any great, global organization, the Church must have a full, or nearly full, complement of staff to carry out its mission. But the decline in the number of persons in religious life, which began in the 1950s, has greatly diminished the capacity of the Church both to minister to the liturgical and ritual needs of the laity and to meet the growing demands on the Church's resources for social missions. The shortage is particularly acute in the advanced nations of Europe and North America, but it is not restricted to those continents. At first glance, the principal consequence would seem to be the abandonment or curtailment of many Church-supported activities. The Catholic schools in the United States, for example, have only a small percentage of teachers and administrators who belong to the religious orders which founded those schools and staffed them for decades. In fact, the larger issue is that the lower population of priests and religious has forced the Church to be more liberal and accepting of those few who do come forward with religious vocations. The centuries-long aphorism about those who wish to enter the life of the Church, ". . . many are called, but few are chosen,"[3] has, all too often, been revised out of necessity into "few are called, and most are chosen." This has led the Church into accepting candidates for religious life who would not have been permitted to enter in former times, when the larger pool of applicants gave bishops and religious superiors the chance to be highly selective. The recent scandals in the West about misappropriated monies, heterosexual misconduct, and active homosexuality and pedophilia, all point to a decline in the qualities, moral and spiritual, of the men who embrace a clerical life. The scandals, which already have brought down an Austrian cardinal and an American bishop, have illuminated the need for strong corrective action. But what can be done, in practical terms, since the need to staff the Church continues?

John Paul II has reacted, in part, by advancing older and older churchmen to offices of high responsibility, including the cardinalate—drawing personnel for the curia and the ordinariates disproportionately from the men who rose to the priesthood during a time when the crisis was less severe and the pathway to the altar longer and more difficult. At the end of 1998, of the one hundred one living cardinal-electors appointed by John Paul II only four were ordained after the end of the Second Vatican Council—Rivera Carrera, Pengo, Schönborn, and Puljic—which closed nearly three-and-a-half decades ago. The next pope will not have the option of concentrating the cardinalate, and much of the archiepiscopate, in the hands of a Tridentine, pre-conciliar clergy. Both the curia and the bishops know that the new pope must establish some method which will ensure that standards are raised again and that only more suitable candidates will achieve the priesthood, and, ultimately, the episcopate and the cardinalate. This difficulty in finding such a method is exacerbated by the closure of most minor seminaries and the rise in the number of three-year priests whose behavior has not been scrutinized in detail over many years by watchful superiors.

CONTRACEPTION

The Church's teachings on both abortion and contraception have been well established for hundreds of years, but modern popes chose not to address the issue of the latter in definite terms until Pius XI issued the encyclical, *Casti Connubii*, on December 31, 1930. His thundering condemnation of contraception, in chapters fifty-three through fifty-six of the document, left his successors with a heavy burden to uphold after the invention of modern medications and procedures made child-bearing a matter of easy choice:

> First consideration is due to the offspring, which many have the boldness to call the disagreeable burden of matrimony and which they say is to be carefully avoided by married people . . . by frustrating the marriage act. Since, therefore, the conjugal act is destined primarily by nature for the begetting of children, those who . . . frustrate its natural power and purpose sin against nature and commit a deed which is shameful and intrinsically vicious. . . . Any use whatsoever of matrimony exercised in such a way that the act is deliberately frustrated in its natural power to generate life is an offense against the law of God and of nature, and those who indulge in such are branded with the guilt of a grave sin.

When some of the council fathers proposed a rethinking of the question in the 1960s, and saw the establishment of a commission to investigate the question, there seemed as if there might be some means of ameliorating the blanket condemnation of Pius XI. The report of the commission, submitted to Paul VI early in 1968, took the position that some clarification of the earlier doctrine which admitted some contraceptive practices, beyond what had been permitted by Pius XII, who yielded on the question of the rhythm method, was possible. Paul VI, of course, rejected the report altogether and responded with the even-stronger encyclical, *Humanæ Vitæ*, on July 25, 1968. Today, especially in much of the developed world, the position taken by Pius XI and Paul VI seems no longer tenable. John Paul I was said to have been readying a new teaching on the subject when he died; but whether he was or not sets no precedent for the successor of John Paul II—other than to indicate that at least one other modern pope had thought the teaching worthy of clarification and elaboration. Privately, many prelates in responsible positions in the United States and Europe have argued that some change must be made, not just to acknowledge the crushing economic and financial burden that large numbers of children impose on Catholic married couples in the industrialized and post-industrial world, but also to free the moral strength of the Church for the even greater combat against the rising acceptance of abortion, which is viewed as a far graver threat to the integrity of moral teaching than contraception. Some cite one opinion poll in the United States, by the Associated Press, which found that eighty percent of Catholic couples were willing to admit that they used some form of artificial birth control.[4] Several have argued that divorcing the theological and moral imperatives of contraception and abortion from one another is a prerequisite to mustering the forces of the Church for a successful combat against abortion, where the link to infanticide is regarded as absolute. The cardinal-electors are well aware that great majorities of Catholics in even the most Catholic nations, like Poland and Ireland, as well as more religiously plural cultures, like the United States, simply ignore the teachings in *Casti Connubii* and *Humanæ Vitæ*, which does not bode well for having the laity acknowledge the authority of Rome on other matters which apply to their daily life in the future. The new pope will make some change in the current doctrine, or be faced with defending a teaching—more and more rejected—which places an interference with *chance* on the same theological and moral plane as an interference with *certainty*.

WOMEN AS PRIESTS AND BISHOPS

Catholicism now is the only major branch of Western Christianity not to have admitted women to its sacerdotal, ministerial, and teaching functions. While its failure to do so has little effect in many parts of the Catholic world, Latin America and Africa most notably, it has stirred increasing resentment in the more developed and historically ancient European world, including the United States.

John Paul II, in *Ordinatio Sacerdotalis*, in May, 1994, made his views quite clear—there will never be women in the priesthood. "In order that all doubt may be removed regarding a matter of great importance, I declare that the Church has no authority whatsoever to confer priestly ordination on women and that this judgment is to be definitively held by all the Church's faithful," he proclaimed.

As if this were not clear, it was followed, in December, 1995, by a *responsum ad dubium* from the Congregation for the Doctrine of the Faith which stated that there could be no doubt that this teaching now belonged to the deposit of the faith, and from it there could be no legitimate dissent: "This doctrine demands a definitive assent since it has been founded on the written Word of God and constantly preserved and applied by the Church since the beginning, and set forth infallibly by the ordinary and universal magisterium." This statement leaves the pope's decree just one step short of an infallible statement made *ex cathedra*.

The next pope will not see this issue disappear, in spite of John Paul's order to sweep it away. One solution, already rejected by John Paul II, but not so definitely, is a revival of the office of deaconess, which has a solid foundation in the New Testament. Such an action might prove an intermediate step to change, if the question of women's equality in the Church eventually becomes too great to ignore.

COLLEGIALITY AND PLURALISM

The local destabilization of the Church which has happened in many places in the past thirty years reflects, many cardinal-ordinaries believe, the errors made by the curia in simply ordering certain policies or events without regard to the wishes of the local bishop, who is far more likely to be better informed about issues in controversy than some cleric on the staff of a congregation or council in Rome. The huge centralization of authority achieved in Paul VI's revolution was not intended, most cardinals believe, to be turned into an autocratic establishment for the imposition of papal will, without consultation—but this is precisely what John Paul II has done with his inheritance of power.

The new pope must decide how much of the episcopal power that was reaffirmed by the Second Vatican Council will be returned to local ordinaries. This question of episcopal authority sometimes is the paramount point of discussion in the early stages of the *prattiche*, because many residential cardinals are well aware that not only they, but also the great majority of bishops under, or near, them, regard the rôle of messengers for the Roman curia as theologically unorthodox and politically impractical. In the age of rapid and mass communication, the Curia cannot simply dispatch orders, as they did in the time of Pius IX or Pius X, and then expect the Catholic faithful to fall quiescently into order behind the Roman banner.

FINANCE AND REVENUE

It is no secret that the financial status of the Vatican has been marginal for years. When Mussolini paid the settlement for which the Lateran Treaties of 1929 provided, the Church's administration was on a firmer financial footing than it had been at any time since at least the mid-eighteenth century. Indeed, at times earlier in this century, the Vatican was almost destitute, particularly in the reign of Benedict XV, who was notoriously improvident, especially in doling out large sums of cash to missionary bishops, or anyone else who pleaded with him for money for good works. He forestalled efforts by the curia to curtail his proverbial generosity by having his staff convert ready assets into cash, which he kept in the drawers of his desk, ready to be handed in wads to anyone who touched him with a plea.

Three successive popes—Pius XI, Pius XII, and John XXIII—were happy to leave the settlement payments in the hands of Nicola Canali, a supporter of Fascism and a genuinely cold and hard financier, who received the cardinalate for his financial wizardry. Under his guidance, the

Vatican's finances were handled carefully for long-term growth, and Paul VI inherited a treasury that was as full and solid as that of any well-managed government in the world. Unfortunately for Paul VI, Canali had died on August 3, 1961, and no one emerged with the same sort of expertise to do the job of financial management so well. In the vacuum, Paul was persuaded to allow a more risky—some might even say highly unethical—managerial style. The consequence was the Vatican's involvement in a whole series of questionable monetary transactions and scandals which brought its whole financial edifice very close to complete ruin. In fairness to Paul VI, it needs to be said that he wanted a larger flow of ready cash to be able to fund many new projects and bureaus in the Vatican that were devoted to implementing the wishes of Vatican II.

John Paul II inherited a nearly bankrupt treasury and a financial system that was both mismanaged and scandal-plagued. For the first dozen years of his reign, John Paul II struggled to achieve some fiscal stability. Part of his program for doing this was a series of meetings, like the plenary sessions of the College of Cardinals and assemblies with the presidents of the episcopal conferences, in which he pleaded for more revenues to be sent to Rome from the wealthier Catholic communities in the United States and Europe. To the pope's regret, these appeals came just at a time when Sunday collections and other monetary contributions by the laity in these developed nations were in sharp decline, partly because its opposition to *Humanæ Vitæ* and other papal pronouncements and partly because of the public reaction to the Vatican's financial scandals. Finally, in 1991, John Paul summoned Edmund Casimir Szoka, archbishop of Detroit, to assume control of the entire fiscal apparatus of the Vatican. Almost immediately, Szoka brought the Vatican's books back into the black for the first time in twenty-three years. Displaying much of the same native skill with money that seemed inborn in Canali—but without the latter's extremist politics or his personal nastiness—Szoka managed to build the financial stability of the system from a point at the close of his first year in office when the surplus was a few thousand dollars to a surplus of eleven million dollars in 1997, after six years of sound management. The short-term problem seems to be solved, but still greater needs for money, particularly to fund the Jubilee of the Year 2000, and to fund a better standard of living for the Vatican's employees, persist. The new pope will need to have a sound understanding of at least the fundamentals of fiscal management in order to choose what course will be taken in the future to ensure the Vatican's long-term stability.

IV. The Prattiche

The preliminary discussions among the cardinals about who may be the next pope begin as soon as physical signs of the pope's deteriorating health make it clear that a conclave cannot be far in the future. Some preliminary discussions can be very long—those that preceded the death of Leo XIII went on for nearly a decade, and were conducted in full measure for almost five years before he died at the age of ninety-three; those which preceded the death of Pius X in 1914 had hardly begun when he died. In modern times, only the death of John Paul I in 1978 came so suddenly that there were no preliminary discussions at all. Most, however, begin about three or four years before the pope's death. The *prattiche* of 1939 began in 1936, as soon as it became clear that Pius XI's worsening circulatory condition would be mortal. In the case of John XXIII, it can almost be said that it began on the day of his election, since he was chosen to be a transitional pope, to give the cardinals time to settle their differences before the next election. It certainly began in earnest during the second month of the reign, after Giovanni Battista Montini was elevated to the cardinalate on December 15, 1958, only one month and seventeen days after John was chosen. For the first conclave of 1978, it began just at the time Paul's favorite, Giovanni Benelli, was made archbishop of Florence, and then cardinal, in the spring of 1977, a year and a half before the pope died.

Because the pope is an absolute monarch, both spiritually and temporally, and because there is no heir apparent to his throne, popes have inveighed against the early *prattiche* in almost the same strong terms they have used to protect the secrecy of the conclave. Consequently, officially at least, the early evolutions of the process never happen. Cardinals whose names appear in the early discussions always deny, often genuinely, any ambition for the throne—Carlo Maria Martini, whose name is heard often today, offers that denial in the form of the statement that the only city for which he would leave Milan is Jerusalem, which obviously precludes Rome. The current preliminary discussions began soon after the consistory for the naming of new cardinals that John Paul II held in November, 1994. Many cardinals, as well as many hasty observers, were sure that this creation would be John Paul's last, and that the College had taken the general form it would have in the next election. The elevation of nineteen new electors in February, 1998, changed the direction of the *prattiche* by introducing Dionigi Tettamanzi as a major focus of discussion, but it did not slow the process down, or derail it in any significant way.

Today, the *prattiche* is more direct and more efficient than it has ever been before. From the later Middle Ages to the twentieth century, almost all of the early stages were carried out in Rome itself, because the curial cardinals made up so large a percentage of the College and because they were gathered together in the same city to work for the same bureaucracy. Other Italian cardinals were involved, somewhat more peripherally, since they were not too far away in their archdioceses scattered in the great Italian peninsula. Transalpine and, later, transoceanic cardinals knew little about the conversations of their colleagues in Italy. Often, they would arrive at the conclave with a need to be briefed on just who the principal candidates were. In 1939, and again in 1958, the telephone was used to some extent by "foreign" cardinals to keep abreast of the early electoral developments in Rome; as airplane travel became easier and more reliable, some cardinals began to make frequent visits to Rome for face-to-face meetings with their curial colleagues—in the 1950s, Francis Joseph Spellman of New York was a master of both devices. But it was only with the *prattiche* of 1963 that modern technologies really began to have an effect on the way in which the cardinals explore the possibilities for the next reign. The telephone, in particular, was the common device in the *prattiche* which led to the election of Montini as Paul VI. So effective was this form of long-distance negotiation that Montini himself only appeared in Rome in time to enter the conclave—most of the preparatory negotiations had been left in the hands of Archbishop Angelo Dell'Acqua in the curia. By 1978, Giovanni Benelli twice led almost all the *prattiche* by telephone from Florence and only a few, late meetings actually were held in Rome, in the days which led to the opening of the conclave. At century's end, the telefacsimile and electronic mail have been added to the tools of the *prattiche*, and these devices have made it possible for those whose health or age does not permit them to travel to participate, as well—Franz König, the emeritus archbishop of Vienna, remains a part of the series of conversations even though he became ninety-three on August 3, 1998. He still resides in the archbishop's residence in the Wollzeile, just behind the cathedral, and, presciently, just a few steps away from the Österreichische Computer Gesellschaft (Austrian Computer Association).[5]

In the current *prattiche*, the regional or national alignments which played so important a part in former times largely are absent, and such traditional groups are likely to have little effect in the coming election. When communication and travel were slow, the cardinals tended to group themselves according to their geography or language, because their neighbors were the other electors they knew best, and with whom they shared common interests, at least in some measure. By voting as blocs, such national groups often had a profound influence on conclaves—in 1914, the German cardinals were essential, as a bloc, to the outcome, while, in 1958, the

French cardinals led the way in electing John XXIII, largely because they had been impressed by his performance when he was nuncio to Paris during the late 1940s and early 1950s. By contrast, many of the present geographical groups of cardinals have no cohesive bond of any kind. Perhaps the American cardinals come closest to a traditional bloc; but other groups, like the Brazilians, for example, are divided radically along ideological lines: men like Lorscheider and Arns are the archconciliarists in the College, while their compatriot, Moreira Neves, is a leading conservative in doctrine and policy.

Instead of regional blocs, the College today has had a chance to align itself more firmly into ideological groups based on the interpretation of doctrine and on ways of understanding the Second Vatican Council. One innovation which has facilitated this realignment was the reestablishment of the College as a type of supercabinet of the pope. When John Paul II came to the throne in 1978, the whole College of Cardinals had not met as a body for advisory purposes since the late sixteenth century. For centuries, the only time that a large majority of the cardinals were gathered together in one place for one purpose was the conclave. John Paul decided to return to the practice of medieval popes in gathering the cardinals together to advise him formally on matters that he viewed as being of great importance—"to join them more closely to the pastoral mission of Peter," was his phrase to describe the cardinals in what were, in fact, large formal consistories. John Paul II has done this five times in his pontificate, beginning with the meeting of November 4–9, 1979. At that plenary session of the College, the paramount question was the Vatican's financial situation, which Paul VI had left in a very precarious state. Essentially, John Paul wanted the residential cardinals—the leading archbishops in their respective nations—to announce, in a somewhat competitive atmosphere, what steps they would take to alleviate the crisis. With considerably less interest, he also asked them for suggestions on the reform of the curia and to advise him on how the Church in wealthy nations could aid Catholicism in poorer countries more effectively—a purely pastoral question. The second plenary meeting, November 23–26, 1982, was convoked formally to discuss the reform of the curia, but was, in reality, another consultation on the matter of the Vatican's finances, which were now on the edge of collapse, in large measure because of the Vatican's involvement in the scandal of the Banco Ambrosiano in Milan.[6] The third, held November 20–22, 1985, was titled, like the extraordinary session of the Synod of Bishops which followed it immediately, "The Twentieth Anniversary of the Conclusion of the Second Vatican Council." It was less consultative than monitory. In it, the pope made it clear that episcopal conferences had only a limited consultative power, and were not, in any way, to be seen as collective extensions of individual episcopal power; and that the curia's dicta superseded all local decisions on matters of doctrine, government, and policy. This meeting was supposed to reflect on Vatican II, to determine the progress of the council's reforms, and to chart a further course based on the council's pronouncements. In fact, John Paul made the sessions an opportunity to reverse many of the council's reforms and to signal that the conciliar age, as most Catholics saw it, was over. The meeting of April 4–6, 1991, "The Church Facing the Threat Against Human Life and the Challenge of Sects," was called to consider the question of the failure of modern evangelism and the loss of large numbers of Catholic communicants to other Christian teachings, especially in Latin America, where Pentecostal and evangelical Protestants have made great inroads into a hitherto solid Catholic population; and to discuss a concerted, global front of Catholicism against both abortion and birth control. In other meetings at the same time, however, John Paul again pressed cardinals for more financial aid for the Vatican, as he did in his meeting with the presidents of episcopal conferences which followed it on April 8–9, and which also included many cardinals. The fifth, and probably last, plenary meeting of the College of Cardinals, June 13–14, 1995, was called to discuss how the Church would prepare for, and then celebrate, the Jubilee of the Third Millennium in the year 2000.

In these sessions, the cardinals had a substantial opportunity to hear the views of their colleagues on a wide variety of questions, from the pastoral to the financial, and to prepare, based on those collegial exchanges of views, estimates of *papabili* in the next election. The assemblies of the Synod of Bishops, of which there have been twelve in the present reign,[7] often have been described in the press as "dress rehearsals for the conclave," because so many cardinals have attended their sessions. In fact, the plenary meetings of the College can be described that way more accurately, at least for the groundwork of the *prattiche*.

The cardinals have begun each *prattiche* in modern times with a generalized idea of some of the characteristics that the new pope should possess. He should be a man in his middle sixties; a man of pastoral experience, but also with some curial work in his background; an apparently friendly and open man, with a personality in keeping with the expectations of the Catholics of his time; and an Italian. From Leo XIII to John Paul II, almost every pope has failed one, and sometimes two, of these five criteria, but never more than two. On the criterion of age, nine of the fourteen popes elected in the past two centuries have been between sixty-three and sixty-eight when they achieved the throne; three others were in their late 50s: Pius VI (57), John Paul II (58), and Pius VII (59); while Pius IX was only 54. By contrast, only one pope in that span of years was older when he was elected: John XXIII at 76.[8] On the question of experience, eleven of the popes who have been elected since the loss of States of the Church in 1870—Leo XIII and his successors—have had both curial and pastoral experience, while two, John Paul I and John Paul II, have had only pastoral experience. Only Pius XII came from an entirely curial background. Catholics under eleven of these fourteen popes generally have regarded the pontiff as warm, sympathetic, and apparently approachable—although not, obviously, to the same degree. Only three of the modern popes have been regarded as cold or distant, or both—Benedict XV, who never could project the attitude of sympathy and friendliness of his two predecessors, Leo XIII and Pius X; Pius XII, who compensated for his apparent coldness by a reputation for both personal sanctity and great intellect; and Paul VI, who was regarded as caring, but not warm or kindly, and who enjoyed instead the reputation of being a skilled, if sometimes vacillating, administrator who was devoted to implementing the wishes of Vatican II. Finally, of course, thirteen of the fourteen were Italian—as all forty-fives popes had been from 1523 to 1978.

Although John Paul II has continued and expanded the policy of Paul VI to widen the geographic and cultural representation of the College, in another sense the coming conclave will be the narrowest in history. In the next election, the cardinals, as a body, will come from the smallest span of age ever. If one assumes that the youngest cardinal at the present time, Vinko Puljic, archbishop of Sarajevo—born on September 8, 1945—also will be the youngest cardinal in the conclave, then all the electors will have lifespans between fifty-three and seventy-nine years. Indeed, only sixteen of the electors will be younger than sixty-five,[9] and only four of those are in their fifties—Rivera Carrera, Pengo, Schönborn, and Puljic. Thus, the great majority of the electors will fall within the extraordinarily narrow span of fourteen years in age. Even in 1978, under the provisions of *Romano Pontifici Eligendo*, the cardinals spanned ages from fifty to seventy-nine, and the population was shifted somewhat more in favor of younger cardinals than is the case today. Consequently, John Paul II's College of older cardinals may discount the criterion of age more than the cardinals have done in earlier conclaves. If they do, Carlo Maria Martini's chances for election are improved.

The cardinals in the most recent series of preliminary discussions, however, still have the fundamental résumé in mind—which is why three of the five prominent *papabili* discussed here are Italian; and two, Tettamanzi and Danneels, are *papabile* partly because they meet the traditional age qualification.[10] But, indeed, the one criterion that seems to have diminished in importance in recent conversations is that of age. This can be explained partly because the median age of the electors at the close of 1998 is seventy-two, and seventy-six of the one hundred fourteen electors are themselves over seventy; and partly by the dearth of candidates who are acceptable in other regards whose age approximates the ideal.

October 16, 1998, marked the twentieth anniversary of John Paul II's election to the papal chair. Already, on the preceding May 26, the length of his reign eclipsed the nineteen years, seven months, and seven days that Pius XII occupied the throne, making John Paul II the longest reigning pope of the twentieth century. That moment also made him the twelfth longest reigning pope of more than two hundred fifty bishops of Rome.[11] Should his reign extend to the beginning of 2000, it will exceed those of four more popes and make John Paul II the eighth longest serving pontiff. Some, perhaps most, of the cardinals think that this is unlikely to happen. One prelate has said that the pope's insistence of reaching the goal of the millennium is, itself, a form of tragic *hubris* that is doomed to fail for that precise reason.

In any case, the current *prattiche* is moving, just now, from early exploratory conversations and exchanges of views to a more positive examination of policies and programs which the leading cardinals espouse today, and the possibilities which may follow if one of them is elected to the papacy in the near future.

V. Papabili

LUCAS MOREIRA NEVES

Neves, the eldest of ten children, was born in São João del Rei, Brazil, on September 16, 1925. His paternal grandfather was the son of slaves, so Neves is one-fourth African, a fact in which he takes great pride. Interestingly, his African ancestors are reputed to have come from the Dahomey coast, now Benin, so he may be a distant relative of the man whom he succeeded, in 1998, as prefect of the Congregation of Bishops, Bernardin Gantin, whose geographical origins also are in the same region.

Neves became a Dominican, made his vows on March 7, 1948, and was ordained on July 9, 1950. He was soon transferred to Rio de Janeiro to become editor-in-chief of *Mensagero do Santo Rosario*, and later, he became head of religious education for the Brazilian Bishops' Conference. On June 9, 1967, he was made titular bishop of Feradi Major and auxiliary bishop of São Paulo. His work for the bishops' conference brought him to the attention of Pope Paul VI. Consequently, in 1974 he was summoned to Rome as vice president of the Pontifical Commission for the Laity. On October 15, 1979, Pope John Paul II made him titular archbishop, and, on the same date, he became secretary of the Congregation of Bishops.

After years of disagreement with the prefect of the Congregation, Sebastiano Baggio, the tension eventually became too great to continue without seriously affecting the work of the bureaucracy. In response to growing complaints, on January 3, 1987, John Paul made him titular archbishop of Vescovio, and then, six months later, made him archbishop of São Salvador da Bahia and primate of Brazil, on July 9, 1987, in succession to Avelar Brandão Vilela, who had died on December 19, 1986. This appointment moved him out of the curia and gave him the opportunity to gain the pastoral experience that is essential for a successful candidate for the throne.

After he returned to Brazil, Neves became a leader in opposing reform movements, both agrarian and social, which did not endear him to the majority of the laity there. An example of his consideration for reformers was his peremptory handling of the representatives of a leading organization for agrarian reform. In July, 1991, he was asked by representatives of the Sem Terra Movement to intercede on their behalf for a papal audience with John Paul when he visited Brazil, between October 12 and October 21 of that year. Neves said that he would forward the request, but only if the leaders of Sem Terra promised that "they [would] not ask the Holy Father to intercede with the government for land reform, but only seek to inform him of the poor conditions in which their people live in rural Latin America."

John Paul II, who always has respected his strong doctrinal conservatism, recalled him to Rome after ten years as archbishop. On June 25, 1998, John Paul II named the Brazilian to be the new prefect of the Congregation of Bishops and president of the Pontifical Commission for Latin America, in succession to Bernardin Gantin, the dean of the College, who retired because of age. At the same time, Neves was made cardinal-bishop of Sabina in succession to Eduardo Pironio.

In his favor, he projects warmth and modesty, and prefers a very informal style of life—he does not have a secretary, and prefers to write his letters by himself.

One of the principal problems Neves will face in the opening days of the formal *prattiche*, after John Paul dies, is the open hostility of Paulo Evaristo Arns, now the emeritus archbishop of São Paulo. The two Brazilians have never been friends, since Arns is one of the most vocal defenders of both Vatican II and Paul VI, while Neves is an archconservative who is associated closely, and personally, with John Paul II.

On the Brazilian stage, often in public and sometimes loudly, they have played out their version of the age-old rivalry between the Franciscans and the Dominicans. The most recent open rupture between the two occurred when Arns submitted his resignation as archbishop on the occasion of his seventy-fifth birthday, September 14, 1996. Arns, who is a strong supporter of dissenting theologians, such as Leonardo Boff, said that he expected his resignation to be accepted immediately, because "the Pope has totally turned his power over to the Roman Curia." Arns continued, in an interview printed in *O Estado de São Paulo*: "Since 1978, when Pope Paul VI died, I have been the victim of hostility from the Roman Curia because of my positions, . . . John Paul is a great person himself, but. . . he does not agree with me." Neves, then the primate of Brazil, took the opportunity to respond with a sharply worded statement, seemingly just for the sake of exacerbating old wounds:

> Several times we have heard reports insisting that the pope is sick or that he is not in control of the government of the Church. The truth, nevertheless, is that the Holy Father is the true pontiff that leads the destiny of the Church. . . . Stories about the opposition or tension between the curia and the pope are inaccurate, since, at present, the whole curia has been appointed personally by the pope himself.

An interesting riposte, since Arns was not attacking John Paul II. In any case, Arns' resignation was not taken up until 1998.

Neves' early work in favor of the Christian Family Movement, *Sacerdotes a Servico da Familia: un Manual para os Assistentes Eclesiasticos do MFC*, was so popular in Brazil that it quickly achieved a second edition a year after its first publication.[12] The book's success warranted a second volume in the series, *Restaurar a Familia em Cristo: O Movimento Familiar Cristao: o Que E, Como se Organiza, o Que Pretende*, which also went through a number of editions.[13] These works paved the way for his career as a priest-journalist and for his initial appointment with the Brazilian Conference of Bishops. More recently, while archbishop of São Salvador da Bahia, he published volumes of essays which were collected from articles he had written for *A Tarde* and *Jornal do Brasil*: *Vigilante Desde a Aurora* appeared in 1989,[14] *Como Olhar de Pastor* in 1990,[15] *Por-do-sol em Reritiba e Outras Cronicas* in 1992,[16] and *O Homem Descartavel e Outras Cronicas*[17] and *O Alferes e o Presidente e Outras Cronicas*, both in 1995.[18] In addition, after the meeting of the fourth General Conference of the Latin American Episcopate in Santo Domingo in 1992, he edited a volume of analysis and commentary on it, *Santo Domingo: Analisis y Comentarios*.[19]

Though Neves' name is spoken frequently as *papabile*, and though he is discussed widely in the *prattiche*, he is the least likely of the prominent candidates to win the throne. The strong conservatives are the largest single bloc of voters who will enter the next conclave, and Neves is their candidate—he also is said to be the favorite of John Paul II for the succession. Neves, however, is severely diabetic, with growing problems caused by the disease, and he was seventy-three years old on September 16, 1998. If the party that supports him can rush him forward on the first or second ballot, by gathering enough moderate conservatives to support him, based on an appeal to the memory of John Paul II, he may just barely win the throne. If not, most observers think that his candidacy will fade quickly; although he may, thereby, become a grand elector by urging his supporters to vote for another candidate who is more moderate in outlook, like Tettamanzi, or even Danneels.

SILVANO PIOVANELLI

If the conclave becomes deadlocked between two irreconcilable parties early in the election, the cardinals may turn to a transitional candidate—a cardinal of more advanced age who is thought to be a capable administrator but one whose papal reign is likely to be short and whose penchant for innovation is thought to be small. This can lead to serious miscalculation, of course, because some of the most dramatically individual popes have been elected as transitional pontiffs, like Sixtus V in 1585 and John XXIII in 1958. Should the cardinals decide to take this course, their first choice probably will be Silvano Piovanelli, archbishop of Florence.

Piovanelli, a native Tuscan, was seventy-five on February 21, 1999, and submitted his resignation as archbishop. After he was ordained on July 13, 1947, he had a modest career in the clergy of the archdiocese of Florence, until Giovanni Benelli accepted him as an auxiliary bishop in May, 1982. Benelli, already ill from the heart condition which would kill him within months, badly needed an auxiliary to relieve him of some of his archiepiscopal functions, and Piovanelli seemed the right man to deal in a workmanlike manner with day-to-day affairs.

When Benelli died, on the following October 26, Piovanelli became his successor on the grounds of his conservative credentials and his limited experience as auxiliary, largely because there did not seem to be another suitable candidate for the position. His appointment as archbishop was issued on March 18, 1983.

Piovanelli, who has not been particularly outspoken on public affairs, even though he is vice president of the Italian Episcopal Conference, had an easy opportunity to reinforce his conservative reputation in 1998.

When he returned from a visit to Africa in July, he was surprised to find that Florence's city council had passed an act which opened the city's common-law marriage rolls to homosexuals. Like an earlier action by the Pisan city government, the act has no legal force, because the register is symbolic and those who enroll are not regarded as having been legally married because they have done so. Piovanelli was publicly outraged, however, and took the opportunity to publish a short riposte to the council of his city in *L'Osservatore Romano* on July 31. Most of the essay consisted of restatements of the obvious; the step "is against the teachings of the Church, that does not correspond to our society's or to traditional Christianity's concept of family." He went on to add: "The registry—to my way of seeing—does not alleviate the suffering and the possible marginalization of those who might be, and often are, the victims of homosexuality." Unlike the other papabili, Piovanelli has published little in his career. One small contribution was a seventy-page tract, *Andiamo alla Casa del Signore!: Lettera Pastorale, 1996.*[20]

GODFRIED DANNEELS

Godfried Danneels was born on June 4, 1933, in Kanegem, in western Flanders, and was ordained on August 17, 1957. In 1959, he was made spiritual director of the major seminary at Brugge (Bruges), but he soon left that position to study theology at the Gregorianum. In 1969, he was appointed professor of Liturgy and Sacramental Theology at the Catholic University of Louvain. After years in academia, he was made him bishop of Antwerpen (Antwerp) by Paul VI on November 4, 1977, and was consecrated on the following December 18. John Paul II speedily advanced him to be Suenens's successor as archbishop of Mechelen-Brusell (Malines-Bruxelles) on December 19, 1979. He also became president of the Belgian Episcopal Conference at about the same time. His metropolitan see includes, as suffragans, the linguistically and culturally diverse dioceses of Antwerpen, Brugge, Ghent, Hasselt, Liege, Namur, and Tournai—about as diverse a group of jurisdictions as it is possible to find in one small region of Europe.

In Rome, he is given credit for having defused much of the anti-Roman sentiment of the Belgian clergy, which had developed under the open rule of his predecessor, Leo Suenens. He accomplished this difficult task by adopting the position of a quiet mediator, rather than of a more autocratic primate.

Although a conservative in his outlook, he is not nearly as inflexible as John Paul II. In one recent interview, he commented:

> People do not want a strict, authoritarian line. They want a pastor.

> They want a bridge back to the Church that is deep in them, a Church they are away from. I have tried to be a bridge. . . . Truth— Too much we are stressing the truth, absolute truth. In the future, I would say we should not be so much in the truth as in the mercy. There are exceptions for everything; every human being knows that.

And, in speaking of the next conclave, he added:

> If you are a bishop, you hear the cries of the world, and these cries I know will be ringing in your ears when the Sistine Chapel is sealed. And whether I am alive to be there or not, those walls must hear not talk of laws but of evangelization, to make Catholicism radical in its love and outreach and compassion—not in its unbending adherence to laws. . . . Any man who enters the conclave desiring to be pope must either be mad or unconscious. He should be forced, dragged to the chair of Saint Peter. A good pope should never have thought of himself as pope in the first place. And once elected, a good pope should never think of himself as pope.

He also said bluntly that John Paul II's encyclical, *Veritatis Splendor,* "is not the best of the encyclicals, but it is an important document."

Significantly, Danneels was asked not long ago to preside over a day-long retreat with the bishops of the United States. This is just the sort of signal that episcopal conferences give when the cardinals who are members wish to vet a prospective pope.

Unlike the present pope, however, Danneels does not project exceptional warmth or sympathy, for he is basically a quiet and reserved man, although he has been known to give a spirited speech when moved. One commentator has said of him, "Danneels [offers] all the charisma of an over-cooked turnip." But the same writer also emphasized that Danneels

> has earned great admiration from his fellow cardinals, who look upon him as a well-travelled intellectual, aware of global differences within the Church and not frightened by them. [He] has a reputation as an excellent consensus builder and a tough voice for moderation.

Like many of the influential cardinals today, Danneels has written a large number of works, from reference works to spiritual tracts. Perhaps the best-known of his popular writings are on the development of faith, including *Les Saisons de la Vie.*[21] He also has published a number of short essays, sermons, and lectures, of which the best are *Devenir des Hommes Nouveaux: Lettres d'Esperance*[22] and *Words of Life.*[23] But perhaps his most important recent work is a small tract on the New Age Movement, which originally was published by his archdiocese, but has been translated into both

Spanish and English, *Christ or Aquarius? Exploring the New Age Movement*.[24] There also is a work with biographical commentary, *De Mensliev-endheid van God: gesprekken met Gwendoline Jarczyk*,[25] which also has appeared in French as *L'Humanité de Dieu*.[26]

Although he underwent triple-bypass surgery in April, 1996, his recovery was complete, and he is said to be far stronger today than he was before his circulatory condition was repaired. Danneels is not being overlooked in the *prattiche*, and he has gained a quiet following on every side of the political spectrum. Should the moderate conservatives fail to succeed with Dionigi Tettamanzi, who has emerged as their strongest candidate, they may well turn to Danneels, who will appeal more strongly to both the pragmatists and the conciliarists than the Genoese archbishop.

DIONIGI TETTAMANZI

Tettamanzi, a native Lombard, became sixty-four on March 14, 1998.[27] After he received his doctorate from the Gregorianum in 1959, he receded into academic obscurity. In 1987, he became rector of the Pontifical Lombard Seminary in Rome. Then, two years later, he joined the staff of the Congregation for the Doctrine of the Faith. Once John Paul II had identified him as a loyal conservative who might well provide an alternative to a more liberal Italian in the future conclave, his rise was swift. From 1989 to 1991, he was archbishop of Ancona-Osimo. Then he was made secretary general of the Italian Episcopal Conference, a papal appointment rather than an elective office. Finally, in 1995, he became archbishop of Genoa, with the assurance of the cardinalate in the next consistory, and vice president of the Italian Episcopal Conference. On February 28, seven days after he was made a cardinal, John Paul enhanced his relationship with the curia by appointing him a member of the Congregation for the Doctrine of the Faith, the Congregation for Catholic Education, and the Pontifical Council for Social Communications, three of the most powerful elements of the Vatican's bureaucracy.

No one argues that Tettamanzi's breadth of intellect or depth of scholarship rivals that of his neighbor, Carlo Maria Martini of Milan. Nevertheless, he has published more than twenty books and collections of essays which have had a significant effect on Church thought on bioethics, medical ethics, and the responsibilities of physicians. Tettamanzi first made his mark with a long tract on the council's pastoral constitution on the Church in the modern world, *La Chiesa Incontro al Mondo*,[28] and a little tract on the laity in the Church, in the spirit of the council, *Il Laico Rivive nella*

Chiesa il Mistero di Cristo.[29] However, he quickly turned his attention to a spirited defense of *Humanæ Vitæ*, which he has maintained undiminished ever since.

Beginning with *Humanæ Vitæ: Commento all'Enciclica sulla Regolazione delle Nascite,*[30] *and continuing through La Risposta dei Vescovi all'Humanæ Vitæ,*[31] *La Famiglia Via della Chiesa,*[32] *Un'Enciclica Profetica: la Humanæ Vitæ Vent'anni Dopo,*[33] and, most recently, *Alle Sorgenti della Vita: Humanæ Vitæ, Attualita di un'Enciclica,*[34] he has always defended Paul VI's principles. But his most important contributions to modern Church thinking have been in bioethics and medical ethics, beginning with articles he wrote between 1981 and 1986 which were revised and collected as *Bioetica: Nuove Sfide per l'Uomo.*[35] Other works in the field include *Custodi e Servitori della Vita: Problemi Medico-morali,*[36] *Bambini Fabbricati: Fertilizzazione in vitro, Embryo Transfer,*[37] and *Eutanasia: l'Illusione della Buona Morte.*[38] He also has contributed large modern tracts on general Christian ethics, *Verita e Liberta: Temi e Prospettive di Morale Cristiana*[39] and *Temi di Morale Fondamentale.*[40] While all of his works hew close to the official teachings of the Church in the time of John Paul II, he does consistently display a real spirit of sympathetic understanding and careful thought which may make him attractive as a candidate for the throne who could bring about some change in the policy on contraception, for example.[41] In January, 1998, Tettamanzi became the national ecclesiastical assistant, or principal clerical advisor, of the Associazione Medici Cattolici Italiani, in recognition of his contributions.

Surprisingly, perhaps because of his long studies in bioethics in which he has learned much about medical and scientific evidence, Tettamanzi has adopted a more conciliatory attitude toward homosexuality than many of his colleagues, and has been rather clear in expressing his opinions. In the spring of 1997, *L'Osservatore Romano* ran a series of fourteen articles which discussed homosexuality from a variety of points of view—historical, philosophical, theological, and pastoral. Tettamanzi wrote the leading contribution to the series, in which he took as his point of departure, the statement in the new catechism:

> The number of men and women who have deep-seated homosexual tendencies is not negligible. They do not choose their homosexual condition; for most of them it is a trial. They must be accepted with respect, compassion and sensitivity. Every sign of unjust discrimination in their regard should be avoided. These persons are called to fulfill God's will in their lives and, if they are Christians, to unite to the sacrifice of the Lord's cross the difficulties they may encounter from their condition (2358).

In that light, Tettamanzi's critical statement in his essay embodied a much less severe view than Catholic tradition dictates. While he condemned licentious behavior, both heterosexual and otherwise, he went on to express an understanding which seems quite advanced for an Italian archbishop:

> The Catholic Church does not have a separate set of criteria for judging the morality of heterosexual and homosexual activity. . . . All questions about sexual morality, including those related to homosexual acts, must be judged in the light of human dignity and the God-given human vocation to love and be loved.

He pointed out that dealing with the topic requires avoiding the danger of forgetting that the same moral principles apply to both heterosexuality and homosexuality; and that the dignity, identity, and final destiny of the person must be the criteria on which the judgment of the morality of all sexual acts is based.[42]

In November, 1995, in Palermo, the Italian Episcopal Conference held a national meeting called "The Gospel of Charity for a New Society in Italy," to deal with the political reality which followed the Mani Pulite campaign and the collapse of the Christian Democrats. The meeting was designed to be exceptionally practical, as John Paul II acknowledged when he said that its object was to "redefine the Church's identity and presence in the present historical context." Tettamanzi was a leader both in organizing the meeting, as the new vice president of the Italian Episcopal Conference, and in conducting its sessions. He broke new ground in the religious life of Italy by having the sessions include important representatives of non-Catholic religious organizations, including the Orthodox Metropolitan Papagheorghiuo Spiridion; the influential evangelical pastor, Domenico Tomasetto; Rabbi Giuseppe Laras; and Abdel El Kettani, the director of the Islamic Institute in Rome.

At the conference, in reference to the political future of the Church in Italy in the *dopodemocristiani*, Tettamanzi said, "It is a question of referring to indisputable principles such as the promotion of everyone's personal dignity, particularly for the poor and the needy in a context and a style of mutual respect."

For the first time, at least in the present reign, there was a final summary and a vote on the conference's conclusions, the central one of which was that each individual was free to find his or her own solutions to each "novel situation" in the context of the "various challenges" offered by the modern world. This conclusion, which Tettamanzi backed to the fullest, marked the Church's final political liberation of the faithful in Italy, as well as the official end of the decades-long connection between the Church and the Christian Democrats. It also heightened Tettamanzi's reputation as a more moderate prelate.

Some observers of the *prattiche* believe that Tettamanzi, who has a broad spectrum of personal respect from both progressive and conservative cardinals, was appointed to Genoa and then elevated to the College specifically to be an alternative to Martini in the next conclave, if the cardinals determine that the time has come for another Italian pope. Those who see him as that alternative, however, believe that he may have difficulty in developing support from both pragmatists and conciliarists because of his ties to Opus Dei.

CARLO MARIA MARTINI

Carlo Maria Martini, Giovanni Colombo's successor at Milan, is the principal pragmatist candidate in the next conclave. Although he is now older than the usual candidate—he was born in Turin on February 15, 1927—he has an intellectual and pastoral background with which few of his colleagues can compete. He joined the Jesuits in 1944 and was ordained in 1952, when he was only twenty-five, very young for a Jesuit. By 1969, he was the rector of the Pontifical Biblical Institute, and, in 1978, he became rector of the Gregorianum. On the strong recommendation of Sebastiano Baggio, then the prefect of the Congregation of Bishops, he was made archbishop of Milan on December 29, 1979, even though he had no earlier curial or pastoral experience.

He speaks eleven languages and has written more than forty books, both monographs and scholarly translations. More interesting in recent times have been the number of books written about him, anticipating perhaps his further rise in the Church. The first was Vittorio De Luca's *Un Vescovo, una Citta: Carlo Maria Martini*[43] which was followed quickly by Giovanni Valentini's *Un Certo, Carlo Maria Martini*[44] and Marco Garzonio's *Cardinale a Milano in un Mondo Che Cambia nella Testimonianza di Carlo Maria Martini*, which included commentary on Martini's understanding of doctrine as well as biographical material.[45] Most recently came Marco Garzonio's *Carlo Maria Martini.*[46] The subtitle of the last work called special attention both to Martini's fifteen years of archiepiscopal experience and to his position as the successor of Saint Ambrose, one of the great Church fathers and Milan's most famous bishop. In addition, several volumes of his correspondence and sermons have been published, which adds to, and complements, his large body of scholarly work. In all, he has written more, and had more published about him, than any other modern cardinal.

There is no doubt that outside the ecclesial community Martini is the favorite candidate. Chancellor Helmut Kohl clearly hopes that Martini will be the next pope: "Europe needs more than ever a spirit of dialogue, beyond the limits of religion and confessional belief. One of the great merits of Martini is that of having for a long time underlined this need with great insistence." Aleksei II, the Russian Orthodox patriarch, also shares that hope: "He [Martini] keeps alive in us the hope for the possibility of dialogue between two apostolic Churches that were so tragically divided a long time ago . . . Never have we heard from him ambiguous theological declarations, similar to those that have come from other sources, regarding the 'non fullness' or a certain 'lacking' on the part of the churches that are not under the jurisdiction of Rome."

But Martini is not well loved by the conservatives, including John Paul II. When asked to comment on the man, his intellect, and his character, Joseph Ratzinger, prefect of the Congregation for the Doctrine of the Faith, simply said that Martini was an "untiring master of the *lectio divina*," but, he added, "no one will be surprised if I say that we have not always been of the same opinion. . . by temperament and by formation we are very different one from the other."

Martini is not shy about expressing his views on the major issues which confront the Church today. Sometimes he is a bit elliptical, as when he said that he thought the Church's position on contraception had not been explained as well as it could be—an oblique reference to the need for change. On other matters, he has been more forthright. When he visited Harvard Divinity School, some time ago, Martini noted that the critical shortage of priests has grown worse in the past two decades. He suggested that a solution may be to expand the rôle of deacons, and ordaining women as deacons, he continued, would be "a good step" even though John Paul II had opposed this idea. "The Holy Father had good reasons," Martini commented. "I don't see the same reasons, but I accept what he said." Sometimes, he added, "a stop sign in traffic does not only mean to stop. It also can mean to try another way."

Martini also opposes excesses in liturgy and rite, which puts him at odds with Opus Dei and other new movements of archconservative Catholicism. He signalled again his resistance to popular enthusiasms that lie outside the message of the Gospel when he forbade the "healing exorcist," Emmanuel Milingo, the exiled Zambian archbishop of Lusaka—appointed by Paul VI in 1969 to succeed Adam Kozlowiecki, now a cardinal—who has been preaching in Italy for many years, to conduct his services in the archdiocese of Milan. Martini's announcement, while largely overlooked outside Italy, made headlines in almost every Italian newspaper.

He is a leader in the Jewish–Christian dialogue, which has prompted one Jewish authority, Rabbi David Rosen, to comment, when he discussed the "powerful and common bonds" which Judaism and Christianity share, and how they are to be translated into a closer relationship, that he had to single out "Cardinal Carlo Maria Martini, [who has] been very dedicated in his attempts to renew and reinvigorate Catholic–Jewish relations."

He is the acknowledged leader for a wider ecumenism from within the Catholic Church. When the ecumenical theologian and general secretary of the World Council of Churches, Konrad Raiser, suggested that perhaps the world's principal Christian traditions should use the year 2000 to start a "conciliar process" to prepare for a universal council, Martini reacted with some alacrity: "We must all move towards a time when it will be possible for all to celebrate in peace such a universal council. It is a profound Christian idea which corresponds to the Council of Jerusalem." This was in sharp contrast to the response of Joseph Ratzinger, who said that only the Petrine principle of papal supremacy, and not "conciliarity," could restore the unity of the Christian Church. To consider any other way would be, continued Ratzinger, "a romantic, unrealistic dream."

Martini is popular, respected, admired—and some might say loved—in the archdiocese of Milan, where his style is very different from the autocratic one of John Paul II. If the precedent of alternation is maintained in the next election, then he may well be the next pope. Milan, Europe's largest diocese, already has provided the pastoral experience for two of the last six popes, Pius XI and Paul VI, so it will come as no surprise, especially to Italian Catholics, if it does so again in the near future.

Martini's views on the acceptance of married priests, women in the Church, contraception, ecumenism, and collegiality reflect, for the most part, the prevailing informed opinion among Catholics in the developed world, at least.

Finally, no book on conclaves can end without a mention of the spurious "Prophecies of Saint Malachy," which were concocted near the end of the sixteenth century to support the candidacy of Cardinal Girolamo Simoncelli, the great-nephew of Julius III. The prophecy attached to the next reign is *Gloria olivæ* (*The glory of the olive*). One commentator, who unabashedly hopes for the election of Martini, points out that no one could fit the prophecy better than Milan's archbishop, since the true "glory of the olive" comes when it rests comfortably at the bottom of the glass that holds a serving of Europe's most famous cocktail.

VI. The Next Pope

The situation in the *prattiche* today suggests that Carlo Maria Martini of Milan will enter a conclave in 1999 with a larger, more committed body of supporters than any other candidate—much as Giovanni Battista Montini, his second predecessor at Milan, did in the conclave of 1963. It seems clear that he will be supported by a mixed group of pragmatists, conciliarists, and even some moderate conservatives who will give him perhaps as many as fifty votes on the first ballot. His principal strengths lie in his very successful pastoral experience in Milan, Europe's largest diocese; and his unquestioned reputation as the foremost scholar, especially in matters of the New Testament, not only in the College of Cardinals but more broadly in the hierarchy and the Church. Even his age of seventy-two may work in his favor, since his pontificate certainly will be expected to be shorter than average, and much shorter than that of John Paul II—although he will not be a transitional pope in the traditional sense of the word, a caretaker pontiff who will make few alterations in the nature or conduct of papal government while the cardinals continue with the informal *prattiche*. The cardinals who elect Martini, if they do, will have no illusions about that—after all, the last pope chosen as transitional was John XXIII, and he proved to be the most determined and masterful pope of the century.

Of course, there is considerable truth in the old Roman maxim that he who enters the conclave a pope, emerges as a cardinal. While Martini's candidacy is discussed perhaps more than that of any other cardinal, he certainly cannot be regarded as the certain pope. He is widely opposed by a large number of strong conservatives who are wary of his frank liberal expressions on some of the leading issues in the Church today—certainly both Ratzinger and Neves, both leading figures of the curia today, will work hard to forestall Martini's election.

One tradition that Martini's supporters will have to overcome is that a Jesuit cardinal is never elected pope. This will be hard to do, because John Paul II has had such a stormy relationship with the order that some strong conservatives may think that Martini will exert himself to overturn or revise many of the present pope's most cherished policies out of some sense of revenge. But only the bitterest enemies of Martini and some of the most conservative adherents of John Paul II are likely to entertain these thoughts after the balloting begins. It does not seem as if the College today has so formidable a conservative leader as Siri was in 1963 and 1978.

The sense of crisis which pervades the College today is strikingly similar in its tone to that in 1878, when Pecci became Leo XIII, and 1963, when Montini became Paul VI. Martini's candidacy, too, has parallels with the pre-conclave discussions about Pecci and Montini. Milan's archbishop has a substantial and dedicated following, but not the necessary majority to ensure election. The majority of the curial cardinals do not support his views or his cause, but a few influential members of the curia—Achille Silvestrini, for one—will work strenuously to promote his election, much as Bartolini worked to secure the accession of Pecci and Angelo Dell'Acqua worked for Montini. A number of the residential cardinal archbishops in Italy also support him, or would be willing to do so with some persuasion, perhaps even his chief rival in the *prattiche*, Dionigi Tettamanzi of Genoa.

A man who can conciliate and unite such disparate views as those of Hume and Lorscheider, Silvestrini and Cé, and perhaps Tettamanzi and Lustiger, should be able to win the throne in a measured and methodical progression of compromise and negotiation. With that in mind, Carlo Maria Martini probably will be the next pope.

What name will the next pope choose? The custom that a man takes a new name when he accedes as bishop of Rome begins only in the tenth century, with one earlier example.[47] Since that time, the great majority of the popes have chosen to reign with a name other than their baptismal one, although nothing prevents a pontiff from retaining his original name—the last to do so was Marcello Cervini degli Spannochi, one of the first three presidents of the Council of Trent, who became Marcellus II, but reigned only from April 9 to May 1, 1555.

Popes weigh the choice of their names carefully, although often quickly. Some have wished to commemorate an earlier pope who had been a friend and patron, as Pius XII did to memorialize Pius XI. Some have chosen the name of an earlier pope whose acts and person they admire—Benedict XV, who had been archbishop of Bologna before he became pope, chose his name because he admired Benedict XIV (August 17, 1740–May 3, 1758), who had been the next earlier archbishop of Bologna to ascend the throne. Some have grounded their choices on historical, philosophical, or literary images. Cardinal Enea Silvio Bartolommeo de' Piccolomini chose to be Pius II when he was elected on August 19, 1458. He did this not from admiration for the shadowy figure of Pius I (140–155), but because his baptismal name was Æneas and the epithet that Vergil uses most in the *Æneid* to describe the Trojan hero and founder of Latium is *Pius* (*dutiful*). Something of a profligate humanist before he was chosen, Pius II said to the cardinals on announcing his name, "Reject Æneas, accept Pius." Pius III (September 22–October 18, 1503) was the nephew of Pius II.[48] By contrast, when Pietro Barbo was elected Pius II's successor on August 30, 1464, he announced that he would be called Formosus II. The word *formosus* means *handsome* in Latin, and the new pope was regarded by his contemporaries as strikingly good looking. The cardinals, knowing that the new pope had gone too far, persuaded him to select another name. He became Paul II.

John XXIII expected a short reign, and recalled to the cardinals how most of the popes with that name likewise lasted only short periods of time. He had other commemorations, as well, which he explained in his somewhat lengthy speech on his election. Paul VI gave no direct explanation for choosing the name he did, but the association of Paul III (1534–1549) with the convocation of the Council of Trent may have suggested to Montini a similar parallel between himself and the Second Vatican Council, to which he genuinely was devoted.

John Paul I said that he wished to commemorate both of the popes of the council, John XXIII and Paul VI, the earlier of whom had made him a bishop, and the latter, a cardinal. Moreover, the dual name is one epithet, *Gianpaolo* or *Giampaolo*, in the dialect of the Veneto, from which John Paul I came. John Paul II wished to be called Stanislas, but was told, bluntly, by Franz König, one of the grand electors of the conclave, that he would be called John Paul II—the Austrian cardinal knew well the value of continuing the precedent of John Paul I, after the short but hopeful and exciting reign of Albino Luciani. Few popes have chosen their names because of public expectations, but John Paul II did.

If Carlo Maria Martini is elected, the names Paul VII (for the great figure of the New Testament, which Martini has studied all his life, as well as for Paul VI and the associations with Vatican II) or Ignatius (the *man of fire*, for Iñigo Yañez de Oñez y Loyola y Saenz de Lieona y Balda, the founder of the Society of Jesus) may occur to him. But if he wishes to revive hope among the world's Catholics, he will revive the most common of all papal names and become John XXIV.

NOTES

1. Ignoring the principle of alternation in papal elections—and the possibilites of *papabile* like Carlo Maria Martini, Godfried Danneels, and even Dionigi Tettamanzi—Jeffery L. Sheler and Eleni Dimmler write "The next pope. . . will not be a clone of John Paul II, but he likely will be a man after John Paul's own heart: as beholden to tradition, as resistant to altering controversial teachings on human sexuality and the role of women in the church, and as committed to strengthening the spiritual discipline of the faithful throughout the world." Their commentary on the pope's health in 1998, however, does reflect the consensus of opinion: ". . . it appears certain that John Paul II, besides bearing the signs of six surgeries and the 1981 attempt on his life, also suffers from Parkinson's disease or a comparable disorder. The telltale symptoms—a slow, shuffling walk, hand tremors, and occasional slurring of speech—have become increasingly apparent." Among other contributions to speculation on the radio was the offering of the BBC World Service, "The Man Who Would Be Pope," by Jane Little,

which admiringly touted the chances of Nigeria's curial cardinal, Francis Arinze. Then there are the collection of television commentaries, of which perhaps the most exhaustive to date was "The Men Who Would Be Pope," a co-production of the Arts & Entertainment Network and the BBC. This hour-long program was first broadcast in the United States on December 27, 1997, as a part of the "Investigative Reports" series. Another speculative article is "The Men Who Would Be Pope" by Tom Fennell and Philip Willan, which appeared in the Febriary 2, 1998, issue of *Maclean's*. In addition to this sort of material, there are the usual "summings up" of the pontificate of John Paul II, anticipating its closure. Of many such offerings, one was Breffni O'Rourke's "A Record Papacy Bears John Paul II's Special Imprint," which was broadcast by Radio Free Europe on May 20, 1998, as a commemoration of the pope's seventy-eighth birthday.

2. The traditional image that the Romans themselves use to illustrate the principle is not that a conservative pope often is followed by a liberal one (Pius IX by Leo XIII, Pius X by Benedict XV) or that a liberal one is succeeded by a conservative, but rather that a thin pope is followed by a fat one in precise alternation. This view, still widely heard and taken seriously in Rome, calls for the next pope to be distinctly endomorphic.

3. Matt. 22:14.

4. At the same time, the poll revealed that most of these respondents also said that they went to Mass regularly, and that they admired Pope John Paul II

5. The cardinals have no difficulty in finding one another. The Annuario Pontificio, the annual almanac of offices and persons published by the Vatican, lists the addresses, telephone numbers, and fax numbers of all the cardinals. In 1998, only eleven cardinals have unlisted numbers, while a twelfth Adam Kozlowiecki in Zambia, has no telephone at all. Forty-two of the cardinals have listed fax numbers, including all of the most influential leaders of groups and parties, including Arns, Lorscheider, Hume, Lustiger, Martini, Neves, and even Puljic, in war-damaged Sarajevo.

6. As a direct consequence of the plenary meeting in 1981, on May 31, 1982, John Paul II created the Council of Cardinals specifically for the study of the Vatican's organizational and economic problems.

7. January 14–31, 1980: Special Assembly for the Netherlands, on "The Pastoral Action of the Church in the Netherlands in the Present Situation"; September 26–October 25, 1980: fifth ordinary General Assembly, on "The Role of the Christian Family in the Modern World"; September 29–October 29, 1983: sixth ordinary General Assembly, on "Penance and Reconciliation in the Mission of the Church"; November 25–December 8, 1985: second Extraordinary General Assembly, on "The Twentieth Anniversary of the Conclusion of the Second Vatican Council"; October 1–30, 1987: seventh ordinary General Assembly, on "The Vocation and Mission of the Lay Faithful in the Church and in the World"; September 30–October 28, 1990: eighth ordinary General Assembly, on "The Formation of Priests in Circumstances of the Present Day"; November 28–December 14, 1991: Special Assembly for Europe, on the theme: "So that we might be witnesses of Christ who has set us free"; April 10–May 8, 1994: Special Assembly for Africa, on "The Church in Africa and Her Evangelizing Mission Towards the Year 2000: 'You Shall Be My Witnesses'"; October 2–29. 1994: ninth ordinary General Assembly, on "The Consecrated Life and Its Role in the Church and in the World"; November 26–December 14, 1995: Special Assembly for Lebanon; November 16–December 12, 1997: Special Assembly for America, on "The Encounter with the Living Jesus Christ: the Way to Conversion, Communion, and Solidarity in America"; April 19, 1998: Special Assembly for Asia, on "Jesus Christ the Savior and His Mission of Love and Service in Asia."

8. Of the forty-five popes who have reigned since 1534, when Paul III was elected and began to move towards an ecumenical council to conduct fundamental reform in the Church—which became the Council of Trent—thirty-five have been between the age of fifty-four and seventy when they were chosen. Nine of them have been in their seventies, including the oldest, Clement X, who was 79 years, 290 days old when he was elected in 1670, and John XXIII, who was 76 years, 336 days old when he became pope. Only one, Clement XI, was younger than fifty-four. He was 51 years, 122 days old when he was chosen in 1700.

9. Joachim Meisner of Köln (born December 25, 1933), Dionigi Tettamanzi of Genoa (born March 14, 1934), Pierre Eyt of Bordeaux (born June 4, 1934), Julius Riyadi Darmaatmadja of

Jakarta (born December 20, 1934), Alfonso López Trujillo (born November 8, 1935), Georg Maximilian Sterzinsky of Berlin (born February 9, 1936), Roger Michael Mahony of Los Angeles (born February 27, 1936), Jean Claude Turcotte of Montréal (born June 26, 1936), Antonio María Rouco Varela of Madrid (born August 24, 1936), Jaime Lucas Ortega y Alamino of Havana (born October 18, 1936), Nicolas Lopez Rodriguez of Santo Domingo (born October 31, 1936), Francis Eugene George of Chicago (born January 16, 1937), Norberto Rivera Carrera of Mexico City (born June 4, 1942), Polycarp Pengo of Dar-Es-Salaam (born August 5, 1944), Christoph von Schönborn of Vienna (born January 22, 1945), and Vinko Puljic of Vrbosna (Sarajevo) (born September 8, 1945).

10. Peter Hebblethwaite, before his untimely death, expressed his opinion in *The Next Pope* that the election of another Italian was, by far, the probability, and that (p. 109) ". . . the pontificate of Pope John Paul II will appear to history as a Polish interlude."

11. The longest reigning popes have been: Pius IX (31 y., 7 m., 22 d.); Leo XIII (25 y., 5 m.); Pius VI (24 y., 6 m., 14 d.); Silvester I (23 y., 10 m., 27 d.); Hadrian I (23 y., 10 m., 17 d.); Pius VII (23 y., 5 m., 6 d.); Alexander III (21 y., 11 m., 22 d.); Leo I (21 y., 1 m., 13 d.); Urban VIII (20 y., 11 m., 21 d.); Leo III (20 y., 5 m., 16 d.); and Clement XI (20 y., 3 m., 25 d.).

12. Rio de Janeiro: AGIR, 1962, vol. 1 in the series *Coleção "Forma Gregis";* 2. ed. Rio de Janeiro: AGIR, 1963.

13. 3. ed. rev., Rio de Janeiro: AGIR, 1965.

14. Rio de Janeiro: Editora Record, 1989, in the series *Coleção Universidade Catolica do Salvador.*

15. Rio de Janeiro: Editora Record, 1990, in the series *Coleção Universidade Catolica do Salvador.*

16. Rio de Janeiro: Editora Record, 1992, in the series *Coleção Universidade Catolica do Salvador.*

17. Rio de Janeiro: Editora Record, 1995, in the series *Coleção Universidade Catolica do Salvador.*

18. Rio de Janeiro: Editora Record, 1995, in the series *Coleção Universidade Catolica do Salvador.*

19. Lima: Vida y Espiritualidad, 1994, vol. 18 of the series *Ediciones VE Libros.*

20. Firenze: Cooperativa Firenze 2000, 1996.

21. [Paris]: Editions du Cerf, 1995.

22. Paris: Centurion, 1993, in the series *Spiritualité.*

23. Kansas City, Missouri: Sheed and Ward, 1990.

24. Dublin: Veritas, 1992.

25. Averbode Baarn: Altiora; Gooi en Sticht, 1994.

26. Paris: Desclée de Brouwer, 1994.

27. He comes from the same family as Maria Tettamanzi, the resistance leader during the War, whose diary, *Diario di un due di Briscola: Ricordi Autobiografici, 1943-1945* (Brescia: La Scuola, 1977, L'Alfiere, series 3, vol. 11), is a valuable narrative of the underground movement.

28. Milano: Massimo, 1967.

29. Milano: Opera della Regalita di N[ostro] S[ignore] Gesu Cristo, 1968.

30. Milano: Ancora, 1968, in the series *Collana Cristianesimo Aperto.*

31. Milano: Ancora, 1969.

32. Milano: Massimo, 1991, vol. 51 of the series *Sussidi Pastorali e Liturgici,* first published in a shorter form in 1987.

33. Milano: Editrice Ancora Milano, 1988.

34. Casale Monferrato: Piemme, 1993.

35. Casale Monferrato: Piemme, 1987.

36. Brezzo di Bedero: Edizioni Salcom, 1985.

37. Casale Monferrato: Edizioni Piemme di Pietro Marietti, 1985, vol. 5 of the series *Collana Azione Pastorale.*

38. Casale Monferrato: Edizioni Piemme di Pietro Marietti, 1985, vol. 6 of the series *Collana Azione Pastorale.*

39. Casale Monferrato: Piemme, 1993.

40. Milano: Edizioni OR, 1975.

41. Recently, there has been a dissertation which explores trends of thinking on morality and conscience since Vatican II, including Tettamanzi's thought and writing. Cataldo Zuccaro, "Ordine Morale Oggettivo E Coscienza: Tendenze Dei Moralisti Italiani Del Dopo Concilio," Unpublished Th.D. dissertation, Pontificia Universitas Gregoriana 1992. See also the abstract in *Dissertations Abstracts International,* 54-02C:397.

42. The articles subsequently were collected under the editorship of Mario Agnes and reprinted under the title *Antropologia Cristiana e Omosessualita* (Citta del Vaticano: L'Osservatore Romano, 1997) as vol. 38 of the series *Quaderni dell'Osservatore Romano.* An English translation also was published as *Christian Anthropology and Homosexuality* (Vatican City:

L'Osservatore Romano, 1997).

43. Roma: Citta Nuova, 1986.

44. Milano: Sperling & Kupfer, 1984.

45. Milano: Rizzoli, 1985.

46. Torino: Edizioni San Paolo, 1993.

47. Mercurius, cardinal-priest of the title of San Clemente, chose to be called John II when he was acclaimed as pope on January 2, 533. He made the alteration because he did not think it seemly for a bishop to bear the name of a pagan god. The second pope to change his name was John XII (December 16, 955–May 14, 964), who was Octavianus, of the family of the counts of Tusculum (Frascati), before he ascended the throne.

48. Pius IV (Giovanni Angelo Medici, 1559–1565) seems to have chosen the name specifically because of its meaning—he would be a *dutiful* pope. Pius V (1566–1572), his successor, wished to commemorate Pius IV. Pius VI (Giovanni Angelo Braschi, 1775–1799) admired Pius V, while Pius VII (1800–1823) was the cousin and successor of Pius VI. Pius VIII (1829–1830) wished to commemorate his patron, Pius VII, and Pius IX (1846–1878) followed the same principle with regard to Pius VIII). Pius X (1903–1914) admired Pius IX, while Pius XI (1922–1939) commemorated Pius X—a remarkable trail of personal tributes.

APPENDIX A:

Apostolic Constitution *Universi Dominici Gregis*

February 22, 1996

Table of Contents

Introduction

The shepherd of the Lord's whole flock is the Bishop of the Church of Rome, where the Blessed Apostle Peter, by sovereign disposition of divine Providence, offered to Christ the supreme witness of martyrdom by the shedding of his blood. It is therefore understandable that the lawful apostolic succession in this See, with which "because of its great preeminence every Church must agree,"[1] has always been the object of particular attention.

Precisely for this reason, down the centuries the Supreme Pontiffs have deemed it their special duty, as well as their specific right, to establish fitting norms to regulate the orderly election of their Successor. Thus, also in more recent times, my Predecessors Saint Pius X,[2] Pius XI,[3] Pius XII,[4] John XXIII[5] and lastly Paul VI,[6] each with the intention of responding to the needs of the particular historical moment, issued wise and appropriate regulations in order to ensure the suitable preparation and orderly gathering of the electors charged, at the vacancy of the Apostolic See, with the important and weighty duty of electing the Roman Pontiff.

If I too now turn to this matter, it is certainly not because of any lack of esteem for those norms, for which I have great respect and which I intend for the most part to confirm, at least with regard to their substance and the basic principles which inspired them. What leads me to take this step is awareness of the Church's changed situation today and the need to take into consideration the general revision of Canon Law which took place, to the satisfaction of the whole Episcopate, with the publication and promulgation first of the *Code of Canon Law* and subsequently of the *Code of Canons of the Eastern Churches*. In conformity with this revision, itself inspired by the Second Vatican Ecumenical Council, I then took up the reform of the Roman Curia in the Apostolic Constitution *Pastor Bonus*.[7] Furthermore, Canon 335 of the *Code of Canon Law*, restated in Canon 47 of the *Code of Canons of the Eastern Churches*, makes clear the need to issue and constantly update the specific laws regulating the canonical provision for the Roman See, when for any reason it becomes vacant.

While keeping in mind present-day requirements, I have been careful, in formulating the new discipline, not to depart in substance from the wise and venerable tradition already established.

It is in fact an indisputable principle that the Roman Pontiff has the right to define and adapt to changing times the manner of designating the person called to assume the Petrine succession in the Roman See. This regards, first of all, the body entrusted with providing for the election of the Roman Pontiff: based on a millennial practice sanctioned by specific canonical norms and confirmed by an explicit provision of the current *Code of Canon Law* (Canon 349), this body is made up of the College of Cardinals of Holy Roman Church. While it is indeed a doctrine of faith that the power of the Supreme Pontiff derives directly from Christ, whose earthly Vicar he is,[8] it is also certain that this supreme power in the Church is granted to him "by means of lawful election accepted by him, together with episcopal consecration."[9] A most serious duty is thus incumbent upon the body responsible for this election.

Consequently, the norms which regulate its activity need to be very precise and clear, so that the election itself will take place in a most worthy manner, as befits the office of utmost responsibility which the person elected will have to assume, by divine mandate, at the moment of his assent.

Confirming therefore the norm of the current *Code of Canon Law* (*cf.* Canon 349), which reflects the millennial practice of the Church, I once more affirm that the College of electors of the Supreme Pontiff is composed solely of the Cardinals of Holy Roman Church. In them one finds expressed in a remarkable synthesis the two aspects which characterize the figure and office of the Roman Pontiff: Roman, because identified with the Bishop of the Church in Rome and thus closely linked to the clergy of this City, represented by the Cardinals of the presbyterial and diaconal titles of Rome, and to the Cardinal Bishops of the suburbicarian Sees; Pontiff of the universal Church, because called to represent visibly the unseen Pastor who leads his whole flock to the pastures of eternal life. The universality of the Church is clearly expressed in the very composition of the College of Cardinals, whose members come from every continent.

In the present historical circumstances, the universality of the Church is sufficiently expressed by the College of one hundred and twenty electors, made up of Cardinals coming from all parts of the world and from very different cultures. I therefore confirm that this is to be the maximum number of Cardinal electors, while at the same time indicating that it is in no way meant as a sign of less respect that the provision laid down by my predecessor Pope Paul VI has been retained, namely, that those Cardinals who celebrate their eightieth birthday before the day when the Apostolic See becomes vacant do not take part in the election.[10] The reason for this provision is the desire not to add to the weight of such venerable age the further burden of responsibility for choosing the one who will have to lead Christ's flock in ways adapted to the needs of the times. This does not however mean that the Cardinals over eighty years of age cannot take part in the preparatory meetings of the Conclave, in conformity with the norms set forth below. During the vacancy of the Apostolic See, and especially during the election of the Supreme Pontiff, they in particular should lead the People of God assembled in the Patriarchal Basilicas of Rome and in other churches in the Dioceses throughout the world, supporting the work of the electors with fervent prayers and supplications to the Holy Spirit and imploring for them the light needed to make their choice before God alone and with concern only for the "salvation of souls, which in the Church must always be the supreme law."[11]

It has been my wish to give particular attention to the age-old institution of the Conclave, the rules and procedures of which have been established and defined by the solemn ordinances of a number of my Predecessors. A careful historical examination confirms both the appropriateness of this institution, given the circumstances in which it originated and gradually took definitive shape, and its continued usefulness for the orderly, expeditious and proper functioning of the election itself, especially in times of tension and upheaval.

Precisely for this reason, while recognizing that theologians and canonists of all times agree that this institution is not of its nature necessary for the valid election of the Roman Pontiff, I confirm by this Constitution that the Conclave is to continue in its essential structure; at the same time, I have made some modifications in order to adapt its procedures to present-day circumstances. Specifically, I have considered it appropriate to decree that for the whole duration of the election the living-quarters of the Cardinal electors and of those called to assist in the orderly process of the election itself are to be located in suitable places within Vatican City State. Although small, the State is large enough to ensure within its walls, with the help of the appropriate measures indicated below, the seclusion and resulting concentration which an act so vital to the whole Church requires of the electors.

At the same time, in view of the sacredness of the act of election and thus the need for it to be carried out in an appropriate setting where, on the one hand, liturgical actions can be readily combined with juridical formalities, and where, on the other, the electors can more easily dispose themselves to accept the interior movements of the Holy Spirit, I decree that the election will continue to take place in the Sistine Chapel, where everything is conducive to an awareness of the presence of God, in whose sight each person will one day be judged.

I further confirm, by my apostolic authority, the duty of maintaining the strictest secrecy with regard to everything that directly or indirectly concerns the election process itself. Here too, though, I have wished to simplify the relative norms, reducing them to their essentials, in order to avoid confusion, doubts and even eventual problems of conscience on the part of those who have taken part in the election.

Finally, I have deemed it necessary to revise the form of the election itself in the light of the present-day needs of the Church and the usages of modern society. I have thus considered it fitting not to retain election by acclamation *quasi ex inspiratione*, judging that it is no longer an apt means of interpreting the thought of an electoral college so great in number and so diverse in origin. It also appeared necessary to eliminate election *per compromissum*, not only because of the difficulty of the procedure, evident from the unwieldy accumulation of rules issued in the past, but also because by its very nature it tends to lessen the responsibility of the individual electors who, in this case, would not be required to express their choice personally.

After careful reflection I have therefore decided that the only form by which the electors can manifest their vote in the election of the Roman Pontiff is by secret ballot, in accordance with the rules set forth below. This form offers the greatest guarantee of clarity, straightforwardness, simplicity, openness and, above all, an effective and fruitful participation on the part of the Cardinals who, individually and as a group, are called to make up the assembly which elects the Successor of Peter.

With these intentions, I promulgate the present Apostolic Constitution containing the norms which, when the Roman See becomes vacant, are to be strictly followed by the Cardinals whose right and duty it is to elect the Successor of Peter, the visible Head of the whole Church and the Servant of the servants of God.

Part One: The vacancy of the apostolic see

Chapter I—The powers of the College of Cardinals during the vacancy of the Apostolic See.

1. During the vacancy of the Apostolic See, the College of Cardinals has no power or jurisdiction in matters which pertain to the Supreme Pontiff during his lifetime or in the exercise of his office; such matters are to be reserved completely and exclusively to the future Pope. I therefore declare null and void any act of power or jurisdiction pertaining to the Roman Pontiff during his lifetime or in the exercise of his office which the College of Cardinals might see fit to exercise, beyond the limits expressly permitted in this Constitution.

2. During the vacancy of the Apostolic See, the government of the Church is entrusted to the College of Cardinals solely for the dispatch of ordinary business and of matters which cannot be postponed (*cf.* No. 6),

and for the preparation of everything necessary for the election of the new Pope. This task must be carried out in the ways and within the limits set down by this Constitution: consequently, those matters are to be absolutely excluded which, whether by law or by practice, come under the power of the Roman Pontiff alone or concern the norms for the election of the new Pope laid down in the present Constitution.

3. I further establish that the College of Cardinals may make no dispositions whatsoever concerning the rights of the Apostolic See and of the Roman Church, much less allow any of these rights to lapse, either directly or indirectly, even though it be to resolve disputes or to prosecute actions perpetrated against these same rights after the death or valid resignation of the Pope.[12] All the Cardinals are obliged to defend these rights.

4. During the vacancy of the Apostolic See, laws issued by the Roman Pontiffs can in no way be corrected or modified, nor can anything be added or subtracted, nor a dispensation be given even from a part of them, especially with regard to the procedures governing the election of the Supreme Pontiff. Indeed, should anything be done or even attempted against this prescription, by my supreme authority I declare it null and void.

5. Should doubts arise concerning the prescriptions contained in this Constitution, or concerning the manner of putting them into effect, I decree that all power of issuing a judgment in this regard belongs to the College of Cardinals, to which I grant the faculty of interpreting doubtful or controverted points. I also establish that should it be necessary to discuss these or other similar questions, except the act of election, it suffices that the majority of the Cardinals present should concur in the same opinion.

6. In the same way, should there be a problem which, in the view of the majority of the assembled Cardinals, cannot be postponed until another time, the College of Cardinals may act according to the majority opinion.

Chapter II—The Congregations of the Cardinals in preparation for the election of the Supreme Pontiff.

7. While the See is vacant, there are two kinds of Congregations of the Cardinals: General Congregations, which include the whole College and are held before the beginning of the election, and Particular Congregations. All the Cardinals who are not legitimately impeded must attend the General Congregations, once they have been informed of the vacancy of the Apostolic See. Cardinals who, by virtue of No. 33 of this Constitution, do not enjoy the right of electing the Pope are granted the faculty of not attending these General Congregations, should they prefer.

The Particular Congregation is made up of the Cardinal Camerlengo of Holy Roman Church and three Cardinals, one from each Order, chosen by lot from among the Cardinal electors already present in Rome. The office of these Cardinals, called Assistants, ceases at the conclusion of the third full day, and their place is taken by others, also chosen by lot and having the same term of office, also after the election has begun.

During the time of the election, more important matters are, if necessary, dealt with by the assembly of the Cardinal electors, while ordinary affairs continue to be dealt with by the Particular Congregation of Cardinals. In the General and Particular Congregations, during the vacancy of the Apostolic See, the Cardinals are to wear the usual black cassock with piping and the red sash, with skull-cap, pectoral cross and ring.

8. The Particular Congregations are to deal only with questions of lesser importance which arise on a daily basis or from time to time. But should there arise more serious questions deserving fuller examination, these must be submitted to the General Congregation. Moreover, anything decided, resolved or refused in one Particular Congregation cannot be revoked, altered or granted in another; the right to do this belongs solely to the General Congregation, and by a majority vote.

9. The General Congregations of Cardinals are to be held in the Apostolic Palace in the Vatican or, if circumstances demand it, in another place judged more suitable by the Cardinals. At these Congregations the Dean of the College presides or, should he be absent or lawfully impeded, the Subdean. If one or both of these, in accordance with No. 33 of this Constitution, no longer enjoy the right of electing the Pope, the assembly of the Cardinal electors will be presided over by the senior Cardinal elector, according to the customary order of precedence.

10. Votes in the Congregations of Cardinals, when more important matters are concerned, are not to be expressed by word of mouth but in a way which ensures secrecy.

11. The General Congregations preceding the beginning of the election, which are therefore called "preparatory," are to be held daily, beginning on the day which shall be fixed by the Camerlengo of Holy Roman Church and the senior Cardinal of each of the three Orders among the electors, and including the days on which the funeral rites for the deceased Pope are celebrated. In this way the Cardinal Camerlengo can hear the opinion of the College and communicate whatever is considered necessary or appropriate, while the individual Cardinals can express their views on possible problems, ask for explanations in case of doubt and make suggestions.

12. In the first General Congregations provision is to be made for each Cardinal to have available a copy of this Constitution and at the same time

to have an opportunity to raise questions about the meaning and the implementation of its norms. The part of the present Constitution regarding the vacancy of the Apostolic See should also be read aloud. At the same time the Cardinals present are to swear an oath to observe the prescriptions contained herein and to maintain secrecy. This oath, which shall also be taken by Cardinals who arrive late and subsequently take part in these Congregations, is to be read aloud by the Cardinal Dean or by whoever else presides over the College by virtue of No. 9 of this Constitution, in the presence of the other Cardinals and according to the following formula:

We, the Cardinals of Holy Roman Church, of the Order of Bishops, of Priests and of Deacons, promise, pledge and swear, as a body and individually, to observe exactly and faithfully all the norms contained in the Apostolic Constitution Universi Dominici Gregis of the Supreme Pontiff John Paul II, and to maintain rigorous secrecy with regard to all matters in any way related to the election of the Roman Pontiff or those which, by their very nature, during the vacancy of the Apostolic See, call for the same secrecy.

Next, each Cardinal shall add: And I, N. Cardinal N., so promise, pledge and swear. And, placing his hand on the Gospels, he will add: So help me God and these Holy Gospels which I now touch with my hand.

13. In one of the Congregations immediately following, the Cardinals, on the basis of a prearranged agenda, shall take the more urgent decisions regarding the beginning of the election. In other words:

a) they shall fix the day, hour and manner in which the body of the deceased Pope shall be brought to the Vatican Basilica in order to be exposed for the homage of the faithful;

b) they shall make all necessary arrangements for the funeral rites of the deceased Pope, to be celebrated for nine consecutive days, determining when they are to begin, in such a way that burial will take place, except for special reasons, between the fourth and sixth day after death;

c) they shall see to it that the Commission, made up of the Cardinal Camerlengo and the Cardinals who had formerly held the offices of Secretary of State and President of the Pontifical Commission for Vatican City State, ensures that the rooms of the Domus Sanctæ Marthæ are made ready for the suitable lodging of the Cardinal electors, that rooms suitable for those persons mentioned in Section Number 46 of the present Constitution are also made ready, and that all necessary arrangements are made to prepare the Sistine Chapel so that the election process can be carried out in a smooth and orderly manner and with maximum discretion, according to the provisions laid down in this Constitution;

d) they shall entrust to two ecclesiastics known for their sound doctrine, wisdom and moral authority the task of presenting to the Cardinals two well-prepared meditations on the problems facing the Church at the time and on the need for careful discernment in choosing the new Pope; at the same time, without prejudice to the provisions of Section Number 52 of this Constitution, they shall fix the day and the time when the first of these meditations is to be given;

e) they shall approve—at the proposal of the Administration of the Apostolic See or, within its competence, of the Governatorato of Vatican City State—expenses incurred from the death of the Pope until the election of his successor;

f) they shall read any documents left by the deceased Pope for the College of Cardinals;

g) they shall arrange for the destruction of the Fisherman's Ring and of the lead seal with which Apostolic Letters are despatched;

h) they shall make provision for the assignment of rooms by lot to the Cardinal electors;

i) they shall set the day and hour of the beginning of the voting process.

Chapter III—Concerning certain offices during the vacancy of the Apostolic See.

14. According to the provisions of Article 6 of the Apostolic Constitution *Pastor Bonus*,[13] at the death of the Pope all the heads of the Dicasteries of the Roman Curia—the Cardinal Secretary of State and the Cardinal Prefects, the Archbishop Presidents, together with members of those Dicasteries—cease to exercise their office. An exception is made for the Camerlengo of Holy Roman Church and the Major Penitentiary, who continue to exercise their ordinary functions, submitting to the College of Cardinals matters that would have had to be referred to the Supreme Pontiff.

Likewise, in conformity with the Apostolic Constitution *Vicariæ Potestatis* (No. 2 §1),[14] the Cardinal Vicar General for the Diocese of Rome continues in office during the vacancy of the Apostolic See, as does the Cardinal Archpriest of the Vatican Basilica and Vicar General for Vatican City for his jurisdiction.

15. Should the offices of Camerlengo of Holy Roman Church or of Major Penitentiary be vacant at the time of the Pope's death, or should they become vacant before the election of his successor, the College of Cardinals shall as soon as possible elect the Cardinal, or Cardinals as the case may be, who shall hold these offices until the election of the new Pope. In each of the two cases mentioned, election takes place by a secret vote of all

the Cardinal electors present, with the use of ballots distributed and collected by the Masters of Ceremonies. The ballots are then opened in the presence of the Camerlengo and of the three Cardinal Assistants, if it is a matter of electing the Major Penitentiary; if it is a matter of electing the Camerlengo, they are opened in the presence of the said three Cardinals and of the Secretary of the College of Cardinals. Whoever receives the greatest number of votes shall be elected and shall ipso facto enjoy all the relevant faculties. In the case of an equal number of votes, the Cardinal belonging to the higher Order or, if both are in the same Order, the one first created a Cardinal, shall be appointed. Until the Camerlengo is elected, his functions are carried out by the Dean of the College or, if he is absent or lawfully impeded, by the Subdean or by the senior Cardinal according to the usual order of precedence, in conformity with No. 9 of this Constitution, who can without delay take the decisions that circumstances dictate.

16. If during the vacancy of the Apostolic See the Vicar General for the Diocese of Rome should die, the Vicegerent in office at the time shall also exercise the office proper to the Cardinal Vicar in addition to the ordinary vicarious jurisdiction which he already holds.[15] Should there not be a Vicegerent, the Auxiliary Bishop who is senior by appointment will carry out his functions.

17. As soon as he is informed of the death of the Supreme Pontiff, the Camerlengo of Holy Roman Church must officially ascertain the Pope's death, in the presence of the Master of Papal Liturgical Celebrations, of the Cleric Prelates of the Apostolic Camera and of the Secretary and Chancellor of the same; the latter shall draw up the official death certificate. The Camerlengo must also place seals on the Pope's study and bedroom, making provision that the personnel who ordinarily reside in the private apartment can remain there until after the burial of the Pope, at which time the entire papal apartment will be sealed; he must notify the Cardinal Vicar for Rome of the Pope's death, whereupon the latter shall inform the People of Rome by a special announcement; he shall notify the Cardinal Archpriest of the Vatican Basilica; he shall take possession of the Apostolic Palace in the Vatican and, either in person or through a delegate, of the Palaces of the Lateran and of Castel Gandolfo, and exercise custody and administration of the same; he shall determine, after consulting the heads of the three Orders of Cardinals, all matters concerning the Pope's burial, unless during his lifetime the latter had made known his wishes in this regard; and he shall deal, in the name of and with the consent of the College of Cardinals, with all matters that circumstances suggest for safeguarding the rights of the Apostolic See and for its proper administration. During the vacancy of the Apostolic See, the Camerlengo of Holy Roman

Church has the duty of safeguarding and administering the goods and temporal rights of the Holy See, with the help of the three Cardinal Assistants, having sought the views of the College of Cardinals, once only for less important matters, and on each occasion when more serious matters arise.

18. The Cardinal Major Penitentiary and his Officials, during the vacancy of the Apostolic See, can carry out the duties laid down by my Predecessor Pius XI in the Apostolic Constitution *Quæ Divinitus* of 25 March 1935,[16] and by myself in the Apostolic Constitution *Pastor Bonus*.[17]

19. The Dean of the College of Cardinals, for his part, as soon as he has been informed of the Pope's death by the Cardinal Camerlengo or the Prefect of the Papal Household, shall inform all the Cardinals and convoke them for the Congregations of the College. He shall also communicate news of the Pope's death to the Diplomatic Corps accredited to the Holy See and to the Heads of the respective Nations.

20. During the vacancy of the Apostolic See, the Substitute of the Secretariat of State, the Secretary for Relations with States and the Secretaries of the Dicasteries of the Roman Curia remain in charge of their respective offices, and are responsible to the College of Cardinals.

21. In the same way, the office and attendant powers of Papal Representatives do not lapse.

22. The Almoner of His Holiness will also continue to carry out works of charity in accordance with the criteria employed during the Pope's lifetime. He will be dependent upon the College of Cardinals until the election of the new Pope.

23. During the vacancy of the Apostolic See, all the civil power of the Supreme Pontiff concerning the government of Vatican City State belongs to the College of Cardinals, which however will be unable to issue decrees except in cases of urgent necessity and solely for the time in which the Holy See is vacant. Such decrees will be valid for the future only if the new Pope confirms them.

Chapter IV—Faculties of the Dicasteries of the Roman Curia during the vacancy of the Apostolic See.

24. During the period of vacancy, the Dicasteries of the Roman Curia, with the exception of those mentioned in Section Number 26 of this Constitution, have no faculty in matters which, *Sede plena*, they can only deal with or carry out *facto verbo cum Sanctissimo* or *ex Audientia Sanctissimi* or *vigore spectalium et extraordinariarum facultatum* which the Roman

Pontiff is accustomed to grant to the Prefects, Presidents or Secretaries of those Dicasteries.

25. The ordinary faculties proper to each Dicastery do not, however, cease at the death of the Pope. Nevertheless, I decree that the Dicasteries are only to make use of these faculties for the granting of favors of lesser importance, while more serious or controverted matters, if they can be postponed, shall be exclusively reserved to the future Pope. If such matters admit of no delay (as for example in the case of dispensations which the Supreme Pontiff usually grants in articulo mortis), they can be entrusted by the College of Cardinals to the Cardinal who was Prefect until the Pope's death, or to the Archbishop who was then President, and to the other Cardinals of the same Dicastery, to whose examination the deceased Supreme Pontiff would probably have entrusted them. In such circumstances, they will be able to decide per modum provisionis, until the election of the Pope, what they judge to be most fitting and appropriate for the preservation and defense of ecclesiastical rights and traditions.

26. The Supreme Tribunal of the Apostolic Signatura and the Tribunal of the Roman Rota, during the vacancy of the Holy See, continue to deal with cases in accordance with their proper laws, with due regard for the prescriptions of Article 18, paragraphs 1 and 3 of the Apostolic Constitution *Pastor Bonus*.[18]

Chapter V—The funeral rites of the Roman Pontiff.

27. After the death of the Roman Pontiff, the Cardinals will celebrate the funeral rites for the repose of his soul for nine consecutive days, in accordance with the *Ordo Exsequiarum Romani Pontificis*, the norms of which, together with those of the *Ordo Rituum Conclavis*, they are to observe faithfully.

28. If burial takes place in the Vatican Basilica, the relevant official document is drawn up by the Notary of the Chapter of the Basilica or by the Canon Archivist. Subsequently, a delegate of the Cardinal Camerlengo and a delegate of the Prefect of the Papal Household shall separately draw up documents certifying that burial has taken place. The former shall do so in the presence of the members of the Apostolic Camera and the latter in the presence of the Prefect of the Papal Household.

29. If the Roman Pontiff should die outside Rome, it is the task of the College of Cardinals to make all necessary arrangements for the dignified and reverent transfer of the body to the Basilica of Saint Peter's in the Vatican.

30. No one is permitted to use any means whatsoever in order to photograph or film the Supreme Pontiff either on his sickbed or after death, or to record his words for subsequent reproduction. If after the Pope's death anyone should wish to take photographs of him for documentary purposes, he must ask permission from the Cardinal Camerlengo of Holy Roman Church who will not however permit the taking of photographs of the Supreme Pontiff except attired in pontifical vestments.

31. After the burial of the Supreme Pontiff and during the election of the new Pope, no part of the private apartment of the Supreme Pontiff is to be lived in.

32. If the deceased Supreme Pontiff has made a will concerning his belongings, bequeathing letters and private documents, and has named an executor thereof, it is the responsibility of the latter to determine and execute, in accordance with the mandate received from the testator, matters concerning the private property and writings of the deceased Pope. The executor will give an account of his activities only to the new Supreme Pontiff.

Part Two: The election of the Roman Pontiff

Chapter I—The electors of the Roman Pontiff.

33. The right to elect the Roman Pontiff belongs exclusively to the Cardinals of Holy Roman Church, with the exception of those who have reached their eightieth birthday before the day of the Roman Pontiff's death or the day when the Apostolic See becomes vacant. The maximum number of Cardinal electors must not exceed one hundred and twenty. The right of active election by any other ecclesiastical dignitary or the intervention of any lay power of whatsoever grade or order is absolutely excluded.

34. If the Apostolic See should become vacant during the celebration of an Ecumenical Council or of a Synod of Bishops being held in Rome or in any other place in the world, the election of the new Pope is to be carried out solely and exclusively by the Cardinal electors indicated in Section Number 33, and not by the Council or the Synod of Bishops. For this reason I declare null and void acts which would in any way temerariously presume to modify the regulations concerning the election or the college of electors. Moreover, in confirmation of the provisions of Canons 340 and 347 n. 2 of the *Code of Canon Law* and of Canon 53 of the *Code of Canons of the Eastern Churches* in this regard, a Council or Synod of Bishops, at whatever point they have reached, must be considered immediately sus-

pended ipso iure, once notification is received of the vacancy of the Apostolic See. Therefore without any delay all meetings, congregations or sessions must be interrupted, and the preparation of any decrees or canons, together with the promulgation of those already confirmed, must be suspended, under pain of nullity of the same. Neither the Council nor the Synod can continue for any reason, even though it be most serious or worthy of special mention, until the new Pope, canonically elected, orders their resumption or continuation.

35. No Cardinal elector can be excluded from active or passive voice in the election of the Supreme Pontiff, for any reason or pretext, with due regard for the provisions of Section Number 40 of this Constitution.

36. A Cardinal of the Holy Roman Church who has been created and published before the College of Cardinals thereby has the right to elect the Pope, in accordance with the norm of Section Number 33 of the present Constitution, even if he has not yet received the red hat or the ring, or sworn the oath. On the other hand, Cardinals who have been canonically deposed or who with the consent of the Roman Pontiff have renounced the cardinalate do not have this right. Moreover, during the period of vacancy the College of Cardinals cannot readmit or rehabilitate them.

37. I furthermore decree that, from the moment when the Apostolic See is lawfully vacant, the Cardinal electors who are present must wait fifteen full days for those who are absent; the College of Cardinals is also granted the faculty to defer, for serious reasons, the beginning of the election for a few days more. But when a maximum of twenty days have elapsed from the beginning of the vacancy of the See, all the Cardinal electors present are obliged to proceed to the election.

38. All the Cardinal electors, convoked for the election of the new Pope by the Cardinal Dean, or by another Cardinal in his name, are required, in virtue of holy obedience, to obey the announcement of convocation and to proceed to the place designated for this purpose, unless they are hindered by sickness or by some other grave impediment, which however must be recognized as such by the College of Cardinals.

39. However, should any Cardinal electors arrive *re integra*, that is, before the new Pastor of the Church has been elected, they shall be allowed to take part in the election at the stage which it has reached.

40. If a Cardinal with the right to vote should refuse to enter Vatican City in order to take part in the election, or subsequently, once the election has begun, should refuse to remain in order to discharge his office, without manifest reason of illness attested to under oath by doctors and confirmed by the majority of the electors, the other Cardinals shall proceed freely with the election, without waiting for him or readmitting him. If on

the other hand a Cardinal elector is constrained to leave Vatican City because of illness, the election can proceed without asking for his vote; if however he desires to return to the place of the election, once his health is restored or even before, he must be readmitted.

Furthermore, if a Cardinal elector leaves Vatican City for some grave reason, acknowledged as such by the majority of the electors, he can return, in order once again to take part in the election.

Chapter II—The place of the election and those admitted to it by reason of their office.

41. The Conclave for the election of the Supreme Pontiff shall take place within the territory of Vatican City, in determined areas and buildings, closed to unauthorized persons in such a way as to ensure suitable accommodation for the Cardinal electors and all those legitimately called to cooperate in the orderly functioning of the election.

42. By the time fixed for the beginning of the election of the Supreme Pontiff, all the Cardinal electors must have been assigned and must have taken up suitable lodging in the Domus Sanctæ Marthæ, recently built in Vatican City.

If reasons of health, previously confirmed by the appropriate Congregation of Cardinals, require that a Cardinal elector should have a nurse in attendance, even during the period of the election, arrangements must be made to provide suitable accommodation for the latter.

43. From the beginning of the electoral process until the public announcement that the election of the Supreme Pontiff has taken place, or in any case until the new Pope so disposes, the rooms of the Domus Sanctæ Marthæ, and in particular the Sistine Chapel and the areas reserved for liturgical celebrations are to be closed to unauthorized persons, by the authority of the Cardinal Camerlengo and with the outside assistance of the Substitute of the Secretariat of State, in accordance with the provisions set forth in the following Numbers.

During this period, the entire territory of Vatican City and the ordinary activity of the offices located therein shall be regulated in a way which permits the election of the Supreme Pontiff to be carried out with due privacy and freedom. In particular, provision shall be made to ensure that no one approaches the Cardinal electors while they are being transported from the Domus Sanctæ Marthæ to the Apostolic Vatican Palace.

44. The Cardinal electors, from the beginning of the election until its conclusion and the public announcement of its outcome, are not to communicate—whether by writing, by telephone or by any other means of

communication—with persons outside the area where the election is taking place, except in cases of proven and urgent necessity, duly acknowledged by the Particular Congregation mentioned in Section Number 7. It is also the competence of the Particular Congregation to recognize the necessity and urgency of any communication with their respective offices on the part of the Cardinal Major Penitentiary, the Cardinal Vicar General for the Diocese of Rome and the Cardinal Archpriest of the Vatican Basilica.

45. Anyone not indicated in Section Number 46 below and who, while legitimately present in Vatican City in accordance with Section Number 43 of this Constitution, should happen to meet one of the Cardinal electors during the time of the election, is absolutely forbidden to engage in conversation of any sort, by whatever means and for whatever reason, with that Cardinal.

46. In order to meet the personal and official needs connected with the election process, the following individuals must be available and therefore properly lodged in suitable areas within the confines mentioned in Section Number 43 of this Constitution: the Secretary of the College of Cardinals, who acts as Secretary of the electoral assembly; the Master of Papal Liturgical Celebrations with two Masters of Ceremonies and two Religious attached to the Papal Sacristy; and an ecclesiastic chosen by the Cardinal Dean or by the Cardinal taking his place, in order to assist him in his duties.

There must also be available a number of priests from the regular clergy for hearing confessions in the different languages, and two medical doctors for possible emergencies.

Appropriate provisions must also be made beforehand for a suitable number of persons to be available for preparing and serving meals and for housekeeping.

All the persons indicated here must receive prior approval from the Cardinal Camerlengo and the three Cardinal Assistants.

47. All the persons listed in Section Number 46 of this Constitution who in any way or at any time should come to learn anything from any source, directly or indirectly, regarding the election process, and in particular regarding the voting which took place in the election itself, are obliged to maintain strict secrecy with all persons extraneous to the College of Cardinal electors: accordingly, before the election begins, they shall take an oath in the form and using the formula indicated in Section Number 48.

48. At a suitable time before the beginning of the election, the persons indicated in Section Number 46 of this Constitution, having been duly warned about the meaning and extent of the oath which they are to take, shall, in the presence of the Cardinal Camerlengo or another Cardinal del-

egated by him, and of two Masters of Ceremonies, swear and sign the oath according to the following formula:

I, N.N., promise and swear that, unless I should receive a special faculty given expressly by the newly elected Pontiff or by his successors, I will observe absolute and perpetual secrecy with all who are not part of the College of Cardinal electors concerning all matters directly or indirectly related to the ballots cast and their scrutiny for the election of the Supreme Pontiff.

I likewise promise and swear to refrain from using any audio or video equipment capable of recording anything which takes place during the period of the election within Vatican City, and in particular anything which in any way, directly or indirectly, is related to the process of the election itself: I declare that I take this oath fully aware that an infraction thereof will make me subject to the spiritual and canonical penalties which the future Supreme Pontiff will see fit to adopt, in accordance with Canon 1399 of the *Code of Canon Law.*

So help me God and these Holy Gospels which I touch with my hand.

Chapter III—The beginning of the election.

49. When the funeral rites for the deceased Pope have been celebrated according to the prescribed ritual, and everything necessary for the regular functioning of the election has been prepared, on the appointed day, and thus on the fifteenth day after the death of the Pope or, in conformity with the provisions of Section Number 37 of the present Constitution, not later than the twentieth, the Cardinal electors shall meet in the Basilica of Saint Peter's in the Vatican, or elsewhere, should circumstances warrant it, in order to take part in a solemn Eucharistic celebration with the Votive Mass *Pro Eligendo Papa.*[19] This celebration should preferably take place at a suitable hour in the morning, so that in the afternoon the prescriptions of the following Numbers of this Constitution can be carried out.

50. From the Pauline Chapel of the Apostolic Palace, where they will assemble at a suitable hour in the afternoon, the Cardinal electors, in choir dress, and invoking the assistance of the Holy Spirit with the chant of the *Veni Creator,* will solemnly process to the Sistine Chapel of the Apostolic Palace, where the election will be held.

51. Retaining the essential elements of the Conclave, but modifying some less important elements which, because of changed circumstances, no longer serve their original purpose, I establish and decree by the present Constitution that the election of the Supreme Pontiff, in conformity with the prescriptions contained in the following Numbers, is to take

place exclusively in the Sistine Chapel of the Apostolic Palace in the Vatican. The Sistine Chapel is therefore to remain an absolutely enclosed area until the conclusion of the election, so that total secrecy may be ensured with regard to everything said or done there in any way pertaining, directly or indirectly, to the election of the Supreme Pontiff.

It will therefore be the responsibility of the College of Cardinals, operating under the authority and responsibility of the Camerlengo, assisted by the Particular Congregation mentioned in Section Number 7 of the present Constitution, and with the outside assistance of the Substitute of the Secretariat of State, to make all prior arrangements for the interior of the Sistine Chapel and adjacent areas to be prepared, so that the orderly election and its privacy will be ensured.

In a special way, careful and stringent checks must be made, with the help of trustworthy individuals of proven technical ability, in order to ensure that no audiovisual equipment has been secretly installed in these areas for recording and transmission to the outside.

52. When the Cardinal electors have arrived in the Sistine Chapel, in accordance with the provisions of Section Number 50, and still in the presence of those who took part in the solemn procession, they shall take the oath, reading aloud the formula indicated in Section Number 53.

The Cardinal Dean, or the Cardinal who has precedence by order and seniority in accordance with the provisions of Section Number 9 of the present Constitution, will read the formula aloud; then each of the Cardinal electors, touching the Holy Gospels, will read and recite the formula, as indicated in the following Number.

When the last of the Cardinal electors has taken the oath, the Master of Papal Liturgical Celebrations will give the order *Extra omnes*, and all those not taking part in the Conclave must leave the Sistine Chapel.

The only ones to remain in the Chapel are the Master of Papal Liturgical Celebrations and the ecclesiastic previously chosen to preach to the Cardinal electors the second meditation, mentioned in Section Number 13d, concerning the grave duty incumbent on them and thus on the need to act with right intention for the good of the Universal Church, *solum Deum præ oculis habentes.*

53. In conformity with the provisions of Section Number 52, the Cardinal Dean or the Cardinal who has precedence by order and seniority, will read aloud the following formula of the oath:

We, the Cardinal electors present in this election of the Supreme Pontiff promise, pledge and swear, as individuals and as a group, to observe faithfully and scrupulously the prescriptions contained in the Apostolic Constitution of the Supreme Pontiff John Paul II, *Universi Dominici Gregis,* published on 22 February 1996. We likewise promise, pledge and swear that whichever of us by divine disposition is elected Roman Pontiff will commit himself faithfully to carrying out the *munus Petrinum* of Pastor of the Universal Church and will not fail to affirm and defend strenuously the spiritual and temporal rights and the liberty of the Holy See. In a particular way, we promise and swear to observe with the greatest fidelity and with all persons, clerical or lay, secrecy regarding everything that in any way relates to the election of the Roman Pontiff and regarding what occurs in the place of the election, directly or indirectly related to the results of the voting, we promise and swear not to break this secret in any way, either during or after the election of the new Pontiff, unless explicit authorization is granted by the same Pontiff; and never to lend support or favor to any interference, opposition or any other form of intervention, whereby secular authorities of whatever order and degree or any group of people or individuals might wish to intervene in the election of the Roman Pontiff.

Each of the Cardinal electors, according to the order of precedence, will then take the oath according to the following formula:

And I, N. Cardinal N., do so promise, pledge and swear. Placing his hand on the Gospels, he will add: So help me God and these Holy Gospels which I touch with my hand.

54. When the ecclesiastic who gives the meditation has concluded, he leaves the Sistine Chapel together with the Master of Papal Liturgical Celebrations. The Cardinal electors, after reciting the prayers found in the relative *Ordo*, listen to the Cardinal Dean (or the one taking his place), who begins by asking the College of electors whether the election can begin, or whether there still remain doubts which need to be clarified concerning the norms and procedures laid down in this Constitution. It is not however permitted, even if the electors are unanimously agreed, to modify or replace any of the norms and procedures which are a substantial part of the election process, under penalty of the nullity of the same deliberation.

If, in the judgment of the majority of the electors, there is nothing to prevent the election process from beginning, it shall start immediately, in accordance with the procedures indicated in this Constitution.

Chapter IV—Observance of secrecy on all matters concerning the election.

55. The Cardinal Camerlengo and the three Cardinal Assistants pro tempore are obliged to be especially vigilant in ensuring that there is absolutely no violation of secrecy with regard to the events occurring in the Sistine Chapel, where the voting takes place, and in the adjacent areas, before, as well as during and after the voting.

In particular, relying upon the expertise of two trustworthy technicians, they shall make every effort to preserve that secrecy by ensuring that no audiovisual equipment for recording or transmitting has been installed by anyone in the areas mentioned, and particularly in the Sistine Chapel itself, where the acts of the election are carried out.

Should any infraction whatsoever of this norm occur and be discovered, those responsible should know that they will be subject to grave penalties according to the judgment of the future Pope.

56. For the whole duration of the election, the Cardinal electors are required to refrain from written correspondence and from all conversations, including those by telephone or radio, with persons who have not been duly admitted to the buildings set aside for their use.

Such conversations shall be permitted only for the most grave and urgent reasons, confirmed by the Particular Congregation of Cardinals mentioned in Section Number 7.

It shall therefore be the duty of the Cardinal electors to make necessary arrangements, before the beginning of the election, for the handling of all non-deferrable official or personal business, so that there will be no need for conversations of this sort to take place.

57. The Cardinal electors are likewise to refrain from receiving or sending messages of any kind outside Vatican City; naturally it is prohibited for any person legitimately present in Vatican City to deliver such messages. It is specifically prohibited to the Cardinal electors, for the entire duration of the election, to receive newspapers or periodicals of any sort, to listen to the radio or to watch television.

58. Those who, in accordance with the prescriptions of Section Number 46 of the present Constitution, carry out any functions associated with the election, and who directly or indirectly could in any way violate secrecy—whether by words or writing, by signs or in any other way—are absolutely obliged to avoid this, lest they incur the penalty of excommunication *latæ sententiæ* reserved to the Apostolic See.

59. In particular, the Cardinal electors are forbidden to reveal to any other person, directly or indirectly, information about the voting and about matters discussed or decided concerning the election of the Pope in the meetings of Cardinals, both before and during the time of the election. This obligation of secrecy also applies to the Cardinals who are not electors but who take part in the General Congregations in accordance with Section Number 7 of the present Constitution.

60. I further order the Cardinal electors, *graviter onerata ipsorum conscientia*, to maintain secrecy concerning these matters also after the election of the new Pope has taken place, and I remind them that it is not licit

to break the secret in any way unless a special and explicit permission has been granted by the Pope himself.

61. Finally, in order that the Cardinal electors may be protected from the indiscretion of others and from possible threats to their independence of judgment and freedom of decision, I absolutely forbid the introduction into the place of the election, under whatsoever pretext, or the use, should they have been introduced, of technical instruments of any kind for the recording, reproducing or transmitting of sound, visual images or writing.

Chapter V—The election procedure.

62. Since the forms of election known as *per acclamationem seu inspirationem* and *per compromissum* are abolished, the form of electing the Roman Pontiff shall henceforth be *per scrutinium* alone. I therefore decree that for the valid election of the Roman Pontiff two thirds of the votes are required, calculated on the basis of the total number of electors present. Should it be impossible to divide the number of Cardinals present into three equal parts, for the validity of the election of the Supreme Pontiff one additional vote is required.

63. The election is to begin immediately after the provisions of Section Number 54 of the present Constitution have been duly carried out. Should the election begin on the afternoon of the first day, only one ballot is to be held; then, on the following days, if no one was elected on the first ballot, two ballots shall be held in the morning and two in the afternoon. The voting is to begin at a time which shall have been determined earlier, either in the preparatory Congregations or during the election period, but in accordance with the procedures laid down in Section Numbers 64ff of the present Constitution.

64. The voting process is carried out in three phases. The first phase, which can be called the pre-scrutiny, comprises: 1) the preparation and distribution of the ballot papers by the Masters of Ceremonies, who give at least two or three to each Cardinal elector; 2) the drawing by lot, from among all the Cardinal electors, of three Scrutineers, of three persons charged with collecting the votes of the sick, called for the sake of brevity Infirmarii; and of three Revisers; this drawing is carried out in public by the junior Cardinal Deacon, who draws out nine names, one after another, of those who shall carry out these tasks; 3) if, in the drawing of lots for the Scrutineers, Infirmarii and Revisers, there should come out the names of Cardinal electors who because of infirmity or other reasons are unable to carry out these tasks, the names of others who are not impeded are to be drawn in their place. The first three drawn will act as Scrutineers, the sec-

ond three as Infirmarii and the last three as Revisers.

65. For this phase of the voting process the following norms must be observed: 1) the ballot paper must be rectangular in shape and must bear in the upper half, in print if possible, the words *Eligo in Summum Pontificem*; on the lower half there must be a space left for writing the name of the person chosen; thus the ballot is made in such a way that it can be folded in two; 2) the completion of the ballot must be done in secret by each Cardinal elector, who will write down legibly, as far as possible in handwriting that cannot be identified as his, the name of the person he chooses, taking care not to write other names as well, since this would make the ballot null; he will then fold the ballot twice; 3) during the voting, the Cardinal electors are to remain alone in the Sistine Chapel; therefore, immediately after the distribution of the ballots and before the electors begin to write, the Secretary of the College of Cardinals, the Master of Papal Liturgical Celebrations and the Masters of Ceremonies must leave the Chapel. After they have left, the junior Cardinal Deacon shall close the door, opening and closing it again each time this is necessary, as for example when the Infirmarii go to collect the votes of the sick and when they return to the Chapel.

66. The second phase, the scrutiny proper, comprises: 1) the placing of the ballots in the appropriate receptacle; 2) the mixing and counting of the ballots; 3) the opening of the votes. Each Cardinal elector, in order of precedence, having completed and folded his ballot, holds it up so that it can be seen and carries it to the altar, at which the Scrutineers stand and upon which there is placed a receptacle, covered by a plate, for receiving the ballots. Having reached the altar, the Cardinal elector says aloud the words of the following oath: I call as my witness Christ the Lord who will be my judge, that my vote is given to the one who before God I think should be elected. He then places the ballot on the plate, with which he drops it into the receptacle. Having done this, he bows to the altar and returns to his place.

If any of the Cardinal electors present in the Chapel is unable to go to the altar because of infirmity, the last of the Scrutineers goes to him. The infirm elector, having pronounced the above oath, hands the folded ballot to the Scrutineer, who carries it in full view to the altar and omitting the oath, places it on the plate, with which he drops it into the receptacle.

67. If there are Cardinal electors who are sick and confined to their rooms, referred to in Section Numbers 41ff of this Constitution, the three Infirmarii go to them with a box which has an opening in the top through which a folded ballot can be inserted. Before giving the box to the Infirmarii, the Scrutineers open it publicly, so that the other electors can see that it

is empty; they are then to lock it and place the key on the altar. The Infirmarii, taking the locked box and a sufficient number of ballot papers on a small tray, then go, duly accompanied, to the Domus Sanctæ Marthæ to each sick elector, who takes a ballot, writes his vote in secret, folds the ballot and, after taking the above-mentioned oath, puts it through the opening in the box. If any of the electors who are sick is unable to write, one of the three Infirmarii or another Cardinal elector chosen by the sick man, having taken an oath before the Infirmarii concerning the observance of secrecy, carries out the above procedure. The Infirmarii then take the box back into the Chapel, where it shall be opened by the Scrutineers after the Cardinals present have cast their votes. The Scrutineers then count the ballots in the box and, having ascertained that their number corresponds to the number of those who are sick, place them one by one on the plate and then drop them all together into the receptacle. In order not to prolong the voting process unduly, the Infirmarii may complete their own ballots and place them in the receptable immediately after the senior Cardinal, and then go to collect the votes of the sick in the manner indicated above while the other electors are casting their votes.

68. After all the ballots of the Cardinal electors have been placed in the receptacle, the first Scrutineer shakes it several times in order to mix them, and immediately afterwards the last Scrutineer proceeds to count them, picking them out of the urn in full view and placing them in another empty receptacle previously prepared for this purpose. If the number of ballots does not correspond to the number of electors, the ballots must all be burned and a second vote taken at once; if however their number does correspond to the number of electors, the opening of the ballots then takes place in the following manner.

69. The Scrutineers sit at a table placed in front of the altar. The first of them takes a ballot, unfolds it, notes the name of the person chosen and passes the ballot to the second Scrutineer, who in his turn notes the name of the person chosen and passes the ballot to the third, who reads it out in a loud and clear voice, so that all the electors present can record the vote on a sheet of paper prepared for that purpose. He himself writes down the name read from the ballot. If during the opening of the ballots the Scrutineers should discover two ballots folded in such a way that they appear to have been completed by one elector, if these ballots bear the same name they are counted as one vote; if however they bear two different names, neither vote will be valid; however, in neither of the two cases is the voting session annulled.

When all the ballots have been opened, the Scrutineers add up the sum of the votes obtained by the different names and write them down on a separate sheet of paper. The last Scrutineer, as he reads out the individual ballots, pierces each one with a needle through the word Eligo and places it on a thread, so that the ballots can be more securely preserved. After the names have been read out, the ends of the thread are tied in a knot, and the ballots thus joined together are placed in a receptacle or on one side of the table.

70. There then follows the third and last phase, also known as the post-scrutiny, which comprises: 1) the counting of the votes; 2) the checking of the same; 3) the burning of the ballots.

The Scrutineers add up all the votes that each individual has received, and if no one has obtained two thirds of the votes on that ballot, the Pope has not been elected; if however it turns out that someone has obtained two thirds of the votes, the canonically valid election of the Roman Pontiff has taken place.

In either case, that is, whether the election has occurred or not, the Revisers must proceed to check both the ballots and the notes made by the Scrutineers, in order to make sure that these latter have performed their task exactly and faithfully.

Immediately after the checking has taken place, and before the Cardinal electors leave the Sistine Chapel, all the ballots are to be burnt by the Scrutineers, with the assistance of the Secretary of the Conclave and the Masters of Ceremonies who in the meantime have been summoned by the junior Cardinal Deacon. If however a second vote is to take place immediately, the ballots from the first vote will be burned only at the end, together with those from the second vote.

71. In order that secrecy may be better observed, I order each and every Cardinal elector to hand over to the Cardinal Camerlengo or to one of the three Cardinal Assistants any notes which he may have in his possession concerning the results of each ballot. These notes are to be burnt together with the ballots.

I further lay down that at the end of the election the Cardinal Camerlengo of Holy Roman Church shall draw up a document, to be approved also by the three Cardinal Assistants, declaring the result of the voting at each session. This document is to be given to the Pope and will thereafter be kept in a designated archive, enclosed in a sealed envelope, which may be opened by no one unless the Supreme Pontiff gives explicit permission.

72. Confirming the dispositions of my Predecessors, Saint Pius X,[20] Pius XII,[21] and Paul VI,[22] I decree that—except for the afternoon of the entrance into the Conclave—both in the morning and in the afternoon, after a ballot which does not result in an election, the Cardinal electors shall proceed immediately to a second one, in which they are to express their vote

anew. In this second ballot all the formalities of the previous one are to be observed, with the difference that the electors are not bound to take a new oath or to choose new Scrutineers, Infirmarii and Revisers. Everything done in this regard for the first ballot will be valid for the second one, without the need for any repetition.

73. Everything that has been laid down above concerning the voting procedures must be diligently observed by the Cardinal electors in all the ballots, which are to take place each day in the morning and in the afternoon, after the celebration of the sacred rites or prayers laid down in the *Ordo Rituum Conclavis*.

74. In the event that the Cardinal electors find it difficult to agree on the person to be elected, after balloting has been carried out for three days in the form described above (in Section Numbers 62ff) without result, voting is to be suspended for a maximum of one day in order to allow a pause for prayer, informal discussion among the voters, and a brief spiritual exhortation given by the senior Cardinal in the Order of Deacons. Voting is then resumed in the usual manner, and after seven ballots, if the election has not taken place, there is another pause for prayer, discussion and an exhortation given by the senior Cardinal in the Order of Priests. Another series of seven ballots is then held and, if there has still been no election, this is followed by a further pause for prayer, discussion and an exhortation given by the senior Cardinal in the Order of Bishops. Voting is then resumed in the usual manner and, unless the election occurs, it is to continue for seven ballots.

75. If the balloting does not result in an election, even after the provisions of Section Number 74 have been fulfilled, the Cardinal electors shall be invited by the Camerlengo to express an opinion about the manner of proceeding. The election will then proceed in accordance with what the absolute majority of the electors decides.

Nevertheless, there can be no waiving of the requirement that a valid election takes place only by an absolute majority of the votes or else by voting only on the two names which in the ballot immediately preceding have received the greatest number of votes; also in this second case only an absolute majority is required.

76. Should the election take place in a way other than that prescribed in the present Constitution, or should the conditions laid down here not be observed, the election is for this very reason null and void, without any need for a declaration on the matter; consequently, it confers no right on the one elected.

77. I decree that the dispositions concerning everything that precedes the election of the Roman Pontiff and the carrying out of the election itself

must be observed in full, even if the vacancy of the Apostolic See should occur as a result of the resignation of the Supreme Pontiff, in accordance with the provisions of Canon 333 §2 of the *Code of Canon Law* and Canon 44 §2 of the *Code of Canons of the Eastern Churches.*

Chapter VI—Matters to be observed or avoided in the election of the Roman Pontiff.

78. If—God forbid—in the election of the Roman Pontiff the crime of simony were to be perpetrated, I decree and declare that all those guilty thereof shall incur excommunication *latæ sententiæ*. At the same time I remove the nullity or invalidity of the same simoniacal provision, in order that—as was already established by my Predecessors—the validity of the election of the Roman Pontiff may not for this reason be challenged.[23]

79. Confirming the prescriptions of my Predecessors, I likewise forbid anyone, even if he is a Cardinal, during the Pope's lifetime and without having consulted him, to make plans concerning the election of his successor, or to promise votes, or to make decisions in this regard in private gatherings.

80. In the same way, I wish to confirm the provisions made by my Predecessors for the purpose of excluding any external interference in the election of the Supreme Pontiff. Therefore, in virtue of holy obedience and under pain of excommunication *latæ sententiæ*, I again forbid each and every Cardinal elector, present and future, as also the Secretary of the College of Cardinals and all other persons taking part in the preparation and carrying out of everything necessary for the election, to accept under any pretext whatsoever, from any civil authority whatsoever, the task of proposing the veto or the so-called *exclusiva*, even under the guise of a simple desire, or to reveal such either to the entire electoral body assembled together or to individual electors, in writing or by word of mouth, either directly and personally or indirectly and through others, both before the election begins and for its duration. I intend this prohibition to include all possible forms of interference, opposition and suggestion whereby secular authorities of whatever order and degree, or any individual or group, might attempt to exercise influence on the election of the Pope.

81. The Cardinal electors shall further abstain from any form of pact, agreement, promise or other commitment of any kind which could oblige them to give or deny their vote to a person or persons. If this were in fact done, even under oath, I decree that such a commitment shall be null and void and that no one shall be bound to observe it; and I hereby impose the penalty of excommunication *latæ sententiæ* upon those who violate this

prohibition. It is not my intention however to forbid, during the period in which the See is vacant, the exchange of views concerning the election.

82. I likewise forbid the Cardinals before the election to enter into any stipulations, committing themselves of common accord to a certain course of action should one of them be elevated to the Pontificate. These promises too, should any in fact be made, even under oath, I also declare null and void.

83. With the same insistence shown by my Predecessors, I earnestly exhort the Cardinal electors not to allow themselves to be guided, in choosing the Pope, by friendship or aversion, or to be influenced by favor or personal relationships towards anyone, or to be constrained by the interference of persons in authority or by pressure groups, by the suggestions of the mass media, or by force, fear or the pursuit of popularity. Rather, having before their eyes solely the glory of God and the good of the Church, and having prayed for divine assistance, they shall give their vote to the person, even outside the College of Cardinals, who in their judgment is most suited to govern the universal Church in a fruitful and beneficial way.

84. During the vacancy of the Apostolic See, and above all during the time of the election of the Successor of Peter, the Church is united in a very special way with her Pastors and particularly with the Cardinal electors of the Supreme Pontiff, and she asks God to grant her a new Pope as a gift of his goodness and providence. Indeed, following the example of the first Christian community spoken of in the *Acts of the Apostles* (*cf.* 1:14), the universal Church, spiritually united with Mary, the Mother of Jesus, should persevere with one heart in prayer; thus the election of the new Pope will not be something unconnected with the People of God and concerning the College of electors alone, but will be in a certain sense an act of the whole Church. I therefore lay down that in all cities and other places, at least the more important ones, as soon as news is received of the vacancy of the Apostolic See and, in particular, of the death of the Pope, and following the celebration of his solemn funeral rites, humble and persevering prayers are to be offered to the Lord (*cf.* Mt 21:22; Mk 11:24), that he may enlighten the electors and make them so like-minded in their task that a speedy, harmonious and fruitful election may take place, as the salvation of souls and the good of the whole People of God demand.

85. In a most earnest and heartfelt way I recommend this prayer to the venerable Cardinals who, by reason of age, no longer enjoy the right to take part in the election of the Supreme Pontiff. By virtue of the singular bond with the Apostolic See which the Cardinalate represents, let them lead the prayer of the People of God, whether gathered in the Patriarchal

Basilicas of the city of Rome or in places of worship in other particular Churches, fervently imploring the assistance of Almighty God and the enlightenment of the Holy Spirit for the Cardinal electors, especially at the time of the election itself. They will thereby participate in an effective and real way in the difficult task of providing a Pastor for the universal Church.

86. I also ask the one who is elected not to refuse, for fear of its weight, the office to which he has been called, but to submit humbly to the design of the divine will. God who imposes the burden will sustain him with his hand, so that he will be able to bear it. In conferring the heavy task upon him, God will also help him to accomplish it and, in giving him the dignity, he will grant him the strength not to be overwhelmed by the weight of his office.

Chapter VII—The acceptance and proclamation of the new pope and the beginning of his ministry.

87. When the election has canonically taken place, the junior Cardinal Deacon summons into the hall of election the Secretary of the College of Cardinals and the Master of Papal Liturgical Celebrations. The Cardinal Dean, or the Cardinal who is first in order and seniority, in the name of the whole College of electors, then asks the consent of the one elected in the following words: Do you accept your canonical election as Supreme Pontiff? And, as soon as he has received the consent, he asks him: By what name do you wish to be called? Then the Master of Papal Liturgical Celebrations, acting as notary and having as witnesses two Masters of Ceremonies, who are to be summoned at that moment, draws up a document certifying acceptance by the new Pope and the name taken by him.

88. After his acceptance, the person elected, if he has already received episcopal ordination, is immediately Bishop of the Church of Rome, true Pope and Head of the College of Bishops. He thus acquires and can exercise full and supreme power over the universal Church.

If the person elected is not already a Bishop, he shall immediately be ordained Bishop.

89. When the other formalities provided for in the *Ordo Rituum Conclavis* have been carried out, the Cardinal electors approach the newly elected Pope in the prescribed manner, in order to make an act of homage and obedience. An act of thanksgiving to God is then made, after which the senior Cardinal Deacon announces to the waiting people that the election has taken place and proclaims the name of the new Pope, who immediately thereafter imparts the Apostolic Blessing *Urbi et Orbi* from the balcony of the Vatican Basilica.

If the person elected is not already a Bishop, homage is paid to him and the announcement of his election is made only after he has been solemnly ordained Bishop.

90. If the person elected resides outside Vatican City, the norms contained in the *Ordo Rituum Conclavis* are to be observed.

If the newly elected Supreme Pontiff is not already a Bishop, his episcopal ordination, referred to in Section Numbers 88 and 89 of the present Constitution, shall be carried out according to the usage of the Church by the Dean of the College of Cardinals or, in his absence, by the Subdean or, should he too be prevented from doing so, by the senior Cardinal Bishop.

91. The Conclave ends immediately after the new Supreme Pontiff assents to his election, unless he should determine otherwise. From that moment the new Pope can be approached by the Substitute of the Secretariat of State, the Secretary for Relations with States, the Prefect of the Papal Household and by anyone else needing to discuss with him matters of importance at the time.

92. After the solemn ceremony of the inauguration of the Pontificate and within an appropriate time, the Pope will take possession of the Patriarchal Archbasilica of the Lateran, according to the prescribed ritual.

Promulgation

Wherefore, after mature reflection and following the example of my Predecessors, I lay down and prescribe these norms and I order that no one shall presume to contest the present Constitution and anything contained herein for any reason whatsoever. This Constitution is to be completely observed by all, notwithstanding any disposition to the contrary, even if worthy of special mention. It is to be fully and integrally implemented and is to serve as a guide for all to whom it refers.

As determined above, I hereby declare abrogated all Constitutions and Orders issued in this regard by the Roman Pontiffs, and at the same time I declare completely null and void anything done by any person, whatever his authority, knowingly or unknowingly, in any way contrary to this Constitution.

Given in Rome, at Saint Peter's, on 22 February, the Feast of the Chair of Saint Peter, Apostle, in the year 1996, the eighteenth of my Pontificate.

Joannes Paulus PP II

NOTES

1. St Irenæus, *Adversus Hæreses*, III, 3, 2: SCh 211, 33.

2. *Cf.* Apostolic Constitution *Vacante Sede Apostolica* (25 December 1904): *Pii X Pontificis Maximi Acta*, III (1908), 239–288.

3. *Cf.* Motu Proprio *Cum Proxime* (1 March 1922): *AAS* 14 (1922), 145–146; Apostolic Constitution *Quæ Divinitus* (25 March 1935): *AAS* 27 (1935), 97–113.

4. *Cf.* Apostolic Constitution *Vacantis Apostolicæ Sedis* (8 December 1945): *AAS* 38 (1946), 65–99.

5. *Cf.* Motu Proprio *Summi Pontificis Electio* (5 September 1962): *AAS* 54 (1962), 632–640.

6. *Cf.* Apostolic Constitution *Regimini Ecclesiæ Universæ* (15 August 1967): *AAS* 59 (1967), 885–928; Motu Proprio *Ingravescentem Ætatem* (21 November 1970): *AAS* 62 (1970), 810–813; Apostolic Constitution *Romano Pontifici Eligendo* (1 October 1975): *AAS* 67 (1975), 609–645.

7. *Cf. AAS* 80 (1988), 841–912.

8. *Cf.* First Vatican Ecumenical Council, Dogmatic Constitution on the Church of Christ *Pastor Æternus*, III; Second First Vatican Ecumenical Council, Dogmatic Constitution on the Church *Lumen Gentium*, 18.

9. Canon 332 §1 *CIC*; Canon 44 §1 *CCEO*.

10. *Cf.* Motu Proprio *Ingravescentem Ætatem* (21 November 1970), II, 2: *AAS* 62 (1970), 811; Apostolic Constitution *Romano Pontifici Eli-* *gendo* (1 October 1975), 33: *AAS* 67 (1975), 622.

11. Code of Canon Law, Canon 1752.

12. *Cf.* Code of Canon Law, Canon 332 §2, Code of Canons of the Eastern Churches, Canon 47 §2.

13. *Cf. AAS* 80 (1988), 860.

14. *Cf. AAS* 69 (1977), 9–10.

15. *Cf.* Apostolic Constitution *Vicariæ Potestatis* (6 January 1977), 2 : *AAS* 69 (1977), 10.

16. *Cf.* No. 12: *AAS* 27 (1935), 112–113.

17. *Cf.* Art. 117: *AAS* 80 (1988), 905.

18. *Cf. AAS* 80 (1988), 864.

19. *Missale Romanum* No. 4, p. 795.

20. *Cf.* Apostolic Constitution *Vacante Sede Apostolica* (25 December 1904), 76: *Pii X Pontificis Maximi Acta*, III (1908), 280–281.

21. *Cf.* Apostolic Constitution *Vacantis Apostolicæ Sedis* (8 December 1945), 88: *AAS* 38 (1946), 93.

22. *Cf.* Apostolic Constitution *Romano Pontifici Eligendo* (1 October 1975), 74: *AAS* 67 (1975), 639.

23. *Cf.* Saint Pius X, Apostolic Constitution *Vacante Sede Apostolica* (25 December 1904), 79: *Pii X Pontificis Maximi Acta*, III (1908), 282; Pius XII, Apostolic Constitution *Vacantis Apostolicæ Sedis* (8 December 1945), 92: *AAS* 38 (1946), 94; Paul VI, Apostolic Constitution *Romano Pontifici Eligendo* (1 October 1975), 79: *AAS* 67 (1975), 611.

Romano Pontifici Eligendo
Apostolic Constitution on the Election of the Roman Pontiff

October 1, 1975

Introduction

Since the Roman Pontiff, as successor of St. Peter in the See of Rome, is Vicar of Christ on earth as well as supreme Shepherd and visible head of the universal Church, his election has always been an object of special attention. Careful measures have always been taken to assure a legitimate election and the freedom of those who cast a vote.

Over the centuries the Supreme Pontiffs have regarded it as their prerogative, right and duty to make the provisions they think best for the election of their successor. They have resisted all views that ecclesiastical practice should be changed and that the Popes should lose the right to determine, entirely on their own, the composition of the electoral college and the manner in which the college carries out its task. At the same time, however, although the manner of election retains important primitive elements that at one time were characteristic of the election of bishops, it has nonetheless gradually undergone changes as a result of the constant concern already mentioned, that is, the concern to prevent illegitimate interference and to safeguard a proper procedure. Through this process of gradual change, the most important rôle in the election of the Pope has been assigned to the three major orders of the Roman clergy—bishops, priests and deacons—who are called the Cardinals of the Holy Roman Church. Their primary rôle in the election of the Roman Pontiff was set forth in the well-known decree *In nomine Domini* which Nicholas II promulgated at the Roman synod of 1059.[1] At the Third Lateran Council (1179) Alexander III published the Constitution *Licet de vitanda* which definitely established that the election is the prerogative solely of the College of Cardinals who represent the Roman Church and that all other participants are to be

467

excluded.[2] All later provisions have had as their sole purpose to assure the effectiveness of this original manner of electing the Roman Pontiff or to adapt it to new circumstances. The tradition of the Roman Church makes it likewise clear that the college to which is entrusted the duty of electing the Pontiff is permanent and so constituted that if the Apostolic See happens to be vacant, the college can continue to act. It cannot be denied that a previously established body of electors is still required and that this body should not have so many members that it cannot easily and quickly be assembled (as becomes necessary at times in periods of difficulty for the Church and the Supreme Pontificate). It is not permissible, therefore, that the electors of the Pope should themselves be elected or deputed only when the Apostolic See has become vacant. Guided by these various considerations, Our recent predecessors have preserved this ancient manner of election in all its important fundamental aspects and have safeguarded its exercise. At the same time, however, they have striven to improve it by adapting it to new conditions. This is what Pius XII did, for example, when he added a number of Fathers to the College of Cardinals so that it might be more representative of the various nations and Churches of the Catholic world. John XXIII had the same end in view when he increased the number of members in the College and decreed that they should all receive the rank of bishop.[3] We Ourselves have already acted in this area by publishing norms for the Sacred College of Cardinals, especially the norms contained in the Apostolic Letter Motu Proprio *Ingravescentem Ætatem*.[4] We now judge it necessary to revise some points relating to the election of a Pontiff, so that they may be appropriate in the present situation and truly contribute to the good of the Church. We also reassert, however, the principle that, in accordance with long-standing tradition, the election of the Roman Pontiff is the prerogative of the Church of Rome as represented by the Sacred College of Cardinals. Therefore, following the example of Our predecessors, on the basis of such knowledge and careful reflection, and in an exercise of the fullness of apostolic authority, We have determined to publish the norms contained in this constitution. This constitution replaces the constitution *Vacantis Apostolicæ Sedis* of Pius XII (December 8, 1945)[5] and the prescriptions which John XXIII promulgated in his Apostolic Letter Motu Proprio *Summi Pontificis Electio* (September 5, 1962).[6]

Part 1: On the Vacancy of the Apostolic See

Chapter 1

The Power of the Sacred College of Cardinals When the Apostolic See Is Vacant

THE COLLEGE GOVERNS THE CHURCH

1. While the Apostolic See is vacant, the government of the Church is in the hands of the Sacred College of Cardinals but only for ordinary business and other matters that cannot be postponed and for the preparations required for the election of a new Pontiff. In making such preparations, the College is bound by the provisions of this constitution and by the limitations it imposes.

2. During the period in question, therefore, the Sacred College has no authority or jurisdiction in questions that were reserved to the Supreme Pontiff while he was alive; decisions in all such matters must be left solely to the future Pontiff. We therefore proclaim invalid and void any exercise by the college of authority or jurisdiction which belongs to the Pope when he is alive, except to the extent that such an exercise is explicitly permitted by this constitution.

3. We also decree that the Sacred College of Cardinals may not in any way dispose of any rights of the Apostolic See and the Church of Rome nor derogate from them directly or indirectly, even when it is a question of resolving disputes or prosecuting actions contrary to these rights after the death of the pope. All must be concerned to protect these rights.

4. Neither is it legitimate, while the Apostolic See is vacant, to amend the laws made by the Roman Pontiffs or to add anything to them or to dispense from sections of them, especially sections having to do with arrangements for the election of the Supreme Pontiff. By Our supreme authority We now declare null and void anything done or attempted contrary to this decree.

RESOLUTION OF DOUBTS

5. If doubts arise about the meaning of prescriptions in this constitution or about the way they are to be implemented, We declare and decree that on these points the Sacred College of Cardinals has the power to decide. Therefore, We grant the Sacred College of Cardinals the authority to interpret doubtful or disputed passages. In this regard, We decree that if deci-

sions must be made on these or similar points (except on the act of election itself), it is enough if the majority of the assembled cardinals is of the same opinion.

6. Similarly, if some matter must be expedited which according to the majority of the assembled cardinals cannot be postponed, the Sacred College of Cardinals is to act in accordance with the majority view.

Chapter 2

Meetings of the Cardinals

TWO TYPES OF MEETINGS

7. While the See is vacant and before the entry into the conclave, two types of meetings of the cardinals, and the cardinals alone, are to be held One is a general meeting of the whole college; the other, a special meeting. All cardinals not legitimately prevented are to attend the general meetings as soon as they have been informed that the apostolic see is vacant. Cardinals who have completed their eightieth year are free to attend or not attend.

The special meeting is attended by the Cardinal Camerlengo of the Holy Roman Church and three other cardinals, one from each order, who are chosen by lot from among all who, in accordance with number 33 of this constitution, have the right to cast a vote in electing the Pontiff. The office of these three cardinals, called assistants, is terminated on the third day after the beginning of the conclave. They are replaced then, and every third day thereafter, by three others, also chosen by lot. During the conclave, more serious matters, should they arise, are settled at the general meeting of the cardinal electors. Ordinary business continues to be handled at the special meetings. During the general and special meetings, while the see is vacant, the cardinals wear the customary black cassock with red piping and red sash.

THE SPECIAL MEETINGS

8. During the special meetings, only business of lesser moment is to be dispatched, such as occurs daily or constantly. If anything arises of a more serious nature or requiring more thorough examination, it is to be presented to the general meeting. In addition, if a decision, solution or refusal of a request is reached during one special meeting, it cannot be withdrawn, amended or granted in another. The right to take a changed posi-

tion rests solely with the general meeting. At the latter a change can be made only by a plurality or majority of votes.

9. General meetings of the Cardinals are to take place in the Apostolic Vatican Palace or, if circumstances require, in some place the Cardinals themselves judge more suitable. The dean of the sacred college presides at these meetings or, in his absence, the subdean. If, however, one or other or both of these Cardinals is not to enter the conclave because he has completed his eightieth year, the cardinal who ranks highest in the general order of precedence is to preside over any general meeting of the Cardinals that may take place within the conclave (in accordance with number 7).

SECRET BALLOT ON IMPORTANT BUSINESS

10. When business of greater moment is being handled, the votes at the meetings of the cardinals are to be taken by a secret ballot rather than by voice.

11. The general meetings that precede the conclave and are therefore called preparatory are to be held daily, from the day determined by the Camerlengo of the Holy Roman Church together with the three senior cardinals of each order; the meetings are to be held even on the days when the rites for the dead pontiff are being celebrated. The reason for the meetings is twofold: to allow the Cardinal Camerlengo to inquire into the views of the Sacred College, as he communicates to it matters he thinks necessary or timely, and to afford each Cardinal the opportunity to make known his views on current business, to seek an explanation of doubtful points and to propose subjects for discussion.

OATH ON OBSERVING PART I OF THIS CONSTITUTION

12. At the first general meeting Part I of this constitution, *Romano Pontifici Eligendo*, is to be read. After the reading, all the cardinals present are to take an oath to observe its prescriptions and to maintain secrecy. The oath is also to be taken by cardinals who arrive later on and are in attendance at subsequent meetings. The formula of the oath which is to be read by the Cardinal Dean in the presence of the other cardinals, is as follows:

"We, the Cardinal Bishops, Priests and Deacons of the Holy Roman Church, promise and swear on oath that we will, each and all of us, observe exactly all that is set down in the Apostolic Constitution *Romano Pontifici Eligendo* of the Supreme Pontiff Paul VI, and that we will maintain a scrupulous secrecy concerning everything discussed in the meetings of the cardinals whether before or during the conclave, and concerning everything that in any way relates to the election of the Roman Pontiff."

Then each Cardinal is to say: "And I, . . . Cardinal . . . , solemnly promise and swear on oath." Laying his hand on the Gospel, each is to add: "So help me God and these holy Gospels of God which I touch with my hand."

PREPARATIONS FOR THE CONCLAVE

13. At one of the meetings and at those immediately subsequent to it, the Cardinals, following a prescribed agenda, are to reach decisions on matters of greater urgency as regards beginning the conclave; namely:

a) They are to decide on the day, hour, and manner in which the body of the dead pontiff is to be carried to the Vatican Basilica and exposed for the homage of the faithful;

b) They are to see to all necessary preparations for the funeral rites of the dead pontiff, which shall last for nine successive days, and they are to determine when the rites are to begin;

c) They are to appoint two committees or commissions, with three Cardinals on each. One of these commissions shall designate those who are to enter the conclave and perform various services, as well as the person who is to be in charge of these individuals. It is also to consider carefully whether any conclavist or private servant is to be admitted to the conclave, in accordance with number 45 of this constitution. The other commission is to oversee the building and enclosing of the conclave, and the arrangement of the cells, or private rooms, in it;

d) They are to estimate and approve the expenses of the conclave;

e) They are to read the documents left for the Sacred College of Cardinals by the dead pontiff, if there be any such documents;

f) They are to see to the breaking of the Fisherman's Ring and the lead seal under which apostolic letters are sent;

g) Cells in the conclave are to be assigned to the electors by lot, unless the poor health of an elector makes some other arrangement advisable;

h) They are to set the day and the hour for entering the conclave.

Chapter 3

Various Offices during the Vacancy of the Apostolic See

RESIGNATION OF OFFICES; EXCEPTIONS TO THIS RULE

14. In accordance with the Apostolic Constitution *Regimini Ecclesiæ Universæ*, all Cardinals who are prefects of the agencies of the Roman Curia, including the Cardinal Secretary of State, are to resign their offices at the death of the pontiff. Exceptions are the Camerlengo of the Holy Roman Church, the Major Penitentiary and the Vicar General of the Diocese of Rome; these are to handle ordinary business and bring before the Sacred College of Cardinals matters requiring referral to the Supreme Pontiff.[7]

15. If the office of Camerlengo of the Holy Roman Church or that of Major Penitentiary should happen to be vacant when the pope dies or should fall vacant before his successor is elected, the Sacred College of Cardinals should, as soon as possible, elect a cardinal (or cardinals) to fill the office (offices) until the election of a new pontiff. In each of these cases, the election is to be by secret vote of all the Cardinals present. Votes are to be cast by means of ballots which are distributed and collected by the masters of ceremonies who shall open them in the presence of the Camerlengo of the Holy Roman Church and the three cardinal assistants, if the vote is for Major Penitentiary, or in the presence of the three cardinal assistants and the secretary of the sacred college, if the vote is for Camerlengo. The individual who receives the majority of votes is elected and automatically receives all faculties for the office. If the votes should be equal in number for two individuals, he is elected who belongs to the higher order, or who, if both are of the same order, was admitted earlier into the sacred college. Until a Camerlengo is elected, his duties are to be performed by the dean of the sacred college, who has power to make decisions without delay, as circumstances require.

VICAR GENERAL OF THE DIOCESE OF ROME

16. If the vicar general of the Diocese of Rome should die while the see is vacant, the assistant vicar then in office has all the faculties, authority and powers which the vicar himself had been given for his office, and which the pope himself customarily gives the assistant vicar when there is no vicar and until he appoints a new vicar. If there is no assistant vicar or if

he is prevented, the auxiliary bishop appointed the longest is to take over the duties.

17. While the see is vacant, it shall be the duty of the Cardinal Camerlengo of the Holy Roman Church to protect the rights of the Holy See, with the help of the three cardinal assistants. He is to obtain the approval of the Sacred College once and for all for matters of lesser moment but in each case for business of greater moment. It is therefore, the duty of the Camerlengo of the Holy Roman Church, as soon as he has received word of the pontiff's death from the prefect of the pontifical household, to verify the pope's death legally, in the presence of the pontifical master of ceremonies, the clerical prelates of the reverend apostolic chamber, and the secretary-chancellor of the same. The latter shall draw up an authentic record of the death. The Camerlengo is then to seal up the private apartments of the pontiff; to announce the pope's death to the cardinal vicar of the city, who will in turn make a special announcement of it to the people of Rome; to go to the Apostolic Vatican Palace and take possession of it, either in person or through a delegate, as well as of the palaces at the Lateran and at Castel Gandolfo, and to see to the protection and administration of these premises; with the advice of the cardinals present from the three orders, to determine everything relating to the pope's burial, unless the pope himself during his lifetime indicated his own wishes in the matter; and, in the name and with the consent of the sacred college, to see to whatever the circumstances of the moment suggest with regard to protecting the rights of the Apostolic See and properly administering its business.

THE MAJOR PENITENTIARY

18. While the see is vacant, the Major Penitentiary and his officials have the power to do and expedite what Our predecessor Pius XI laid down in his Apostolic Constitution *Quæ divinitus* of March 25, 1935.[8]

19 As soon as the dean of the sacred college learns of the pope's death from the prefect of the pontifical household, he is to relay the news to all the cardinals and summon them to attend the meetings of the sacred college and, if they enjoy the right, to take part in the conclave at the proper time. He shall also communicate the news of the pope's death to the ambassadors or representatives of the various nations to the Apostolic See, as well as to the highest authorities in their countries.

20. As is provided in the Apostolic Constitution *Regimini Ecclesiæ Universæ* the substitute secretary of state (substitute papal secretary) is to continue the duties of his office while the see is vacant; he is responsible the Sacred College of Cardinals.[9]

PAPAL LEGATES

21. The office and powers of the papal legates likewise continue while the see is vacant.

22. The almoner of His Holiness also continues his works of charity, in the manner in which he was accustomed while the pontiff was alive. He is subordinate, however, to the Sacred College of Cardinals and dependent on them from the time of the pope's death to the election of a new pontiff. It is the duty of the Camerlengo of the Holy Roman Church to issue any instructions in this area.

23. While the apostolic see is vacant, the civil power of the Supreme Pontiff in the government of Vatican City passes in its entirety to the Sacred College of Cardinals. The college cannot issue decrees, however, except in cases of urgent need, and then only for the period of the see's vacancy. These decrees will be valid thereafter only if the new pontiff confirms them.

Chapter 4

The Faculties of the Sacred Congregations and Tribunals of the Roman Curia, While the Apostolic See Is Vacant

NO EXTRAORDINARY FACULTIES

24. While the apostolic see is vacant, the sacred congregations have no power in matters in which they cannot act and do business, while the see is occupied, except "after having spoken with His Holiness" or "as a result of an audience with His Holiness" or "in virtue of special and extraordinary faculties" which the Roman Pontiff customarily grants to the prefects of these congregations.

25. The ordinary faculties granted to each congregation do not cease at the pope's death. We decree, however, that the congregations are to use these faculties only to grant favors of lesser moment, while reserving for the future pontiff matters of greater importance or matters in dispute, provided a decision on these can be postponed. If a decision cannot be postponed, the Sacred College of Cardinals can entrust it to the cardinal who was prefect up to the pope's death,[10] and to the other cardinals, of the agency to which the Supreme Pontiff would probably have committed the matter for examination. In these circumstances, and until a pontiff is elected, the cardinals in question can make the provisional decision which

they judge best suited to guarding and protecting the rights and traditions of the Church.

26. While the see is vacant, the Supreme Tribunal of the Apostolic Signatura and the Tribunal of the Sacred Roman Rota are to carry on their business according to their own regulations, while observing the prescriptions of Canons 244.1 and 1603.

Chapter 5

The Funeral Rites for the Roman Pontiff: Norms To Be followed

27. When the Roman Pontiff dies, the cardinals are to celebrate the rites for his soul on nine successive days, according to the *Order of Funeral Rites for a Deceased Roman Pontiff*, which, like the *Order of Sacred Rites for a Conclave*, is to be made an appendix to this constitution.

28. If interment is to be in the Vatican Basilica, an authentic record of it is to be drawn up by the notary of the Chapter of the Basilica. Afterward, a delegate of the Cardinal Camerlengo and a delegate of the prefect of the pontifical household will separately sign the documents which attest to the interment. The former delegate shall sign in the presence of the reverend apostolic chamber, the latter in the presence of the prefect of the pontifical household.

DEATH OUTSIDE ROME

29. If the Roman Pontiff dies outside the city, the Sacred College of Cardinals shall take all the measures necessary to assure that the corpse is transferred in a worthy and fitting manner to the Vatican Basilica.

30. No one may photograph a dying or dead Supreme Pontiff in his apartments or record his words for later transmission. If, when the pope has died, anyone wants to take a picture for probative testimony, he must request permission of the Cardinal Camerlengo of the Holy Roman Church; the latter is not to allow such a picture of the Supreme Pontiff to be taken unless the body is clad in pontifical vestments.

31. No part of the Supreme Pontiff's apartments is to be used as living quarters before or during the conclave.

32. If the deceased Supreme Pontiff has made a will concerning his possessions and his private letters and documents and has appointed an exec-

utor, the latter, in accordance with the powers assigned him by the testator, is to decide upon and carry out what should be done with these private possessions and writings. The executor shall render an account of his office only to the new Supreme Pontiff.

Part II: On the Election of the Roman Pontiff

Chapter 1

The Electors of the Roman Pontiff

THE CARDINALS ALONE ELECT

33. The right to elect the Roman Pontiff belongs exclusively to the cardinals of the Holy Roman Church, except for those of them who, in accordance with the norm previously established,[11] shall have completed their eightieth year when the time comes for entering into the conclave; the number of cardinal electors shall not, however, exceed one hundred twenty. Excluded from among the electors, therefore, is any person of any other ecclesiastical rank and any layperson of whatever rank and order.

34. If it should happen that the Roman Pontiff dies during the celebration of a general council or a synod of bishops, whether at Rome or anywhere else in the world, the election of the new pontiff is to be carried out solely and exclusively by the cardinal electors just mentioned, and not by the council of the synod of bishops. We, therefore, declare null and void any acts which rashly presume to change either the manner of election or the college of electors. Moreover, the general council or the synod of bishops, no matter what point it may have reached, is to be understood as automatically suspended immediately upon sure notice that the pope has died. Without any delay, the council or synod is to suspend all meetings, congregations and sessions and to cease drawing up or preparing any decrees or canons, under pain of their nullity. Nor may the council or synod proceed further, for any reason whatsoever, no matter how serious and deserving of special consideration, until a canonically elected new pope bids the council or synod take up and continue its work.

NO CARDINAL EXCLUDED

35. No cardinal elector may be excluded from active and passive participation in the election of the Supreme Pontiff because of or on pretext of any excommunication, suspension, interdict or other ecclesiastical imped-

iment. Any such censures are to be regarded as suspended as far as the effect of the election is concerned.

36. A cardinal of the Holy Roman Church, once he is appointed in a consistory and his name is published, automatically has the right to vote for a pontiff, even though he has not yet received his biretta and has not been sent his cardinal's ring and has not yet taken the customary oath of fidelity. However, cardinals who have been canonically deposed or who have, with the consent of the Roman Pontiff, renounced the cardinalitial dignity do not have the right to vote; nor while the see is vacant may the Sacred College of Cardinals readmit such cardinals and restore this right to them.

WAITING FOR CARDINALS TO ARRIVE

37. We also prescribe that after the death of the pontiff the cardinals present are to wait 15 full days for the absent cardinals. Permission is granted the Sacred College of Cardinals to delay the beginning of the conclave for a few more days; however, once 20 days at most have passed, the cardinal electors present are to enter the conclave and proceed to the business of the election.

38. If other cardinal electors arrive before the matter has been expedited, that is, before the Church has been given a new pastor, they are to be admitted to the electoral process at the point it has already reached.

39. All the cardinal electors, when summoned to the election of a new pontiff by the dean or by some other cardinal acting in his name, are obliged in virtue of holy obedience to obey the summons and go to the place appointed for the election, unless they are prevented by ill health or some other serious obstacle. The impediment must, however, be acknowledged by the Sacred College of Cardinals.

ENTERING AND LEAVING THE CONCLAVE

40. If a cardinal with the right to vote refuses to enter the conclave or, having entered it, leaves it except for reason of manifest ill health (a reason which must be supported by the sworn testimony of the doctors and accepted by the majority of the electors), there is to be no waiting for him nor is he to be admitted again to the election but the others are to proceed freely to the election of a Supreme Pontiff. If a cardinal elector is forced to leave the conclave because of illness, the others are to proceed to the election without asking for his vote; if he wishes to return to the conclave after recovering his health or even before, he is to be readmitted. If a cardinal

leaves the conclave for some other serious reason which is approved by the majority of the electors, he can return to it while the election is still going on.

Chapter 2

The Conclave and Those Who Participate in It

NECESSITY OF A "CONCLAVE"

41. The election of the Supreme Pontiff is to be held in the conclave, once the latter has been closed off this conclave being established either in the Vatican Palace, as is customary, or elsewhere for some special reason. However, this is not to be considered a condition for the validity of the election, as prescribed by Gregory XV or any other pontifical decree.

42. "Conclave" means the carefully determined place, a kind of sacred retreat, where, after asking the Holy Spirit to enlighten them, the cardinal electors choose the Supreme Pontiff, and where the cardinals and other officials and staff, together with the conclavists, if there be any, remain day and night until the election is complete, and do not communicate with persons and things outside, in accordance with the following modalities and norms.

43. In addition to the cardinal electors, the following enter the conclave: the secretary of the Sacred College of Cardinals, who acts as secretary of the conclave; the vicar general of the Roman Pontiff for Vatican City, along with one or more assistants for the sacristy; the master of pontifical ceremonies and the papal masters of ceremonies for the duties proper to them. It is also licit for the cardinal dean or the cardinal who replaces him to bring an ecclesiastic as his assistant.

44. Also to be present are to be some priests from the religious orders, so that there may be a sufficient number of confessors in the various languages; two doctors, one of them a surgeon, the other a general practitioner, and one or two male nurses; the architect of the conclave with two experts in technological matters (*cf.* numbers 55 and 61). All of these are to be nominated by the Camerlengo of the Holy Roman Church and his cardinal assistants, and approved by a majority of the cardinals. To these are to be added others in suitable numbers who will minister to the needs of the conclave; they are appointed by the committee for commission of cardinals established for the purpose (*cf.* number 13c).

45. The cardinal electors may not bring with them conclavists, or private servants, clerical or lay. This can be permitted only by way of excep-

tion in the special case of serious ill health. The cardinal in question shall submit an express request, with his reasons, to the Cardinal Camerlengo who in turn will propose it to the committee or commission of cardinals appointed for the purpose. The latter are to decide and, if they think the request should be granted, they are to investigate very carefully the character of the person admitted as a servant.

46. All the officials and staff, clerical or lay, of the conclave, as well as all the conclavists, if there are any, are to take an oath, in Latin or some other language; it is to be administered by the Camerlengo of the Holy Roman Church, once he has made sure that each of them clearly understands the importance of the oath and the meaning of the formula. One or two days before entering into the conclave, in the presence of the secretary of the conclave and the master of pontifical ceremonies, who have been delegated for the purpose by the Camerlengo (in whose presence they themselves had earlier taken the oath,[12] the officials and others are to pronounce the following formula in the national language suitable for them:

"I, . . . , promise and swear that I will preserve an inviolate secrecy concerning each and every action taken and decree passed in the meetings of the cardinals with regard to the election of the new pontiff, and concerning everything done in the conclave or place of election that directly or indirectly has to do with the balloting, and concerning everything that I shall in any way come to know. Neither directly nor indirectly, by gesture or word or writing or in any other way, shall I violate this secrecy. I also promise and swear that in the conclave I shall not use any kind of transmitter or receiver or any photographic equipment—this under pain of automatic excommunication reserved in a very special way to the Apostolic See, if I violate this precept. I shall preserve this secrecy with scrupulous care even after the election of the new pontiff, unless he grants me special permission and explicit authorization. I likewise promise and swear that I shall in no way aid in or favor any interference, protest or other action by which civil authorities of any order or rank or any groups of persons or any individuals try to take a hand in the election of the pontiff. So help me God and these holy Gospels of God which I touch with my hand."

47. Lay officials and other lay staff members who leave the conclave are not permitted to return. They may leave only for reason of evident and notable ill health that is attested on oath by the doctors and with the consent of the Cardinal Camerlengo and the three cardinal assistants who must be acting in good conscience in this matter. If the need arises, substitutes may enter to take the place of those who leave on account of illness. These substitutes must be legitimately approved and accepted and must already have taken the oath.

48. If a cardinal elector who has brought a conclavist with him should die in the conclave, the conclavist is to leave immediately and may not be taken into the service of any other cardinal elector in the same conclave.

Chapter 3

Entry into the Conclave

INITIAL RITES; OATH OF THE ELECTORS

49. When the funeral rites for the deceased pontiff have been duly carried out and the conclave has meanwhile been prepared, the cardinal electors gather on the appointed day in the Vatican Basilica of St. Peter or elsewhere as the circumstances of time and place dictate. Here the ceremonies take place that are appointed in the *Order of Sacred Rites for a Conclave*. Immediately after morning Mass, or in the afternoon of that day if it seems preferable, the electors enter the conclave. When they reach the chapel, a suitable prayer is recited, and the "Extra omnes" is proclaimed. Then part II of this constitution, *Romano Pontifici Eligendo*, is to be read, after which the cardinal electors take an oath according to the following formula which the dean or the cardinal who is senior in rank and age is to recite in a loud voice:

"Each and all of us, the cardinal electors present in this conclave, promise and swear on oath that we will observe faithfully and to the letter all the prescriptions contained in the Apostolic Constitution *Romano Pontifici Eligendo* of the Supreme Pontiff Paul VI, dated October 1, 1975. We also promise and swear on oath that whoever of us in God's providence is elected Roman Pontiff will fully and zealously assert and defend the spiritual and temporal rights and freedom of the Holy See, and, if need arises, will lay unyielding claim to them. Above all, we promise and swear on oath that all of us, and even our conclavists if there be any, will preserve a scrupulous secrecy regarding everything that relates in any way to the election of the Roman Pontiff and everything that goes on in the conclave and relates directly or indirectly to the voting. Moreover, we will never in any way break that secrecy whether during the conclave or after the election of the new pontiff, unless that same pontiff gives us special permission and explicit authorization. In addition, we will under no conditions accept from any civil power, under any pretext, a commission to propose a veto or "exclusion," even in the form of a simple wish; nor will we manifest such a desired veto, should we in any way come to know of one, or give aid or favor to any interference, protest or other form of intervention, by which secular authorities of any order or rank or any groups of persons or any individuals try to take a hand in the election of the pontiff."

Then each cardinal elector is to say: "And I, . . . Cardinal . . ., promise and swear on oath"; whereupon he is to place his hand on the Gospel and add: "So help me God and these holy Gospels of God which I touch with my hand."

Afterward, the Cardinal Dean or the Cardinal senior in rank and age shall exhort those present, in a brief and suitable discourse, to take up the business of the election in the proper way and with a right intention, looking solely to the good of the universal Church.

THE OATH TAKEN BY OTHERS PRESENT

50. When all this has been done, the prefect of the pontifical household, the special delegate of the pontifical commission for Vatican City, and the prefect of the Papal Swiss Guards, to whom this constitution assigns the duty of protecting the conclave, are to take their oath, according to the prescribed formula,[13] in the presence of the cardinal dean or the first-ranking cardinal and all the cardinal electors. The oath is also to be taken by the clerical prelates of the Reverend Apostolic Chamber, the participant protonotaries apostolic, and the auditors of the Sacred Roman Rota, all of whom are charged to maintain a watchful guard over everything that is brought into the conclave or taken from it. They are assisted by the papal masters of ceremonies.

51. All the cardinal electors now go to the cells assigned them, except for the Cardinal Camerlengo and the three cardinal assistants, who remain in the chapel and proceed to the closing off of the conclave. Meanwhile, the officials of the conclave and the other staff members take the above mentioned oath as soon as possible (if they have not already done so), in the presence of the secretary of the conclave and the master of pontifical ceremonies, who are delegated for this purpose by the Camerlengo of the Holy Roman Church.

SEARCH OF THE PREMISES

52. Finally, after a suitable signal has been given at the order of the cardinal dean or the first-ranking cardinal, the Camerlengo and the three cardinal assistants, together with the master of pontifical ceremonies and the other masters of ceremonies, the architect of the conclave and the two technicians, shall carefully search the premises to see that no one barred from the conclave is still there. For the same reason, they shall go over the

list of the staff for the conclave, including any conclavists who may be serving the cardinal electors, lest an outsider have made his way among them; in order to conduct this check, all are bidden to enter the chapel where each answers to his name.

53. After a careful examination, the conclave is locked from the outside and the inside by the prefect of the pontifical household, the special delegate of the pontifical commission for Vatican City, and the prefect of the Papal Swiss Guards, in the presence of the dean of the clerical prelates of the Reverend Apostolic Chamber, as well as of the secretary-chancellor of the latter (who is deputed for the purpose by Cardinal Camerlengo of the Holy Roman Church) and the masters of ceremonies and the architects. The keys are entrusted to the special delegate of the pontifical commission for Vatican City.

RECORDS OF THE LOCKING OF THE CONCLAVE

54. Separate records are made of the exterior and interior lockings. One is drawn up by the master of pontifical ceremonies and signed by the secretary of the conclave and the master of pontifical ceremonies himself (acting as notary), with two masters of ceremonies as witnesses. The other record is drawn up by one of the clerical prelates of the Reverend Apostolic Chamber, who is deputed for this by the Cardinal Camerlengo of the Holy Roman Church; this is done in the office of the special delegate of the pontifical commission for Vatican City, and signed by the prefect of the pontifical household, the special delegate himself, and the prefect of the Papal Swiss Guards.

Chapter 4

The Observance of Secrecy Concerning All That Happens in the Conclave

GUARDING OF THE PREMISES

55. The Cardinal Camerlengo and the three cardinals who are his assistants at any given time are bound to keep careful watch and to visit the entire premises frequently, in person or through delegates, in order to see that the conclave enclosure is in no way breached. At these visitations, the two technicians are always to be present and, if necessary, to use the apt means our age provides for detecting the possible presence of the instruments mentioned below in number 61. If any such instruments be found, those responsible for them are to be expelled from the conclave and be

subject to serious penalties as the future pontiff shall judge fit.

56. Once the conclave is locked, no one is to be admitted to speak to the cardinal electors or others in the conclave, except in the presence of the prelates charged with guarding the conclave and they may only speak aloud so that others can understand what they say. If any one should enter the conclave by stealth, he is automatically deprived of every ecclesiastical honor, rank, office and benefice and, according to who he is, subjected to other suitable punishments.

COMMUNICATION BY LETTER AND IN OTHER WAYS

57. We also decree that no letters or writings of any kind, even printed, are to be sent either to those in the conclave, including the cardinal electors, or especially from the conclave to persons outside, unless they have in each and every case been carefully examined by the secretary of the conclave and the prelate assigned to guard the conclave. The only exception to this rule is the correspondence between the Tribunal of the Sacred Apostolic Penitentiary and the Cardinal Major Penitentiary who is in the conclave; such correspondence is to be free and unhindered, and the letters, bearing the seal of office, are not subject to examination and inspection. We also explicitly forbid the sending of newspapers and periodicals into or out of the conclave.

58. The staff of the conclave must also carefully avoid anything that would in any way, directly or indirectly, by word, writing, sign or in any other manner, violate secrecy—this, under pain of automatic excommunication reserved to the Apostolic See.

59. In particular, We forbid the cardinal electors to make known to servants they may have with them or to anyone else anything that directly or indirectly relates to the voting or that is done or decreed with regard to the election of the pontiff in the meetings of the cardinals either before or during the conclave.

SECRECY OF ELECTORS AFTER THE CONCLAVE

60. In addition, We order the cardinal electors, under serious obligation in conscience, to observe this secrecy even after the election of the new pontiff. They must remember that they may in no way break the secrecy unless the new pontiff gives special and explicit permission to do so. We extend this prohibition to all who are present in the conclave, should any of them, innocently or otherwise, gain knowledge of what has been done in the conclave.

61. Finally, in order to protect the cardinal electors against the indiscretion of others and against insidious attempts to limit their independence of judgment and freedom of decision, We entirely forbid the introduction into the conclave, under any pretext, or the use, should these already be there, of any equipment for recording, playing back or transmitting voices or pictures.

Chapter 5

The Method of Election

THREE METHODS OF ELECTION

62. On the morning of the day after the conclave has been locked, the cardinal electors who are not prevented by ill health shall, at a signal, assemble in the appointed chapel and concelebrate, or be present at, the Eucharistic sacrifice. When Mass is over and the Holy Spirit has been invoked, they shall immediately proceed to the election. The election must be conducted according to one or other of the three methods or forms described below, otherwise the election is null and void, except as provided for in no. 76.

METHOD OF ACCLAMATION

63. The first method can be called the method of acclamation or inspiration; it is used when the cardinal electors, as though inspired by the Holy Spirit, freely and spontaneously proclaim one man Supreme Pontiff, acclaiming him unanimously. This method can be used only in the closed conclave and must involve the use of the word *eligo*, pronounced intelligibly or written if the elector is unable to use his voice. A further requirement is that the method be accepted by each and every cardinal elector present, including those who may have remained in their cells because of ill health. There can be no dissenting voice and care must be taken to see that no special negotiations are carried on with regard to the name of the person to be elected. Consequently, if, for example, one of the cardinal electors, speaking spontaneously and without any special negotiations having taken place, should say, "Father Eminences, in view of the singular virtue and probity of the Very Reverend . . . , I judge him worthy of being elected Roman Pontiff, and I myself vote for him as pope"; and if, then, the other Fathers without exception accept the view of the first and unanimously vote for the same man, using the verb *eligo* and pronouncing it in-

telligibly or, if need be, writing it down: then the man is canonically elected by this method.

METHOD OF COMPROMISE

64. The second method is called the method of compromise and is used when in special circumstances the cardinal electors give some of their number authority to act in the name of all and elect a pastor for the Catholic Church. In this case, too, each and every cardinal elector present in the closed conclave, without any dissenting voice, must agree to the concession of authority and put the election into the hands of a limited number of the fathers. This group must have an uneven number of members, at least nine and at most fifteen. The cardinal electors are to sign some such formula as this: "In the name of the Lord. Amen. On the . . . day of the . . . month of the year . . . , we, the cardinal electors present at the conclave [a complete list of names follows], have determined and now determine, with no dissenting voice, to proceed to an election using the method of compromise. Therefore, in full and unanimous agreement, with no one dissenting, we choose as our representatives the Most Eminent Fathers, . . . , and give them full power and authority to provide a pastor for the Holy Roman Church. They are to act in the following manner . . ." Here the cardinal electors who are handing over the authority shall clearly set down the method and form their representatives are to use in electing a pontiff. The cardinal electors must determine what they require for the election to be valid, for example, whether the representatives must first propose the person of their choice to the whole college, or may simply proceed to elect him without further ado; whether all the representatives must agree on the same person or a two-thirds majority is enough; whether they must choose someone from the electoral college or may choose someone from outside it; and so on. Also to be included in the instructions is the length of time for which the cardinal electors wish their representatives to have the power of electing. Finally, they must add words to this effect: "And we promise that we will accept as Roman Pontiff the person whom our representatives shall think worthy of being elected according to the above-described method."

Once the representatives have accepted their mandate and the prescriptions governing its exercise, they are to assemble in a separate closed place. In order that they may talk more freely among themselves, they are to make it clear that they do not intend to give their consent by a verbal formula alone but must also put it in writing. When the representatives have finally carried out the election according to the form prescribed for them and have made their choice known in the conclave, the person thus elected is the true canonical pope.

METHOD OF BALLOTING

65. The third and ordinary method or form for electing a Roman Pontiff is by casting ballots. Here We fully confirm the rule determined long ago and subsequently observed with scrupulous care, that a two-thirds majority is required for the valid election of a Roman Pontiff. We also wish to keep in force the norm established by Our predecessor Pius XII, that the majority must always be two-thirds plus one.[14]

66. Balloting involves three stages. The first, or prescrutinial, stage includes:

(1) the preparation and distribution of ballots; this is done by the masters of ceremonies who are to give at least two or three ballots to each cardinal elector;

(2) the choice by lot (with all the cardinal electors participating) of three examiners (*scrutatores*), three deputies to take care of the votes cast by the sick (*infirmarii*), and three controllers (*recognitores*); the lots are to be drawn by the lowest-ranking cardinal deacon who shall pull in order the names of the nine who are to be assigned these various duties;

(3) the writing of the ballots, which is to be done secretly by each cardinal elector; he shall write down the name of his choice, making his handwriting unrecognizable as far as possible; he must not write more than one name on a ballot or his vote is nullified;

(4) the folding of the ballot in half, so that it is reduced in width to about an inch.

NORMS FOR THE FIRST STAGE

67. In dispatching this first stage of the balloting process, the following norms are to be observed.

a) The ballot should be rectangular in shape, longer than it is wide; at the upper center should appear the words (printed, if possible): *Eligo in Summum Pontificem* (I choose as Supreme Pontiff), with room below for writing a name; thus, the ballot is so arranged that it can be folded in two

(b) If, in choosing the examiners, deputies for the sick and controllers. the names of cardinal electors are drawn who for reason of sickness or some other impediment cannot carry out the duties, the names of others not so prevented must be drawn. The first three names drawn are the examiners, the next three the deputies for the sick and the final three the controllers.

(c) While votes are being cast, the cardinal electors must be alone in the chapel; therefore, immediately after the ballots have been distributed and before the electors begin to write on them, the secretary of the conclave, the master of pontifical ceremonies, and the masters of ceremonies are to leave. When they have left, the lowest-ranking cardinal deacon is to close the door; he is to open and close it as often as is necessary, for example when the deputies for the sick leave to collect the ballots of the sick and when they return to the chapel.

THE SECOND STAGE

68. The second stage is that of the balloting proper. It comprises (1) the placing of the ballots in an urn, (2) the mixing and counting of the ballots and (3) the announcement of the vote. After writing and folding his ballot, each Cardinal elector, in order of precedence, shall raise his hand so that he may be seen and take his ballot to the altar where the examiners are stationed and on which stands an urn, covered with a dish, ready to receive the ballots. At the altar the cardinal elector is to kneel, pray for a moment, rise and in a loud voice swear: "I call Christ the Lord, my judge, to witness that I am voting for the one whom, in the Lord, I think should be elected." Then he puts the ballot on the plate and slides it into the urn; whereupon he bows to the altar and returns to his place. If a cardinal elector present in the chapel is hindered by weakness from going to the altar, the last-chosen examiner goes to him. The elector, having taken the oath, gives the folded ballot to the examiner who carries it so that all can see it, takes it to the altar and, without any prayer or oath, puts it on the dish and slides it into the urn.

VOTING BY THE SICK

69. If any cardinal electors are ill in their rooms, the three deputies for the sick go to them with a small box that has a slit in the top through which the folded ballot can be inserted. Before the examiners give the box to the deputies, they open it and show the other electors that it is empty, then lock it and place the key on the altar. The deputies take the locked box and a plate containing the necessary number of ballots to each elector who is ill. The elector takes a ballot, secretly writes a name, folds the ballot and, after taking the oath, inserts it into the box. If the sick person cannot write, one of the three deputies, or some other cardinal elector whom the sick

person deputes, takes an oath before the deputies that he will observe secrecy and then goes through the previous steps on behalf of the sick elector. The deputies then take the box to the chapel where it is opened by the examiners who count the number of ballots in it; having ascertained that there are as many ballots as there are sick electors, they put the ballots on the dish one by one and finally slide them all together into the urn. Lest the balloting take too long, immediately after the senior cardinal elector has cast his vote the deputies can finish their own ballots and place them in the urn, then, while the other electors are voting, they can go for the ballots of the sick electors, as described above.

COUNTING THE NUMBER OF BALLOTS

70. After all the cardinal electors have placed their ballots in the urn, the first examiner shakes it several times to mix up the ballots, then the third examiner immediately counts them, drawing them one by one from the urn and placing them in an empty receptacle set there for the purpose. If the number of ballots does not correspond to the number of electors, they are all to be burned and a second balloting is to be begun. If the number of ballots is correct, the results of the balloting are made known in the following manner.

71. The examiners sit at a table in front of the altar. The first examiner takes a ballot, opens it and, having seen the name written on it, hands it to the second examiner, who in turn sees the name and hands the ballot to the third examiner. The latter reads the name aloud in a clear voice so that all the electors present can record the vote on a sheet of paper ready for the purpose. The third examiner also records the name he has read from the ballot. If, in making the results of the voting known, the examiners find two ballots so folded in together that they appear to have been put into the urn by the same person, the two votes are to be regarded as one if they are for the same person. Neither is valid if they are for different persons. In any case, the balloting as a whole is not invalidated. Once the ballots have been made public, the examiners total up the votes received by each candidate and record them on a separate page.

The third examiner, as he reads each ballot, puts a threaded needle through it at the word *eligo*, as a way of carefully preserving each in turn. Once all the names have been read, the ends of the thread are knotted together and the ballots thus tied in a bunch are placed in an empty urn or at one side of the table.

72. The third and last stage is the postscrutinial stage. It includes (1) the counting of the total votes for each candidate, (2) the verification of the votes, (3) the burning of the ballots. The examiners count up the votes each candidate has received. If no one receives two thirds of the votes plus one, no Pope is elected on that ballot. If someone does receive two thirds plus one, there has been a canonically valid election of a Roman Pontiff. Whether or not there has been an election, the controllers must inspect both the ballots and the listing of the votes by the examiners, so as to determine whether the latter have faithfully and accurately carried out their duties. Immediately after this verification and before the cardinal electors leave the room, all the ballots are to be burned by the examiners with the help of the secretary of the conclave and the masters of ceremonies, whom the junior cardinal deacon has meanwhile summoned for the purpose. If however, a second balloting is to take place immediately, the first set of the ballots is to be burned at the end, that is, along with the second set of ballots.

RECORDS OF THE VOTING

73. In order that secrecy may be better guaranteed, We order each and all of the cardinal electors to hand over any notes dealing with the outcome of each balloting, to the Cardinal Camerlengo or one of the three cardinal assistants so that the notes may be burned along with the ballots. We also decree that once the conclave is finished the Cardinal Camerlengo of the Holy Roman Church is to draw up a report, approved by the three cardinal assistants, which records the outcome of each balloting. This report, to be kept in the archives, is to be placed in a sealed envelope that may not be opened without the express permission of the Supreme Pontiff.

74. In confirmation of the norms established by Our predecessors, Saint Pius X[15] and Pius XII,[16] We prescribe that at both the morning and evening sessions, immediately after a balloting that has not resulted in an election the cardinal electors are to proceed to another balloting and vote again; the votes cast on the previous ballots are not to be taken into account in the new balloting. In this second round of voting the same procedure is to be followed as in the first except that the electors need not repeat the oath or elect new examiners; the oaths taken and the examiners chosen for the first vote suffice.

75. The whole procedure for balloting is to be carefully observed by the cardinal electors at each round of votes which takes place daily in the

morning and evening. All the sacred rites and prayers prescribed in the *Order of Sacred Rites for a Conclave* are to be followed.

REGULATIONS FOR PROTRACTED VOTING

76. If the cardinal electors cannot agree on the person to be elected, then, after they have cast their votes in vain for three days according to the prescribed manner (numbers 65 *ff.*), one day is to be allowed to pass without voting. The purpose is that the electors may pray to God and converse freely among themselves and that the senior cardinal deacon may deliver a short spiritual exhortation. The balloting is then begun anew, following the same method. If no election occurs, seven ballotings are to be conducted. Then there is to be another interruption for prayer, discussion and an exhortation by the senior cardinal priest. Seven more ballotings, according to the prescribed manner, are then to be conducted if seven are needed. If these fail to produce an election, prayers are once more offered to God, the electors are to discuss the matter and the senior cardinal bishop is to deliver an exhortation to the electors. At this point, the Camerlengo of the Holy Roman Church is to consult with the electors on procedure. The usual plan requiring two thirds of the votes plus one for a successful balloting is not to be abandoned unless the cardinal electors unanimously, without any dissenting voice, agree to another plan. This other plan may be the method of compromise (*cf.* number 64) which requires only an absolute majority plus one or else a vote in which there are only two candidates, namely, the two who received the most votes in the immediately preceding balloting.

NULLITY OF AN ELECTION

77. If an election is conducted according to some method other than the three listed above (numbers 63 *ff.*) or if the regulations governing each method are not followed, the election is automatically null and void (*cf.* number 62). No further declaration of invalidity is needed and no power is bestowed on the man elected.

78. We declare that the norms thus far set down for the steps to be taken before the election and for the election itself of the Roman Pontiff are to be followed even if the vacancy in the Apostolic See should occur because the Supreme Pontiff has resigned.

Chapter 6

What Is to Be Observed and Avoided During the Election of the Roman Pontiff

SIMONY WRONG BUT NOT INVALIDATING

79. Like Our predecessors, We reject and condemn the detestable sin of simony in the election of the Roman Pontiff and We impose an automatic excommunication on all who are guilty of this sin. At the same time, however, We also confirm the act of Our predecessor Saint Pius X in canceling the invalidity of a simoniacal election as established by Julius II or any other pontifical decree. This We do lest the validity of the election of the Roman Pontiff be attacked.[17]

80. We also confirm the prescriptions of Our predecessors which command that no one, even a cardinal, may, during the Roman Pontiff's lifetime and without having consulted him, enter into consultations about his successor or promise a vote or make decisions regarding it in secret meetings.

EXCLUSION OF OUTSIDE INTERVENTION

81. We also confirm the decrees which Our predecessors issued with a view to excluding all external intervention in the election of the Supreme Pontiff. Therefore, again in virtue of holy obedience and under pain of automatic excommunication We forbid the cardinal electors, all and singly, present and future, as well as the secretary of the conclave and all other participants in the conclave to accept from any civil authority whosoever and under any pretext the commission to propose a veto or "exclusion," even in the form of a simple wish or to make such a veto known to the whole college assembled or to individual electors, either in writing or orally, either directly and in person or indirectly and through others, either before the conclave or during it. We intend this prohibition to extend to every form of interference, protest and wish by which secular authorities of any order or rank or any groups of persons or any individuals may try to take a hand in the election of a pontiff.

FREEDOM OF THE ELECTORS TO VOTE

82. The cardinal electors are also to avoid all pacts, agreements, promises or any other commitments by which they can be bound to vote or not

vote for any individual or individuals. We decree that any such agreements, even if made under oath, are null and void and that no one is bound to honor them; and We now impose an automatic excommunication on those who act against this prohibition. We do not intend, however, to forbid the electors to communicate their views on the election to one another while the see is vacant.

83. We also forbid the cardinals to make concessions before the election, that is, to enter upon agreements which each party binds himself to honor should he be elevated to the papacy. Again, We declare any such promises to be null and void, even if made under oath.

84. Like Our predecessors, We strongly exhort the cardinal electors not to be guided by likes or dislikes in electing the pope, nor influenced by the favor or compliance of anyone, nor moved by the interference of persons . . . [in] high places or pressure groups, or by the suasive language of the masters of the communications media, or by violence or fear or love of popularity. Instead, with God's glory and the good of the Church as their sole guide, and having asked for divine help, let them vote for him whom they judge most fit to rule the universal Church in a fruitful and useful way.

85. During the conclave, the church is united in a very special way with its sacred pastors and, in particular, with the cardinals who are electing a Supreme Pontiff and she asks God for a new leader as a gift of his providential goodness. For, like the first Christian community of which we read in the *Acts of the Apostles*,[18] the universal Church assembled in spirit with Mary the Mother of Jesus, must persevere in prayer. In consequence, the election of the new pontiff will not be the action solely of the electoral college, independent of any connection with the people of God but will, in a sense, be an action of the entire Church. For this reason, We decree that in every city and in other places as well, at least in the more important ones, as soon as news of the pope's death arrives and again after his solemn funeral rites have been celebrated humble and persevering prayers should be offered to God that he would enlighten the minds of the electors and bring them into an agreement which will result in a quick, unanimous and fruitful election, such as the salvation of souls and the good of the whole Catholic world require.

LET THE MAN ELECTED NOT BE DAUNTED

86. We ask him who shall be elected not to be frightened by the seriousness of the office into refusing it when he is called to it but to bow humbly to the divine will and plan. For God who lays the burden on him also supports him so that he can carry the burden. He who is the source of the bur-

den also helps a man to cope with it. He who bestows the dignity gives the weak man strength lest he falter before the magnitude of the task.

Chapter 7

Acceptance and Proclamation of the Election

CORONATION OF THE NEW POPE

87. After a canonically valid election, the junior cardinal deacon summons into the conclave assembly hall the secretary of the conclave, the master of pontifical ceremonies and the masters of ceremonies. The cardinal dean or the cardinal senior in order and age, acting in the name of the whole electoral college, asks the consent of the person elected, in these words: "Do you accept your canonical election as Supreme Pontiff?" As soon as the person elected declares his consent, he is asked: "What name do you wish to bear?" Then the master of pontifical ceremonies, acting as notary, with two masters of ceremonies as witnesses, makes a record of the new pope's acceptance and his choice of name.

88. After his acceptance, the person elected, if he be a bishop, is straightway bishop of Rome, true pope, and head of the episcopal college. He possesses and can exercise full and supreme power over the universal Church. If, however, the elected person does not possess the episcopal character, he is to be immediately ordained a bishop.

HOMAGE OF THE ELECTORS

89. Once the formalities have been observed in accordance with the *Order of Sacred Rites for a Conclave*, the cardinal electors come forward in their proper order to offer homage and obedience to the newly elected Supreme Pontiff. When this has been done, thanks are given to God. The senior cardinal deacon tells the waiting people of the new pope, and the latter immediately gives the Apostolic Blessing *Urbi et Orbi*. If the newly elected pope lacks the episcopal character, homage and obedience is offered to him, but the people are told of the election only after he has been ordained a bishop.

90. If the elected person is not at the conclave, the regulations set down in the *Order of the Sacred Rites for a Conclave* are to be observed. The episcopal Conclave of a Supreme Pontiff who is not yet a bishop (*cf.* numbers 88 and 89) is celebrated, according to Church usage, by the dean of

the sacred college or, in his absence, the subdean or, if he too is prevented by the oldest cardinal bishop.

THE CONCLAVE ENDED

91. We decree that immediately after the new Supreme Pontiff has been elected and has given his assent, and after he has been ordained a bishop if need be (*cf.* numbers 88 and 89) the conclave is ended as far as its canonical effects are concerned (*cf.* number 56). Therefore We decree that the newly elected Supreme Pontiff may now be approached by the substitute secretary of state (papal secretary), the secretary of the council for the public affairs of the Church, the prefect of the pontifical household, and others who must consult with the new pope on immediately pressing matters.

CROWNING OF THE NEW PONTIFF

92. Finally, the new pontiff is to be crowned by the senior cardinal deacon. Within a suitable period, he is also to take possession, in the prescribed manner, of the Patriarchal Archbasilica of the Lateran.

Conclusion

After serious and lengthy consideration, We decree and prescribe these norms. We declare abrogated, as provided for above, the apostolic constitutions and ordinations issued on these matters by other Roman pontiffs, and We will that this constitution take full effect now and in the future. All of its explanations and determinations are to be carefully observed and fulfilled by all whom they affect, anything to the contrary notwithstanding, even if it be worthy of very special consideration. If anyone, knowingly or unknowingly, acts otherwise than We have prescribed, We declare his acts null and void.

Rome, at Saint Peter's, October 1, 1975, the thirteenth year of Our pontificate.
Paulus P P VI

NOTES

1. Gratian, *Decretum*, Dist. 23, c. 1.

2. See Mansi, *Conciliorum amplissima collectio*, 23:217–218.

3. See Motu Proprio *Cum gravissima* (April 15, 1962) *AAS* 54 (1962).

4. See *AAS* 62 (1970), 810–813.

5. See *AAS* 38 (1946), 65–99.

6. See *AAS* 54 (1962), 632–640.

7. See *Prooeminum* and number 2, paragraph 6: *AAS* 59 (1967), 889, 891.

8. See No. 12: *AAS* 27 (1935), 112–113.

9. See No. 19, paragraph 2: *AAS* 59 (1967), 895.

10. *Cf.* Paul VI, *Regimini Ecclesiæ universæ*, prooemium: *AAS* 59 (1967), 889.

11. Paul VI, Motu Proprio *Ingravescentem Ætatem*, II, 2: *AAS* 62 (1970), 811.

12. Formula of the oath to be taken by the secretary of the conclave and the master of pontifical ceremonies: "I, . . . , promise and swear that I will faithfully observe each and every decree of the sacred college and that I will execute the duties of my office in a diligent and conscientious way. I also promise and swear that I will preserve an inviolate secrecy . . ." (continuing with the oath taken by the officials of the conclave, which follows immediately in the text).

13. Formula of their oath: "I, . . . , promise and swear that I will execute the duties of my office in a diligent and conscientious way, according to the norms established by the Supreme Pontiffs and the prescriptions of the Sacred College of Cardinals. So help me God and these holy Gospels of God which I touch with my hand."

14. See Pius XII, *Vacantis Apostolicæ Sedis*, No. 68: *AAS* 38 (1946), 87.

15. See Pius X, *Vacante Sede Apostolica*, No. 68, in *Pii X Pontificis Maximi Acta* 3: 280–281.

16. See Pius XII, *Vacantis Apostolicæ Sedis*, No. 88: *AAS* 38 (1946). 93.

17. See Pius X, *Vacante Sede Apostolica*, No. 79, in *Pii X Pontificis Maximi Acta* 3:282.

18. See *Acts* 1, 14.

APPENDIX C:
Motu Proprio *Ingravescentem Ætatem*

November 21, 1970

The natural relationship between the increasing burden of age and the ability to perform certain major offices, such as those of diocesan bishop and parish priest, was dealt with by the Second Vatican Ecumenical Council in the Decree *Christus Dominus* (21 and 31).

Implementing the wishes of the Council Fathers, we, by our Apostolic Letter *Ecclesiae Sanctae* of 6 August 1966, called on bishops and parish priests voluntarily to submit their resignation not later than their seventy-fifth birthday (11 and 20, paragraph 3).

The same question of age was touched on by the general regulations of the Roman Curia, issued under the title *Regolamento Generale della Curia Romana*, which we approved and ordered to be published on 22 February 1968. It is laid down therein that major and minor officials should retire from office on the completion of their seventieth year, and higher prelates at the beginning of their seventy-fifth year of age (article 101, paragraph 1).

It seems to us now that the good of the Church demands that the increasing burden of age should be taken into consideration also for the illustrious office of the cardinalate, to which we have on several occasions given special attention. It is in fact a particularly important office which demands great prudence, both for its quite unique connection with our supreme office at the service of the whole Church and because of the high importance it has for all the Church when the Apostolic See falls vacant.

Accordingly, after long and mature consideration of the whole question, and continuing to trust for the future in the unceasing counsel and prayers of all the cardinals without distinction, we decree:

I. Cardinals in charge of departments of the Roman Curia (listed in article 1 of the *Regolamento Generale*) or to the other permanent institutions of the Apostolic See and Vatican City are requested to submit their resignation voluntarily to the Pope on the completion of their seventy-fifth year of age. After due consideration of all the circumstances of each case, he will judge whether it is fitting to accept the resignation immediately.

497

II. On the completion of eighty years of age, cardinals:

1. cease to be members of the departments of the Roman Curia and of the other institutions mentioned in the above article;

2. lose the right to elect the Pope and consequently also that of entering the conclave. If, however, a cardinal completes his eightieth year after the beginning of the conclave, he continues to enjoy the right of electing the Pope on that occasion.

III. The arrangements in articles I and II.1 take effect even when the five-year term dealt with in article 2, paragraph 5, of the Apostolic Constitution *Regimini Ecclesiae Universae* is not yet completed.

IV. What is laid down in article II above applies no less to cardinals who, by exception, continue in charge of a diocese, or keep its title without the function of governing it, after their eightieth year.

V. Even after completing their eightieth year, cardinals continue to be members of the Sacred College in all other respects. They retain all the other rights and prerogatives connected with the office of cardinal, including the faculty of taking part in any General or Special Congregation which may be held during a vacancy of the Apostolic See before the beginning of the conclave.

VI. If it should happen, because of unusual circumstances, that the Cardinal Camerlengo or the Cardinal Major Penitentiary should continue in office until his eightieth year, the following procedure is decreed:

1. If he completes his eightieth year before the death of a Pope, and if a successor has not been appointed by then, or if he should do so between a Pope's death and the beginning of a conclave, then, during the vacancy of the Apostolic See, a regular Congregation of the Sacred College will vote to elect a successor to remain in office until the new Pope's election;

2. If he completes his eightieth year after the beginning of the conclave, his term of office is by law extended up to the election of the new Pope.

VII. If the Dean of the Sacred College is not present at the conclave because of having completed his eightieth year, the duties of his office are performed within the conclave by the Subdean, or, if he too should be absent, by another of the more senior cardinals in accordance with the general order of precedence.

VIII. A system similar to that laid down in article VII is to be followed, if necessary, in the performance of the duties in the conclave assigned by law to the three cardinals who are at the head of the orders.

INTERIM ARRANGEMENT

Those who are now members of the Sacred College and have completed their eightieth year of age on the date of coming into force of this Apostolic Letter may continue, if they so wish, to take part, with voting rights, in the Plenary and Ordinary Congregations of departments of the Roman Curia.

We decree that what is laid down by this Apostolic Letter should come into force on 1 January 1971.

We order that all the things decreed in this letter issued motu proprio be regarded as established and ratified, notwithstanding anything to the contrary, even if worthy of very special notice.

Given in Rome at Saint Peter's, on the twenty-first day of November in the year 1970, the eighth of our pontificate.
Paulus PP VI

[From *L'Osservatore Romano*, December 3, 1970.]

For Further Reading

I. General and Reference Works for the Cardinalate and Conclaves

Battandier, Albert. "Essai de Liste Général des Cardinaux." *Annuaire Pontifical Catholique* (1922–1939). Paris: La Bonne Presse, 1898–1939.

B[erton], C[harles]. *Dictionnaire des Cardinaux: Contenant des Notions Générales sur le Cardinalat, la Nomenclature Complète, par ordre Alphabétique, des Cardinaux de Tous les Temps et de Tous le Pays; la Même Nomenclature par ordre Chronologique; les Détails Biographiques Essentiels sur Tous les Cardinaux sans Exception; de Longues Études sur les Cardinaux Célèbres, qui, en Si Grand Nombre, ont rempli un Rôle Supérieur dans l'Église, dans la Politique ou dans les Lettres.* Tome Unique, vol. 31 of J[acques]-P[aul] Migne, ed. *Troisième et Dernière Encyclopédie Théologique: ou Troisième et Dernière Série de Dictionnaires sur Toutes les Parties de la Science Religieuse, offrant en Français, et par Ordre Alphabétique, la Plus Claire, la Plus Facile, la Plus Commode, la Plus Variée et la Plus Complète des Théologies,* 65 vols., itself vol. 133 of *Encyclopédie Théologique: ou Troisième et Dernière Série de Dictionnaires sur Toutes les Parties de la Science Religieuse,* 168 vols. in 171 [1845–1873]. Paris: s'imprime et se vend chez J.-P. Migne, éditeur, aux Ateliers Catholiques, Rue d'Amboise, au Petit-Montrouge, Barrière d'Enfer de Paris, 1857.

Cardella, Lorenzo. *Memorie Storiche de' Cardinali,* 9 vols. Rome: Pagliacine, 1792–1797.

Cartwright, W[illiam] C[ornwallis]. *On Papal Conclaves.* Edinburgh: Edmonston and Douglas, 1868.

Ciaconius, Alphonsus [Alphonso Ciaconio]. *Vitæ et Res Gestæ Pontificum Romanorum et S[anctæ] R[omanæ] E[cclesiæ] Cardinalium ab Initio Nascentis Ecclesiæ, usque ad Urbanum VIII Pont[ifex] Max[imus] Auctoribus.* Roma: Typis Vaticanis, MDCXXX.

Cristofori, [Conte] Francesco. *Storia dei Cardinali di Santa Romana Chiesa dal Secolo V all'Anno del Signore MDCCCLXXXVIII.* Roma: Tipografia de Propaganda Fide, 1888.

Dizionario Biografico Degli Italiani. Alberto Maria Ghisalberti and successors, gen. eds. Roma: Instituto della Enciclopedia Italiana, 1960– .

Dizionario Enciclopedico Italiano. Domenico Bartolini, direttore generale. Roma: Instituto della Enciclopedia Italiana, 1958.

Gams, Pius Bonifacius. *Series Episcoporum Ecclesiæ Catholicæ.* Regensburg: Verlag Josef Manz, 1873; reprinted, Graz: Akademische Druck- U. Verlagsanstalt, 1957.

Hierarchia Catholica Medii [et Recentioris] Ævi: sive, Summorum Pontificum, S[anctæ] R[omanæ] E[cclesiæ] Cardinalium, Ecclesiarum Antistitum Series. E Documentis Tabularii Præsertim Vaticani Collecta, Digesta, Edita. 8 vols. Patavii

[Padua]: Typis Librariæ "Il Messaggero di S[an] Antonio" apud Basilicam S[ancti] Antonii, 1952–1969. Vols. 1–2 have the title: Hierarchia Catholica Medii Ævi. Vols. 1–4 are reprints of the 2d ed., with reproductions of original title pages. That imprint reads: Monasterii [Munich] Sumptibus et typis Librariæ Regensbergianæ, 1913–35. [v. 1] *Ab anno 1198 usque ad annum 1431 perducta*, per Conradus Eubel.; [v. 2] *Ab anno 1431 usque ad annum 1503 perducta*, per Conradus Eubel.; v. 3. *Sæculum XVI ab anno 1503 complectens: Volumen tertium sæculum XVI ab anno 1503 complectens quod cum Societatis Goerresianæ subsidio*, quod inchoavit G. [Wilhelm Heinrich Hubert] van Gulik, absolvit C[onradus] Eubel.; v. 4 (1935, reprinted 1960) *A pontificatu Clementis Pp. VIII (1592) usque ad pontificatum Alexandri Pp. VII (1667)* per P[atritium] Gauchat.; v. 5 (1952) *A pontificatu Clementis Pp. IX (1667) usque ad pontificatum Benedicti Pp. XIII (1730)* per R[emigius] Ritzler et Pirminus] Sefrin.; v. 6 (1958) *A pontificatu Clementis Pp. XII (1730) usque ad pontificatum Pii VI (1799)* per R[emigius] Ritzler et P[irminus] Sefrin; v. 7 (1968). *A pontificatu Pii Pp. VII (1800) usque ad pontificatum Gregorii Pp. XVI (1846)* per R[emigius] Ritzler et P[irminus] Sefrin; v. 8 (1978). A pontificatu Pii Pp. IX (1846) usque ad pontificatum Leonis Pp. XIII (1903) per R[emigius] Ritzler et P[irminus] Sefrin.

Isenburg, Wilhelm Karl von. *Stammtafeln der Geschichte der Europäischen Staaten (Europäischen Stammtafeln), band II: Die ausserdeutchen Staaten*. Marburg: Verlag von J. A. Stargardt, 1956.

Kelly, J[ohn] N[orman] D[avidson]. *The Oxford Dictionary of the Popes*. Oxford: Oxford University Press, 1986.

Litta, [*Conte*] Pompeo and successors, Federico Oderici, Luigi Passerini, and Federico Stefani. *Famiglie Celebri Italiane*, 185 fascicles in various bindings and pagings. Milano: Typografia del [P. E.] Giusti, 1819–1885.

Moroni, Gaetano. *Dizionario di Erudizioni Storico-Ecclesiastici*. Rome: Tipografia Emiliana, 1847.

Panvinius, Onuphrius [Onofrio Panvinio]. *Epitome Pontificvm Romanorvm a S. Petro usque ad Paulum IIII. Gestorum (videlicet) electionisque singulorum, & conclauium compendiaria narratio. Cardinalium item nomina, dignitatum tituli, insignia legationes, patria & obitus*. Edited by Jacobus de Strada. Venetiis [Venice]: Imp[r]ensis I. Stradæ, 1557.

Pastor, Ludwig, Freiherr von. *History of the Popes*. 40 vols., translated and edited by Ralph Francis Kerr, et al.. London: Routledge & Kegan Paul Ltd., 1923–1951.

Pirie, Valerie. *The Triple Crown: an Account of Papal Conclaves from the Fifteenth Century to the Present Day*. Wilmington, North Carolina: Consortium Books, 1976.

II. Materials on the Modern College, Cardinals, and Conclaves

Alberigo, Giuseppe, and Andrea Riccardi. *Chiesa e Papato nel Mondo Contemporaneo*. Roma: Editori Laterza, 1990.

Alexander, Stella. *Trostruki mit Zivot Zagrebackog Nadbiskupa Alojzija Stepinca*. Zagreb: Biblioteka Golia, 1990.

Alfaric, Prosper. *Como Se Fizeram Papas*. Lisboa: Delfos, 1972.

Anstruther, George Elliot. *The Election of a Pope*. London: Catholic Truth Society,

1936.

Aradi, Zsolt. *The Popes: The History of How They are Chosen, Elected and Crowned.* London: Macmillan, 1956.

Archdiocese of Chicago. Commission on Clerical Sexual Misconduct with Minors. "Report to Joseph Cardinal Bernardin Archbishop of Chicago." The Cardinal's Commission on Clerical Sexual Misconduct with Minors. S.l. [Chicago, Illinois]: s.n., June, 1992.

Aschoff, Hans-Georg. *Kirchenfürst im Kaiserreich: Georg Kardinal Kopp.* Hildesheim: Bernward, 1987.

Baart, Peter A.. *The Roman Court, or, A Treatise on the Cardinals, Roman Congregations and Tribunals, Legates, Apostolic Vicars, Protonotaries, and other Prelates of the Holy Roman Church.* 4th ed. New York: F. Pustet, 1895.

Barbier, Jean. *Le Cardinal Gerlier.* Roanne/Le Coteau: Horvath, 1987.

Barbier de Montault, X[avier]. *Le Conclave et le Pape.* 2d ed. Paris: Oudin, 1878.

Baudrillart, Alfred (Cardinal). *Les Carnets du Cardinal Baudrillart (20 novembre 1935–11 avril 1939).* Paris: Editions du Cerf, 1996.

Bautista, Felix B. *Cardinal Sin and the Miracle of Asia: a Biography.* Manila: Vera-Reyes, Inc., 1987.

Belardo, Marius. *De Iuribus S[anctæ] R[omanæ] E[cclesiæ] Cardinalium in Titulus.* [Romæ]: Typis Polyglottis Vaticanis, 1939.

Berthelet, Giovanni. *Muss der Päpst ein Italiener sein? Das Italienertum der Päpste, seine Ursachen und seine Wirkungen.* Leipzig: Rengersche Buchhandlung, 1894.

————. *Storia e Rivelazioni sul Conclave del 1903 Elezione di Pio X.* Roma-Torino: Casa Editrice Nazionale, Roux e Viarengo, 1904.

Berthod, Bernard. *Cardinal Gerlier (1880–1965).* Lyon: LUGD, 1995.

Bonghi, Ruggiero. *Pio IX e il Papa Futuro.* Milano: Treves, 1877.

Boudens, Robrecht. *Kardinaal Van Roey en de Tweede Wereldoorlog.* Averbode: Altiora, 1997.

Bowen, Desmond. *Paul Cardinal Cullen and the Shaping of Modern Irish Catholicism.* Waterloo, Ontario, Canada: Wilfrid Laurier University Press, 1983.

Breyer, Richard. *Der Papst polnischer Nation: zum Widerhall seiner Wahl in Ostmitteleuropa.* Marburg an der Lahn: Johann-Gottfried-Herder-Institut, 1979. *Dokumentation Ostmitteleuropa*, N.F., Jahrg. 5 (29), Heft 3 (Juni 1979).

Broucker, Jose de. *The Suenens Dossier: The Case for Collegiality.* Dublin: Gill and Macmillan, 1970.

Bull, George Anthony. *Inside the Vatican.* New York: St. Martin's Press, 1983.

Il Cardinale Alfredo Ildefonso Schuster, Avvio allo Studio. Milano: Nuove Edizioni Duomo, 1979. *Archivio Ambrosiano*, no. 38.

Castle, Tony, ed. *Basil Hume: A Portrait.* London: Collins, 1987.

Ceccaroni, Agostino. *Il Conclave: Storia, Costituzioni, Ceremonie.* Torino: G. Marietti, 1901.

Le Ceremonie dei Funerali del Papa, il Conclave, Cenni Biografici dei Cardinali. Roma: Desclée, Lefebvre, 1903.

Cesare, Raffáel de. *Le Conclave de Leon XIII.* Rome: Loreto Pasqualucci, 1888.

Chelini, Jean. *Jean-Paul II au Vatican.* [Paris]: Hachette, 1995.

Cochlovius, Klaus. *Die Papstwahl und das Veto der katholischen Staaten.* Greifswald: Abel, 1910.

Commeaux, Charles. *Les Conclaves Contemporains, ou, Les Aléas de l'Inspiration.* Paris: France-Empire, 1985.

Congar, Yves (Cardinal). *La Collegialité Episcopale: Histoire et Théologie.* Paris: Editions du Cerf, 1965.

Congregation Consistorialis. *Le Consistoire et la Creation de Nouveaux Cardinaux.* Edition Reservee au Corps Diplomatitique. [Roma]: Imprimerie Polyglotte Vaticane, 1946.

Cooney, John. *The American Pope: The Life and Times of Francis Cardinal Spellman.* New York: Dell, 1986.

Cornwell, John. *A Thief in the Night: The Death of Pope John Paul I.* New York: Viking Press, 1989.

Croaty, A. *Cardinal Agagianian, Papal Legate: a Profile.* Dublin: J. Duffy, 1961.

Cutter, George W. *Three American Cardinals.* Boston: Ellis, 1912.

Cvitkovic, Ivan. *Ko je bio Alojzije Stepinac.* 2d ed., Sarajevo: NISRO "Oslobodenje," OOUR Izdavacka Djelatnost, 1986.

[Dearden, John Francis (Cardinal)]. *Cardinal John Francis Dearden, 1907–1988.* [Detroit, Michigan]: The Michigan Catholic, 1988. Supplement to the *Michigan Catholic,* August 12, 1988.

[Decourtray, Albert (Cardinal)]. *Les Dix Commandements par Dix Cardinaux.* Paris: Editions du Cerf, 1987.

De Luca, Vittorio. *Un Vescovo, una Città: Carlo Maria Martini.* Roma: Città Nuova, 1986.

Del Papa Montini al Papa Wojtyla los 75 dias que estremecieron a la Iglesia. Bilbao, Espana: Mensajero, 1979.

Duffy, Leonard T. "Historical Development of the Mode of Papal Elections." Unpublished thesis (M.A.), St. Bonaventure University, 1956.

Ebers, Godehard Josef, ed. *Der Papst und die Römische Kurie.* Paderborn: F. Schöningh, 1916. *Quellensammlung zur kirchlichen Rechtsgeschichte und zum Kirchenrecht,* no. 3.

Edmund C. Szoka, Cardinal of Detroit. Detroit, Michigan: The Michigan Catholic Company, 1988.

Elvins, Mark Turnham. *Cardinals and Heraldry.* London: Buckland, 1988.

Encyclopedia of the Catholic Bishops in America 1789–1989. 10 vols., S.l.: s.n., 1984.

Fappani, Antonio. *Padre Giulio Bevilacqua, il Cardinale-Parroco.* Brescia: Queriniana, 1979.

Fede è Chiesa. Trento: Reverdito, 1993. Collana la Coce della Chiesa.

Felice Cardot, Carlos. *La Labor Histórica y Humanistica del Cardenal Quintero.* Caracas: Instituto Panamericano de Geografia e Historia, Comisión de Historia, Comité Origenes de la Emancipación, s.d. *Serie Opusculos,* no. 18

Finn, Brendan A. *Twenty-four American Cardinals: Biographical Sketches of those Princes of the Catholic Church who either were born in America or served there at some time.* Boston: B. Humphries, 1947.

Fitzgerald, Billy. *Father Tom.* [London]: Fount, 1991.

Fraccaroli, Arnaldo. *Il Cardinale Che Io Ho Conosciuto: Giacomo Lercaro.* Cinisello Balsamo (Milano): Paoline, 1992.

Frei, Peter. *Die Papstwahl des Jahres 1903, unter besonderer Berücksichtigung des österreichisch-ungarischen Vetos.* Bern: Peter Lang, 1977. Geist und Werk der Zeiten,

Heft 49.

Frisón, Basilio. *Cardenal Larraona*. Madrid: Instituto Teológico de Vida Religiosa, 1979.

Galeazzi-Lisi, Riccardo. *Dans l'Ombre et dans la Lumière de Pie XII*. Paris: Flammarion, 1960.

Garzonio, Marco. *Cardinale a Milano in un Mondo che Cambia nella Testimonianza di Carlo Maria Martini*. Milano: Rizzoli, 1985.

Gaugusch, Ludwig. *Das Rechtsinstitut der Papstwahl: eine historisch-kanonistische Studie*. Wien: Manzsche k.u.k.hof-Verlags- und Universitäts-buchhandlung, 1905.

Giese, Friedrich, ed. *Die Geltenden Papstwahlgesetze*. Bonn: A. Marcus und E. Weber, 1912.

Giraldo, Roberto. *Problematica sul Rapporto tra Poteri Papali e Consacrazione Episcopale*. Roma: s. n., 1978. *Pontificium Atenæum Antonianum. Facultas theologica, sectio dogmatica. Thesis ad doctoratum*, no. 248.

Giuliani, D. *Un mois à Rome: la Mort de Léon XIII, l'Élection de Pie X: Impressions, Souvenirs, Anecdotes*. Lyon: E. Vitte, 1982.

Glemp, Jozef. *W teczy Frankow orzel i krzyz wizyta duszpasterska we Francji, 1986*. [Poznan]: Pallottinum, 1987.

Goyau, Georges, and Paul Lesourd. *Comment on élit un pape*. [Paris]: Flammarion, 1935.

Greeley, Andrew M. *The Making of the Popes 1978: The Politics of Intrigue in the Vatican*. Kansas City, Kansas: Andrews and McMeel, 1979.

Grissell, Hartwell de la Garde. *Sede Vacante: being a diary written during the conclave of 1903, with additional notes on the accession and coronation of Pius X*. Oxford: J. Parker, 1903.

Gury, Christian. *Le Cardinal Grente des Maisons Closes à l'Academie Française*. Paris: Kimé, 1995.

Hartmann, Jan, Bohumil Svoboda, and Vaclav Vasko, eds. *Kardinal Tomasek: Svedectvi o Dobrem Katechetovi Bojacnem Biskupovi a Statecnem Kardinalovi*. Praha: Zvon Æterna, 1994.

Hebblethwaite, Peter. *In the Vatican*. London: Sidgwick & Jackson, 1986.

———. *John XXIII: Pope of the Council*. Revised ed., London: Fount, 1994.

———. *The Next Pope*. [San Francisco, California]: HarperSanFrancisco, 1995.

———. *The New Inquisition? Schillebeeckx and Küng*. London: Collins, 1980.

———. *Paul VI: The First Modern Pope*. London: HarperCollins, 1993.

———. *Pope John Paul II and the Church*. Kansas City: Sheed & Ward, 1995. A collection of articles that were published originally in The National Catholic Reporter between 1978 and 1994.

———. *The Runaway Church*. Revised ed., [London]: Fount Paperbacks, 1978.

———. *Synod Extraordinary: the Inside Story of the Rome Synod, November–December, 1985*. London: Darton, Longman and Todd, 1986.

———. *The Year of the Three Popes*. London: Collins, 1978.

Heiderscheid, Andre. *Rom 1978: Paul VI., Jean Paul I., Jean Paul II: Berichte, Kommentare, Skizzen*. Luxembourg: Verlag der St.-Paulusdruckerei, Aktiengesellschaft, 1979.

Hierzenberger, Gottfried, ed. *Franz König: Appelle an Gewissen und Vernunft*. Innsbruck: Tyrolia-Verlag, 1995.

[Höffner, Joseph (Cardinal)]. *Begegnungen in Mittelamerika: Kardinal Joseph Höffner in Nicaragua, Costa Rica, El Salvador, Guatemala, Honduras; 6 bis 12 Dezember 1986.* Bonn: Sekretariat der Deutschen Bischofskonferenz, 1987.

Homenaje de la Universidad de Los Andes al Primer Cardenal de Venezuela, Su Eminencia José Humberto Quintero. Mérida, Venezuela: Universidad de Los Andes, Ediciones del Rectorado, 1985.

Hynes, Harry Gerard. *The Privileges of Cardinals: Commentary with Historical Notes.* Washington, D.C.: Catholic University of America Press, 1945. *Catholic University of America. Canon Law Studies,* no. 217

Iannotta, Antonio M.. *Lucubratio Theologica de Ecclesia et Primatu Romani Pontificis Vacante Sede Apostolica Collata etiam Codicis Juris Canonici Doctrina.* Editio altera emendata et aucta, Roma: Tipografia dell'Unione Editrice, 1919.

John Paul I. *Pope John Paul I: First Address—Address to College of Cardinals—Purposes of Vatican Diplomacy—Address to Journalists—Installation Homily—Address to Group of Visiting U. S. Bishops—Sermon Given at Funeral Mass for Pope John Paul I by Cardinal-Dean Carlo Confalonieri.* Washington, D.C.: United States Catholic Conference, 1979.

Jos, En. Ke. *Karddinal Josaph Parekkattil Ente Drstiyil.* Vaikkam: Hobi Pablisels, 1988.

Kakol, Kazimierz. *Kardynal Stefan Wyszynski Jakim go Znalem.* Warszawa: Instytut Wydawniczy Zwiazkow Zawodowych, 1985.

Kant, Bronislaw. *Sztygar Bozej kopalni obrazki z zycia ks. Kardynala Augusta Hlonda.* 2d ed., Lodz: Wydawnictwo Salezjanskie, 1983.

Kaspar, Peter Paul. *Das Schweigen des Kardinals und das Begehren des Kirchenvolks.* Thaur: Kulturverlag, 1995. *Reihe der Plattform "Wir sind Kirche,"* Bd. 1.

Keller, Joseph Edward. *The Life and Acts of Pope Leo XIII.* New York: Benziger Brothers, 1879.

Kennedy, Eugene C. *Bernardin: Life to the Full.* Chicago: Bonus Books, 1997.

Kilumanga, Raphael, ed. *Mwadhama Kardinali Rugambwa, Miaka 25 Ya Uaskofu, 1952–1977.* [Dar es Salaam]: Jimbo Kuu la Dar es Salaam, 1977.

Kittler, Glenn D. *The Papal Princes: a History of the Sacred College of Cardinals.* New York: Funk & Wagnalls, 1960.

Komar, Edward. *Kardynal Puzyna, Moje Wspomnienia.* Krakow: Nakl. autora, 1912.

Kozi-Horvath, Jozsef. *Cardinal Mindszenty: Confessor and Martyr of Our Time.* Chichester: Augustine, 1979. trans. of *Ostpriesterhilfe Kirche in Not,* 1979.

Laicus, Philipp. *Die Papstwahl: nach authentischen Quellen dargestellt nebst einem kurzen Abriss der letzten Lebenstage Papst Pius IX.* Einsiedeln: C. und N. Benziger, 1878.

Lector, Lucius [pseud. of Joseph Guthlin]. *Le Conclave: Origines—Histoire, Organisation, Législation, ancienne et moderne.* Paris: P. Lethielleux, 1894.

Lesourd, Paul. *Comment le pape est élu?* Paris: Éditions de Paris, 1954.

Lesourd, Paul, and Claude Paillat. *Dossier Secret des Conclaves.* Paris: Presses de la Cité, 1969.

Leufkens, Joseph, ed. *Clemens August Kardinal von Galen.* Münster, Westfalen: Aschendorff, 1946.

Life of His Holiness Pope Pius X. New York: Benziger, 1904.

Locigno, Joseph P. *We Have a Pope.* New York: Manor Books, 1978.

Lustiger, Jean-Marie (Cardinal). *Le Choix de Dieu: Entretiens avec Jean-Louis Missika et Dominique Wolton*. Paris: Éditions de Fallois, 1987.

MacEoin, Gary. *The Inner Elite: Dossiers of Papal Candidates*. Kansas City: S. Andrews and McMeel, 1978.

Majo, Angelo, ed. *Cardinale a Milano: l'Episcopato di Giovanni Colombo*. [Milano]: N E D, 1982.

Malula, Joseph (Cardinal). *L'Eveque Africain aujourd'hui et demain: Reflexions Personnelles et Méditations de 20 Ans d'Episcopat*. [Kinshasa]: Société Missionnaire de St-Paul, 1979.

Martin, Jacques (Cardinal). *Mes Six Papes, Souvenirs Romains*. S. l., Mame, 1993.

Martin, Victor. *Les cardinaux et la Curie: Tribunaux et Offices, la Vacance du Siège Apostolique*. [Paris]: Bloud & Gay, 1930.

Marty, François (Cardinal). *Chronique Vécue de l'Église en France*. Paris: Le Centurion, 1980.

Matt, Leonard von. *Sedisvakanz*. Würzburg: Echter Verlag, 1959.

Meluzzi, Luciano. *Gli Arcivescovi di Westminster*. Bologna: s.n., 1975.

Mesa, Carlos E. *El Cardenal Tabera: Semblanza Biográfica del Emminentisimo Señor Cardenal Arturo Tabera Araoz, C. M. F.*. Medellin, Colombia: Consorcio Editorial, 1982.

Mindszenty, Jozsef (Cardinal). *Memoirs [of] Jozsef, Cardinal Mindszenty*. London: Weidenfeld and Nicolson, 1974. Trans. of: *Erinnerungen*. Frankfurt am Main: Verlag Ullstein.

Miranda, Francisco. *Pablo Muñoz Vega: Expresión de Humanismo Eclesial en Servicio*. Quito: Ediciones de la Universidad Católica, 1984. *Cuadernos universitarios (Pontificia Universidad Católica del Ecuador)*, no. 5.

Myshanych, Oleksii Vasylovych. *Mytropolyt Iosyf Slipyi pered "sudom" KGB za arkhivnymy dzherelamy*. Kyiv: s.n., 1993.

Natanson, Phoebe, et al. *The Papal Handbook*. Revised and expanded edition, [New York]: Distributed by ABC News, Special Events, 1996.

Nikolic, Vinko, ed. *Stepinac mu je ime Zbornik Uspomena, Svjedocanstava i Dokumenata*. 2 vols., Zagreb: Krscanska sadasnjost, 1991. *Izvan nizova Biblioteka Centra za koncilska istrazivanja, dokumentaciju i informacije "Krscanska sadasnjost."* Reprint of the first edition, Barcelona: "Knjiznica Hrvatske revije," 1978.

O'Connell, William H[enry] (Cardinal). *A Memorable Voyage*. [Boston, Massachusetts]: 1939.

Oddi, Silvio (Cardinal). Ed. Lucio Brunelli. *Il Tenero Mastino di Dio: Memorie del Cardinale Silvio Oddi*. Roma: Progetti Museali Editore ENEL, 1995.

O'Neil, Robert J. *Cardinal Herbert Vaughan: Archbishop of Westminster, Bishop of Salford, Founder of the Mill Hill Missionaries*. Tunbridge Wells, Kent: Burns & Oates, 1995.

Packard, Jerrold M. *Peter's Kingdom: Inside the Papal City*. New York: Charles Scribner's Sons, 1985.

Pastor Poloniæ: Stefan Kardynal Wyszynski. London: Wyd. przez O. O. Marianow, 1982.

Paulus VI. *Pauli VI Summi Pontificis Constitutio Apostolica de Sede Apostolica Vacante deque Electione Romani Pontificis*. [Civitas Vaticana]: Typis Polyglottis Vaticanis, 1975.

Pavicic, Darko. *Razgovori S Kardinalom.* Zagreb: Teovizija, 1995.

Pelikan, Jaroslav Jan. *Confessor between East and West: a Portrait of Ukrainian Cardinal Josyf Slipyj.* Grand Rapids, Michigan: W. B. Eerdmans, 1989.

Pennington, Arthur Robert. *The Papal Conclaves.* New York: E. & J.B. Young, 1897.

Peries, G[eorge]. *L'Intervention du Pape dans l'Élection de Son Successeur.* Paris: A. Roger & F. Chernoviz, 1902.

Peszkowski, Zdzislaw. *Ojciej.* S. l.: Veritas, 1987.

Petralia, Giuseppe. *Il Cardinale Ernesto Ruffini, Arcivescovo di Palermo.* Città del Vaticano: Libreria Editrice Vaticana, 1989.

Peyrefitte, Roger. *Les Secrets des Conclaves.* Paris: Flammarion, 1964.

Pichon, Charles. *Le Pape: le Conclave, l'Élection, et les Cardinaux.* Paris: A. Fayard, 1955.

Pillon, Adrien. *Biographies des Cardinaux et des Prélats Contemporains.* Paris: Librairie du Rosier de Marie, 1861.

Pinochet de la Barra, Oscar. *El Cardenal Silva Henriquez: Luchador por la Justicia.* Santiago, Chile: Editorial Salesiana, 1987.

Pius XII. *Sanctissimi Domini nostri Pii divina providencia Papæ XII Constitutio de sede apostolica vacante et de Romani pontificis electione.* [Roma]: Typis Polyglottis Vaticanis, 1946.

Pope Pius XII: His Life and Work. Articles reprinted from *The Tablet,* October, 1958. London: Burns & Oates, 1958.

Prati, Carlo. *Papes et Cardinaux dans la Rome Moderne.* Paris: Librairie Plon, 1925.

Proces Alojziju Stepincu: Dokumenti. Zagreb: Krscanska Sadasnjost, 1997. *Croatica Christiana*: Fontes, sv. 13.

Pronzato, Alessandro. *Cardinali: Tre Modi di Servire il Vangelo: Guglielmo Massaia, Giuseppe Gamba, Angelo Sodano.* Casale Monferrato [Alessandria]: Piemme, 1996.

Raina, Peter K. *Kardynal Wyszynski.* 6 vols., Warszawa: Ksiazka Polska, n d.

_____. *Stefan Wyszynski, Prymas Polski.* Londyn: Oficyna Poetów i Malarzy, 1979.

Reese, Thomas J. *Archbishop: Inside the Power Structure of the American Catholic Church.* San Francisco: Harper & Row, 1989.

_____. *Inside the Vatican: The Politics and Organization of the Catholic Church.* Cambridge, Massachusetts: Harvard University Press, 1996.

Reese, Thomas J., ed. *Episcopal Conferences: Historical, Canonical, and Theological Studies.* Washington, D.C.: Georgetown University Press, 1989.

Ribeiro, Helcion, ed. *Paulo Evaristo Arns: Cardeal da Esperança e Pastor da Igreja de São Paulo.* São Paulo: Ediçaoes Paulinas, 1989. *Série Teologia em Diálogo.*

Robillard, Denise. *Paul-Emile Léger: Evolution de Sa Pensée, 1950–1967.* Ville La Salle, Québec, Canada: Éditions Hurtubise, 1993. *Cahiers du Québec, Collection Sociologie*, no. 105.

Rola, Zygmunt. *Ucz sie umierac: gnieznienska nekropolia prymasów Polski.* Poznan: "Lawica," 1994.

Rossi, Agnelo (Cardinal). *Il Collegio Cardinalizio.* Città del Vaticano: Libreria Editrice Vaticana, 1990.

_____. *La Diocesi di Ostia e i Cardinali Decani.* Roma: Pontificia Universitas Urbaniana, 1993. *Pontificia Universitas Urbaniana*, no. 55.

Rota, Livio. *Le Nomine Vescovili e Cardinalizie in Francia.* Roma: Pontificia Università Gregoriana, 1996. *Miscellanea Historiæ Pontificiæ*, v. 62.

Sagmüller, Johannes Baptist. *Die Papstwahlbullen und das staatliche Recht der Exklusive*. Tübingen: H. Laupp, 1892.

Salazar Palacio, Hernando. *La Guerra Secreta del Cardenal López Trujillo*. Santa Fe de Bogota, Colombia: Temas de Hoy, 1996.

Sandstede-Auzelle, Marie-Corentine. *Clemens August Graf von Galen, Bischof von Münster im Dritten Reich*. Münster: Aschendorff, 1986.

Santos, José António. *António Ribeiro, Patriarca de Lisboa*. Lisboa: Editorial Notícias, 1996.

Sapag Chain, Reinaldo. *Mi Amigo, El Cardenal*. Santiago: Ediciones Copygraph, 1996.

Schifferle, Alois, ed. *Geduld und Vertrauen: Franz Kardinal Konig—Texte und Gespräche*. Freiburg, Schweiz: Paulusverlag, 1995.

Schlichte, George A. *Politics in the Purple Kingdom: The Derailment of Vatican II*. Kansas City: Sheed & Ward, 1993.

Schmidt, Stjepan, ed. *Augustin Cardinal Bea: Spiritual Profile: Notes from the Cardinal's Diary, with a Commentary*. London: G. Chapman, 1971.

Schmidt, Stjepan. *Augustin Bea: der Kardinal der Einheit*. Graz, 1989. Trans. of: *Agostino Bea, Il Cardinale dell'Unita*.

Schuster e Lazzati. Roma: A. V. E., 1994. *Dossier Lazzati*, v. 7.

Schweizerische Kärdinale: Das apostolische Gesandtschaftswesen in der Schweiz, Erzbistümer und Bistümer I. Bern: Francke, 1972. *Helvetia Sacra*, Abt. 1, Bd. 1.

Secretariat of State. *Instruction on the Dress of Cardinals, Bishops and Other Prelates*. [Washington, D.C.]: United States Catholic Conference, 1969.

Serrou, Robert. *Lustiger: "Cardinal, Juif et Fils d'Immigré."* Paris: Perrin, 1996.

Siri, Giuseppe (Cardinal). *Un Vescovo ai Vescovi: Memorie, Discorsi e Documenti sul Ministero Episcopale*. Pisa: Giardini Editori e Stampatori, 1991.

Sladen, Douglas Brooks Wheelton. *The Pope at Home*. London: Hurst and Blackett, 1913.

Stanford, Peter. *Cardinal Hume and the Changing Face of English Catholicism*. London: G. Chapman, 1993.

Suenens, Léon Joseph (Cardinal). *Memories and Hopes*. Dublin: Veritas, 1992. Originally published: Paris: Fayard, 1991.

Suhard, Emmanuel-Célestin (Cardinal). *Carnets du Cardinal Suhard: Pensées Extraites de Ses Notes de Retraite et de Son Journal*. Paris: Bonne Press, 1951.

Taschereau, Elzear-Alexandre (Cardinal). *Mandement de Monseigneur E.-A. Taschereau, archevêque de Québec, sur l'élection de Notre Saint-Père le pape Léon XIII, 20 février 1878*. S.l.: s.n., 1878.

Theorêt, Chantal, comp; Brenda O'Brien, trans. *In Remembrance—1904–1991, Cardinal Paul-Emile Léger*. [Outremont, Québec]: Partnership Publishers, 1992.

Thils, Gustave. *Choisir les évêques? Élire le pape?* Paris: P. Lethielleux, 1970.

Thompson, Donald. *Le Cardinal Léger, c'est un saint: un aperçu de la vie et de l'oeuvre du Cardinal Paul-Emile Léger*. Montreal: Édimag, 1992.

Turnbull, Michael. *Cardinal Gordon Joseph Gray: a Biography*. Edinburgh: Saint Andrew, 1994.

Unsworth, Tim. *I Am Your Brother Joseph: Cardinal Bernardin of Chicago*. New York: Crossroad, 1987.

Villaflor-Venago, Maria Luisa. *Christendom's Malayan Prince*. Pasay City: Venago, 1970.

Vinatier, Jean. *Le Cardinal Suhard (1874–1949): l'Évêque du Renouveau Missionnaire en France*. Paris: Le Centurion, 1983.

Volk, Hermann. *Hermann Volk im Gesprach mit Michael Albus in Zusammenarbeit mit dem ZDF*. Stuttgart: J. F. Steinkopf Verlag, 1988.

Washburn, Henry Bradford. *The College of Cardinals and the Veto*. S.l.: s.n., 1914; reprinted from the *Papers of the American Society of Church History*, Second Series, v. IV, 1914.

Wayman, Dorothy G[odfrey]. *Cardinal O'Connell of Boston: a Biography of William Henry O'Connell, 1859–1944*. New York: Farrar, Straus and Young, 1955.

Weber, Francis J. *A Cardinal for California's Southland*. Pasadena, California: Castle Press, 1991.

————. *His Eminence of Los Angeles: James Francis Cardinal McIntyre*. 2 vols., Mission Hills, California: Saint Francis Historical Society, 1996.

————. *Magnificat: The Life and Times of Timothy Cardinal Manning*. Santa Barbara, California: McNally & Loftin, 1998.

White, John H. *The Final Journey of Joseph Cardinal Bernardin*. Chicago, Illinois: Loyola Press, 1997.

Who is Cardinal Sin? S.l., s. n., s. d. An interesting collection of essays on the life of Cardinal Jaime L. Sin.

Wurm, Hermann Joseph. *Die Papstwahl: ihre Geschichte und Gebräuche*. Köln: J. P. Bachem, 1902.

Zdzarski, Jan. *Z orlem i z krzyzem duszpasterskie podroze Prymasa Polski*. Warszawa: Instytut Wydawniczy PAX, 1991.

Zizola, Giancarlo. *La Chiesa nei Media*. Torino: Società Editrice Internazionale, 1996.

————. *Il Conclave: Storia e Segreti l'Elezione Papale da San Pietro a Giovanni Paolo II*. Roma: Newton Compton, 1993.

————. *Geopolitica Mediterranea: il Mare Nostrum dall'Egemonia al Dialogo*. Soveria Mannelli (Catanzaro): Rubbettino, 1997.

————. *Giovanni XXIII: la Fede e la Politica*. Roma: Laterza, 1988.

————. *Il Microfono di Dio: Pio XII, Padre Lombardi e i Cattolici Italiani*. Milano: A. Mondadori, 1990.

————. *Les Papes du XXe siécle*. Paris: Desclée de Brouwer, 1996.

————. *Quale papa? Analisi delle Strutture Elettorali e Governative del Papato*. Romano. Roma: Borla, 1977.

————. *La Restaurazione di Papa Wojtyla*. Roma: Laterza, 1985.

————. *Il Sinodo dei Vescovi: Cronaca, Bilancio, Documentazione*. Torino: Borla, 1968.

————. *Le Successeur*. Paris: Desclée de Brouwer, 1995.

————. *Il Successore*. Roma: Laterza, 1997. An Italian edition of *Le Successeur*, but with some new items.

————. *The Utopia of Pope John XXIII*. Maryknoll, New York: Orbis Books, 1978. trans. of the 2d ed. of *L'Utopia di Papa Giovanni*.

III. Frequently Consulted Serials and Newspapers

Annuario Pontificio. (Title varies: *Notizie per l'anno* . . . [1716–1858]; *Annuario Pontificio* [1860–1871]; *Gerarchia Cattolica* [1872–1911]; *Annuario Pontificio* [1912–]). Città del Vaticano: Tipografia Poliglotta Vaticana, 1716– (Imprint varies: Original imprint: Roma: G. F. Chracas).

Archivum Historiæ Pontificiæ. Editum a Facultate Historiæ Ecclesiastica in Pontificia Universitate Gregoriana. Romæ: s.n., 1963– .

Catholic Almanac. (Title varies: 1904–1910, *St. Anthony's Almanac*; 1911, *Franciscan Almanac*; 1912–1929, *St Anthony's Almanac*; 1931–1933, *The Franciscan: Almanac Edition*; 1936–1939, *The Franciscan Almanac*; 1940–1968, *The National Catholic Almanac.*) Felician A. Foy, ed. (1969–). Huntington, Indiana: Our Sunday Vistor, Inc., annual. (Imprint varies in editions before 1968).

The Catholic Year Book for . . . (Title varies: *Catholic Year Book*; *Catholic Almanac and Year Book*). London: Burns Oates & Washbourne, 1951– (annual).

The New York Times.

L'Osservatore Romano (Citta del Vaticano). Frequency had varied: weekly, 1849–1851 (Anno 1., no. 1 [5 sett. 1849]–); three times a week, 1852–1859; daily (except Sunday) 1861– (Anno 1, num. 1 [1 luglio 1861]–).

L'Osservatore Romano. Weekly Edition in English. (Vatican City). 1st year, no. 1 (Apr. 4, 1968)–

The Tablet. London: The Tablet Publishing Company, 1840– . Weekly, May 16, 1840– .

The Times (London).

The Washington Post (Washington, D.C.).

IV. Selected Electronic Resources.

Den Katolske Kirke: http://www.katolsk.no
New Advent: http://www.sni.net/advent
Aquinas Multimedia: http://www.aquinas-multimedia.com
Christus Rex: http://christusrex.org
ANSA News Service in English: http://www.ansa.it/inglese2.html
Saint Michael's Depot: http://abbey.apana.org.au
Catholic Information Network (CIN): http://www.cin.org
Chiesa Cattolica Italiana: http://www.chiesacattolica.it
The Holy See: http://www.vatican.va
130 Catholic Newspapers: http://www.catholic.org/media/news/features.htm
National Conference of Catholic Bishops: http://www.nccbuscc.org
L'Osservatore Romano, English: http://www.vatican.va/news_services/or/or_eng/or_
  eng.htm
Woodstock Theological Center: http://guweb.georgetown.edu/woodstock
Catholic World News: http://www.cwnews.com
The Tablet: http://www.thetablet.co.uk
VIS—Vatican Information Service: http://www.ugkc.lviv.ua/CDHN/visindex.html
Catholic News Service: http://www.catholicnews.com
Documents of the Ecumenical Councils: http://catholic.net/RCC/Indices/subs/coun-

cils.html
ZENIT: http://www.zenit.org/weekly/index.htm
Aciprensa: http://www.aciprensa.com/index.htm

Index

This is an index of personal names, papal documents, and Church councils.

About the Author

Francis A. Burkle-Young, a native of Pittsburgh, is the son of the late Ellen Louise Burkle Young, a historian of manufactures and a former newspaper publisher and editor.

He spent his youth in private study at the Library of Congress in Washington. Guided by Fra Raphael Brown, a senior reference specialist at the Library, he began his work on the history of the College of Cardinals in 1958, at the age of thirteen. After study in Rome and Mainz under the late Professor Hermann E. Schuessler, Burkle-Young received his Ph.D. in history from the University of Maryland at College Park in 1978 with a dissertation on the cardinals of the fifteenth century. Besides *Passing the Keys*, his most recent book is *The Life of Cardinal Innocenzo del Monte: A Scandal in Scarlet.*

He has taught both history and English, including appointments at the University of Maryland, the University of Akron, Gettysburg College, and the George Washington University.

Among his recent publications are two books on research and writing techniques: *The Art of the Footnote: The Intelligent Student's Guide to the Art and Science of Annotating Texts* and *The Research Guide for the Digital Age: A New Handbook to Research and Writing for the Serious Student.*

Today, Burkle-Young is a senior consultant in the technical documentation for telecommunication and other electronic systems and in techniques of online research. He lives in Arlington, Virginia.